Consumer Behavior

sixth edition

Consumer Behavior

Leon G. Schiffman
Baruch College
City University of New York

Leslie Lazar Kanuk
Baruch College
City University of New York

Prentice Hall, Upper Saddle River, New Jersey 07458

Acquisitions Editor: David Borkowsky
Associate Editor: John Larkin
Editorial Assistant: Theresa Festa
Editor-in-Chief: James Boyd
Marketing Manager: John Chillingworth
Senior Project Manager/Liaison: Linda M. DeLorenzo
Production Editor: Neil Saunders, Monotype Editorial Services
Production Coordinator: Renee Pelletier
Managing Editor: Valerie Q. Lentz
Manufacturing Supervisor: Arnold Vila
Manufacturing Manager: Vincent Scelta
Senior Designer: Ann France
Interior Design: Ginider Marshall
Illustrator (Interior):   Dartmouth Publishing, Inc.
Composition: Monotype Composition Company, Inc.

 Copyright © 1997, 1994, 1991, 1987, 1983, 1978 by Prentice-Hall, Inc.
A Simon & Schuster Company
Upper Saddle River, New Jersey 07458

Library of Congress Cataloging-in-Publication Data
Schiffman, Leon G.
    Consumer behavior / Leon G. Schiffman, Leslie Lazar Kanuk. — 6th
ed.
        p.   cm.
    Includes bibliographical references and index.
    ISBN 0-13-372988-5
    1. Consumer behavior.   2. Motivation research (Marketing)
I. Kanuk, Leslie Lazar.   II. Title.
HF5415.32.S35   1997
658.8342—dc21   96-47756
                                                                                                                              CIP

Prentice-Hall International (UK) Limited, London
Prentice-Hall of Australia Pty. Limited, Sydney
Prentice-Hall Canada, Inc., Toronto
Prentice-Hall Hispanoamericana, S.A., Mexico
Prentice-Hall of India Private Limited, New Delhi
Prentice-Hall of Japan, Inc., Tokyo
Simon & Schuster Asia Pte. Ltd., Singapore
Editora Prentice-Hall do Brasil, Ltda., Rio de Janeiro

Printed in the United States of America

10   9   8   7   6   5   4   3   2

Contents

10 COMMUNICATION AND PERSUASION

PART III CONSUMERS IN THEIR SOCIAL AND CULTURAL SETTINGS

11 GROUP DYNAMICS AND CONSUMER REFERENCE GROUPS

12 THE FAMILY

13 SOCIAL CLASS AND CONSUMER BEHAVIOR

18 DIFFUSION OF INNOVATIONS

19 CONSUMER DECISION MAKING: CHOOSING AND CONSUMING

PART V CONSUMER BEHAVIOR AND SOCIETY

20 CONSUMER BEHAVIOR APPLICATIONS TO PROFIT AND NOT-FOR-PROFIT MARKETING

Part of the challenge in preparing this revision (as well as the five editions that preceded it) was the fact that the field of consumer behavior is so dynamic and its researchers so prolific. With this in mind, the sixth edition of *Consumer Behavior* is committed to the "spirit of diversity"—diversity of viewpoints (distinctive theories and concepts), diversity of focus (strategic vs. consumer), diversity of methods (qualitative vs. quantitative), and diversity of consumers.

Given the *diversity* of consumer behavior research, we have worked particularly hard in this edition to achieve an appropriate balance between our ongoing commitment to strategic consumer behavior (i.e., using consumer behavior principles to make strategic marketing decisions) and the broader postmodern perspective that focuses on individual consumption experience. We have continued our efforts to update our endnotes to include the most up-to-date citations possible.

As true believers in the marketing concept, we have always tried our best to meet the needs of our consumers—students, practitioners, and professors of consumer behavior—by providing a text that is highly readable and that clearly explains the relevant concepts upon which the discipline of consumer behavior is based. We have supplemented this material with a great many "real-world" examples in order to demonstrate how consumer behavior concepts are used by marketing practitioners to develop and implement effective marketing strategies.

Our aim in the sixth edition, as in earlier editions, was to write a book that was complete and comprehensive without being encyclopedic. To make it as useful as possible to both graduate and undergraduate students, we have sought to maintain an even balance of basic behavioral concepts, research findings, and applied marketing examples. We are convinced that a major contribution of consumer behavior studies to the practice of marketing is the provision of structure and direction for effective market segmentation. To this end, we have paid particular attention to revising and refining the discussion on market segmentation.

This sixth edition of *Consumer Behavior* is divided into five parts, consisting of twenty-one chapters. Part I provides the background and the tools for a strong and comprehensive understanding of the consumer behavior principles that follow. Chapter 1 introduces the reader to the study of consumer behavior, its diversity, its development, and the role of consumer research. It concludes with a detailed discussion of ethical considerations in marketing and consumer practices. Chapter 2 provides readers with a detailed overview of the critical research process and the techniques associated with consumer behavior research, including a discussion of positivist and interpretivist research methods. Chapter 3 presents a comprehensive examination of market segmentation.

Part II discusses the consumer as an individual. It begins with an exploration of consumer needs and *motivations*, recognizing both the rational and emotional bases of many consumer actions. Chapter 5 discusses the impact of a full range of *personality* theories (e.g., Freudian theory, Neo-Freudian theory, Jungian theory, and trait and cognitive theory) on consumer behavior, explores consumer materialism, fixated consumption, and compulsive consumption behavior, and considers the related concepts of "self" and "self-image." This chapter is followed by a comprehensive examination of the impact of consumer *perception* on marketing strategy, and includes a discussion of product positioning and repositioning. The discussion of consumer *learning* focuses on limited and extensive information processing, including an evaluation of involvement theory and its applications to marketing practice. After an in-depth examination of consumer *attitudes*, Part II concludes with a discussion of *communication* and persuasion, and links consumers as individuals to the world and people around them.

Part III is concerned with the social and cultural dimensions of consumer behavior. It begins with a discussion of *group dynamics* and consumer reference groups, followed by an examination of new *family* role orientations and changing family lifestyles. It presents consumers in their *social* and *cultural* milieus, and investigates the impact of societal and subcultural values, beliefs, and customs on consumer behavior. This section includes an expanded discussion of geodemographic clustering and examines such *subcultures* as Generation X, the affluent and non-affluent, and the Asian-American consumer. Part III concludes with an extended discussion of *cross-cultural* consumer behavior within an increasingly global marketplace.

Part IV explores various aspects of consumer decision making. It begins with a discussion of *personal influence* and *opinion leadership*, followed by an examination of the *diffusion of innovations*. Next, it describes how consumers make product decisions, and explores the newly important practice of relationship marketing. This section offers the reader a simple model of *consumer decision making* that ties together the psychological, social, and cultural concepts examined throughout the book, a greatly expanded exploration of consumer gifting behavior, and concludes with an examination of the expanding research focus on understanding individual consumption and the symbolic meanings of possessions.

Part V addresses the role of consumer behavior in our society. It demonstrates the *application of consumer behavior principles* to the marketing of profit and not-for-profit services, including health care marketing, political marketing, environmental marketing, and the marketing of social causes. The book concludes with an examination of *public policy issues* and a discussion of consumer behavior research priorities for the next decade.

Supplements

For the sixth edition of *Consumer Behavior,* a state-of-the-art new supplements package has been created to support your teaching. The following materials are available upon adoption of the text.

An **Instructor's Resource Manual and Video Guide** includes extensive chapter overviews, learning objectives, and outlines as well as applications exercises. Discussion questions and answers are presented in detail. A separate section in the manual includes the On Location! at Lands' End video cases and provides answers to the discussion questions.

A new **Test Item File** with more than 100 questions per chapter has been created. The multiple choice, true/false, and essay questions are presented with three levels of difficulty and are page referenced. **Prentice Hall Custom Test**, a computerized test management system, is available in DOS and Windows.

A set of **Color Transparencies** has been created to present the concepts found throughout the book, and an additional disk of electronic transparencies is available in **PowerPoint**.

Prentice Hall Presents: Multimedia Presentations for Marketing and Advertising is also available to adopters of Schiffman and Kanuk. This brand new CD-ROM is a compilation of nearly 300 media objects, which range from EFFIE award-winning TV and print advertisements to On Location! video case clips and dozens upon dozens of concept illustrations taken from seven Prentice Hall marketing and advertising texts. All of the media are organized in a presentation program that makes arranging

multimedia lectures simple. Create your presentation by choosing from a list of the media by topic or run premade chapter-by-chapter multimedia lectures for *Consumer Behavior* from a template that already exists on the CD. Contact your local sales representative for a demonstration.

On Location! at Lands' End is a series of custom case videos created especially to accompany *Consumer Behavior.* A relevant videocase and questions designed to provide the students with an opportunity to apply the concepts learned has been written to correspond to each of the five parts of the text. For each videocase there is an 8 to 10 minute custom-produced video segment that presents background information and interviews with Lands' End marketing executives on the issues and topics discussed in that section. The written video case studies and the answers to the accompanying discussion questions are continued in the *Instructor's Resource Manual.* This new feature of *Consumer Behavior* is designed to provide focused case studies for professors who wish to use dynamic case materials as part of their teaching.

Acknowledgments

Of the many people who have been enormously helpful in the preparation of this sixth edition of *Consumer Behavior*, we are especially grateful to our own consumers—the graduate and undergraduate students of consumer behavior, and their professors, who have provided us with invaluable experiential feedback to our earlier editions.

We would particularly like to thank our close friends and colleagues in the Department of Marketing at Baruch College for their continued support, encouragement, and friendship. We are grateful to the following professors for their continuous suggestions and highly constructive comments: Steve Schnaars, Baruch College; Benny Barak, Hofstra University; Elaine Sherman, Hofstra University; Martin Topol, Pace University; Harold Kassarjian, UCLA; David Brinberg, Virginia Polytechnic Institute; John Holmes, Simmons College; Joel Saegert, The University of Texas at San Antonio; Lewis Hershey, Eastern Missouri State College; William R. Dillon, Southern Methodist University; Havva J. Meric, East Carolina University; Ron Goldsmith, Florida State University; Richard Yalch, University of Washington; Mark Young, Winona State University; Michael Taylor, Marietta College; Daniel Johnson, Radford University; Bob Settle, San Diego State University; Gerald Cavallo, Fairfield University; Kristina Cannon-Bonventre, Northeastern University; Kathy Pettit, University of Idaho; Douglas W. Mellott, Jr., Radford University; Darvin R. Hoffman, Texas A & I; David Shepherd, University of Tennessee at Chatanooga; John T. Shaw, Providence College; Janet G. Hibbard, Eastern Kentucky University; Ron Lennon, Barry University; Jeanne Mueller, Cornell University; Charles Gulas, Wright State University; James W. Cagley, University of Tulsa; Kenneth R. Lord, Niagara University; Paul Chao, University of Northern Iowa; John H. Holmes, Skidmore College; Donna Frick, Maine Maritime Academy; Sheri Zeigler, University of Hawaii; Christina Goulding, Wolverhampton University, United Kingdom; U. B. Bradley, London Guildhall University, United Kingdom; Adrienne Czerwin-Abbott, Dublin Institute of Technology, Ireland; and Bernard A. Delagneau, The University of Wales, Aberystwyth, United Kingdom.

Professor Steve Gould, our Baruch colleague, has always been forthcoming with valuable insights, suggestions and advice. We would also like to acknowledge the support and friendship of Professor Joseph Wisenblit of Seton Hall University. Alan Pollack provided invaluable legal insights into the marketing process. Many other professors, students, and colleagues have made a contribution to our thinking; among these are Martha Cook of Baruch College, Mark Kay of Montclair State University, Mary Long of Drexel University, and Charles McMellon of Pennsylvania State University. Deborah Y. Cohn provided original thinking and an interesting perspective on consumer gifting.

We would also like to acknowledge Don Siebert of Fruit of the Loom, Ross Copper of Clarion Marketing and Communications, Larry Chiagouris of Creamer Dickson Besford, Jerry Lott, an independent marketing consultant, and Walter McCullough of Monroe Mendelsohn Research. We are grateful to the executives and staff of the following research firms for their continuous flow of interesting illustrative materials: Claritas Corporation, Simmons Market Research Bureau, Donnelley Marketing Information Services, SRI International, and Mediamark Research.

Our thanks also go to the many people at Prentice Hall who aided and supported us in the editorial and production processes of this sixth edition, including our editor David Borkowsky, the marketing manager John Chillingworth, and the senior production editor Linda DeLorenzo. We also want to acknowledge the caring and careful work of the Permissions Group (in particular Cheryl and Joe Besenjak and Sherry Hoesly) and the professionalism and concern of Neil Saunders of Monotype Editorial Services.

Finally, we would like to give very special recognition to Professor Stanley Garfunkel of CUNY for his untiring assistance, encouragement and friendship, and to Randi Dauler for her invaluable contributions and insights into the application of consumer behavior principles to not-for-profit marketing.

To the countless other people who have been generous with their time, their support and encouragement, please know we think of you, we thank you, and we love you.

Leon G. Schiffman
Leslie Lazar Kanuk

PART ONE

Introduction

PART 1 PROVIDES

THE BACKGROUND &

THE TOOLS FOR A

STRONG & COMPREHENSIVE

UNDERSTANDING OF

CONSUMER

BEHAVIOR.

CHAPTER ONE INTRODUCES THE READER TO THE STUDY OF consumer

behavior, its diversity, its development, and the role of consumer

research. It concludes with a detailed discussion of ethical

considerations in marketing and consumer practices. Chapter 2

provides a detailed overview of the critical research process and the

techniques associated with consumer behavior research, including a

discussion of positivist and interpretivist research methods. Chapter 3

presents a comprehensive examination of market segmentation and

demonstrates how consumer behavior provides both the conceptual

framework and the strategic direction for the practical segmentation

of markets.

THE DIVERSITY OF
CONSUMER BEHAVIOR

As the twentieth century draws to a close, the United States is a celebration in diversity. Its people differ not only in the usual ways— by age and gender, by race and nationality, by education and occupation, by marital status and living arrangements—but also in their activities and interests, their preferences and opinions. They differ in the music they like, the television shows they watch, the political beliefs they hold, the clothing they wear.

Indeed, there has never been a better time for people-watching. Just stand on a street corner during the afternoon in any medium-sized city. The diversity in dress—in fashion, if you will—is astounding. Women's hemlines may vary from just below the hips to just below the ankle, with any and every length in between. Their trousers may range from short-shorts to tailored slacks, from spandex bicycle pants to flowing pajamas, from bell-bottom hip huggers to jeans. Men's clothing may vary from traditional

There never was in the world two opinions alike, no more than two hairs or two grains; the most universal quality is diversity.

—Michel De Montaigne, 1533–1592

3

business suits to sport jackets, from baseball jackets to un-structured jackets, from tee shirts to sport shirts to dress shirts. Department stores feature tattered clothing; the "grunge" look is still "in"; alligator logos are out; and unisex clothing abounds. And everybody is in style (see Figure 1-1).

Or look at hairdos—on men and women alike, regardless of age and regardless of stage. They may range from the shaved head to the flowing mane, from the clipped bob to the ubiquitous ponytail, from straight hair to curly hair, from frizz to cornrows to perms. In America in the late 1990s, we are all free to express our tastes and our personalities in any way that we wish, and the wonderful news is that we all fit in.

In addition to the *diversity* among consumers, there is also tremendous diversity among marketers. Traditional retailers, from department stores to mom-and-pop stores, are still around. So are the mass merchandisers, the discount stores, and the off-price stores. However, the 1990s also have seen a tremendous increase in outlet malls, as well as a shift from mass marketing to niche marketing to direct marketing, from showrooms to custom catalogs, from selling through direct mail to selling through television shopping networks. Catalog items range in price from 59-cent kitchen utensils to a $100,000, fully operative, solid-gold miniature train carrying rubies, diamonds, sapphires, and emeralds around a 41-foot track. In addition to the continued interest in *value pricing*, which stresses high quality at the lowest possible price, many marketers are concerned with *relationship marketing*—developing a close affiliation with the consumer that results in brand or store loyalty. Some consumers prefer to shop at stores that offer large selections of merchandise and low prices, while others prefer stores where they can get in and out quickly and to which they are willing to pay a premium to save time.

Manufacturers sell through traditional distribution channels, through custom-designed channels, and directly to the consumer. Where United States producers once focused almost exclusively on the domestic market, the larger global market now beckons, and marketers are designing marketing strategies that they hope will be as effective in Bombay as they are in Boston.

There is great diversity in advertising media. We still have the traditional broadcast and print media, but cable TV has made enormous inroads on network advertising, and marketers of every size and every product or service are rushing on to the Internet and World Wide Web. We have become accustomed to seeing advertising on bus shelters, on municipal trash baskets, on shopping carts and cabs, and now marketers can even buy advertising space on the hull of a rocket from NASA.

With all of the diversity that surrounds us, the profusion of goods and services offered to us, and the freedom of choice available to us, one may wonder how individual marketers actually reach us with their highly specific marketing messages. How do they know which people to target, where to reach them, and what message would be most persuasive to that target audience?

The answer, of course, is that despite the diversity among us, there are also many similarities—constants that can be found among many peoples of the world. For example, we all have the same set of biological needs, no matter where we were born. These needs include the need for food, for nourishment, for water, for air, for shelter from the elements. We also acquire needs *after* we are born. These needs often are shaped by the environment and the culture in which we live, and by our education and the experiences we have had. For example, if we are brought up in a culture that values exercise and physical fitness, we

FIGURE 1-1

might make it a point to jog every day before work or school. If we experience a euphoric "high" after jogging for a while, we may acquire the *need* to jog daily to maintain a sense of well-being. The interesting thing about acquired needs is that there are usually many people who experience the same needs, despite the individual nature of such needs. Remember, if you're "one in a million," there may be 4000 people just like you.

One of the few common denominators among all of us, despite our differences, is that above all, we are consumers. That is, we use or consume on a regular basis food, clothing, shelter, transportation, education, brooms, dishes, vacations, necessities, luxuries, services, even ideas. And as consumers, we play a vital role in the health of the economy—local, national, and international. The decisions that we make concerning our consumption behavior affect the demand for basic raw materials, for transportation, for production, for banking; they affect the employment of workers and the deployment of resources, the success of some industries and the failure of others. Thus, consumer behavior is an integral factor in the ebb and flow of all business in a consumer-oriented society such as our own.

This chapter introduces the reader to the notion of consumer behavior as an interdisciplinary science that investigates the consumption-related activities of individuals. It describes the reasons for the development of consumer behavior as an academic discipline and an applied science. It discusses the importance of consumer behavior research to marketers and scholars alike, why they want to know everything there is to know about consumers—what they want, what they think, how they work, how they play, and the personal and group influences that affect their consumption decisions.

THE STUDY OF CONSUMER BEHAVIOR

The study of **consumer behavior** is the study of how individuals make decisions to spend their available resources (time, money, effort) on consumption-related items. It includes the study of *what* they buy, *why* they buy it, *when* they buy it, *where* they buy it, *how often* they buy it, and how often they *use* it. Take the simple product *toothpaste*. Consumer researchers want to know what types of toothpaste consumers buy (gel, regular, striped, in a tube, with a pump); what brand (national brand, private brand, generic brand); why they buy it (to prevent cavities, to remove stains, to brighten or whiten teeth, to use as a mouthwash, to attract romance); where they buy it (supermarket, drugstore, convenience store); how often they use it (when they wake up, after each meal, when they go to bed, or any combination thereof); and how often they buy it (weekly, biweekly, monthly).

Consider a more durable product, such as the fax machine. What kinds of consumers buy fax machines for home use? What features do they look for? What benefits do they seek? What types of documents do they fax and for what reasons? How likely are they to replace their old models when new models with added features become available? The answers to these questions can be found through consumer research and can provide fax manufacturers with important input for product scheduling, design modification, and promotional strategy.

Although this book focuses on how and why consumers make decisions to buy goods and services, consumer behavior research goes far beyond these facets of consumer behavior and encompasses all of the behaviors that consumers display in *searching for, purchasing, using, evaluating,* and *disposing* of products and services that they expect will satisfy their needs. For example, a couple may experience dissatisfaction with their choice of an automobile, perhaps because of continuing service problems. They may communicate their dissatisfaction to friends and, in turn, influence their friends' future automobile purchases. They may vow never to buy the same make or model again, limiting their own future selection decisions. Each of these possible consequences of consumer postpurchase dissatisfaction has significant ramifications for automobile marketers, who have to build postpurchase strategies into their promotional campaigns.

In addition to studying consumer uses and postpurchase evaluations of the products they buy, consumer researchers also are interested in how individuals dispose of their once-new purchases. For example, after consumers have used a product, do they store it, throw it or give it away, sell it, rent it, or lend it out? The answers to these questions are important to marketers, because they must match their production to the frequency with which consumers buy replacements. However, the answers are also important to society as a whole, because solid waste disposal has become a major environmental problem that marketers must address in their development of new products and packaging.

The term *consumer* is often used to describe two different kinds of consuming entities: the personal consumer and the organizational consumer. The **personal consumer** buys goods and services for his or her own use (e.g., shaving cream or shampoo), for the use of the household (a VCR), or as a gift for a friend (a book). In each of these contexts, the goods are bought for final use by individuals, who are referred to as *end users* or *ultimate consumers*.

The second category of consumer—the **organizational consumer**—includes profit and not-for-profit businesses, government agencies (local, state, and national), and institutions (e.g., schools, hospitals, prisons), all of which must buy products, equipment, and services in order to run their organizations. Manufacturing companies must buy the raw materials and other components needed to manufacture and sell their own products; service companies must buy the equipment necessary to render the services they sell; government agencies must buy the office products needed to operate their agencies; institutions must buy the materials they need to maintain themselves and their populations.

Despite the importance of both categories of consumers, individuals and organizations, this book will focus on the individual consumer, who purchases for his or her own personal use or for household use. End-use consumption is perhaps the most pervasive of all types of consumer behavior, for it involves every individual, of every age and background, in the role of either *buyer, user,* or both.

The person who makes a product purchase is not always the user, or the only user, of the product in question. Nor is the purchaser necessarily the person who makes the product decision. A mother may buy toys for her children (who are the users); she may buy food for dinner (and be one of the users); she may buy a handbag and be the only user. She may buy a magazine that one of her teenagers requested or rent a video that her husband requested, or she and her husband together may buy a station wagon that they both selected. Clearly, buyers are not always the users, or the only users, of the products they buy, nor do they necessarily make the product selection decisions themselves.

Marketers must decide at whom to direct their promotional efforts: the buyer or the user. For some products, they must identify the person who is most likely to influence the decision—who may be neither the buyer nor the user. For example, as people live longer, they often depend more and more upon the advice and counsel of their children or other caregivers. Should a retirement community advertise to the elderly or to their middle-aged children? Should an emergency response system be targeted to elderly people or to their concerned relatives? Some marketers believe that the *buyer* of the product is the best prospect, others believe it is the *user* of the product, while still others play it safe by directing their promotional efforts to *both* buyers and users.

Why We Study Consumer Behavior

Just as consumers and marketers are diverse, the reasons why people study consumer behavior are also diverse. The field of consumer behavior holds great interest for us as consumers, as marketers, and as students of human behavior.

As *consumers*, we benefit from insights into our own consumption-related decisions: what we buy, why we buy, how we buy, and the promotional influences that persuade us to buy. The study of consumer behavior enables us to become better, that is, wiser, consumers.

As *marketers* and *future marketers*, it is important for us to recognize why and how individuals make their consumption decisions, so that we can make better strategic marketing decisions. If marketers *understand* consumer behavior, they are able to *predict* how consumers are likely to react to various informational and environmental cues, and are able to shape their marketing strategies accordingly. Without doubt, marketers who understand consumer behavior have great competitive advantage in the marketplace.

As *students* of human behavior, we are concerned with understanding consumer behavior; with gaining insights into *why* individuals act in certain consumption-related ways and with learning what internal and external influences impel them to act as they do. Indeed, the desire for understanding consumption-related human behavior has led to a diversity of theoretical approaches to its study.

Consumer behavior was a relatively new field of study in the mid-to-late 1960s. With no history or body of research of its own, the new discipline borrowed heavily from concepts developed in other scientific disciplines, such as *psychology* (the study of the individual), *sociology* (the study of groups), *social psychology* (the study of how an individual operates in groups), *anthropology* (the influence of society on the individual), and *economics*. Many early theories concerning consumer behavior were based on economic theory, on the notion that individuals act rationally to maximize their benefits (satisfactions) in the purchase of goods and services.

The initial thrust of consumer research was from a managerial perspective: marketing managers wanted to know the specific causes of consumer behavior. They also wanted to know how people receive, store, and use consumption-related information, so that they could design marketing strategies to influence consumption decisions. They regarded the consumer behavior discipline as an applied marketing science; if they could *predict* consumer behavior, they could influence it. This approach has come to be known as **positivism**, and consumer researchers primarily concerned with predicting consumer behavior are known as *positivists*.[1]

Given the interdisciplinary background in which the consumer behavior discipline is rooted, it is not surprising that academicians from a variety of contributing disciplines, including marketing itself, have become interested in the study of consumer behavior, not necessarily from a managerial or applied perspective, but simply to understand the consumer better. The study of consumer behavior from the point of view of *understanding* consumption behavior and the meanings behind such behavior is called **interpretivism**, (sometimes referred to as *postmodernism*).[2] Interpretivists have expanded the boundaries of study to include many subjective aspects of consumer behavior, such as the effects of moods, emotions, and types of situations on consumer behavior; the roles of fantasy, of play, of rituals, even of the sensory pleasures that certain products and services provide. (Figure 1-2 is an example of a mood-inducing ad.) Many interpretivists consider each purchase experience unique because of the diverse set of variables at play at that one particular moment in time. Because of its focus on the consumption *experience*, the interpretive approach is also known as **experientalism**.[3]

Despite the apparent diversity of these two major approaches to the study of consumer behavior, each can be seen to complement the other. Although the major focus of this book is on *managerial marketing strategy*, the authors have endeavored to integrate both approaches—**positivism** and **interpretivism**—because of their firm belief that both *prediction* and *understanding* together give a richer and more robust portrait of consumer behavior than either approach used alone. This dual approach to consumer research enables marketers to make better strategic decisions.

Why the Field of Consumer Behavior Developed

There are a number of reasons why the study of consumer behavior developed as a separate marketing discipline. Marketers had long noted that consumers did not always act or react as marketing theory suggested they would. The size of the consumer market in this country was vast and constantly expanding. Billions of dollars were being spent on goods and services by tens of millions of people. Consumer preferences were changing and

FIGURE 1-2 ▼ Mood Inducement
Courtesy of Chic Jeans

LIFE'S AN OPEN ROAD.

MONTANA
5·39459

chic

becoming highly diversified. Even in industrial markets, where needs for goods and services were always more homogeneous than in consumer markets, buyers were exhibiting
diversified preferences and less predictable purchase behavior.

As marketing researchers began to study the buying behavior of consumers, they
soon realized that, despite a sometimes "me too" approach to fads and fashions, many consumers rebelled at using the identical products everyone else used. Instead, they preferred
differentiated products that they felt reflected their own special needs, personalities, and
lifestyles.

To better meet the needs of specific groups of consumers, most marketers adopted a
policy of **market segmentation**, which called for the division of their total potential markets into smaller, homogeneous segments for which they could design specific products
and/or promotional campaigns (see Chapter 3). They also used promotional techniques to
vary the *image* of their products so that they would be perceived as better fulfilling the specific needs of certain target segments—a process now known as **positioning**. Other reasons for the developing interest in consumer behavior included the rate of new product
development, growth of the consumer movement, public policy concerns, environmental
concerns, and the growth of both nonprofit marketing and international marketing.

Indeed, a major stumbling block to many international marketing efforts has been
the general lack of familiarity with the needs, preferences, and consumption habits of consumers in foreign markets. Marketers now use *cross-cultural consumer research* studies as

the basis for product development and promotional strategies to meet the needs of targeted foreign consumers (see Chapter 16).

▲ **Development of the Marketing Concept** The field of consumer behavior is rooted in the **marketing concept**, a marketing strategy that evolved in the late 1950s, after marketers passed through a series of marketing approaches referred to as the *production concept*, the *product concept*, and the *selling concept*.

When World War II ended, marketers found they could sell almost any goods they could produce to consumers who had done without while the nation's manufacturing facilities were dedicated to the production of war materiel. This marketing approach is called a **production orientation**; its implicit marketing objectives are cheap, efficient production and intensive distribution. A production orientation is a feasible marketing strategy when consumers are more interested in obtaining the product than they are in its specific features. When demand exceeds supply, a production orientation can work. Consumers will buy what's available, rather than wait for what they really want.

A production orientation should not be confused with a **product orientation**, which assumes that consumers will buy the product that offers them the highest quality, the best performance, and the most features. A product orientation leads a company to strive constantly to improve the quality of its product, with a result often referred to as "marketing myopia"—that is, a focus on the product, rather than on the consumer needs it presumes to satisfy. A marketer in love with its product may improve it far beyond its worth to the consumer, passing the cost of unneeded quality or special features on to the public. In highly competitive markets, some companies keep adding unnecessary features in hopes of attracting buyers.

A natural evolution from both a production orientation and a product orientation is a **selling orientation**, in which a marketer's primary focus is selling the products that it has unilaterally decided to produce. The implicit assumption in the selling orientation is that consumers are unlikely to buy a product unless they are actively and aggressively persuaded to do so (i.e., through a "hard-sell" approach.) The problem with a selling orientation is that it does not take consumer satisfaction into account. When consumers are induced to buy products that they don't want or need, any resulting unhappiness is likely to be communicated through negative word-of-mouth that may dissuade other potential consumers from making a similar purchase. Furthermore, when the product (or service or political candidate) does not fulfill a consumer need, it is unlikely that a repeat purchase (or donation or vote) will be forthcoming.

In the late 1950s, some marketers began to realize that they could sell more goods, more easily, if they produced only those goods that they had predetermined consumers would buy. Instead of trying to persuade customers to buy what the firm had already produced, marketing-oriented firms endeavored to produce only products that they had first confirmed consumers would buy. Consumer needs and wants became the firm's primary focus. This consumer-oriented marketing philosophy came to be known as the **marketing concept**. The key assumption underlying the marketing concept is that, to be successful, a company must determine the needs and wants of specific target markets, and deliver the desired satisfactions better than the competition. The marketing concept is based on the premise that a marketer should make what it can sell, instead of trying to sell what it has made. While the selling concept focused on the needs of the seller, the marketing concept focuses squarely on the needs of the buyer.

The widespread adoption of the marketing concept by American business provided the impetus for the study of consumer behavior. To identify unsatisfied consumer needs, companies had to engage in extensive marketing research. In so doing, they discovered that consumers were highly complex individuals, subject to a variety of psychological and social needs quite apart from their survival needs. They discovered that the needs and priorities of different consumer segments differed dramatically and that to design new products and marketing strategies that would fulfill consumer needs they had to study consumers and their consumption behavior in depth. Thus, the marketing concept laid the groundwork for the application of consumer behavior principles to marketing strategy.

▲ **The Role of Consumer Research** **Consumer research** is the methodology used to study consumer behavior. Given the fact that there are two major theoretical perspectives concerning the study of consumer behavior, it is not surprising to find that there is a divergence in theoretical assumptions and, to some extent, in research methodology between the *positivist* approach and the *interpretivist* approach. Broadly speaking, positivists tend to be objective and empirical, to seek causes for behavior, and to conduct research studies that can be generalized to larger populations. The early consumer researchers, with their strategic management perspective, were largely *positivist* in their approach.

The research done by *interpretivists*, on the other hand, tends to be qualitative and based on small samples. Although they tend to view each consumption situation as unique and nonreplicable, interpretivists seek to find common patterns of operative values, meanings, and behavior across consumption situations. Chapter 2 explores the basic assumptions and methodology of each approach in some detail, and examines the major variables involved in both types of research.

ETHICS IN MARKETING

The primary purpose for studying consumer behavior as part of a marketing curriculum is to understand why and how consumers make their purchase decisions. These insights enable marketers to design more effective marketing strategies. Some critics are concerned that an in-depth understanding of consumer behavior makes it possible for unethical marketers to exploit human vulnerabilities in the marketplace. In short, they are concerned that a knowledge of consumer behavior gives marketers an unfair advantage.

Newspaper headlines have identified a number of highly unethical, often illegal marketing practices undertaken by seemingly honest, educated, and respectable business people who were obviously caught up in the quest for commercial superiority, for profits, for market share. Unethical marketing practices occur at every level of the marketing mix: in the design of products, in packaging, in pricing practices, in distribution efforts, and in promotional schemes. They also occur at the other side of the marketing equation, with consumers sometimes practicing unethical behavior as well. Although most studies of **marketing ethics** focus on marketers' practices, some researchers are beginning to study consumer ethics.[4] Tables 1-1 and 1-2 on pages 12 and 13 list various types of unethical marketing behavior, together with some blatant examples. Occurrences such as these make it important to reflect on the role of ethics in marketing.

Unfortunately, there is no universally accepted definition for the term *ethics*. A study of ethical philosophies reveals two different groups of theories: teleological theories and deontological theories.[5]

Teleology deals with the moral worth of a behavior as determined by its consequences. One's choice is based on what is best for everyone involved. **Utilitarianism**, a teleological theory, is summarized best by the notion of "the greatest good for the greatest number." According to this theory, it is perfectly ethical for a company to conceal potentially negative consequences of a product trial from early consumers, if a large number of people are likely to benefit once the product is perfected. To utilitarians, ethics are evaluated on the basis of a cost/benefit analysis: as long as the benefits to society (or to a specific segment of society) exceed the costs (e.g., to the same or even other segments of

table 1-1 Unethical Marketing Behavior

TYPES OF UNETHICAL MARKETING BEHAVIOR	EXAMPLES
PRODUCT	
• Safety	Manufacture of flammable stuffed animals
• Shoddy goods	Products that cannot withstand ordinary wear and tear
• Inadequate warranties	Warranties with insufficient time or parts coverage
• Environmental pollution	Manufacture of nonbiodegradable plastic products
• Mislabeled products	Flavored sugar water sold as apple juice for babies
• Development	Bribery of FDA officials to secure agency approval of generic pharmaceuticals
• Manufacturing	Unauthorized substitutions in generic drugs after FDA approval
• Brand "knock-offs"	Counterfeit branded goods sold as genuine brands.
PRICE	
• Excessive markups	High prices used by retailers to connote quality
• Price differentiation	Yield-management pricing of airline tickets, resulting in day-to-day differential pricing of adjacent seats[a]
• Price discrimination	Favored pricing to preferred racial or ethnic groups
PROMOTION	
• Exaggerated claims	Wilkinson Blades claimed its Ultra Glide Razor offered "the smoothest, most comfortable shave known to man"—an assertion challenged by Gillette[b]
• Tasteless advertising	Sexual innuendos and gender disparagement (e.g., Miller Brewing Company targeted college males with ads on "how to scam babes"[c])
• Inappropriate targeting	Inner-city billboards for luxury products (e.g., $125 sneakers targeted to ghetto youth)
• Deceptive advertising	Ads for coach accommodations depicting first-class facilities (e.g., ad for France coach railpass with misleading illustration of all-first-class train)
• Persuasive role models for inappropriate products	Celebrity spokespersons in beer, liquor, and cigarette ads targeted to youths
• Naive audiences	Billboards for cigarettes and alcohol in poor urban neighborhoods, where many people are dying from related causes[d]
	Ads on children's TV for nutritionally unsound products (sugary cereals, candy, etc.)[e]
• Captive audiences	Mandatory viewing of TV commercials by students in schools subscribing to Channel One newscasts
• Telemarketing	Offers of fabulous prizes in return for credit-card purchases of touted goods[f]
DISTRIBUTION	
• Fraudulent sales	Phony markdowns based on "kited" retail list prices
• Bait-and-switch tactics	Luring consumers with ads for low-priced merchandise and switching them to higher-priced models
• Direct marketing	Deceptive, misleading product size and performance claims[g]
PACKAGING	
• Deceptive quantities	Some marketers use "packaging-to-price" tactics that mask a decrease in product quantity while maintaining the same price and traditional package size[h]

Adapted from:

[a]Frank A. Weil, "$540 on Saturday, $1560 on Monday," *The New York Times*, 26 March 1989.

[b]"Close Shaves Battling Blades," *Time*, 5 June 1989, 57.

[c]"Miller Beer Drops Ad After Protest," *The New York Times*, 12 March 1989.

[d]"An Uproar Over Billboards in Poor Areas," *The New York Times*, 1 May 1989, D10.

[e]"What Are Commercials Selling to Children?", *The New York Times*, 6 June 1988, C20.

[f]Janice Castro, "Reach Out and Rob Someone," *Time*, 3 April 1989, 38–39.

[g]"Self-Regulation Will Suppress Direct Marketing's Dark Side," *Marketing News*, 24 April 1989, B4.

[h]John B. Hinge, "Critics Call Cuts in Package Size Deceptive Move," *The Wall Street Journal*, 5 February 1991, B1.

table 1-2   Unethical Consumer Practices

- Shoplifting
- Switching price tags
- Returning clothing that has been worn
- Abusing products and returning them as damaged goods
- Redeeming coupons without the requisite purchase
- Redeeming coupons that have expired
- Returning clothing bought at full-price and demanding a refund for the sales price differential
- Returning products bought at sale and demanding the full-price refund
- Stealing belts from store clothing
- Cutting buttons off store merchandise
- Returning partially used products for full store credit
- Abusing warranty or unconditional guarantee privileges
- Damaging merchandise in a store and then demanding a sales discount
- Copying copyrighted materials (e.g., books, videotapes, or computer software) without permission

society), a behavior is considered ethical. Under this scenario, a company could "justify" concealing from construction workers the dangers involved in removing asbestos from a school building because of the resulting safety benefits to generations of schoolchildren. A number of Environmental Protection Agency decisions are currently being appealed by business people who have complained that the costs of compliance in selected instances are too high for the number of people who may be harmed by, for instance, hazardous wastes or polluted air. It is somewhat unclear how such business people evaluate the cost of a human life versus the costs of environmental compliance.

Ideally, a cost/benefit analysis should explore the human and financial, long- and short-range implications of a business decision. Responsible decisions require that all individuals who may be affected by the decision be correctly identified, and the consequences of the contemplated actions anticipated. It is especially important that ethical decision makers anticipate all negative consequences that may occur, and take actions to avert such outcomes.

Deontology deals with the methods and intentions involved in a particular behavior. Deontological theories focus on the results of a particular action, and they tend to place greater weight on personal and social values than on economic values.

Kant's *categorical imperative* is a deontological theory that suggests that individuals should be willing to have their actions become universal laws that would apply equally to themselves as to all others.[6] The reverse of the "golden rule," which most of us learned in grammar school, aptly expresses the notion of ethical behavior in marketing: *Do not do unto others what you would not have others do unto you (or your loved ones).* Clearly, this is a deontological theory, not a utilitarian theory. Of the two dominant traditions, deontology is favored by most moral philosophers today.[7]

How, then, can we ensure that marketers do practice the golden rule? That they incorporate a strong sense of social responsibility and ethical behavior in all decisions that impact upon consumers? Clearly, adulthood is a little late to start "learning" ethics. Value systems are developed early in life. When marketers have a strong sense of ethics and social responsibility, these values will prevail in all of their business dealings. For a small percentage of marketers, however, strong outside influences are needed to promote more ethical behavior. Similarly, for a small percentage of consumers, strong influences are needed to encourage ethical behavior in the marketplace.[8]

Ethics is clearly a two-way street. For the marketing process to work beneficially for all of society, marketers and consumers alike must understand and *practice* ethical behavior. Once again, the golden rule should prevail. The following section explores the influence of business school education, consumerism, and the corporate environment on ethics in the marketplace.

Business School Education

The Wall Street scandals that erupted in 1986 encouraged many schools of business to incorporate the study of ethics into their graduate curricula, sometimes as components of other courses, sometimes as separate courses. The insider trading disclosures shocked academicians and the general public alike because of the education and status of those involved. It had long been presumed that college students possessed strong internal ethical values developed in early childhood through family and religious training, and that it was unnecessary to reinforce those values in college or graduate school. Needless to say, this presumption was not universally valid. Furthermore, business school training traditionally placed heavy, if not total, emphasis on the bottom line. The achievement of profits and market share was the goal, and the means became secondary to the ends. And, according to utilitarian theory, if the benefits (i.e., dividends) to a large number of stockholders exceed the aggregate cost of injury suffered by consumers (or employees) as the result of a business decision, then the action could be justified as ethical.

The Wall Street scandals led the academic community to reevaluate their original assumptions. Although it generally is agreed that ethical values are internalized best through childhood socialization (see Chapter 12), it is clear that case studies involving ethical business decisions and classroom discussions of ethical issues reinforce earlier training, and make explicit some of the implicit values developed early in life. For example, case studies in global business ethics explore the differences between *cultural relativism* (which holds that no culture's ethical beliefs are superior to any other culture's ethical beliefs) and *moral absolutism* (which measures all moral issues against a rigid, universal yardstick, regardless of cultural differences.)[9] Under moral relativism, no nation has the right to impose its own ethical values on another nation. Under moral absolutism, moral values transcend national boundaries. The problem is: Which country's moral values should prevail? If China sees no problem with the piracy of intellectual work, why should they adhere to principles espoused by other nations? If the United States Food & Drug Administration rejects certain foods because of stringent health standards, should U.S. marketers ship these same foods to needy Third World countries with less rigorous health standards? For some students, classroom discussions such as these are true eye-openers, in that they raise issues that otherwise would receive little consideration. In some cases, classroom dissection of ethical issues results in *selective perception* (see Chapter 6) among young business executives; suddenly, they see the ethical dilemmas that certain business decisions pose, situations they would not have recognized without explicit discussion.

The Consumer Movement

In 1962, President John Kennedy declared that consumers had the rights to *safety,* to *be informed*, and to *be heard*. This **Consumers' Bill of Rights** (subsequently expanded to include the rights to *recourse* and *redress* and to a *physical environment that enhances the quality of life*) set the stage for a consumer movement that started around 1964, triggered by widespread consumer discontent with shoddy merchandise, inadequate warranties, arrogant marketers, and widespread abuses in the marketplace. The consumer movement tried to correct the imbalance that had developed between buyers and sellers. Consumers complained of poorly made, hazardous products. In response to consumer complaints, Congress enacted several major pieces of legislation designed to protect consumers (see Table 1-3 on page 16), and dozens more were enacted by state and local governments.

Ultimately, consumers express their approval or disapproval of a company's policies by their actions in the marketplace. In an effort to systematize such marketplace activity, some consumer groups have urged their members and other consumers to take concerted action against specific marketers in the form of **consumer boycotts**. The purpose of a *boycott*, defined as *the concerted refusal by a group of consumers to do business with one or more companies*, is to express disapproval of certain company policies and to attempt to coerce the target companies to modify those policies.[10] Under appropriate circumstances, consumer boycotts can be very effective. For example, a consumer boycott by animal rights advocates resulted in the gradual elimination of product testing on animals by cosmetic companies. For a boycott to be successful, the consumer group must accurately assess the commitment of the target company to the disputed policy, and its own ability to generate sufficient economic pressure and negative publicity to accomplish its objective effectively.

Ethics and the Corporate Environment

The corporate environment and corporate philosophy are crucial determinants of ethical behavior among an organization's employees. Many companies have developed explicit codes of ethics that set the tone for decision making throughout the organization. The New York Life Insurance Company, for example, distributes to its employees a *Statement of Purpose*, which includes the following: "We adhere to the highest ethical standards in all of our business dealings." Research shows that ethical practices by employees are very much a product of the corporate environment. Employee surveys suggest that those who engage in unethical practices often are coerced into doing so by their superiors.[11] A highly ethical environment, on the other hand—one that espouses a strong moral code—encourages ethical practices among its employees.

▲ **Ethics and Social Responsibility** A number of companies have incorporated specific social goals into their mission statements and include programs in support of these goals as integral components of their strategic planning. Research shows that marketers generally believe that ethics and social responsibility are important components of organizational effectiveness.[12]

Most companies recognize that socially responsible activities improve their image among consumers, stockholders, the financial community, and other relevant publics. They have found that ethical and socially responsible practices are simply good business, resulting in a favorable image and, ultimately, in increased sales. The converse is also true: Perceptions of a company's lack of social responsibility negatively affect consumer purchase decisions. Examples of company policies that influence consumer patronage include corporate environmental concerns, political activities, the company's reputation for fairness,

table 1-3 Some Consumer-Oriented Federal Laws

STATUTE	PURPOSE
National Traffic and Safety Act (1958)	Provides for the creation of compulsory safety standards for automobiles and tires.
Fair Packaging and Labeling Act (1966)	Provides for the regulation of the packaging and labeling of consumer goods. Requires manufacturers to state what the package contains, who made it, and how much it contains. Permits industries' voluntary adoption of uniform packaging standards.
Child Protection Act (1966)	Bans sale of hazardous toys and articles. Amended in 1969 to include articles that pose electrical, mechanical, or thermal hazards.
Federal Cigarette Labeling and Advertising Act (1967)	Requires that cigarette packages contain the statement "Warning: The Surgeon General Has Determined That Cigarette Smoking Is Dangerous to Your Health."
Truth-in-Lending Act (1968)	Requires lenders to state the true costs of a credit transaction, outlaws the use of actual or threatened violence in collecting loans, and restricts the amount of garnishments. Establishes a National Commission on Consumer Finance.
National Environmental Policy Act (1969)	Establishes a national policy on the environment and provides for the establishment of the Council on Environmental Quality. The Environmental Protection Agency was established in 1970 by Reorganization Plan No. 3.
Fair Credit Reporting Act (1970)	Ensures that a consumer's credit report contains only accurate, relevant, and recent information and remains confidential unless requested for an appropriate reason by a proper party.
Consumer Product Safety Act (1972)	Establishes the Consumer Product Safety Commission and authorizes it to set safety standards for consumer products and penalize failures to uphold the standards.
Consumer Goods Pricing Act (1975)	Prohibits the use of price maintenance agreements among manufacturers and resellers in interstate commerce.
Magnuson-Moss Warranty/FTC Improvement Act (1975)	Authorizes the FTC to determine rules concerning consumer warranties and provides for consumer redress, such as class action suits. Expands FTC regulatory powers over unfair or deceptive acts or practices.
Equal Credit Opportunity Act (1975)	Prohibits credit discrimination on the basis of sex, marital status, race, national origin, religion, age, or receipt of public assistance.
Fair Debt Collection Practice Act (1978)	Makes it illegal to harass or abuse any person and make false statements or use unfair methods when collecting a debt.
Toy Safety Act (1984)	Gives the government the power to recall dangerous toys quickly when they are found.
Nutritional Labeling and Education Act (1990)	Makes labeling mandatory for all processed foods and stipulates the type of nutritional information required.
Truth-in-Savings Act (1991)	Requires banks to furnish information on fees imposed and the annual percentage yield earned.

Source: Adapted in part from Philip Kotler, *Marketing Management: Analysis, Planning, Implementation, and Control*, 8th ed., © 1994. Reprinted by permission of Prentice Hall, Inc., Englewood Cliffs, New Jersey.

sexism, equality, and downsizing approaches.[13] For example, the consumer boycott of Exxon products following the Alaskan oil spill damage has been attributed to consumer perceptions that Exxon executives displayed little concern for the environment and showed a lack of social responsibility in their delayed reaction to this environmental disaster. Many trade associations have developed industry-wide codes of ethics, because they recognize that industry-wide self-regulation is in every member's best interests, in that it deters government from imposing its own regulations on the industry.

▲ **The Societal Marketing Concept** Given the fact that all companies prosper when society prospers, many people believe that all of us, companies as well as individuals, would be better off if social responsibility was an integral component of every marketing decision. Indeed, in an era of environmental deterioration, abject poverty, homelessness, drug addiction, AIDS, rampant crime, casual gun use, and countless other societal ills, the marketing concept as we know it—fulfilling the needs of target audiences—is sometimes inappropriate. This is particularly true in situations in which the means for need satisfaction—the product or service provided (e.g., drugs or prostitution)—can be harmful to the individual or to society.

A reassessment of the traditional marketing concept suggests that a more appropriate conceptualization for the times in which we live would balance the needs of society with the needs of the individual and the organization. The **societal marketing concept** requires that all marketers adhere to principles of social responsibility in the marketing of their goods and services; that is, they must endeavor to satisfy the needs and wants of their target markets in ways that preserve and enhance the well-being of consumers and society as a whole. Thus, a restructured definition of the marketing concept calls on marketers to *fulfill the needs of the target audience in ways that improve society as a whole, while fulfilling the objectives of the organization.*[14]

According to the societal marketing concept, fast-food restaurants would not sell hamburgers, or fries, or pies that are high in fat and starch and low in nutrients, despite strong consumer acceptance of these products. Nor would marketers advertise alcoholic beverages to young people, or use young models or professional athletes in liquor or tobacco advertisements, because they so often serve as role models for the young.

A serious deterrent to widespread implementation of the societal marketing concept is the short-term orientation embraced by most business managers in their drive for increased market share and quick profits. This short-term orientation is understandable in light of the fact that managerial performance usually is evaluated on the basis of short-term results. When personal advancement is based on short-term profits, marketing decisions tend to be based on anticipated short-term economic results.

The societal marketing concept necessarily requires a long-term perspective. It recognizes that all companies would be better off in a stronger, healthier society, and that companies that incorporate ethical behavior and social responsibility in all of their business dealings attract and maintain loyal consumer support over the long term.

PLAN OF THE BOOK

In an effort to build a useful conceptual framework that both enhances understanding and permits practical application of consumer behavior principles to marketing strategy, this book is divided into five parts: Introduction to the Study of Consumer Behavior, The Consumer as an Individual, Consumers in Their Social and Cultural Settings, The Consumer Decision-Making Process, and Consumer Behavior and Society. Chapter 2 examines the methodology of consumer research studies, including the assumptions underlying the various theoretical research approaches. Chapter 3 discusses the process of market segmentation, including the demographic, sociocultural, and psychographic bases for segmenting markets.

Part II focuses on the consumer as an individual. It discusses how individuals are motivated (Chapter 4), the impact of individual personality characteristics on consumer behavior (Chapter 5), the process and importance of perception (Chapter 6), learning (Chapter 7), and consumer attitudes (Chapters 8 and 9). This part concludes with an examination of the communications process as it influences consumer behavior (Chapter 10).

Part III focuses on consumers as members of society, subject to varying external influences on their buying behavior, such as their group memberships (Chapter 11), families (Chapter 12), social class (Chapter 13), and the broad cultural and specific subcultural groups to which they belong (Chapters 14 and 15). The importance of cross-cultural consumer research to international marketing is explored in Chapter 16.

Part IV examines the consumer decision-making process. It explores the impact of others on consumer choices (Chapter 17) and describes the process by which new products are adopted by consumers and diffused throughout the target population (Chapter 18). The various steps in the consumer decision-making process are examined in Chapter 19.

Part V focuses on broad issues of consumer behavior and society. Chapter 20 describes consumers behavior applications to specific profit and not-for-profit marketing sectors, and Chapter 21 concludes with a discussion of public policy issues and consumer research priorities.

summary

Our society is a study in diversity. We see diversity among consumers, among marketers, among customs, among nations, even among consumer behavior theoretical perspectives. However, despite prevailing diversity in our society, there also are many similarities. Segmenting target audiences on the basis of such similarities makes it possible for marketers to design marketing strategies with which consumers will identify.

The study of consumer behavior enables marketers to understand and predict consumer behavior in the marketplace; it also promotes understanding of the role that consumption plays in the lives of individuals.

Consumer behavior is defined as the behavior that consumers display in searching for, purchasing, using, evaluating, and disposing of products, services, and ideas that they expect will satisfy their needs. The study of consumer behavior is concerned not only with what consumers buy, but also with why they buy it, when and where and how they buy it, and how often they buy it. It is concerned with learning the specific meanings that products hold for consumers. Consumer research takes place at every phase of the consumption process: before the purchase, during the purchase, and after the purchase.

Consumer behavior is interdisciplinary; that is, it is based on concepts and theories about people that have been developed by scientists in such diverse disciplines as psychology, sociology, social psychology, cultural anthropology, and economics. Consumer research is the methodology used to study consumer behavior.

Consumer research designed to predict consumer behavior is called positivism; research designed to understand consumption behavior is called interpretivism. Rather than take a polar approach to the study of consumer behavior, this book explores both approaches, because it recognizes the dual importance of both understanding and prediction in making strategic marketing decisions.

Consumer behavior has become an integral part of strategic market planning. The belief that ethics and social responsibility should also be integral components of every marketing decision is embodied in a revised marketing concept—the societal marketing concept—which calls on marketers to fulfill the needs of their target markets in ways that improve society as a whole.

There is no universally accepted definition of the term ethics. Of the two major groups of ethical philosophies, however, deontological theories are favored over teleological theories by most moral philosophers today. Deontology places greater weight on personal and social values than on economic values. For marketers, deontology is best encapsulated in a revised golden rule: Do not do unto others what you would not have others do unto you.

Although ethics and morality are usually learned early in life, the explicit study of ethical issues within a business school curriculum serves to focus the attention of future marketers on moral issues and ethical behavior in the marketplace.

1. Describe the interrelationship between the consumer behavior discipline and the marketing concept.

2. Explain the difference(s) between personal and organizational consumers. Discuss the differences involved in marketing fax machines to personal consumers and to organizational consumers.

3. In the 1920s, Henry Ford remarked that his customers could have any color car they wanted, as long as it was black. Could the president of Ford Motor Company make the same statement today? In your answer, discuss the changes in marketing philosophy that have occurred since the 1920s.

4. How can the study of consumer behavior assist marketers in segmenting markets and positioning products?

5. Compare the positivist and interpretivist perspectives to the study and analysis of consumption behavior.

6. You are the brand manager of a new line of biodegradable diapers that includes separate versions for boys and girls. Describe how an understanding of consumer behavior is useful to you in terms of: (a) market segmentation strategy, (b) new product introduction, (c) product life-cycle strategy, and (d) societal issues.

7. Among animals, chimpanzees are man's closest genetic relative and are frequently used in medical research to test new drugs against AIDS. This process often involves infecting chimpanzees with the AIDS virus. Evaluate this practice in terms of the teleological and deontological ethical philosophies discussed in this chapter.

8. The upper-lower and lower-lower social classes together constitute more than half the United States population. Is it ethical for marketers and the mass media to promote products that most members of the lower classes cannot afford? Explain your answer.

9. A well-known electronics company is introducing a new smoke detector with a special feature that makes the alarm beep once a minute when the detector's batteries are weak and need to be replaced. Assume that the company discovers that in many detectors, the batteries can be too weak to properly operate the alarm for some time before the beep feature is activated. Should the manufacturer: (a) recall and redesign the smoke detector, (b) stop making the alarm without recall and inform current owners of the problem by mail, or (c) continue marketing the smoke detector while informing buyers of the need to change batteries regularly? How can an understanding of consumer behavior help the company select the most effective strategy to handle this situation?

10. Compare the marketing concept with the societal marketing concept. Do you think marketers should adopt the societal marketing concept? What arguments can you suggest against the practice of societal marketing? In which industries does the immediate adoption of the societal marketing concept appear to be necessary?

1. Select a product you bought that has features you never used. Which one of the business orientations discussed in the text may have guided the development of this product?

2. Select a product, brand, or service that you bought or used because it was particularly suitable for your needs. Would you say that the development of this product or service was guided by the marketing concept? If so, how?

3. Find an advertisement for a new product. Identify the psychological, sociological, and cultural factors that may influence consumers' decisions regarding the purchase of this product. In your opinion, will this product succeed or fail in the marketplace? Explain your answer.

4. Give an example of what you believe to be an unethical marketing practice. How can this practice be stopped through government regulation? Can the industry stop this practice? If so, how?

key words

- **Anthropology**
- **Consumer behavior**
- **Consumers' Bill of Rights**
- **Consumer boycotts**
- **Consumer diversity**
- **Consumerism**
- **Consumer-oriented legislation**
- **Consumer research**
- **Deontology**
- **Experientialism**
- **Interpretivism**
- **Market segmentation**
- **Marketing concept**
- **Marketing ethics**
- **Marketing myopia**
- **Organizational consumer**
- **Personal consumer**
- **Positioning**
- **Positivism**
- **Product orientation**
- **Production orientation**
- **Psychology**
- **Selling orientation**
- **Societal marketing concept**
- **Sociology**
- **Teleology**
- **Utilitarianism**

end notes

1. See, for example, JOHN F. SHERRY, JR. "Postmodern Alternatives: The Interpretive Turn in Consumer Research," in H. Kassarjian and T. Robertson, eds., *Handbook of Consumer Behavior* (Englewood Cliffs, NJ: Prentice Hall, 1991), 548–91.

2. See BOBBY CALDER and ALICE TYBOUT, "Interpretive, Qualitative and Traditional Scientific Empirical Consumer Behavior Research," in Elizabeth Hirschman, ed., *Interpretive Consumer Research* (Provo, UT: Association for Consumer Research, 1989), 199–208; MORRIS HOLBROOK and JOHN O'SHAUGHNESSY, "On the Scientific Status of Consumer Research and the Need for an Interpretive Approach to Studying Consumption Behavior," *Journal of Consumer Research* 15(3), September 1988, 398–402; and JULIE L. OZANNE and LAUREL A. HUDSON, "Exploring Diversity in Consumer Research," in Elizabeth Hirschman, ed., *Interpretive Consumer Research* (Provo, UT: Association for Consumer Research, 1989), 1–9.

3. RICHARD LUTZ, "Positivism, Naturalism and Pluralism in Consumer Research: Paradigms in Paradise," in Thomas Srull, ed., *Advances in Consumer Research* 16 (Provo, UT: Association for Consumer Research, 1989), 1–7; SHELBY HUNT, "Naturalistic, Humanistic and Interpretive Inquiry: Challenges and Ultimate Potential," in Elizabeth Hirschman, ed., *Interpretive Consumer Research* (Provo, UT: Association for Consumer Research, 1989), 185–98.

4. ELIZABETH COOPER-MARTIN and MORRIS B. HOLBROOK, "Ethical Consumption Experiences and Ethical Space," *Advances in Consumer Research* 20, 1993, 113–118.

5. See, for example, O. C. FERRELL, LARRY G. GRESHAM, and JOHN FRAEDRICH, "A Synthesis of Ethical Decision Models for Marketing," *Journal of Macromarketing* 11, Fall 1989, 55–64; MICHAEL A. MAYO and LAWRENCE J. MARKS, "An Empirical Investigation of a General Theory of Marketing Ethics," *Journal of the Academy of Marketing Science* 18, Spring 1990, 163–71; and SHELBY D. HUNT and SCOTT VITELL, "A General Theory of Marketing Ethics," *Journal of Macromarketing* 6, Spring 1986, 5–16.

6. IMMANUEL KANT, *Groundwork of the Metaphysics of Morals*, translated by H. J. Paton (New York: Harper & Row, 1964).

7. DONALD P. ROBIN and R. ERIC REIDENBACK, "Social Responsibility, Ethics, and Marketing Strategy: Closing the Gap Between Concept and Application," *Journal of Marketing* 51, January 1987, 44–53.

8. LAWRENCE J. MARKS and MICHAEL A. MAYO, "Modeling Consumer Ethical Dilemmas: A Preliminary Investigation," *AMA Conference Proceedings,* Bearden et al., eds., 1990, 121. See also DENA COX, ANTHONY D. COX, GEORGE P. MOSCHIS, "When Consumer Behavior Goes Bad: An Investigation of Adolescent Shoplifting," *Journal of Consumer Research* 17, September 1990, 149–59; JON BERRY, "The Fix and Patch Society," *Brandweek*, July 27, 1992, 23.

9. THOMAS DONALDSON, "Global Business Must Mind Its Morals," *The New York Times*, February 13, 1994, D1; also LAWRENCE B. CHONKO, *Ethical Decision Making in Marketing* (California: Sage Publications, 1995).

10. DENNIS E. GARRETT, "The Effectiveness of Marketing Policy Boycotts: Environmental Opposition to Marketing," *Journal of Marketing* 51, April 1987, 46–57; CALVIN SIMS, "The Politics of Dealing with the Threat of Boycott," *The New York Times*, March 14, 1993, 2E; ARTHUR S. HAYES and JOSEPH PEREIRA, "Facing a Boycott, Many Companies Bend," *The Wall Street Journal*, November 6, 1990, B1.

11. See, for example, GENE R. LACZNIAK and PATRICK E. MURPHY, *Marketing Ethics* (Lexington, MA: Lexington Books, 1985), 36.

12. A. SINGHAPAKDI, KENNETH L. KRAFT, SCOTT J. VITELL, and KUMAR C. RALLAPALLI, "The Perceived Importance of Ethics and Social Responsibility on Organizational Effectiveness: A Survey of Marketers," *Journal of the Academy of Marketing Science*, 23(1), 1995, 49–56.

13. KIM A. NELSON, "The Role of Cognitive Moral Development in Socially Responsible Consumer Choice," *American Marketing Association Proceedings* 14, Winter 1993, 165–71.

14. PHILIP KOTLER, *Marketing Management Analysis, Planning and Control*, 9th ed. (Englewood Cliffs, NJ: Prentice Hall, 1997).

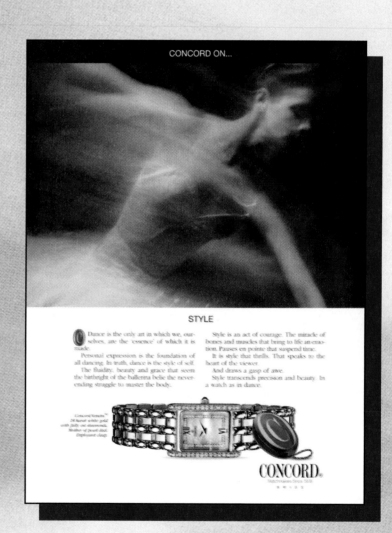

The marketing concept is built on the premise that marketers first identify consumer needs and then develop products and services to satisfy those needs. Consumer research offers a set of diverse methods to identify such needs. Consumer research also is used to better understand consumption behavior. It is used to identify and locate appropriate target markets and to learn the targets' media habits. It is used to identify both felt and unfelt (latent) needs, to learn how consumers perceive products and brands and stores, what their attitudes are before and after promotional campaigns, and how and why they make their consumption decisions. Many of these applications of consumer research are managerial in perspective: they are designed to help a marketer make specific marketing decisions concerning product, price, promotion, and distribution.

The product of the scientific imagination is a new vision of relations—like that of the artistic imagination.

—Edmund Wilson
in a letter to Allen Tate,
July 20, 1931, quoted in
Letters on Literature and Politics, 1912–1972, 1977

Consumer research provides the basis for the development of new product and service concepts to meet targeted consumer needs. It also enables the marketer to build consumer "meaning" into the product or service by discovering which attributes are most important to the target market and integrating them into the product or service design.

History of Consumer Research

The field of consumer research developed as an extension of the field of marketing research, focusing almost exclusively on consumer behavior rather than on other aspects of the marketing process. Just as the findings of marketing research were used to improve managerial decision making, so too were the findings of consumer research. The initial reason for studying consumer behavior was to enable marketers to *predict* how consumers would react to promotional messages, and to understand *why* they made the purchase decisions they did. Marketers assumed that if they knew everything there was to know about the consumer decision-making process, they could design marketing strategies and promotional messages that would influence the consumer in the desired way (i.e., to purchase the marketer's product or service). In the belief that marketing was simply applied economics, the *economic man* theory prevailed—the assumption that consumers are rational decision makers who objectively evaluate the goods and services available to them and select only those that give them the highest utility (satisfaction) at the lowest cost.

The Modernist Era

The era in which the field of consumer research developed is known as the **modernist era**.[1] Researchers who endorse the assumptions upon which modernism is based are called **positivists**. (Other terms used to describe the positivist research paradigm include *logical positivism, logical empiricism, operationalism,* and *objectivism*.)[2]

The research methods used in positivist research are borrowed primarily from the natural sciences and consist of experiments, survey techniques, and observation. The findings are descriptive, empirical, and if collected randomly, can be generalized to larger populations. The data collected are *quantitative* in nature and lend themselves to sophisticated statistical analysis.

The Development of Motivational Research Despite their assumptions that consumers were logical problem solvers who engaged in careful thought processes (i.e., information processing) to arrive at their consumption decisions, researchers soon realized that consumers were not always consciously aware of why they made the decisions they did. Even when they were aware of their basic motivations, consumers were not always willing to reveal these reasons.

As early as 1939, a Viennese psychoanalyst named Ernest Dichter began to use Freudian psychoanalytic techniques to uncover the hidden motivations of consumers. By the late 1950s, his research methodology, which has come to be known as **motivational research**, was widely adopted by marketers and advertising agencies. Motivational research methods consist of projective techniques and depth interviews (discussed later in the chapter). Motivational research requires highly trained interviewer-analysts to collect data and to analyze research findings. Because sample sizes are necessarily small, findings cannot be generalized to larger populations. Motivational research findings are highly subjective, because they are based on analyst interpretation. Used primarily to obtain new ideas for promotional campaigns, motivational research is considered to be *qualitative* research. (Chapter 4 discusses the uses and limitations of motivational research in greater detail.)

▲ **Combining Quantitative and Qualitative Research for Strategic Marketing Decisions** Aware of the limitations of motivational research findings, some marketers use a combination of quantitative and qualitative research to help make strategic marketing decisions. They use qualitative research findings to discover new ideas and consumer insights, and quantitative research findings to predict consumer actions based on various promotional inputs. Sometimes ideas stemming from qualitative research are tested empirically (i.e., they become the basis for the design of quantitative studies).

Postmodernism

A number of academicians from the field of consumer behavior, as well as from other social science disciplines from which the consumer behavior field developed, have become more interested in the act of *consumption* than in the act of *buying* (i.e., decision making). They view consumer behavior as a subset of human behavior, and increased understanding as a key to reducing some of the ills associated with consumer behavior (the so-called "dark side" of consumer behavior), such as drug addiction, shoplifting, alcoholism, and compulsive buying behavior. Interest in consumer *experiences* has led to the term **experientialism**, and the researchers who adopt this paradigm are known as *experientialists, postmodernists,* or *interpretivists.*[3] (Other terms used to describe this approach to consumer behavior include *naturalism, humanism,* and *postpositivism.*)[4]

▲ **Interpretivist Research** Interpretivists engage in qualitative research. Among the research methodologies they use are ethnography, semiotics, and depth interviews. *Ethnography* is a technique borrowed from cultural anthropology, in which the researchers place themselves in the society under study in an effort to absorb the meaning of various cultural practices. Ethnography lends itself easily to the study of all kinds of consumer behavior, including how individuals buy products and services.[5] (For example, in shopping for a car, do consumers kick the tires, or look under the hood? Do they bring the family with them?) Ethnography has been used in interpretivist studies to discover the meanings of objects accumulated by the homeless. Interpretivists are also very interested in *semiotics*—the study of symbols and the meanings they convey.[6] Consumer researchers use semiotics to discover the meanings of various consumption behaviors and rituals. It is important to understand the meanings that nonverbal symbols may hold for the target audience to be certain that the symbols enhance, rather than inhibit, the persuasiveness of the message. The illustration in Figure 2-1 on page 26 symbolizes—and thus underscores—the gracefulness of the watch that the marketer wishes to convey. *Depth interviews* are an important part of the interpretivist research process. However, interpretive research findings are often unique to the specific researcher/consumer interaction, because sometimes the researcher plays an active role in the interview process. Both interpretive research and positivist research are often used to help make business decisions. Table 2-1 on page 26 compares the purposes and assumptions of positivist research and interpretivist research.

Combining Positivist and Interpretivist Research Findings

Marketers have discovered that rather than conflicting, these two research paradigms—*positivism* and *interpretivism*—are really complementary in nature. The *prediction* made possible by positivist research and the insightful *understanding* provided by interpretivist

FIGURE 2-1

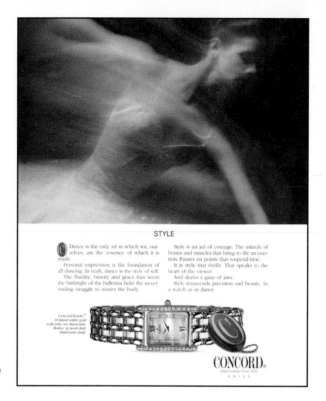

Nonverbal Symbolism
Enhances the Message
Courtesy of Concord Watch

table 2-1   Comparisons between Positivism and Interpretivism

PURPOSE	
Positivism	Prediction of consumer actions
Interpretivism	Understanding consumption practices
METHODOLOGY	
Positivism	Quantitative
Interpretivism	Qualitative
ASSUMPTIONS	
Positivism	• Rationality: consumers make decisions after weighing alternatives • The causes and effects of behavior can be identified and isolated • Individuals are problem solvers who engage in information processing • A single reality exists • Events can be objectively measured • Causes of behavior can be identified; by manipulating causes (i.e., inputs), the marketer can influence behavior (i.e., outcomes) • Findings can be generalized to larger populations
Interpretivism	• There is no single, objective, truth • Reality is subjective • Cause and effect cannot be isolated • Each consumption experience is unique • Researcher/respondent interactions affect research findings • Findings are often not generalized to larger populations

research together produce a richer and more robust profile of consumer behavior, and enable the marketer to design more meaningful and effective marketing strategies. Furthermore, positivist and interpretivist research findings, used together, provide a firmer basis for nonprofit marketing strategies and for public policy decisions, than either research approach used alone.[7]

THE CONSUMER RESEARCH PROCESS

The major steps in the consumer research process include (1) defining the objectives of the research, (2) collecting and evaluating secondary data, (3) designing a primary research study (unless the secondary data provide sufficient information to meet the study objectives), (4) collecting primary data, (5) analyzing the data, and (6) preparing a report on the findings. Figure 2-2 depicts a model of the consumer research process.

Developing Research Objectives

The first step in the consumer research process is to define carefully the objectives of the study. Is it to segment the market for wide-screen television? To find out consumer attitudes about cellular phones? To determine what percentage of men use cologne? It is important for the marketing manager and the researcher to agree at the outset on the purposes and ob-

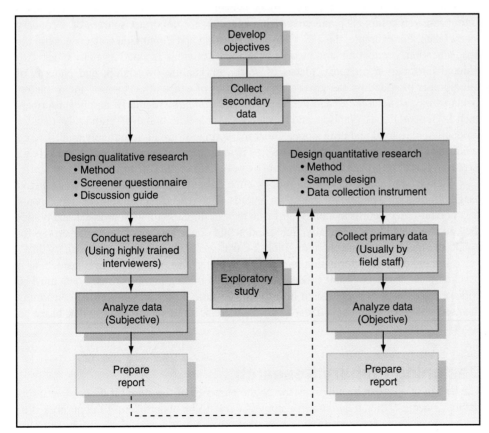

FIGURE 2-2

The Consumer Research Process

jectives of the study to ensure that the research design is appropriate. A carefully thought-out statement of objectives helps to define the type and level of information needed.

For example, if the purpose of the study is to come up with new ideas for products or promotional campaigns, then a *qualitative* study is usually undertaken, in which respondents spend a significant amount of time face-to-face with a highly trained professional moderator who also does the analysis. Because of the high costs of each interview, a fairly small sample of respondents is studied; thus, the findings are not projectable to the marketplace. If the purpose of the study is to find out how many people in the population (i.e., what percentage) use certain products and how frequently they use them, then a *quantitative* study that can be computer-analyzed is undertaken. Sometimes, in designing a quantitative study, the researcher may not know what questions to ask. In such cases, before undertaking a full-scale study, the researcher is likely to conduct a small-scale *exploratory* study to identify the critical issues to include in the data collection instrument (e.g., questionnaire).

Collecting Secondary Data

A search for *secondary information* generally follows the statement of objectives. Secondary information is any data originally generated for some purpose other than the present research objectives. It includes findings based on research done by outside organizations as well as data generated in-house for earlier studies, or even customer information collected by the firm's sales or credit departments. Locating secondary data is called *secondary research.* (Original research performed by individual researchers or organizations to meet specific objectives is called *primary research.*)

Secondary research sometimes provides sufficient insight into the problem at hand to eliminate the need for primary research. Most often, it provides clues and direction for the design of primary research. Government agencies, private population data firms, marketing research companies, and advertising agencies are important sources of secondary market data. For example, the U.S. Census of Housing and Population collects data on the age, education, occupation, and income of residents of areas as small as a city block. Additional information on rents, places of work, automobile ownership, and patterns of migration is provided by the government in studies of census tracts within major metropolitan areas. *Behaviorscan* and the *A. C. Nielsen Company* regularly supply subscribers such as General Foods, Nabisco, and Procter & Gamble with brand-by-brand sales data for products sold in food and drug stores. Other marketing information routinely published by syndicated market research firms shows key demographic changes by census tracts (e.g., *Census Update*) or breaks down such data by postal zip codes (*ZIProfile*).

Retailers and nonprofit organizations often have directly relevant demographic and usage information available in their own records. They can use credit and charge account data or mail-order records to identify just who their customers are, what products and brands they purchase, and how frequently. Subscription and donor lists serve the same purpose for nonprofit organizations and charities. Table 2-2 lists some major sources of secondary data.

If more detailed information on purchasing patterns or product usage is needed, or if psychological or sociocultural consumer information is sought, then primary data must be collected. Research to secure such information is more costly and more time-consuming than secondary research but is likely to yield a more accurate picture than studies based on secondary data alone.

Designing Primary Research

The design of a research study is based on the purposes of the study: if descriptive information is needed, then a *quantitative* study is likely to be undertaken; if the purpose is to get new ideas (e.g., for repositioning a product), then a *qualitative* study may be in order.

table 2-2   Major Sources of Secondary Data

INTERNAL SOURCES	Internal sources include company profit-loss statements, balance sheets, sales figures, sales-call reports, invoices, inventory records, and prior research reports.
GOVERNMENT PUBLICATIONS	*Statistical Abstract of the U.S.*, updated annually, provides summary data on demographic, economic, social, and other aspects of the American economy and society.
	County and City Data Book, updated every three years, presents statistical information for counties, cities, and other geographical units on population, education, employment, aggregate and median income, housing, bank deposits, retail sales, etc.
	U.S. Industrial Outlook provides projections of industrial activity by industry and includes data on production, sales, shipments, employment, etc.
	Marketing Information Guide provides a monthly annotated bibliography of marketing information.
	Other government publications include the *Annual Survey of Manufacturers; Business Statistics; Census of Manufacturers; Census of Population; Census of Retail Trade, Wholesale Trade, and Selected Service Industries; Census of Transportation; Federal Reserve Bulletin; Monthly Labor Review; Survey of Current Business;* and *Vital Statistics Report.*
PERIODICALS AND BOOKS	*Business Periodicals Index*, a monthly, lists business articles appearing in a wide variety of business publications.
	Standard and Poor's Industry Surveys provides updated statistics and analyses of industries.
	Moody's Manuals provide financial data and names of executives in major companies.
	Encyclopedia of Associations provides information on every major trade and professional association in the United States.
	Marketing journals include the *Journal of Marketing, Journal of Marketing Research,* and *Journal of Consumer Research.*
	Useful trade magazines include *Advertising Age, Chain Store Age, Progressive Grocer, Sales and Marketing Management,* and *Stores.*
	Useful general business magazines include *Business Week, Fortune, Forbes,* and *Harvard Business Review.*
COMMERCIAL DATA	A. C. Nielsen Company provides data on products and brands sold through retail outlets (Retail Index Services), data on television audiences (Media Research Services), magazine circulation data (Neodata Services, Inc.), etc.
	Market Research Corporation of America provides data on weekly family purchases of consumer products (National Consumer Panel), data on home food consumption (National Menu Census), and data on 6000 retail, drug, and discount retailers in various geographical areas (Metro Trade Audits).
	Selling Areas-Marketing, Inc., provides reports on warehouse withdrawals to food stores in selected market areas (SAMI reports).
	Simmons Market Research Bureau provides annual reports covering television markets, sporting goods, proprietary drugs, etc., giving demographic data by sex, income, age, and brand preferences (selective markets and media reaching them).
	Burke Marketing Services, Inc., provides TV campaign testing in controlled marketing labs, marketing modeling, retail store audits, physiological measures of advertising stimuli, pre- and post-TV copy testing, and custom survey research.
	Markets Facts, Inc. provides consumer mail panel, market test-store audit services, shopping mall facilities, WATS telephone interviewing, and ad hoc survey research.
	Other commercial research houses selling data to subscribers include the Audit Bureau of Circulation, Audits and Surveys, Dun and Bradstreet, Opinion Research, Roper-Starch, and Arbitron.

Source: Adapted from Philip Kotler, *Marketing Management: Analysis, Planning, and Control*, 9th ed. (Englewood Cliffs, NJ: Prentice Hall, 1997)

Because the approach for each type of research differs in terms of method of data collection, sample design, and type of data collection instrument used, each research approach is discussed separately below.

▲ **Qualitative Research Designs** In selecting the appropriate research format for a qualitative study, the researcher takes into consideration the purpose of the study and the type of data needed. The choice of data collection techniques for qualitative studies includes depth interviews, focus groups, and projective techniques.

Although these research methods may differ in composition, they all have roots in psychoanalytic and clinical aspects of psychology, and they stress open-ended and free-response types of questions to stimulate respondents to reveal their innermost thoughts and beliefs.

These techniques are regularly used in the early stages of attitude research to pinpoint relevant product-related beliefs or attributes and to develop an initial picture of consumer attitudes (especially the beliefs and attributes that they associate with particular products and services).

DEPTH INTERVIEWS A *depth interview* is a lengthy (generally 30 minutes to an hour), nonstructured interview between a respondent and a highly trained interviewer, who minimizes his or her own participation in the discussion after establishing the general subject to be discussed.[8] (However, interpretative researchers often take a more active role in the discussion.) Respondents are encouraged to talk freely about their activities, attitudes, and interests, in addition to the product category or brand under study. Transcripts, videotapes, or audiotape recordings of interviews are then carefully studied, together with reports of respondents' moods and any gestures or "body language" that they might have used to convey attitudes or motives. Such studies provide marketers with valuable ideas about product design or redesign and provide insights for positioning or repositioning the product. For purposes of copytesting, respondents might be asked to describe in depth various ads that they are shown.

New techniques for probing consumers and new methods of interpretation are always being tried to improve the results of qualitative research. For example, a new technique called *autodriving* involves exposing respondents to photographs, videos, and audiorecordings of their own behavior, thus giving them the opportunity to explicitly comment on their consumption actions, thereby enriching the interpretation of qualitative data.[9]

FOCUS GROUPS A *focus group* consists of eight to ten respondents who meet with a moderator/analyst for a group discussion "focused" on a particular product or product category (or any other subject of research interest). Respondents are encouraged to discuss their interests, attitudes, reactions, motives, lifestyles, feelings about the product or product category, usage experience, and so forth. Because a focus group takes about two hours to complete, a researcher can easily conduct two or three focus groups (with a total of thirty respondents) in one day, while it might take that same researcher five or six days to conduct thirty individual depth interviews. Analysis of responses in both depth interviews and focus groups requires a great deal of skill on the part of the researcher. A multinational study of focus group moderators found that the moderators themselves—as well as the objectives of the research—play important roles in the interpretation of focus group research, and that these effects do not differ by country.[10]

Focus group sessions are invariably taped, and sometimes videotaped, to assist in the analysis. Interviews are usually held in specially designed conference rooms with one-way mirrors that allow marketers and advertising agency staff to observe the sessions without disrupting or inhibiting the responses. Respondents are recruited on the basis of a carefully drawn consumer profile (called a *screener questionnaire*) based on specifications defined by marketing management, and usually are paid a fee for their participation. Sometimes users of the company's brands are interviewed in one or more groups, and their responses are compared to those of nonusers interviewed in other groups.

Some focus groups take the form of *collage focus research*, in which the participants are given scissors, paste, paper, and magazines, and asked to make a collage representing themselves, as well as their relationship with the product category under study. Collage research findings inspired the marketers of the Cadillac Eldorado to take a more "emotional" approach in its advertising, replacing previous campaigns that stressed luxury and specific vehicle features.[11]

Some marketers prefer individual depth interviews because they feel that respondents are free of group pressure, are less likely to give socially acceptable (and not necessarily truthful) responses, are more likely to remain attentive during the entire interview, and—because of the greater personal attention received—are more likely to reveal private thoughts. Other marketers prefer focus groups because it takes them less time overall to complete the study, and they feel that the free-wheeling group discussions and group dynamics tend to yield a greater number of new ideas and insights.

Figure 2-3 presents a portion of a discussion guide that might be used in a focus-group session to gain insights into the attitudes of brokerage customers toward various brokerage firms and a proposed new investment service.

PROJECTIVE TECHNIQUES *Projective techniques* are designed to tap the underlying motives of individuals despite their unconscious rationalizations or efforts at conscious concealment. They consist of a variety of disguised tests that contain ambiguous stimuli, such as incomplete sentences, untitled pictures or cartoons, ink blots, word-association tests, and other-person characterizations. Figures 2-4 and 2-5 on pages 32 and 33 present examples of projective techniques used in consumer research. The respondent is asked to complete, describe, or explain the meaning of various stimuli. The theory behind projective tests is that respondents' inner feelings influence how they perceive ambiguous stimuli. The stories they tell or the sentences they complete are actually projections of their

---

FIGURE 2-3

Selected Portions of a Discussion Guide

PERSONAL FINANCIAL SERVICES STUDY

I. INTRODUCTION

    A. What do you like and dislike about the various financial services that you have accounts with? Which is your primary brokerage house? Why?

    B. What would it take to get you to change brokers?

    C. List the services and accounts that a "perfect" or "ideal" brokerage house would provide you.

              •
              •
              •

V. REACTIONS TO THE PROPOSED BROKERAGE SERVICE

    A. Does anything need clarification?

    B. What is your overall reaction?

    C. What do you specifically like or dislike about this service?

    D. What improvements/modifications would make it better?

    E. When and how often would you use it?

    F. Which brokerage houses in this area would be most likely to offer this service? Why?

    G. Would it encourage you to switch brokerage houses? Why/why not?

VI. OTHER SECTIONS OF THE GUIDE
          •
          •
          •

FIGURE 2-4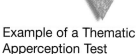

Example of a Thematic
Apperception Test

inner thoughts, even though subjects may attribute their responses to something or some-one else. Thus, their responses are likely to reveal their underlying needs, wants, fears, as-pirations, and motives, whether or not the respondents are fully aware of them. For example, if a subject looks at a picture of a mature woman speaking to a teenager (see Fig-ure 2-4 again) and describes her as lecturing or scolding the girl, the analyst may infer that the subject is resentful of parental or adult control.

The basic assumption underlying projective techniques is that respondents are un-aware that they are exposing their own feelings. This is sometimes illustrated by the old joke about a researcher who shows his subject a series of geometric figures and asks him to describe what he sees. In each case, the subject reports seeing a highly erotic scene. When the researcher comments that the subject has an obvious sexual fixation, the subject retorts: "It's not *my* fixation; after all, it's *you* who's showing me the dirty pictures."

▲ **Quantitative Research Designs** The design of a quantitative research study includes the method for collecting the data, the sample design, and construction of the data collec-tion instrument.

DATA COLLECTION METHODS There are three basic ways to collect primary data in quantitative research: by observing behavior, by experimentation (in a laboratory or in the field, e.g., a supermarket), or by survey (that is, by questioning people).

Observational Research Observational research is an important method of con-sumer research, because marketers recognize that the best way to gain an in-depth under-standing of the relationship between people and products is by watching them in the process of buying and using products. Many large corporations and advertising agencies use cultural anthropologists to observe and often videotape consumers in stores, malls, and their own homes (i.e., to engage in *ethnographic* research). By watching people, observa-tional researchers gain a better understanding of what a product symbolizes to a consumer and greater insight into the bond between people and products that is the essence of brand loyalty. Observational research also provides valuable input into product advertising. For example, when observational research showed that many customers saw cars as art ob-jects, Toyota worked that theme into early ads for its Lexus automobile. Observational re-search is widely used by interpretivist researchers to understand the buying and consumption process.

Experimentation It is possible to test the relative sales appeal of many types of variables—such as package designs, prices, promotional offers, or copy themes—through experiments designed to identify cause and effect. In such experiments (called **causal**

WORD ASSOCIATION

Respondents are presented with a series of words or phrases and are asked to answer quickly with the first word that comes to mind after hearing each stimulus word.

Application: AT&T used this approach to choose the name for long-distance direct dialing from among several alternatives. Respondents interpreted the name "Nationwide Dialing" as "worldwide" dialing. The name "Custom Toll Dialing" was associated with "money," "charges," and the cost of a long-distance phone call. The name "Direct Distance Dialing" was chosen by AT&T because it communicated to respondents the notion of long-distance dialing without operator assistance and had no unfavorable associations.[a]

SENTENCE COMPLETION

The beginning of a sentence is read to the respondent, who is asked to complete it with the first thought that comes to mind.

Application: In an effort to create more effective advertising, a study was conducted to probe the motivation for buying cars. The results indicated that men and women view automobiles differently. When women were asked to complete the sentence, "When you first get a car,...," their responses were in the direction of "You can't wait till you drive" and "You would go for a ride." Men's responses to the same sentence stem were in the direction of "You take good care of it," "Check the engine," and "Polish it." These results indicate that for women a car is something to use, whereas men view a car as something for which they should be protective and responsible.[b]

THE THIRD-PERSON TECHNIQUE

Respondents are asked to describe a third person about whom they are given some information.

Application: When instant coffee was introduced in 1950, a study was conducted to identify the symbolic meaning of the new product. Two groups of homemaker respondents were each given a shopping list that was identical except for the type of coffee listed. The first group's shopping list included instant coffee; the other group's list included drip grind coffee. Respondents were asked to describe the woman whose shopping list they saw, and the differences in their descriptions were attributed to the only experimental variable: the type of coffee listed. Homemakers perceived women who used instant coffee as lazy housekeepers and poor wives, and users of regular grind coffee as thrifty and good wives. In 1950, this research suggested that convenience foods evoked a feeling of guilt and skepticism. However, a 1970 replication of this study indicated that the stigma associated with instant coffee had disappeared; this was attributed to the general acceptance of instant coffee and convenience foods that had taken place since the original study was conducted.[c]

THEMATIC APPERCEPTION TEST

Respondents are asked to interpret one or more pictures or cartoons relating to the product or topic under study.

Application: A study was designed to measure the price/quality perception of women regarding cosmetics. One-half of the respondents were shown a cartoon of a woman buying a 49-cent beauty cream; the other half were presented with a picture of a woman buying a $5 beauty cream. Both groups were asked to describe the beauty cream. The 49-cent product was perceived as "greasy and oily" and bought by someone who "falls for advertising claims and doesn't have too much money to spend on cosmetics." The $5 cream was viewed as leaving the skin "clear, refreshed and young-looking," "softening and cleansing the skin," and purchased by "someone who cares what she looks like—possibly a business woman." The results demonstrate that women consider more expensive cosmetics to be of higher quality.[d]

[a] Paul E. Green and Donald S. Tull, *Research for Marketing Decisions*, 3rd ed. (Englewood Cliffs, NJ: Prentice-Hall), 1975, pp. 141-43.
[b] J. W. Newman, *Motivation Research and Marketing Management* (Cambridge, Mass.: Harvard University Graduate School of Administration), 1957, pp. 227-28.
[c] Mason Haire, "Projective Techniques in Marketing Research," *Journal of Marketing* 14, April 1950, pp. 649-50; and Frederick E. Jr., and Frederick Von Pechmann, "A Replication of the 'Shopping List' Study," *Journal of Marketing* 34, April 1970, pp. 61-63.
[d] Green and Tull, *op.cit.*

FIGURE 2-5

Examples of Projective Techniques

research), only one variable is manipulated at a time (the *independent variable*), while all other elements are kept constant. A controlled experiment of this type ensures that any difference in results (the *dependent variable*) is due to different treatments of the variable under study and not to extraneous factors. For example, if a marketer wanted to test the sales appeal of three different-colored packages, he or she might select three supermarkets (or groups of supermarkets) matched in terms of size, appearance, and type of neighborhood and place a display of green packages in one, blue packages in the second, and red packages in the third. In each instance, the design of the package is held constant. If one store sells significantly more units of the product than the others during a specific time frame, the researcher could conclude that the difference in sales was due solely to the specific color of the package, because all other factors (such as price, type of customer, type of promotional appeal) were kept constant. Experiments could also be conducted in a laboratory with the use of special instrumentation, such as eye cameras that study the eye movement of subjects as they view competitive advertisements. For complex situations, researchers use computer-generated research designs.[12]

Surveys If researchers wish to ask consumers about their purchase preferences, they can do so in person, by mail, or by telephone. Each of these survey methods has certain advantages and certain disadvantages that the researcher must weigh in selecting the method of contact (see Table 2-3).

Personal interview surveys most often take place in the home or in retail shopping areas. The latter, referred to as *mall intercepts,* have become much more frequent of late because of the high incidence of not-at-home working women and, among those who do not work, because of fears of allowing a stranger into the home.

Telephone surveys are often used to collect consumer data, although the high incidence of working women has limited their use. Evenings and weekends are often the only times to reach the working homemaker, who tends to be less responsive to calls that interrupt dinner, television viewing, or general relaxation. The difficulties of reaching people who have unlisted telephone numbers have been solved through random-digit dialing, and the costs of a widespread telephone survey are often reduced by using toll-free telephone lines. Other problems arise, however, from the increased use of answering machines to screen calls, especially among the young affluent market segment.

Mail surveys are conducted by sending questionnaires directly to individuals at their home. A number of commercial research firms that specialize in consumer surveys have

table 2-3   Comparative Advantages of Mail, Telephone, and Personal Interview Surveys

	MAIL	TELEPHONE	PERSONAL INTERVIEW
Cost	Low	Moderate	High
Speed	Slow	Immediate	Slow
Response rate	Low	Moderate	High
Geographic flexibility	Excellent	Good	Difficult
Interviewer bias	N/A	Moderate	Problematic
Interviewer supervision	N/A	Easy	Difficult
Quality of response	Limited	Limited	Excellent

set up "panels" of consumers who, for a token fee, agree to complete the research company's mail questionnaires on a regular basis. Sometimes panel members are also asked to keep diaries of their purchases.

DATA COLLECTION INSTRUMENTS For quantitative research, the primary data collection instrument is the *questionnaire,* which can be sent through the mail to selected respondents for self-administration, or can be administered by a trained interviewer in person or by telephone.

Consumers are often reluctant to take the time to respond to surveys. For this reason, researchers have found that questionnaires must be interesting, objective, unambiguous, easy to complete, and generally not burdensome to motivate respondents to answer truthfully and completely. To enhance the analysis and facilitate the classification of responses into meaningful categories, questionnaires include both questions that are relevant to the purposes of the study as well as pertinent demographic questions. To ensure validity, questionnaires are pretested and "debugged" before widespread distribution. The format of the questionnaire, and the wording and sequence of the questions, affect the validity of the responses and, in the case of mail questionnaires, the number (rate) of responses received.

The questionnaire itself can be *disguised* or *undisguised* as to its true purpose; a disguised questionnaire sometimes yields more truthful answers and avoids responses that respondents may think are expected or sought. Questions can be *open-ended* (requiring answers in the respondent's own words) or *closed-ended* (the respondent merely checks the appropriate answer from a list of options). Open-ended questions yield more insightful information but are more difficult to code and analyze; closed-ended questions are relatively simple to tabulate and analyze, but the answers are limited to the alternative responses provided (i.e., to the existing insights of the questionnaire designer). Great care must be taken in wording each question to avoid biasing the responses. The sequence of questions is also important: the opening questions must be interesting enough to "draw" the respondent into participating, they must proceed in a logical order, and classification questions should be placed at the end, where they are more likely to be answered. Questionnaires usually offer respondents confidentiality or anonymity to dispel any reluctance about self-disclosure.

Sometimes, instead of a list of questions, the data collection instrument presents a series of statements for which respondents are asked to indicate their degree of agreement or disagreement; these are often called **inventories**. Researchers sometimes present respondents with a list of products or product attributes for which they are asked to indicate their relative feelings or evaluations. The instruments most frequently used to capture this evaluative data are called **attitude scales**; they include Likert scales, semantic differential scales, and rank-order scales.

The **Likert scale** is by far the most popular form of attitude scale because it is easy for researchers to prepare and to interpret, and simple for consumers to answer. They check or write the number corresponding to their level of "agreement" or "disagreement" with each of a series of statements that describe the attitude-object under investigation. Figure 2-6 on page 36 presents an example of a five-point Likert scale. Note that the scale consists of an equal number of agreement/disagreement choices on either side of a neutral choice. A principal benefit of the Likert scale is that it gives the researcher the option of considering the responses to each statement separately, or of combining the responses to produce an overall, summated score. Because of this property, the Likert scale is often called a *summated* scale.

Like the Likert scale, the **semantic differential scale** is relatively easy to construct and administer. The scale typically consists of a series of bipolar adjectives (such as good/bad, hot/cold, like/dislike, expensive/inexpensive) that are anchored at the ends of an odd-numbered (e.g., five- or seven-point) continuum. Respondents are asked to evaluate a concept (or a product or company) on the basis of each attribute by checking the point on the continuum that best reflects their feelings or beliefs. Sometimes an even-numbered

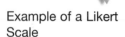
Instructions:

Please place the number which best indicates how strongly you agree or disagree with each of the following statements about shopping at flea markets in the space to the left of the statement.

1. Agree Strongly
2. Agree
3. Neither Agree nor Disagree
4. Disagree
5. Disagree Strongly

_____ a. It is fun to shop at a flea market.

_____ b. Products often cost more than they are worth.

_____ c. It is a good place to meet friends and neighbors.

_____ d. Many of the sellers are rude and aggressive.

_____ e. There is no waiting for delivery.

_____ f. Most flea markets are difficult to reach.

_____ g. There are no taxes to be paid.

scale is used to eliminate the option of a neutral answer. An important feature of the semantic differential is that it can be used to develop graphic consumer profiles of the concept under study. Figure 2-7 depicts semantic differential profiles of three retail stores. Semantic differential profiles are also used to compare consumer perceptions of competitive products, and to indicate areas for product improvement when perceptions of the existing product are measured against perceptions of the "ideal" product.

With **rank-order scales,** subjects are asked to rank items such as products (or retail stores or companies) in order of preference in terms of some criterion, such as overall quality or value for the money. Rank-order scaling procedures provide important competitive information and enable marketers to identify needed areas of improvement in product design or product positioning. Figure 2-8 illustrates how rank-order scales can be utilized in consumer research.

SAMPLING An integral component of a research design is the sampling plan. Specifically, it addresses three questions: whom to survey (the sampling *unit*), how many to survey (the sample *size*), and how to select them (the sampling *procedure*).

Deciding *whom to survey* requires that the *universe* or boundaries of the market from which data is sought be defined so that an appropriate sample can be selected (e.g., working mothers). Interviewing the correct target market or potential target market is basic to the validity of the study.

The *size of the sample* is dependent both on the size of the budget and the degree of confidence that the marketer wants to place in the findings. The larger the sample, the more likely the responses will reflect the total universe under study. It is interesting to note, however, that a small sample can often provide highly reliable findings, depending on the sampling procedure adopted. (The exact number needed to achieve a specific level of confidence in the accuracy of the findings can be computed with a mathematical formula that is beyond the scope of this discussion.)

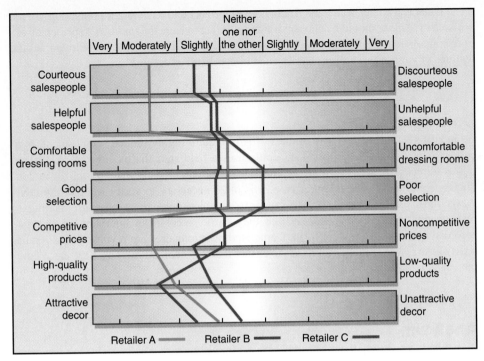

Neither
one nor
| Very | Moderately | Slightly | the other | Slightly | Moderately | Very |

Courteous salespeople								Discourteous salespeople
Helpful salespeople								Unhelpful salespeople
Comfortable dressing rooms								Uncomfortable dressing rooms
Good selection								Poor selection
Competitive prices								Noncompetitive prices
High-quality products								Low-quality products
Attractive decor								Unattractive decor

Retailer A ——— Retailer B ——— Retailer C ———

FIGURE 2-7

A Comparison of Retail Store Profiles Based on Semantic Differential Scales
Source: Adapted from G. H. G. McDougall and J. N. Fry, "Combining Two Methods of Image Measurement," *Journal of Retailing* 50 (Winter 1974–75), 60. Reprinted by permission.

FIGURE 2-8

Rank-Order Scales

A. The following are six brands of candy bars. We are interested in learning your preference for each of these brands. Place a **1** alongside the brand you would be most likely to buy, a **2** alongside the brand you would next be most likely to buy. Continue doing this until you have ranked all six brands.

_____ Hershey chocolate bar

_____ Snickers

_____ Three Musketeers

_____ M&Ms

_____ Mounds

_____ Twix

B. Rank the following electric razors from 1 to 6 in terms of closeness of shave.

_____ Remington

_____ Norelco

_____ Schick

_____ Braun

_____ Panasonic

_____ Ronson

C. We're interested in knowing how much you enjoy each of the following four types of TV professional sports programs. Please rank them from 1 to 4, where **1** means you enjoy it the most and **4** means that you enjoy it the least.

_____ Baseball

_____ Football

_____ Basketball

_____ Hockey

If the researcher wants the findings to be projectable to the total population, then a *probability sample* should be chosen; if it is sufficient to have the findings "representative" of the population, then a *nonprobability sample* can be selected. Table 2-4 summarizes the features of various types of probability and nonprobability designs.

Data Collection

As indicated earlier, qualitative studies usually require highly trained social scientists to collect data. A quantitative study generally uses a field staff that is either recruited and trained directly by the researcher or contracted from a company that specializes in conducting field interviews. In either case, it is often necessary to verify whether the interviews have, in fact, taken place. This is sometimes done by a postcard mailing to respondents asking them to verify that they participated in an interview on the date recorded on the questionnaire form. Completed questionnaires are reviewed on a regular basis as the research study progresses to ensure that the recorded responses are clear, complete, and legible.

Analysis

In qualitative research, the moderator or test administrator usually analyzes the responses received. In quantitative research, the researcher supervises the analysis. Open-ended responses are first coded and quantified (i.e., converted into numerical scores); then all of the

table 2-4   Probability and Nonprobability Sampling Designs

PROBABILITY SAMPLE	
Simple random sample	Every member of the population has a known and equal chance of being selected.
Stratified random sample	The population is divided into mutually exclusive groups (such as age groups), and random samples are drawn from each group.
Cluster (area) sample	The population is divided into mutually exclusive groups (such as blocks), and the researcher draws a sample of the groups to interview.
NONPROBABILITY SAMPLE	
Convenience sample	The researcher selects the most accessible population members from whom to obtain information (e.g., students in a classroom).
Judgment sample	The researcher uses his or her judgment to select population members who are good sources for accurate information (e.g., experts in the relevant field of study).
Quota sample	The researcher interviews a prescribed number of people in each of several categories (e.g., 50 men and 50 women).

responses are tabulated and analyzed. Although it is possible to tabulate and analyze up to 200 responses without the use of a computer, most surveys are computer-analyzed using sophisticated analytical techniques. The computer can process multiple correlations and cluster the data by selected demographic characteristics.

Report Preparation

In both qualitative and quantitative research, the research report includes a brief executive summary of the findings. Depending on the assignment from marketing management, the research report may or may not include recommendations for marketing action. The body of the report includes a full description of the methodology used and, for quantitative research, also includes tables and graphics to support the findings. A sample of the questionnaire is usually included in the appendix to enable management to evaluate the objectivity of the findings.

CONDUCTING A RESEARCH STUDY

In designing a research study, researchers adapt the research process described in the sections above to the special needs of the study. For example, if a researcher is told that the *purpose* of the study is to develop a segmentation strategy for coffee, he or she would first collect *secondary data*. Then, together with the marketing manager, the researcher would specify the parameters (i.e., define the *sampling unit*) of the coffee market to be studied (e.g., instant coffee drinkers, decaffeinated coffee drinkers, regular ground coffee drinkers). A *qualitative study* might be undertaken first to gather ideas about consumer needs, motivations, perceptions, benefits sought, and attitudes toward coffee drinking in general, and toward specific brands. This might be done through a series of *focus groups* conducted in several areas of the country. This phase of the research should result in tentative generalizations about the product qualities that consumers prefer.

The marketing manager then might instruct the researcher to conduct a *quantitative study* to confirm and attach "hard " numbers (percentages) to the findings that emerged from the focus groups. The first-phase study should have provided sufficient insights to develop a research design and to launch directly into a large-scale survey. If, however, there is still doubt about any element of the research design, such as question wording or format, they might decide first to do a small-scale *exploratory study* of representative consumers. After refining the questionnaire and any other needed elements of the research design, they would launch a full-scale quantitative survey, using a *probability sample* that would allow them to project the findings to the total population of coffee drinkers (as originally defined). The analysis should cluster consumers into segments based on relevant sociocultural or life-style characteristics and on media habits, attitudes, perceptions, and geodemographic characteristics.

Research Methods and Tools

The same basic research methods are used to measure a variety of consumer behavior variables. Table 2-5 on page 40 presents a matrix indicating which research methods are most applicable in measuring specific consumer behavior constructs that are examined in the following chapters. Table 2-6 on page 40 indicates the research tools used in each research methodology.

table 2-5   Primary Research Methods for Selected Consumer Behavior Variables

	EXPERIMENTATION	OBSERVATION AND INFERENCE	SELF REPORTS (SURVEYS)	PROJECTIVE TESTS	FOCUS GROUPS/ DEPTH INTERVIEWS
Motivation		✔	✔	✔	✔
Personality			✔	✔	
Segmentation			✔		✔
Perception			✔	✔	✔
Attitudes		✔	✔	✔	✔
Communication	✔		✔	✔	✔
Family Decisions		✔	✔		✔
Social Class			✔		✔
Culture and Subculture		✔	✔		✔
Opinion Leadership	✔	✔	✔		

table 2-6   Types of Research Tools Used in Consumer Research Studies

	RESEARCH METHODS				
	EXPERIMENTATION	OBSERVATION AND INFERENCE	SELF REPORTS (SURVEYS)	PROJECTIVE TESTS	FOCUS GROUPS/ DEPTH INTERVIEWS

RESEARCH TOOLS	• copy pretests
	• split cable
	• tachistoscopes
		• cameras
		• camcorders
		• recorders
		• product scanners
		• people meters
		• content analysis
		• ethnography
			• questionnaires
			• inventories
			• attitude scales
			  –Likert scales
			  –semantic differential scales
			  –rank-order scales
			• value survey instruments
				• word association
				• sentence completion
				• figure drawings
				• picture sorting
				• ink blots
				• cartoons (TAT)
				• other-person characterizations
					• screener questionnaires
					• discussion guides

The field of consumer research developed as an extension of the field of marketing research to enable marketers to predict how consumers would react in the marketplace and to understand the reasons they made the purchase decisions they did. Consumer research undertaken from a managerial perspective to improve strategic marketing decisions is known as positivism. It is generally quantitative in approach, and tries to identify cause-and-effect relationships in buying situations. It is often supplemented with qualitative research.

A second research perspective, called interpretivism, is generally more concerned with understanding the act of consumption itself rather than the act of buying (i.e., consumer decision making). Interpretivists view consumer behavior as a subset of human behavior, and increased understanding as a key to eliminating some of the ills associated with destructive consumer behavior.

Each theoretical perspective is based on its own specific assumptions and uses its own research methodologies. Positivists generally use quantitative studies that can be generalized to larger populations. Interpretivists often use subjective studies that view consumption experiences as unique situations that occur at specific moments in time. The two theoretical research orientations, used together, provide a deeper and more insightful understanding of consumer behavior than either approach used alone.

The consumer research process—whether quantitative or qualitative in approach—generally consists of six steps: defining objectives, collecting secondary data, developing a research design, collecting primary data, analyzing the data, and preparing a report of the findings.

discussion questions

1. Compare qualitative and quantitative consumer research in terms of: (a) the purpose of the study, (b) the data collection methods available, (c) analysis of the data, and (d) using the findings to make marketing decisions.

2. Why should every consumer research study include a search for secondary information *before* the collection of primary data? What are the major sources of secondary data?

3. What are the advantages and disadvantages of using qualitative research in the study of consumer behavior?

4. a. Select one of the projective techniques discussed in the textbook. Illustrate how it is applied in consumer research and discuss the advantages and limitations of this method.

   b. Describe the barriers to consumer responsiveness that can be overcome by using projective techniques.

5. Secondary data in the form of information about consumers' buying habits is collected by many research firms and sold to marketers. Some people believe that collecting and selling such data is unethical and constitutes invasion of privacy. Do you agree or disagree? Why?

6. A cereal marketer is using observational research to study consumer buying habits. The research design consists of observing shoppers in 16 supermarkets throughout the country and recording the sex and approximate ages of the consumers who buy cereal. (a) Is observation the best research technique to use in studying this type of consumer behavior? If not, which method(s) would you use? Why? (b) What sampling method is the researcher using? Is this technique appropriate for this situation? If not, which sampling method would you use and why?

7. What type of research—qualitative or quantitative—would you use in each of the following situations, and why? How would you contact respondents? What type of sample would be best? Explain. (a) Procter & Gamble wants to determine whether a new line of plaque-preventing toothpaste would be profitable. (b) Anheuser-Busch wants to obtain some insights into the attitudes of college students regarding low-alcohol beer. (c) LA Gear—a sneaker manufacturer—wants to find out which colors to use in a new line it is introducing.

exercises

1. Have you ever been selected as a respondent in a marketing research survey? If yes, how were you contacted? Why do you think you, in particular, were selected? Do you know or can you guess the purpose of the survey? Do you know the name of the company or brand involved in the survey?

2. Identify a purchase you have made that was motivated primarily by your desire to obtain a special "feeling" or an "experience." Would the positivist or interpretivist research paradigm be a more appropriate approach to study your consumption behavior? Explain your answer.

3. a. Develop a questionnaire to measure students' attitudes toward the instructor in this course. (a) Prepare five statements to be evaluated on a Likert scale. (b) Prepare five semantic differential scales to measure student attitudes. Can the *same* dimensions be measured by using either scaling technique? Explain your answer.

   b. Administer the questionnaire you developed to several students in your class. Discuss any response-related problems you encountered.

key words

- Consumer panels
- Depth interview
- Disguised or undisguised questions
- Experimentation
- Focus group
- Interpretivist research
- Likert scale
- Mail and telephone surveys
- Nonprobability sample
- Observation
- Personal interviews
- Positivist research
- Primary research
- Probability sample
- Projective techniques
- Qualitative research
- Quantitative research
- Rank-order scale
- Reliability
- Secondary data
- Semantic differential scale
- Validity

end notes

1. ALLADI VENKATESH, "Postmodernism, Consumer Culture and the Society of the Spectacle," in John F. Sherry, Jr. and Brian Sternthal, eds., *Advances in Consumer Research* 19 (Provo, UT: Association for Consumer Research, 1992), 199–202.

2. RICHARD LUTZ, "Positivism, Naturalism, and Pluralism in Consumer Research: Paradigms in Paradise," *Advances in Consumer Research* 16 (Provo, UT: Association for Consumer Research, 1989), 1–7; BOBBY J. CALDER and ALICE M. TYBOUT, "Interpretive, Qualitative, and Traditional Scientific Empirical Consumer Behavior Research," in Elizabeth Hirschman, ed., *Interpretive Consumer Research* (Provo, UT: Association for Consumer Research, 1989), 199–208.

3. JOHN SHERRY, "Postmodern Alternatives: The Interpretive Turn in Consumer Research," in H. Kassarjian and T. Robertson, eds., *Handbook of Consumer Behavior* (Englewood Cliffs, NJ: Prentice-Hall, 1991); MORRIS B. HOLBROOK and JOHN O'SHAUGHNESSY, "On the Scientific Status of Consumer Research and the Need for an Interpretive Approach to Studying Consumption Behavior," *Journal of Consumer Research* 15, December 1988, 398–402; MORRIS HOLBROOK and ELIZABETH HIRSCHMAN, "The Experiential Aspects of Consumption: Consumer Fantasies, Feelings, and Fun," *Journal of Consumer Research* 9(2), 1982, 132–40; JULIE L. OZANNE and LAUREL ANDERSON HUDSON, "Exploring Diversity in Consumer Research," in Elizabeth Hirschman, ed., *Interpretive Consumer Research* (Provo, UT: Association for Consumer Research, 1989), 1–9; and LAUREL ANDERSON HUDSON and JULIE L. OZANNE, "Alternative Ways of Seeking Knowledge in Consumer Research," *Journal of Consumer Research* 14, March 1988, 508–21.

4. See, for example, SHELBY D. HUNT, "Naturalistic, Humanistic, and Interpretive Inquiry: Challenges and Ultimate Potential," in Elizabeth C. Hirschman, ed.,

Interpretive Consumer Research (Provo, UT: Association for Consumer Research, 1989), 185–98; MELANIE WALLENDORF and RUSSELL BELK, "Assessing Trustworthiness in Naturalistic Consumer Research," in Elizabeth C. Hirschman, ed., *Interpretive Consumer Research* (Provo, UT: Association for Consumer Research, 1989), 69–84; ELIZABETH C. HIRSCHMAN, "Humanistic Inquiry in Marketing Research, Philosophy, Method, and Criteria," *Journal of Marketing Research* 23, August 1986, 237–49; PAUL F. ANDERSON, "On Method in Consumer Research: A Critical Relativist Perspective," *Journal of Consumer Research* 13, September 1986, 155–73; and TIMOTHY B. HEATH, "The Reconciliation of Humanism and Positivism in the Practice of Consumer Research: A View from the Trenches," *Journal of the Academy of Marketing Science* 20(2), 1992, 107–18.

5. See RONALD PAUL HILL, "Ethnography and Marketing Research: A Postmodern Perspective," *Proceedings*, AMA Educators' Conference, V. 4, 1993, 257–261; also ERIC J. ARNOULD and MELANIE WALLENDORF, "Market-Oriented Ethnography: Interpretation Building and Marketing Strategy Formulation," *Journal of Marketing Research* 31, November 1994, 484–504.

6. ANIL PANDYA and A. VENKATESH, "Symbolic Communication among Consumers in Self-Consumption and Gift Giving: A Semiotic Approach," in John F. Sherry and Brian Sternthal, eds., *Advances in Consumer Research* 19 (Provo, UT: Association for Consumer Research, 1992), 147–54; DAVID MICK, "Consumer Research and Semi-

otics: Exploring the Morphology of Signs, Symbols, and Significance," *Journal of Consumer Research* 13(2), 1986, 196–213; and WINFRED NOTH, "The Language of Commodities: Groundwork for a Semiotics of Consumer Goods," *International Journal of Research in Marketing* 4(3), 1988, 173–86.

7. Not all researchers agree that interpretive research enhances traditional quantitative and qualitative market research. See, for example, STEPHEN BROWN, "No Representation without Taxation: Postmodern Marketing Research," *Proceedings*, American Marketing Association Educators' Conference, Summer, 1995, 256–262.

8. SUSAN SPIGGLE, "Analysis and Interpretation of Qualitative Data in Consumer Research, *Journal of Consumer Research* 21, December 1994, 491–503.

9. DEBORAH D. HEISLEY and SIDNEY J. LEVY, "Autodriving: A Photoelicitation Technique" *Journal of Consumer Research* 18, December 1991, 257–272.

10. WILLIAM J. MCDONALD, "Provider Perceptions of Focus Group Research Use: A Multicountry Perspective," *Journal of the Academy of Marketing Science* 22(3), 1994, 265–273.

11. LEAH RICKARD, "Focus Groups Go to Collage," *Advertising Age*, November 14, 1994, 39.

12. WARREN F. KUHFELD, RANDALL D. TOBIAS, and MARK GARRATT, "Efficient Experimental Design with Marketing Research Applications," *Journal of Marketing Research* 31, November 1994, 545–57.

Market segmentation and diversity are in natural harmony. Without a diverse marketplace, composed of many different peoples, with different backgrounds and countries of origin, different interests, and different needs and wants, there would be little reason to segment markets. Diversity in the global marketplace makes market segmentation an attractive, viable, and potentially highly profitable strategy. The necessary conditions for successful segmentation are: a large enough population with sufficient money to spend (general affluence) and sufficient diversity to be capable of being partitioned into sizable segments on the basis of demographic, psychological, or other strategic variables. The presence of these conditions in the United States, Canada, Western Europe, Japan, Australia, and other highly industrialized nations makes these marketplaces extremely attractive to global marketers.

The optimist proclaims that we live in the best of all possible worlds; and the pessimist fears this is true.

—James Branch Cabell
The Silver Stallion, 1926

45

When marketers provide a range of product or service choices to meet diverse consumer interests, consumers are better satisfied, and their overall happiness, satisfaction, and *quality of life* are ultimately enhanced. Thus, market segmentation is a positive force for both consumers and marketers alike.

WHAT IS MARKET SEGMENTATION?

Market segmentation can be defined as the *process of dividing a market into distinct subsets of consumers with common needs or characteristics and selecting one or more segments to target with a distinct marketing mix*. Before the widespread acceptance of market segmentation, the prevailing way of doing business with consumers was through **mass marketing**—that is, offering the same product and marketing mix to all consumers. The essence of this strategy was summed up by the entrepreneur Henry Ford, who offered the Model T automobile to the public "in any color they wanted, as long as it was black."

If all consumers were alike, if they all had the same needs, wants, and desires, and the same background, education, and experience, mass (undifferentiated) marketing would be a logical strategy. Its primary advantage is that it costs less: One advertising campaign is all that is needed, one marketing strategy is all that is developed, and one standardized product is usually all that is offered. Some companies, primarily those that deal in agricultural products or very basic manufactured goods, successfully follow a mass marketing strategy. Other marketers, however, see major drawbacks in an undifferentiated marketing approach. When trying to sell the same product to every prospect with a single advertising campaign, the marketer must portray its product as a means for satisfying a common or generic need and, often, ends up appealing to no one. A washing machine may fulfill a widespread need to clean dirty laundry, but a standard-sized washing machine may be too big for a grandmother who lives alone and too small for a family of six. Without market differentiation, both the grandmother and the family of six would have to make do with the very same model and, as we all know, "making do" is a far cry from being satisfied.

The strategy of segmentation allows producers to avoid head-on competition in the marketplace by differentiating their offerings, not only on the basis of price, but also through styling, packaging, promotional appeal, method of distribution, and superior service. Marketers have found that the costs of consumer segmentation research, shorter production runs, and differentiated promotional campaigns are usually more than offset by increased sales. In most cases, consumers readily accept the passed-through cost increases for products that more closely satisfy their specific needs.

Market segmentation is just the first step in a three-phase marketing strategy. After *segmenting* the market into homogeneous clusters, the marketer then must select one or more segments to *target*. To accomplish this the marketer must decide on a specific product, price, channel and/or promotional appeal for each distinct segment. The third step is **positioning** the product so that it is perceived by each target market as satisfying that market's needs better than other competitive offerings.

Who Uses Market Segmentation?

Because the strategy of **market segmentation** benefits both sides of the marketplace, marketers of consumer goods are eager practitioners. For example, Swatch has continuously employed market segmentation to expand its offerings of inexpensive and fashionable watches for men and women. Today, the company—which distributes its watches through department stores, better jewelers, specialty watch stores, and franchised Swatch stores—

markets a wide range of wristwatches designed to cater to the interests and lifestyles of different segments of consumers. While Swatch still offers consumers conservative watches to wear to work and funky watches for leisure use, it now also features several distinctive lines: scuba or diving watches for the sports-minded individual, chronographic watches with stopwatches and other technofeatures for wristwatch enthusiasts, pager watches to eliminate the need to carry a separate pager, art and limited-edition watches for Swatch collectors (there is even a worldwide Swatch collectors' club), children's watches for toddlers first learning to tell time and, now, metal models for those who want a watch case made of metal rather than plastic (Figure 3-1).

Market segmentation also has been adopted by retailers. For instance, *The Gap* targets different age, income, and lifestyle segments in a diversity of retail outlets. *The Gap*, *Super Gap*, and *Gap Shoe* stores are designed to attract a wide age range of consumers who prefer a casual and relaxed style of dress. *The Gap* also targets more upscale consumers through its chain of *Banana Republic* stores, young parents (who also are likely to be *Gap* shoppers) at its *Baby Gap* and *Gap Kids* stores, and less upscale customers with its *Old Navy Clothing Company* stores.[1]

Hotels also segment their markets and target different chains to different market segments. For example, Marriott operates the *Fairfield Inns* (short stay) and *Residence Inns* (apartment-like accommodations for extended stays) for the value- or budget-oriented traveler, *Courtyard* for the price-conscious businessperson, *Marriott Hotels* for full-service business travelers, *Marriott Resorts* for leisure and vacation guests, *Marriott Time*

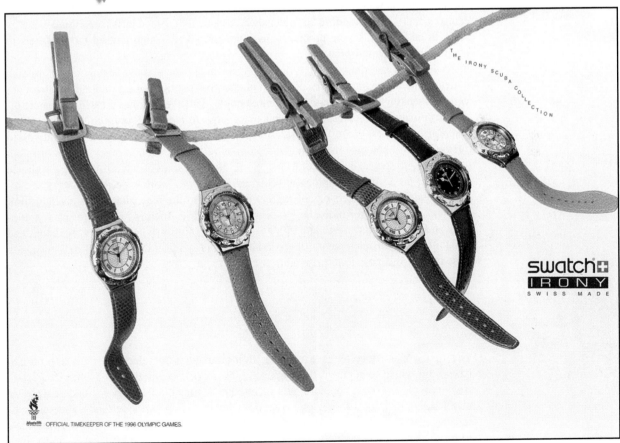

Sharing for those seeking affordable resort ownership, and *Marriott Senior Living* environments for elderly people. Marriott also owns an interest in the luxury upmarket *Ritz Carlton* hotel chain.

Industrial manufacturers also segment their markets, as do not-for-profit organizations and the media. For example, Boeing produces different models of aircraft to meet the needs of the airlines, air charter services, the military, and air freight companies. Charities such as the Heart Fund or the Red Cross frequently focus their fund-raising efforts on "heavy givers." Some Performing Arts Centers segment their subscribers on the basis of *benefits sought* in subscribing and have succeeded in increasing attendance through specialized promotional appeals.

How Market Segmentation Operates

Segmentation studies are designed to discover the needs and wants of specific groups of consumers, so that specialized goods and services can be developed and promoted to satisfy each group's needs. Many new products have been developed to fill gaps in the marketplace revealed by segmentation research. For instance, One–A–Day vitamins has developed a variety of products that are designed to appeal directly to different age and gender market segments, in terms of their specific vitamin requirements.

Segmentation studies also are used to guide the redesign, the **repositioning**, or the extending of the product targeting to a new consumer segment. For example, Nintendo, very successful in capturing a large share of the children's market for its electronic games, now seeks to attract adult users. The ongoing ad campaign appeals to potential adult game players by promising them "kid-like" fun, a notion that many adults find appealing. In a similar fashion, Sharp has been very success in selling its organizers to busy business executives and is now targeting busy teenagers, especially teenage girls (see Figure 3-2).

In addition to filling product gaps, segmentation research is used by marketers to identify the most appropriate media in which to place advertisements. Almost all media vehicles from TV and radio stations to newspapers and magazines use segmentation research to determine the characteristics of their audience and publicize their findings to attract advertisers seeking a similar audience. For example, Time Warner has created a separate division to market magazines to baby boomers (e.g., *In Health, Parenting, Cooking Light,* and *Martha Stewart Living*).[2] The titles reveal why these magazines would be of interest to "aging" baby boomers. In a somewhat similar fashion, *Business Week* targets different segments with special editions of its magazine. Not only does an advertiser have the choice of placing an ad in geographically based editions (e.g., worldwide, North America, regional, state, and city versions of each issue), but also the magazine offers an Industrial/ Technology edition (for individuals working in industries such as manufacturing and mining), an Elite edition (targeted to 250,000 subscribers living in high-income zip codes and $50,000+ senior management titles receiving the magazine at their offices), and a recently added Small Business Enterprise edition.

BASES FOR SEGMENTATION

The first step in developing a segmentation strategy is to select the most appropriate base(s) on which to segment the market. Eight major categories of consumer characteristics provide the most popular bases for market segmentation. They include geographic factors, demographic factors, psychological characteristics, sociocultural variables, use-related characteristics, use-situation factors, benefits sought, and hybrid segmentation forms such as demographic/psychographic profiles, geodemographic factors, and values

FIGURE 3-2

Sharp Branches Out
from Traditional Market
Segments
Courtesy of Sharp Electronics
Corporation

and lifestyles. Hybrid segmentation formats each use a combination of several segmentation bases to create rich and comprehensive profiles of particular consumer segments (e.g., a specific age range, income, lifestyle, and profession). A number of products that by their very nature appear to serve as examples of hybrid segmentation are presented in Table 3-1.

table 3-1   Examples of Hybrid Segmentation

PRODUCT	SEGMENTATION BASES
Ladies Gold Rolex Wristwatch	Sex: female Income: high Psychographic: status seeker Benefit: prestige
Gentle-Treatment Creme Hair Relaxer	Sex: female Subculture: Black
Coach Leather Briefcase	Sex: male Income: high Benefit: durable Usage/location: work Occupation: professional
Toyota Celica	Age: under 35 Income: moderate Marital status: singles/young married couples (no children)

All eight segmentation bases are divided into specific variables, with examples for each, in Table 3-2. The following section discusses each of the eight segmentation bases. (Various psychological and sociocultural segmentation variables are also examined in greater depth in Parts II and III.)

Geographic Segmentation

In **geographic segmentation**, the market is divided by location. The theory behind this strategy is that people who live in the same area share some similar needs and wants and that these needs and wants differ from those of people living in other areas. For example, certain food products sell better in one region than in others (e.g., cream cheese and frozen waffles tend to sell better in the Northeast, Japanese food and soy sauce in the Northwest, and cake mixes and cottage cheese in the Midwest and mountain states).

Some regional consumption differences can be accounted for by climate. The Sunbelt regions of the South and West represent better opportunities for selling bathing suits and in-ground pools than the snowbelt regions of the North and East, where snowblowers and children's sleds are likely to be better sellers.

Some marketing theorists and marketing practitioners believe that worldwide satellite television transmission and global communication networks have erased all regional boundaries and, therefore, that geographic segmentation should be replaced by a single global marketing strategy. Other marketers have, for a number of years, been moving in the opposite direction and developing highly regionalized marketing strategies. For example, Campbell's Soup segments its domestic market into more than twenty regions, each with its own advertising and promotion budget. Within each region, Campbell's sales managers have the authority to develop advertising and promotional campaigns geared to local market needs and conditions, using local media ranging from newspapers to church bulletins. They work closely with local retailers on displays and promotions and report that their **micromarketing** strategy has won strong consumer support. Similarly, Coca-Cola, which is known for its global advertising orientation, has also launched a number of micromarketing campaigns.[3] In one campaign, targeted to Texans, Coca-Cola uses outdoor and broadcast media to say: "Coca-Cola, Texas Home of the Real Thing."

Marketers have observed divergent consumer purchasing patterns among urban, suburban, and rural areas. Throughout the United States, more furs and expensive jewelry are sold in cities than in small towns. Even within a large metropolitan area, different types of household furnishings and leisure products are sold in the central city and in the suburbs. Convertible sofas and small appliances are more likely to be bought by city apartment dwellers (see Figure 3-3 on page 52); suburban homeowners are better prospects for barbecue grills and home freezers. Probably the best example of successful segmentation based on geographic density is the giant Wal-Mart operation. Wal-Mart's basic marketing strategy was to locate discount stores in small towns (often in rural areas) that other major retail chain operations were ignoring at the time.

In summary, geographic segmentation is a useful strategy for many marketers. It is relatively easy to find geographically based differences for many products. In addition, geographic segments can be easily reached through the local media, including newspapers, TV, and radio, and through regional editions of magazines.

Demographic Segmentation

Demographic characteristics, such as age, sex, marital status, income, occupation, and education, are most often used as the basis for market segmentation. Demography refers to the vital and measurable statistics of a population. Demographics help to *locate* a target market, whereas psychological and sociocultural characteristics help to *describe* how its

table 3-2 Market Segmentation Categories and Selected Variables

SEGMENTATION BASE	SELECTED SEGMENTATION VARIABLES
GEOGRAPHIC SEGMENTATION	
Region	North, South, East, West
City Size	Major metropolitan areas, small cities, towns
Density of area	Urban, suburban, exurban, rural
Climate	Temperate, hot, humid
DEMOGRAPHIC SEGMENTATION	
Age	Under 11, 12–17, 18–34, 35–49, 50–64, 65–74, 75–99, 100+
Sex	Male, female
Marital status	Single, married, divorced, living together, widowed
Income	Under $15,000, $15,000–$24,999, $25,000–$39,999, $40,000–$54,999, $55,000–$69,999, $70,000 and over
Education	Some high school, high school graduate, some college, college graduate, postgraduate
Occupation	Professional, blue-collar, white-collar, agricultural, military
PSYCHOLOGICAL/PSYCHOGRAPHIC SEGMENTATION	
Needs-motivation	Shelter, safety, security, affection, sense of self-worth
Personality	Extroverts, novelty seeker, aggressives, low dogmatics
Perception	low-risk, moderate-risk, high-risk
Learning-involvement	Low-involvement, high-involvement
Attitudes	Positive attitude, negative attitude
Psychographic (lifestyle)	Economy-minded, status seekers, outdoors enthusiasts, status seekers
SOCIOCULTURAL SEGMENTATION	
Culture/Subculture	American, Italian, Chinese, Mexican
Religion	Catholic, Protestant, Jewish, other
Race/ethnic	Black, Caucasian, Oriental, Hispanic
Social class	Lower, middle, upper
Family life cycle	Bachelors, young marrieds, full nesters, empty nesters
USE-RELATED SEGMENTATION	
Usage rate	Heavy users, medium users, light users, nonusers
Awareness status	Unaware, aware, interested, enthusiastic
Brand loyalty	None, some, strong
USE-SITUATION SEGMENTATION	
Time	Leisure, work, rush, morning, night
Objective	Personal, gift, snack, fun, achievement
Location	Home, work, friend's home, in-store
Person	Self, family members, friends, boss, peer
BENEFIT SEGMENTATION	Convenience, social acceptance, long lasting, economy, value-for-the-money
HYBRID SEGMENTATION	
Demographic/psychographic profiles	Combination of demographic and psychographic profiles of consumer segments
Geodemographics	"Latino America," "Young Literati," Suburbia, Blue-Blood Estates
SRI VALS™ 2	Actualizer, fulfilled, believer, achiever, striver, experiencer, maker, struggler

VALS™ 2 is an example of a demographic/psychographic profile. GeoVALS is an example of a geodemopsychographic profile. PRIZM is an example of a geodemographic profile.

FIGURE 3-3

Appealing to a City
Apartment Dweller
Courtesy of Jennifer Convertibles

members think and how they feel. Demographic information is the most accessible and
cost-effective way to identify a target market. Indeed, most secondary data, including census data, are expressed in demographic terms. Demographics are easier to measure than
other segmentation variables; they are invariably included in psychographic and sociocultural studies, because they add meaning to the findings. For example, if you were in the
business of selling either fine wristwatches or writing instruments, it would be useful to
know that the overlap between individuals who collect wristwatches and those who collect
fountain pens is very high—as much as seventy percent. *American Demographics Magazine* each month publishes research dealing with demographic issues, and a number of its
articles relate demographic variables to other segmentation bases.

Demographic variables reveal ongoing trends, such as shifts in age, sex (gender),
and income distributions, that signal business opportunities. For example, demographic
studies consistently show that the "mature–adult market"—the fifty-plus market—has a

much greater proportion of disposable income than its younger counterparts. This factor alone makes consumers over age 50 a critical market for products and services that they might buy for themselves or for their adult children, who are more likely to be facing major purchase decisions (such as home ownership) with fewer financial resources.

▲ **Age** Because product needs and interest often vary with consumer age, marketers have found age to be a particularly useful demographic variable for distinguishing segments. Many marketers have carved themselves a niche in the marketplace by concentrating on a specific age segment. For example, while your present cable TV company may be offering you the Disney Channel with its programming aimed at children, Our Time Television is planning to offer a new cable TV channel aimed at the over–49-year-old crowd. Referring to their target audience as "boomovers" (i.e., baby boomers over the 49-year-old age line), the founders of this channel note that 76 million baby boomers will be turning 50 in the coming years, while most TV is now aimed at 18–49 year olds.[4]

As baby boomers push toward middle age, "youth-driven" marketing and advertising executives are beginning to court the 46 million-plus 18–29 year olds who constitute the "**Xers**" (also referred to as Generation X or *baby busters*). For example, WordPerfect Corporation, in an attempt to gain recognition for its software among Generation Xers, was an official sponsor of Tony Bennett's recent 40–city tour of the United States and Canada. Each time Tony Bennett performed, an on–stage banner plugged WordPerfect.[5]

Age, especially chronological age, implies a number of underlying forces. In particular, demographers has drawn an important distinction between *age effects* (occurrences due to age, e.g., "how old a person is") and *cohort affects* (individuals born during a certain time period and who grew up sharing a similar environment). To illustrate the nature of an *age effect*, Table 3-3 shows how women's attraction or motivation to use fragrances shifts with age.[6] In contrast, the qualities of *cohort affects* are captured by the idea that if ten years from today it is determined that a lot of people over fifty years of age are rock-and-roll fans, it would not be because older people have suddenly altered their musical tastes. Instead, it will be because the baby boomers who grew up with rock and roll have become older.[7] It is important for marketers to be aware of the distinction between these two age–related effects: one stresses the impact of aging, whereas the second stresses the influence of the period when one is born and related shared experiences.

table 3-3   The Five Age Stages of Women's Fragrance

STAGE	APPROXIMATE AGE DURING STAGE (YR)	REASON FOR USING FRAGRANCE
Stage 1	Puberty through teens	Define personal territory; cope with new body odors; define self as woman
Stage 2	Late teens through 20s	Same as in teens, plus to attract men and to feel feminine, fresh, and happy
Stage 3	30s	To attract men, for special occasions, to feel special
Stage 4	40s	To attract men and please self
Stage 5	50-plus	For social reasons (the appropriate thing to do)

Source: Maxine Wilkie, "Scent of a Market," *American Demographics*, August 1995, 42. © 1995 American Demographics Magazine. Reprinted with permission.

Of course, defining market segments in strictly chronological terms can sometimes be stereotypical and misleading, particularly because many adult consumers have a perceived age (i.e., *cognitive age*) about 10 to 15 years younger than their chronological age. A useful segmentation approach categorizes older consumers in terms of their cognitive age rather than chronological age.

▲ **Sex** Gender has always been a distinguishing segmentation variable. Women have traditionally been the main users of such products as hair coloring and cosmetics, and men have been the main users of tools and shaving preparations. However, sex roles have blurred, and gender is no longer an accurate way of distinguishing consumers in some product categories. For example, women are buying household repair tools, and men have become significant users of skin care and hair products. It is becoming increasingly common to see magazine ads and TV commercials that depict men and women in roles traditionally occupied by the opposite sex. For example, many ads reflect the expanded child-nurturing roles of young fathers in today's society.

Much of the change in sex roles has occurred because of the continued impact of dual-income households (see Chapter 15). One consequence for marketers is that women are not so readily accessible through traditional media as they once were. Because working women do not have much time to watch TV or listen to the radio, many advertisers now emphasize magazines in their media schedules, especially those specifically aimed at working women (e.g., *Working Woman* and *Working Mother*). Direct marketers also have been targeting time–pressured working women who use their catalogs and convenient 800 numbers as ways of shopping for personal clothing and accessories, as well as many household and family needs.

In addition to the impact of more women working and dual-income households, male homemakers are expected to become an increasingly important target market in the future. As Table 3-4 indicates, the overall demographic characteristics of male homemakers are different from those of female homemakers, a factor that marketers must take into consideration when developing their marketing strategies.

table 3-4   Demographic Profiles of Male Homemakers versus Female Homemakers

	MALE HOMEMAKERS*	FEMALE HOMEMAKERS
Total number (in '000s)	27,469	87,017
Size of household		
1 person	35.2%	16.8%
2+ persons	64.8%	83.2%
Number of children		
None	80.3%	55.1%
1 or more	19.8%	45.0%
Employed	69.3%	55.8%
Median age	40.4	43.5
Median household income	$33,162	$32,396

*In particular, male homemakers are found in nonfamily-type situations, mostly as single persons or, if more than one person, in single-sex households. They also tend to be concentrated in the under-35 and over-65 age groups. Use of food and other household products reflect these underlying differences.

Source: Mediamark Research Product Summary Report, Spring 1995 (New York: Mediamark Research, Inc., 1995). Reprinted by permission.

▲ **Marital Status** Traditionally, the family has been the focus of most marketing efforts, and for many products and services, the household continues to be the relevant consuming unit. Marketers are interested in the number and kinds of households that own and/or buy certain products. They also are interested in determining the demographic and media profiles of household decision makers (the persons involved in the actual selection of the product) to develop appropriate marketing strategies.

Marketers also have discovered the benefits of targeting specific marital status grouping, e.g., singles and divorced individuals, as well as single parents and dual–income married couples. For instance, targeting singles, especially one–person households with incomes greater than $35,000, yields a market group that tends to be above average in their usage of products not traditionally associated with supermarkets (e.g., cognac, books, loose tea) and below average in their consumption of traditional supermarket products (e.g., catsup, peanut butter, mayonnaise). For a supermarket operating in a neighborhood of one-person households, such insights can be particularly useful when one is deciding on the merchandise mix for the store. Some marketers target one-person households with single-serving prepared foods (e.g., Lipton Cup-a-Soup) and others with miniappliances such as small microwave ovens and two-cup coffee makers. (The family as a consuming unit is discussed in greater detail in Chapter 12.)

▲ **Income, Education, and Occupation** Although income has long been an important variable for distinguishing market segments, a major problem with segmenting the market on the basis of income alone is that income simply indicates the ability (or inability) to pay for a product. For this reason, marketers often combine income with some other demographic variable(s) to define their target markets more accurately. To illustrate, high income has been combined with age to identify the important *affluent elderly* segment. It also has been combined with age and occupational status to produce the so-called *yuppie* segment, a sought-after subgroup of the baby boomer market. College students (a kind of educational-occupational grouping) are also a highly sought after segment. Figure 3-4 on page 56 shows an ad for the U.S. Army Reserve, which suggests that outstanding students who need to supplement their incomes to pay for college should consider joining up.

Education, occupation, and income tend to be closely correlated in almost a cause-and-effect relationship. High-level occupations that produce high incomes usually require advanced educational training. Individuals with little education rarely qualify for high-level jobs. Insights on media preferences tend to support the close relationship among income, occupation, and education. Specifically, prime–time TV watching appears to be strongest in those households whose members have incomes of less than $20,000, have less than high school educations, and are not employed, whereas newspaper readership is strongest among those with household incomes of $75,000 or more, among college graduates, and among those in executive/managerial professions.[8]

Because of the interrelationship among these three variables, education, occupation, and income are combined into a composite index of social class (described in detail in Chapter 13) that is useful in that it reflects values, attitudes, tastes, and lifestyle.

Psychological/Psychographic Segmentation

Psychological characteristics refer to the inner or intrinsic qualities of the individual consumer. Consumer segmentation strategies are often based on specific psychological variables. For instance, consumers may be segmented in terms of their *needs* and *motivations*, *personality*, *perceptions*, *learning*, *level of involvement*, and *attitudes*. (Part II more fully examines the wide range of psychological variables that influence consumer decision making and consumption behavior.)

FIGURE 3-4

Appealing to
College Students—
an Educational-
Occupational Segment
Courtesy of the Department of the
U.S. Army and Army Reserve

▲ **Psychographics** *Psychographic research*, also commonly referred to as lifestyle analysis, has been heartily embraced by marketing practitioners in the promotion of such a diverse group of products as Colgate-Palmolive's Irish Spring soap, Jack Daniel's Whiskey, Peter Paul's Mounds, TUMS, AT&T services, the *Los Angeles Times*, Lava Soap, Union 76 gasoline, Kentucky Fried Chicken, Nescafe coffee, *People*, Greyhound Bus Company, and Dewar's White Label Scotch. With involving names like "Marathon Man," "Perpetual

Student," and "Netman," Visa U.S.A. is featuring a series of advertisements that is humorously capturing and **targeting** a variety of contemporary lifestyles (see Figure 3-5). Marketers conduct psychographic research to capture insights and create profiles of the consumers they wish to target. Table 3-5 on the next page contains a hypothetical psychographic profile of American Airlines loyal frequent business flyers. The appeal of psychographic research lies in the frequently vivid and practical profiles of consumer segments that it can produce (which will be illustrated later in this chapter).

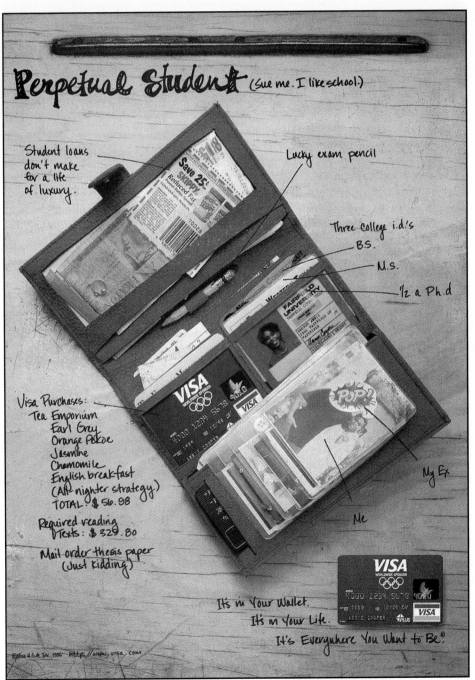

FIGURE 3-5

Visa Targets Lifestyle Types
Courtesy of VISA USA, Inc.

table 3-5
A Hypothetical Psychographic Profile of an American Airlines Loyal Frequent Business Flyer

—Loyal to one airline
—Willing to make a stopover to earn points in a particular frequent flyer program
—Happy with lot in life
—Flying adds to the quality of his/her life
—Frequent flyer benefits add to the quality of life
—Using a frequent flyer program makes him/her feel special
—Accruing frequent flyer points provides a sense of accomplishment

Source: Mary Long and Leon Schiffman, "On the Road Again: Frequent Flyer Programs and Quality of Life among Road Warriors," working paper.

Psychographics are often referred to as **AIOs**, for much psychographic research focuses on the measurement of **activities** (i.e., how the consumer or family spends time, e.g., working, vacationing, hiking), **interests** (the consumer's or family's preferences and priorities, e.g., home, fashion, food), and **opinions** (how the consumer feels about a wide variety of events and political issues, social issues, the state of education, the future). In their most common form, psychographic studies use a battery of statements designed to identify relevant aspects of a consumer's personality, buying motives, interests, attitudes, beliefs, and values. Table 3-6 presents a portion of a psychographic inventory from a recently de-

table 3-6
A Portion of an Actual Psychographic Inventory

	STRONGLY AGREE						STRONGLY DISAGREE
People sometimes have quite definite feelings and emotions about frequent flyer programs. To understand your personal experience with belonging to frequent flyer programs, please indicate how strongly you "agree" or "disagree" with the following statements by placing an X in the box that corresponds to your opinions or feelings.							
I feel *good* when I look at my statement showing the number of mileage points earned.	[1]	[2]	[3]	[4]	[5]	[6]	[7]
When I receive upgrade coupons or special offers, I feel as if the airline is trying to keep me satisfied.	[1]	[2]	[3]	[4]	[5]	[6]	[7]
Once you start accruing miles, it's *addictive*; you just want to keep getting more.	[1]	[2]	[3]	[4]	[5]	[6]	[7]
Using a frequent flyer program makes me feel *special.*	[1]	[2]	[3]	[4]	[5]	[6]	[7]
When I receive my statement showing the number of points accumulated, I feel *disappointed* that I have so few points accumulated.	[1]	[2]	[3]	[4]	[5]	[6]	[7]
I feel *bad* if I miss an opportunity to get mileage points.	[1]	[2]	[3]	[4]	[5]	[6]	[7]
Accruing a lot of points in a frequent flyer program gives me a feeling of accomplishment.	[1]	[2]	[3]	[4]	[5]	[6]	[7]
My use of frequent flyer programs gives me a chance to show off to other people.	[1]	[2]	[3]	[4]	[5]	[6]	[7]

Source: Mary M. Long, *The Ties that Bind: An Examination of Consumption Values at Various Stages of a Relationship Marketing Program* (New York: The City University of New York, 1995). Dissertation Abstracts International, UMI.

signed study of frequent air travelers. (The discussion of psychographic segmentation is continued in the latter half of this chapter, where we consider how psychographic and demographic variables are combined to create descriptive profiles of consumer segments.)

Sociocultural Segmentation

Sociological (i.e., group) and *anthropological* (i.e., cultural) variables—that is, **sociocultural variables**—provide further bases for market segmentation. For example, consumer markets have been successfully subdivided into segments on the basis of *stage in the family life-cycle*, *social class*, *core cultural values*, *subcultural memberships*, and *cross-cultural affiliation*.

▲ **Family Life Cycle** Family life-cycle segmentation is based on the premise that many families pass through similar phases in their formation, growth, and final dissolution. At each phase, the family unit needs different products and services. Young single people, for example, need basic furniture for their first apartment, while their parents, finally free of child rearing, often refurnish their homes with more elaborate pieces. Family life cycle is a composite variable based explicitly on *marital* and *family status*, but implicitly including relative *age*, *income*, and *employment status*. Each of the stages in the traditional family-life cycle (i.e., *bachelorhood*, *honeymooners*, *parenthood*, *postparenthood*, and *dissolution*) represents an important target segment to a variety of marketers. (Chapter 12 discusses the family life cycle in greater depth and shows how marketers cater to the needs and wishes of consumers in each stage of the life cycle.)

▲ **Social Class** Social class (or relative status in the community) is a potential market segmentation variable. It is traditionally "measured" by a weighted index of several demographic variables, such as education, occupation, and income (as discussed in the section on demographic segmentation). The concept of *social class* implies a hierarchy in which individuals in the same class generally have the same degree of status, while members of other classes have either higher or lower status. Studies have shown that consumers in different social classes vary in terms of values, product preferences, and buying habits. For example, a recent study found that 80 percent of upper management workers use toll–free 800 numbers "often," compared with only 32 percent of blue collar workers.[9]

Marketers regularly have used their knowledge of social class differences to appeal to specific segments. Many major banks, for example, offer a variety of different levels of service to people of different social classes (e.g., private banking services to the upper classes). Figure 3-6 on page 60 illustrates how one bank appeals to upper class customers. Chapter 13 discusses in depth the use of social class as a segmentation variable.

▲ **Culture, Subculture, and Cross-Culture** Some marketers have found it useful to segment their domestic and international markets on the basis of cultural heritage, because members of the same culture tend to share the same values, beliefs, and customs. Marketers who use cultural segmentation stress specific, widely held cultural values with which they hope consumers will identify (e.g., for American consumers, *youthfulness* and *fitness and health*). Cultural segmentation is particularly successful in international marketing, but in such instances, it is important for the marketer to understand fully the beliefs, values, and customs of the countries in which the product is marketed (i.e., the cross-cultural context).

Within the larger culture, distinct subgroups (subcultures) often are united by certain experiences, values, or beliefs that make effective market segments. These groupings could be based on a specific demographic characteristic (e.g., race, religion, ethnicity, or age) or lifestyle characteristic (working women, golfers). In the United States, African-Americans,

FIGURE 3-6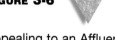

Appealing to an Affluent
Social Class Segment
Courtesy of Huntington
Bancshares, Inc.

Hispanic-Americans, Asian-Americans, and the elderly are important subcultural market segments. For example, advertisers use a variety of Spanish-language and English-language print and broadcast media through which they target the Hispanic market.

Culturally distinct segments can be prospects for the same product but often are targeted more efficiently with different promotional appeals. For example, a bicycle might be promoted as an efficient means of transportation in Asia and as a health-and-fitness product in the United States. Refrigerators are sold in Arctic regions as a way of keeping food from freezing and in temperate and tropical climates as a way of keeping food cold. (Chapters 14, 15, and 16 examine cultural, subcultural, and cross-cultural bases of market segmentation in greater detail.)

Use-Related Segmentation

An extremely popular and effective form of segmentation categorizes consumers in terms of product, service, or brand *usage* characteristics, such as usage rate, awareness status, and degree of brand loyalty.

Rate of usage segmentation differentiates among heavy users, medium users, light users, and nonusers of a specific product, service, or brand. For example, research has consistently indicated that between twenty-five and thirty-five percent of beer drinkers account for more than seventy percent of all beer consumed. For this reason, most marketers prefer to target campaigns to the heavy users, rather than spend considerably more money trying to attract light users. This also explains the successful targeting of light beer to heavy drinkers on the basis that it is less filling (and thus can be consumed in greater quantities) than regular beer.

Marketers of a host of other products have also found that a relatively small group of heavy users accounts for a disproportionately large percentage of product usage and that targeting these heavy users has become the basis of their marketing strategy. Other marketers take note of the gaps in market coverage for light and medium users and profitably target these segments.

Awareness status encompasses the notion of consumer awareness, interest level, or buyer readiness. Marketers have to determine whether potential consumers are aware of the product, interested in the product, or need to be informed about the product. Figure 3-7 on page 62 presents an ad for the Omega Seamaster Professional Chronograph that is designed to create both awareness and interest for this new model wristwatch.

Sometimes, *brand loyalty* is used as the basis for segmentation. Marketers often try to identify the characteristics of their brand-loyal consumers so that they can direct their promotional efforts to people with similar characteristics in the larger population. Other marketers target consumers who show no brand loyalty (i.e., "brand switchers"), in the belief that such people represent greater market potential than consumers who are loyal to competing brands. Also, almost by definition, consumer innovators—often a prime target for new products—tend *not* to be brand loyal. (Chapter 18 discusses the characteristics of consumer innovators.)

Increasingly, marketers stimulate and reward brand loyalty by offering special benefits to consistent or frequent customers. Such frequent usage or relationship programs often take the form of a membership "club" (e.g., Hertz Number 1 Club Gold, American Airlines Platinum Level, or Marriott's Club Marquis Program). Relationship programs tend to provide special accommodations and services, as well as free extras, to keep these frequent customers loyal and happy.

Usage-Situation Segmentation

Marketers recognize that the occasion or situation often determines what consumers will purchase or consume. For this reason, they sometimes focus on the **usage situation** as a segmentation variable.

The following three statements reveal the potential of situation segmentation: "When Elizabeth gets a promotion, I always take her out for a lobster dinner"; "When I'm away on business for a week or more, I always stay at an Embassy Suites hotel"; "I always buy my wife roses on her birthday." Under other circumstances, in other situations, and on other occasions, the same consumer might make other choices. Some situational factors that might influence a purchase or consumption choice include weekday or workday (e.g., going to a movie), on time or in a rush (e.g., use of express mail), whether it is a gift for a girlfriend or parent, or even a self–gift (as a reward to one's self).

The following advertisement appears as a full-page figure:

What you should know about the new
Omega Seamaster Professional Chronograph

Omega Seamaster Professional Chronograph.
Automatic diver chronograph with date.
Titanium with tantalum and 18K gold.
Chronometer certificate.
Push-buttons functional underwater.
Screw-down crown and helium escape valve.
Waterproof to 300 m/1000 ft.
Pat. pending.
Swiss made since 1848.

Symbolizing tradition, know how, research and the spirit of innovation, the Omega Seamaster combines state-of-the-art technology and handsome styling.

Since William Beebe wore one of the first Seamasters in 1934 during a diving-bell expedition, scientists, adventurers and sportsmen alike have placed their confidence in this watch.

With a Seamaster on their wrist, pioneers like Jaques Yves Cousteau and Jaques Mayol pushed the limits of underwater performance, writing new chapters in the history of the oceans.

The new Omega Seamaster Chronograph is an exclusive world first, designed to meet the demands of professional divers. It is the only chronograph in the world which can function underwater to a depth of 300 meters/1000 feet with a push of a button. The materials, titanium and tantalum, utilized in the Omega Seamaster Chronograph are state-of-the-art.

The Seamaster Chronograph is also available in all stainless steel.

The Omega Seamaster Chronograph will be the new benchmark to which all other dive watches are judged.

Liljenquist & Beckstead
JEWELERS
Gold Coast Mall, Ocean City, MD, (410) 524-0979
Annapolis Mall, Annapolis, MD, (410) 224-4787
Montgomery Mall, Bethesda, MD, (301) 469-7575
The Galleria at Tysons II, McLean, VA, (703) 448-6731

Ω
OMEGA®
The sign of excellence

©1993 Omega, a division of SMH (US) Inc.

FIGURE 3-7

Ad Designed to Create Awareness and Interest for a New Product
Courtesy of Omega

Some marketers try to instill the notion of the suitability of certain products for certain situations; others try to break consumer habits. In an effort to challenge the customary usage of coffee as a breakfast and midmorning adult drink, the Pepsi-Cola Company has test-marketed Pepsi AM (which is high in caffeine) as a "wakeup" and midmorning drink. Similarly, Coca-Cola has promoted the idea of its popular Coke Classic as a morning drink.

Many products are promoted for special usage occasions. The greeting card industry, for example, stresses special cards for a variety of occasions, which seem to be increasing almost daily (Grandparents' Day, Secretaries' Day, etc.). The florist and candy industries promote their products for Valentine's Day and Mother's Day, the diamond industry promotes diamond rings as an engagement symbol, and the wristwatch industry promotes its products as graduation gifts. Figure 3-8 suggests that a 25th wedding anniversary is the perfect time for a man to buy his wife a diamond necklace.

Benefit Segmentation

Marketing and advertising executives constantly attempt to isolate the one particular benefit that they should communicate to consumers. Examples of benefits that are commonly used include: *financial security* (Met Life), *reduced calories* (Amstel Light), *comfort* (Bausch & Lomb disposable contact lenses), *good health* (Egg Beaters egg substitute), *proper fit* (Wrangler women's jeans), and *backache relief* (Advil).

FIGURE 3-8

Ad Asking Consumers to Celebrate the Occasion by Buying a Diamond Necklace
Courtesy of J. Walter Thompson Agency

Changing lifestyles play a major role in determining the product benefits that are important to consumers and provide marketers with opportunities for new products and services. For example, the microwave oven was the perfect solution to the needs of dual-income households, where neither the husband nor the wife have the time for lengthy meal preparation. Also, food marketers, like Quaker Oats are offering busy families the *benefit* of breakfast products requiring only 90 seconds to prepare.

Benefit segmentation can be used to position various brands within the same product category.[10] The classic case of successful benefit segmentation is the market for toothpaste: Close-up, with a social appeal that stresses bright teeth, is targeted to young people; Aim is targeted to parents as a good-tasting toothpaste that will encourage children to brush longer; Viadent is targeted to adults as a means of removing tartar (a cosmetic benefit) and plaque (a health benefit).

Hybrid Segmentation Approaches

Marketers commonly segment markets by combining several segmentation variables rather than relying on a single segmentation base. This section examines three hybrid segmentation approaches psychographic/demographic profiles, geodemographics, and VALS 2 that provide marketers with more accurately defined consumer segments than can be derived from using a single segmentation variable.

▲ **Psychographic-Demographic Profiles** Psychographic and demographic profiles are highly complementary approaches that work best when used together. By combining the knowledge gained from both demographic and psychographic studies, marketers are provided with powerful information about their target markets. Tables 3-7 and 3-8 are examples of the very different types of information that marketers can gain from demographic and psychographic profiles of a geographic market area. The demographics presented in Table 3-7 enable a marketer to compare the Phoenix, Arizona market with alternative market areas and with the firm's prototypical target market in terms of socioeconomic traits. In contrast, the psychographic details in Table 3-8 on page 66 provide a useful sense of how the residents of Phoenix spend their time and what they value.

Applications of Psychographic/Demographic Profiles

Psychographic/demographic profiling is particularly useful in two closely related tasks: creating **customer profiles** (for product and service marketers) and creating **audience profiles** (for mass and special interest media to attract advertisers).

Used together, demographics and psychographics provide meaningful insights for segmenting mass markets, providing direction as to which promotional appeals to use, and selecting advertising media that is most likely to reach the target market.

Demographic/psychographic profiling has been widely used in the development of advertising campaigns to answer three questions: "Whom should we target?" "What should we say?" "Where should we say it?" To help advertisers answer the third question, many advertising media vehicles sponsor demographic/psychographic research on which they base carefully detailed *audience profiles*. Table 3-9 on page 67 presents a selected demographic and psychographic profile of the readership of *Popular Science*. By offering media buyers such dual profiles of their audiences, mass media publishers and broadcasters make it possible for advertisers to select media whose audiences most closely resemble their target markets. Advertisers are increasingly designing ads that depict in words and/or pictures the essence of a particular target-market lifestyle or segment that they want to cater to. In this spirit, Timex makes wristwatches designed to meet the need of specific active and outdoors lifestyles (Figure 3-9 on page 68).

table 3-7

Selected Demographic Profile Information of the Phoenix, AZ, Market (Base Index: United States = 100)

OCCUPATION	POPULATION	%	INDEX
Administrative	244,142	10.7	92
Blue Collar	180,255	7.9	84
Clerical	177,973	7.8	100
Homemaker	305,748	13.4	95
Professional/Technical	536,200	23.5	95
Retired	545,327	23.9	117
Sales/Marketing	146,029	6.4	116
Self Employed	88,705	3.8	95
Student	61,605	2.7	117

EDUCATION (1990 CENSUS)

	POPULATION	%	INDEX
Elementary (0-8 years)	144,201	8.4	81
High School (1-3 years)	212,868	12.4	86
High School (4 years)	453,203	26.4	88
College (1-3 years)	559,637	32.6	131
College (4+ years)	345,052	20.1	99

RACE/ETHNICITY

	POPULATION	%	INDEX
White	1,645,108	72.1	98
Black	68,451	3.0	25
Asian	38,789	1.7	50
Hispanic	412,988	18.1	179
American Indian	114,085	5.0	714
Other	2,282	0.1	100

TOTAL HOUSEHOLDS   1,174,535

AGE OF HEAD OF HOUSEHOLD

	HOUSEHOLDS	%	INDEX
18-24 years old	73,986	6.3	121
25-34 years old	236,082	20.1	106
35-44 years old	259,572	22.1	97
45-54 years old	206,718	17.6	97
55-64 years old	140,944	12.0	94
65-74 years old	144,468	12.3	103
75 years and older	112,755	9.6	95
Median Age	45.8 years		

SEX/MARITAL STATUS

	HOUSEHOLDS	%	INDEX
Single Male	240,780	20.5	101
Single Female	266,445	22.6	93
Married	668,310	56.9	103

CHILDREN AT HOME

	HOUSEHOLDS	%	INDEX
At Least One Child	339,441	28.9	96
Child Age Under 2	48,156	4.1	111
Child Age 2-4	96,312	8.2	106
Child Age 5-7	91,614	7.8	103
Child Age 8-10	89,265	7.6	97
Child Age 11-12	63,425	5.4	95
Child Age 13-15	89,265	7.6	93
Child Age 16-18	73,996	6.3	84

HOME OWNERSHIP

	HOUSEHOLDS	%	INDEX
Owner	768,146	65.4	101
Renter	406,389	34.6	98

STAGE IN FAMILY LIFE CYCLE

	HOUSEHOLDS	%	INDEX
Single, 18-34. No Children	137,421	11.7	105
Single, 35-44. No Children	76,345	6.5	105
Single, 45-64. No Children	108,057	9.2	97
Single, 65+. No Children	93,963	8.0	79
Married, 18-34. No Children	56,378	4.8	104
Married, 35-44. No Children	42,283	3.6	106
Married, 45-64. No Children	170,308	14.5	101
Married, 65+. No Children	149,166	12.7	120
Single. Any Child at Home	90,439	7.7	101
Married. Child Age Under 13	150,340	12.8	100
Married. Child Age 13-18	98,661	8.4	87

HOUSEHOLD INCOME

	HOUSEHOLDS	%	INDEX
Under $20,000	346,488	29.5	106
$20,000-$29,999	203,195	17.3	114
$30,000-$39,999	172,657	14.7	110
$40,000-$49,999	131,548	11.2	101
$50,000-$74,999	189,100	16.1	89
$75,000-$99,999	71,647	6.1	80
$100,000 and over	59,901	5.1	75
Median Income	$32,185		

INCOME EARNERS

	HOUSEHOLDS	%	INDEX
Married, One income	368,804	31.4	113
Married, Two Incomes	299,506	25.5	92
Single	506,225	43.1	97

DUAL INCOME HOUSEHOLDS

	HOUSEHOLDS	%	INDEX
Children Age Under 13 years	79,868	6.8	92
Children Age 13-18 years	62,250	5.3	83
No Children	157,388	13.4	96

AGE BY INCOME

	HOUSEHOLDS	%	INDEX
18-34, Income under $30,000	170,306	14.5	123
35-44, Income under $30,000	86,916	7.4	116
45-64, Income under $30,000	123,325	10.5	109
65+, Income under $30,000	169,133	14.4	85
18-34, Income $30,000-$49,999	79,868	6.8	105
35-44, Income $30,000-$49,999	75,170	6.4	102
45-64, Income $30,000-$49,999	92,788	7.9	103
65+, Income $30,000-$49,999	57,552	4.9	120
18-34, Income $50,000-$74,999	41,109	3.5	80
35-44, Income $50,000-$74,999	57,552	4.9	89
45-64, Income $50,000-$74,999	71,647	6.1	88
65+, Income $50,000-$74,999	18,793	1.6	94
18-34, Income $75,000 and over	19,967	1.7	81
35-44, Income $75,000 and over	41,109	3.5	78
45-64, Income $75,000 and over	58,727	5.0	77
65+, Income $75,000 and over	11,745	1.0	83

CREDIT CARD USAGE

	HOUSEHOLDS	%	INDEX
Travel/Entertainment	152,690	13.0	94
Bank Card	882,076	75.1	100
Gas/Department Store	372,328	31.7	82
No Credit Cards	219,638	18.7	106

From THE LIFESTYLE MARKET ANALYST 1996. Data provided by National Demographics and Lifestyles. Published by SRDS. Copyright © 1996 by SRDS. Reprinted by permission.

table 3-8
Selected Psychographic Profile Information of the Phoenix, AZ, Market (Base Index United States = 100)

THE TOP TEN LIFESTYLES RANKED BY INDEX

CASINO GAMBLING	162	OWN A DOG	116
CAMPING/HIKING	146	SCIENCE FICTION	116
RECREATIONAL VEHICLES	143	GOLF	115
BICYCLING FREQUENTLY	121	HEALTH/NATURAL FOODS	114
MOTORCYCLES	119	SELF-IMPROVEMENT	113

HOME LIFE

HOME LIFE	HOUSEHOLDS	%	INDEX	RANK
Avid Book Reading	460,418	39.2	104	49
Bible/Devotional Reading	214,940	18.3	94	150
Flower Gardening	280,714	23.9	73	208
Grandchildren	256,049	21.8	94	175
Home Furnishing/Decorating	236,082	20.1	99	86
House Plants	318,299	27.1	83	209
Own a Cat	300,681	25.6	97	145
Own a Dog	463,941	39.5	116	95
Subscribe to Cable TV	684,754	58.3	90	187
Vegetable Gardening	177,355	15.1	68	201

GOOD LIFE

GOOD LIFE	HOUSEHOLDS	%	INDEX	RANK
Attend Cultural/Arts Events	187,959	14.3	103	41
Fashion Clothing	143,293	12.2	95	82
Fine Art/Antiques	123,326	10.5	102	43
Foreign Travel	157,388	13.4	86	46
Frequent Flyer	267,794	22.8	107	31
Gourmet Cooking/Fine Foods	200,845	17.1	102	47
Own a Vacation Home/ Property	138,595	11.8	110	47
Travel for Business	220,813	18.8	95	71
Travel for Pleasure/Vacation	448,323	38.0	101	46
Travel in USA	422,833	36.0	104	30
Wines	140,944	12.0	99	47

INVESTING & MONEY

INVESTING & MONEY	HOUSEHOLDS	%	INDEX	RANK
Casino Gambling	230,208	19.6	162	7
Entering Sweepstakes	167,958	14.3	105	101
Moneymaking Opportunities	142,119	12.1	104	66
Real Estate Investments	79,868	6.8	111	37
Stock/Bond Investments	187,926	16.0	99	49

GREAT OUTDOORS

GREAT OUTDOORS	HOUSEHOLDS	%	INDEX	RANK
Boating/Sailing	106,883	9.1	88	117
Camping/Hiking	388,771	33.1	146	31
Fishing Frequently	245,478	20.9	90	181
Hunting/Shooting	180,878	15.4	101	156
Motorcycles	102,185	8.7	119	55
Recreational Vehicles	139,770	11.9	143	45
Wildlife/Environmental	189,100	15.1	99	89

SPORTS, FITNESS & HEALTH

SPORTS, FITNESS & HEALTH	HOUSEHOLDS	%	INDEX	RANK
Bicycling Frequently	237,256	20.2	121	36
Dieting/Weight Control	241,954	20.6	100	106
Golf	264,270	22.5	115	45
Health/Natural Foods	205,544	17.5	114	24
Improving Your Health	293,634	25.0	104	36
Physical Fitness/Exercise	425,182	36.2	106	29
Running/Jogging	125,675	10.7	96	67
Snow Skiing Frequently	88,265	7.6	107	63
Tennis Frequently	57,552	4.9	91	55
Walking for Health	394,644	33.6	89	138
Watching Sports on TV	478,036	40.7	108	20

HOBBIES & INTERESTS

HOBBIES & INTERESTS	HOUSEHOLDS	%	INDEX	RANK
Automotive Work	196,147	16.7	111	77
Buy Pre-Recorded Videos	230,209	18.6	109	24
Career-Oriented Activities	109,232	9.3	101	51
Coin/Stamp Collecting	77,519	8.8	97	161
Collectibles/Collections	133,897	11.4	100	128
Crafts	351,185	29.9	109	99
Current Affairs/Politics	189,100	16.1	101	48
Home Workshop	308,903	26.3	104	106
Military Veteran in Household	318,299	27.1	108	78
Needlework/Knitting	189,100	16.1	98	156
Our Nation's Heritage	57,552	4.9	98	134
Self-Improvement	247,827	21.1	113	11
Sewing	221,987	18.9	103	142
Supports Health Charities	157,388	13.4	86	119

HIGH TECH ACTIVITIES

HIGH TECH ACTIVITIES	HOUSEHOLDS	%	INDEX	RANK
Electronics	140,944	12.0	107	43
Home Video Games	143,293	12.2	103	98
Listen to Records/Tapes/CDs	618,980	52.7	104	27
Own a CD Player	680,056	57.9	103	34
Photography	211,416	18.0	101	54
Science Fiction	125,675	10.7	116	20
Science/New Technology	112,733	9.6	103	35
Use a Personal Computer	489,781	41.7	105	39
Use an Apple/Macintosh	110,408	9.4	103	44
Use an IBM Compatible	419,309	35.7	106	38
VCR Recording	221,987	18.9	103	52

From THE LIFESTYLE MARKET ANALYST 1996. Data provided by National Demographics and Lifestyles. Published by SRDS. Copyright © 1996 by SRDS. Reprinted by permission.

▲ **Geodemographic Segmentation** This type of hybrid segmentation scheme is based on the notion that people who live close to one another are likely to have similar financial means, tastes, preferences, lifestyles, and consumption habits (i.e., "Birds of a feather flock together"). Syndicated market research firms specialize in producing computer-generated geodemographic market "clusters" of like consumers. Specifically, these firms have clustered the nation's 250,000-plus neighborhoods into 8–10 lifestyle groupings based on

table 3-9 Selected Psychographic/Demographic Characteristics of the *Popular Science* Reader

DEMOGRAPHICS		PSYCHOGRAPHICS	
SEX (BASE 4,541)		Enjoy working with computers	82.4%
		Friends think I'm a good source of computer information	46.9%
Men	83.6%	Welcome technological changes in my work situation	91.0%
Women	16.4%	Gave opinion/advice to others regarding . . .	
AGE		Automobiles	71.3%
		Home Improvements/Do-it-Yourself	61.5%
18–24	12.6%	Home Electronics	54.9%
25–34	21.4%	Computer Equipment/Services	52.5%
35–44	24.6%	Audio/Video Equipment	44.5%
45–54	18.3%	Participated in Past Year (Index United States = 100)	
55-plus	23.1%	Target Shooting	223
	Median Age 41.3 yrs.	Hunting	189
		Weight Training	157
		Golf	153
EDUCATION		Hiking/Backpacking	153
		Motorcycling	132
Graduated College	27.5%	Racquetball	129
Attended/Graduated College	57.1%	Fishing	128
OCCUPATION			
Professional	12.9%		
Professional/Managerial	22.2%		
Professional/Technical	17.3%		
HOUSEHOLD INCOME (HHI)			
$75,000+	18.4%		
$60,000+	29.6%		
$50,000+	44.8%		
$40,000+	59.5%		
$30,000+	71.5%		
	Median HHI $47,120		
HOME OWNERSHIP			
Own Home	77.1%		
Value of Home $100,000+	38.9%		
Value of Home $70,000+	53.4%		

Source: From *1994–1995 Popular Science Subscriber Study*, conducted by Simmons, with materials from SMRB Adults. Reprinted by permission of Simmons Study of Media and Markets, 1995.

the nation's more than 38,000 zip codes. Clusters are based on consumer lifestyles, and a specific cluster includes similar neighborhoods, that is, neighborhoods composed of people with similar lifestyles widely scattered throughout the country. Marketers use the cluster data for direct-mail campaigns, to select retail sites and appropriate merchandise mixes, to locate banks and restaurants, and to design marketing strategies for specific market segments. Indeed, the college you are presently attending may have used geodemographics to prune the list of high school students it purchased from the College Board (including zip code and SAT performance information). Knowing that students with similar geodemographic backgrounds tend to be attracted to the same schools, this technique helps colleges save money on mailings to prospective students—they target high school students living in the same clusters as their present undergraduate students.[11] Table 3-10 on page 69 presents five examples of geodemographic clusters.

Geodemographic segmentation is most useful when an advertiser's best prospects (in terms of personalities, goals, and interests) can be isolated in terms of where they live. However, for products and services used by a broad cross-section of the American public, other segmentation schemes may be more productive.

FIGURE 3-9

Timex Appeals to
Specific Active and
Outdoor Lifestyles
Courtesy of Timex

▲ **SRI Values and Lifestyle Program (VALS™ 2)** Drawing on Maslow's need hierarchy
(see Chapter 4) and the concept of social character, researchers at SRI in the late 1970s developed a generalized segmentation scheme of the American population known as the values and lifestyle (VALS) program. This original system was designed to better explain the
dynamics of societal change but was quickly adapted as a marketing tool. In the past
decade, a number of marketers have reported using the VALS typology to segment markets
and to target their promotional efforts.

In 1989 SRI revised the VALS 2 system to focus more explicitly on explaining consumer purchase behavior. The current VALS 2 typology classifies the American population

table 3-10   Sample Geodemographic Clusters

LATINO AMERICA

1.3% of United States households

Median household income: $30,100

Adult age range: under 24, 25–34

Hispanic middle-class families

Characteristics: Dominated by Latin Americans with the nation's highest index for foreign-born immigrants, "Latino America" is a giant step in achievement. These families are concentrated in New York, Miami, Chicago, and the Southwest. They are young families with lots of children. Although they live in rented houses and have blue-collar jobs, they are moving up and are college-bound. They go to boxing matches, bank by mail, eat Mexican foods, listen to Spanish radio, and read lifestyle/fashion magazines.

GRAY COLLARS

2.1% of United States households

Median household income: $31,400

Adult age range: 55–64, 65+

Aging couples in inner suburbs

Characteristics: For nearly two decades, we read about the decline of the Great Lakes industrial "Rust Belt." Decimated by foreign takeovers in the steel and automobile industries, the area lost a million jobs. Although most of the kids left, their highly skilled parents stayed, and are now benefitting from a major U.S. industrial resurgence. They buy 1950's nostalgia, own CDs, eat canned cooked hams, listen to radio football, and read health/fitness magazines.

YOUNG LITERATI

1.0%of United States households

Median household income: $52,100

Adult age range: 25–34, 35–44

Upscale urban singles and couples

Characteristics: This cluster leads in education, although it is below other clusters in affluence. A younger mix of executives, professionals, and students live in multi-unit apartments, condos, and townhouses near private urban universities. Having few children, these bon vivants are free to pursue their interests in art, fitness, and travel. They travel to Japan and Asia, own tax exempt funds, buy a Montblanc/Waterman pen, listen to urban contemporary radio, and read style/fashion magazines.

SHOTGUNS AND PICKUPS

1.6% of United States households

Median household income: $33,300

Adult age range: 35–44, 45–54

Rural blue-collar workers and families

Characteristics: The least affluent of the "Country Families" clusters, members of this group are found in the Northeast, the Southeast, in the Great Lakes and Piedmont industrial regions. They lead the "Country Families" Group in blue-collar jobs; the majority are married with school-age children. They are church-goers who also enjoy bowling, hunting, sewing, and attending auto races, smoke pipe tobacco, have medical loss of income insurance, drink Canadian whisky, listen to country radio, and read hunting/car & truck magazines.

BLUE BLOOD ESTATES

0.8% of United States households

Median household income: $113,000

Adult age range: 35–44, 45–54, 55–64

Elite super-rich families

Characteristics: America's wealthiest suburbs are populated by established executives, professionals, and heirs to "old money." These people are accustomed to privilege and live in luxury, often surrounded by servants. A tenth of this group are multi-millionaires. The next level of affluence is a sharp drop from this pinnacle. Blue blood estate people belong to a country club, own mutual funds ($10,000+), purchase a car phone, watch TV golf, and read business magazines.

Source: Courtesy of Claritas Inc. (PRIZM and 62 Cluster nicknames are registered trademark of Claritas Inc.) Reprinted by permission.

into eight distinctive subgroups or segments based on their answers to 35 attitudinal and 4 demographic questions. Figure 3-10 depicts the VALS 2 classification scheme and offers a brief profile of the consumer traits of each of the VALS 2 segments. The major groupings (from left to right in Figure 3-10) are defined in terms of three major **self-orientations** and a new definition of resources: the *principle-oriented* (consumers whose choices are motivated by their beliefs, rather than by desires for approval), the *status-oriented* (consumers whose choices are guided by the actions, approval, and opinions of others), and the *action-oriented* (consumers who are motivated by a desire for social or physical activity, variety, and risk taking). Each of these three major self-orientations has distinct attitudes, lifestyles, and deci-

FIGURE 3-10

SRI VALS 2 Segments
Source: Reprinted with permission of SRI International

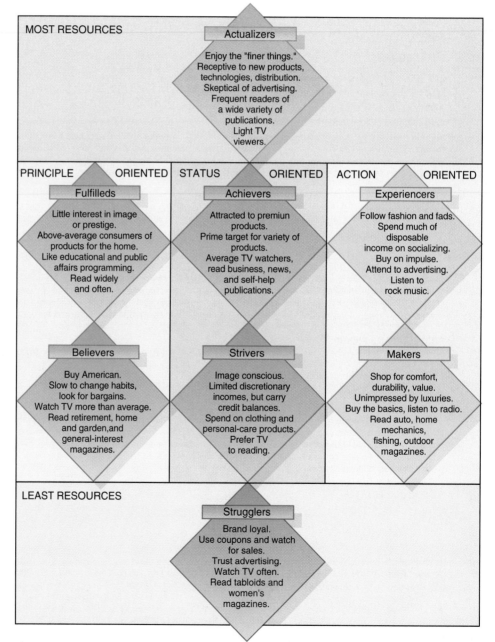

table 3-11 A Brief Demographic/Socioeconomic Profile of the Eight VALS 2 Segments

SEGMENT	PERCENT OF POPULATION	SEX (M)	MEDIAN AGE	MEDIAN INCOME	EDUCATION (SOME COLLEGE OR GRADUATED COLLEGE)	OCCUPATION WHITE COLLAR	MARRIED
Actualizer	10%	68%	42%	$74,000	89%	63%	67%
Fulfilled	10	53	55	54,000	86	46	71
Believer	17	37	58	25,000	2	17	59
Achiever	14	34	39	59,000	85	58	71
Striver	14	60	36	34,000	25	24	60
Experiencer	13	54	24	36,000	32	20	35
Maker	12	55	35	24,000	6	11	53
Struggler	10	33	67	13,500	6	7	50

Source: VALS 2/Simmons 1994.

sion-making styles. Resources refers to the range of psychological, physical, demographic, and material means and capacities consumers have to draw upon. It encompasses education, income, self-confidence, health, eagerness to buy, and energy level. Table 3-11 presents a brief demographic and socioeconomic profile of each of the eight segments that make up the VALS 2 model.

In terms of consumer characteristics, the eight VALS 2 segments differ in some important ways. For instance, *Believers* tend to buy American-made products and are slow to alter their consumption-related habits, while *Actualizers* are drawn to top-of-the-line products and to new products, especially innovative technologies (e.g., they might be early buyers of such products as tiny palm-held computers). National product service and media data for each VALS consumer segment is available through VALS linkages with the Simmons' annual survey of the American Household and other databases. Table 3-12 on page 72 presents the top five metropolitan areas for each of the eight VALS 2 segments, according to percentage of households.[12] GeoVALS™, a sister program, provides the percent of each VALS consumer type in each residential ZIP code to help marketers identify where concentrations of their customers live.

CRITERIA FOR EFFECTIVE TARGETING OF MARKET SEGMENTS

The previous sections have described various bases on which consumers can be clustered into homogeneous market segments. The next challenge for the marketer is to select one or more segments to target with an appropriate marketing mix. To be an effective target, a market segment should be (1) identifiable, (2) sufficient (in terms of size), (3) stable or growing, and (4) reachable (accessible) in terms of media and cost.

ACTUALIZERS

rank	metropolitan area	percent
1	Honolulu, HI	17.4%
2	Ventura, CA	16.5
3	Orange County, CA	16.4
4	Anchorage, AK	16.0
5	San Jose, CA	15.8
	U.S. AVERAGE	8.2

FULFILLEDS

rank	metropolitan area	percent
1	Ventura, CA	17.0%
2	Honolulu, HI	16.8
3	Orange County, CA	16.5
4	Bridgeport, CT	16.4
5	San Jose, CA	16.2
	U.S. AVERAGE	12.3

ACHIEVERS

rank	metropolitan area	percent
1	Manchester-Nashua, NH	23.2%
2	Portsmouth-Rochester, NH	22.1
3	Bridgeport, CT	21.1
4	Hartford, CT	20.2
5	Middlesex-Somerset-Hunterdon, NJ	19.7
	U.S. AVERAGE	10.1

EXPERIENCERS

rank	metropolitan area	percent
1	Bryan-College Station, TX	18.3%
2	Provo-Orem, UT	16.3
3	Yolo, CA	16.0
4	Gainesville, FL	15.5
5	Anchorage, AK	15.4
	U.S. AVERAGE	10.6

BELIEVERS

rank	metropolitan area	percent
1	Punta Gorda, Fl	26.2%
2	Sarasota-Bradenton, FL	24.3
3	Johnstown, PA	23.2
4	Fort Myers-Cape Coral, FL	23.1
5	Ocala, FL	23.1
	U.S. AVERAGE	17.3

STRIVERS

rank	metropolitan area	percent
1	Jacksonville, NC	20.2%
2	State College, PA	20.0
3	Jamestown, NY	19.1
4	Fayetteville, NC	19.0
5	Killeen-Temple, TX	18.7
	U.S. AVERAGE	14.0

MAKERS

rank	metropolitan area	percent
1	Bloomington, IN	17.6%
2	Lawrence, KS	17.3
3	Grand Forks, ND-MN	17.0
4	Columbia, MO	17.0
5	St. Cloud, MN	16.9
	U.S. AVERAGE	11.9

STRUGGLERS

rank	metropolitan area	percent
1	Cumberland, MD-WV	27.0%
2	McAllen-Edinburg-Mission, TX	26.7
3	Brownsville-Harlingen-San Benito, TX	26.6
4	Gadsden, AL	26.3
5	Ocala, FL	25.5
	U.S. AVERAGE	15.7

Source: GeoVALS™, SRI Consulting, and Judith Waldrop, "Markets with Attitude," *American Demographics*, July 1994, 30–31.

Identification

To divide the market into separate segments on the basis of a common need or characteristic that is relevant to the product or service, marketers must be able to identify the relevant characteristic. Some segmentation variables, such as *geography* (location) or *demographics* (age, gender, occupation, race), are relatively easy to identify or are even observable. Others, such as *education*, *income*, or *marital status*, can be determined through questionnaires. Still other characteristics, such as *benefits sought* or *lifestyle*, are more difficult to identify. A knowledge of consumer behavior is especially useful to marketers who use such intangible consumer characteristics as the basis for market segmentation.

Sufficiency

For a market segment to be a worthwhile target, it must have a sufficient number of people to warrant tailoring a product or promotional campaign to its specific needs or interests. To estimate the size of each segment under consideration, marketers often use secondary demographic data, such as that provided by the United States Census Bureau (and available at most local libraries), or undertake a probability survey whose findings can be projected to the total market. (Consumer research methodology was described in Chapter 2.)

Stability

Most marketers prefer to target consumer segments that are relatively stable in terms of demographic and psychological factors and needs and that are likely to grow larger over time. They prefer to avoid "fickle" segments that are unpredictable in embracing fads. For example, teens are a sizeable and easily identifiable market segment, eager to buy, able to spend, and easily reached. Yet, by the time a marketer produces merchandise for a popular teenage fad, interest in it may have waned. The popularity among teenagers of Batman merchandise (T-shirts and caps) during the highly successful run of *Batman* (the first movie) was not repeated during *Batman Returns*, when much of the tie-in promotional merchandise remained unsold.

Accessibility

A fourth requirement for effective targeting is accessibility, which means that marketers must be able to reach the market segments they want to target in an economical way. Despite the wide availability of special-interest magazines and cable TV programs, marketers are constantly looking for new media that will enable them to reach their target markets with a minimum of waste circulation and competition. One innovative communications company has devised an advertiser's dream: it created a cable television channel that provides a captive audience of junior and senior high school students daily with 2 minutes of commercials. Each school showing the 12-minute news and information report and the 2 minutes of commercials receives $50,000 worth of free satellite dishes, television sets, and VCRs.[13] The same company offers a set of six glossy magazines for display in doctors' waiting rooms to 15,000 physicians who agree to cancel all but two other publications. Advertisers are offered a large captive audience and a pledge of exclusivity: All six magazines feature only one brand in any product category.[14]

IMPLEMENTING SEGMENTATION STRATEGIES

Firms that use market segmentation can pursue a *concentrated* marketing strategy or a *differentiated* marketing strategy. In certain instances, they might use a *countersegmentation* strategy.

Concentrated versus Differentiated Marketing

Once an organization has identified its most promising market segments, it must decide whether to target one segment or several. The premise behind market segmentation is that each targeted segment receives a specially designed marketing mix, that is, a specially tailored product, price, distribution network, and/or promotional campaign. Targeting several segments using individual marketing mixes is called **differentiated marketing**; targeting just one segment with a unique marketing mix is called **concentrated marketing**.

Differentiated marketing is a highly appropriate segmentation strategy for financially strong companies that are well established in a product category and competitive with other firms that also are strong in the category (e.g., soft drinks, automobiles, detergents). However, if a company is small or new to the field, concentrated marketing is probably a better bet. A company can survive and prosper by filling a niche not occupied by stronger competitors. For example, Viadent toothpaste has become a leader in the small but increasingly important submarket of the overall tooth care market that focuses on products that fight gingivitis and other gum diseases.

Countersegmentation

Sometimes, companies find that they must reconsider a highly differentiated marketing strategy. They might find that some segments, although still worthwhile, have contracted over time to the point that they do not warrant an individually designed marketing program. In such cases, the company seeks to discover a more generic need or consumer characteristic that would apply to the members of two or more segments and recombine those segments into a single segment that could be targeted with an individually tailored product or promotional campaign. This is called a **countersegmentation** strategy. Some business schools with wide course offerings in each department were forced to adopt a countersegmentation strategy when they discovered that students simply did not have enough available credits to take a full spectrum of in-depth courses in their major area of study. As a result, some courses had to be canceled each semester because of inadequate registration. For some schools, a countersegmentation strategy effectively solved the problem (e.g., by combining *advertising*, *publicity*, *sales promotion*, and *personal selling* courses into a single course called *promotion*).

summary

Market segmentation and diversity are in natural harmony. Without a diverse marketplace, composed of many different peoples, with different backgrounds and countries of origin, different interests, different needs and wants, there really would be little reason to segment markets.

Before the widespread adoption of the marketing concept, mass marketing offering the same product or marketing mix to everyone was the marketing strategy most widely used. Market segmentation followed as a more logical way to meet consumer needs. Segmentation is defined as the process of dividing a potential market into distinct subsets of consumers with a common need or characteristic and selecting one or more segments to target with a specially designed marketing mix. Besides aiding in the development of new products, segmentation studies assist in the redesign and repositioning of existing products and the creation of promotional appeals and the selection of advertising media.

Because segmentation strategies benefit both marketers and consumers, they have received wide support from both sides of the marketplace. Market segmentation now is widely used by manufacturers, by retailers, and by the nonprofit sector.

Eight major classes of consumer characteristics serve as the most common bases for market segmentation. These include geographic factors, demographic factors, psychological-psychographic characteristics, sociocultural variables, use-related characteristics, use-situation factors, benefits sought, and hybrid forms of segmentation (e.g., psychographic-demographic profiles, such as VALS^{TM} 2, and geodemographic factors, such as PRIZM^{TM} or GeoVALS^{TM}). Important criteria for targeting market segments include identification, sufficiency, stability, and accessibility. Once an organization has identified promising target markets, it must decide whether to pursue several segments (differentiated marketing) or just one segment (concentrated marketing). It then develops a positioning strategy for each targeted segment. In certain instances, a company might decide to follow a countersegmentation strategy in which it combines two or more segments.

discussion questions

1. What is market segmentation? How is the practice of market segmentation related to the marketing concept?

2. Are market segmentation, targeting, and positioning interrelated? Illustrate how these three concepts can be used to develop a marketing strategy for a product of your choice.

3. Discuss the advantages and disadvantages of using demographics as a basis for segmentation. Can demographics and psychographics be used together to segment markets? Illustrate your answer with a specific example.

4. Many marketers have found that a relatively small group of heavy users accounts for a disproportionately large amount of the total product consumed. What are the advantages and disadvantages of targeting these heavy users?

5. Under which circumstances and for what types of products should a marketer segment the market on the basis of: (a) awareness status, (b) brand loyalty, or (c) use-situation?

6. Some marketers consider benefit segmentation as the segmentation approach most consistent with the marketing concept. Do you agree or disagree with this view? Why?

7. Club Med is a prominent company in the vacation and travel industry. Describe how the company can use demographics and psychographics to identify TV shows and magazines in which to place its advertisements.

8. How can a marketer use the VALS 2 segmentation profiles to develop an advertising campaign for a chain of health clubs? Which segments should be targeted? How should the health club be positioned to each of these segments?

9. For each of the following products, identify the segmentation base that you consider best for targeting consumers: (a) coffee, (b) soups, (c) home exercise equipment, (d) portable telephones, and (e) nonfat frozen yogurt. Explain your choices.

10. Apply the criteria for effective segmentation to marketing a product of your choice to college students.

exercises

1. Select a product and brand that you use frequently and list the benefits you receive from using it. Without disclosing your list, ask a fellow student who uses a different brand in this product category (preferably, a friend of the opposite sex) to make a similar list for his or her brand. Compare the two lists and identify the implications for using benefit segmentation to market the two brands.

2. Does your lifestyle differ significantly from your parents lifestyle? If so, how are the two lifestyles different? What factors cause these differences?

3. Do you anticipate any major changes in your lifestyle in the next 5 years? If so, into which VALS 2 segment are you likely to belong five years from now? Explain.

4. The owners of a local health-food restaurant have asked you to prepare a psychographic profile of families living in the community surrounding the restaurant's location. Construct a 10-question psychographic inventory appropriate for segmenting families on the basis of their dining-out preferences.

5. Find three print advertisements that you believe are targeted at a particular psychographic segment. How effective do you think each ad is in terms of achieving its objective? Why?

key words

- AIOs (i.e., Activities, Interests, Opinions)
- Audience profiles
- Benefit segmentation
- Concentrated marketing
- Customer profiles
- Countersegmentation
- Demographic characteristics
- Demographic segmentation
- Differentiated marketing
- Generation X
- Geographic segmentation
- Hybrid Segmentation
- Mass marketing
- Market segmentation
- Micromarketing
- Positioning
- Psychographic inventory
- Psychological characteristics
- Psychographic segmentation
- Psychological/Psychographic segmentation
- Repositioning
- Self-orientation
- Segmentation criteria
- Sociocultural segmentation
- Sociocultural variables
- Targeting
- Use-related segmentation
- Use-situation segmentation
- VALS 2
- Xers

1. STEPHANIE STROM, "How Gap, Inc. Spells Revenge," *The New York Times*, April 24, 1994, Business Section, 1; and "For a Gap Sibling, the Fun Begins," *The New York Times*, November 2, 1995, C1.

2. SCOTT DONATON, "Media Reassess as Boomers Age," *Advertising Age*, July 15, 1991, 13.

3. CARA APPELBAUM, "Forget About Global, Coke's Gone Texan," *Adweek's Marketing Week*, March 9, 1992, 10.

4. LAWRIE MIFFLIN, "New Cable Programming for the Over–49 Crowd," *The New York Times*, September 11, 1995, D9.

5. CYNDEE MILLER, "Bennett Redefines 'Cool' as Endorser," *Marketing News*, September 28, 1994, 6.

6. MAXINE WILKIE, "Scent of a Market," *American Demographics*, August 1995, 42.

7. GEOFFREY MEREDITH and CHARLES SCHEWE, "The Power of Cohorts," *American Demographics*, December 1994, 22–31.

8. REBECCA PIIRTO, "Cable TV," *American Demographics*, June 1995, 42.

9. KATHLEEN MORROW and CLINT B. TANKERSLEY, "An Exploratory Study of Consumer Usage and Satisfaction with 800 and 900 Numbers," *Journal of Direct Marketing* 8, Autumn 1994, 54.

10. RUSSELL HALEY, "Benefit Segmentation: A Decision-Oriented Research Tool," *Marketing Management* 4, Summer 1995, 59–62; DIANNE CERMAK, KAREN MARU FILE, and RUSS ALAN PRINCE, "A Benefit Segmentation of the Major Donor Market," *Journal of Business Research*, February 1994, 121–30; GORDON MCDOUGALL and TERRENCE LEVESQUE "Benefit Segmentation Using Service Quality Dimensions: An Investigation in Retail Banking," *International Journal of Bank Marketing*, 1994, 15–23; and JOEL S. DUBOW, "Occasion-Based Versus User-Based Benefit Segmentation: A Case Study," *Journal of Advertising Research*, March/April 1992, 11–18.

11. ALVIN P. SANOFF, "The Consulting Game," *U.S. News & World Report*, September 18, 1995, 119–20.

12. JUDITH WALDROP, "Markets with Attitude," *American Demographics*, July 1994, 30–31.

13. N. R. KLEINFIELD, "In Search of the Next Medium," *The New York Times*, March 19, 1989, 1.

14. LAWRENCE ZUCKERMAN, "Targeting the Waiting Room," *Time*, March 21, 1988, 56.

PART TWO

The Consumer as an Individual

PART 2 DISCUSSES THE CONSUMER AS AN INDIVIDUAL.

CHAPTERS 4 THROUGH 9 PROVIDE THE READER with a comprehen-

sive picture of consumer psychology. These chapters explain the basic

psychological concepts that account for individual behavior and

demonstrate how these concepts influence the individual's consumption-

related behavior. Chapter 10 shows how communication links

consumers as individuals to the world and people around them.

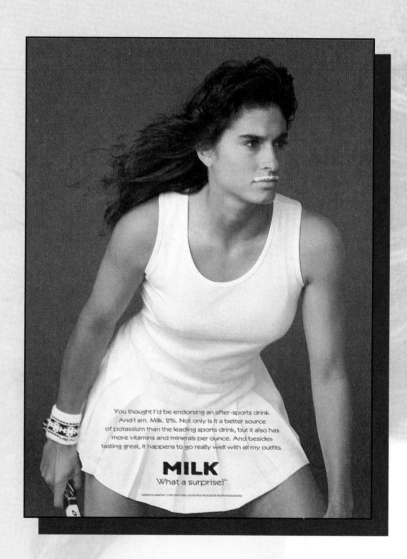

You thought I'd be endorsing an after-sports drink. And I am. Milk. 2%. Not only is it a better source of potassium than the leading sports drink, but it also has more vitamins and minerals per ounce. And besides tasting great, it happens to go really well with all my outfits.

MILK
What a surprise!™

Diversity is not a new phenomenon. We all seek different pleasures and spend our money in different ways. One husband and wife may spend their vacation on a cruise to Alaska; their friends may prefer to lie on a beach and watch the sea. One father may buy his young son a set of electric trains; another may buy his son a personal computer. One woman may spend her Christmas bonus on a new washer/dryer; her neighbor may spend hers to join a health club.

Diversity in consumer behavior—different ways of spending money—does not surprise us. We have been brought up to believe that the differences among people are what make life truly interesting. However, the diversity in human behavior often causes us to overlook the fact that people are really very much alike. There are underlying similarities—constants that tend to operate across many types of people—that serve to explain and clarify consumption behavior. Psychologists

Understanding human needs is half the job of meeting them.

—Adlai Stevenson
Speech, Columbus, Ohio,
October 3, 1952

81

and consumer behaviorists agree that most people tend to experience the same kinds of needs and motives; they simply express these motives in different ways. For this reason, an understanding of human motives is very important to marketers; it enables them to understand and to predict human behavior in the marketplace.

Human needs—consumer needs—are the basis of all modern marketing. Needs are the essence of the marketing concept. The key to a company's survival, profitability, and growth in a highly competitive marketing environment is its ability to identify and satisfy unfulfilled consumer needs better and sooner than the competition.

Marketers do not create needs, although in some instances they may make consumers more keenly aware of unfelt needs. Successful marketers define their markets in terms of the needs they presume to satisfy, rather than in terms of the products they sell. This is a **market-oriented**, rather than a **production-oriented** approach to marketing. A marketing orientation focuses on the needs of the buyer; a production orientation focuses on the needs of the seller. The marketing concept implies that the manufacturer will make only what it knows people will buy; a production orientation implies that the manufacturer will try to sell what it decides to make. This difference in orientation can readily be seen in Eastern Europe, where Western marketers are producing products that people want to buy, rather than "the old way" of making products and then trying to sell them.[1]

Marketers who base their offerings on a recognition of consumer needs find a ready market for their products. The popularity of farmers' markets in the United States is grounded in their appeal to consumers' needs for flavor, quality, and freshness, needs that too often are not met by large food marketers who focus on appearance and convenience. The success of Merrill Lynch's Cash Management Account is based on its fulfillment of consumers' expressed needs for bank accounts that eliminate idle funds, provide access to credit, and compile consolidated information about their total financial picture.[2]

There are countless examples of products that have succeeded in the marketplace because they fulfilled consumer needs; there are even more examples of products and companies that have failed because they did not recognize or understand consumer needs.

This chapter discusses basic needs that operate in most people to motivate behavior. It explores the influence such needs have on consumption behavior. Later chapters in Part II explain why and how these basic human motives are expressed in so many diverse ways.

WHAT IS MOTIVATION?

Several basic concepts are integral to an understanding of human motivation. Before we discuss these, it is necessary to agree on some basic definitions.

Motivation

Motivation can be described as the driving force within individuals that impels them to action. This driving force is produced by a state of tension, which exists as the result of an unfulfilled need. Individuals strive—both consciously and subconsciously—to reduce this tension through behavior that they anticipate will fulfill their needs and thus relieve them of the stress they feel. The specific goals they select and the patterns of action they undertake to achieve their goals are the results of individual thinking and learning. Figure 4-1 presents a model of the motivational process. It portrays motivation as a state of need-induced tension that exerts a "push" on the individual to engage in behavior that he or she expects will gratify a need and thus reduce the tension. Whether gratification is actually achieved depends on the course of action being pursued. (If a high school girl expects to become a great tennis player by wearing the same brand of sneakers that Jennifer Capriati wears, she is likely to be disappointed; if she takes tennis lessons and practices diligently, she may succeed.)

The specific courses of action that consumers pursue and their special goals are selected on the basis of their thinking processes (i.e., cognition) and previous learning. For that reason, marketers who understand motivational theory attempt to influence the consumer's cognitive processes.

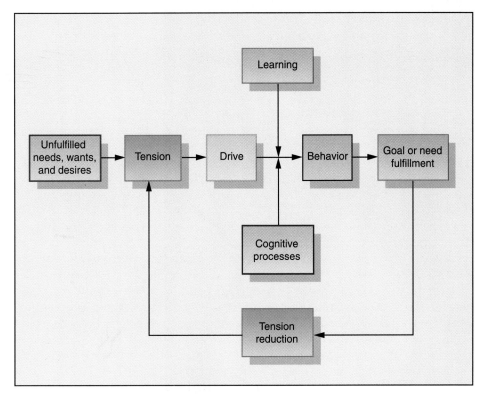

FIGURE 4-1

Model of the Motivation Process

Needs

Every individual has needs: some are innate, others are acquired. Innate needs are *physiological* (i.e., biogenic); they include the needs for food, for water, for air, for clothing, for shelter, and for sex. Because they are needed to sustain biological life, the biogenic needs are considered **primary needs** or motives.

Acquired needs are needs that we learn in response to our culture or environment. These may include needs for self-esteem, for prestige, for affection, for power, and for learning. Because acquired needs are generally *psychological* (i.e., psychogenic), they are considered **secondary needs** or motives. They result from the individual's subjective psychological state and from relationships with others. For example, all individuals need shelter from the elements; thus, finding a place to live fulfills an important *primary* need for a newly transferred executive. However, the kind of residence she rents or buys may be the result of *secondary* needs. She may seek a place in which she and her husband can entertain large groups of people (and fulfill social needs); she may want to live in an exclusive community to impress her friends and family (and fulfill ego needs). The house an individual ultimately purchases thus may serve to fulfill both primary and secondary needs.

Goals

Goals are the sought-after results of motivated behavior. As Figure 4-1 indicated, all behavior is goal oriented. Our discussion of motivation in this chapter is in part concerned with **generic goals**—that is, the general classes or categories of goals that consumers select to fulfill their needs. Figure 4-2 illustrates a generic goal. Marketers are even more

FIGURE 4-2

A Generic Appeal Designed to Promote Milk Consumption
Courtesy of Bozell Worldwide Inc., as agent for National Fluid Milk Processor Promotion Board

You thought I'd be endorsing an after-sports drink. And I am. Milk. 2%. Not only is it a better source of potassium than the leading sports drink, but it also has more vitamins and minerals per ounce. And besides tasting great, it happens to go really well with all my outfits.

MILK
What a surprise!

concerned with consumers' **product-specific goals**—that is, the specifically branded or labeled products they select to fulfill their needs. For example, the Thomas J. Lipton Company wants consumers to view iced tea as a good way to quench summer thirst (i.e., as a generic goal). However, it is even more interested in having consumers view Lipton's Iced Tea as the *best* way to quench summer thirst (i.e., as a product-specific goal). Marketers who support their trade association advertising recognize the importance of promoting both types of goals.

▲ **The Selection of Goals** For any given need, there are many different and appropriate goals. The goals selected by individuals depend on their *personal experiences, physical capacity*, prevailing *cultural norms and values*, and the goal's *accessibility* in the physical and social environment. For example, an individual may have a strong hunger need. If he is a young college athlete, he may envision a thick sirloin steak as his goal object; if his doctor has advised him to avoid red meat, he may settle for a thick tuna steak instead. If he has a toothache, he may not be able to chew a steak; he may have to select hamburger. If he has never tasted steak, if it is outside his realm of personal experience, he probably would not even think of steak but instead would select a food that has previously satisfied his hunger.

Finally, the goal object has to be both socially acceptable and physically accessible. If our college athlete was having dinner with his mother, she might frown on his eating red meat and insist he eat fish or chicken instead. If he were shipwrecked on an island with no food provisions or living animals, he could not realistically select steak as his goal object, although he might fantasize about it. If he were in India, where cows are considered sacred, he would not be able to eat steak, because to do so would be considered a sacrilege. He would have to select a substitute goal more appropriate to the social environment.

An individual's own perception of himself or herself also serves to influence the specific goals selected. The products a person owns, would like to own, or would not like to own are often perceived in terms of how closely they reflect (are congruent with) the person's **self-image**. A product that is perceived as matching a consumer's self-image has a greater probability of being selected than one that is not. Thus, a man who perceives himself as young and "with it" may drive a Porsche; a woman who perceives herself as rich and conservative may drive a Mercedes. The types of houses people live in, the cars they drive, the clothes they wear, the very foods they eat—these specific goal objects are often chosen because they symbolically reflect the individual's self-image while they satisfy specific needs. (The relationship of self-concept to product choice is explained more fully in Chapters 5 and 6.)

▲ **Interdependence of Needs and Goals** Needs and goals are interdependent; neither exists without the other. However, people are often not as aware of their needs as they are of their goals. For example, a teenager may not consciously be aware of his social needs but may join a photography club to meet new friends. A local politician may not consciously be aware of a power need but may regularly run for public office. A woman may not recognize her achievement needs but may strive to have the most successful real estate office in town.

Individuals are usually somewhat more aware of their physiological needs than they are of their psychological needs. Most people know when they are hungry or thirsty or cold, and they take appropriate steps to satisfy these needs. The same people may not consciously be aware of their needs for acceptance, for self-esteem, for status. They may, however, subconsciously engage in behavior that satisfies these psychological (acquired) needs.

Positive and Negative Motivation

Motivation can be **positive** or **negative** in direction. We may feel a driving force *toward* some object or condition, or a driving force *away* from some object or condition. For example, a person may be impelled toward a restaurant to fulfill a hunger need and away from motorcycle transportation to fulfill a safety need.

Some psychologists refer to positive drives as needs, wants, or desires, and to negative drives as fears or aversions. However, although positive and negative motivational forces seem to differ dramatically in terms of physical (and sometimes emotional) activity, they are basically similar in that both serve to initiate and sustain human behavior. For this reason, researchers often refer to both kinds of drives or motives as needs, wants, and desires. Some theorists distinguish *wants* from *needs* by defining wants as product-specific needs. Thus, to use an earlier example, a person may experience thirst (a *need*); she may *want* Lipton's Iced Tea as a means of alleviating her thirst.

Goals, too, can be positive or negative. A positive goal is one toward which behavior is directed and thus is often referred to as an **approach object**. A negative goal is one from which behavior is directed away and thus is sometimes referred to as an **avoidance object**. Since both approach and avoidance goals can be considered objects of motivated behavior, most researchers refer to both simply as *goals*. Consider this example: A middle-aged woman may have a *positive* goal of fitness, and so she joins a health club to work out regularly. Her husband may view getting fat as a *negative* goal, and so he joins a road runners club. In the former case, the wife's actions are designed to achieve a positive goal—health and fitness; in the latter case, her husband's action is designed to avoid a negative goal—a flabby physique. Figures 4–3A and B present two ads by Neutrogena; one offers readers a positive goal (Figure 4-3A) and the other offers a negative goal (Figure 4-3B).

Sometimes people become motivationally aroused by a threat to or elimination of a behavioral freedom (e.g., the freedom to make a product choice without undue influence from a retailer). This motivational state is called *psychological reactance* and is usually manifested by a negative consumer response.[3] For example, in 1985 when the Coca-Cola company changed its traditional formula and introduced "New Coke," many people reacted negatively to the fact that their "freedom to choose" had been taken away, and refused to buy the New Coke. Coca-Cola management responded to this unexpected psychological reaction by reintroducing the original formula as "Classic Coke."

Rational versus Emotional Motives

Some consumer behaviorists distinguish between so-called **rational motives** and **emotional** (or nonrational) **motives**. They use the term *rationality* in the traditional economic sense, which assumes that consumers behave rationally when they carefully consider all alternatives and choose those that give them the greatest utility. In a marketing context, the term *rationality* implies that consumers elect goals based on totally objective criteria, such as size, weight, price, or miles per gallon. *Emotional* motives imply the selection of goals according to personal or subjective criteria (e.g., the desire for individuality, pride, fear, affection, status).

The assumption underlying this distinction is that subjective or emotional criteria do not maximize utility or satisfaction. However, it is reasonable to assume that consumers always attempt to select alternatives that, *in their view*, serve to maximize satisfaction. Obviously, the assessment of satisfaction is a very personal process, based on the individual's own need structure, as well as on past behavioral and social (or learned) experiences. What may appear irrational to an outside observer may be perfectly rational in the context of the consumer's own psychological field. For example, a product purchased to enhance self-image (such as a fragrance) is a perfectly rational form of consumer behavior. If behavior does not appear rational to the person at the time it is undertaken, obviously he or she

FIGURE 4-3A Positive Motivation
Courtesy of Neutrogena, a Beiersdorf
Company

FIGURE 4-3B Negative Motivation
Courtesy of Neutrogena, a Beiersdorf
Company

would not do it. Therefore, the distinction between rational and emotional consumption motives is not always warranted.

Consumer researchers who subscribe to the **positivist perspective** tend to view all consumer behavior as rationally motivated, and they try to isolate the causes of such behavior so that they can predict, and thus influence, future behavior. **Experientialists** are interested in studying the hedonistic pleasures that consumption behavior provides, such as fun, or fantasy, or sensuality. They study consumer behavior to gain insights and understanding of the consumer in his or her own unique circumstances.

THE DYNAMIC NATURE OF MOTIVATION

Motivation is a highly dynamic construct that is constantly changing in reaction to life experiences.

Needs and Goals Are Constantly Changing

Needs and goals are constantly growing and changing in response to an individual's physical condition, environment, interactions with others, and experiences. As individuals attain their goals, they develop new ones. If they do not attain their goals, they continue to strive for old goals, or they develop substitute goals. Some of the reasons why need-driven human activity never ceases include the following: (1) Existing needs are never completely satisfied; they continually impel activity designed to attain or maintain satisfaction. (2) As needs become satisfied, new and higher-order needs emerge that cause tension. (3) People who achieve their goals set new and higher goals for themselves. Figure 4-4 suggests the anticipation of new and higher goals.

FIGURE 4-4

New and Higher Goals
Motivate Behavior
Reprinted with the permission
of The Prudential Insurance
Company of America. All rights
reserved.

"Prudential's size is a real plus.

It gives me room to expand my horizons."

A company as large and diverse as The Prudential has plenty of job opportunities. What we need are more talented people to fill them.

Mark Miller, a CPA in the Comptroller's Office, answered our call. He not only found a job, he found the kind of environment that challenges his skills and his intellect.

Mark and all Prudential employees benefit from our job diversity. We have training programs that let you explore a variety of positions so you can find a job that suits you best. Your options can range from finance and real estate to securities and insurance.

The Prudential is a big company, not only in size, but also in job opportunities.

If you're interested in exploring a wide range of opportunities at The Prudential, write to: Ms. Conic, College Relations, The Prudential Employment Center, Dept. B , 56 Livingston Avenue, Roseland, NJ 07068. An equal opportunity employer.

The biggest is looking for the best.

▲ **Needs Are Never Fully Satisfied** Most human needs are never fully or permanently satisfied. For example, at fairly regular intervals people experience hunger needs that must be satisfied. Most people regularly seek companionship and approval from others to satisfy their social needs. Even more complex psychological needs are rarely satisfied. For example, a person may partially or temporarily satisfy a *power* need by working as assistant to the CEO of a Fortune 500 company, but this small taste of power may not sufficiently satisfy her need, and so she may strive for her own decision-making position in the company. In this instance, temporary goal achievement does not adequately satisfy the need for power, and the individual strives harder in an effort to satisfy the need more fully.

▲ **New Needs Emerge as Old Needs Are Satisfied** Some motivational theorists believe that a hierarchy of needs exists and that new, higher-order needs emerge as lower-order needs are fulfilled.[4] For example, a man who has largely satisfied his basic psychological needs may turn his efforts to achieving *acceptance* among his new neighbors by joining their political clubs and supporting their candidates. Having achieved acceptance, he then may seek *recognition* by giving lavish parties or making large charitable contributions.

Marketers must be attuned to changing needs. Car manufacturers who stress the prestige value of their automobiles may fail to recognize that many consumers now look elsewhere to satisfy needs for prestige—for example, through charitable gift giving or public service. For this reason, manufacturers of prestige cars might do better if they stressed other need satisfactions (e.g., family enjoyment or safety) as reasons for buying a new model.

▲ **Success and Failure Influence Goals** A number of researchers have explored the nature of the goals that individuals set for themselves.[5] In general, they have concluded that individuals who successfully achieve their goals usually set new and higher goals for themselves; that is, they raise their **levels of aspiration**. This is probably due to the fact that success makes them more confident of their ability to reach higher goals. Conversely, those who do not reach their goals sometimes lower their levels of aspiration. Thus, goal selection is often a function of success and failure. For example, a college senior who is not accepted into medical school may try instead to enter dental school; failing that, he may study to be a pharmacist.

The nature and persistence of an individual's behavior are often influenced by expectations of success or failure in reaching certain goals. Those expectations, in turn, are often based on past experience. A person who takes good snapshots with an inexpensive camera may be motivated to buy a more sophisticated camera in the belief that it will enable her to take even better photographs. In this way, she eventually may upgrade her camera by several hundred dollars. On the other hand, a person who has not been able to take good photographs is just as likely to keep the same camera or even to lose all interest in photography.

These effects of success and failure on goal selection have strategy implications for marketers. Goals should be reasonably attainable. Advertisements should not promise more than the product will deliver. Even a good product will not be repurchased if it fails to live up to expectations. A consumer is likely to regard a disappointing product with even less satisfaction than its objective performance warrants. Advertisers who create unrealistic expectations for their products are likely to cause dissatisfaction among consumers. The frustrations and disappointments that result from consumer dissatisfaction have helped fuel the driving force behind consumerism.

▲ **Substitute Goals** When an individual cannot attain a specific goal or type of goal that he or she anticipates will satisfy certain needs, behavior may be directed to a **substitute goal**. Although the substitute goal may not be as satisfactory as the primary goal, it may be sufficient to dispel uncomfortable tension. Continued deprivation of a primary goal may result in the substitute goal assuming primary-goal status. A man who has stopped drinking whole milk because he is dieting may actually begin to prefer skim milk. A woman who cannot afford a BMW may convince herself that a Mazda Miata has an image she clearly prefers. Of course, in this instance, the substitute goal may be a defensive reaction to frustration.

Frustration

Failure to achieve a goal often results in feelings of **frustration**. At one time or another, everyone has experienced the frustration that comes from the inability to attain a goal. The barrier that prevents attainment of a goal may be personal to the individual (e.g., limited physical or financial resources), or it can be an obstacle in the physical or social environment. Regardless of the cause, individuals react differently to frustrating situations. Some people are adaptive and manage to cope by finding their way around the obstacle or, if that fails, by selecting a substitute goal. Others are less adaptive and may regard their inability to achieve a goal as a personal failure and experience feelings of anxiety. An example of adaptive behavior would be the college student who would prefer to own a sports car but settles for a used minivan.

▲ **Defense Mechanisms** People who cannot cope with frustration often mentally redefine their frustrating situations in order to protect their self-images and defend their self-esteem. For example, a young woman may yearn for a European vacation she cannot afford. The coping individual may select a less expensive vacation trip to Disneyland or a national park. The person who cannot cope may react with anger toward her boss for not paying her enough money to afford the vacation she prefers, or she may persuade herself that Europe is unreasonably expensive for Americans this year. These last two possibilities are examples, respectively, of *aggression* and *rationalization*, defense mechanisms people sometimes adopt to protect their egos from feelings of failure when they do not attain their goals. Other defense mechanisms include *regression, withdrawal, projection, autism, identification*, and *repression*.

AGGRESSION Individuals who experience frustration may resort to aggressive behavior in attempting to protect their self-esteem. This was aptly illustrated by two British yachtsmen who, disappointed at their poor showing in a sailing competition, burned their boat and swam ashore. Frustrated consumers have boycotted manufacturers in an effort to improve product quality, and have boycotted retailers in an effort to have prices lowered.

RATIONALIZATION Sometimes, individuals redefine a frustrating situation by inventing plausible reasons for being unable to attain their goals. Or, they may decide that the goal really is not worth pursuing. Rationalizations are not deliberate lies, since the individual is not fully aware of the cognitive distortion that occurs as a result of the frustrating situation.

REGRESSION Sometimes people react to frustrating situations with childish or immature behavior. A shopper attending a bargain sale, for example, may fight over merchandise and resort to tearing a garment that another shopper will not relinquish, rather than allow the other person to have it.

WITHDRAWAL Frustration is often resolved by simply withdrawing from the situation. A person who has difficulty achieving officer status in an organization may simply quit that organization. Furthermore, he may rationalize his resignation by deciding the organization is not true to its stated ideals and that its other members are somewhat shallow. In addition, he may decide he can use his time more constructively in other activities.

PROJECTION An individual may redefine a frustrating situation by projecting blame for his or her own failures and inabilities on other objects or persons. Thus, the golfer who misses a stroke may blame the caddie or the golf clubs; the driver who has an automobile accident may blame the other driver or the condition of the road.

AUTISM Autism, or autistic thinking, refers to thinking that is almost completely dominated by needs and emotions, with little effort made to relate to reality. Such daydreaming, or fantasizing, enables the individual to attain imaginary gratification of unfulfilled needs. A person who is shy and lonely, for example, may daydream about a romantic love affair.

IDENTIFICATION Sometimes people resolve their feelings of frustration by subconsciously identifying with other persons or situations that they consider relevant. Marketers have long recognized the importance of this defense mechanism and often use it as the basis for advertising appeals. That is why slice-of-life commercials and advertisements are so popular. Such advertisements usually portray a stereotypical situation in which an individual experiences a frustration and then overcomes the problem that has caused the frustration by using the advertised product. If the viewer can identify with the frustrating situation, he or she may very likely adopt the proposed solution and buy the product advertised. For example, a fellow who has difficulty in attracting dates may decide to use the same mouthwash, shampoo, or clothing that "worked" for the man in the commercial. Interestingly enough, use of the product may increase his self-confidence sufficiently to enable him to achieve his goal. Figures 4-5A and B invite readers frustrated with their aging appearance to identify with people who have had cosmetic surgery.

REPRESSION Another way that individuals avoid the tension arising from frustration is by repressing the unsatisfied need. Thus, individuals may "forget" a need; that is, they force the need out of their conscious awareness. Sometimes repressed needs manifest themselves indirectly. A couple who cannot have children may surround themselves with plants or pets. The wife may teach school or work in a library; the husband may do volunteer work in a

FIGURES 4-5A and B Identification with Cosmetic Surgery Patients
Courtesy of The Austin-Weston Center for Cosmetic Surgery

Judy Katter:

Entrepreneur. Grandmother. Pasta lover. Cosmetic surgery patient.

Judy Katter loves being a grandmother as much as she loves not looking like one. She decided a year ago that she had the right to look as young as she feels. At the Austin-Weston Center for Cosmetic Surgery, we specialize in helping people's bodies match their souls. Call us for a free consultation. Because cosmetic surgery can be for everyone. Including you.

The
AUSTIN-WESTON
CENTER
for
COSMETIC SURGERY
1776 Old Meadow Rd., McLean, VA 22102

703-893-6168

Harvey Austin:

Plastic surgeon. Movie buff. Fly fisherman for life. Cosmetic surgery patient.

Harvey Austin, M.D. knows what it's like to be a cosmetic surgery patient. He is one. So is his partner, George Weston, M.D. So are both of their wives. At the Austin-Weston Center for Cosmetic Surgery, improving self images isn't just our practice. It's our lives. Call us for a free consultation. Because cosmetic surgery can be for everyone. Including you.

The
AUSTIN-WESTON
CENTER
for
COSMETIC SURGERY
1776 Old Meadow Rd., McLean, VA 22102

703-893-6168

boys' club. The manifestation of repressed needs in a socially acceptable form is called **sublimation**, another type of defense mechanism.

This listing of defense mechanisms is far from exhaustive. People have virtually limitless ways of redefining frustrating situations to protect their self-esteem from the anxieties that result from experiencing failure. Based on their early experiences, individuals tend to develop their own characteristic ways of handling frustration. Marketers often consider this fact in their selection of advertising appeals. For example, a flour manufacturer may try to convince consumers that previous baking failures were caused by the ingredients they used, rather than the ineptness of their efforts. (See *attribution theory* in Chapter 9.)

▲ **Multiplicity of Needs** A consumer's behavior often fulfills more than one need. In fact, it is more likely that specific goals are selected because they fulfill several needs. We buy clothing for protection and for modesty; in addition, our clothing fulfills an enormous range of personal and social needs. Usually, however, there is one overriding (i.e., prepotent) need that initiates behavior. For example, a woman may want to lose weight because she wants to wear more stylish clothing; she also may be concerned about high blood pressure. In addition, she has noticed her husband admiring slimmer girls on the beach. If the cumulative amount of tension produced by each of these three reasons is sufficiently strong, she will truly diet. However, just one of the reasons (e.g., her husband's straying eye) may serve as the triggering mechanism; that would be the **prepotent need**.

▲ **Needs and Goals Vary among Individuals** One cannot accurately infer motives from behavior. People with different needs may seek fulfillment through selection of the same goals, while people with the same needs may seek fulfillment through different goals. Consider the following examples. Five people who are active in a consumer advocacy organization may each belong for a different reason. The first may be genuinely concerned with protecting consumer interests; the second may be concerned about an increase in counterfeit merchandise; the third may seek social contacts from organizational meetings; the fourth may enjoy the power of directing a large group; and the fifth may enjoy the status provided by membership in a powerful organization.

Similarly, five people may be driven by the same need (e.g., an ego need) to seek fulfillment in different ways. The first may seek advancement and recognition through a professional career; the second may become active in the League of Women Voters; the third may join a health club; the fourth may take professional dance lessons; and the fifth may seek attention by monopolizing classroom discussions.

Arousal of Motives

Most of an individual's specific needs are dormant much of the time. The arousal of any particular set of needs at a specific point in time may be caused by internal stimuli found in the individual's *physiological* condition, *emotional* or *cognitive* processes, or by stimuli in the outside *environment*.

▲ **Physiological Arousal** Bodily needs at any one specific moment in time are rooted in an individual's physiological condition at that moment. A drop in blood sugar level or stomach contractions will trigger awareness of a hunger need. Secretion of sex hormones will awaken the sex need. A decrease in body temperature will induce shivering, which makes the individual aware of the need for warmth. Most of these physiological cues are involuntary; however, they arouse related needs that cause uncomfortable tensions until they are satisfied. For example, a shivering man may turn up the heat in his home to relieve his discomfort; he also may make a mental note to buy flannel pajamas. Research suggests that television programs often generate physiological arousal in viewers that affects the impact of ensuing commercials.[6]

▲ **Emotional Arousal** Sometimes daydreaming results in the arousal or stimulation of latent needs. People who are bored or frustrated in attempts to achieve their goals often engage in daydreaming (autistic thinking), in which they imagine themselves in all sorts of desirable situations. These thoughts tend to arouse dormant needs, which may produce uncomfortable tensions that "push" them into goal-oriented behavior. A young woman who dreams of becoming a successful business leader may enroll in graduate business school. A young man who dreams of becoming a novelist may sign up for a writing workshop.

An advertising campaign for Calvin Klein's perfume, Obsession, relied on the emotional arousal of needs. A series of 30-second TV commercials portrayed men and women in situations of feverish, all-consuming intensity. Although most perfume advertising talks about the fragrance or scent of the product, these commercials were capped with the phrase, "Ahhh . . . the smell of it," further stressing the all-consuming lust portrayed.[7]

▲ **Cognitive Arousal** Sometimes, random thoughts or personal achievement can lead to a cognitive awareness of needs. An advertisement that provides reminders of home might trigger instant yearning to speak with one's parents. This is the basis for many long distance telephone company campaigns that stress the low cost of international long-distance rates. Figure 4-6 on page 94 depicts an ad seeking cognitive arousal of the "need" for executive education.

▲ **Environmental Arousal** The set of needs activated at a particular time are often determined by specific cues in the environment. Without these cues, the needs might remain dormant. For example, the 6 o'clock news, the sight or smell of bakery goods, fast-food commercials on television, the end of the school day—all of these may arouse the "need" for food. In such cases, modification of the environment may be necessary to reduce the arousal of hunger.

A most potent form of situational cue is the goal object itself. A woman may experience an overwhelming need for a new sofa when she sees her neighbor's new sofa; a man may suddenly experience a "need" for a new car when passing a dealer's display window. Sometimes, an advertisement or other environmental cue produces a psychological imbalance in the viewer's mind. For example, a man who prides himself on his gardening may see an advertisement for a tractor mower that apparently works more efficiently than his own rotary mower. The ad may make him so unhappy with his old mower that he experiences severe tension until he buys himself a new tractor model.

When people live in a complex and highly varied environment, they experience many opportunities for need arousal. Conversely, when their environment is poor or deprived, fewer needs are activated. This explains why television has had such a mixed effect on the lives of people in underdeveloped countries. It exposes them to various lifestyles and expensive products that they would not otherwise see, and it awakens wants and desires which they have little opportunity or even hope of satisfying. Thus, while television enriches many lives, it also serves to frustrate people with little money or education or hope, and may result in the adoption of such aggressive defense mechanisms as robbery, boycotts, or even revolts.

There are two opposing philosophies concerned with the arousal of human motives. The **behaviorist** school considers motivation to be a mechanical process; behavior is seen as the response to a stimulus, and elements of conscious thought are ignored. An extreme example of this stimulus-response theory of motivation is the impulse buyer who reacts largely to external stimuli in the buying situation. According to this theory, the consumer's cognitive control is limited; he or she does not *act*, but *reacts* to stimuli in the marketplace.[8] The **cognitive** school believes that all behavior is directed at goal achievement.

FIGURE 4-6

Cognitive Arousal of Needs
Courtesy of The Wharton School

Needs and past experiences are reasoned, categorized, and transformed into attitudes and beliefs that act as predispositions to behavior. These predispositions are aimed at helping the individual satisfy needs, and they determine the direction that he or she takes to achieve this satisfaction.

TYPES AND SYSTEMS OF NEEDS

For many years, psychologists and others interested in human behavior have attempted to develop exhaustive lists of human needs or motives.

Diversity of Need Systems

Most lists of human needs tend to be diverse in content as well as in length. Although there is little disagreement about specific **physiological** needs, there is considerable disagreement about specific **psychological** (i.e., psychogenic) **needs**. Table 4-1 presents a list of forty-four human motives compiled in 1923 by Professor Daniel Starch of the Harvard Business School for use as copy appeals.

In 1938, the psychologist Henry Murray prepared a detailed list of twenty-eight psychogenic needs that have served as the basic constructs for a number of widely used personality tests (e.g., the Edwards Personal Preference Schedule). Murray believed that everyone has the same basic set of needs, but that individuals differ in their priority ranking of these needs. Murray's basic needs include many motives that are assumed to play an important role in consumer behavior, such as *acquisition, achievement, recognition*, and *exhibition* (see Table 4-2 on page 96).

Lists of human motives often are too long to be of practical use to marketers. The most useful kind of list is a limited one in which needs are sufficiently generic in title to subsume more detailed human needs. Although some psychologists have suggested that people have different need priorities based on their personalities, their experiences, their environments, and so forth, others believe that most human beings experience the same basic needs, to which they assign a similar priority ranking.

▲ **Hierarchy of Needs** Dr. Abraham Maslow, a clinical psychologist, formulated a widely accepted theory of human motivation based on the notion of a universal **hierarchy of human needs**.[9] Maslow's theory postulates five basic levels of human needs, which rank

table 4-1   Motives in Male and Female Adults: A 1923 Compilation

Appetite—hunger	Respect for deity
Love of offspring	Sympathy for others
Health	Protection of others
Sex attraction	Domesticity
Parental affection	Social distinction
Ambition	Devotion to others
Pleasure	Hospitality
Bodily comfort	Warmth
Possession	Imitation
Approval of others	Courtesy
Gregariousness	Play—sport
Taste	Managing others
Personal appearance	Coolness
Safety	Fear—caution
Cleanliness	Physical activity
Rest—sleep	Manipulation
Home comfort	Construction
Economy	Style
Curiosity	Humor
Efficiency	Amusement
Competition	Shyness
Cooperation	Teasing

Source: Daniel Starch, *Principles of Advertising* (Chicago: A.W. Shaw & Co., 1923), 273.

table 4-2   Murray's List of Psychogenic Needs

NEEDS ASSOCIATED WITH INANIMATE OBJECTS

Acquisition
Conservancy
Order
Retention
Construction

NEEDS THAT REFLECT AMBITION, POWER, ACCOMPLISHMENT, AND PRESTIGE

Superiority
Achievement
Recognition
Exhibition
Inviolacy (inviolate attitude)
Infavoidance (to avoid shame, failure, humiliation, ridicule)
Defendance (defensive attitude)
Counteraction (counteractive attitude)

NEEDS CONCERNED WITH HUMAN POWER

Dominance
Deference
Similance (suggestible attitude)
Autonomy
Contrarience (to act differently from others)

SADO-MASOCHISTIC NEEDS

Aggression
Abasement

NEEDS CONCERNED WITH AFFECTION BETWEEN PEOPLE

Affiliation
Rejection
Nurturance (to nourish, aid, or protect the helpless)
Succorance (to seek aid, protection, or sympathy)
Play

NEEDS CONCERNED WITH SOCIAL INTERCOURSE (THE NEEDS TO ASK AND TELL)

Cognizance (inquiring attitude)
Exposition (expositive attitude)

Source: Adapted from Henry A. Murray, "Types of Human Needs," in David C. McClelland, *Studies in Motivation* (New York: Appleton-Century-Crofts, 1955), 63–66. Reprinted by permission of Irvington Publishers, Inc.

in order of importance from lower-level (biogenic) needs to higher-level (psychogenic) needs. It suggests that individuals seek to satisfy lower-level needs before higher-level needs emerge. The lowest level of chronically unsatisfied need that an individual experiences serves to motivate his or her behavior. When that need is fairly well satisfied, a new (and higher) need emerges that the individual is motivated to fulfill. When this need is satisfied, a new (and still higher) need emerges, and so on. Of course, if a lower-level need experiences some renewed deprivation, it may temporarily become dominant again.

Figure 4-7 presents Maslow's hierarchy of needs in diagrammatic form. For clarity, each level is depicted as mutually exclusive. According to the theory, however, there is some overlap between each level, as no need is ever completely satisfied. For this reason, although all levels of need below the dominant level continue to motivate behavior to some extent, the prime motivator—the major driving force within the individual—is the lowest level of need that remains largely unsatisfied.

PHYSIOLOGICAL NEEDS In the hierarchy-of-needs theory, the first and most basic level of needs is *physiological*. These needs, which are required to sustain biological life, include food, water, air, shelter, clothing, sex—all the biogenic needs, in fact, that were listed as primary needs earlier.

According to Maslow, physiological needs are dominant when they are chronically unsatisfied: "For the man who is extremely and dangerously hungry, no other interest exists but food. He dreams food, he remembers food, he thinks about food, he emotes only about food, he perceives only food, and he wants only food."[10] For many citizens of this country, the biogenic needs are generally satisfied, and the higher-level needs are dominant. Unfortunately, however, the lives of a large and growing population found in many of our major cities are focused almost entirely on biogenic needs: the needs for food, for clothing, and for shelter from the elements in freezing weather.

SAFETY NEEDS After the first level of needs is satisfied, *safety* and *security* needs become the driving force behind an individual's behavior. These needs are concerned with much more than physical safety. They include order, stability, routine, familiarity, control over one's life and environment, and certainty—the knowledge, for example, that the individual will eat dinner not only that day and the following day but also every day far into the future. Health is also a safety concern.

Savings accounts, insurance policies, education, and vocational training are all means by which individuals satisfy the need for security (see Figure 4-8 on page 98). The high crime rate in the 1990s has caused safety needs—in all of their ramifications—to become prominent once again. The personal protection business has grown by leaps and bounds, and companies are offering self-defense products (e.g., pepper sprays, handguns, mace, personal bodyguards) as ways of expressing love and holiday cheer.[11]

SOCIAL NEEDS The third level of Maslow's hierarchy includes such needs as *love, affection, belonging*, and *acceptance*. People seek warm and satisfying human relationships with other people and are motivated by love for their families (see Figure 4-9 on page 99).

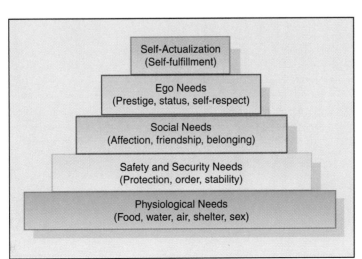

FIGURE 4-7

Maslow's Hierarchy of Human Needs

ONLY YOUR MOTHER IS MORE OBSESSED WITH YOUR SAFETY.

Ford Safety Engineers: Karin H. Przybylo, Steve Pingston, Mike Foster.

Where would we be without our mothers? They take care of us and protect us. So, we're proud to say, when it comes to safeguarding drivers, at FORD MOTOR COMPANY our maternal instinct becomes very apparent. You can feel it in our TRACTION CONTROL system. And in our ANTI-LOCK BRAKES. It's why DUAL-AIR BAGS* are standard in all our cars. And why ROADSIDE ASSISTANCE is available 24 hours a day. We're also developing a Vision Enhancement System — to help drivers when "mother" nature acts up. All this might be considered obsessive. But at Ford Motor Company, we believe such commitments to safety and security will enhance the quality of all our lives. Besides, it's for your own good.

• FORD • FORD TRUCKS • • LINCOLN • MERCURY •

QUALITY IS JOB 1.

*Always wear your safety belt.

Of course it's a family car. Who do you think will be driving it years from now?

The C-Class.
Starting at $31,545.*

The Mercedes-Benz C-Class is built to take care of your growing family. It is also built with the durability for which Mercedes is legendary.

Test-drive the C-Class at your Mercedes-Benz dealer, and who knows? Your children may be sitting in an heirloom. Mercedes-Benz

Why not bring the whole family to your Mercedes-Benz dealer?

*MSRP for a C220 includes $595 transportation charge. Excludes all taxes, title/documentary fees, registration, tags, dealer prep charges, insurance, optional equipme[nt] [c]ertificate of compliance or noncompliance fees, and finance charges. Prices may vary by dealer.   ©1995 Authorized Mercedes-Benz Deal[er]

FIGURE 4-9

Appealing to the Social
Need
Courtesy of Mercedes-Benz AG
and Mercedes-Benz of North
America, Inc.

Because of the importance of social motives in our society, advertisers of personal care products often emphasize this appeal in their advertisements.

EGOISTIC NEEDS When social needs are more or less satisfied, the fourth level of Maslow's hierarchy becomes operative. This level is concerned with *egoistic needs*. These needs can take either an inward or an outward orientation, or both. **Inwardly-directed ego needs** reflect an individual's need for self-acceptance, for self-esteem, for success, for independence, for personal satisfaction with a job well done. **Outwardly-directed ego needs** include the needs for prestige, for reputation, for status, for recognition from others. The presumed desire to "keep up with the Jones's" is a reflection of an outwardly-oriented ego need.

Unfortunately, the ego need is sometimes fulfilled in dysfunctional ways. Poverty-stricken youngsters may value expensive sneakers as symbols of status, and steal in order to acquire them. The incredible increase in gun possession among teenagers in inner city schools has been attributed to the need for status and "respect" from their peers. It seems that the bigger the gun, the more respect they believe they command. It is a societal responsibility to change this perception of gun possession among the young.

NEED FOR SELF-ACTUALIZATION According to Maslow, most people do not satisfy their ego needs sufficiently to ever move to the fifth level—the need for *self-actualization* (self-fulfillment). This need refers to an individual's desire to fulfill his or her potential—to become everything he or she is capable of becoming. In Maslow's words, "What a man can be, he must be."[12] This need is expressed in different ways by different people (see Figure 4-10 on page 100). A young man may desire to be an Olympic star and work single-mindedly for years to become the best in his sport. An artist may need to express herself on canvas; a research scientist may strive to find a new drug to eradicate disease. Maslow noted that the self-actualization need is not necessarily a creative urge, but

FIGURE 4-10

Appealing to the Self-
Actualization Need—
"Be All You Can Be"
Courtesy of The Department of
the U.S. Army and Army Reserve

that in people with some capacity for creativity, it is likely to take that form. Advertisements for art lessons, for banking services, and even for military recruitment often try to appeal to the self-actualization need. Figure 4-11 shows an ad for shoes based on a self-actualization appeal.

In summary, the hierarchy-of-needs theory postulates a five-level hierarchy of prepotent human needs. Higher-order needs become the driving force behind human behavior as lower-level needs are satisfied. The theory says, in effect, that dissatisfaction, not satisfaction, motivates behavior.

▲ **An Evaluation of the Need Hierarchy** The need hierarchy has received wide acceptance in many social disciplines because it appears to reflect the assumed or inferred motivations of many people in our society. The five levels of need postulated by the hierarchy are sufficiently generic to encompass most lists of individual needs. Some critics, however, maintain that Maslow's concepts are too general. To say that hunger and self-esteem are similar, in that both are needs, is to obscure the urgent, involuntary nature of the former and the largely conscious, voluntary nature of the latter. The major problem with the theory is that it cannot be tested empirically; there is no way to measure precisely how satisfied one need must be before the next higher need becomes operative. The need hierarchy also appears to be very closely bound to our contemporary American culture (i.e., it appears to be both culture- and time-bound).

Despite these criticisms, Maslow's hierarchy is a useful tool for understanding consumer motivations and is readily adaptable to marketing strategy, primarily because consumer goods often serve to satisfy each of the need levels. For example, individuals buy

CABLE & Co.

The Art of Movement. Defined.

*Destination is not a finite place.
Rather, it's a compass by which you judge
how far you've come.
Motion does not scare you.
Indeed, it's where you draw the energy to strive,
to achieve, to explore.
No distance is too great. No territory too vast.*

*No discovery too new.
Space is something you've mastered.
In style.
Because that's the only way you move. Always.
And that's a powerful state.
For if not for men like you, the horizon would
indeed be a place somewhere near.*

CABLE & Co.
The Art of Movement™

The Cable & Co. "Drivers" are designed, constructed and hand finished by the world's finest craftsmen and are available at
SAKS FIFTH AVENUE • BLOOMINGDALES • MACY'S • BULLOCKS • PARISIAN • NEIMAN MARCUS
and other fine specialty and department stores
For the store nearest you please call 1-800-624-2020
©1995 Cable & Co., 39 West 56th St, New York, NY 10019

FIGURE 4-11

A Self-Actualization
Appeal
Courtesy of Cable & Company

houses, food, and clothing to satisfy physiological needs; they buy insurance and radial tires and vocational training to satisfy safety and security needs. Almost all personal care products (cosmetics, mouthwash, shaving cream) are bought to satisfy social needs. Luxury products such as furs, jewels, or big cars are often bought to fulfill ego needs, and college training and financial services are sold as ways of achieving self-fulfillment. Maslow's need hierarchy has been called an "emotional trigger" that enables marketers to communicate with their target audiences on a personal, meaningful level that goes beyond product benefits.[13]

The hierarchy offers a useful, comprehensive framework for marketers trying to develop appropriate advertising appeals for their products. It is adaptable in two ways: first, it enables marketers to focus their advertising appeals on a need level that is likely to be shared by a large segment of the prospective audience; second, it facilitates product positioning or repositioning.

SEGMENTATION APPLICATIONS The need hierarchy is often used as the basis for market segmentation, with specific advertising appeals directed to individuals on one or more need levels. For example, soft drink ads directed to teenagers often stress a social appeal by showing a group of young people sharing good times as well as the advertised product. Research sponsored by the National Spa and Pool Institute found that men and women had different motivations concerning these products. Women saw the purchase of a pool as an enhancement of family life (the social need) but were concerned about the safety of their small children (the safety need). Thus, pool advertisements tend to stress the supervision of children, health, and family enjoyment, and are targeted primarily to women. Because the study found that men were more interested in spas than pools, spa commercials began to stress a more intimate message: relaxation, privacy, time together.[14]

POSITIONING APPLICATIONS Another way to use the need hierarchy is for positioning products—that is, deciding how the product should be perceived by prospective consumers. The key to positioning is to find a niche that is not occupied by a competing product or brand. This application of the need hierarchy relies on the notion that no need is ever fully satisfied, that it always continues to be somewhat motivating. Safety, for example, is a continuing need.

Most manufacturers of luxury cars use status appeals (e.g., "Impress your friends"), self-actualizing appeals ("You deserve the very best"), or even social appeals ("The whole family can ride in luxurious comfort"). To find a unique position among its luxury competitors, some automobile companies have used a safety appeal in advertisements directed to well-to-do executives (see Figure 4-12).

VERSATILITY OF THE NEED HIERARCHY One way to illustrate the usefulness of the need hierarchy in designing promotional programs is to show how workable appeals for a single product can be developed from each level. Consider, for example, the potential promotional appeals for home Nautilus equipment. An appeal to *physiological* needs would show how the home exercise unit can improve body tone and health; a *safety* appeal would demonstrate how safe the equipment is for home (and solo) use. A *social* appeal might show how much fun it can be to exercise with a friend or even how a streamlined figure would encourage social encounters. *Self-esteem* is easily demonstrated through a narcissistic appeal such as "be proud of your body." Finally, an appeal to *self-actualization* may suggest to career couples that they deserve the convenience and the luxury of home exercise after a long and challenging workday.

▲ **A Trio of Needs** Some psychologists believe in the existence of a trio of basic needs: the needs for *power*, for *affiliation*, and for *achievement*. These needs can each be subsumed within Maslow's need hierarchy; considered individually, however, they each have a unique relevance to consumer motivation.

The **power** need relates to an individual's desire to control his or her environment (see Figure 4-13 on page 104). It includes the need to control other persons and various objects. This need appears to be closely related to the ego need, in that many individuals experience increased self-esteem when they exercise power over objects or people. A number of products, such as automobiles, lend themselves to promises of power or superiority for users. The need to control one's environment also can be subsumed under Maslow's *safety* need.

Affiliation is a well-known and well-researched social motive that has far-reaching influence on consumer behavior. The affiliation need suggests that behavior is highly

influenced by the desire for friendship, for acceptance, for belonging. People with high af-filiation needs tend to have strong social dependence on others. They often select goods they feel will meet with the approval of friends. People who go to craft fairs or to garage sales, teenagers who hang out at malls, car buffs who congregate at automobile shows, often do so more for the satisfaction of being with others than for making a purchase. This need is very similar to Maslow's *social* need.

A considerable number of research studies have focused on the **achievement** need.[15] Individuals with a strong need for achievement often regard personal accomplishment as an end in itself. The achievement need is closely related to both the *egoistic* need and the *self-actualization* need. People with a high need for achievement tend to be more self-con-fident, enjoy taking calculated risks, actively research their environments, and are very in-terested in feedback. Monetary rewards, for example, provide an important type of feedback as to how they are doing. People with high achievement needs like situations in which they can take personal responsibility for finding solutions.[16] They prefer activities that allow self-evaluation.[17] They respond well to feedback concerning their own compe-tence.[18] High-achievement people are often good prospects for cleverly presented, innova-tive products, for do-it-yourself projects, for older houses, and even for moderately speculative stock issues. Figure 4-14 on page 105 appeals to the achievement need.

One study showed that individuals' dominant needs may be related to their career progress. *Achievement* was shown to be a dominant need for MBA students and Air Force officers; *power* was a dominant need among partners in a "Big Eight" accounting firm; and

FIGURE 4-13

The Need to Control
One's Environment
Courtesy of GTE

affiliation was a dominant need among high school seniors, freshman cadets at the Air Force Academy, and undergraduate accounting students. Such findings imply that relevant promotional appeals can be targeted to consumers based on their career progress.[19]

In summary, individuals with specific psychological needs tend to be receptive to advertising appeals directed at those needs. They also tend to be receptive to certain kinds of products. Thus, awareness of such needs provides marketers with additional bases on which to segment their markets.

Omega Seamaster Professional chronograph.
Self-winding diver chronometer
in titanium, tantalum 18K gold.
Water-resistant with fully functional
push-buttons to 300m/1000ft.

ROD DAVIS' CHOICE

Battling the elements and winning the Match Race Sailing Championships, the America's Cup, the Whitbread and the BOC Challenge require precision, endurance and a perfect mastery of the course. Qualities Rod Davis - like Peter Blake, Grant Dalton and Isabelle Autissier - finds in his Omega, at the helm of his sailboat and in his daily life. "Trust your judgement, trust Omega" - Rod Davis.

OMEGA®
The sign of excellence

FIGURE 4-14

The Achievement Need
Courtesy of Omega

THE MEASUREMENT OF MOTIVES

How are motives identified? How are they measured? How do researchers know which motives are responsible for certain kinds of behavior? These are difficult questions to answer because motives are hypothetical constructs—that is, they cannot be seen or touched, handled, smelled, or otherwise tangibly observed. For this reason, no single measurement method can be considered a reliable index. Instead, researchers usually rely on a combination of observation and inference, self-reports, and projective techniques to try to establish the presence and/or the strength of various motives. (These techniques have been described in Chapter 2.)

Obviously, the identification and measurement of human motives is an inexact process. Some psychologists are concerned that most measurement techniques do not meet the crucial test criteria of *validity* and *reliability*. (Remember, validity ensures that the technique measures what it purports to measure; reliability refers to the consistency with which the technique measures what it does measure.)

As discussed in Chapter 2, the findings of projective research methods are highly dependent on the analyst; they focus not only on the data themselves but also on what the analyst thinks they imply. Therefore, many consumer behaviorists are reluctant to rely on projective techniques alone. However, by using a combination of assessments (i.e., *triangulation*) based on behavioral data (observation), subjective data (self-reports), and projective tests, many consumer researchers feel more confident of achieving valid insights into consumer motivations than they would by using any one technique alone. Though some marketers are concerned that such research does not produce hard numbers that objectively "prove" a point under investigation, others are convinced that qualitative studies can be just as revealing as quantitative studies. However, there is a clear need for improved methodological procedures for measuring human motives.

MOTIVATIONAL RESEARCH

The term **motivational research**, which should logically include all types of research into human motives, has become a "term of art" used to refer to qualitative research designed to uncover the consumer's subconscious or hidden motivations.[20] Based on the premise that consumers are not always aware of the reasons for their actions, motivational research attempts to discover underlying feelings, attitudes, and emotions concerning product, service, or brand use. Table 4-3 describes the "personalities" consumers have attributed to selected products uncovered through motivational research studies.

Development of Motivational Research

Sigmund Freud's **psychoanalytic theory of personality** (discussed in Chapter 5) provided the basis for the development of motivational research. This theory was built on the premise that unconscious needs or drives—especially biological and sexual drives—are at the heart of human motivation and personality. Freud constructed his theory from patients' recollections of early childhood experiences, analysis of their dreams, and the specific nature of their mental and physical adjustment problems.

▲ **Early Motivational Research** Dr. Ernest Dichter, formerly a psychoanalyst in Vienna, adapted Freud's psychoanalytical techniques to the study of consumer buying habits. Up to this time, marketing research had focused on *what* consumers did (i.e., quantitative, descriptive studies) rather than on *why* they did it. Marketers were quickly fascinated by the glib, entertaining, and usually surprising explanations offered for consumer behavior, especially since many of these explanations were rooted in sex. For example, marketers were told that cigarettes and Lifesaver candies were bought because of their sexual symbolism, that men regarded convertible cars as surrogate mistresses, that women baked cakes to fulfill their reproductive yearnings.[21] Before long, almost every advertising agency on Madison Avenue had a psychologist on staff to conduct motivational research studies.

table 4-3 Selected Product Personality Profiles Uncovered by Motivational Research

BAKING	An expression of femininity and motherhood, baking evokes pleasant, nostalgic memories of the odors pervading the house when one's mother was baking. To many, a woman is subconsciously and symbolically going through the act of giving birth when baking a cake, and the most fertile moment occurs when the baked product is pulled out of the oven.
ICE CREAM	Ice cream is associated with love and affection. It derives particular potency from childhood memories, when it was given to a child for being "good" and withheld as an instrument of punishment. People refer to ice cream as something they "love" to eat. Ice cream is a symbol of abundance; people prefer round packaging with an illustration that runs around the box panel because it suggests unlimited quantity.
POWER TOOLS	Power tools are a symbol of manliness. They represent masculine skill and competence and are often bought more for their symbolic value than for active do-it-yourself applications. Ownership of a good power tool or circular saw provides a man with feelings of omnipotence.
BEER	For most people, beer is an active, alive, sensuous beverage that provides the drinker with a feeling of security. People generally describe the beer they like as "alive," "foamy," and "sparkling," and disliked brands as "flat," "dead," or "stale."

Source: Adapted from *Handbook of Consumer Motivations*, by Ernest Dichter, Copyright 1964, McGraw-Hill Book Company. Used with permission of McGraw-Hill Book Company.

▲ **Limitations of Motivational Research** By the early 1960s, marketers realized that motivational research had some drawbacks. Because of the intensive nature of qualitative research, samples necessarily were small; thus, there was concern about generalizing findings to the total market. Also, marketers soon realized that the analysis of projective tests and depth interviews was highly subjective. The same data given to three different analysts could produce three different reports, each offering its own explanation of the consumer behavior examined. Critics noted that many of the projective tests that were used had originally been developed for clinical purposes, rather than for studies of marketing or consumer behavior. (One of the basic criteria for test development is that tests be developed and validated for the specific purpose and on the specific audience from which information is desired.) Other consumer theorists had noted additional inconsistencies in applying Freudian theory to the study of consumer behavior: first, psychoanalytic theory was structured specifically for use with disturbed people, while consumer behaviorists were interested in explaining the behavior of "typical" consumers. Second, Freudian theory was developed in an entirely different social context (19th century Vienna), while motivational research was introduced in 1950s postwar America.[22]

Finally, too many motivational researchers imputed highly exotic reasons to rather prosaic consumer purchases. Marketers began to question their recommendations (e.g.: Is it better to sell a man a pair of suspenders as a means of holding up his pants or as a "reaction to castration anxiety?" Is it easier to persuade a woman to buy a garden hose to water her lawn or as a symbol of "genital competition for the female?"). Motivational researchers often came up with sexual explanations for the most mundane activities. For example, an ad showing a hostess behind a beverage table filled with large bottles of soft drinks was commended by a leading motivational researcher for its "clever use of phallic symbolism."[23]

Motivational Research Today

Despite these criticisms, motivational research is still regarded as an important tool by marketers who want to gain deeper insights into the whys of consumer behavior than conventional marketing research techniques can yield. There is new and compelling evidence that the unconscious is the site of a far larger portion of mental life than even Freud envisioned. Research studies show that the unconscious mind may understand and respond to nonverbal symbols, form emotional responses, and guide actions largely independent of conscious awareness.[24] The new science of **semiotics** is concerned with the conscious and subconscious meanings of nonverbal symbols to consumers.[25] These insights are usually obtained through motivational research. Table 4-4 lists some psychological meanings ascribed to current advertising symbols.

▲ **Uses of Motivational Research** Since motivational research often reveals unsuspected consumer motivations concerning product or brand usage, its principal use today is in the development of new ideas for promotional campaigns, ideas that can penetrate the consumer's conscious awareness by appealing to unrecognized needs.

Motivational research also provides marketers with a basic orientation for new product categories and enables them to explore consumer reactions to ideas and advertising copy at an early stage so that costly errors can be avoided. Furthermore, motivational research provides consumer researchers with basic insights that enable them to design structured, quantitative marketing research studies to be conducted on larger, more representative samples of consumers.

table 4-4   Psychological Symbolism in Advertising

TEDDY BEAR	A symbol of tamed aggression (Perfect image for a fabric softener that "tames" the rough texture of clothing)
PENGUINS	Symbolize coolness, refreshment, and friendliness (Used in Diet Coke commercials to connote these qualities.)
A MALE BACK	Can be perceived as "rudely giving the consumer the cold shoulder" (Grey Flannel cologne removed this nonverbal symbol from its ads.)
A MALE IN A RUGGED OUTDOOR SITUATION	Symbolizes a "lone wolf" (Schick used this symbol to connote the underlying message "to be touched and loved and be a lover")

Source: Based on Ronald Alsop, "Agencies Scrutinize Their Ads for Psychological Symbolism," *The Wall Street Journal*, 11 June 1987, 27.

Motivational research has also been used to great advantage by nonprofit organizations. For example, Dichter found that people subconsciously resist making charitable donations because they feel that once they have given, they will no longer be the objects of attention. Using that insight, many large charities now spend almost as much time keeping donors advised of accomplishments as soliciting new donations in order to generate goodwill for future campaigns.

Motivational research continues to be a useful tool for many marketers who want to know the actual reasons underlying consumer behavior. For example, in trying to discover why women bought traditional roach sprays rather than a brand packaged in little plastic trays, researchers asked women to draw pictures of roaches and write stories about their sketches. They found that, for many of their respondents, roaches symbolized men who had left them feeling poor and powerless. The women reported that spraying the roaches and "watching them squirm and die" allowed them to express their hostility toward men and gave them feelings of greater control.[26]

Motivational research often suggests new ways for marketers to present their products to the public. For example, in using figure sketches to determine consumers' differing perceptions of American Express gold card and green card holders, researchers found that the gold card user was perceived as a broad-shouldered man standing in an active position, while the green card user was perceived as a "couch potato" in front of a TV set. Based on this and other research, American Express decided to market the gold card as "a symbol of responsibility for people who have control over their lives and finances."[27]

summary

Motivation is the driving force within individuals that impels them to action. This driving force is produced by a state of uncomfortable tension, which exists as the result of an unsatisfied need. All individuals have needs, wants, and desires. The individual's subconscious drive to reduce need-induced tension results in behavior that he or she anticipates will satisfy needs and thus bring about a more comfortable state.

All behavior is goal oriented. Goals are the sought-after results of motivated behavior. The form or direction that behavior takes—the goal that is selected—is a result of thinking processes (cognition) and previous learning. There are two types of goals: generic goals and product-specific goals. A generic goal is a general category of goal that may fulfill a certain need; a product-specific goal is a specifically branded or labeled product that the individual sees as a way to fulfill a need. Product-specific needs are sometimes referred to as wants.

Innate needs—those an individual is born with—are primarily physiological (biogenic); they include all the factors required to sustain physical life (e.g., food, water, clothing, shelter, sex). Acquired needs—those an individual develops after birth—are primarily psychological (psychogenic); they include esteem, fear, love, and acceptance. For any given need, there are many different and appropriate goals. The specific goal selected depends on the individual's experiences, physical capacity, prevailing cultural norms and values, and the goal's accessibility in the physical and social environment.

Needs and goals are interdependent and change in response to the individual's physical condition, environment, interaction with other people, and experiences. As needs become satisfied, new, higher-order needs emerge that must be fulfilled.

Failure to achieve a goal often results in feelings of frustration. Individuals react to frustration in two ways: "fight" or "flight." They may cope by finding a way around the obstacle that prohibits goal attainment or by adopting a substitute goal (fight); or they may adopt a defense mechanism that enables them to protect their self-esteem (flight). Defense mechanisms include aggression, regression, rationalization, withdrawal, projection, autism, identification, and repression.

Motives cannot easily be inferred from consumer behavior. People with different needs may seek fulfillment through selection of the same goals: people with the same needs may seek fulfillment through different goals.

Although some psychologists have suggested that individuals have different need priorities, others believe that most human beings experience the same basic needs, to which they assign a similar priority ranking. Maslow's hierarchy-of-needs theory proposes five levels of prepotent human needs: physiological needs, safety needs, social needs, egoistic needs, and self-actualization needs. Other needs widely used in consumer appeals include the needs for power, affiliation, and achievement.

There are three commonly used methods for identifying and "measuring" human motives: observation and inference, subjective reports, and projective techniques. None of these methods is completely reliable by itself. Therefore, researchers often use a combination of two or three techniques in tandem to assess the presence or strength of consumer motives.

Motivational research is qualitative research designed to delve below the consumer's level of conscious awareness. Despite some shortcomings, motivational research has proved to be of great value to marketers concerned with developing new ideas and new copy appeals.

discussion questions

1. a. "Marketers don't create needs; needs preexist marketers." Discuss this statement.

   b. Can marketing efforts change consumers' needs? Why or why not?

2. Consumers have both innate and acquired needs. Give examples of each kind of need and show how the same purchase can serve to fulfill either or both kinds of needs.

3. Specify the innate and/or acquired needs that would be useful bases for developing promotional strategies for: (a) airbags in cars, (b) vitamins, (c) Harley Davidson motorcycles, and (d) recruiting college seniors to work for a company in the energy field.

4. Why are consumers' needs and goals constantly changing? What factors influence the formation of new goals?

5. How can marketers use consumers' failures at achieving goals to develop advertisements for products and services?

6. Most human needs are dormant much of the time. What factors cause their arousal? Give examples of ads for personal care products that are designed to arouse latent consumer needs.

7. For each of the situations listed in Question 3, select one level from Maslow's hierarchy of human needs that can be used to segment the market and position the product (or the company). Explain your choices. What are the advantages and/or disadvantages of using Maslow's hierarchy in segmentation and positioning?

8. a. What is motivational research?

   b. What are its strengths and weaknesses?

   c. How did Dr. Ernest Dichter apply Freudian theory to consumer behavior?

   d. How was motivational research used in the 1950s?

   e. How do marketers use the technique today?

exercises

1. You are a member of an advertising team assembled to develop a promotional campaign for a new running shoe. Develop three slogans for this campaign, each based on one of the levels in Maslow's need hierarchy.

2. Find an advertisement that depicts a defense mechanism. Present it in class and discuss its effectiveness.

3. Choose three magazine advertisements for different consumer goods. Carefully review Murray's list of human needs (Table 4-2). Through the advertising appeal used, identify which need(s) each product is presumed to satisfy.

4. Explain briefly the needs for power, affiliation, and achievement. Find three advertisements for different products that are designed to appeal to these needs.

key words

- Achievement needs
- Acquired needs
- Affiliation needs
- Aggression
- Approach objects
- Arousal of motives (physiological, emotional, cognitive, environmental)
- Autism
- Avoidance objects
- Defense mechanisms
- Emotional motives
- Frustration
- Generic goals

- Identification
- Levels of aspiration
- Maslow's hierarchy of human needs
- Motivation
- Motivational research
- Negative motivation
- Physiological needs
- Positive motivation
- Power needs
- Prepotent need
- Primary needs
- Product-specific goals
- Projection

- Psychoanalytic theory of personality
- Psychological needs
- Rational motives
- Rationalization
- Regression
- Repression
- Secondary needs
- Self-image
- Semiotics
- Sublimation
- Substitute goals
- Withdrawal

end notes

1. JANE PERLEZ, "The Capitalist Pioneers of Prague", *The New York Times*, July 29, 1995, 35.

2. MARY J. RUDIE, "The CMA Revolution," *Marketing Review* 40(1), September-October 1984, 19–21.

3. JACK W. BREHM, "Psychological Reactance: Theory and Applications," *Advances in Consumer Research* 16, (1989 Association for Consumer Research), 72–75.

4. See ABRAHAM H. MASLOW, "A Theory of Human Motivation," *Psychological Review* 50, 1943, 370–96; Abraham H. MASLOW, *Motivation and Personality* (New York: Harper & Row, 1954); and ABRAHAM H. MASLOW, *Toward a Psychology of Being* (New York: Van Nostrand Reinhold, 1968), 189–215.

5. A number of studies have focused on human levels of aspiration. See, for example, KURT LEWIN et al., "Level of Aspiration," in J. McV. Hunt, *Personality and Behavior Disorders* (New York: Ronald Press, 1944); HOWARD GARLAND, "Goal Levels and Task Performance, a Compelling Replication of Some Compelling Results," *Journal of Applied Psychology* 67, 1982, 245–48; EDWIN A. LOCKE, ELIZABETH FREDERICK, CYNTHIA LEE, and PHILIP BOBKO, "Effect of Self Efficacy, Goals and Task Strategies on Task Performance," *Journal of Applied Psychology* 69(2), 1984, 241–51; EDWIN A. LOCKE, ELIZABETH FREDERICK, ELIZABETH BUCKNER, and PHILIP BOBKO, "Effect of Previously Assigned Goals on Self-Set Goals and Performance," *Journal of Applied Psychology* 72(2), 1987, 204–11; and JOHN R. HOLLENBECK and HOWARD J. KLEIN, "Goal Commitment and the Goal-Setting Process: Problems, Prospects and Proposals for Future Research," *Journal of Applied Psychology* 2, 1987, 212–20.

6. SURENDRA N. SINGH and GILBERT A. CHURCHILL, JR., "Arousal and Advertising Effectiveness," *Journal of Advertising* 16(1), 1987, 4–10.

7. PAT SLOAN, "Klein's Sultry Avedon Ads for Obsession Hit TV," *Advertising Age*, March 25, 1985, 104; and MICHAEL MCWILLIAMS, "Calvin Bests Fellini with Obsession Spots," *Advertising Age*, April 8, 1985, 81.

8. PETER WEINBERG and WOLFGANG GOTTWALD, "Impulsive Consumer Buying as a Result of Emotions," *Journal of Business Research* 10, 1982, 43.

9. MASLOW, "A Theory of Human Motivation," op. cit.

10. Ibid., 380.

11. J. PEDERZANE, "Visions of Perpetrators Dancing in Their Heads," *The New York Times*, December 18, 1994, 2E.

12. MASLOW, op. cit., 380.

13. RUDY SCHROCER, "Maslow's Hierachy of Needs as a Framework for Identifying Emotional Triggers," *Marketing Review* 46(5), February 1991, 26, 28.

14. "Pegging Buyers by Their Gender," *The New York Times*, September 13, 1992, F10.

15. See, for example, DAVID C. MCCLELLAND, *Studies in Motivation* (New York: Appleton-Century-Crofts, 1955).

16. DAVID C. MCCLELLAND, "Business Drive and National Achievement," *Harvard Business Review*, July-August 1962, 99; "Achievement Motivation Can Be Developed," *Harvard Business Review* 5(24), November-December 1965, 18; and ABRAHAM K. KORMAN, *The Psychology of Motivation* (Englewood Cliffs, NJ: Prentice Hall, 1974), 190.

17. A. G. GREENWALD, "Ego Task Analysis: An Integration of Research on Ego-Involvement and Self Awareness," in A. H. Hastorf and A. M. Isen, eds., *Cognitive Social Psychology* (New York: Elsevier-North Holland, 1982), 109–47.

18. JUDITH M. HARACKIEWICZ, CAROL SANSONE, and GEORGE MANDERLINK, "Competence, Achievement Orientation, and Intrinsic Motivation: A Process Analysis," *Journal of Personality and Social Psychology* 48, 1985, 493–508.

19. MICHAEL J. STAHL and ADRIAN M. HARRELL, "Evaluation and Validation of a Behavioral Decision Theory Management Approach to Achievement, Power, and Affiliation," *Journal of Applied Psychology* 67, 1982, 744–51.

20. ERNEST DICHTER, *A Strategy of Desire* (Garden City, NY: Doubleday, 1960).

21. For additional reports of motivational research findings, see DICHTER, *A Strategy of Desire*, op. cit.; VANCE PACKARD, *The Hidden Persuaders* (New York: Pocket Books, 1957); and Pierre Martineau, *Motivation in Advertising* (New York: McGraw-Hill, 1957).

22. JEFF B. MURRAY and DEBORAH J. EVERS, "Theory Borrowing and Reflectivity in Interdisciplinary Fields," *Advances in Consumer Research* 16, 1988, 657–52.

23. LESLIE KANUK, "Emotional Persuasion in Print Advertising" (Masters Thesis, City College of New York, 1964).

24. DANIEL GOLEMAN, "New View of Mind Gives Unconscious an Expanded Role," *The New York Times*, February 7, 1984, C1-2.

25. RONALD ALSOP, "Agencies Scrutinize Their Ads for Psychological Symbolism," *The Wall Street Journal*, June 11, 1987, 27. See also DAVID MICK, "Consumer Research and Semiotics: Exploring the Morphology of Signs, Symbols and Significance," *Journal of Consumer Research* 13, September 1986, 196–213.

26. PAULA DRILLMAN, quoted in Ronald Alsop, "Advertisers Put Consumers on the Couch," *The Wall Street Journal*, May 13, 1988, 21.

27. Ibid.

Marketers have long been intrigued by the possibility of appealing to consumers in terms of personality traits. They have felt that what consumers purchase, and when and how they consume, are likely to be influenced by personality factors. For this reason, advertising and marketing people have frequently depicted (or targeted) specific personality traits or characteristics in their advertising messages. Some recent examples are Nabisco® Frosted Wheat Bites' (cereal) appeal to demanding people (headline: "She's demanding. Uncompromising. And if she's going to eat what you want, it better taste good."), Samsara's (fragrance) appeal to confidence (headline: "A look inside. Serenity born of confidence"), Tiffany's (famous jewelry and giftwear retailer) appeal to individualism (headline: "Every woman has a signature"), Clairol Ultress' (hair color) appeal to the inner self (headline: "New Ultress lets you express your inner self. Or perhaps we

> *Personality is the supreme realization of the innate individuality of a particular living being.*
>
> —Carl Gustav Jung
> 1875–1961, *On the Development of Personality,* 1932, V. 17, 195.

should say selves."), and Miraval's (luxury resort) appeal to introspectionism (headline: "At Miraval, you'll meet someone new. Yourself.").

This chapter is designed to provide the reader with an understanding of the relationship between *personality* and various aspects of consumer behavior. It examines what personality is and how it interrelates with other consumer behavior concepts. It reviews several major personality theories and describes how they have stimulated marketing interest in the study of consumer personality. The chapter also explores how the related concepts of *self* and *self-image* influence consumer attitudes and behavior.

WHAT IS PERSONALITY?

The study of personality has been approached by theorists in a variety of ways. Some have emphasized the dual influence of heredity and early childhood experiences on personality development; others have stressed broader social and environmental influences and the fact that personalities develop continuously over time. Some theorists prefer to view personality as a unified whole; others focus on specific traits. The wide variation in viewpoints makes it difficult to arrive at a single definition. However, we propose that personality be defined as *those inner psychological characteristics that both determine and reflect how a person responds to his or her environment.*

The emphasis in this definition is on *inner characteristics*—those specific qualities, attributes, traits, factors, and mannerisms that distinguish one individual from other individuals. As discussed later in the chapter, the deeply ingrained characteristics that we call personality are likely to influence the individual's product choices (and even certain brand choices); they also affect the way the consumer responds to a firm's promotional efforts, and when, where, and how they consume particular products or services. Therefore, the identification of specific personality characteristics associated with consumer behavior may be highly useful in the development of a firm's market segmentation strategies.

The Nature of Personality

In the study of personality, three distinct properties are of central importance: (1) personality reflects *individual differences*; (2) personality is *consistent and enduring*; and (3) personality can *change.*

▲ **Personality Reflects Individual Differences** Because the inner characteristics that constitute an individual's personality are a unique combination of factors, no two individuals are exactly alike. Nevertheless, many individuals tend to be similar in terms of a single personality characteristic. For instance, many people can be described as "high" in sociability (the degree of interest they display in social or group activities), while others can be described as "low" in sociability. Personality is a useful concept because it enables us to categorize consumers into different groups on the basis of a **single trait** or a few traits. If each person were different in *all* respects, it would be impossible to group consumers into segments, and there would be little reason to develop standardized products and promotional campaigns.

▲ **Personality Is Consistent and Enduring** An individual's personality is commonly thought to be both consistent and enduring. Indeed, the mother who comments that her child "has been stubborn from the day he was born" is supporting the contention that personality has both consistency and endurance. Both qualities are essential for marketers to explain or predict consumer behavior in terms of personality.

The stable nature of personality suggests that it is unreasonable for marketers to attempt to change consumers' personalities to conform to certain products. At best, they may learn which personality characteristics influence specific consumer responses and attempt to appeal to relevant traits inherent in their target group of consumers.

Even though an individual's personality may be consistent, consumption behavior often varies considerably because of psychological, sociocultural, and environmental factors that affect behavior. For instance, while an individual's personality may be largely stable, specific needs or motives, attitudes, reactions to group pressures, and even responses to newly available brands may cause a change in the person's behavior. Personality is only one of a combination of factors that influence how a consumer behaves.

▲ **Personality Can Change** Although personality tends to be consistent and enduring, it may still change under certain circumstances. For instance, an individual's personality may be altered by major life events, such as the birth of a child, the death of a loved one, a divorce, or a major career promotion. An individual's personality changes not only in response to abrupt events, but also as part of a gradual maturing process.

THEORIES OF PERSONALITY

This section briefly reviews four major theories of personality: (1) **Freudian** theory, (2) **Jungian** theory, (3) **neo-Freudian** theory, and (4) **trait theory**. These theories have been chosen for discussion from among many theories of personality because each has played a prominent role in the study of the relationship between consumer behavior and personality.

Freudian Theory

Sigmund Freud's **psychoanalytic theory of personality** is the cornerstone of modern psychology. This theory was built on the premise that *unconscious needs or drives*, especially sexual and other biological drives, are at the heart of human motivation and personality. Freud constructed his theory on the basis of patients' recollections of early childhood experiences, analysis of their dreams, and the specific nature of their mental and physical adjustment problems.

▲ **Id, Superego, and Ego** Based on his analyses, Freud proposed that the human personality consists of three interacting systems: the **id**, the **superego**, and the **ego**. The *id* was conceptualized as a "warehouse" of primitive and impulsive drives—basic physiological needs such as thirst, hunger, and sex—for which the individual seeks immediate satisfaction without concern for the specific means of satisfaction. The ad for Animale fragrance (see Figure 5-1 on page 116) captures the exciting "forces" associated with the primitive drives of the "id." There is a strong emotional sense of "animalism" in the appearance of the female model (her stalking pose and green eyes). Also, the words "pure instinct" give some extra "id-like" punch. (It is also interesting to note that the last four letters of the name spell "male.")

 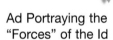
In contrast to the id, the *superego* is conceptualized as the individual's internal expression of society's moral and ethical codes of conduct. The superego's role is to see that the individual satisfies needs in a socially acceptable fashion. Thus, the superego is a kind of "brake" that restrains or inhibits the impulsive forces of the id.

Finally, the *ego* is the individual's conscious control. It functions as an internal monitor that attempts to balance the impulsive demands of the id and the sociocultural constraints of the superego. Figure 5-2 represents the interrelationship among the three interacting systems.

▲ **Stages of Personality Development** In addition to specifying a structure for personality, Freud emphasized that an individual's personality is formed as he or she passes through a number of distinct stages of infant and childhood development. These are the **oral**, **anal**, **phallic**, **latent**, and **genital** stages. Freud labeled four of these stages of development to conform to the area of the body on which he believed the child's sexual instincts are focused at the time.

ORAL STAGE The infant first experiences social contact with the outside world through the mouth (e.g., eating, drinking, sucking). A crisis develops at the end of this stage when the child is weaned from the mother's breast or from the bottle.

ANAL STAGE During this stage, the child's primary source of pleasure is the process of elimination. A second crisis develops at the end of this stage when parents try to toilet train the child.

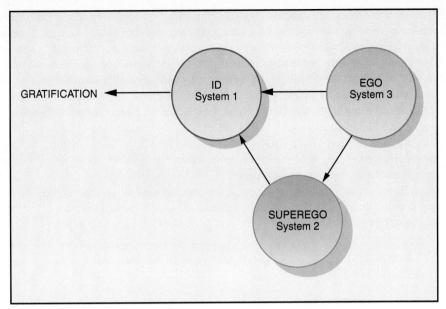

FIGURE 5-2

A Representation of the Interrelationships among the Id, Ego, and Superego

PHALLIC STAGE The child experiences self-oriented sexual pleasure during this phase with the discovery of the sex organs. A third crisis occurs when the child experiences sexual desire for the parent of the opposite sex. How the child resolves this crisis affects later relationships with persons of the opposite sex and with authority figures.

LATENCY STAGE Freud believed that the sexual instincts of the child lie dormant from about age 5 until the beginning of adolescence and that no important personality changes occur during this time.

GENITAL STAGE At adolescence, the individual develops a sexual interest in persons of the opposite sex, beyond self-oriented love and love for parents.

According to Freud, an adult's personality is determined by how well he or she deals with the crises that are experienced while passing through each of these stages (particularly the first three). For instance, if a child's oral needs are not adequately satisfied at the first stage of development, the person may become fixated at this stage and as an adult display a personality that includes such traits as dependence and excessive oral activity (e.g., gum chewing and smoking). When an individual is fixated at the anal stage, the adult personality may display other traits, such as an excessive need for neatness.

▲ **Freudian Theory and "Product Personality"** Researchers who apply Freud's psychoanalytic theory to the study of consumer personality tend to stress the idea that human drives are largely *unconscious* and that consumers are primarily unaware of their true reasons for buying what they buy. These researchers tend to focus on consumer purchases and/or consumption situations, treating them as a reflection and an extension of the consumer's own personality. In other words, one's appearance and possessions—how well groomed one is, what one wears, carries, and displays—are taken to reflect the individual's personality. (The relationship between how consumers see the products or brands they use and how they see themselves is considered later in the chapter as part of the discussion on *self* and *self-images*.)

▲ **Brand Personality** Consumers tend to ascribe various descriptive "personality-like" traits or characteristics—the ingredients of brand personalities—to different brands in a wide variety of product categories. A brief case history of Mr. Coffee, a leading marketer of automatic-drip coffee makers, illustrates this phenomenon. An unexpected bonus from consumer focus groups sponsored by the company was the observation that consumers were referring to Mr. Coffee as if the product were a *person* (e.g., "He makes good coffee." "He's got a lot of different models and prices.")[1] After careful consideration, the marketers decided to explore the possibility of creating a **brand personification** which was already somewhat of a personification, given the "Mr." in the name "Mr. Coffee." Initial consumer research indicated that "Mr. Coffee" was seen as being: "dependable," "friendly," "efficient," and "intelligent/ smart." "Mr. Coffee" was also envisioned as looking like actors Gregory Peck, Robert Young (from "Father Knows Best"), or Andy Griffith; "he" was further envisioned as having a science or mathematics background, possessing an "inventive spirit," and being "practical and prudent."

Based on these and other research insights, as well as product expansion goals, it was decided that Mr. Coffee would be personified as a "practical inventor." The advertising agency even created a biographical profile of Mr. Coffee, which begins:

> *Born September 18, 1938, in Chagrin Falls, Ohio, eldest of three children (two girls, one boy) of Harold and Betty Coffee, second-generation immigrants from France (name changed from DeCouvier at Ellis Island).*[2]

Ultimately the advertising agency, Meldrum & Fewsmith Communications, created a TV advertising campaign that featured family (wife, sister, and parents) and "others" (e.g., his elementary school art teacher), telling the TV audience their memories and reflections of "Mr. Coffee" (see Figure 5-3).

In a somewhat similar fashion, the management of Celestial Seasonings Inc., the leading specialty tea maker in the United States, has "personified and humanized its model consumer." The company claims that it almost never talks about its consumers; instead, it talks about "Tracy Jones." And just who is Tracy Jones? "She's female, upscale, well-educated, and highly involved in life in every way. We sell to smart women. That's who Tracy Jones is."[3]

That Mr. Coffee was given a masculine personality by its creators, and the Celestial tea prototypical consumer has a feminine persona is fully consistent with the marketplace reality that products and services, in general, are viewed by consumers as having a gender-being, either masculine or feminine. Supporting what many marketing practitioners already know, a recent study asked Chinese consumers to place forty-one products and services into one of four categories: masculine (high-masculine, low-feminine), feminine (high-feminine, low-masculine), androgynous (high-masculine and high-feminine), and undifferentiated (low-masculine and low-feminine).[4] The results revealed that none of the products and services studied were judged androgynous or undifferentiated, and that male and female consumers tended to be in agreement regarding the gender of a product or service. Table 5-1 on page 120 presents a list of those products and services perceived by Chinese consumers to have either a decidedly masculine or feminine gender.

Consumers not only ascribe personality traits to products and services, but also they tend to associate personality factors with specific colors. In some cases, various products, even brands, associate a specific color with personality-like connotations. For instance, Coca-Cola is associated with red, which connotes excitement. Yellow is associated with "novelty," and black frequently connotes "sophistication."[5] For this reason, brands wishing to create a sophisticated persona (e.g., Minute Maid juices or Pasta LaBella) or an upscale or premium image (e.g., Miller Beers' Miller Reserve) use labeling or packaging that is primarily black. Still further, a combination of black and white has the power of communicating that a product is carefully engineered, high technology, and sophisticated in design. To illustrate, IBM has consistently used an all-black case with a few selected red buttons and bars to house its very successful Thinkpad laptops; Nike used black, white,

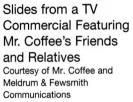

FIGURE 5-3

Slides from a TV
Commercial Featuring
Mr. Coffee's Friends
and Relatives
Courtesy of Mr. Coffee and
Meldrum & Fewsmith
Communications

table 5-1   Products and Services Perceived by Chinese Consumers to Possess a Definite Gender

MASCULINE PRODUCTS/SERVICES	FEMININE PRODUCTS/SERVICES
Beer	Bath soap
Car	Clothes dryer
Cigarettes	Day care
Coffee	Dishwashing liquid
Credit card	Electric iron
Haircut	Facial tissue
Legal services	Hair spray
Long-distance telephone	Shampoo
Restaurant	Washer
Scotch	
Sneakers	
Tennis racquet	
Toothpaste	
Wine	

Source: From Laura M. Milner and Dale Fodness, "Product Gender Perception: The Case of China," in David W. Stewart and Naufel J. Vilcassin, eds., *1995 Winter Educators' Conference* 6 (Chicago: American Marketing Association, 1995), 334. Reprinted by permission of American Marketing Association.

and a touch of red for selected models of its sport shoes to suggest (without even using any words) that it is a leader in advanced-performance sports shoes.

Many fast-food restaurants use combinations of bright colors, like red, yellow, and blue, for their roadside signs and interior designs. These colors have come to be associated with fast service and food being inexpensive. In contrast, fine dining restaurants tend to use sophisticated colors like grey, white, shades of tan, or other soft, pale, or muted colors to reflect fine leisurely service. Furthermore, consumer research performed by the first author of this book, for a marketer of popular-priced casual wear, revealed that dark colors like grey, dark blue, and black continuously outperformed pastel colors, in terms of consumer preference, in wintry Northeastern and Midwestern markets. However, when the multimarket study reached sunny Phoenix, Arizona, a reversal occurred—the darker colors fell into disfavor, and rose, pinks, yellows, and turquoise became the preferred colors. Upon reflection and further questioning, it became clear that many people sought to contrast the somber backdrop of the desert with multicolor pastel clothing and home furnishings. Table 5-2 presents a list of various colors, their personality-like meanings, and associated marketing insights. To discover such insights, researchers use a variety of qualitative measurement techniques, such as *observations*, *focus groups*, *depth interviews*, and *projective techniques* (discussed in Chapter 2).

Jungian Personality Types

Carl Jung was a contemporary and colleague of Freud. His contribution to modern psychology is extensive and his theories and insights pertaining to *personality types* are especially relevant to consumer behavior.[6] Jung's personality types have been made particularly useful for marketers by the Myers-Briggs Type Indicators (a personality inventory) that measures the following *pairs* of Jungian-inspired psychological dimensions:[7] (1) sensing-intuiting, (2) thinking-feeling, (3) extroversion-introversion, and (4) judging-perceiving. Each of these four pairs of dimensions reflects two distinctly different personality characteristics that offer a picture as to how consumers respond to the world around them.

table 5-2   The Personality-like Associations of Selected Colors

COLOR	PERSONALITY LINK	MARKETING INSIGHTS
BLUE	Commands respect, authority	• America's favored color • IBM holds the title to blue • Associated with club soda • Men seek products packaged in blue • Houses painted blue are avoided • Low-calorie, skim milk • Coffee in a blue can perceived as "mild"
YELLOW	Caution, novelty, temporary, warmth	• Eyes register it fastest • Coffee in yellow can tasted "weak" • Stops traffic • Sells a house
GREEN	Secure, natural, relaxed or easy going, living things	• Good work environment • Associated with vegetables and chewing gum • Canada Dry ginger ale sales increased when it changed sugar-free package from red to green and white
RED	Human, exciting, hot, passionate, strong	• Makes food "smell" better • Coffee in a red can perceived as "rich" • Women have a preference for bluish red • Men have a preference for yellowish red • Coca-Cola "owns" red
ORANGE	Powerful, affordable, informal	• Draws attention quickly
BROWN	Informal and relaxed, masculine, nature	• Coffee in a dark-brown can was "too strong" • Men seek products packaged in brown
WHITE	Goodness, purity, chastity, cleanliness, delicacy, refinement, formality	• Suggests reduced calories • Pure and wholesome food • Clean, bath products, feminine
BLACK	Sophistication, power, authority, mystery	• Powerful clothing • High-tech electronics
SILVER, GOLD, PLATINUM	Regal, wealthy, stately	• Suggests premium price

Source: From Bernice Kanner, "Color Schemes," *New York Magazine*, 3 April 1989, 22–23. Copyright, 1996, New York Magazine. Distributed by Los Angeles Times. Reprinted by permission.

The attempt to match each psychological dimension from all pairs with each psychological dimension in all other pairs would result in too many different combinations of personality types for productive study. To avoid this extreme complexity, a consumer researcher recently investigated the consumption relevance of just two pairs of dimensions (i.e., sensing-intuiting and thinking-feeling).[8] The sensing (S) and intuiting (N) dimensions capture how consumers find out about "things" (obtaining and processing information), and the thinking (T) and feeling (F) dimensions are opposite ways of making decisions (decision styles). By cross-tabulating the specific characteristics of the two pairs of psychological dimensions, four possible *personality types* are derived (Table 5-3). Table 5-4 summarizes the main characteristics of each of these four Jungian personality types. Using a psychological inventory, such as the Myers-Briggs Type Indicators, or by creating a consumer-specific personality inventory, it would be possible to learn how these four personality types impact on consumer information processing, consumer decision making, and other consumption-related issues—personality-related insights that would enable marketers to better satisfy consumer needs.

For instance, imagine four individuals (corresponding to the four Jungian personality types) facing the investment decision to purchase some stocks. The ST and SF types (the sensing types) would tend to conscientiously study balance sheets and financial performance to secure their facts. However, the ST (sensing-thinking) consumer would arrive at his or her *own* decision and might eventually use a discount broker. In contrast, the SF (sensing-feeling) consumer would want to include the recommendations of others as part of the decision and would be more likely to use a full-service brokerage house. The NT and NF consumers would be more likely to make their stock selections intuitively or in terms of a "hunch." NT consumers would rely heavily on their imaginations, yet would carefully think out all of the options. Although NF consumers would also rely on their imaginations while considering options, the ultimate decision might be expected to reflect inputs from others (e.g., comments overheard in some social setting, such as a cocktail party).

It is likely that advertising and marketing executives have used some of these Jungian personality types intuitively in creating consumer-targeted messages. For example, Figure 5-4 on page 124 presents an ad apparently aimed at Jungian ST types. The headline for the Principal Financial Group ad "We have the edge you need to meet any financial challenge," addresses many of the characteristics of a ST person. The body copy in the ad reinforces the headline.

Neo-Freudian Personality Theory

Several of Freud's colleagues disagreed with his contention that personality is primarily instinctual and sexual in nature. Instead, these neo-Freudians believed that **social relationships** are fundamental to the formation and development of personality. For instance, Alfred Adler viewed human beings as seeking to attain various rational goals, which he called *style of life*. He also placed much emphasis on the individual's efforts to overcome feelings of *inferiority* (i.e., to strive for superiority).

Harry Stack Sullivan, another neo-Freudian, stressed that people continuously attempt to establish significant and rewarding relationships with others. He was particularly concerned with the individual's efforts to reduce tensions, such as *anxiety*.

table 5-3 Selected Jungian Personality Types

	THINKING (T)	FEELING (F)
SENSING (S)	Sensing-thinking (ST)	Sensing-feeling (SF)
INTUITING (N)	Intuiting-thinking (NT)	Intuiting-feeling (NF)

table 5-4 Summary Characteristics of Selected Jungian Personality Types

SENSING-THINKING (ST)

- Rational in decision making
- Logical and empirical in viewpoint
- Makes decisions following an "objective" orientation
- Heavily weighs economic considerations—most price sensitive
- Will extend considerable effort to search for decision-making information
- Risk avoider
- Materialism reflects personal or private motives (i.e., identifies with material objects or "things")
- Short-time horizon in making decisions

SENSING-FEELING (SF)

- Empirical viewpoint
- Propelled by personal values rather than logic
- Makes decisions following a "subjective" orientation
- Likely to consider others when making a decision
- Shares risk with others
- Materialism reflects how objects will impact on others (i.e., status conscious)
- Short-time horizon in making decisions

INTUITING-THINKING (NT)

- Takes a broad view of personal situation or would
- Relies heavily on imagination, yet uses logic in approaching decisions
- Imagines a wider range of options in making a decision
- Weighs options mentally
- Willing to take risk or be speculative in decisions
- Long-time horizon in making decisions

INTUITING-FEELING (NF)

- Takes a broad view of personal situation or world
- Imagines a wide range of options in making a decision
- Highly "people oriented"—likely to consider others' views
- Makes decisions following a subjective orientation
- Least price sensitive
- Risk seeking (venturesome and novelty seeking)
- Indefinite time horizon in making decisions

Source: Adapted from Stephen J. Gould, "Jungian Analysis and Psychological Types: An Interpretive Approach to Consumer Choice Behavior," *Advances in Consumer Research* 18, Rebecca H. Holman and Michael R. Solomon, eds., (Provo, UT: Association for Consumer Research, 1991), 743–48. Reprinted by permission.

Like Sullivan, Karen Horney was also interested in anxiety. She focused on the impact of *child-parent* relationships, especially the individual's desire to conquer feelings of anxiety. Horney proposed that individuals be classified into three personality groups: **compliant**, **aggressive**, and **detached**.[9]

1. *Compliant individuals are those who move toward others (they desire to be loved, wanted, and appreciated).*

FIGURE 5-4

Ad Aimed at the
Jungian Sensing-
Thinking (ST) Type
Courtesy of Principal Financial
Group

2. *Aggressive individuals are those who move against others (they desire to excel and win admiration).*

3. *Detached individuals are those who move away from others (they desire independence, self-reliance, self-sufficiency, and freedom from obligations).*

A personality test based on Horney's theory (i.e., the CAD) has been developed and tested within the context of consumer behavior.[10] The initial CAD research uncovered a number of tentative relationships between college students' scores and their product and brand usage patterns. For instance, highly *compliant* students were found to prefer name brand products, such as Bayer aspirin; students classified as *aggressive* showed a preference for Old Spice deodorant over other brands (seemingly because of its masculine appeal); and highly *detached* students proved to be heavy tea drinkers (possibly reflecting their desire not to conform). More recent research reveals that children who scored high in self-reliance—who preferred to do things independently of others (which is similar to being a detached person)—were *less* likely to be very brand loyal and, up to a point, were more likely to try different brands.[11]

It is likely that many marketers have used some of these neo-Freudian theories intuitively. For example, marketers who position their products or services as providing an opportunity to belong or be appreciated by others in a group or social setting would seem to be guided by Horney's characterization of a compliant individual. Figure 5-5 shows an ad for Starter active wear; its headline, "It's about team," targets it directly to the compliant individual.

Trait Theory

Trait theory constitutes a major departure from the basically *qualitative* measures that typify the Freudian and neo-Freudian movements (e.g., personal observation, self-reported experiences, dream analysis, projective techniques).

The orientation of trait theory is primarily *quantitative* or *empirical*; it focuses on the measurement of personality in terms of specific psychological characteristics, called traits. A **trait** is defined as "... *any distinguishing, relatively enduring way in which one*

FIGURE 5-5

Ad Targeted to the Compliant Personality
Courtesy of Starter

individual differs from another."[12] Accordingly, trait theorists are concerned with the construction of personality tests (or inventories) that pinpoint individual differences in terms of specific traits.

Selected **single-trait personality** tests (which measure just one trait, such as self-confidence) are increasingly being developed specifically for use in consumer behavior studies. These tailor-made personality tests measure such traits as *consumer innovativeness* (how receptive a person is to new experiences), *consumer susceptibility to interpersonal influence* (SUSCEP gauges how consumers respond to social influence), *consumer materialism* (assesses the degree of consumer's attachment to "world" possessions), and *consumer ethnocentrism* (CETSCALE identifies consumer's likelihood to accept or reject foreign-made products).[13]

Based on experience using personality inventories to understand consumption-related behavior, researchers have learned that it is generally more realistic to expect personality to be linked to how consumers *make their choices* and to the purchase or consumption of a *broad product category*, rather than a specific brand. For example, there is more likely to be a relationship between personality and whether or not an individual *owns* a convertible sports car, than between personality and the *brand* of convertible sports car purchased.

The next section shows how trait measures of personality are used to expand our understanding of consumer behavior.

PERSONALITY AND UNDERSTANDING CONSUMER DIVERSITY

Marketers are interested in understanding how personality influences consumption behavior, because such knowledge enables them to better understand consumers and, more appropriately, to segment and target those consumers who are likely to respond positively to their product or service communications. This section examines some specific personality traits that appear promising for a better understanding of consumer behavior.

Consumer Innovativeness and Related Personality Traits

Marketing practitioners must learn all they can about consumers who are likely to try new products, services, or practices, for the market response of such innovators is often crucial to the ultimate success of a new product or service.

Personality traits that have proved useful in differentiating between **consumer innovators** and **noninnovators** include *consumer innovativeness*, *dogmatism*, *social character*, *optimum stimulation level*, and *variety-novelty seeking*. (Chapter 18 examines additional characteristics that distinguish between consumer innovators and noninnovators.)

▲ **Consumer Innovativeness** How receptive consumers are to new products, new services, or new practices is quite important to both consumers and marketers, for both can benefit from the right innovation. Consumer researchers have endeavored to develop measurement instruments to gauge the level of consumer innovativeness, because such personality trait measures provide insights into the nature and boundaries of a consumer's willingness to innovate.[14] Table 5-5 presents a six-item measure of consumer innovativeness that is specially designed to be flexible in terms of the boundaries or domain being studied (e.g.,

table 5-5 A Consumer Innovativeness Scale*

In general, I am among the last in my circle of friends to buy a new (rock album#) when it appears.**

If I heard that a (new rock album) was available in the store, I would be interested enough to buy it.

Compared to my friends, I own few (rock albums).**

In general, I am the last in my circle of friends to know the (titles of the latest rock albums).**

I will buy a new (rock album), even if I haven't heard it yet.

I know the names of (new rock acts) before other people do.

* Measured on a 5-point "agreement" scale.

\# The product category and related wording is altered to fit the purpose of the researcher.

**Items with an (**) are negatively worded and are scored inversely.

Source: Ronald E. Goldsmith and Charles F. Hofacker, "Measuring Consumer Innovativeness," *Journal of the Academy of Marketing Science* 19 (1991), 212. Copyright © 1991 Academy of Marketing Science. Reprinted by permission.

broad product category, personal computers; *subproduct category*, portable computers; *type*, notebook computers). The important topic of "consumer innovativeness" will be examined in greater detail in Chapter 18.

▲ **Dogmatism** Dogmatism is a personality trait that measures the degree of rigidity individuals display toward the unfamiliar and toward information that is contrary to their own established beliefs.[15] A person who is highly dogmatic approaches the unfamiliar defensively and with considerable discomfort and uncertainty. At the other end of the spectrum, a person who is low in dogmatism will readily consider unfamiliar or opposing beliefs.

Consumers who are low in dogmatism (open-minded) are more likely to prefer innovative products to established or traditional alternatives. In contrast, highly dogmatic (closed-minded) consumers are more likely to choose established, rather than innovative, product alternatives.

It is likely that highly dogmatic consumers will be more accepting of ads for new products or services that contain an *authoritative appeal*. To this end, marketers have used celebrities and experts in their new-product advertising to make it easier for potentially reluctant consumers (noninnovators) to accept the innovation. In contrast, low-dogmatic consumers (who are frequently high in innovativeness) seem to be more receptive to messages that stress factual differences and product benefits.

▲ **Social Character** The personality trait known as *social character* has its origins in sociological research, which focuses on the identification and classification of individuals into distinct sociocultural types. As used in consumer psychology, social character is a personality trait that ranges on a continuum from **inner-directedness** to **other-directedness**. Available evidence indicates that **inner-directed consumers** tend to rely on their own "inner" values or standards in evaluating new products and are likely to be consumer innovators. Conversely, **other-directed consumers** tend to look to others for direction on what is "right" or "wrong"; thus, they are less likely to be consumer innovators.

Inner- and *other-directed* consumers also may be attracted to different types of promotional messages. Inner-directed people seem to prefer ads that stress product features and personal benefits (enabling them to use their own values and standards in evaluating products), while other-directed people seem to prefer ads that feature a social environment or social acceptance (in keeping with their tendency to look to others for direction). Thus, other-directed individuals may be more easily influenced because of their natural inclination to go beyond the content of an ad and think in terms of likely social approval of a potential purchase.

 Optimum Stimulation Level Some people seem to prefer a simple, uncluttered, and calm existence, while others seem to prefer an environment crammed with novel, complex, and unusual experiences. Consumer research has examined how such variations in need for stimulation may be influenced by selected personality traits and how, in turn, specific stimulation levels may be related to consumer behavior. So far, this research has linked high **optimum stimulation levels** (OSLs) with more willingness to take risks, to try new products, to be innovative, to seek purchase-related information, and to accept new retail facilities.

OSL also seems to reflect a person's desired level of lifestyle stimulation.[16] For instance, if consumers' actual lifestyles are equivalent to their OSL scores, then they are likely to be *quite satisfied*. On the other hand, if their lifestyles are understimulated (i.e., their OSL is greater than current reality), they are likely to be *bored*; if their lifestyles are overstimulated (i.e., their OSL is lower than current reality), they are likely to seek *rest* or *relief*. This suggests that the relationship between consumers' lifestyles and their OSLs is likely to influence their choices of products or services and how they manage and spend their time. For instance, a person who feels bored (an understimulated consumer) is likely to be attracted to a vacation that offers much activity and an exciting time. In contrast, a person who feels overwhelmed (an overstimulated consumer) is likely to seek a quiet, isolated, relaxing, and rejuvenating vacation. The message in the magazine ad in Figure 5-6 for The Pointe Hilton Resorts gives readers the choice as to how stimulated they might wish to be, when it says: "Where you can explore endless activities or relax and do absolutely nothing."

 Variety-Novelty Seeking A personality-driven trait quite similar and related to OSL is **variety** or **novelty seeking**.[17] There appear to be many different types of variety seeking:

FIGURE 5-6

A Message for Both High- and Low-OSL Consumers
Courtesy of Pointe Hilton Resorts

exploratory purchase behavior (e.g., switching brands to experience new and possibly better alternatives), *vicarious exploration* (e.g., where the consumer secures information about a new or different alternative and then contemplates or even daydreams about the option), and *use innovativeness* (e.g., where the consumer uses an already adopted product in a new or novel way).[18]

The third form of variety or novelty seeking—use innovativeness—is particularly relevant to technological products (such as home electronics products), where some models offer an abundance of features and functions, while others contain only a few essential features or functions. For example, consumers with higher variety-seeking scores have been found to purchase calculators with more features than consumers with lower variety-seeking scores.[19]

The stream of research examined here indicates that the consumer innovator differs from the noninnovator in terms of personality orientation. A knowledge of such personality differences should help marketers select target segments for new products and design distinctive promotional strategies for specific segments.

Consumer Susceptibility to Interpersonal Influence

Just as consumer researchers are interested in identifying characteristics of consumer innovators, they are also engaged in pinpointing the traits of consumers who are likely to be responsive to the influence of others. To this end, consumer researchers have developed a twelve-item scale (called "SUSCEP") designed to measure consumers' susceptibility to interpersonal influence.[20] SUSCEP is assumed to be a general trait that reflects consumer differences in terms of response to social influence. According to the underlying theory upon which the scale was developed, there are three types of interpersonal influence: (1) *information influence*, which is the tendency to accept information from others as evidence about reality, (2) *value-expressive influence*, which captures consumers desires to enhance their standing with others by being similar to them, and (3) *utilitarian influence*, where consumers conform with the wishes of others to obtain a reward or avoid punishment. The latter two types of influence (i.e., value-expressive and utilitarian) are each *normative* and *subjective* in nature; that is, they reflect the consumer's own expectations of the objectives of others. Testing of the SUSCEP scale shows that individuals who scored *higher* on susceptibility to interpersonal influence were less self-confident than consumers who scored *lower* on susceptibility to interpersonal influence. This was particularly true for the normative factor (a combination of value-expressive and utilitarian influences).

The SUSCEP measure should prove useful in examining how social influence operates to encourage and discourage the acceptance of new products and services. (See Chapter 17 for a detailed discussion of personal influence and opinion leadership.)

Cognitive Personality Factors

Consumer researchers have been increasingly interested in how **cognitive personality** factors influence various aspects of consumer behavior. In particular, two cognitive personality traits **visualizers versus verbalizers** and **need for cognition** have shown signs of being useful in understanding selected aspects of consumer behavior.[21]

▲ **Visualizers versus Verbalizers** One highly promising area of cognitive personality research classifies consumers as *visualizers* (consumers who prefer visual information and products that stress the visual, such as membership in a videotape cassette club) or *verbalizers* (consumers who prefer written or verbal information and products, such as membership in book clubs or audiotape clubs). Some marketers stress strong visual dimensions to attract visualizers (see Figure 5-7); others feature a detailed description or point-by-point explanation to attract verbalizers (see Figure 5-8).

▲ **Need for Cognition** Another promising cognitive personality characteristic is *need for cognition* (NC), which measures a person's craving for or enjoyment of *thinking*. Available research indicates that consumers who are *high* in NC are more likely to be responsive to

FIGURE 5-7

Light n' Lively's® Ad
Targets Visualizers
Courtesy of Kraft Foods

We make it light.

You make it lively.

Light n' Lively® cottage cheese is the healthy fast food you can enjoy many ways. Always low in fat, Light n' Lively is also a delicious source of calcium. So next time you want a quick and easy lunch - or breakfast or dinner or snack - make it Light n' Lively.®

| Serving Size 1/2 cup |
| Total Fat 1.5 g |
| Calories 80 Calcium 10% DV |

The Healthy Fast Food

©1995 Kraft Foods, Inc. Not available in all areas.

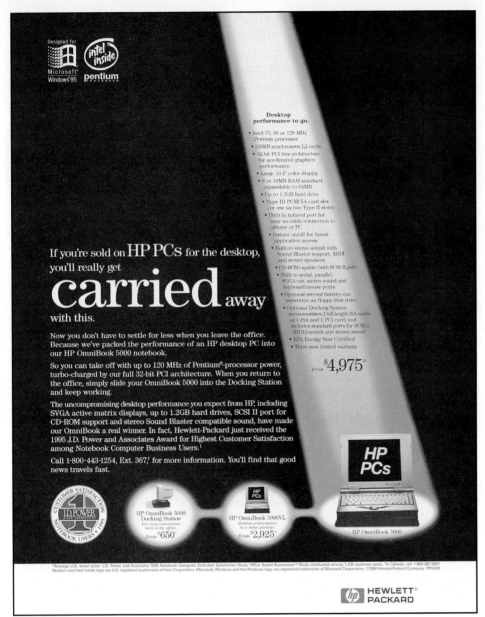

FIGURE 5-8

Hewlett-Packard's Ad Targets Verbalizers
Courtesy of Hewlett-Packard Company

the part of an ad that is rich in product-related information or description and unresponsive to the contextual or peripheral aspects of the ad, such as the presence of a celebrity endorser.[22] In contrast, those consumers who are relatively *low* in NC are more likely to be attracted to the background or peripheral aspects of an ad, such as an attractive model or well-known celebrity. (See also the discussion on central and peripheral routes to persuasion in Chapters 7, 9, and 10.) Other research suggests that consumers who are high in NC are more likely to be partial to cool colors (e.g., blue and green) than those who are low in NC and that individuals with a high need for cognition spend more time processing print advertisements, which results in superior brand and ad claim recall.[23]

If substantiated by future research, such insights should provide advertisers with valuable guidelines for creating advertising messages and supporting art (including color) that appeals to particular target consumers' *need for cognition.*

From Consumer Materialism
to Compulsive Consumption

Consumer researchers have become increasingly interested in exploring several interrelated consumption and possession traits. These traits range from *consumer materialism* to *fixated consumption behavior* to *consumer compulsive behavior*.

▲ **Consumer Materialism** "Materialism" (or people being "materialistic") is a topic frequently discussed in newspapers, magazines, and on TV (e.g., "Americans are very materialistic") and in everyday conversations between friends ("He's so materialistic!"). *Materialism*, as a personality-like trait, distinguishes between individuals who regard possessions as particularly essential to their identities and lives and those for whom possessions are secondary.[24] Researchers testing a new materialism scale have found some general support for the following characteristic observations about materialistic people: (1) They especially value acquiring and showing-off possessions. (2) They are particularly self-centered and selfish. (3) They seek lifestyles full of possessions (e.g., they desire to have lots of "things," rather than a simple uncluttered lifestyle). (4) Their many possessions do not give them greater personal satisfaction (i.e., possessions do not lead to greater happiness).[25] Table 5-6 presents sample items from a materialism scale.

Consistent with their strong status nature, the following seven products were thought to possess characteristics that would made them sought after by highly materialistic consumers: (1) Cadillac El Dorado, (2) Corvette, (3) diamond jewelry, (4) mink and leather jacket, (5) mink coat, (6) sports car, and (7) diamonds.[26]

▲ **Fixated Consumption Behavior** Somewhere between being materialistic and being compulsive or addictive with respect to buying or possessing objects is the notion of being

table 5-6   Sample Items from a Materialism Scale*

SUCCESS

The things I own say a lot about how well I'm doing in life.
I don't place much emphasis on the amount of material objects people own as a
    sign of success.**
I like to own things that impress people.

CENTRALITY

I enjoy spending money on things that aren't practical.
I try to keep my life simple, as far as possessions are concerned.**
Buying things gives me a lot of pleasure.

HAPPINESS

I'd be happier if I could afford to buy more things.
I have all the things I really need to enjoy life.**
It sometimes bothers me quite a bit that I can't afford to buy all the things I'd like.

* Measured on a 5-point "agreement" scale.

** Items with an (**) are negatively worded and are scored inversely.

Source: From Marsha L. Richins and Scott Dawson, "A Consumer Values Orientation for Materialism and Its Measurement: Scale Development and Validation," *Journal of Consumer Research* 19 (December 1992), 310. Reprinted by permission of The University of Chicago Press as publisher.

fixated with regard to consuming or possessing. Like materialism, *fixated consumption behavior* is in the realm of normal and socially acceptable behavior (i.e., fixated consumers do not keep their objects or purchases of interest a secret; rather, they frequently display them, and their involvement is openly shared with others who share a similar interest). For example, 7000 collectors of Zippo cigarette lighters recently spent a day at company headquarters to celebrate National Zippo Day. Collectors of these lighters pay up to $2500 for a mint-condition vintage Zippo.[27]

Fixated consumers typically possess the following characteristics: (1) a deep (possibly "passionate") interest in a particular object or product category; (2) a willingness to go to considerable lengths to secure additional examples of the object or product category of interest; and (3) the dedication of a considerable amount of discretionary time and money to searching out the object or product.[28] This profile of the fixated consumer describes many collectors or hobbyists (e.g., coin, stamp, or antique collectors or vintage wristwatch or fountain pen collectors). Research exploring the dynamics of the fixated consumer (in this case, coin collectors) revealed that, for fixated consumers, there is not only an enduring involvement in the object category itself but also a considerable amount of involvement in the *process of acquiring* the object (sometimes referred to as the "hunt").[29] Indeed, research conducted recently with collectors of previously discarded objects (e.g., old baby boots, glassware) found that "the shopping experience was as important as the items themselves.[30] Figure 5-9 shows the cover of a magazine targeted to collectors of vintage and current wristwatches (an area of interest to one of the "fixated consumers" who authored this book).

▲ **Compulsive Consumption Behavior** Unlike materialism and fixated consumption, **compulsive consumption** is in the realm of abnormal behavior. Consumers who are compulsive have an addiction; in some respects they are out of control, and their actions may

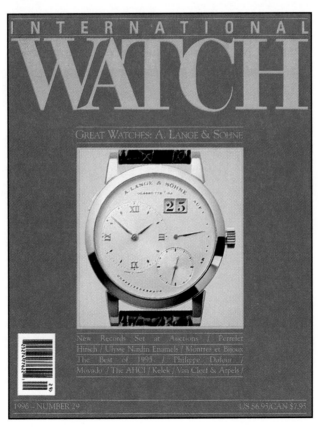

FIGURE 5-9

Cover of a Special-Interest Magazine Frequently Read by "Fixated Consumers"
Courtesy of International Publishers

have damaging consequences to them and those around them. Examples of compulsive consumption problems are: uncontrollable gambling, drug addiction, alcoholism, and various food and eating disorders.[31] From a marketing and consumer behavior perspective, compulsive buying can also be included in any list of "compulsive" activities. To control or possibly eliminate such compulsive problems generally requires some type of therapy or clinical treatment.

There have been some research efforts to develop a screener-inventory to pinpoint compulsive buying behavior. Two such scales were recently compared in a study of college students. Table 5-7 presents sample questions from these scales.[32] There is also evidence to suggest that self-gifting, impulse buying, and compulsive buying may be used by some consumers as a way to influence or manage their moods, i.e., the act of purchasing may alter a negative mood to a more positive one (e.g., "I'm depressed, I'll go out shopping and I'll feel better").[33]

Consumer Ethnocentrism: Responses to Foreign-Made Products

In an effort to distinguish between consumer segments that are likely to be receptive to foreign-made products and those that are not, researchers have developed and tested the **consumer ethnocentrism** scale, called CETSCALE (see Table 5-8).[34] The CETSCALE results have been encouraging in terms of identifying consumers with a predisposition to accept (or reject) foreign-made products. Consumers who are highly *ethnocentric* are likely to feel that it is inappropriate or wrong to purchase foreign-made products because of the economic impact on the domestic economy, whereas nonethnocentric consumers

table 5-7   Sample Items from Scales to Measure Compulsive Buying

VALENCE, D'ASTOUS AND FORTIER COMPULSIVE BUYING SCALE

1. When I have money, I cannot help but spend part or the whole of it.
2. I am often impulsive in my buying behavior.
3. As soon as I enter a shopping center, I have an irresistible urge to go into a shop to buy something.
4. I am one of those people who often responds to direct mail offers (e.g., books or compact discs).
5. I have often bought a product that I did not need, while knowing I had very little money left.

FABER AND O'GUINN COMPULSIVE BUYING SCALE

1. If I have any money left at the end of the pay period, I just have to spend it.
2. I felt others would be horrified if they knew my spending habits.
3. I have bought things though I couldn't afford them.
4. I wrote a check when I knew I didn't have enough money in the bank to cover it.
5. I bought something in order to make myself feel better.

Source: Gilles Valence, Alain d'Astous, and Louis Fortier, "Compulsive Buying: Concept and Measurement," *Journal of Consumer Policy* 11 (1988), 419–433; Ronald J. Faber and Thomas C. O'Guinn, "A Clinical Screener for Compulsive Buying," *Journal of Consumer Research* 19, December 1992, 459–469; and Leslie Cole and Dan Sherrell, "Comparing Scales to Measure Compulsive Buying: An Exploration of Their Dimensionality," in Frank R. Kardes and Mita Sujan, eds., *Advances in Consumer Research* 22 (Provo, UT: Association for Consumer Research, 1995), 419–427.

table 5-8 The Consumer Ethnocentrism Scale—CETSCALE

1. American people should always buy American-made products instead of imports.
2. Only those products that are unavailable in the U.S. should be imported.
3. Buy American-made products. Keep America working.
4. American products, first, last, and foremost.
5. Purchasing foreign-made products is un-American.
6. It is not right to purchase foreign products, because it puts Americans out of jobs.
7. A real American should always buy American-made products.
8. We should purchase products manufactured in America instead of letting other countries get rich off us.
9. It is always best to purchase American products.
10. There should be very little trading or purchasing of goods from other countries unless out of necessity.
11. Americans should not buy foreign products, because this hurts American business and causes unemployment.
12. Curbs should be put on all imports.
13. It may cost me in the long run but I prefer to support American products.
14. Foreigners should not be allowed to put their products on our markets.
15. Foreign products should be taxed heavily to reduce their entry into the United States.
16. We should buy from foreign countries only those products that we cannot obtain within our own country.
17. American consumers who purchase products made in other countries are responsible for putting their fellow Americans out of work.

Response format is a 7-point Likert-type scale (strongly agree =7, strongly disagree =1). Range of scores is from 17 to 119.

Calculated from confirmatory factor analysis of data from 4-area study.

Source: Terence A. Shimp and Subhash Sharma, "Consumer Ethnocentrism: Construction and Validation of the CETSCALE," *Journal of Marketing Research* 24 (August 1987), 282. Reprinted by permission.

tend to evaluate foreign-made products more objectively for their extrinsic characteristics. For example, a recent article suggests that some older American consumers, in remembrance of World War II, may refuse to purchase German- and/or Japanese-made products, while their German and Japanese counterpart consumers may feel similarly about American-made products.[35] Additionally, there is evidence to suggest that Jungian personality types (discussed earlier in this chapter) are associated with consumers' tendency toward ethnocentrism.[36] For instance, ST (sensing-thinking) consumers, who tend to arrive at their own decisions, were found to feel the strongest that it is wrong to purchase foreign-made products (i.e., score highest on ethnocentricism).

Thus, domestic marketers can attract ethnocentric consumers by stressing a nationalistic theme in their promotional appeals (e.g., "Made in America" or "Made in France"), because this segment is predisposed to buy products made in their native land. Honda's advertisement for its Accord wagon uses an ethnocentric appeal with its "Exported from America" photo caption (see Figure 5-10 on the next page).

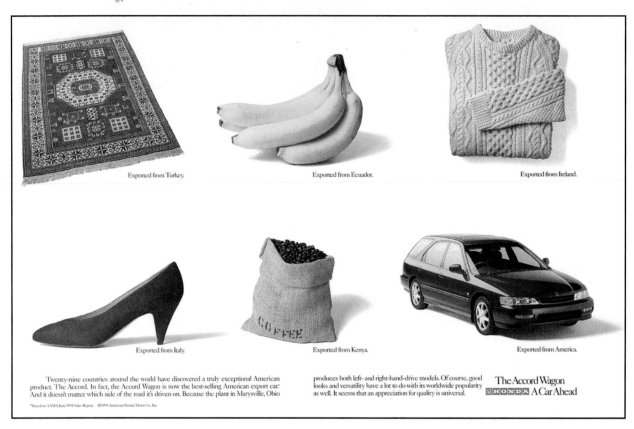

SELF AND SELF-IMAGE

Consumers have a number of enduring images of themselves. These self-images, or "perceptions of self," are very closely associated with personality in that individuals tend to buy products and services, and patronize retailers, with images or "personalities" that closely correspond to their own self-images. In this final section, we examine the issue of *one* or *multiple* selves, explore the *makeup* of the self-image, the notion of *extended self*, and the possibilities of *altering the self-image*.

One or Multiple Selves

Historically, individual consumers have been thought to have "a single self" and to be interested in products and services that satisfy that single self. However, research indicates that it is more accurate to think of the consumer in terms of a **multiple self** or **multiple selves**.[37] The change in thinking reflects the understanding that a single consumer is actually quite likely to act quite differently with different people and in different situations. For instance, a person is likely to behave differently at a museum opening, at school, at work, with parents, or with friends at a night club. The healthy or normal person is likely to be a somewhat different person in each of these different situations or social **roles**. In fact, acting exactly the same in all situations or roles is likely to be a sign of an abnormal or unhealthy person.

In terms of consumer behavior, the idea that an individual embodies a number of different "selves" (i.e., has multiple self-images) suggests that marketers should target their products and services to consumers *within the context of a particular "self."* (The notion of a consumer having multiple selves or multiple roles is consistent with the idea of use-situation segmentation discussed in Chapter 3.)

The Makeup of the Self-Image

Consistent with the idea of multiple self-images, each individual has an image of himself or herself as a certain kind of person, with certain traits, habits, possessions, relationships, and ways of behaving. As with other types of images and personality, the individual's self-image is unique, the outgrowth of that person's background and experience. Individuals develop their self-images through interactions with other people: initially their parents and then other individuals or groups with whom they relate over the years.

Products and brands have symbolic value for individuals, who evaluate them on the basis of their consistency (i.e., congruence) with their personal pictures or images of themselves. Some products seem to match one or more of an individual's self-images; others seem totally alien. It is generally held that consumers attempt to preserve or enhance their self-images by selecting products with "images" or "personalities" they believe are congruent with their own self-images and avoiding products that are not.[38]

A variety of different self-images have been identified in the consumer behavior literature. One popular model depicts four specific kinds of self-image: (1) **actual self-image** (e.g., how consumers in fact see themselves), (2) **ideal self-image** (e.g., how consumers would like to see themselves), (3) **social self-image** (e.g., how consumers feel others see them), and (4) **ideal social self-image** (e.g., how consumers would like others to see them).[39] Other research has identified a fifth type of self-image, **expected self-image** (e.g., how consumers expect to see themselves at some specified future time). The *expected* self-image is somewhere between the *actual* and *ideal* self-images. It is somewhat like a future-oriented combination of "what is" (the actual self-image) and what consumers would like "to be" (the ideal self-image). Moreover, because the expected self-image provides consumers with a realistic "opportunity" to change the "self," it is likely to be more valuable to marketers than the actual or ideal self-image as a guide for designing and promoting products.

In different contexts (i.e., in different situations and/or with respect to different products), consumers might select a different self-image to guide their attitudes or behavior. For instance, with some everyday household products, consumers might be guided by their *actual self-images*; whereas, for some socially enhancing or socially conspicuous products, they might be guided by their *social self-image*. When it comes to a so-called fantasy product, they might be guided by either their ideal self-images or ideal social self-images.

The concept of self-image has strategic implications for marketers. For example, marketers can segment their markets on the basis of relevant consumer self-images and then position their products or services as symbols of such self-images. Such a strategy is fully consistent with the marketing concept in that the marketer first assesses the needs of a consumer segment (with respect to both the product category and to an appropriate symbol of self-image) and then proceeds to develop and market a product or service that meets both criteria.

The Extended Self

The interrelationship between consumers' self-images and their possessions (i.e., objects they call their "own") is an exciting topic for consumer research. Specifically, consumers' possessions can be seen to "confirm" or "extend" their self-images. For instance, acquiring a desired or sought-after tennis racquet might serve to expand or enrich Mary's image of "self." Mary might now see herself as "being more competitive, more fit, and more successful," because she has added the tennis racquet to her "inventory" of self-enhancing possessions. In a similar manner, if the fountain pen that Steve received as a gift from his grandfather were stolen, Steve is likely to feel diminished in some way. Indeed, the loss of a prized possession may lead Steve to "grieve" and to experience a variety of emotions such as frustration, loss of control, the feeling of being "violated," even the loss of magical protection.

The above examples suggest that much human emotion can be connected to valued possessions. In such cases, possessions can be considered extensions of the self.[40] It has been proposed that possessions can extend the self in a number of ways: (1) actually, by allowing the person to do things that otherwise would be very difficult or impossible to accomplish (e.g., problem-solving using a computer); (2) symbolically, by making the person feel better or "bigger" (e.g., receiving an employee award for excellence); (3) by conferring status or rank (e.g., status among collectors of rare works of art because of the ownership of a particular masterpiece); (4) by bestowing feelings of immortality, by leaving valued possessions to young family members (this also has the potential of extending the recipients' "selves"); and (5) by endowing with magical powers (e.g., a cameo pin inherited from one's aunt might be perceived as a magic amulet bestowing good luck when it is worn).[41]

Altering the Self

Sometimes consumers wish to change themselves to become a different or "improved" self. Clothing, grooming aids, and all kinds of accessories (e.g., cosmetics, jewelry) offer consumers the opportunity to modify their appearances and thereby to alter their "selves." In using "self-altering products," consumers are frequently attempting to express their individualism or uniqueness by *creating a new self*, *maintaining the existing self* (or preventing the loss of self), and *extending the self* (modifying or changing the self). Sometimes, consumers use self-altering products or services to conform to or take on the appearance of a particular type of person (e.g., a military person, a physician, a business executive, or a college professor).

Altering one's self, particularly one's appearance or body parts, can be accomplished by cosmetics, hair restyling or coloring, switching from eye glasses to contact lenses (or the reverse), or undergoing cosmetic surgery.[42] Figure 5-11 presents an ad for Clairol's new Ultress hair color. The headline declares that "New Ultress Lets You Express Your Inner Self. Or Perhaps We Should Say Selves." The visual depicts a well-known model "wearing" different hair colors.

When it comes to altering one's self, both male and female consumers are open to the idea. According to a *Psychology Today* study, 45 percent of women and 33 percent of men would consider cosmetic surgery.[43] By using these options, it is possible to create a "new" or "improved" person. Some people also call upon *image consultants* to achieve an appropriate and mutually agreed-upon self-image.[44] Image consultants provide clients with advice on such personal attributes as clothing, color, presentation, appearance, posture, speaking, and media skills.

▲ **Vanity and Consumer Behavior** Closely related to self-image is the idea of personal vanity. Using a recently developed vanity scale (Table 5-9), researchers have investigated both *physical vanity* (an excessive concern for and/or a positive or even inflated view of one's physical appearance) and *achievement vanity* (an excessive concern for and/or a positive or even inflated view of one's personal achievements). Thus far they have found these two ideas related to materialism, use of cosmetics, concern with clothing, and country club membership.[45]

"Ultress Lets You Express Your Inner Self.

Or Perhaps I Should Say Selves." —LINDA EVANGELISTA

With color this expressive, there's no limit to who you can be. Because Ultress, with Color Maximizing Gel, is no ordinary color. It's the ultimate color. No wonder Ultress is the favorite of those, like Linda, who have a passion for coloring their hair.

ULTRESS
CLAIROL
Feel The Power Of Color.

table 5-9   Sample Items from a Vanity Scale

PHYSICAL-CONCERN ITEMS

1. The way I look is extremely important to me.
2. I am very concerned with my appearance.
3. It is important that I always look good.

PHYSICAL-VIEW ITEMS

1. People notice how attractive I am.
2. People are envious of my good looks.
3. My body is sexually appealing.

ACHIEVEMENT-CONCERN ITEMS

1. Professional achievements are an obsession with me.
2. Achieving greater success than my peers is important to me.
3. I want my achievements to be recognized by others.

ACHIEVEMENT-VIEW ITEMS

1. My achievements are highly regarded by others.
2. I am a good example of professional success.
3. Others wish they were as successful as me.

Source: Richard G. Netemeyer, Scot Burton, and Donald R. Lichtenstein, "Trait Aspects of Vanity: Measurement and Relevance to Consumer Behavior," *Journal of Consumer Research* 21, March 1995, 624. Reprinted by permission of The University of Chicago Press as publisher.

summary

Personality can be described as the psychological characteristics that both determine and reflect how a person responds to his or her environment. Although personality tends to be consistent and enduring, it may change abruptly in response to major life events, as well as gradually over time.

Four theories of personality are prominent in the study of consumer behavior: psychoanalytic theory, Jungian theory, neo-Freudian theory, and trait theory. Freud's psychoanalytic theory provides the foundation for the study of motivational research, which operates on the premise that human drives are largely unconscious in nature and serve to motivate many consumer actions. Jungian theory focuses on personality types. Consumer researchers are interested in four pairs of personality types: sensing-intuiting, thinking-feeling, extroversion-introversion, and judging-perceiving. Each of these four pairs of dimensions reflects two distinctly different personality characteristics that influence consumer responses to the world around them.

Neo-Freudian theory tends to emphasize the fundamental role of social relationships in the formation and development of personality. Alfred Adler viewed human beings as seeking to overcome feelings of inferiority. Harry Stack Sullivan believed that people attempt to establish significant and rewarding relationships with others. Karen Horney saw individuals as trying to overcome feelings of anxiety and categorized them as compliant, aggressive, or detached.

Trait theory is a major departure from the qualitative or subjective approach to personality measurement. It postulates that individuals possess innate psychological traits (e.g., innovativeness, novelty seeking, need for cognition, materialism) to a greater or lesser degree, and that these traits can be measured by specially designed scales or inventories. Because they are simple to use and to score and can be self-administered, personality inventories are the preferred method for many researchers in the assessment of consumer personality.

Each individual has a perceived self-image (or multiple self-images) as a certain kind of person with certain traits, habits, possessions, relationships, and ways of behaving. Consumers frequently attempt to preserve, enhance, alter, or extend their self-images by purchasing products or services and shopping at stores believed to be consistent with the relevant self-image and by avoiding products and stores that are not.

discussion questions

1. How would you explain the fact that, although no two individuals have identical personalities, personality is sometimes used in consumer research to identify distinct and sizable market segments?

2. Contrast the major characteristics of the following personality theories: (a) Freudian theory, (b) Jungian theory, (c) Neo-Freudian theory, and (d) trait theory. In your answer, illustrate how each theory is applied to the understanding of consumer behavior.

3. Describe personality trait theory. Give five examples of how personality traits can be used in consumer research.

4. How can a marketer of cameras use the research findings that the target market consists primarily of inner-directed or other-directed consumers? Of consumers who are high (or low) on innovativeness?

5. Describe the type of promotional message that would be most suitable for each of the following personality market segments and give an example of each: (a) highly dogmatic consumers, (b) inner-directed consumers, (c) consumers with high optimum stimulation levels, (d) consumers with high need for recognition, and (e) consumers who are visualizers versus consumers who are verbalizers.

6. Is there likely to be a difference in personality traits between individuals who readily purchase foreign-made products and those who prefer American-made products? How can marketers use the consumer ethnocentrism scale to segment consumers?

7. A marketer of health foods is attempting to segment his or her market on the basis of consumer self-image. Describe the four types of consumer self-image and discuss which one(s) would be most effective for the stated purpose.

exercises

1. How do your clothing preferences differ from those of your friends? What personality differences might explain why your preferences are different from those of other people?

2. Find three print advertisements based on Freudian personality theory. Discuss how Freudian concepts are used in these ads. Do any of the ads personify a brand? If so, how?

3. Find print ads for (a) a domestic airline, and (b) a foreign airline. Compare the contents of the ads with the Jungian personality types listed in Table 5-4. Identify the personality type that each ad targets. Explain your choices.

4. Administer the nine items from the materialism scale (listed in Table 5-6) to two of your friends. In your view, are their consumption behaviors consistent with their scores on the scale? Why or why not?

- Actual self-image
- Brand personification
- Cognitive personality
- Compliant, aggressive, and detached personality groups
- Compulsive consumption
- Consumer ethnocentrism
- Consumer innovativeness
- Consumer innovators
- Consumer materialism
- Consumer susceptibility to interpersonal influence
- Dogmatism
- Expected self-image
- Extended self
- Freudian theory

- Freud's stages of personality development
- Id, superego, and ego
- Ideal self-image
- Ideal social self-image
- Inner-directed consumers
- Inner-directedness
- Jungian personality types
- Jungian theory
- Multiple self or multiple selves
- Need for cognition
- Neo-Freudian personality theory
- Noninnovators
- Optimum stimulation levels

- Oral, anal, phallic, latent, and genital stages
- Other-directed consumers
- Other-directedness
- Personality
- Psychoanalytic theory of personality
- Roles
- Single-trait personality
- Social relationships
- Social self-image
- Trait
- Trait theory
- Variety- or novelty-seeking trait
- Visualizers vs. verbalizers

1. DAVID M. MORAWSKI and LACEY J. ZACHARY, "Making Mr. Coffee," *Quirk's Marketing Research Review* 6, March 1992, 6–7, 29–33.

2. Ibid., 31.

3. TIM TRIPLETT, "When Tracy Speaks, Celestial Listens," *Marketing News*, October 24, 1994, 14.

4. LAURA M. MILNER and DALE FODNESS, "Product Gender Perception: The Case of China," in David W. Stewart and Naufel J. Vilcassin, eds., *1995 Winter Educators' Conference* 6 (Chicago: American Marketing Association, 1995), 331–36.

5. PAMELA S. SCHINDLER, "Color and Contrast in Magazine Advertising," *Psychology & Marketing* 3, 1986, 69–78.

6. CARL G. JUNG, *Collected Works Volume 6: Psychological Types* (Princeton, NJ: Princeton University Press, 1921/1977).

7. ISABEL B. MYERS, *Introduction to Type* (Palo Alto, CA: Consulting Psychologists Press, 1980); and ISABEL B. MYERS and MARY H. MCCAULLEY, *Manual: A Guide to the Development and Use of the Myers-Briggs Type Indicator* (Palo Alto, CA: Consulting Psychologists Press, 1985).

8. STEPHEN J. GOULD, "Jungian Analysis and Psychological Types: An Interpretive Approach to Consumer Choice Behavior," in Rebecca H. Holman and Michael R. Solomon, eds., *Advances in Consumer Research* 18

(Provo, UT: Association for Consumer Research, 1991), 743–48.

9. For example, see KAREN HORNEY, *The Neurotic Personality of Our Time* (New York: Norton, 1937).

10. JOEL B. COHEN, "An Interpersonal Orientation to the Study of Consumer Behavior," *Journal of Marketing Research* 6, August 1967, 270–78; ARCH G. WOODSIDE and RUTH ANDRESS, "CAD Eight Years Later," *Journal of the Academy of Marketing Science* 3, Summer-Fall 1975, 309–13; see also JON P. NOERAGER, "An Assessment of CAD A Personality Instrument Developed Specifically for Marketing Research," *Journal of Marketing Research* 16, February 1979, 53–59; and PRADEEP K. TYAGI, "Validation of the CAD Instrument: A Replication," in Richard P. Bagozzi and Alice M. Tybout, eds., *Advances in Consumer Research* 10 (Ann Arbor: Association for Consumer Research, 1983), 112–14.

11. MORTON I. JAFFE, "Brand-Loyalty/Variety-Seeking and the Consumer's Personality: Comparing Children and Young Adults," in Scott B. MacKenzie and Douglas M. Stayman, eds., *Proceedings of the Society for Consumer Psychology* (LaJolla, CA: American Psychological Association, 1995), 144–51.

12. J. P. GUILFORD, *Personality* (New York: McGraw-Hill, 1959), 6.

13. RONALD E. GOLDSMITH and CHARLES F. HOFACKER, "Measuring Consumer Innovativeness," *Journal of the Academy of Marketing Science* 19, 1991, 209–21; WILLIAM O. BEARDEN, RICHARD G. NETEMEYER, and JESSE E. TEEL, "Further Validation of the Consumer Susceptibility to Interpersonal Influence Scale," in Marvin E. Goldberg, Gerald Gorn, and Richard W. Pollay, eds., *Advances in Consumer Research* 17 (Provo, UT: Association for Consumer Research, 1990), 770–76; RUSSELL W. BELK, "Three Scales to Measure Constructs Related to Materialism: Reliability, Validity, and Relationships to Measures of Happiness," in Thomas C. Kinnear, ed., *Advances in Consumer Research* 11 (Ann Arbor: Association for Consumer Research, 1984), 291–97; and TERENCE A. SHIMP and SUBHASH SHARMA, "Consumer Ethnocentrism: Construction and Validation of the CETSCALE," *Journal of Marketing Research* 24, August 1987, 280–89.

14. Also see: SURESH SUBRAMANIAN and ROBERT A. MITTELSTAEDT, "Conceptualizing Innovativeness as a Consumer Trait: Consequences and Alternatives," in Mary C. Gilly and F. Robert Dwyer, et al., eds., *1991 AMA Educators' Proceedings* (Chicago: American Marketing Association, 1991), 352–60; and "Reconceptualizing and Measuring Consumer Innovativeness," in ROBERT P. LEONE and V. KUMOR, et al., eds., *1992 AMA Educators' Proceedings* (Chicago: American Marketing Association, 1992), 300–307.

15. MILTON ROKEACH, *The Open and Closed Mind* (New York: Basic Books, 1960).

16. P. S. RAJU, "Optimum Stimulation Level: Its Relationship to Personality, Demographics, and Exploratory Behavior," *Journal of Consumer Research* 7, December 1980, 272–82; LEIGH MCALISTER and EDGAR PESSEMIER, "Variety Seeking Behavior: An Interdisciplinary Review," *Journal of Consumer Research* 9, December 1982, 311–22; EDGAR PESSEMIER and MOSHE HANDELSMAN, "Temporal Variety in Consumer Behavior," *Journal of Marketing Research* 21, November 1984, 435-44; ERICH A. JOACHIMSTHALER and JOHN L. LASTOVICKA, "Optimal Stimulation Level-Exploratory Behavior Models," *Journal of Consumer Research* 11, December 1984, 830-35; ELIZABETH C. HIRSCHMAN, "Experience Seeking: A Subjectivist Perspective of Consumption," *Journal of Business Research* 12, 1984, 115–36; JAN-BENEDICT E. M. STEENKAMP and HANS BAUMGARTNER, "The Role of Optimum Stimulation Level in Exploratory Consumer Behavior," *Journal of Consumer Research* 19, December 1992, 434; and RUSSELL G. WAHLERS and MICHAEL J. ETZEL, "A Consumer Response to Incongruity between Optimal Stimulation and Life Style Satisfaction," in Elizabeth C. Hirschman and Morris B. Holbrook, eds., *Advances in Consumer Research* 12 (Provo, UT: Association for Consumer Research, 1985), 97–101.

17. SATYA MENON and BARBARA E. KAHN, "The Impact of Context on Variety Seeking in Product Choices," *Journal of Consumer Research* 22, December 1995, 285–95.

18. ELIZABETH C. HIRSCHMAN, "Innovativeness, Novelty Seeking and Consumer Creativity," *Journal of Consumer Research* 7, 1980, 283–95; and WAYNE HOYER and NANCY M. RIDGWAY, "Variety Seeking as an Explanation for Exploratory Purchase Behavior: A Theoretical Model," in Thomas C. Kinnear, ed., *Advances in Consumer Research* 17 (Provo, UT: Association for Consumer Research, 1984), 114–19.

19. S. RAM and HYUNG-SHIK JUNG, "How Does Variety Seeking Affect Product Usage?" in Jon M. Hawes and George B. Gilsan, eds., *Developments in Marketing Science* 10 (Akron, OH: Academy of Marketing Science, 1987), 85-89.

20. WILLIAM O. BEARDEN, RICHARD G. NETEMEYER, and JESSE E. TEEL, "Measurement of Consumer Susceptibility to Interpersonal Influence," *Journal of Consumer Research* 15, March 1989, 473–81; and "Further Validation of the Consumer Susceptibility to Interpersonal Influence Scale," in Marvin E. Goldberg, Gerald Gorn, and Richard W. Pollay, eds., *Advances in Consumer Research* 17 (Provo, UT: Association for Consumer Research, 1990), 770–76.

21. MORRIS B. HOLBROOK, et al., "Play as a Consumption Experience: The Roles of Emotions, Performance, and Personality in the Enjoyment of Games," *Journal of Consumer Research* 11, September 1984, 728–39; and MORRIS B. HOLBROOK, "Aims, Concepts, and Methods for Representation of Individual Differences in Esthetic Responses to Design Features," *Journal of Consumer Research* 13, December 1986, 337–47.

22. RICHARD PETTY, et al., "Personality and Ad Effectiveness: Exploring the Utility of Need for Cognition," in Michael Houston, ed., *Advances in Consumer Research* 15 (Ann Arbor: Association for Consumer Research, 1988), 209–12.

23. AYN E. CROWLEY and WAYNE D. HOYER "The Relationship Between Need for Cognition and Other Individual Difference Variables: A Two-Dimensional Framework," in Thomas K. Srull, ed., *Advances in Consumer Research* 16 (Provo, UT: Association for Consumer Research, 1989), 37–43; and JAMES W. PELTIER and JOHN A. SCHIBROWSKY, "Need for Cognition, Advertisement Viewing Time and Memory for Advertising Stimuli," *Advances in Consumer Research* 21, 1994, 244–50.

24. RUSSELL W. BELK, "Three Scales to Measure Constructs Related to Materialism," op. cit.; and RUSSELL W. BELK, "Materialism: Trait Aspects of Living in the Material World," *Journal of Consumer Research* 12, December 1985, 265–80.

25. MARSHA L. RICHINS and SCOTT DAWSON, "A Consumer Values Orientation for Materialism and Its Measurement: Scale Development and Validation," *Journal of Consumer Research* 19, December 1992, 303–16.

26. MARSHA L. RICHINS, "Special Possessions and the Expression of Material Values," *Journal of Consumer Research* 21, December 1994, 531.

27. ALESSANDRA GALLONI, "Lighter Lovers Flip Their Tops at a Zippo Collectors' Convention," *The Wall Street Journal*, August 4, 1995, B4.

28. RONALD J. FABER and THOMAS C. O'GUINN, "A Clinical Screener for Compulsive Buying," *Journal of Consumer Research* 19, December 1992, 459–69.

29. Ibid.

30. STACEY MENZEL BAKER and ROBERT A. MITTELSTAEDT, "The Meaning of the Search, Evaluation, and Selection of 'Yesterday's Cast-Offs:' A Phenomenological Study into the Acquisition of the Collection," in Barbara B. Stern and George M. Zinkan, eds., *1995 AMA Educators' Proceedings* (Chicago: American Marketing Association, 1995), 152.

31. ELIZABETH C. HIRSCHMAN, "The Consciousness of Addiction: Toward a General Theory of Compulsive Consumption," *Journal of Consumer Research* 19, September 1992, 155–79.

32. LESLIE COLE and DAN SHERRELL, "Comparing Scales to Measure Compulsive Buying: An Exploration of Their Dimensionality," in Frank R. Kardes and Mita Sujan, eds., *Advances in Consumer Research* 22 (Provo, UT: Association for Consumer Research 1995), 419–27.

33. RONALD J. FABER and GARY A. CHRISTENSON, "Can You Buy Happiness?: A Comparison of the Antecedent and Concurrent Moods Associated with the Shopping of Compulsive and Non-Compulsive Buyers," in David W. Stewart and Naufel J. Vilcassin, eds., *1995 Winter Educator's Conference* 6 (Chicago: American Marketing Association, 1995), 378–79.

34. TERENCE A. SHIMP and SUBHASH SHARMA, "Consumer Ethnocentrism: Construction and Validation of the CETSCALE," op. cit.; and RICHARD G. NETEMEYER, SRINIVAS DURVAULA, and DONALD R. LICHTENSTEIN, "A Cross-National Assessment of the Reliability and Validity of the CETSCALE," *Journal of Marketing Research* 28, August 1991, 320–27.

35. SUBHARSH SHARMA, TERENCE A. SHIMP, and JEONGSHIN SHIN, "Consumer Ethnocentrism: A Test of Antecedents and Moderators," *Journal of the Academy of Marketing Science* 23, 1995, 27.

36. ROGER P. MCINTYRE and HAVVA J. MERIC, "Cognitive Style and Consumers' Ethnocentrism," in Michael Levy and Dhruv Grewal, eds., *Developments in Marketing Science* (Coral Gables, FL: Academy of Marketing Science, 1993), 46.

37. HAZEL MARKUS and PAULA NURIUS, "Possible Selves," *American Psychologist,* 1986, 954–69.

38. For a detailed discussion of self-images and congruence, see: M. JOSEPH SIRGY, "Self-Concept in Consumer Behavior: A Critical Review," *Journal of Consumer Research* 9, December 1992, 287–300; C. B. CLAIBORNE and M. JOSEPH SIRGY, "Self-Image Congruence as a Model of Consumer Attitude Formation and Behavior: A Conceptual Review and Guide for Future Research," in B. J. Dunlap, ed., *Developments in Marketing Science* 13 (Cullowhee, NC: Academy of Marketing Science, 1990), 1–7; and J. S. JOHAR and M. JOSEPH SIRGY, "Value-Expressive versus Utilitarian Advertising Appeals: When and Why to Use Which Appeal," *Journal of Advertising* 20, September 1991, 23–33.

39. Ibid.

40. RUSSELL W. BELK, "Possessions and the Extended Self," *Journal of Consumer Research* 15, September 1988, 139–68; and AMY J. MORGAN, "The Evolving Self in Consumer Behavior: Exploring Possible Selves," in Leigh McAlister and Michael L. Rothschild, eds., *Advances in Consumer Research* 20 (Provo, UT: Association for Consumer Research 1992), 429–32.

41. Ibid.

42. JOHN W. SCHOUTEN, "Selves in Transition: Symbolic Consumption in Personal Rites of Page and Identity Reconstruction," *Journal of Consumer Research* 17, March 1991, 412–25; and STACEY M. FABRICANT and STEPHEN J. GOULD, "Women's Makeup Careers: An Interpretive Study of Color Cosmetic Use and 'Face Value,'" *Psychology and Marketing* 10, November–December 1993, 531–48.

43. RICHARD G. NETEMEYER, SCOT BURTON, and DONALD R. LICHTENSTEIN, "Trait Aspects of Vanity: Measurement and Relevance to Consumer Behavior," *Journal of Consumer Research* 21, March 1995, 613.

44. JOSEPH Z. WISENBLIT, "Person Positioning: Empirical Evidence and a Paradigm," *Journal of Professional Services Marketing* 4, 1989, 53–84; and BETSY WIESENDANCER, "Do You Need an Image Consultant?" *Sales & Marketing Management*, May 1992, 30–36.

45. Op. cit., RICHARD G. NETEMEYER, SCOT BURTON, and DONALD R. LICHTENSTEIN, "Trait Aspects of Vanity: Measurement and Relevance to Consumer Behavior," *Journal of Consumer Research* 21, March 1995, 612–26.

THE ART OF REFRESHMENT™

THE ART OF

perrier

BOTTLED IN FRANCE

SPARKLING
MINERAL
WATER

REFRESHMENT

Swing

Mingle

Charm

Delight

Smile

Toast

Perrier

REFRES

As diverse individuals, we all tend to see the world in our own special ways. Four people can view the same event at the same time, and each will report in total honesty a story different from all the others. For example, the classic Japanese film *Rashomon* tells the story of the abduction and rape of a woodcutter's wife and the murder of her husband, first from the point of view of the bandit, then that of the wife, then the husband and, finally, that of a hidden bystander. Each story varied because each participant perceived the events that occurred in a different way. Hard to believe? Not really. For each individual, reality is a totally personal phenomenon, based on that person's needs, wants, values, and personal experiences.

Reality to an individual is merely that individual's perception of what is "out there"—of what has taken place. Individuals act and react on the basis of their perceptions, not on the basis of objective reality. Thus, to the

> *The illusion that times that were are better than those that are, has probably pervaded all ages.*
>
> —Horace Greeley

marketer, consumers' perceptions are much more important than their knowledge of objective reality. For if one thinks about it, it's not what *actually* is so, but what consumers *think* is so, that affects their actions, their buying habits, their leisure habits, and so forth. And, because individuals make decisions and take actions based on what they perceive to be reality, it is important that marketers understand the whole notion of perception and its related concepts, so they can more readily determine what factors influence consumers to buy.

This chapter examines the psychological and physiological bases of human perception and discusses the principles that control our perception and interpretation of the world we see. Knowledge of these principles enables astute marketers to develop advertisements that have a good chance of being seen and remembered by their target consumers.

WHAT IS PERCEPTION?

Perception can be described as "how we see the world around us." Two individuals may be subject to the same stimuli under the same apparent conditions, but how each person recognizes them, selects them, organizes them, and interprets them is a highly individual process based on each person's own needs, values, and expectations. The influence that each of these variables has on the perceptual process, and its relevance to marketing, will be explored in some detail. First, however, we will examine some of the basic concepts that underlie the perceptual process. These will be discussed within the framework of consumer behavior.

Perception

Perception is defined as the *process by which an individual selects, organizes, and interprets stimuli into a meaningful and coherent picture of the world*. A **stimulus** is any unit of input to any of the senses. Examples of stimuli (i.e., sensory input) include products, packages, brand names, advertisements, and commercials. **Sensory receptors** are the human organs (i.e., the eyes, ears, nose, mouth, and skin) that receive sensory inputs. Their sensory functions are to see, hear, smell, taste, and feel. All of these functions are called into play either singly or in combination in the evaluation and use of most consumer products.

The study of perception is largely the study of what we subconsciously add to or subtract from raw sensory inputs to produce our own private picture of the world. Figure 6-1 shows an advertisement for the Lexus automobile that specifically addresses the five senses.

Sensation

Sensation is the immediate and direct response of the sensory organs to simple stimuli (an advertisement, a package, a brand name). Human sensitivity refers to the experience of sensation. Sensitivity to stimuli varies with the quality of an individual's sensory receptors (e.g., eyesight or hearing) and the amount or intensity of the stimuli to which he or she is

FIGURE 6-1 ▼ Appealing to the Senses

Courtesy of Lexus, a Division of Toyota Motor Sales, U.S.A., Inc.

You Might Expect A Luxury Sedan To Cater To Your Senses. But All Six Of Them?

The sixth sense is a keen, highly intuitive power – a power of perception – that goes far beyond the five senses. That's according to the dictionary. According to our engineers, it comes standard with every Lexus ES 300. Let us explain. Have you ever been in a new place and felt like you had been there before? Some call it déjà vu, but we call it ergonomics: the uncanny ability of our cabin to have everything in exactly the place you would most likely want it. So whether it's the knob for the climate control system or the switch for the power window or the buttons for the optional six-disc CD auto-changer, or whatever – the first time you reach for it, the very first time, it will be there, as if you had placed it there yourself. Kind of spooky. Of course, we also do a lot for your other senses: the look of a sleek, aerodynamic body, the feel of gentle lumbar support, the smell of available handcrafted leather upholstery, and the soothing sound of eight strategically placed speakers. As for taste, it's in everything we do. Figuratively speaking, of course.

LEXUS *The Relentless Pursuit Of Perfection.*

© 1993 Lexus, A Division Of Toyota Motor Sales, U.S.A., Inc. Lexus reminds you to wear seat belts and obey all speed laws. For more information, call 800-872-5398 (800-USA-LEXUS). For the hearing impaired, call 800-443-4999.

exposed. For example, a blind person may have a more highly developed sense of hearing than the average sighted person and may be able to hear sounds that the average person cannot. Smell is the sense most closely tied to memory. Some adults, for example, relate the smell of crayola crayons to their childhood days.

Sensation itself depends on energy change (i.e., differentiation of input). A perfectly bland or unchanging environment—regardless of the strength of the sensory input—provides little or no sensation at all. Thus, a person who lives on a busy street in midtown Manhattan would probably receive little or no sensation from the inputs of such noisy stimuli as horns honking, tires screeching, and fire engines clanging, because such sounds are so commonplace in New York City. One honking horn more or less would never be noticed. In situations in which there is a great deal of sensory input, the senses do not detect small intensities or differences in input.

As sensory input decreases, however, our ability to detect changes in input or intensity increases, to the point that we attain maximum sensitivity under conditions of minimal stimulation. This accounts for the statement, "It was so quiet I could hear a pin drop." It also accounts for the increased attention given to a commercial that appears alone during a program break, or to a black-and-white advertisement in a magazine full of four-color advertisements. This ability of the human organism to accommodate itself to varying levels of sensitivity as external conditions vary not only provides more sensitivity when it is needed, but also serves to protect us from damaging, disruptive, or irrelevant bombardment when the input level is high.

The Absolute Threshold

The lowest level at which an individual can experience a sensation is called the **absolute threshold**. The point at which a person can detect a difference between "something" and "nothing" is that person's absolute threshold for that stimulus. To illustrate, the distance at which a driver can note a specific billboard on a highway is that individual's absolute threshold. Two people riding together may first spot the billboard at different times (i.e., at different distances); thus, they appear to have different absolute thresholds.

Under conditions of constant stimulation, such as driving through a "corridor" of billboards, the absolute threshold increases (that is, the senses tend to become increasingly dulled). After an hour of driving through billboards, it is doubtful that any one billboard will make an impression. Hence, we often speak of "getting used to" a hot bath, a cold shower, the bright sun, or even the odor in a college locker room. In the field of perception, the term *adaptation* refers specifically to "getting used to" certain sensations, becoming accommodated to a certain level of stimulation.

Sensory adaptation is a problem that concerns many TV advertisers, which is why they try to change their advertising campaigns regularly. They are concerned that consumers will get so used to their current print ads and TV commercials that they will no longer "see" them; that is, the ads will no longer provide sufficient sensory input to be noted.

In an effort to cut through the advertising "clutter" and ensure that consumers note their ads, some marketers try to increase sensory input. For example, Apple Computer once bought all the advertising space in an issue of *Newsweek* magazine to ensure that readers would note its ads. For the three weeks preceding the introduction of WINDOWS 95, Microsoft saturated the airwaves with advertising and, on the day of introduction, distributed all copies of the *London Times* (which contained an advertising insert describing the new software program) at no cost to British readers. Other advertisers try to attract attention by *decreasing* sensory input. Recent studies suggest that some advertisers use silence (the absence of music or other audio effects) to generate attention.[1]

Some marketers seek unusual media in which to place their advertisements in an effort to gain attention. Some have advertised their products on bus shelters; others have used parking meters and shopping carts; still others pay to have their products appear on TV shows and in movies. Fragrance marketers often include fragrance samples in their direct mail and magazine advertisements through sealed perfume inserts. (Because of frequent scent "leakage" from these perfume inserts, many readers have begun to object to this practice.) McDonald's once sent plastic records to consumers as part of a contest that required them to play the entire record in order to participate. Table 6-1 lists various ways in which marketers have tried to increase sensory inputs to consumers.

Some marketers have retained scent researchers to develop specially engineered smells to enhance their products and entice consumers to buy. For example, a new-car spray gives used vehicles the smell of new plastic and carpeting. A "fresh linen" scent has been added to a line of plastic trash bags to make consumers feel "healthy and clean."[2] Package designers try to determine consumers' absolute thresholds to make sure that their new product designs will stand out from those of the competition on retailers' shelves. Marketers use packaging consultants and marketing research to develop up-to-date, visual marketing strategies.

The Differential Threshold

The minimal difference that can be detected between two similar stimuli is called the **differential threshold**, or the **j.n.d.** (for *just noticeable difference*). A 19th century German scientist named Ernst Weber discovered that the just noticeable difference between two stimuli was not an absolute amount, but an amount relative to the intensity of the first stim-

table 6-1   Advertisers Attempt to Increase Sensory Input

MAGAZINE INSERTS

- Perfume manufacturers, such as Giorgio of Beverly Hills, Calvin Klein, Fendi, and Fabergé, use scent strips in magazines and direct mail to bring the smell of their perfumes directly to the consumer.
- Procter & Gamble used a "scratch-and-sniff" sticker in ads for one of its detergents to evoke the perception of sun-dried clothes.
- Rolls Royce put the aroma of its leather upholstery on a scent strip in Architectural Digest.
- Absolut vodka magazine advertisements contained microchips that played "Jingle Bells" and "Santa Claus Is Coming to Town."
- Toyota bound 3-D glasses into magazine ads for its Corolla automobile.
- Revlon and Estee Lauder offer eye shadow and blusher samples bound into fashion magazines.

POINT-OF-PURCHASE DISPLAYS

- Kraft has developed an electronic kiosk that responds to consumers' questions by printing out recipes that call for Kraft products along with cents-off coupons for Kraft ingredients.
- Store displays for Nabisco's Fruit Wheats cereal emit the scent of fresh rasberries.
- Interactive computers are programmed to give cosmetic product advice to consumers who input information about their eye, hair, and skin coloring.
- Orville Redenbacher packages popcorn in packets designed to resemble videocassettes and distributes them through video rental stores.
- Store customers are invited to press buttons that activate minirecorders that play a stream of product messages.

ulus. **Weber's law**, as it has come to be known, states that the stronger the initial stimulus, the greater the additional intensity needed for the second stimulus to be perceived as different. For example, if the price of an automobile was increased by $100, it would probably not be noticed (i.e., the increment would fall below the j.n.d.). It may take an increase of $200 or more before a differential in price would be noticed. However, a one-dollar increase in the price of gasoline would be noticed very quickly by consumers, because it is a significant percentage of the initial (i.e., base) cost of the gasoline.

According to Weber's law, an additional level of stimulus equivalent to the j.n.d. must be added for the majority of people to perceive a difference between the resulting stimulus and the initial stimulus. Weber's law holds for all the senses and for almost all intensities.[3]

Let us say that a manufacturer of silver polish wants to improve the product sufficiently to claim that it retards tarnish longer than the leading competitive brand. In a series of experiments, the company has determined that the j.n.d. for its present polish (which now gives a shine that lasts about 20 days) is 5 days, or one-fourth longer. That means that the shine given by the improved silver polish must last at least one-fourth longer than that of the present polish if it is to be perceived by the majority of users as, in fact, improved. By finding this j.n.d. of 5 days, the company has isolated the minimum amount of time necessary to make its claim of "lasts longer" believable to the majority of consumers.

If the company had decided to make the silver polish effective for 40 days, it would have sacrificed a good deal of repeat purchase frequency. If it had decided to make the polish effective for 23 days (just 3 extra days of product life), its claim of "lasts longer" would not be perceived as true by most consumers. Making the product improvement just equal to the j.n.d. thus becomes the most efficient decision that management can make.

The j.n.d. has other uses as well. For example, retailers have long made use of a general rule of thumb that markdowns of merchandise must amount to at least twenty percent of the old price, since a smaller amount often goes unnoticed. They recognize that the just noticeable difference is not an absolute amount, but rather a relative amount contingent upon the level of the initial price.

▲ **Marketing Applications of the j.n.d.** Weber's law has important applications in marketing. Manufacturers and marketers endeavor to determine the relevant j.n.d. for their products for two very different reasons: (1) so that negative changes (e.g., reductions in product size, increases in product price, or reduced quality) are not readily discernible to the public and (2) so that product improvements (such as improved or updated packaging, larger size, lower price) are very apparent to consumers without being wastefully extravagant. For example, because of rising costs, many manufacturers are faced with the choice of increasing prices or reducing the quantity of the product offered at the existing price. Some companies have done both, keeping the increased cost or the reduced size just under the j.n.d. to avoid negative consumer reaction.

Manufacturers who choose to reduce the quality of their products also try to ensure that product changes remain just under the point of just noticeable difference. For example, when the price of coffee beans goes up, coffee processors often downgrade quality by adding inferior beans to the mix, up to but not including the j.n.d.—the point at which the consumer will notice a difference in taste. Another example: to meet current nutritional concerns, a number of food processors have adjusted their recipes to substitute unsaturated fats for the animal fats and the coconut and palm oils previously used, with the intention of keeping any differences in taste under the j.n.d. A number of well-known food companies have been "downsizing" their packaging—that is, decreasing the package size or even maintaining the package size but decreasing the contents. By charging the same price, they are in fact achieving a price increase that is "invisible" to the consumer. To illustrate, Starkist Tuna traditionally put 6½ ounces of tuna into its regular-sized can. When it decreased this quantity to 6⅛ ounces while maintaining the same price, it actually realized a 5.8 percent price increase. Both Procter & Gamble and Kimberly-Clark have decreased the number of diapers in their packages. By downsizing the box of 88 to 80, and leaving the price the same, they effected a 9.1 percent price increase. The former 28-diaper box downsized to 26 diapers resulted in a 7.1 percent increase.

Consumer Reports magazine reported that for five rolls of Procter & Gamble's Bounty paper towels bought in succession, the contents dropped steadily from 85 to 70 square feet.[4] Despite the fact that the adjusted quantity is usually listed on the package label, most consumers do not notice it, because the package size remains the same. (This practice is referred to as *packaging-to-price* or *packaging-to-size*.)

Marketers often want to update existing packaging without losing the ready recognition by consumers who have been exposed to years of cumulative advertising impact. In such cases, they usually make a number of small changes, each carefully designed to fall below the j.n.d., so that consumers will not perceive any difference. For example, Betty Crocker, the General Mills symbol, has been updated seven times since it first appeared in 1936.

Since 1921, General Mills has used the name "Betty Crocker" to symbolize its Gold Medal flour and other food products. In 1936, it commissioned a well-known artist to draw a "portrait" of Betty Crocker with whom homemakers would identify. The artist blended the features of women employed in the company's Home Service Department into a warm, motherly image, which remained the fictitious Betty Crocker's official "portrait" for almost 20 years. In 1955, this image was updated into a soft, smiling version of the original portrait, and it was updated again in 1964 and 1968 to reflect the changing times.

In 1972, as women's roles in society evolved, the "portrait" was again updated to reflect a much more businesslike Betty. In 1980, a new portrait gave the always-poised Betty a softer image and slightly more casual dress, so that more women would identify with her. In 1986 her image was again updated to show a more professional and approachable Betty Crocker, as comfortable in the board room as in the kitchen. In 1996, her portrait was updated once again to reflect contemporary women from all walks of life and ethnic backgrounds. This last portrait was based on a computer-generated image of 75 different women which was combined with the 1986 rendition, to enable an even wider audience of women to identify with her.[5] As Figure 6-2 indicates, in all of her incarnations, Betty is portrayed in a red dress or jacket with white at her neck, wearing a hairstyle and clothing which reflect the current fashions of the times. Despite the dramatic differences between the 1936 and 1996 versions, each successive change remained below the j.n.d., enabling Betty Crocker to remain a current, familiar, and valuable symbol of quality for General Mills products.

The Campbell Soup Company traditionally has been extremely subtle in changing its package. An alteration here, a slight typographic change there, a refinement of its logotype, have all combined to keep the product looking up-to-date without losing any of the valuable Campbell image. However, the company recently decided to re-engineer its classic red and white packaging, updating the traditional packaging with high-gloss color pictures. They also changed the company's time-honored slogan from "M'm-m'm good" to "M'm-m'm better"—all in an effort, in the words of its president, "to get noticed in a new way . . . to break through."[6]

Lexmark International Inc., which bought the office supplies and equipment line from the International Business Machine Corporation in March 1991, agreed to relinquish the IBM name by 1996. Recognizing the need to build a brand image for Lexmark while they moved away from the well-known IBM name, Lexmark officials conducted a four-stage campaign for phasing in the Lexmark name on products. As Figure 6-3 on page 152 indicates, Stage 1 carried only the IBM name, Stage 2 featured the IBM name and downplayed

FIGURE 6-2

Sequential Changes in the Betty Crocker Symbol Fall Below the j.n.d.
Source: Used with the permission of General Mills, Inc.

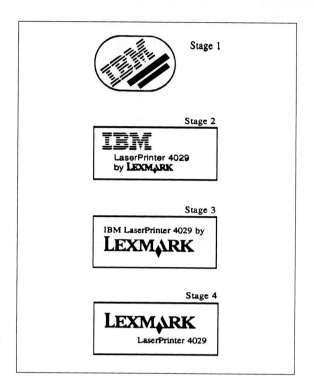

Lexmark, Stage 3 featured the Lexmark name and downplayed IBM, and Stage 4 features only the Lexmark name. Figure 6-4 shows a Lexmark ad with the transition complete.

Another interesting example is Ivory soap, which was introduced in 1879. The subtle packaging changes Ivory introduced over the years were each small enough to avoid notice, but the package managed to retain a contemporary look. The latest Ivory package is considerably different from the original, but the changes made at each step of the way were designed so skillfully that the transition has been hardly noticeable to consumers.

When the Coors Brewing Company changed its packaging *above* the j.n.d. by adding the words "original draft" to its label, it received hundreds of complaints from drinkers who believed the product itself had been changed, thus forcing the company to bring back the old label. Similarly, when the Kellogg Company decided to change the color and the illustration on its well-known Corn Flakes box to celebrate its 90th birthday, loyal consumers were confused into thinking the new box was a different product.

When it comes to product improvements, marketers very much want to meet or exceed the consumer's *differential threshold*; that is, they want consumers to readily perceive any improvements made in the original product. Marketers can use the j.n.d. to determine the amount of improvement they should make in their products. Less than the j.n.d. is wasted effort because the improvement will not be perceived; more than the j.n.d. may be wasteful by reducing the level of repeat sales.

Subliminal Perception

In Chapter 4, we spoke of people being *motivated* below their level of conscious awareness. People are also *stimulated* below their level of conscious awareness; that is, they can perceive stimuli without being consciously aware that they are doing so. The threshold for conscious awareness or conscious recognition appears to be higher than the *absolute threshold* for effective perception. Stimuli that are too weak or too brief to be consciously seen or heard may nevertheless be strong enough to be perceived by one or more receptor

cells. This process is called **subliminal perception** because the stimulus is beneath the threshold, or "limen," of awareness, though obviously not beneath the absolute threshold of the receptors involved. (Perception of stimuli that are above the level of conscious awareness is called *supraliminal perception*.)

In general, there are three types of subliminal perception: (1) briefly presented visual stimuli, (2) accelerated speech in low-volume auditory messages, and (3) embedded or hidden imagery or words (often of a sexual nature) in print ads or on product labels. **Embeds** are defined as *disguised stimuli not readily recognized by readers* that are "planted" in print advertisements to persuade consumers to buy their products.

Subliminal perception created a great furor in the late 1950s, when it was reported that consumers were being exposed to subliminal advertising messages they were not aware of receiving. These messages purportedly were persuading people to buy goods and services without being aware of why they were motivated to do so. The effectiveness of so-called subliminal advertising was reportedly tested at a drive-in movie in New Jersey in 1957, where the words "Eat popcorn" and "Drink Coca-Cola" were flashed on the screen during the movie.[7] Exposure times were so short that viewers were unaware of seeing a message. It was reported that during the 6-week test period, popcorn sales increased 58 percent and Coca-Cola sales increased 18 percent. However, no scientific controls were used, and researchers were never able to replicate the results. Nevertheless, public indignation at the possibility of such manipulation was so widespread that both the Federal Communications Commission and the United States Congress conducted hearings to determine whether subliminal advertising should be outlawed. The resultant publicity reawakened academic interest in the subject of subliminal perception.

▲ Research Studies of Subliminal Persuasion

A series of highly imaginative laboratory experiments that followed the public hearings gave some support to the notion that individuals could perceive below the level of their conscious awareness, but found no evidence that they could be persuaded to act in response to such subliminal stimulation. For example, one researcher found that while the simple subliminal stimulus *COKE* served to arouse thirst in subjects, the subliminal command, *DRINK COKE*, did not have a greater effect, nor did it have any behavioral consequences. However, a replication of this study by the original researcher in 1989 cast doubt on the earlier findings.[8] Other experiments had similar results; they supported the finding that individuals could *perceive* below their level of conscious awareness, but that subliminal stimuli did not affect their purchase intentions.

Interest in the field of subliminal perception was renewed in the mid-1970s with the charge that advertisers were using subliminal *embeds* in their print ads to persuade consumers to buy their advertised brands. It was alleged, for example, that liquor advertisers try to increase the subconscious appeal of their products by embedding sexually suggestive symbols in ice cubes floating in a pictured drink.[9] Seagram's Gin ran a series of ads that poked fun at subliminal embeds in liquor advertisements while cleverly inviting readers to study each ad closely.

Several studies suggest that individuals differ in their susceptibility to subliminal stimuli.[10] Some research indicates that subliminal messages can stimulate basic drives, such as hunger, but these messages do not appear to work equally well on everyone, and stimulation does not necessarily trigger action. In one study, for example, people were visually exposed to the word "beef" for 1/200th of a second every seven seconds. At the end of the experiment, the people in the test group reported being hungrier than those in the control group, who did not receive the messages. When asked to choose from a menu, however, few chose beef.[11] Another study found that subjects' attitudes toward the subliminal stimuli became significantly more positive with repeated exposures, even when they were unaware that exposures had occurred.[12] Other studies have found that sexually oriented embeds did not influence consumer preferences.[13]

Two recent experiments into the effectiveness of subliminal messages in television commercials concluded that it not only would be very difficult to use the technique on television, but even if it were to have "some influence," it would be much less effective than overt advertising and would likely interfere with consumers' memory for a brand name.[14]

Despite the fact that research suggests that subliminal *auditory* stimuli have an even lower probability of being cognitively processed than *visual* stimuli, a whole new industry seems to have been built on the basis of subliminal *audioperception*.[15] For example, self-help audiocassettes are a rapidly growing industry built on the premise of subliminal persuasion. Consumers are spending millions of dollars annually on self-help tapes in the belief that they can learn a foreign language, break a bad habit, improve their willpower or their memory, or take off weight. The tapes play relaxing music (or the sound of ocean waves) and contain subliminal messages not perceptible to the ear but supposedly recognizable to the subconscious mind. Most of the tapes come with a written script of the subliminal messages (e.g., "I chew slowly," "I eat less," "I am capable," "I act decisively"). One series of subliminal tapes is targeted at parents of young children so that the children may be exposed to "constructive messages" while they are involved in other activities. The producers advise parents not to expect results "immediately"; the caveat is in order, because there is no scientific evidence to support industry claims that the tapes work.[16]

Department stores are incorporating subliminal messages in musical soundtracks played on their public address systems to motivate employees and to discourage shoplifting. Subliminal messages, such as "I am honest," "I won't steal," and "Stealing is dishonest," have reportedly brought about significant decreases in shoplifting and inventory shrinkage.[17]

▲ Evaluating the Effectiveness of Subliminal Persuasion

Despite the many studies undertaken by academicians and researchers since the 1950s, there is no evidence that subliminal advertising persuades people to buy goods or services. A review of the literature indicates that subliminal perception research is based on two theoretical approaches. According to the first theory, constant repetition of very weak (e.g., subthreshold) stimuli has an incremental effect that enables such stimuli to build response strength over many presentations. This would be the operative theory when weak stimuli are flashed repeatedly on a movie screen or played on a soundtrack or audiocassette. The second approach is based on the theory that subliminal sexual stimuli arouse unconscious sexual motivations.[18] This is the theory behind the use of sexual embeds in print advertising. But no studies have yet indicated that either of these theoretical approaches have been effectively used by advertisers to increase sales. However, there is some indication that subliminal advertising may provide new opportunities for modifying antisocial behavior through public awareness campaigns that call for individuals to make generalized responses to suggestions that enhance their personal performance or improve their attitudes.[19]

One researcher pointed out that many studies of subliminal perception are flawed because the investigators assumed that some specific exposure duration or stimulus intensity automatically guaranteed that the stimulus would be sufficiently below the threshold to be undetected by experimental subjects. However, because perceptual thresholds differ widely among individuals, and even for the same individuals from day-to-day and minute-to-minute, there is no absolute cutoff point in stimulus intensity below which stimulation is imperceptible, and above which it is perceived.

In summary, although there is some evidence that subliminal stimuli may influence affective reactions, there is no evidence that subliminal stimulation can influence consumption motives or actions. There continues to be a big gap between perception and persuasion. A recent review of the evidence on subliminal persuasion indicates that the only way for subliminal techniques to have a significant persuasive effect would be through long-term repeated exposure under a limited set of circumstances, which would not be economically feasible or practical within an advertising context.[20]

As to sexual embeds, most researchers are of the opinion that "What you see is what you get"; that is, a vivid imagination can see whatever it wants to see in just about any situation, including any illustration. And that pretty much sums up the whole notion of perception: individuals see what they want to see (e.g., what they are motivated to see) and what they expect to see. To correct any misperceptions among the public that subliminal advertising does in fact exist, the advertising community occasionally sponsors ads like the one depicted in Figure 6-5 on page 156, which ridicule the notion that subliminal techniques are effective or used in advertising applications.

Several studies concerned with public awareness of subliminal advertising found that a large percentage of Americans know what subliminal advertising is, they believe that it is used by advertisers and that it is effective.[21] This should be a concern to marketers because, true or not, these beliefs influence consumer attitudes toward advertising.

Because of the absence of any evidence that subliminal persuasion really works, no state or federal laws have been enacted to restrict the use of subliminal advertising. The Federal Communications Commission has adopted the position that "covert messages by their very nature are against the public interest."[22] Clearly, that position covers both paid (commercial) subliminal advertisements and unpaid (public service) subliminal messages.

DYNAMICS OF PERCEPTION

The preceding section explained how the individual receives sensations from stimuli in the outside environment and how the human organism adapts to the level and intensity of sensory input. We now come to one of the major principles of perception: Raw sensory input

PEOPLE HAVE BEEN TRYING TO FIND THE BREASTS IN THESE ICE CUBES SINCE 1957.

The advertising industry is sometimes charged with sneaking seductive little pictures into ads.

Supposedly, these pictures can get you to buy a product without your even seeing them.

Consider the photograph above. According to some people, there's a pair of female breasts hidden in the patterns of light refracted by the ice cubes.

Well, if you really searched you probably *could* see the breasts. For that matter, you could also see Millard Fillmore, a stuffed pork chop and a 1946 Dodge.

The point is that so-called "subliminal advertising" simply doesn't exist. Overactive imaginations, however, most certainly do.

So if anyone claims to see breasts in that drink up there, they aren't in the ice cubes.

They're in the eye of the beholder.

ADVERTISING
ANOTHER WORD FOR FREEDOM OF CHOICE.
American Association of Advertising Agencies

FIGURE 6-5

Subliminal Embeds Are in the Eye of the Beholder.
Courtesy of American Association of Advertising Agencies

by itself does not produce or explain the coherent picture of the world that most adults possess.

Human beings are constantly bombarded with stimuli during every minute and every hour of every day. The sensory world is made up of an almost infinite number of discrete sensations that are constantly and subtly changing. According to the principles of sensation, intensive stimulation "turns off" most individuals, who subconsciously block the receipt of a heavy bombardment of stimuli. Otherwise, the billions of different stimuli to which we are constantly exposed might serve to confuse us totally and keep us perpetually disoriented in a constantly changing environment. However, neither of these consequences tend to occur, because perception is not a function of sensory input alone. Rather, perception is the result of two different kinds of inputs that interact to form the personal pictures—the perceptions—that each individual experiences.

One type of input is *physical stimuli* from the outside environment; the other type of input is provided by individuals themselves in the form of certain predispositions (e.g., expectations, motives, and learning) based on *previous experience*. The combination of these two very different kinds of inputs produces for each of us a very private, very personal picture of the world. Because each person is a unique individual, with unique experiences, wants, needs, wishes, and expectations, it follows that each individual's perceptions are also unique. This explains why no two people see the world in precisely the same way.

Individuals are very *selective* as to which stimuli they "recognize"; they subconsciously *organize* the stimuli they do recognize according to widely held psychological principles, and they *interpret* such stimuli (i.e., they give meaning to them) subjectively in accordance with their needs, expectations, and experiences. Let us examine in some detail each of these three aspects of perception: the **selection, organization**, and **interpretation** of stimuli.

Perceptual Selection

Consumers subconsciously exercise a great deal of selectivity as to which aspects of the environment—which stimuli—they perceive. An individual may look at some things, ignore others, and turn away from still others. In actuality, people receive—or perceive—only a small fraction of the stimuli to which they are exposed. Consider, for example, a woman in a supermarket. She may be exposed to over 20,000 products of different colors, sizes, and shapes; to perhaps 100 people (looking, walking, searching, talking); to smells (from fruit, from meat, from disinfectant, from people); to sounds within the store (cash registers ringing, shopping carts rolling, air conditioners humming, and clerks sweeping, mopping aisles, stocking shelves); and to sounds from outside the store (planes passing, cars honking, tires screeching, children shouting, car doors slamming). Yet she manages on a regular basis to visit her local supermarket, select the items she needs, pay for them, and leave, all within a relatively brief time, without losing her sanity or her personal orientation to the world around her. This is because she exercises *selectivity* in perception.

Which stimuli get selected depends on two major factors in addition to the nature of the stimulus itself: consumers' previous experience as it affects their expectations (what they are prepared, or "set", to see) and their motives at the time (their needs, desires, interests, and so on.) Each of these factors can serve to increase or decrease the probability that a stimulus will be perceived.

▲ **Nature of the Stimulus** Marketing stimuli include an enormous number of variables that affect the consumer's perception, such as the nature of the product, its physical attributes, the package design, the brand name, the advertisements and commercials (including copy claims, choice and sex of model, positioning of model, size of ad, and typography), the position of a print ad or the time of a commercial, and the editorial environment.

In general, **contrast** is one of the most attention-compelling attributes of a stimulus. Advertisers often use extreme attention-getting devices to achieve maximum contrast and thus penetrate the consumer's perceptual "screen." For example, a growing number of magazines and newspapers are carrying ads that readers can unfold to reveal oversized, poster-like advertisements for products ranging from cosmetics to automobiles, because of the "stopping power" of giant ads among more traditional sizes. However, advertising does not have to be unique to achieve a high degree of differentiation; it simply has to contrast with the environment in which it is run. The use of lots of white space in a print advertisement, the absence of sound in a commercial's opening scene, a 60-second commercial within a string of 20-second spots—all offer sufficient contrast from their environments to achieve differentiation and merit the consumer's attention. Figure 6-6 illustrates the

The new Mita AF-1000 is four machines in one. It has more capabilities than any multi-function machine in its class. It's a whole office in two square feet. To learn more call 1-800-495-MITA. The times demand Mita. **mita** ™
Available only in selected areas.

attention-getting nature of white space in an advertisement. In an effort to achieve contrast, advertisers are also using splashes of color in black-and-white print ads to highlight the advertised product. As shown in Figure 6-7, Levi Strauss produced an entire series of black and white ads simulating Matisse paintings, highlighting just the color of the jeans. Eye-catching ads, some using surrealistic imagery for either humorous effect or mood enhancement, attract attention because of their contrast to consumer expectations (see Figures 6-8A and B on page 160). The campaign for the TAGHeuer line of sports watches carries the theme "Success. It's a mind game." The ads make use of breathtaking visuals to attract the consumer's attention and dramatically communicate the message that mental edge and imagination make a winner. The ads in the campaign vary: One shows a swimmer racing a

A

"Woman At Ease"

Levi's® 501®, 512™ and 550™ Jeans. Now Cut, Styled and Sized for Women.

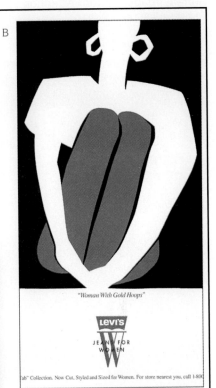

B

"Woman With Gold Hoops"

ab™ Collection. Now Cut, Styled and Sized for Women. For store nearest you, call 1-800

"Woman Combing Hair"

Levi's 900 Series® Now Cut, Styled and Sized for Women.

C

"Woman In Repose"

Levi's® 501®, 512™ and 550™ Jeans. Now Cut, Styled and Sized for Women.

D

"Woman Reading Sunday Paper"

Series® Now Cut, Styled and Sized for Women. For store nearest you, call 1-800-US

E

FIGURE 6-8A ▼

Surreal Images Attract Attention
Courtesy of Erox Corporation

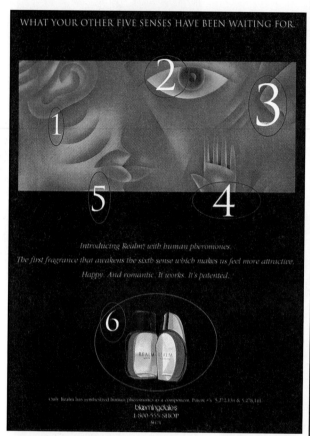

FIGURE 6-8B ▼

Provocative Collages Attract Attention
Courtesy of Schieffelin & Somerset Company

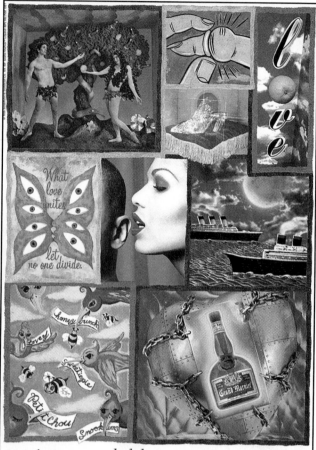

Grand Marnier, *slightly* less mysterious than love.

shark in an olympic-sized pool; another shows a relay racer holding a lighted stick of dynamite as a baton (see Figure 6-9).

With respect to packaging, astute marketers usually try to differentiate their packages to ensure rapid consumer perception. Since the average package on the supermarket shelf has about 1/10th of a second to make an impression on the consumer, it is important that every aspect of the package—the name, shape, color, label, and copy—provide sufficient sensory stimulation to be noted and remembered.

Sometimes advertisers capitalize on the *lack* of contrast. For example, a technique that has been used effectively in TV commercials is to position the commercial so close to the storyline of a program that viewers are unaware they are watching an ad until they are well into it. In the case of children's programming, the Federal Trade Commission has strictly limited the use of this technique. TV stars or cartoon characters are prohibited from promoting products during children's shows in which they appear.

Advertisers are producing 30-minute commercials (called *infomercials*) that appear to the average viewer as documentaries and thus command more attentive viewing than obvious commercials would receive. Advertisers are also running print ads (called *adver-*

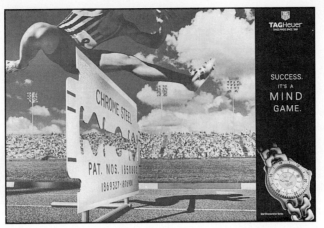

FIGURE 6-9

Breathtaking Imagery Attracts Attention
Courtesy of TAGHeuer

torials) that so closely resemble editorial material that it has become increasingly difficult for readers to tell them apart.

▲ **Expectations** People usually see what they expect to see, and what they expect to see is usually based on familiarity, previous experience, or preconditioned *set*. In a marketing context, people tend to perceive products and product attributes according to their own expectations. A man who has been told by his friends that a new brand of Scotch has a bitter taste will probably perceive the taste to be bitter; a teenager who attends a horror movie that has been billed as terrifying will probably find it so. On the other hand, stimuli that conflict sharply with expectations often receive more attention than those that conform to expectations (see Figure 6-10 on page 162).

For years, certain advertisers have used blatant sexuality in advertisements for products to which sex was not relevant, in the belief that such advertisements would attract a high degree of attention. However, ads with irrelevant sexuality often defeat the marketer's purpose because readers tend to remember the sexual aspects of the ad (e.g., the innuendo or the model), not the product or brand. Nevertheless, some advertisers continue to use erotic appeals in promoting a wide variety of products, from office furniture to jeans. (The use of sex in advertising is discussed in Chapter 10.)

Another advertising technique designed to attract the reader's attention is the so-called topsy-turvy ad, in which the top half is printed right side up, while the bottom half is printed upside down. The goal of marketers such as Quaker Oats, Clorox, and McDonald's is to attract the attention of readers who are glancing rapidly through the paper or magazine, and provoke them into spending a little extra time studying the ad. Figure 6-11 on page 163 is a variation of the topsy-turvy ad, with just the body copy upside down.

▲ **Motives** People tend to perceive things they need or want; the stronger the need, the greater the tendency to ignore unrelated stimuli in the environment. A woman interested in a portable computer is more likely to notice and to read carefully ads for computer laptops than her neighbor, who does not use a computer. In general, there is a heightened awareness of stimuli that are relevant to one's needs and interests, and a decreased awareness of stimuli that are irrelevant to those needs. An individual's perceptual process simply attunes itself more closely to those elements in the environment that are important to that person. Someone who is hungry is more likely to spot a restaurant sign; a sexually repressed person may perceive sexual symbolism where none exists.

Marketing managers recognize the efficiency of targeting their products to the perceived needs of consumers. In this way, they help to ensure that their products will be

Bye-Bye, Crocodile.

The LUBRIDERM® Body Bar and
LUBRIDERM Lotion. Think of them as Shampoo
and Conditioner for your skin.

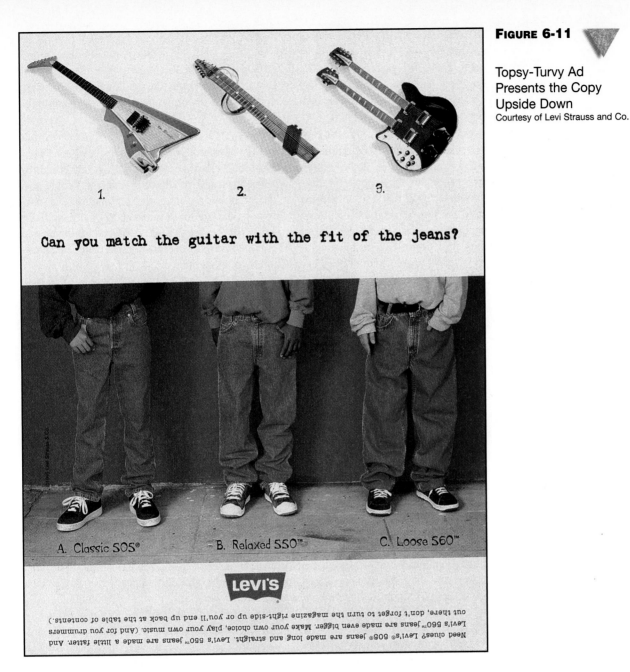

FIGURE 6-11

Topsy-Turvy Ad
Presents the Copy
Upside Down
Courtesy of Levi Strauss and Co.

Can you match the guitar with the fit of the jeans?

A. Classic 505®   B. Relaxed 550™   C. Loose 560™

LEVI'S

(Need clues? Levi's® 505® jeans are made long and straight. Levi's 550™ jeans are made a little fatter. And
Levi's 560™ jeans are made even bigger. Make your own choice, play your own music. (And for you drummers
out there, don't forget to turn the magazine right-side up or you'll end up back at the table of contents.)

perceived by potential prospects. For example, a marketer can determine through market-ing research what consumers consider to be the ideal attributes of the product category, or what consumers perceive their needs to be in relation to the product category. The mar-keter can then segment the market on the basis of those needs and vary the product adver-tising so that consumers in each segment will perceive the product as meeting their own specific needs, wants, and interests.

▲ **Important Selective Perception Concepts** As the preceding discussion illustrates, the consumer's "selection" of stimuli from the environment is based on the interaction of ex-pectations and motives with the stimulus itself. These factors give rise to a number of im-portant concepts concerning perception.

SELECTIVE EXPOSURE Consumers actively seek out messages that they find pleasant or with which they are sympathetic, and they actively avoid painful or threatening ones. Thus, heavy smokers avoid articles that link cigarette smoking to cancer. Instead, they note (and even quote) the relatively few articles that deny the relationship. Consumers also selectively expose themselves to advertisements that reassure them of the wisdom of their purchase decisions.

SELECTIVE ATTENTION Consumers tend to have a heightened awareness of stimuli that meet their needs or interests and minimal awareness of stimuli irrelevant to their needs. Thus, they are likely to note ads for products that would satisfy their needs and for stores in which they shop, and disregard those in which they have no interest. People also vary in terms of the kind of information in which they are interested and the form of message and type of medium they prefer. Some people are more interested in price, some in appearance, and some in social acceptability. Some people like complex, sophisticated messages; others like simple graphics. Clearly, consumers exercise a great deal of selectivity in terms of the attention they give to commercial stimuli.

PERCEPTUAL DEFENSE Consumers subconsciously screen out stimuli that they would find psychologically threatening, even though exposure has already taken place. Thus, threatening or otherwise damaging stimuli are less likely to be consciously perceived than are neutral stimuli at the same level of exposure.[23] Furthermore, individuals unconsciously may distort information that is not consistent with their needs, values, and beliefs.

PERCEPTUAL BLOCKING Consumers protect themselves from being bombarded with stimuli by simply "tuning out"—blocking such stimuli from conscious awareness. Research shows that enormous amounts of advertising are screened out by consumers; they mentally tune out because of the visually overstimulating nature of the world in which we live. This perceptual blocking-out is similar to consumers "zapping" commercials using remote controls.

Perceptual Organization

People do not experience the numerous stimuli they select from the environment as separate and discrete sensations; rather, they tend to organize them into groups and perceive them as unified wholes. Thus, the perceived characteristics of even the simplest stimulus are viewed as a function of the whole to which the stimulus appears to belong. This method of perceptual organization simplifies life considerably for the individual.

The specific principles underlying perceptual organization are often referred to by the name given the school of psychology that first developed it: **Gestalt psychology**. (Gestalt, in German, means *pattern* or *configuration*.) Three of the most basic principles of perceptual organization are **figure and ground, grouping**, and **closure**.

▲ **Figure and Ground** As was noted earlier, stimuli that contrast with their environment are more likely to be noticed. A sound must be louder or softer, a color brighter or paler. The simplest visual illustration consists of a *figure* on a *ground* (i.e., background). The figure is usually perceived clearly because, in contrast to its ground, it appears to be well defined, solid, and in the forefront. The ground, however, is usually perceived as indefinite, hazy, and continuous. The common line that separates the figure and the ground is perceived as belonging to the figure, rather than to the ground, which helps give the figure greater definition. Consider the stimulus of music. People can either "bathe" in music or listen to music. In the first case, music is simply *ground* to other activities; in the second, it is *figure*. Figure is more clearly perceived because it appears to be dominant; in contrast, ground appears to be subordinate and, therefore, less important.

People have a tendency to organize their perceptions into figure-and-ground relationships. However, learning affects which stimuli are perceived as *figure* and which as *ground*. We are all familiar with reversible figure-ground patterns, such as the picture of the woman in Figure 6-12. How old would you say she is? Look again, very carefully. Depending on how you perceived *figure* and how you perceived *ground*, she can be either in her early twenties or her late seventies.

Like perceptual selection, perceptual organization is affected by *motives* and by *expectations* based on experience. How a reversible figure-ground pattern is perceived can be influenced by prior pleasant or painful associations with one or the other element in isolation. The consumer's physical state can also affect how he or she perceives reversible figure-ground illustrations. For example, after returning to work following an automobile accident and resultant brain concussion, the 35-year-old secretary of one of the authors remarked about the unfamiliar picture of the old woman shown in Figure 6-12. It took a great deal of concentrated effort for her to recognize the picture of the smartly dressed young woman that she had been accustomed to seeing on the author's desk.

Advertisers have to plan their advertisements carefully to make sure that the stimulus they want noted is seen as figure and not as ground. The musical background must not overwhelm the jingle; the background of an advertisement must not detract from the product. Print advertisers often silhouette their products against a white background to make sure that the features they want noted are clearly perceived (see Figure 6-13 on page 166). Others use reverse lettering (white letters on a black background) to achieve contrast; however, in such cases they are flirting with the problem of figure-ground reversal.

Marketers sometimes run advertisements that confuse the consumer because there is no clear indication of which is figure and which is ground. Of course, in some cases, the blurring of figure and ground is deliberate. The well-known Absolut Vodka campaign—which started in 1981—often runs print ads in which the figure (the shape of the Absolut bottle) is poorly delineated against its ground, but readers are conditioned to search for the

FIGURE 6-12

Figure-Ground Reversal

FIGURE 6-13

Readers Focus on
Details When Products
Are Silhouetted
Courtesy of Tencel

shape of the Absolut bottle, which is usually cleverly hidden in the ad. Figures 6-14A and B are just two examples in the highly celebrated campaign that has made many consumers collectors of the ads.[24]

▲ **Grouping** Individuals tend to group stimuli so that they form a unified picture or impression. The perception of stimuli as *groups* or *chunks* of information, rather than as discrete bits of information, facilitates their memory and recall.

    Grouping can be used advantageously by marketers to imply certain desired meanings in connection with their products. For example, an advertisement for tea may show a young man and woman sipping tea in a beautifully appointed room before a blazing hearth. The overall mood implied by the grouping of stimuli leads the consumer to associate the drinking of tea with romance, fine living, and winter warmth.

    Most of us can remember and repeat our Social Security numbers because we automatically group them into three "chunks," rather than try to remember nine separate numbers. When AT&T introduced the idea of all-digit telephone numbers, consumers objected strenuously on the grounds that they would not be able to recall or repeat a long string of numbers. However, because we automatically group telephone numbers into two chunks (or three, with the area code), the anticipated problems never occurred.

▲ **Closure** Individuals have a need for closure. They express this need by organizing their perceptions so that they form a complete picture. If the pattern of stimuli to which they are exposed is incomplete, they tend to perceive it, nevertheless, as complete; that is, they consciously or subconsciously fill in the missing pieces. Thus, a circle with a section of its pe-

riphery missing is invariably perceived as a circle, not as an arc. The need for closure is
also seen in the tension an individual experiences when a task is incomplete, and the satisfaction and relief that come with its completion.

A classic study reported in 1972 found that incomplete tasks are better remembered
than complete tasks. One explanation for this phenomenon is that the person who begins a
task develops a need to complete it. If he or she is prevented from doing so, a state of tension is created that manifests itself in improved memory for the incomplete task (the
Zeigernik effect). Hearing the beginning of a message leads to the need to hear the rest of
it—like waiting for the second shoe to drop.[25] The Absolut vodka campaign has conditioned readers to search for closure by finding the outline of the Absolut bottle. (Study Figures 6-14 A and B again.)

The tension created by an incomplete message leads to improvement in memory for
that part of the message that has already been heard. There are numerous examples of such
concept closure, where viewers react to background cues by "filling in" more information
than the commercial provides. For example, a TV commercial for Cudahy Bar S bacon
showed a close-up of bacon frying in an iron skillet while a voice-over in a deep cowboy
twang said what a fine bacon it was. Beneath the laid-back delivery was the sound of a har-
monica playing a soft, mournful cowboy tune. A telephone survey 24 hours later found that
people remembered far more than the simple commercial had shown them. One respondent recalled bacon frying on a campfire with cowboys sitting around; another recalled
horses standing in the background and the light of the campfire reflecting on the faces of
the cowboys eating bacon. The viewers filled in the story "painted" by the background
cues, in effect creating their own more effective, more memorable commercial.[26]

The need for closure has some interesting implications for marketers. The presentation of an incomplete advertising message "begs" for completion by consumers, and the very act of completion serves to involve them more deeply in the message itself. In a related vein, advertisers have discovered that they can achieve excellent results by using the soundtrack of a frequently shown television commercial on radio. Consumers who are familiar with the TV commercial perceive the audio track alone as incomplete; in their need for completion, they mentally play back the visual content from memory.

In summary, it is clear that perceptions are not equivalent to the raw sensory input of discrete stimuli, nor to the sum total of discrete stimuli. Rather, people tend to add to or subtract from stimuli to which they are exposed according to their expectations and motives, using generalized principles of organization based on Gestalt theory.

Perceptual Interpretation

The preceding discussion has emphasized that perception is a personal phenomenon. People exercise selectivity as to which stimuli they perceive, and they organize these stimuli on the basis of certain psychological principles. The **interpretation** of stimuli is also uniquely individual, because it is based on what individuals expect to see in light of their previous experience, on the number of plausible explanations they can envision, and on their motives and interests at the time of perception.

Stimuli are often highly ambiguous. Some stimuli are weak because of such factors as poor visibility, brief exposure, high noise level, or constant fluctuation. Even stimuli that are strong tend to fluctuate dramatically because of such factors as different angles of viewing, varying distances, and changing levels of illumination.

Consumers usually attribute the sensory input they receive to sources they consider most likely to have caused the specific pattern of stimuli. Past experiences and social interactions help to form certain expectations that provide categories (or alternative explanations) that individuals use in interpreting stimuli. The narrower the individual's experience, the more limited the access to alternative categories.

When stimuli are highly ambiguous, an individual will usually interpret them in such a way that they serve to fulfill personal needs, wishes, interests, and so on. It is this principle that provides the rationale for the projective tests discussed in Chapter 2. Such tests provide ambiguous stimuli (such as incomplete sentences, unclear pictures, untitled cartoons, or ink blots) to respondents who are asked to interpret them. How a person describes a vague illustration, what meaning the individual ascribes to an ink blot, is a reflection not of the stimulus itself, but of the subject's own needs, wants, and desires. Through the interpretation of ambiguous stimuli, respondents reveal a great deal about themselves.

How close a person's interpretations are to reality, then, depends on the clarity of the stimulus, the past experiences of the perceiver, and his or her motives and interests at the time of perception.

▲ **Distorting Influences** Individuals are subject to a number of influences that tend to distort their perceptions; some of these are discussed below.

PHYSICAL APPEARANCES People tend to attribute the qualities they associate with certain people to others who may resemble them, whether or not they consciously recognize the similarity. For this reason, the selection of models for advertisements and for television commercials can be a key element in their ultimate persuasiveness. Studies on physical appearance have found that attractive models are more persuasive and have a more positive influence on consumer attitudes and behavior than average-looking models; attractive men are perceived as more successful businessmen than average-looking men; more attractive women are perceived as less able in business; and women wearing severely tailored clothing are more likely to be hired.[27]

STEREOTYPES Individuals tend to carry "pictures" in their minds of the meanings of various kinds of stimuli. These stereotypes serve as expectations of what specific situations, people, or events will be like, and they are important determinants of how such stimuli are subsequently perceived. For example, Figure 6-15 presents a stereotypical authority figure with which parochial school alumni can identify.

IRRELEVANT CUES When required to form a difficult perceptual judgment, consumers often respond to irrelevant stimuli. For example, many high-priced automobiles are

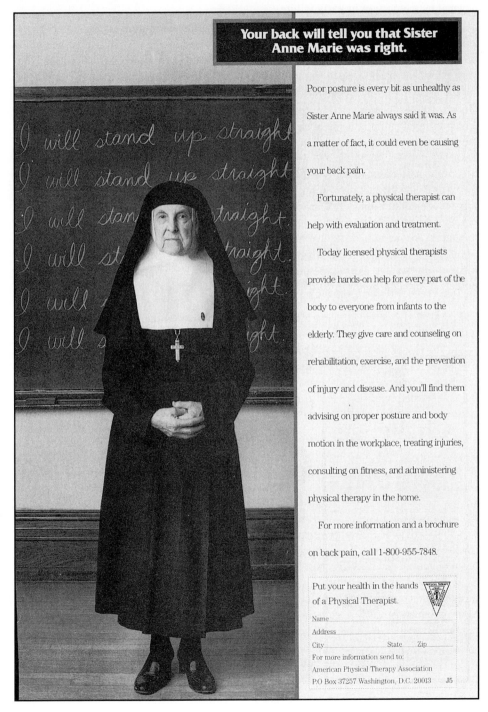

Your back will tell you that Sister Anne Marie was right.

Poor posture is every bit as unhealthy as Sister Anne Marie always said it was. As a matter of fact, it could even be causing your back pain.

Fortunately, a physical therapist can help with evaluation and treatment.

Today licensed physical therapists provide hands-on help for every part of the body to everyone from infants to the elderly. They give care and counseling on rehabilitation, exercise, and the prevention of injury and disease. And you'll find them advising on proper posture and body motion in the workplace, treating injuries, consulting on fitness, and administering physical therapy in the home.

For more information and a brochure on back pain, call 1-800-955-7848.

Put your health in the hands of a Physical Therapist.

Name

Address

City   State   Zip

For more information send to:
American Physical Therapy Association
P.O. Box 37257 Washington, D.C. 20013   J5

FIGURE 6-15

Ad Using a Stereotypical Authority Figure
Reprinted with the permission of the APTA

purchased because of their color or because of luxury options like retractable headlights or leather upholstery, rather than on the basis of mechanical or technical superiority.

FIRST IMPRESSIONS First impressions tend to be lasting; yet, in forming such impressions, the perceiver does not yet know which stimuli are relevant, important, or predictive of later behavior. A shampoo commercial effectively used the line "You'll never have a second chance to make a first impression." Since first impressions are often lasting, introducing a new product before it has been perfected may prove fatal to its ultimate success, because subsequent information about its advantages, even if true, will often be negated by memory of its early failure.

JUMPING TO CONCLUSIONS Many people tend to jump to conclusions before examining all the relevant evidence. For example, the consumer may hear just the beginning of a commercial message and draw conclusions regarding the product or service being advertised on the basis of such limited information. For this reason, some copywriters are careful *not* to save their most persuasive arguments for last.

HALO EFFECT Historically, the halo effect has been used to describe situations in which the evaluation of a single object or person on a multitude of dimensions is based on the evaluation of just one or a few dimensions (e.g., a man is trustworthy, fine, and noble because he looks you in the eye when he speaks). Consumer behaviorists broaden the notion of the halo effect to include the evaluation of multiple objects (e.g., a product line) on the basis of the evaluation of just one dimension (a brand name or a spokesperson). Using this broader definition, marketers take advantage of the halo effect when they extend a brand name associated with one line of products to another. For example, building on its reputation for manufacturing inexpensive, reliable, disposable pens, BIC successfully introduced a line of disposable razors under the BIC name. Consumers bought the new BIC razor on the basis of their favorable evaluation of the BIC pen. (An extension of this phenomenon, *stimulus generalization*, is discussed in Chapter 7.)

The mushrooming field of **licensing** also is based on the halo effect. Manufacturers and retailers hope to acquire instant recognition and status for their products by association with a well-known celebrity or designer name.

The reader may well ask how "realistic" perception can be, given the many subjective influences on perceptual interpretation. It is somewhat reassuring to remember that previous experiences usually serve to resolve stimulus ambiguity in a realistic way and to help in its interpretation. Only in situations of unusual or changing stimulus conditions do expectations lead to wrong interpretations.

CONSUMER IMAGERY

Consumers have a number of enduring perceptions, or **images**, that are particularly relevant to the study of consumer behavior. Chapter 5 discussed consumer self-images; the following section examines consumers' perceived images of products and services, of prices, product quality, retail stores, manufacturers, and of brands.

Products and brands have symbolic value for individuals, who evaluate them on the basis of their consistency (i.e., congruence) with their personal pictures of themselves. Some products seem to match an individual's self-image; others do not. Consumers attempt to preserve or enhance their self-images by buying products that they believe are congruent with their self-images, and by avoiding products that are not.[28]

Retail stores select mannequins that they feel reflect the store's image as well as the targeted consumer's self-image. In the 1970s, for example, some female mannequins were made in bold, upright stances with tightly clenched fists to reflect women's fight for equality; today, they have a confident, outgoing but softer appearance. Some mannequins also have a more athletic look in response to the health and fitness concerns of the 90s and are shown running, diving, and jumping, in addition to more traditional poses. It is generally believed that if the customer identifies with the mannequin, he or she is more likely to purchase the product.

Consumers also tend to shop in stores that have images consistent with their own self-images. Major department store chains have begun to focus on the need to build a strong image for their stores. They recognize the importance of building an identity to attract loyal consumers. A number of chains are increasingly stressing customer service and the provision of a pleasant shopping experience, rather than focusing on price promotions.

Product and Service Images

The image that a product or service has in the mind of the consumer—that is, its **positioning**—is probably more important to its ultimate success than are its actual characteristics. Marketers try to position their brands so that they are perceived by the consumer as fitting into a distinctive niche in the marketplace—a niche occupied by no other product. They try to differentiate their products by stressing attributes that they claim will fulfill the consumer's needs better than competing brands. They strive to create a product image consistent with the relevant self-image of the targeted consumer segment.

▲ **Positioning Strategy** Positioning strategy is the essence of the marketing mix; it complements the company's segmentation strategy and selection of target markets. Positioning conveys the concept, or meaning, of the product or service in terms of how it fulfills a consumer need. Different consumer meanings (i.e., product images) are sometimes assigned to the same product or service. Thus, a product (or service) can be *positioned* differently to different market segments, or can be *repositioned* to the same audience, without actually being physically changed.

In our overcommunicated society, the marketer must create a distinctive product image in the mind of the consumer. When Avis challenged Hertz by saying "We're number two. We try harder," it distinguished itself in the consumer's mind as the underdog—a clever marketing strategy, because many Americans tend to favor the underdog. With its brilliantly colored illustrations and the tag line "Find your own road"™, Saab positions its automobiles as cars for individualists (see Figures 6-16A, B, and C on page 172).

The result of successful positioning strategy is a distinctive brand image on which consumers rely in making product choices. In today's highly competitive environment, a distinctive product image is most important. As products become more complex and the marketplace more crowded, consumers rely more on the product's image than on its actual attributes in making purchase decisions.

PERCEPTUAL MAPPING The technique of perceptual mapping helps marketers to determine just how their products or services appear to consumers in relation to competitive brands on one or more relevant characteristics. It enables them to see gaps in the positioning of all brands in the product or service class and to identify areas in which consumer needs are not being adequately met. For example, a magazine publisher may discover that consumers perceive its magazine (let's call it *Splash*) to be very similar in editorial content and format to its closest competitors, *Bash* and *Crash* (see Figure 6-17 on page 173). By changing the focus of its editorial features to appeal to a new market niche, the publisher can reposition the magazine (e.g., from *Splash* to *Fashion Splash*).

POSITIONING OF SERVICES Compared with manufacturing firms, service marketers face several unique problems in positioning and promoting their offerings. Because services are intangible, *image* becomes a key factor in differentiating a service from its

FIGURE 6-16A, B, and C

Saab Positions Its Cars for
Individualists with the Slogan:
Find Your Own Road™
Courtesy of Saab

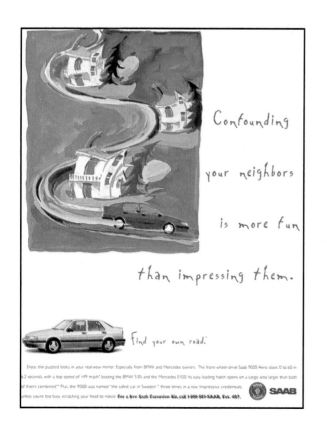

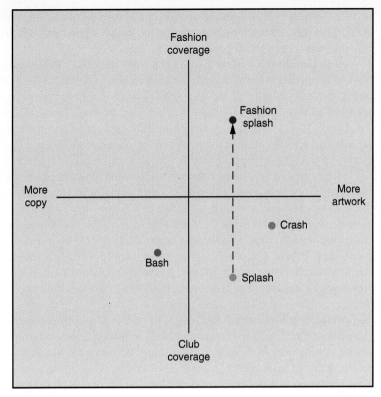

FIGURE 6-17

Perceptual Map of
Competitors Facilitates
Magazine Repositioning

competition. Thus, the marketing objective is to enable the consumer to link a specific image with a specific brand name. Many service marketers have developed strategies to provide customers with visual images and tangible reminders of their service offerings. These include painted delivery vehicles, restaurant matchbooks, packaged hotel soaps and shampoos, and a variety of other specialty items. Some financial companies try to associate their services with tangible objects. The Prudential Insurance Company invites consumers to "get a piece of the rock." Travelers, the financial services giant formed when Primerica acquired the Travelers Insurance Company, introduced a corporate identity and brand-image program that uses the familiar Travelers Insurance umbrella as a logo for the entire company and its new name, the Travelers Group, which emphasizes its multiple services. The company has adopted the new *positioning* line, "The symbol of financial leadership."

Sometimes companies market several versions of their service to different market segments by using a differentiated positioning strategy. However, they must be careful to avoid perceptual confusion among their customers. The American Express Company offers its regular (green) card to consumers as a short-term credit instrument, the True Grace card for long-term credit, and the prestigious Gold and Platinum cards, each with increased services, to the affluent cardholder. Private banks that target affluent consumers focus on estate planning, investments, and trust funds to maintain an exclusive image; commercial banks stress cash machines and overdraft privileges to consumers with more modest financial means.

The Service Environment The design of the *service environment* is an important aspect of service positioning strategy and sharply influences consumer impressions and consumer and employee behavior. The physical environment is particularly important in creating a favorable impression for such services as banks, retail stores, and professional offices, because there are so few objective criteria by which consumers can judge the quality of the services they receive.[29] The service environment conveys the image of the service provider with whom the service is so closely linked. Thus, at the Chase Private Banking offices, expensive mahogany desks, leather chairs, and silk draperies project stability, solidity, wealth, and power.

The Polo/Ralph Lauren store in the renovated 1895 Rhinelander mansion in New York is the embodiment of the image Lauren wants to create for his clothes: traditionalism and Old World values. All the trappings of what one imagines to be the high-class and well-heeled ways of the very, very rich are here, from the baronial, hand-carved staircase lined with "family" portraits to the plush sitting rooms with working fireplaces. The Polo store image artfully extends the image of the clothing it sells, and projects an Old World quality of living and shopping that its upscale target market finds appealing.

One study of service environments identified the environmental variables most important to bank customers: (1) *privacy* (both visually and verbally, such as enclosed offices, transaction privacy, etc.); (2) *efficiency/convenience* (transaction areas that are easy to find, directional signs, etc.); (3) *ambient background conditions* (temperature, lighting, noise, music); (4) *social conditions* (the appearance of other people in the bank environment, such as bank customers and bank personnel); and (5) *aesthetics* (e.g., color, style, use of materials, artworks).[30] Clearly, a favorable service environment creates the perception among consumers that the service itself better satisfies their needs.

▲ **Repositioning Strategies** Regardless of how well positioned a product appears to be, the marketer may be forced to reposition it in response to *market events*, such as a competitor cutting into the brand's market share. For example, rather than trying to meet the lower prices of high-quality private label competition, some premium brand marketers have repositioned their brands to justify their higher prices, playing up brand attributes that had previously been ignored.

When Revlon decided to change the image of Revlon cosmetics to attract a younger, more diverse audience, its repositioning strategy involved changing its copy appeals, changing its advertising media (to youth-oriented TV shows), and changing its distribution channels (from higher-priced department stores to lower-priced retail outlets such as drugstores and supermarkets.)

Another reason to reposition a product or service is *changing consumer preferences*. For example, as consumers became aware of the dangers of intense suntanning, alert cosmetic companies began to add sunscreens to lipsticks, moisturizers, and foundation creams, and to promote this new benefit as a major attribute, thus repositioning specific product lines. They also created a new and highly profitable product category: self-tanners that required no sun exposure whatever. When health-oriented consumers began to avoid high-fat foods, many fast-food chains acted swiftly to reposition their images by offering salad bars and other health-oriented foods. Kentucky Fried Chicken changed its well-known corporate name to KFC in order to omit the dread word "fried" from its advertising. Weight Watchers repositioned its line of frozen foods from "dietetic" to "healthy," maintaining its diet-thin imagery while responding to a perceived shift in consumer values.

Perceived Price

How a consumer perceives a price—as high, as low, as fair—has a strong influence on both purchase intentions and purchase satisfaction. Consider perception of *price fairness*, for example. There is some evidence that customers do pay attention to the prices paid by other customers (e.g., senior citizens, frequent fliers, affinity club members), and that the differential pricing strategies used by some marketers are perceived as unfair by customers not eligible for the special prices. No one is happy knowing they paid twice as much for their airline ticket as the person in the next seat. Perceptions of price unfairness affect consumers' perceptions of product value, and ultimately, their willingness to patronize a store or a service. Strategies that reduce perceived price unfairness ultimately enhance perceived product value.[31]

Products advertised as "on sale" tend to create enhanced customer perceptions of savings and value. Different formats used in sales advertisements have differing impacts, based on consumer **reference prices**. A reference price is any price that a consumer uses as a basis for comparison in judging another price. Reference prices can be external or internal.[32] An advertiser generally uses a higher *external reference price* (sold elsewhere at . . .) in an ad in which a lower sales price is being offered, to persuade the consumer that the product advertised is a really good buy.

Internal reference prices are those prices (or price ranges) retrieved by the consumer from memory. Internal reference points are thought to play a major role in consumers' evaluations and perceptions of value of an advertised price deal, as well as in the believability of any advertised reference price. According to **acquisition-transaction utility theory**, two types of utility are associated with consumer purchases: *acquisition utility* and *transaction utility*. Acquisition utility represents the perceived economic gain or loss associated with a purchase, and is a function of product utility and purchase price. Transaction utility concerns the perceived pleasure or displeasure associated with the financial aspect of the purchase, and is determined by the difference between the internal reference price and the purchase price.[33] For example, if a consumer wants to purchase a television set for which her internal reference price is approximately $500, and she buys a set that is sale-priced at $500, she receives no transaction utility. However, if either her internal reference price is increased or the sale price of the set is decreased, she will receive positive transaction utility, which increases the total utility she experiences with the purchase.

Several recent studies have investigated the effects on consumer price perceptions of three types of advertised reference prices: *plausible low, plausible high*, and *implausible high*. Plausible low prices are well within the range of acceptable market prices; plausible high are near the outer limits of the range but not beyond the realm of believability, and implausible high are well above the consumer's perceived range of acceptable market prices. As long as an advertised reference price is within a given consumer's acceptable price range, the external reference price is considered plausible and is *assimilated*. (See *assimilation-contrast theory* in Chapter 9.) If the advertised reference point is outside the range of acceptable prices ((i.e., implausible), it will be *contrasted* and thus will not be perceived as a valid reference point.[34] Findings show that an implausible high reference price can affect consumer evaluations, as well as the advertiser's image of credibility. By setting the reference price at the highest price recently offered for identical or comparable merchandise, the advertiser can enhance consumer perceptions of value while minimizing negative effects.

The semantic cues (i.e., specific wording) of the phrase used to communicate the price-related information may affect consumers' price perceptions. **Tensile price claims** (e.g., "save 10 to 40%," "save up to 60%," "save 20% or more") are used to promote a range of price discounts for a product line, an entire department, or sometimes an entire store. In contrast with *tensile cues*, **objective price claims** provide a single discount level (e.g., "save 25%.") Because of the broader range of sale merchandise that is covered by tensile and objective price discounts, they potentially have a greater effect on consumer shopping and on store traffic than a reference price advertisement that promotes a single product.[35]

Consumer evaluations and shopping intentions are least favorable for advertisements stating the minimum discount level (save 10% or more). Ads that state a maximum discount *level* (save up to 40%) either equal or exceed the effectiveness of ads stating a discount *range* (save 10 to 40%.) When different levels of savings are advertised across a product line, the maximum discount level has been found to be the most effective at influencing consumers' perceptions of savings.

Consumer reactions to tensile price claims are affected by the *width* of the discount range. Two studies that examined the effects of the three forms of tensile price claims (i.e., advertising a minimum, a maximum, or a range of savings) on consumers' price perceptions and their search and shopping intentions found that, for broader discount ranges, tensile claims stating the maximum level of savings have more positive effects than those stating the minimum level or the entire savings range. For more narrow discount ranges, tensile claims stating the maximum level of savings appear to be no more effective than claims stating the minimum level or the entire savings range.[36]

An experiment examining the effects of a "bundle price" (i.e., the marketing of two or more products and/or services in a single package for a special price) on consumer price perceptions found that additional savings offered directly on the bundle have a greater relative impact on buyers' perceptions of transaction value than savings offered on the bundle's individual items.[37]

Perceived Quality

Consumers often judge the quality of a product or service on the basis of a variety of informational cues that they associate with the product. Some of these cues are **intrinsic** to the product or service, others are **extrinsic**. Either singly or in composite, such cues provide the basis for perceptions of product and service quality.

▲ **Perceived Quality of Products** Cues that are *intrinsic* concern physical characteristics of the product itself, such as size, color, flavor, or aroma. In some cases, consumers use physical characteristics to judge product quality. For example, consumers often judge the flavor of ice cream or cake by color cues. Even the perceived quality of laundry detergents is affected by color cues. For example, many detergents are traditionally colored blue, in the hopes that housewives will associate the color with the "bluing" their grandmothers used to add to whiten and brighten their laundry.

Consumers like to believe that they base their evaluations of product quality on intrinsic cues, because that enables them to justify their product decisions (either positive or negative) as being "rational" or "objective" product choices. More often than not, however, the physical characteristics they use to judge quality have no intrinsic relationship to the product's quality. For example, though many consumers claim they buy a brand because of its superior taste, they are often unable to identify that brand in blind taste tests. *Consumer Reports* found that consumers often cannot differentiate among various cola beverages and base their preferences on such extrinsic cues as pricing, packaging, advertising, and even peer pressure.[38]

In the absence of actual experience with a product, consumers often "evaluate" quality on the basis of *extrinsic* cues—cues that are external to the product itself, such as price, brand image, manufacturer's image, retail store image, or even the country of origin. Many consumers use country-of-origin stereotypes to evaluate products (e.g., "German engineering is excellent," "Japanese cars are reliable.")[39] Inexperienced consumers tend to use country of origin as a surrogate for product quality, regardless of whether or not product attributes are ambiguous; knowledgeable consumers tend to use country of origin to judge quality only when information about an attribute is ambiguous.[40] Figure 6-18 presents the findings of a survey in which respondents were asked to evaluate the quality of products based on their country of origin. Ninety-three percent of the respondents said that a "Made in the U.S.A." label means a product is "superior" or "fairly good."[41] Yet for food products, a foreign image is often more enticing. For example, the elegant image of Vichysoisse, a soup created in New York in 1917, is based on the perception that it is a French delicacy. Häagen-Dazs, an American-made ice cream, has been incredibly successful with its made-up (and meaningless) Scandinavian-sounding name. The success of

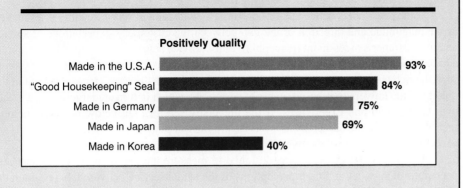

CONSUMER DATA

Positively Quality

Made in the U.S.A. — 93%
"Good Housekeeping" Seal — 84%
Made in Germany — 75%
Made in Japan — 69%
Made in Korea — 40%

FIGURE 6-18

Perceived Quality Based on Country of Origin
Source: Adweek's Marketing Week (August 20, 1990), 10. Reprinted by permission of Roper Starch Worldwide.

Smirnoff Vodka, made in Connecticut, can be related to its so-called Russian derivation. Sorbet has become a very popular and chic dessert, now that it is no longer called sherbet. There are many other examples that support the notion that American consumers are much more impressed with foreign foods than they are with domestic foods.[42]

▲ **Perceived Quality of Services** It is more difficult for consumers to evaluate the quality of services than the quality of products. This is true because of certain distinctive characteristics of services: they are *intangible*, they are *variable*, they are *perishable*, and they are *simultaneously produced and consumed*.

To overcome the fact that consumers are unable to compare services side-by-side as they do competing products, consumers rely on *surrogate cues* (i.e., extrinsic cues) to evaluate service quality. In evaluating a doctor's services, for example, they note the quality of the office and examining room furnishings, the number (and source) of framed degrees on the wall, the pleasantness of the receptionist, and the professionalism of the nurse; all contribute to the consumer's overall evaluation of service quality.

Because the actual quality of services can vary from day to day, from service employee to service employee, and from customer to customer (e.g., in food, in waiter service, in haircuts, even in classes taught by the same professor), marketers try to standardize their services in order to provide *consistency of quality*. The downside of service standardization, unfortunately, is the loss of customized services, which many consumers value.

Unlike products, which are first produced, then sold, then consumed, most services are first sold, then produced and consumed simultaneously. While a defective product is likely to be detected by factory quality control inspectors before it ever reaches the consumer, a "defective" service is consumed as it is being produced; thus there is little opportunity to correct it. For example, a defective haircut is difficult to correct, just as the negative impression caused by an argument between two service employees in the presence of a customer is difficult to correct.

During peak demand hours, the interactive quality of services often declines, because both the customer and the service provider are hurried and under stress. Without special effort by the marketer to ensure consistency of services during peak hours, service image is likely to decline. Some marketers try to change demand patterns in order to "distribute" the service more equally over time. Long-distance telephone services, for instance, offer a discount on telephone calls placed after 11:00 p.m. or on weekends; some restaurants offer a significantly less expensive "early-bird" dinner for consumers who come in before 6:00 p.m. Research suggests that service providers can reduce the perceived wait time and consequent negative service evaluation by filling the consumer's time. Diners may be invited to study the menu while waiting for a table; patients can view informative videos in the doctor's waiting room.[43]

Some researchers believe that a consumer's evaluation of service quality is a function of the magnitude and direction of the *gap* between the customer's expectations of service and the customer's assessment (perception) of the service actually delivered.[44] For example, a brand new graduate student may have certain expectations about the quality of her professors, the richness of classroom discussions, and the school's libraries. Her assessment of the quality of the university is based on her expectations, which in turn are largely based on her own background and experiences. If the university services fall below her expectations, then she will view the university as a service provider of poor quality. If her expectations are exceeded, she will view the university as a high-quality educational institution.

The **SERVQUAL** scale was designed to measure the gap between customers' expectations of services and their perceptions of the actual service delivered, based upon the following five dimensions: tangibles, reliability, responsiveness, assurance, and empathy.[45] Table 6-2 presents a description of these factors. Since its development, the SERVQUAL scale has been used in numerous studies, though not all of its empirical findings correspond precisely to the five dimensions that the scale is designed to measure.[46] Furthermore, some researchers believe that there are problems in conceptualizing service quality as a "difference" score.[47]

Another scale that measures service quality, called **SERVPERF**, is based on the consumer's perception of service performance. The SERVPERF scale results in a summated overall service quality score that can be plotted relative to time and specific consumer subgroups (e.g., demographic segments.)[48]

Recent research divides the dimensions along which consumers evaluate service quality into two groups: the *outcome* dimension (which focuses on the reliable delivery of the core service) and the *process* dimension (which focuses on how the core service is delivered).[49] The process dimension offers the service provider a significant opportunity to exceed customer expectations. For example, while Federal Express provides the same core service as other couriers (the *outcome* dimension), it provides a superior *process* dimension through its highly advanced tracking system which can provide customers with in-

table 6-2   SERVQUAL Dimensions for Measuring Service Quality

DIMENSION	DESCRIPTION
• Tangibles	Appearance of physical facilities, equipment, personnel, and communication materials
• Reliability	Ability to perform the promised service dependably and accurately
• Responsiveness	Willingness to help customers and provide prompt service
• Assurance	Knowledge and courtesy of employees and their ability to convey trust and confidence
• Empathy	Caring, individualized attention the firm provides its customers.

Source: Adapted with permission of The Free Press, a division of Simon & Schuster, from VALARIE A. ZEITHAML, A. PARASURAMAN, and LEONARD L. BERRY, *Delivering Quality Service: Balancing Customer Perceptions and Expectations* (New York: The Free Press, 1990). Copyright 1990 by The Free Press.

stant information about the status of their packages at any time between pickup and delivery. Thus, Fedex uses the process dimension to exceed customers' expectations, and has acquired the image of a company that has an important, customer-focused competitive advantage among the many companies providing the same core service.[50]

Researchers have tried to integrate the concepts of *product quality* and *service quality* into an overall **transaction satisfaction index**, on the basis that all product (i.e., tangible) purchases contain some element of service. For example, satisfaction with a retail purchase would include evaluation of the helpfulness and efficiency of the salesperson. Figure 6-19 presents a conceptual model that proposes that the consumer's overall satisfaction with the transaction is based on evaluation of service quality, product quality, and price.[51] A study of the relationship between *service quality, consumer satisfaction*, and *purchase intentions* found that perceptions of high service quality and high service satisfaction result in a very high level of purchase intentions.[52]

▲ **Price/Quality Relationship** Perceived product value has been described as a trade-off between the product's perceived benefits (or quality) and the perceived sacrifice—both monetary and nonmonetary—required to acquire it.[53] A number of research studies support the view that consumers rely on price as an indicator of product quality. Several studies have shown that consumers attribute different qualities to identical products that carry different price labels. Other studies suggest that consumers using a price/quality relationship are actually relying on a well-known (and hence more expensive) brand name as an indicator of quality, without actually relying directly on price per se.[54] Because price is so often considered to be an indicator of quality, some product advertisements deliberately emphasize a high price to underscore the marketers' claims of quality. One of the dangers of sales pricing for retailers is that products with lower prices may be interpreted as reduced quality. For that reason, it is important to include other information associated with perceived quality (e.g., brand and specific attribute information) to counter any perceptions of negative quality associated with the lower price.[55]

Real estate developers often use the price/quality relationship in positioning their offerings. For example, the Trump Tower apartments in New York were deliberately priced much higher preconstruction than other nearby luxury apartment buildings in the belief that the most expensive apartments would be identified by the targeted consumers as the "best" apartments. The strategy worked: almost all of the units were sold before construction was completed. Another real estate developer who had a half-dozen luxury homes

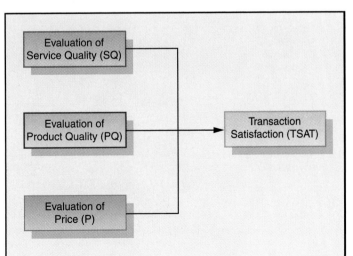

FIGURE 6-19

A Conceptual Model of the Components of Transaction Satisfaction

Source: A. PARASURAMAN, VALARIE A. ZEITHAML, and LEONARD L. BERRY, "Reassessment of Expectations as a Comparison Standard in Measuring Service Quality," *Journal of Marketing* 58 (January 1994), 121. Reprinted by permission of the American Marketing Association.

under construction at the time of a market downturn reported that he "just kept raising the prices until they all were sold."

Other marketers have successfully used the price/quality relationship to position their products as the top-quality offerings in their product categories. For example, Chock Full O' Nuts coffee was originally introduced as a high-priced coffee that was "worth the difference" in cost because of its allegedly superior flavor and taste.

A comprehensive review of the literature confirms the existence of a positive price/quality relationship. However, when other cues are available (e.g., brand name, store image), they are sometimes more influential than price in determining perceived quality. A study that investigated the effects of the extrinsic cues of price, brand, and store information on consumers' perceptions of product quality found that *price* had a positive effect on perceived quality but a negative effect on perceived value and respondents' willingness to buy. *Brand* and *store information* also had a positive effect on perceived quality, but in addition they had a positive effect on perceived value and willingness to buy.[56] Figure 6-20 presents a conceptual model of the effects of price, brand name, and store name on perceived product quality.

Consumers use price as a surrogate indicator of quality if they have little information to go on, or if they have little confidence in their own ability to make the choice on other

FIGURE 6-20

Conceptual Model of the Effects of Price, Brand Name, and Store Name on Perceived Value
Source: W. B. DODDS, K. B. MONROE, and DHRUV GREWEL, "Effects of Price, Brand and Store Information on Buyers' Product Evaluations," *Journal of Marketing Research* 28 (August 1991), 308. Reprinted by permission.

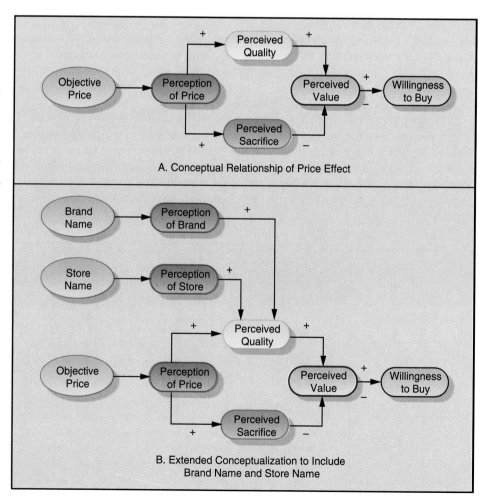

grounds. When the consumer is familiar with a brand name or has experience with a product, price declines as a factor in product selection. The price/quality relationship also extends into the realm of consumer services, though the extent of positive price/quality perceptions varies across service categories.[57]

Retail Store Image

Retail stores have images of their own that serve to influence the perceived quality of products they carry and the decisions of consumers as to where to shop. In order to create a distinctive identity, many retailers put their own labels on the clothes of popular designers. Such private-label clothing has been successful because consumers perceive high quality and value in clothing that bears a well-known retail name. Because of this trend, private-label fashions in many cases are squeezing well-known designer clothing off the racks.

A study of retail store image based on comparative pricing strategies found that consumers tend to perceive stores that offer a small discount on a large number of items (i.e., *frequency* of price advantage) as having lower prices overall than competing stores which offer larger discounts on a smaller number of products (i.e., *magnitude* of price advantage.)[58] This finding has important implications for retailers' positioning strategies in this era of value-pricing. One study showed that frequent advertising that presents large numbers of price specials reinforces consumer beliefs about the competitiveness of a store's prices.[59] The downside of constant advertising of sale prices can be an unwanted change in store image. For example, the Lord & Taylor's department store chain long carried an upscale fashion image. In recent years, however, this image has been negatively affected by consistent advertising focused on storewide sales prices.

The type of product the consumer wishes to buy influences his or her selection of retail outlet; conversely, the consumer's evaluation of a product often is influenced by the knowledge of where it was bought. A consumer wishing to buy an elegant dress for a special occasion may go to a store with an elegant, high-fashion image, such as Saks Fifth Avenue in New York. Regardless of what she actually pays for the dress she selects (regular price or marked-down price), she will probably perceive its quality to be high. However, she may perceive the quality of the same dress to be much lower if she buys it in an off-price store with a low-price image. A study that examined the effects of specific store environmental factors on quality inferences found that consumer perceptions were more heavily influenced by ambient factors (i.e., the people within the store's environment: the number, type, and behavior of other customers and sales personnel) than by store design features.[60] A recent study found that both the store environment, and perceptions of merchandise and service quality, are actually antecedents of store image, rather than components of store image.[61]

Most studies of the effects of extrinsic cues on perceived product quality have focused on just one variable—either price or store image. However, when a second extrinsic cue is available (e.g., price *and* store image), perceived quality is sometimes a function of the interaction of both cues on the consumer. For example, a study found that when brand and retailer images become associated, the less favorable image becomes enhanced at the expense of the more favorable image. Thus, when a low-priced store carries a brand with a high-priced image, the image of the store will improve, while the image of the brand will be adversely affected.[62]

Manufacturer's Image

Consumer imagery extends beyond perceived price and store image to the producers themselves. Manufacturers who enjoy a favorable image generally find that their new products are accepted more readily than those of manufacturers who have a less favorable or even a "neutral" image. Researchers have found that consumers generally have favorable perceptions of *pioneer brands* (the first in a product category), even after *follower brands* become available. They also found a positive correlation between pioneer brand image and an individual's ideal self-image, which suggests that positive perceptions toward pioneer brands lead to positive purchase intentions.[63]

Some major marketers are introducing new products under the guise of supposedly smaller, pioneering (and presumably more forward-thinking) companies. The goal of this so-called *stealth* (or *faux*) *parentage* is to persuade consumers (particularly those in their twenties and thirties) that the new brands are produced by independent, nonconformist free spirits, rather than by giant corporate entities such as their parents might patronize. Examples of stealth parentage include Bartles & Jaymes, which is owned, not by Frank and Ed, but by the huge E & J Gallo Winery. Red Dog beer is marketed by the Miller Brewing Company under the name "Plank Road Brewery," the name it operated under from 1855 to 1873.[64] Stealth parentage also enables a mainstream brand to go after a special niche without endangering its base market. For example, Toyota entered the luxury automobile market with the name Lexus.

Companies sometimes use stealth parentage when they enter a product category totally unrelated to the one with which their corporate name has become synonymous. For example, the Clorox Company decided not to attach the name Clorox to its food-related products, since the Clorox name is so closely identified with laundry and cleaning products. Its Hidden Valley Ranch dressings are marketed under the name of the HVR Company, while its KC Masterpiece barbecue sauce is marketed by Kingsford Products, both divisions of the Clorox Company.[65]

Today, companies are using advertising, exhibits, and sponsorship of community events to enhance their images. While some marketers argue that product and service advertising do more to boost the corporate image than institutional (i.e., image) advertising does, others see both types of advertising—product and institutional—as integral and complementary components of a total corporate communications program.

Brand Image

Brand image is defined as *the set of associations linked to the brand that consumers hold in memory.*[66] Positive brand image is associated with consumer loyalty, consumer beliefs about positive brand value, and a willingness to search for the brand. A positive brand image helps the consumer to be favorably inclined toward future brand promotions and to resist competitors' marketing activities.

Advertising plays an important role in establishing a favorable brand image. For example, a Perrier campaign provides very favorable associations with the product through words and illustrations (see Figures 6-21A and B). In the absence of other information about a new brand, people sometimes use the volume of advertising as a signal of brand quality.[67] Products that are not new but are heavily advertised often are perceived as higher in quality than nonadvertised brands.[68] Consumer satisfaction or dissatisfaction with price promotions (e.g., discounts, coupons, manufacturer rebates) can influence brand image. Short-term price promotion decisions affect the brand's long-term future image. Consumers update their brand images to reflect new information—both positive and negative (i.e., higher or lower brand value). Brand managers who wish to establish a "value" image for their brands must be careful to avoid price promotion strategies that instead create a discount image for the brand.[69]

Figure 6-21A and B ▼ Perrier Ads Provide a Set of Positive
Associations for the Brand
Courtesy of Perrier

PERCEIVED RISK

Consumers must constantly make decisions regarding what products or services to buy and
where to buy them. Because the outcomes (or consequences) of such decisions are often
uncertain, the consumer perceives some degree of "risk" in making a purchase decision.
Perceived risk is defined as *the uncertainty that consumers face when they cannot foresee
the consequences of their purchase decisions*. This definition highlights two relevant dimensions of perceived risk: uncertainty and consequences.

The degree of risk that consumers perceive and their own tolerance for risk taking
are factors that influence their purchase strategies. It should be stressed that consumers are
influenced by risk that they *perceive*, whether or not such risk actually exists. Risk that is
not perceived—no matter how real or how dangerous—will not influence consumer behavior. Furthermore, the amount of money involved in the purchase is not directly related
to the amount of risk perceived. Selecting the right mouthwash may present as great a risk
to a consumer as selecting a new television set.

Types of Perceived Risk

The major types of risks that consumers perceive when making product decisions include
functional risk, physical risk, financial risk, social risk, psychological risk, and *time risk.*

1. **Functional Risk** is the risk that the product will not perform as expected. ("Will the new electric car operate a full day without needing to be recharged?")

2. **Physical Risk** is the risk to self and others that the product may pose. ("Is a cellular phone really safe, or does it emit harmful radiation?")

3. **Financial Risk** is the risk that the product will not be worth its cost. ("Will art school really help me become an artist?")

4. **Social Risk** is the risk that a poor product choice may result in social embarrassment. ("Will that new deodorant really eliminate perspiration odor?")

5. **Psychological Risk** is the risk that a poor product choice will bruise the consumer's ego. ("Will I really be proud to invite friends to this house?")

6. **Time Risk** is the risk that the time spent in product search may be wasted if the product does not perform as expected. ("Will I have to go through the shopping effort all over again?")

Perception of Risk Varies

Consumer perception of risk varies, depending on the person, the product, the situation, and the culture.

The *amount* of risk perceived depends on the specific consumer. Some consumers tend to perceive high degrees of risk in various consumption situations; others tend to perceive little risk. For example, studies of risk perception among adolescents have found that adolescents who engage in high-risk consumption activities (e.g., drug use) differ significantly from those who do not engage in frequent high-risk activities.[70] **High-risk perceivers** are often described as *narrow categorizers* because they limit their choices (e.g., product choices) to a few safe alternatives. They would rather exclude some perfectly good alternatives than chance a poor selection. **Low-risk perceivers** have been described as *broad categorizers* because they tend to make their choices from a much wider range of alternatives. They would rather risk a poor selection than limit the number of alternatives from which they can choose.

An individual's perception of risk varies with *product categories*. For example, consumers are likely to perceive a higher degree of risk in the purchase of a large screen television set (e.g., functional risk, financial risk, time risk) than in the purchase of a cordless telephone. In addition to product-category risk, researchers have identified product-specific perceived risk.[71] A recent study showed that consumers perceive service decisions to be riskier that product decisions, particularly in terms of social risk, physical risk, and psychological risk.[72]

The degree of risk perceived by a consumer is also affected by the *shopping situation* (e.g., a traditional retailer, by mail or telephone, from catalogs or direct-mail solicitations, or from door-to-door salespeople.) The sharp increase in mail-order catalog sales in recent years suggests that on the basis of positive experiences and word of mouth, consumers now tend to perceive less risk in mail-order shopping than they once did, despite their inability to physically inspect the merchandise before ordering.

Not all people around the world exhibit the same level of risk perception. For this reason, marketers who do business in several countries cannot generalize the results of consumer behavior studies conducted in one country to other countries without additional research.

How Consumers Handle Risk

Consumers characteristically develop their own strategies for reducing perceived risk. These risk-reduction strategies enable them to act with increased confidence when making product decisions, even though the consequences of such decisions are still somewhat uncertain. Some of the more common risk-reduction strategies are discussed below.

▲ **Consumers Seek Information** Consumers seek information about the product and product class through *word-of-mouth* communication (from friends and family and from other people whose opinions they value), from salespeople, and from the general media. They spend more time thinking about their choice and search for more information about the product alternatives when they associate a high degree of risk with the purchase. This strategy is straightforward and logical, because the more information the consumer has about the product and the product category, the more predictable the probable consequences, and thus the lower the perceived risk.

▲ **Consumers Are Brand Loyal** Consumers can avoid risk by remaining loyal to a brand with which they have been satisfied instead of purchasing new or untried brands. High-risk perceivers, for example, are more likely to be loyal to their old brands and less likely to purchase newly introduced products.

▲ **Consumers Select by Brand Image** When consumers have had no experience with a product, they tend to "trust" a favored or well-known brand name. Consumers often think well-known brands are better and are worth buying for the implied assurance of quality, dependability, performance, and service. Marketers' promotional efforts supplement the perceived quality of their products by helping to build and sustain a favorable brand image.

▲ **Consumers Rely on Store Image** If consumers have no other information about a product, they often trust the judgment of the merchandise buyers of a reputable store and depend on them to have made careful decisions in selecting products for resale. Store image also imparts the implication of product testing and the assurance of service, return privileges, and adjustment in case of dissatisfaction.

▲ **Consumers Buy the Most Expensive Model** When in doubt, consumers may feel that the most expensive model is probably the best in terms of quality; that is, they equate price with quality. (The price/quality relationship was discussed earlier in this chapter.)

▲ **Consumers Seek Reassurance** Consumers who are uncertain about the wisdom of a product choice seek reassurance through money-back guarantees, government and private laboratory test results, warranties, and prepurchase trial (through free samples or limited free trials.) For example, it is unlikely that anyone would buy a new model car without a "test drive." Products that do not easily lend themselves to free trial present a challenge to marketers.

The concept of perceived risk has major implications for the introduction of new products. Because high-risk perceivers are less likely to purchase new or innovative products than low-risk perceivers, it is important for marketers to provide such consumers with persuasive risk-reduction strategies, such as a well-known brand name (sometimes achieved through licensing), distribution through reputable retail outlets, informative advertising, publicity stories in the media, impartial test results, free samples, and money-back guarantees. Figure 6-22 on page 186 presents an ad for disposable contact lenses designed to reduce consumers' perceived risk.

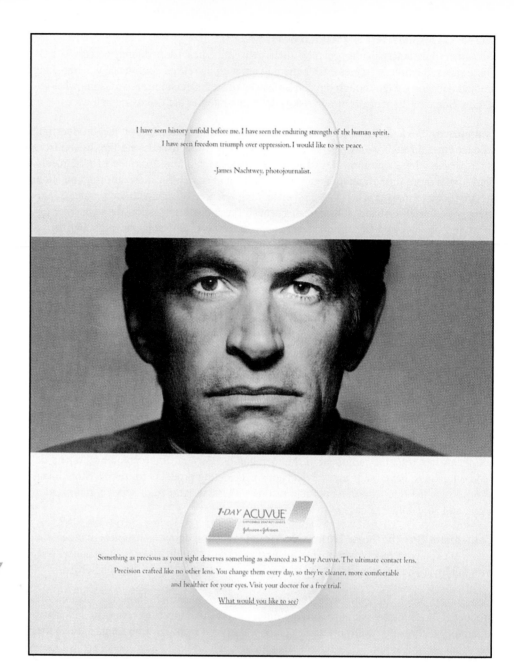

FIGURE 6-22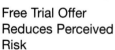

Free Trial Offer
Reduces Perceived
Risk
Courtesy of Vista Con

Inside the ad image:

> I have seen history unfold before me. I have seen the enduring strength of the human spirit.
> I have seen freedom triumph over oppression. I would like to see peace.
>
> -James Nachtwey, photojournalist.

1-DAY ACUVUE
DISPOSABLE CONTACT LENSES
Johnson & Johnson

Something as precious as your sight deserves something as advanced as 1-Day Acuvue. The ultimate contact lens.
Precision crafted like no other lens. You change them every day, so they're cleaner, more comfortable
and healthier for your eyes. Visit your doctor for a free trial.

What would you like to see?

summary

Perception is the process by which individuals select, organize, and interpret stimuli into a meaningful and coherent picture of the world. Perception has strategy implications for marketers, because consumers make decisions based on what they perceive, rather than on the basis of objective reality.

The lowest level at which an individual can perceive a specific stimulus is that person's absolute threshold. The mini-mal difference that can be perceived between two stimuli is called the differential threshold, or just noticeable difference (j.n.d.). Most stimuli are perceived by consumers above the level of their conscious awareness; however, weak stimuli can be perceived below the level of conscious awareness (i.e., subliminally). Research does not support the contention that subliminal stimuli affect consumer buying decisions.

Consumers' selections of stimuli from the environment are based on the interaction of their expectations and motives with the stimulus itself. The principle of selective perception includes the following concepts: selective exposure, selective attention, perceptual defense, and perceptual blocking. People usually perceive things they need or want and block the perception of unnecessary, unfavorable, or painful stimuli. Consumers organize their perceptions into unified wholes according to the principles of Gestalt psychology: figure and ground, grouping, and closure.

The interpretation of stimuli is highly subjective and is based on what the consumer expects to see in light of previous experience, on the number of plausible explanations he or she can envision, on motives and interests at the time of perception, and on the clarity of the stimulus itself. Influences that tend to distort objective interpretation include physical appearances, stereotypes, halo effects, irrelevant cues, first impressions, and the tendency to jump to conclusions.

Just as individuals have perceived images of themselves, they also have perceived images of products and brands. The perceived image of a product or service (i.e., its symbolic meaning) is probably more important to its ultimate success than are its actual physical characteristics. Products and services that are perceived favorably have a much better chance of being purchased than products or services with unfavorable or neutral images.

Compared with manufacturing firms, service marketers face several unique problems in positioning and promoting their offerings, including the service environment and service characteristics (e.g., services are intangible, variable, perishable, and are simultaneously produced and consumed. Regardless of how well positioned a product or service appears to be,

the marketer may be forced to reposition it in response to market events, such as new competitive strategies or changing consumer preferences.

Consumers often judge the quality of a product or service on the basis of a variety of informational cues; some are intrinsic to the product (e.g., color, size, flavor, aroma), while others are extrinsic (e.g., price, store image, brand image, service environment). In the absence of direct experience or other information, consumers often rely on price as an indicator of quality. The images of retail stores influence the perceived quality of products they carry, as well as the decisions of consumers as to where to shop.

Consumer imagery extends beyond perceived price and store image to the producers themselves. Manufacturers who enjoy a favorable image generally find that their new products are accepted more readily than those of manufacturers with less favorable or even neutral images.

Consumers often perceive risk in making product selections because of uncertainty as to the consequences of their product decisions. The most frequent types of risk that consumers perceive are functional risk, physical risk, financial risk, social risk, psychological risk, and time risk.

Consumer strategies for reducing perceived risk include increased information search, brand loyalty, buying a well-known brand, buying from a reputable retailer, buying the most expensive brand, and seeking reassurance in the form of money-back guarantees, warranties, and prepurchase trial. The concept of perceived risk has important implications for marketers, who can facilitate the acceptance of new products by incorporating risk reduction strategies in their new product promotional campaigns.

discussion questions

1. How does sensory adaptation affect advertising effectiveness? How can marketers overcome sensory adaptation?

2. Describe how manufacturers of chocolate bars can apply their knowledge of differential threshold to packages and prices during periods of: (a) rising ingredient costs, (b) increasing competition, and (c) consumer nutrition concerns.

3. Does subliminal advertising work? Support your view.

4. How do advertisers use contrast to make sure that their ads are noticed? Would the lack of contrast between the ad and the medium in which it appears help or hinder the effectiveness of the ad? What are the ethical considerations in employing such strategies?

5. Martha Brown is a 29-year-old, single investment banker who lives in an apartment in a large city. After a particularly difficult, long workday, she relaxed in her apartment by reading several magazines. When questioned by a researcher the next day, she could clearly recall seeing two vacation ads and vaguely remembered one ad for a personal computer from among the nearly 100 ads she

had seen in the three magazines. However, she could repeat the articles which she read in detail and even recalled the titles of articles which she did not read. How can you explain this?

6. a. Discuss the differences between the absolute threshold and the differential threshold.

   b. What is consumer reality?

7. What are the implications of figure-ground relationships for print ads and for TV ads? How can the figure-ground construct help or interfere with the communication of advertising messages?

8. How is perceptual mapping used in consumer research? Why are marketers sometimes forced to reposition their products or services? Illustrate your answers with examples.

9. Why is it more difficult for consumers to evaluate the quality of services than the quality of products?

10. Discuss the roles of extrinsic cues and intrinsic cues in the perceived quality of: (a) wines, (b) restaurants, (c) shampoo, (d) medical services, and (e) graduate education.

exercises

1. Find five examples of print advertisements or packages that use stimulus factors to create attention. For each example, evaluate the effectiveness of the stimulus factors used. Also, identify the principles of perceptual organization which are integrated into these ads.

2. Using Weber's law as a guideline, develop a reasonable j.n.d. for the sales price of: (a) a car, (b) a personal computer, (c) a pair of denim jeans, and (d) a tube of toothpaste. Explain your choices.

3. What roles do actual product attributes and perceptions of attributes play in positioning a product? Find three different toothpaste advertisements which stress different product attributes and discuss whether each marketer has effectively positioned its product to communicate a specific image.

4. Construct a two-dimensional perceptual map of your college using the two attributes that were most important to you in selecting it rather than other colleges in your area. Then, mark the position of your school on the diagram relative to that of another school you considered. Discuss the implications of this perceptual map for the student recruitment function of the university that you did *not* choose.

5. Conduct interviews with five of your fellow students in this class. On what dimensions do they evaluate this course? Which intrinsic and extrinsic cues do they use as indicators of quality? Do your observations support the concepts discussed in the chapter? Explain.

6. Select a restaurant where you have recently eaten. Analyze the atmosphere and physical environment of this service establishment. What image does the environment convey? Should the owner change anything to make the environment more appealing to customers? Explain.

key words

- **Absolute threshold**
- **Acquisition utility**
- **Broad categorizers**
- **Closure**
- **Consumer imagery**
- **Contrast**
- **Differential threshold**
- **Embeds**
- **Extrinsic cues**
- **Figure and ground**
- **Gestalt psychology**
- **Grouping**
- **Halo effect**
- **High-risk perceivers**
- **Intrinsic cues**

- **j.n.d.**
- **Low-risk perceivers**
- **Narrow categorizers**
- **Objective price cues**
- **Perceived quality**
- **Perceived risk**
- **Perception**
- **Perceptual blocking**
- **Perceptual defense**
- **Perceptual interpretation**
- **Perceptual mapping**
- **Perceptual organization**
- **Positioning**
- **Price/quality relationship**
- **Reference prices**

- **Repositioning**
- **Selective attention**
- **Selective exposure**
- **Selective perception**
- **Sensation**
- **Sensory adaptation**
- **Sensory receptors**
- **Stereotypes**
- **Stimulus**
- **Subliminal perception**
- **Tensile price cues**
- **Transaction satisfaction index**
- **Transaction utility**
- **Weber's law**
- **Zeigernik effect**

end notes

1. C. DOUGLAS OLSEN, "Observations: The Sound of Silence: Functions and Use of Silence in Television Advertising," *Journal of Advertising Research*, September/October 1994, 89–95.

2. N. R. KLEINFIELD, "The Smell of Money," *The New York Times*, November 25, 1992, B1.

3. BERNARD BERELSON and GARY A. STEINER, *Human Behavior: An Inventory of Scientific Findings* (New York: Harcourt, Brace & World, 1964), 87–130.

4. JOHN B. HINGE, "Critics Call Cuts in Package Size Deceptive Move," *The Wall Street Journal*, February 5, 1991, B1.

5. BARRY WEGENER, General Mills, Inc., March 19, 1996.

6. GLENN COLLINS, "Updating an Icon, Carefully," *The New York Times*, November 17, 1995, D1.

7. W. BEVAN, "Subliminal Stimulation: A Pervasive Problem for Psychology," *Psychological Bulletin* 61(2), 1964, 81–99.

8. SHARON E. BEATTY and DEL I. HAWKINS, "Subliminal Stimulation: Some New Data and Interpretation," *Journal of Advertising* 18, 1989, 4–8.

9. WILSON BRYAN KEY, *Subliminal Seduction* (New York: New American Library, 1973).

10. PHILIP M. MERIKLE and JIM CHEESMAN, "Current Status of Research on Subliminal Perception," in M. Wallendorf and P. F. Anderson, eds., *Association for Consumer Research* 14, 1987, 298–302.

11. JO ANNA NATALE, "Are You Open to Suggestion?" *Psychology Today*, September 1988, 28–30.

12. ROBERT BORNSTEIN, et al., "The Generalizability of Subliminal Mere Exposure Effects: Influence of Stimuli Perceived without Awareness on Social Behavior," *Journal of Personality and Social Psychology* 53(6), 1987, 1070–79.

13. MYRON GABLE, HENRY T. WILKENS, LYNN HARRIS, and RICHARD FEINBERG, "An Evaluation of Subliminally Embedded Sexual Stimuli in Graphics," *Journal of Advertising* 16(1), 1987, 26–31.

14. KIRK H. SMITH and MARTHA ROGERS, "Effectiveness of Subliminal Messages in Television Commercials: Two Experiments," *Journal of Applied Psychology* 19(6) 1994, 866–74.

15. KATHRYN T. THEUS, "Subliminal Advertising and the Psychology of Processing Unconscious Stimuli: A Review of Research," *Psychology and Marketing* 11(3), May/June 1994, 271–90.

16. JOHN LOFFLIN, "Help from the Hidden Persuaders," *The New York Times*, March 20, 1988, D17.

17. MARY ALICE CRAWFORD, "A 50s Technology Enjoys a Rebirth," *Security Management*, August 1985, 54–56.

18. JOEL SAEGERT, "Why Marketing Should Quit Giving Subliminal Advertising the Benefit of the Doubt," *Psychology and Marketing* 4(2), Summer 1987, 107–13.

19. THEUS, op. cit. See also DENNIS L. ROSEN and SURENRA N. SINGH, "An Investigation of Subliminal Embed Effect on Multiple Measures of Advertising Effectiveness," *Psychology and Marketing* 9(2), March/April 1992, 157–73.

20. CARL L. WITTE, MADHAVAN PARTHASARATHY, and JAMES W. GENTRY, "Subliminal Perception Versus Subliminal Persuasion: A Re-Examination of the Basic Issues," *American Marketing Association*, Summer 1995, 133–38.

21. MARTHA ROGERS and CHRISTINE A. SEILER, "The Answer Is No: A National Survey of Advertising Practitioners and Their Clients about Whether They Use Subliminal Advertising," *Journal of Advertising Research*, March/April 1994, 36–45; MARTHA ROGERS and KIRK H. SMITH, "Public Perceptions of Subliminal Advertising: Why Practitioners Shouldn't Ignore This Issue," *Journal of Advertising Research*, March/April 1993, 10–18. See also NICOLAS E. SYNODINOS, "Subliminal Stimulation: What Does the Public Think about It?" *Current Issues and Research in Advertising*, James H. Leigh and Claude R. Martin Jr., eds., 11(1 and 2), 1988, 157–87.

22. LOFFLIN, op. cit.

23. THEUS, op. cit., 273–4.

24. ROBIN POGREBIN, "By Design or Not, an Ad Becomes a Fad," *The New York Times*, December 24, 1995, E3.

25. JAMES T. HEIMBACH and JACOB JACOBY, "The Zeigernik Effect in Advertising," in M. Venkatesan, ed., *Proceedings of the Third Annual Conference* (Association for Consumer Research, 1972), 746–58.

26. JULIUS HARBURGER, "Concept Closure," *Advertising Age*, January 12, 1987, 18.

27. KATHLEEN DEBEVEC and JEROME B. KERNAN, "More Evidence on the Effects of a Presenter's Physical Attractiveness: Some Cognitive, Affective, and Behavioral Consequences," in Thomas C. Kinnear, ed., *Advances in Consumer Research* 11 (Association for Consumer Research, 1983), 127–32; and GORDON L. PATZER, "An Experiment Investigating the Influence of Communicator Physical Attractiveness on Attitudes," in Patrick E. Murphy, O. C. Ferrell, Gene R. Laczniak, Robert F. Lurch, Paul F. Anderson, Terence A. Shimp, Russell W. Belk, and Charles B. Weinberg, eds., *1983 American Marketing Association Educators' Proceedings* 49 (Chicago: American Marketing Association, 1983), 25–29. See also MADELINE H. STOPECK, "Attractiveness and Corporate Success: Different Causal Attributions for Males and Females," *Journal of Applied Psychology* 70, 1985, 379–88; and SANDRA FORSYTHE, MARY FRANCES DRAKE, and CHARLES E. COX, "Influence of Applicant's Dress on Interviewer's Selection Decisions," *Journal of Applied Psychology* 70, 1985, 374–78.

28. RUSSELL W. BELK, "Possessions and the Extended Self," *Journal of Consumer Research* 15, September 1988, 139–68.

29. MARY JO BITNER, "Servicescapes: The Impact of Physical Surroundings on Customers and Employees," *Journal of Marketing* 56, April 1992, 57–71.

30. JULIE BAKER, LEONARD L. BERRY, and A. PARASURAMAN, "The Marketing Impact of Branch Facility Design," *Journal of Retail Banking* 10(2), Summer 1988, 33–42.

31. MARIELZA MARTINS and KENT B. MONROE, "Perceived Price Fairness: A New Look at an Old Construct," *Advances in Consumer Research* 21, 1994, 75–78.

32. ABHIJIT BISWAS and EDWARD A. BLAIR, "Contextual Effects of Reference Prices in Retail Advertisements," *Journal of Marketing* 55, July 1991, 1–12; ABHIJIT BISWAS, "The Moderating Role of Brand Familiarity in Reference Price Perceptions," *Journal of Business Research* 25, 1992, 251–62.

33. KATHERINE FRACCASTORO, SCOT BURTON, and ABHIJIT BISWAS, "Effective Use of Advertisements Promoting Sales Prices," *Journal of Consumer Marketing* 10(1), 1993, 61–79.

34. Ibid.

35. Ibid.

36. ABHIJIT BISWAS and SCOT BURTON, "Consumer Perceptions of Tensile Price Claims in Advertisements: An Assessment of Claim Types Across Different Discount Levels," *Journal of the Academy of Marketing Science* 21(3), 217–29.

37. MANJIT S. YADAV and KENT B. MONROE, "How Buyers Perceive Savings in a Bundle Price: An Examination of a Bundle's Transaction Value," *Journal of Marketing Research* 30, August 1993, 350–58.

38. MICHAEL J. MCCARTHY, "Forget the Ads: Cola Is Cola, Magazine Finds," *The Wall Street Journal*, February 24, 1991, B1.

39. DURAIRAJ MAHASWARON, "Country of Origin as a Stereotype: Effects of Consumer Expertise and Attribute Strength on Product Evaluations," *Journal of Consumer Research* 21, September 1994, 354–65.

40. It is interesting to note that, prior to World War II, anything "made in Japan" was stereotyped as "junk."

41. The Roper Organization, "Consumer Data," *Adweek's Marketing Week*, August 20, 1990, 10.

42. RUTH REICHL, "The Vichyssoise of Ice Cream," *The New York Times Magazine*, January 1, 1995, 29.

43. SHIRLEY TAYLOR, "Waiting for Service: The Relationship Between Delay and Evaluations of Service," *Journal of Marketing* 58, April 1994, 56–69.

44. VALARIE A. ZEITHAML, A. PARASURAMAN, and LEONARD L. BERRY, "Delivering Quality Service: Balancing Customer Perceptions and Expectations" (New York: The Free Press, 1990).

45. A. PARASURAMAN, LEONARD L. BERRY, and VALARIE A. ZEITHAML, "Refinement and Reassessment of the SERVQUAL Scale," *Journal of Retailing* 67(4), Winter 1991, 420–50. See also JAMES M. CARMAN, "Consumer Perceptions of Service Quality: An Assessment of the SERVQUAL Dimensions," *Journal of Retailing* 66(1), Spring 1990, 33–55.

46. See, for example, J. JOSEPH CRONIN, JR. and STEVEN A. TAYLOR, "Measuring Service Quality: A Reexamination and Extension," *Journal of Marketing* 56, July 1992, 55–68.

47. J. JOSEPH CRONIN, JR. and STEVEN A. TAYLOR, "SERVPERF Versus SERVQUAL: Reconciling Performance-Based and Perceptions-Minus-Expectations Measurement of Service Quality," *Journal of Marketing* 58, January 1994, 125–31; also WILLIAM BOULDING, AJAY KALRA, RICHARD STAELIN, and VALARIE ZEITHAML, "A Dynamic Process Model of Service Quality: From Expectations to Behavioral Intentions," *Journal of Marketing Research* 30, February 1993, 7–27; and KENNETH TEAS, "Expectations as a Comparison Standard in Measuring Service Quality: An Assessment of a Reassessment," *Journal of Marketing* 58, January 1994, 132–39.

48. CRONIN and TAYLOR, 1994, op. cit. 130.

49. ZEITHAML, PARASURAMAN, and BERRY, 1990, op. cit. Chapters 4, 5, 6, 7.

50. A. PARASURAMAN, LEONARD L. BERRY, and VALARIE A. ZEITHAML, "Understanding Customer Expectations of Service," *Sloan Management Review*, Spring 1991, 39–48.

51. A. PARASURAMAN, VALARIE A. ZEITHAML, and LEONARD L. BERRY, "Reassessment of Expectations as a Comparison Standard in Measuring Service Quality: Implications for Further Research," *Journal of Marketing* 58, January 1994, 111–24.

52. STEVEN A. TAYLOR and THOMAS L. BAKER, "An Assessment of the Relationship Between Service Quality and Customer Satisfaction in the Formation of Consumers' Purchase Intentions," *Journal of Retailing* 70(2), 163–78.

53. WILLIAM DODDS, KENT MONROE, and DHRUV GREWAL, "Effects of Price, Brand, and Store Information on Buyers' Product Evaluations," *Journal of Marketing Research* 28, August 1991, 307–19; KENT MONROE, *Pricing: Making Profitable Decisions*, 2nd edition (New York: McGraw-Hill, 1990). See also TUNG-ZONG CHANG and ALBERT R. WILDT, "Price, Product Information, and Purchase Intention: An Empirical Study," *Journal of the Academy of Marketing Science* 22(1), 1994, 16–27.

54. DONALD R. LIECHTENSTEIN, MANCY M. RIDGWAY, and RICHARD G. NITEMEYER, "Price Perception and Consumer Shopping Behavior: A Field Study," *Journal of Marketing Research* 30, May 1993, 242.

55. FRACCASTORRO, op. cit.

56. DODDS, MONROE, and GREWEL, op. cit. See also NOEL MARK LAVENKA, "Measurement of Consumers' Perceptions of Product Quality, Brand Name and Packaging: Candy Bar Comparisons by Magnitude Estimation," *Marketing Research* 3(2), June 1991, 38–45.

57. ROSE L. JOHNSON and JAMES J. KELLARIES, "An

Exploratory Study of Price/Perceived Quality Relationships Among Consumer Services," in Michael Housten, ed., *Advances in Consumer Research* 15, 1988, 316–22.

58. JOSEPH W. ALBA, SUSAN M. BRONIARCZYK, TERENCE A. SHIMP, and JOEL E. URBANY, "The Influence of Prior Beliefs, Frequency Cues, and Magnitude Cues on Consumers' Perceptions of Comparative Price Data," *Journal of Consumer Research* 21, September 1994, 219–35.

59. Ibid.

60. JULIE BAKER, DHRUV GREWEL, and A. PARASURAMAN, "The Influence of Store Environment on Quality Inferences and Store Image," *Journal of the Academy of Marketing Science* 22(4), 328–39.

61. Ibid.

62. JACOB JACOBY and DAVID MAZURSK, "Linking Brand and Retailer Images: Do the Potential Risks Outweigh the Potential Benefits?" *Journal of Retailing* 60, Summer 1984, 105–22.

63. FRANK H. ALPERT and MICHAEL A. KAMINS, "An Empirical Investigation of Consumer Memory, Attitude and Perceptions Toward Pioneer and Follower Brands," *Journal of Marketing* 59, October 1995, 34–45.

64. STUARD ELLIOTT, "In the Quest for Niches, Some Companies Discover that Good Things Come from Smaller Packaging," *The New York Times*, March 29, 1994, D20.

65. Ibid.

66. K. L. KELLER, "Conceptualizing and Measuring Customer-Based Brand Equity," *Journal of Marketing* 57, January 1993, 1–22.

67. AMA CARMINE, "The Effect of Perceived Advertising Costs on Brand Perceptions," *Journal of Consumer Research* 17, September 1990, 160–71.

68. Ibid.

69. KENNETH A. HUNT and SUSAN M. KEAVENEY, "A Process Model of the Effects of Price Promotions on Brand Image," *Psychology and Marketing* 11(6), November/December 1994, 511–32; P. R. DICKSON and A. G. SAWYER, "The Price Knowledge and Search of Supermarket Shoppers," *Journal of Marketing* 54, July 1990, 42–53.

70. HERBERT H. SEVERSON, PAUL SLOVIC, and SARAH HAMPSON, "Adolescents' Perception of Risk: Understanding and Preventing High Risk Behavior," *Advances in Consumer Research* 20, 1993, 177–82.

71. GRAHAME R. DOWLING and RICHARD STAELIN, "A Model of Perceived Risk and Intended Risk-Handling Activity," *Journal of Consumer Research* 21, June 1994, 119–34.

72. KEITH B. MURRAY and JOHN L. SCHLACTER, "The Impact of Services versus Goods on Consumers' Assessment of Perceived Risk and Variability," *Journal of the Academy of Marketing Sciences* 18, Winter 1990, 51–65.

How individuals learn is a matter of great interest and importance to academicians, to psychologists, to consumer researchers, and to marketers. The reason that marketers are so concerned with how individuals learn is that they are vitally interested in teaching them, in their roles as consumers, about products, product attributes and potential consumer benefits; about where to buy their products, how to use them, how to maintain them, even how to dispose of them.

Marketing strategies are based on communicating with the consumer: directly, through advertisements, and indirectly, through product appearance, packaging, price, and distribution channels. Marketers want their communications to be noted, believed, remembered, and recalled. For these reasons, they are interested in every aspect of the learning process.

However, despite the fact that learning is all-pervasive in our lives, there is no single,

I am always ready to learn, although I do not always like being taught.

—Winston Churchill

universal theory of how people learn. Instead, there are two major schools of thought concerning the learning process: one consists of behavioral theories, the other of cognitive theories. Cognitive theorists view learning as a function of purely mental processes, while behavioral theorists focus almost exclusively on observable behaviors (responses) that occur as the result of exposure to stimuli.

In this chapter, we examine the two general categories of learning theory: **behavioral learning theory** and **cognitive learning theory**. Although these theories differ markedly in a number of essentials, each theory offers insights to marketers on how to shape their messages to consumers to bring about desired purchase behavior. We also discuss how consumers store, retain, and retrieve information, how learning is measured, and how marketers use learning theories in their marketing strategies. The chapter concludes with a discussion of an important type of learned consumer behavior—brand loyalty.

What is Learning?

Since learning theorists do not agree on how learning takes place, it is difficult to come up with a generally acceptable definition of learning. From a marketing perspective, however, consumer learning can be thought of as *the process by which individuals acquire the purchase and consumption knowledge and experience that they apply to future related behavior.* Several points in this definition are worth noting.

First, consumer learning is a **process**; that is, it continually evolves and changes as a result of newly acquired **knowledge** (which may be gained from reading, from discussions, from observation, from thinking) or from actual **experience**. Both newly acquired knowledge and experience serve as feedback to the individual and provide the basis for future behavior in similar situations. The definition makes clear that learning results from *acquired* knowledge and/or experience. This qualification distinguishes learning from instinctive behavior, such as sucking in infants.

The role of experience in learning does not mean that all learning is deliberately sought. Much learning is *intentional*—that is, it is acquired as the result of a careful search for information. However, a great deal of learning is also *incidental,* acquired by accident or without much effort. For example, some ads may induce learning (e.g., of brand names), even though the consumer's attention is elsewhere (on a magazine article rather than on the advertisement on the facing page). Other ads are sought out and carefully read by consumers contemplating an important purchase decision.

The term *learning* encompasses the total range of learning, from simple, almost reflexive responses to the learning of abstract concepts and complex problem solving. Most learning theorists recognize the existence of different types of learning and explain the differences through the use of distinctive models of learning.

Despite their different viewpoints, learning theorists in general agree that in order for learning to occur, certain basic elements must be present. The elements included in most learning theories are **motivation**, **cues**, **response**, and **reinforcement**. These concepts are discussed first because they tend to recur in the theories discussed later in this chapter.

Motivation

The concept of *motivation* is important to learning theory. Remember, motivation is based on needs and goals. Motivation acts as a spur to learning. For example, men and women who want to become good tennis players are motivated to learn all they can about tennis and to practice whenever they can. They may seek information concerning the prices, quality, and characteristics of tennis racquets if they "learn" that a good racquet is instrumental to playing a good game. Conversely, individuals who are not interested in tennis are likely to ignore all information related to the game. The goal object (proficiency in tennis) simply has no relevance for them. The degree of relevance, or *involvement,* determines the consumer's level of motivation to search for knowledge or information about a product or service. Uncovering consumer motives is one of the prime tasks of marketers, who then try to teach motivated consumer segments why and how their products will fulfill the consumer's needs. (*Involvement theory,* as it has come to be known, will be discussed later in the chapter.)

Cues

If motives serve to stimulate learning, *cues* are the stimuli that give direction to these motives. An advertisement for a tennis camp may serve as a cue for tennis buffs, who may suddenly "recognize" that attending tennis camp is a concentrated way to improve their game while taking a vacation. The ad is the cue, or stimulus, that suggests a specific way to satisfy a salient motive. In the marketplace, price, styling, packaging, advertising, and store displays all serve as cues to help consumers fulfill their needs in product-specific ways.

Cues serve to direct consumer drives when they are consistent with consumer expectations. Marketers must be careful to provide cues that do not upset those expectations. For example, consumers expect designer clothes to be expensive and to be sold in upscale retail stores. Thus, a high-fashion designer should sell his or her clothes only through exclusive stores and advertise only in quality fashion magazines. Each aspect of the marketing mix must reinforce the others if cues are to serve as the stimuli that guide consumer actions in the direction desired by the marketer.

Response

How individuals react to a drive or cue—how they *behave*—constitutes their *response*. Learning can occur even when responses are not overt. The automobile manufacturer who provides consistent cues to a consumer may not always succeed in stimulating a purchase, even if that individual is motivated to buy. However, if the manufacturer succeeds in forming a favorable image of a particular model in the consumer's mind, when the consumer is ready to buy, it is likely he or she will consider that make or model.

A response is not tied to a need in a one-to-one fashion. Indeed, as was discussed in Chapter 4, a need or motive may evoke a whole variety of responses. For example, there are many ways to respond to the need for physical exercise besides tennis playing. Cues provide some direction, but there are many cues competing for the consumer's attention. Which response he or she makes depends heavily on previous learning; that, in turn, may depend on which responses were reinforced in the past.

Reinforcement

Reinforcement increases the likelihood that a specific response will occur in the future as the result of particular cues or stimuli. If a college student finds that an advertised brand of pain remedy has enabled him to run in a marathon despite a knee injury, he is more likely to buy the advertised brand should he suffer another injury. Clearly, through reinforcement, learning has taken place, since the pain remedy lived up to expectations. On the other hand, if the pain remedy had not alleviated his pain the first time, the student would be less likely to buy that brand again, despite extensive advertising or store display cues for the product.

With these basic principles established, we can now discuss some well-known theories or models of how learning occurs.

BEHAVIORAL LEARNING THEORIES

Behavioral learning theories are sometimes referred to as *stimulus-response* theories because they are based on the premise that observable responses to specific external stimuli signal that learning has taken place. When a person acts (i.e., responds) in a predictable way to a known stimulus, he or she is said to have "learned." Behavioral theories are not so much concerned with the *process* of learning as they are with the inputs and outcomes of learning; that is, in the stimuli that consumers select from the environment and the observable behaviors that result. Two behavioral theories with great relevance to marketing are **classical conditioning** and **instrumental** (or *operant*) **conditioning**.

Classical Conditioning

Early classical conditioning theorists regarded all organisms (both animal and human) as relatively passive entities that could be taught certain behaviors through repetition (or "conditioning"). In everyday speech, the word *conditioning* has come to mean a kind of "knee-jerk" or automatic response to a situation built up through repeated exposure. If you get a headache every time you think of visiting your Aunt Gertrude, your reaction may be conditioned from years of boring visits with her.

Ivan Pavlov, a Russian physiologist, was the first to describe conditioning and to propose it as a general model of how learning occurs. According to Pavlovian theory, conditioned learning results when a stimulus that is paired with another stimulus that elicits a known response serves to produce the same response when used alone. In experimental terms, if an unconditioned stimulus (**US**) results in an unconditioned response (**UR**), then the conditioned stimulus (**CS**), after repeated pairings with the unconditioned stimulus, will result in the same response, which is now called a **conditioned response (CR)**.

Pavlov demonstrated what he meant by *conditioned learning* in his studies with dogs. The dogs were hungry and highly motivated to eat. In his experiments, Pavlov sounded a bell and then immediately applied a meat paste to the dogs' tongues, which caused them to salivate. Learning (i.e., conditioning) occurred when, after a sufficient number of repetitions of the bell sound, followed almost immediately by the food, the bell sound alone caused the dogs to salivate. The dogs associated the bell sound (the CS) with the meat paste (the US) and, after a number of pairings, gave the same response (salivation) to the bell alone as they did to the meat paste. The unconditioned response (UR) to the meat paste became the conditioned response (CR) to the bell. Figure 7-1A models this relationship.

An analogous situation would be one in which the smells of dinner cooking would cause your mouth to water. If you usually listen to the 6 o'clock news while waiting for dinner to be served, you would tend to associate the 6 o'clock news with dinner, so that

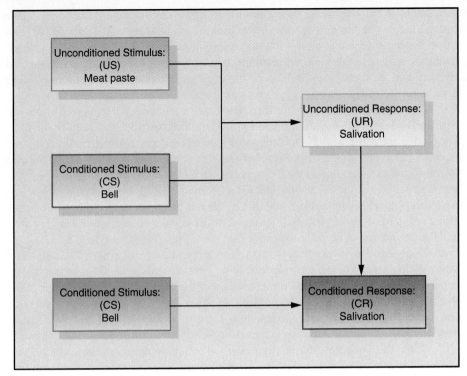

FIGURE 7-1A

Pavlovian Model of Classical Conditioning

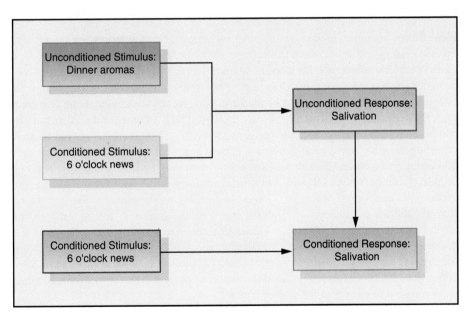

FIGURE 7-1B

Analogous Model of Classical Conditioning

eventually the sounds of the 6 o'clock news alone might cause your mouth to water, even if dinner was not being prepared and even if you were not hungry. Figure 7-1B diagrams this basic relationship. In a consumer behavior context, an *unconditioned stimulus* might consist of a well-known brand label or store; *conditioned stimuli* would consist of products or services bearing the well-known brand label or advertised by the store; and *conditioned responses* would include purchases or store patronage.

A reinterpretation of classical conditioning by learning theorists sees early Pavlovian theory as inadequately characterizing the circumstances that produce conditioned learning, the content of that learning, and the manner in which that learning influences behavior.[1] Instead, recent conditioning theory views classical conditioning as the *learning of associations* among events that allows the organism to anticipate and "represent" its environment.[2] According to this view, the relationship (i.e., contiguity) between the CS and the US (the bell and the meat paste) influenced the dogs' expectations, which in turn influenced their behavior (salivation).

Classical conditioning, then, rather than being a reflexive action, is seen as **cognitive associative learning**; not the acquisition of new reflexes, but the acquisition of new knowledge about the world.[3] According to some researchers, optimal conditioning—that is, the creation of a strong association between the conditioned stimulus and the unconditioned stimulus—requires (1) the CS to precede the US (called *forward conditioning*), (2) repeated pairings of the CS and the US, (3) a CS and US that logically belong together, (4) a CS that is novel and unfamiliar, and (5) a US that is biologically or symbolically salient.[4] Other research suggests that conditioning does not depend on contiguity between the CS and the US, but rather on the information that the CS provides about the US.[5]

Under **neo-Pavlovian theory**, the consumer can be viewed as an *information seeker* who uses logical and perceptual relations among events, along with his or her own preconceptions, to form a sophisticated representation of the world. Conditioning is the learning that results from exposure to relationships among events in the environment; such exposure creates expectations as to the structure of the environment. Studies have found that conditioning encourages attention to the advertised brand in subsequent promotions.[6]

Three basic concepts derive from classical conditioning: *repetition, stimulus generalization,* and *stimulus discrimination.* Each of these concepts is important to an understanding of consumer behavior.

▲ **Repetition** Some researchers believe that repetition works by increasing the strength of the association and by slowing the process of *forgetting,* which is seen as a process of decay. However, there is a limit to the amount of repetition that will aid retention. The evidence suggests that some overlearning, or repetition beyond what is necessary to learn, aids retention. But with exposure beyond a certain point, an individual can become satiated, and attention and retention will decline. This effect, known as **advertising wearout**, can be decreased by varying the advertising message.[7] Some marketers avoid wearout by repeating the same advertising theme in a variety of formats. This type of advertising variation strategy has been described as a *cosmetic variation,* because there is no real change in message content across the ads.[8] Cosmetic variation strategies may use different backgrounds, different print types, or different advertising spokespersons. *Substantive variation* is defined as changes in advertising content across different versions of an advertisement, with no changes in cosmetic features. A recent research study found that individuals exposed to substantively varied ads process more information about product attributes and have more positive thoughts about the product than those exposed to cosmetic variations.[9] Attitudes formed as a result of exposure to substantively varied ads were also more resistant to change in the face of attack.[10]

Although the principle of repetition is well established among advertisers, not everyone agrees on how much repetition is enough. Some researchers maintain that the optimum number of exposures to an advertisement is just three: one to make consumers aware of the product, a second to show consumers the relevance of the product, and a third to remind them of its benefits. According to this *three-hit theory,* all other ad repetitions are wasted effort. Other researchers suggest that an average frequency of eleven to twelve exposures is needed to increase the probability that consumers will actually receive three exposures.

One study that related the viewing of TV commercials to product purchases found that, in the short term, advertising had much greater influence in attracting new buyers (e.g., encouraging brand switching) than encouraging repeat purchases.[11] The study also showed that the greater the number of commercials shown, the more likely a product is to attract new buyers. Generally, the largest incremental value was attributed to the first ad seen, although additional benefits were noted in seeing four or more ads between consecutive purchases of the product category.

▲ **Stimulus Generalization** According to classical conditioning theorists, learning depends not only on repetition, but also on the ability of individuals to generalize. Pavlov found, for example, that a dog could learn to salivate not only to the sound of a bell but also to the somewhat similar sound of jangling keys. If we were not capable of **stimulus generalization**—that is, of making the same response to slightly different stimuli—not much learning would take place.

Stimulus generalization explains why imitative "me too" products succeed in the marketplace: consumers confuse them with the original product they have seen advertised. It also explains why manufacturers of private label brands try to make their packaging resemble the national brand leaders.

PRODUCT LINE EXTENSIONS Another marketing strategy that works on the principle of stimulus generalization is **product line extension**—the practice of adding related products to an already established brand. A 1993 report of leading consumer product companies found that three-quarters of new product introductions were line extensions (such as a new flavor or package size.) For example, Coca-Cola, long a single product, is now available in at least six varieties (Classic Coke, Diet Coke, Caffeine-Free Coke, Caffeine-Free Diet Coke, Cherry Coke, Diet Cherry Coke.) That is because it is significantly cheaper for marketers to associate a new product with a known and trusted brand name than to try to develop a totally new brand.

For a long time, marketers have offered product line extensions that include different sizes, different colors, even different flavors, but now they also offer **product form extensions** (e.g., Ivory bar soap to Ivory liquid soap) and **product category extensions** (disposable BIC pens to disposable BIC razors). The success of this strategy depends on a number of factors. For example, if the image of the parent brand is one of quality, consumers are more likely to bring positive associations to the new category extensions. Consumers tend to relate a given brand extension to other products affiliated with the brand. Tylenol initially introduced line extensions by making its products available in a number of forms (tablets, capsules, gelcaps), strengths (regular, extra-strength, or children's), and package sizes. Since 1987 Tylenol has extended its brand name to a wide range of related remedies for colds, flu, sinus congestion, and allergies, further segmenting the line for adults, children, and infants. Figure 7-2 on page 200 shows an ad for product line extensions; Figure 7-3 on page 201 for product usage extension.

Of course, the process of relating multiple unrelated products to a well-known brand may change the "meaning" of the brand.[12] For example, the brand name Black & Decker was first associated with power tools. When the company bought the small electric appliance division from General Electric, the meaning of the name Black & Decker broadened from "electric power tools" to a more generalized "small powered electric equipment for the home."

Researchers report that the number of different products affiliated with a brand may actually strengthen the brand name, as long as the company manages quality across all brand extensions. Failure to do so is likely, in the long run, to negatively affect consumer confidence and evaluations of all the brand offerings.[13]

FAMILY BRANDING Family branding—the practice of marketing a whole line of company products under the same brand name—is another strategy that capitalizes on the con-

FIGURE 7-2

Product Line Extensions
Courtesy of Panama Jack
International

sumer's ability to generalize favorable brand associations from one product to the next. The Campbell's Soup Company, for example, continues to add new soup entrees to its product line under the Campbell's brand name, achieving ready acceptance for the new products from satisfied consumers of other Campbell's Soup products. The Ralph Lauren designer label on men's and women's clothing helps to achieve ready acceptance for these products in the upscale sportwear market.

You used to just peel it and drink it. Now guess what you can do with it.

Introducing a new way to cook. Florida orange and grapefruit juice are the healthy, creative ways to eliminate oils and fats while giving your meals more flavor. It'll even change the way you barbecue this summer. Check out the Florida Citrus Growers' *Fit, Fresh & Fast* recipe booklet in this magazine. It's full of delicious ideas, like marinating steak with citrus salsa, or spicing up barbecue chicken with a tangy orange glaze. No matter how you choose to cook with orange and grapefruit juice, indoors or out, they're bound to make your meals better than you ever could've guessed.

100% Pure Florida Orange Juice. To Your Health.

© State of Florida, Department of Citrus, 1995

FIGURE 7-3

Product Usage Extension
Courtesy of Florida Department of Citrus

Procter & Gamble (P&G) was built on the strength of its many individual brands in the same product category (e.g., laundry detergents and cleansers.) Now, however, it has begun to focus on the category-wide benefits of its products, using the combined weight of its brands to come up with a more powerful message directed against competitive products. To effectively manage this strategy, P&G is moving from *brand management* to *category management*.[14]

Retail private branding often achieves the same effect as family branding. For example, Wal-Mart used to advertise that its stores carried only "brands you trust." Now, the name Wal-Mart itself has become a "brand" that consumers have confidence in, and the name confers brand value on Wal-Mart's store brands.

LICENSING Licensing—allowing a well-known brand name to be affixed to products of another manufacturer—is a rapidly growing type of marketing strategy that operates on the principle of stimulus generalization. The names of designers, manufacturers, celebrities, and even cartoon characters are attached (i.e., "rented") to a variety of products for a fee, enabling the licensees to achieve instant recognition and implied quality for the licensed products. Some successful licensors include Jordache, Bill Blass, Calvin Klein, and Christian Dior, whose names appear on an exceptionally wide variety of products, from sheets to shoes and luggage to perfume. Figure 7-4 shows an ad for eyeglasses bearing the name of the well-known shoe manufacturer, Kenneth Cole.

Corporations also license their names and trademarks, usually for some form of brand extension, where the name of the corporation is licensed to the maker of a related product and thereby enters a new product category (e.g., Godiva chocolates licensed its name for Godiva Liqueur.) Corporations also license their names for purely promotional licensing, in which popular company logos (e.g., "Always Coca-Cola") are stamped on clothing, toys, mugs, and the like. Viacom, the giant entertainment conglomerate, was astounded by the number of licensing requests generated by the movie *Forrest Gump* for such products as Bubba Gump Shrimp, table-tennis sets, even books of Forrest Gump sayings.[15]

Municipal and state governments have begun licensing their names to achieve new sources of revenue. For example, the city of Atlanta licensed its name to Visa USA, which wanted to offer consumers the "official credit card" of the home of the 1996 Summer Olympics.[16] The Vatican Library has agreed to a lucrative licensing project that involves a variety of products from luggage to bed linens. The Mormon Church has begun expanding

FIGURE 7-4

Shoe Manufacturer
Licenses Its Name
Courtesy of Kenneth Cole Optical
Eyewear

its own licensing activities to apparel and home decorating items, and Britain's Queen Elizabeth II has agreed to extend the licensed name "House of Windsor" to furniture and Scottish throw rugs.[17]

The increase in licensing has made *counterfeiting* a booming business, as counterfeiters add well-known licensor names to a variety of products without benefit of contract or quality control, and then sell them as licensed goods. Aside from their loss of sales revenue because of counterfeiting, marketers also suffer the consequences associated with zero quality control over products that bear their names. For example, a counterfeit beer sold in China under the label Pabst Blue Ribbon was contaminated and resulted in at least one death and dozens of illnesses, thus endangering the quality image of Pabst worldwide.[18] Counterfeiting has spread to many product categories, and a great deal of counterfeit merchandise is virtually identical to the original. The *International Anticounterfeiting Coalition* estimated that counterfeit products accounted for $200 billion in lost sales for United States companies in 1994, up from $60 billion in 1987.[19]

Not only are marketers trying to generalize positive associations for their brand name through product line extensions and product category extensions, but some marketers are also trying to generalize the usage situations of their well-known brands. For example, Kellogg's is trying to persuade consumers that its dry cereals are good snack foods for any time of the day. Similarly, Florida citrus growers tried to persuade consumers that orange juice was "not just for breakfast anymore," and Coca-Cola tried to persuade consumers that Coke provided a good caffeine boost at breakfast.

▲ **Stimulus Discrimination** Stimulus discrimination is the opposite of stimulus generalization and results in the selection of a specific stimulus from among similar stimuli. The consumer's ability to discriminate among similar stimuli is the basis of positioning strategy, which seeks to establish a unique image for a brand in the consumer's mind.

Imitators want consumers to *generalize* their perceptions, but market leaders want to retain the top spot by convincing consumers to *discriminate*. Major marketers are constantly vigilant concerning store brand look-alikes, and they quickly file suit against retailers that they believe are cannibalizing their sales. For example, Chesebrough-Pond's, the Unilever division that markets Vaseline Intensive Care, filed suit against Venture Stores in St. Louis, alleging that the Venture store brand infringed on Vaseline Intensive Care's copyright, trademark, and packaging.

Conventional product differentiation strategies prescribe distinguishing a product or brand from that of competitors on the basis of an attribute that is relevant, meaningful, and valuable to consumers. However, many marketers also successfully differentiate their brands on an attribute that *appears* valuable but on closer examination is actually irrelevant to creating the implied benefit.[20] For example, Procter & Gamble differentiates Folger's instant coffee by its "flaked coffee crystals" created through a "unique, patented process"—implying that the coffee crystals improve the taste of the coffee. However, this "attribute" is irrelevant for instant coffee.

For companies that offer generic-type services (such as supermarkets or airlines, fast-food restaurants or credit card companies), stimulus discrimination is often key to survival.

It often is quite difficult to unseat a brand leader once stimulus discrimination has occurred. One explanation is that the leader is usually first in the market and has had a longer period to "teach" consumers (through advertising and selling) to associate the brand name with the product. In general, the longer the period of learning—of associating a brand name with a product—the more likely the consumer is to discriminate, and the less likely to generalize the stimulus. In our overcommunicated society, a key to stimulus discrimination is effective positioning. Figure 7-5 is an example of stimulus discrimination.

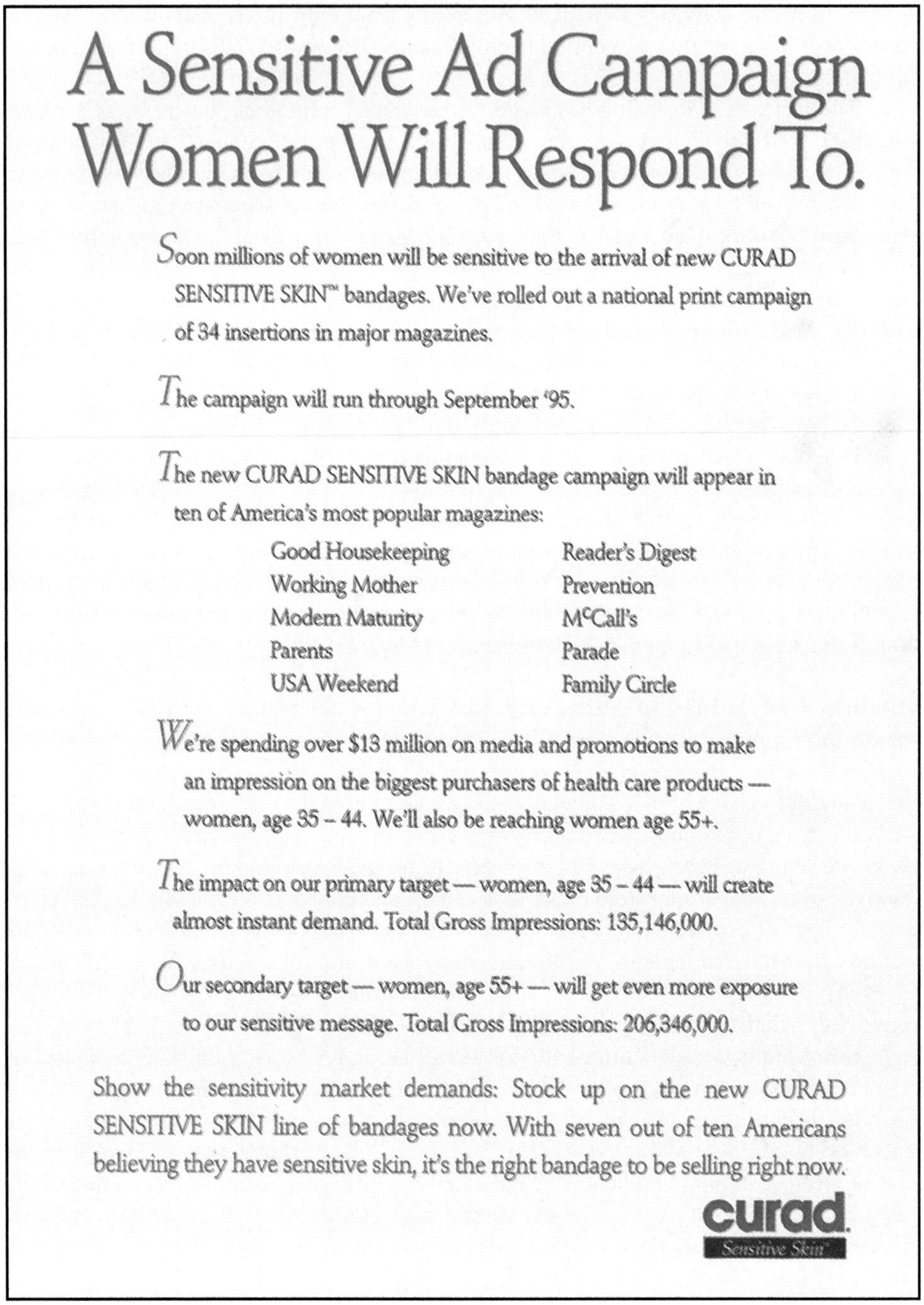

A Sensitive Ad Campaign Women Will Respond To.

Soon millions of women will be sensitive to the arrival of new CURAD SENSITIVE SKIN™ bandages. We've rolled out a national print campaign of 34 insertions in major magazines.

The campaign will run through September '95.

The new CURAD SENSITIVE SKIN bandage campaign will appear in ten of America's most popular magazines:

Good Housekeeping	Reader's Digest
Working Mother	Prevention
Modern Maturity	McCall's
Parents	Parade
USA Weekend	Family Circle

We're spending over $13 million on media and promotions to make an impression on the biggest purchasers of health care products — women, age 35 – 44. We'll also be reaching women age 55+.

The impact on our primary target — women, age 35 – 44 — will create almost instant demand. Total Gross Impressions: 135,146,000.

Our secondary target — women, age 55+ — will get even more exposure to our sensitive message. Total Gross Impressions: 206,346,000.

Show the sensitivity market demands: Stock up on the new CURAD SENSITIVE SKIN line of bandages now. With seven out of ten Americans believing they have sensitive skin, it's the right bandage to be selling right now.

curad.
Sensitive Skin

FIGURE 7-5

Stimulus Discrimination
Courtesy of Curad (Futuro Inc., A Beiersdorf Company)

▲ **Evaluation of Classical Conditioning** The principles of classical conditioning provide the theoretical underpinnings for many marketing applications. Repetition, stimulus generalization, and stimulus discrimination are useful concepts in explaining consumer behavior in the marketplace. However, they do not explain all the activities classified as consumer learning. Traditional classical conditioning assumes that consumers are passive beings who react with predictable responses to stimuli after a number of trials. Neo-Pavlovian theory views individuals as information seekers using logical and perceptual relationships among events, along with their own preconceptions, to form a sophisticated representation of their world. Although some of our purchase behavior—for example, the purchase of branded convenience goods—may have been shaped to some extent by repeated advertising messages, other purchase behavior results from evaluation of product alternatives. Our assessments of products are often based on the rewards we experience as a result of making specific purchases—in other words, from *instrumental conditioning*.

Instrumental Conditioning

The name most closely associated with **instrumental** *(operant)* **conditioning** is that of the American psychologist B. F. Skinner. According to Skinner, most individual learning occurs in a controlled environment in which individuals are "rewarded" for choosing an appropriate behavior. In consumer behavior terms, instrumental conditioning suggests that consumers learn by means of a trial-and-error process in which some purchase behaviors result in more favorable outcomes (i.e., rewards) than other purchase behaviors. A favorable experience is *instrumental* in teaching the individual to repeat a specific behavior.

Like Pavlov, Skinner developed his model of learning by working with animals. Small animals, such as rats and pigeons, were placed in his "Skinner box;" if they made appropriate movements (e.g., if they depressed levers or pecked keys), they received food (a positive reinforcement). Skinner and his many adherents have done amazing things with this simple learning model, including teaching pigeons to play ping-pong, and even to dance. In a marketing context, the consumer who tries several brands and styles of jeans before finding a style that fits her figure (positive reinforcement) has engaged in instrumental learning. Presumably, the brand that fits best is the one she will continue to buy. This model of instrumental conditioning is presented in Figure 7-6.

▲ **Positive and Negative Reinforcement** Skinner distinguished two types of reinforcement (or reward) that influence the likelihood that a response will be repeated. The first type, **positive reinforcement**, consists of events that strengthen the likelihood of a specific

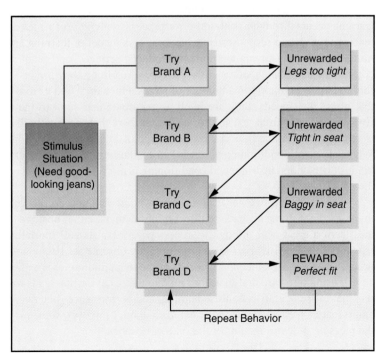

FIGURE 7-6

A Model of Instrumental Conditioning

response. Using a shampoo that leaves your hair feeling silky and clean is likely to result in a repeat purchase of the shampoo. **Negative reinforcement** is an unpleasant or negative outcome that also serves to *encourage* a specific behavior. An advertisement that shows a model with wrinkled skin is designed to encourage consumers to buy and use skin creams. Negative reinforcement should not be confused with **punishment**, which is designed to *discourage* behavior. For example, parking tickets are not negative reinforcement; they are a form of "punishment" designed to discourage drivers from parking illegally.

Fear appeals in ad messages are examples of negative reinforcement. Many life insurance commercials rely on negative reinforcement to encourage the purchase of life insurance: the ads warn husbands of the dire consequences to their wives and children in the event of their sudden death. Marketers of headache remedies use negative reinforcement when they illustrate the unpleasant symptoms of an unrelieved headache, as do marketers of mouthwash when they show the loneliness suffered by someone with bad breath. In each of these cases the consumer is encouraged to avoid the negative consequences by buying the advertised product. Either positive or negative reinforcement can be used to elicit a desired response. When a learned response is no longer reinforced, it diminishes to the point of **extinction**, that is, to the point at which it no longer occurs.

▲ **Massed or Distributed Learning** Another important influence on consumer learning is *timing*. Should a learning schedule be spread out over a period of time (**distributed learning**), or should it be "bunched up" all at once (**massed learning**)? The question is an important one for advertisers planning a media schedule, because massed advertising produces more initial learning, while a distributed schedule usually results in learning that persists longer. When advertisers want an immediate impact (e.g., to introduce a new product or to counter a competitor's blitz campaign), they generally use a massed schedule. However, when the goal is long-term repeat buying on a regular basis, a distributed schedule is preferable. Automobile manufacturers tend to use a combination of the two: they use concentrated (massed) advertising during the first few weeks of a new model introduction, then distributed advertising over the rest of the product year.

▲ **Evaluation of Instrumental Conditioning** Instrumental learning theorists believe that learning occurs through a trial-and-error process, with *habits* formed as a result of rewards received for certain responses or behaviors. This model of learning applies to many situations in which consumers learn about products, services, and retail stores. For example, consumers learn which stores carry the type of clothing they prefer at prices they can afford to pay by shopping in a number of stores. Once they find a store that carries clothing that meets their needs, they are likely to patronize that store to the exclusion of others. Every time they purchase a shirt or a sweater there that they really like, their store loyalty is rewarded (reinforced), and their patronage of that store is more likely to be repeated. While classical conditioning is useful in explaining how consumers learn very simple kinds of behaviors, instrumental conditioning is more helpful in explaining complex, goal-directed activities.

Critics of instrumental learning theory point out that a considerable amount of learning takes place in the absence of direct reinforcement, either positive or negative. Individuals learn a great deal through a process psychologists call **modeling** or **observational learning** (also called *vicarious learning*). They observe the behavior of others, remember it, and imitate it. Instrumental theorists argue that children learn in this way because they can envision a reward and therefore imitate the behavior that leads to it, but critics maintain that instrumentalists confuse learning and performance (behavior). Both children and adults learn a great deal that they do not act upon. Moreover, some people learn merely for the pleasure of learning, not for the sake of rewards.

Some researchers argue that because instrumental learning theory views behavior as a result of environmental manipulation rather than cognitive processes, it is applicable only to products that have little personal relevance or importance to the consumer. Other marketers claim that instrumental learning theory is applicable to products of both high and low relevance to the consumer.[21] (The question of product relevance will be discussed later in this chapter, in connection with *involvement theory.*)

COGNITIVE LEARNING THEORY

Not all learning takes place as the result of repeated trials. A considerable amount of learning takes place as the result of consumer thinking and problem solving. Sudden learning is also a reality. When confronted with a problem, we sometimes see the solution instantly. More often, however, we are likely to search for information on which to base a decision, and we evaluate what we learn carefully in order to make the best decision possible for our purposes. Learning based on mental activity is called **cognitive learning**.

Cognitive learning theory holds that the kind of learning most characteristic of human beings is problem solving, which enables individuals to gain some control over their environment. Unlike behavioral learning theory, cognitive theory holds that learning involves complex mental processing of information. Instead of stressing the importance of repetition or the association of a reward with a specific response, cognitive theorists emphasize the role of motivation and mental processes in producing a desired response.[22] Figure 7-7 on page 208 presents an ad designed to appeal to cognitive processing.

Information Processing

Just as a computer processes information received as input, so too does the human mind process the information it receives as input. **Information processing** is related to both the consumer's cognitive ability and the complexity of the information to be processed. Consumers process product information by attributes, brands, comparisons between brands, or a combination of these factors. While the attributes included in the brand's message and the number of available alternatives influence the intensity or degree of information processing, consumers with higher cognitive ability apparently acquire more product information and are more capable of integrating information on several product attributes than consumers with lesser ability.

Individuals also differ in terms of **imagery**; that is, in their ability to form mental images, and these differences influence their ability to recall information.[23] Individual differences in imagery processing can be measured with tests of *imagery vividness* (the ability to evoke clear images), *processing style* (preference for and frequency of visual versus verbal processing), and tests of *daydream* (fantasy) *content* and *frequency.*[24]

The more experience a consumer has with a product category, the greater his or her ability to make use of product information. Greater familiarity with the product category also increases cognitive ability and learning during a new purchase decision, particularly with regard to technical information.[25] This suggests that advertising of technical features, and technical evaluations of products (e.g., by *Consumer Reports*, have greater impact on the purchase decisions of consumers who are already knowledgeable about the product category than those who are not.

FIGURE 7-7

A Cognitive Appeal
Courtesy, Pharmacia & Upjohn and Ziggy & Friends, Inc.

▲ **How Consumers Store, Retain, and Retrieve Information** Of central importance to the processing of information is the human **memory**. A basic research concern of most cognitive scientists is discovering how information gets stored in memory, how it is retained, and how it is retrieved.

STRUCTURE OF MEMORY Because information processing occurs in stages, it is generally believed that there are separate "storehouses" in memory where information is kept temporarily before further processing: a *sensory store,* a *short-term store,* and a *long-term store.*

Sensory Store All data come to us through our senses; however, the senses do not transmit whole images like a camera; instead, each sense receives a fragmented piece of information (e.g., the smell, the color, the shape, the feel of a flower) and transmits it to the brain in parallel, where the perceptions of a single instant are synchronized and perceived as a single image, in a single moment of time.[26] The image of a sensory input lasts for just a second or two in the mind's **sensory store**. If it is not processed, it is lost immediately. As noted in Chapter 6, we are constantly bombarded with stimuli from the environment, and subconsciously block out a great deal of information that we do not "need" or cannot use. For marketers, this means that although it is relatively easy to get information into the consumer's sensory store, it is difficult to make a lasting impression. Furthermore, studies suggest that the brain automatically and unconsciously "tags" all perceptions with a value, either positive or negative; thus the evaluation, added to the perception in the first microsecond of cognition, tends to remain unless further information is processed.[27] This would explain why first impressions tend to last, and why marketers should not introduce products prematurely into the marketplace.

Short-Term Store The short-term store (now known as the **working memory**) is the stage of real memory in which information is processed and held for just a brief period. Anyone who has ever looked up a number in a telephone book, only to forget it just before dialing, knows how briefly information lasts in short-term storage. If information in the short-term store undergoes the process known as **rehearsal**, it is then transferred to the long-term store. (Rehearsal is defined as *the silent, mental repetition of information.*) The transfer process takes from two to ten seconds. If information is not rehearsed and transferred, it is lost in about 30 seconds or less. The amount of information that can be held in short-term storage is limited to about four or five items.

Long-Term Store In contrast to the short-term store, where information lasts only a few seconds, the long-term store retains information for relatively extended periods of time. Although it is possible to forget something within a few minutes after the information has reached long-term storage, it is more common for data in long-term storage to last for days, weeks, or even years. Almost all of us, for example, can remember the name of our first-grade teacher. Figure 7-8 depicts the transfer of information received by the sensory store, through the short-term store, to long-term storage.

Rehearsal and Encoding The amount of information available for delivery from short-term storage to the long-term store depends on the amount of *rehearsal* an individual gives to it. Failure to rehearse an input, either by repeating it or by relating it to other data, can cause fading and eventual loss of the information. Information can also be lost because of competition for attention. For example, if the short-term store receives a great number of inputs simultaneously from the sensory store, its capacity may be reduced to only two or three pieces of information.

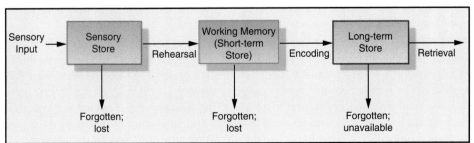

FIGURE 7-8

Information Processing and Memory Stores

The purpose of rehearsal is to hold information in short-term storage long enough for **encoding** to take place. *Encoding* is the process by which we select a word or visual image to represent a perceived object. Marketers, for example, help consumers encode brands by using brand symbols. Morton Salt uses a little girl with an umbrella on its packaging to symbolize its claim that the salt pours easily, even in rainy weather. A memorable brand name, such as Smucker's, can also aid in the consumer's encoding process.

"Learning" a picture takes less time than learning verbal information, but both types of information are important in forming an overall mental image. A print ad with both an illustration and body copy is more likely to be encoded and stored than an illustration without verbal information. A study that examined the effects of visual and verbal advertising found that when advertising copy and illustrations focus on different product attributes, the illustrations disproportionately influence consumer inferences.[28] Another study found that high-imagery copy had greater recall, whether or not it was accompanied by an illustration; for low-imagery copy, illustrations were an important factor in audience recall.[29]

A recent study found that the encoding of a commercial is related to the context of the TV program during which it is shown. Some parts of a program may require viewers to commit a larger portion of their cognitive resources to processing (e.g., when a dramatic event takes place versus a casual conversation). When viewers commit more cognitive resources to the program itself, they encode and store *less* of the information conveyed by a commercial. Thus, ads placed within or adjacent to a dramatic program setting may be more effective with a relatively low level of elaboration.[30]

Men and women exhibit different encoding patterns. For example, although women are more likely than men to recall TV commercials portraying a social relationship theme, there is no difference in recall among men and women for commercials that focus on the product itself.[31] One study showed that a greater number of concrete product attributes (i.e., actual features) rather than abstract attributes can be processed at one time.[32] Another study showed that knowledge concerning the *number* of positive and negative attributes a brand possesses (without going into the nature of the attributes themselves) can influence consumer judgment and choice.[33]

When consumers are presented with too much information (called **information overload**), they may encounter difficulty in encoding and storing it all. Findings suggest that it is difficult for consumers to remember product information from ads for new brands in heavily advertised categories.[34] Consumers can become cognitively overloaded when they are given a lot of information in a limited time. The result of this overload is confusion, resulting in poor purchase decisions. Studies have found that consumers make less effective choices when presented with too much information (also with too much high-quality information).[35] Other studies have found that consumers can handle large amounts of information without experiencing overload.[36] The apparent contradiction between these findings may be due to the absence of a precise definition as to how much information constitutes overload. Is it five items or fifteen items? One experiment that concluded that information overload causes consumers to become confused and make poor choices used ten to twenty-five choice alternatives and provided information on fifteen to twenty-five product attributes.[37] Given the amount of information provided the consumer-subjects, it is not surprising that they became confused. Research is needed to determine at what point information overload sets in for various subsets of consumers.

RETENTION Information does not just sit in long-term storage, waiting to be retrieved. Instead, information is constantly organized and reorganized as new links between chunks of information are forged. In fact, many information-processing theorists view the long-term store as a network consisting of nodes (i.e., concepts), with links among them. Figure 7-9 is a representation of long-term storage of information about personal computers, showing nodes (e.g., the concepts *models, monitors, manufacturers, software, operating systems, printers*) connected by links (e.g., for software: *word processing, data bases,*

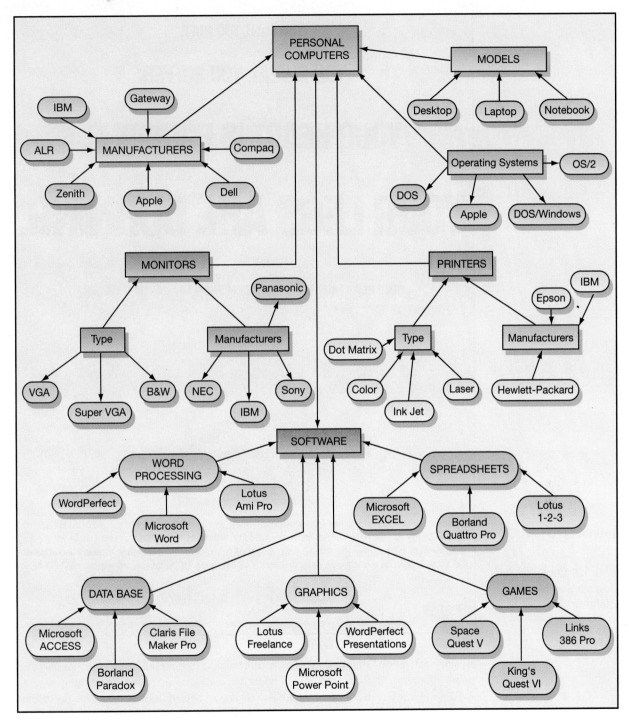

graphics, games, spreadsheets). As individuals gain more knowledge about computers, they expand their network of relationships, and sometimes their search for additional information. This process is known as **activation**, which involves relating new data to old to make the material more meaningful. Figure 7-10 shows an advertisement that encourages

FIGURE 7-10

Advertisement
Encouraging Memory
Activation
Courtesy of Lady Foot Locker/
Kinney Shoes

memory activation—the linking of new information to material already in storage. Consumer memory for the name of a product may also be activated by relating it to the spokesperson used in its advertising. The total package of associations brought to mind when a cue is activated is called a **schema**.

Product information stored in memory tends to be brand-based, and consumers interpret new information in a manner consistent with the way in which it is already organized.[38] Consumers are confronted with thousands of new products each year, and their information search often is dependent upon how similar or dissimilar (discrepant) these products are to product categories already stored in memory. One study found that at a moderate level of discrepancy, consumers are more likely to examine a relevant set of attributes in greater depth than to search for new information on a broader range of attributes.[39] Another study found that consumers have better recall of new product information for familiar brands.[40] This suggests that established brands have important advantages in advertising: consumers are more likely to recall the information they receive on new products bearing a familiar brand name, and their memory is less affected by exposure to competitive ads.

Consumers *recode* what they have already encoded to include larger amounts of information *(chunking).* For example, those individuals new to a computer keyboard must type letter by letter. Those with more experience type in chunks of whole words or phrases. It is important for marketers to discover the kinds and number of groupings (chunks) of information that consumers can handle. Recall may be hampered when the chunks offered in an advertisement do not match those in the consumer's frame of reference. The degree of prior knowledge is an important consideration. Experts can take in more complex chunks of information. Thus, the amount and type of information in a computer ad can be much more detailed in a magazine such as *PC Magazine* or *WIRED* than in a general-interest magazine such as *Time.*

Information is stored in long-term memory in two ways: **episodically** (i.e., by the order in which it is acquired) and **semantically** (according to significant concepts). Thus, we may remember having gone to a movie last Saturday because of our ability to store data *episodically,* and we may remember the plot, the stars, and the director because of our ability to store data *semantically.* A recent study found that when consumers have little knowledge about brands, *sequential exposure* to information about different brands produces different learning, depending on the order in which the information is received. The product attributes of later entries in a product category—although regarded as novel and attention-getting for the initial brand—seem to be redundant and uninteresting for the later entrants.[41] That is why the first brand in a new product category tends to retain the largest market share.

Many learning theorists believe that memories stored *semantically* are organized into frameworks by which we integrate new data with previous experience. For information about a new brand or model of fax machine to enter our memory, for example, we would have to relate it to our previous experience with faxes in terms of such qualities as speed, print quality, resolution, and memory.

RETRIEVAL Retrieval is the process by which we recover information from long-term storage. Most people have had the experience of being unable to remember something with which they are quite familiar. Information-processing theorists look on such **forgetting** as a failure of the retrieval system. A great deal of research is focused on how individuals retrieve information from memory. One study found that consumers tend to remember the product's *benefits,* rather than its *attributes.*[42] These findings suggest that advertising messages are most effective when they link the product's attributes with the benefits that consumers seek from the product.

Motivated consumers are likely to spend time interpreting and elaborating on information they find relevant to their needs; thus, they are likely to activate such relevant knowledge from long-term memory.[43] When consumers lack the ability to engage in extensive information processing, however, relatively low-level information may become influential, particularly when motivation is high.[44] When people retrieve information, they rarely search for negative information, although they sometimes do search for disconfirming information.[45]

The greater the number of competitive ads in a product category, the lower the recall of brand claims in a specific ad. These **interference** effects are caused by confusion with competing ads and result in a failure to retrieve.[46] One study found that ads can act as retrieval cues for a competitive brand.[47] An example of such consumer confusion occurred when consumers attributed the long-running and attention-getting television campaign featuring the Eveready Energizer Bunny to the leader in the field, Duracell.

Advertisements for competing brands or for other products made by the same manufacturer can lower the consumer's ability to remember advertised brand information. Such effects occur in response to even a small amount of advertising for similar products. *Interference* can depend on the consumer's previous experiences, prior knowledge of brand attribute information, and the amount of brand information available at the time of choice.[48] There are actually two kinds of interference. *New learning* can interfere with the retrieval of previously stored material, and *old learning* can interfere with the recall of recently learned material. With both kinds of interference, the problem is the similarity of old and new information. Advertising that creates a distinctive brand image can help consumers better retain and retrieve the message.

One stream of research has investigated the ability of incongruent advertising elements to provoke consumer memory. The findings suggest that incongruent elements—that is, unexpected elements—pierce the perceptual screen of consumers and improve the memorability of an ad when they are relevant to the advertising message.[49] For example, an ad for a brand of stain-resistant, easy-to-clean carpet shows an elegantly dressed couple in a beautiful dining-room setting where the man inadvertently knocks the food, the flowers, and the china crashing to the floor. The elegance of the actors and the upscale setting make the accident totally incongruent and unexpected, while the message remains highly relevant: that the mess can be cleaned up easily from the carpet and will leave no stain. Incongruent elements that are not relevant to an ad also pierce the consumer's perceptual screen but provide no memorability for the product. An ad showing a nude woman sitting on a piece of office furniture would very likely attract the consumer's attention but would provide no memorability for the product or the advertiser because of the irrelevance of the nudity to the advertising message.

There are times when a marketer would prefer that retrieval did not take place. This is particularly true when negative information or an unfounded rumor is publicized. In a laboratory simulation of the rumor that there were worms in McDonald's hamburgers, a refutational message that did not specifically mention the rumor was found to be more effective than a message that did. A refutational comment that specifically denied the allegations actually triggered the retrieval of the original rumor.[50]

Sometimes marketers encourage retrieval of negative information. Recognizing the negative publicity caused by the conviction of Leona Helmsley for income tax evasion, the Helmsley Hotel Corporation ran a series of ads with headlines such as "Say what you want about 'you know who', she runs a helluva hotel." The reader's effort to retrieve the "you know who" from memory brought to mind (i.e., activated) the long-running advertising campaign built on the theme that Mrs. Helmsley paid close attention to even the smallest details in her hotels' services. In this case, retrieval of negative information served to enhance the message.

▲ **Limited and Extensive Information Processing** For a long time, consumer researchers believed that all consumers passed through a complex series of mental and behavioral stages in arriving at a purchase decision. These stages ranged from awareness (exposure to information), to evaluation (preference, attitude formation), to behavior (purchase), to final evaluation (adoption or rejection). This same series of stages often is presented as the *consumer adoption process* (see Chapter 18).

A number of models have been developed over the years to express the same notion of sequential processing of information by consumers (see Figure 7-11). Initially, marketing theorists believed that sequential, extensive, and complex processing of information by consumers was applicable to all purchase decisions. However, on the basis of their own subjective experiences as consumers, some theorists began to realize that there were some

Figure 7-11 ▽ Models of Cognitive Learning

	Tricomponent Model	Promotional Model	Decision-making Model	Innovation Adoption Model	Innovation Decision Process
Sequential Stages of Processing	Cognitive	Attention	Awareness Knowledge	Awareness	Knowledge
	Affective	Interest Desire	Evaluation	Interest Evaluation	Persuasion
	Conative	Action	Purchase Postpurchase Evaluation	Trial Adoption	Decision Confirmation

purchase situations that simply did not call for extensive information processing and evaluation; that sometimes consumers simply went from awareness of a need to a routine purchase, without a whole lot of information search and mental evaluation. Such purchases were considered of minimal personal relevance, as opposed to highly relevant, search-oriented purchases. Purchases of minimal personal importance were called *low-involvement* purchases, and complex, search-oriented purchases were considered *high-involvement* purchases. The following section describes the development of **involvement theory** and discusses its applications to marketing strategy.

Involvement Theory

Involvement theory developed from a stream of research called **hemispheral lateralization,** or *split-brain theory.* The basic premise of split-brain theory is that the right and left hemispheres of the brain "specialize" in the kinds of information they process. The *left hemisphere* is primarily responsible for cognitive activities such as reading, speaking, and attributional information processing. Individuals who are exposed to verbal information cognitively analyze the information through left-brain processing and form mental images. Unlike the left hemisphere, the *right hemisphere* of the brain is concerned with nonverbal, timeless, pictorial, and holistic information.[51] Put another way, the left side of the brain is rational, active, realistic; the right side is emotional, metaphoric, impulsive, and intuitive.

▲ **High- and Low-Involvement Media** Building on the notion of hemispheral lateralization, a pioneer consumer researcher theorized that individuals passively process and store right-brain (i.e., nonverbal, pictorial) information—that is, without active involvement.[52] Because TV is primarily a pictorial medium, TV viewing was considered a right-brain activity (passive and holistic processing of images viewed on the screen), and TV itself was therefore a low-involvement medium. Passive learning was thought to occur through repeated exposures to a TV commercial (i.e., low-involvement information processing,) and to produce a change in consumer behavior (e.g., a product purchase) *prior* to a change in the consumer's attitude toward the product.

To extend this line of reasoning, cognitive (verbal) information is processed by the left side of the brain; thus, print media (i.e., newspapers and magazines) are high-involvement media. According to this theory, print advertising is processed in the complex sequence of cognitive stages depicted in classic models of information processing (i.e., high-involvement information processing.)

The right-brain, passive-processing-of-information theory is consistent with classical conditioning. Through repetition, the product is paired with a visual image (e.g., a distinctive package) to produce the desired response: purchase of the advertised brand. According to this theory, in situations of passive learning (generated by low-involvement media), repetition is all that is needed to produce purchase behavior. This behavior, in turn, is likely to lead to a favorable attitude toward the product.[53] In marketing terms, the theory suggests that television commercials are most effective when they are of short duration and repeated frequently, thus ensuring brand familiarity without provoking detailed evaluation of the message content.

The right-brain processing theory stresses the importance of the visual component of advertising, including the creative use of symbols. Thus, highly visual TV commercials, packaging, and in-store displays generate familiarity with the brand and induce purchase behavior. For example, Procter & Gamble runs brief detergent commercials that contain numerous visual symbols with great repetition. Consumers instantly recognize the P&G packaging they have passively "learned" through TV advertising; the familiar package promotes purchase behavior.

Research evidence confirms the fact that pictorial cues (which activate right-brain processing) are more effective at generating recall and familiarity with the product, while verbal cues (which trigger left-brain processing) generate cognitive activity that encourages consumers to evaluate the advantages and disadvantages of the product.[54]

There are limitations to the application of split-brain theory to media strategy. Research suggests that the right and left hemispheres of the brain do not operate independently of each other, but work together to process information. Some individuals are *integrated processors* (they readily engage both hemispheres during information processing.) Integrated processors show greater overall recall of both the verbal and visual portions of print ads than individuals who exhibit more "specialized" processing (i.e., right *or* left hemispheral processing).[55] Figure 7-12 presents an ad that builds on the notion of integrated processing; it shows an illustration and provocative headline on one page, and a block of body copy explaining the headline on the facing page.

One stream of research suggests that, despite hemispheral specialization, both sides of the brain are capable of high *and* low involvement: the left side of the brain in high and low *cognitive* processing, the right side in high and low *affective* processing.[56] An example of high-involvement affective processing is seen when an individual is exposed to a highly emotional or fantasy-laden stimulus, such as the emotionally arousing ad shown in Figure 7-13 on page 218. An example of low-involvement cognitive processing might involve a simple, single-attribute print advertisement. This theory also suggests that both sides of the brain simultaneously process information, although at different levels of involvement. For example, there is some initial engagement of the right brain in a high-involvement *cognitive* condition and, similarly, some engagement of the left brain in a high-involvement *affective* condition.

▲ **Involvement Theory and Consumer Relevance** From the conceptualization of high- and low-involvement media, involvement theory next focused on the consumer's involvement with products and purchases. It was briefly hypothesized that there are high- and low-involvement consumers; then, that there are high- and low-involvement purchases. These two approaches led to the notion that a consumer's level of involvement depends on the degree of personal relevance that the product holds for that consumer. Under this definition, high-involvement purchases are those that are very important to the consumer (e.g., in terms of *perceived risk*) and thus provoke extensive problem solving (information pro-

cessing). An automobile and a dandruff shampoo both may represent high-involvement purchases under this scenario; the automobile because of high perceived financial risk, the shampoo because of high perceived social risk. Low-involvement purchases are purchases that are not very important to the consumer, hold little relevance and little perceived risk, and thus provoke very limited information processing.

Two theories that illustrate the concepts of extensive and limited problem solving for high- and low-involvement purchase situations are the *central and peripheral routes to persuasion theory* and the *social judgment theory.*

CENTRAL AND PERIPHERAL ROUTES TO PERSUASION The major premise of the *central and peripheral routes to persuasion theory* is that consumers are more likely to weigh information about a product (or service) carefully and to devote considerable cognitive effort to evaluating it when they are highly involved with the product category.[57] The theory suggests that there is a strong likelihood that consumers will carefully evaluate the merits and/or weaknesses of a product when the purchase is of high relevance to them. Conversely, the likelihood is great that consumers will engage in very limited information search and evaluation when the purchase holds little relevance or importance for them. Thus, for *high-involvement* purchases, the **central route to persuasion**—provoking considered thought about the product—is likely to be a highly effective marketing strategy. For *low-involvement* purchases, the **peripheral route to persuasion** is likely to be more effective. In this instance, because the consumer is less motivated to exert cognitive effort,

FIGURE 7-13

Emotionally Arousing
Ads Encourage High-
Involvement Affective
Processing
Courtesy of CompuServe

You can get your feet wet, or plumb unimaginable depths.

In a way, it's a lot like CompuServe.

CompuServe members who join for the basics quickly discover an ocean of opportunity. Like at-home shopping, financial data, travel information and reservations, and entertainment, and free time to sharpen their online skills.

Computer professionals who join to access a wealth of high-tech expertise find much more. Like sophisticated research tools, hardware and software support forums, and lots of free software and share-ware. In fact, no other information service offers the number and quality of choices that CompuServe does.

Now, for just $8.95 a month, and a one-time membership fee, you get all the basics as often as you like: news, sports, weather, shopping, a com-plete encyclopedia, and much more, plus up to 60 E-mail messages a month. And, there are lots of other valuable services available on a nominal pay-as-you-use basis.

To make the right choice in selecting an inter-active service, pick the one that will always help you get the most out of your computer. For more infor-mation or to order CompuServe, see your computer dealer or call 1 800 848-8199. Outside the United States, call 614 457-0802.

CompuServe
The information service you won't outgrow.℠

learning is more likely to occur through repetition, the passive processing of visual cues, and holistic perception.

Various researchers have addressed the relationship between the central and periph-eral routes to persuasion theory and consumer information processing. For example, a number of studies have found that high involvement with an issue produces more exten-sive processing of information. In these situations, the quality of the argument presented in the persuasive message was very influential to the decision outcome.[58] That would explain why highly involved consumers tend to use more attributes to evaluate brands, while less involved consumers apply very simple decision rules.[59]

The Elaboration Likelihood Model The Elaboration Likelihood Model (ELM) suggests that a person's level of involvement during message processing is a critical factor in determining which route to persuasion is likely to be effective. For example, as the mes-sage becomes more personally relevant (that is, as involvement increases), people are more willing to expend the cognitive effort required to process the message arguments.

Thus, when involvement is high, consumers follow the *central route* and base their attitudes or choices on the message arguments. When involvement is low, they follow the *peripheral route* and rely more heavily on other message elements (e.g., spokespersons or background music) to form attitudes or make product choices. Figure 7-14 shows an ad using the central route to persuasion; Figure 7-15 on page 220 shows an ad taking the peripheral route to persuasion. One study found that comparative ads (see Chapter 10) are more likely to be processed centrally (purposeful processing of message arguments) while noncomparative ads are commonly processed peripherally (with little message elaboration, and a response derived from other executional elements in the ad).[60]

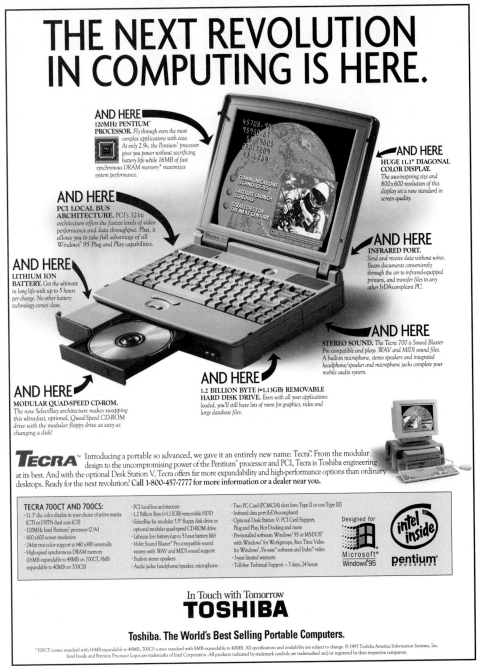

FIGURE 7-14

Ad Using the Central Route to Persuasion
Courtesy of Toshiba

FIGURE 7-15

Ad Using the Peripheral
Route to Persuasion
Courtesy of Sasson Jeans, Inc.

The marketing implications of the *elaboration likelihood model* are clear: for high-involvement purchases, marketers should use arguments stressing the strong, solid, high-quality attributes of their products—thus using the central (i.e., highly cognitive) route. For low-involvement purchases, marketers should use the peripheral route to persuasion, focusing on the method of presentation rather than on the content of the message (e.g., through the use of celebrity spokespersons or highly visual and symbolic advertisements).

SOCIAL JUDGMENT THEORY The central premise of **social judgment theory** is that an individual's processing of information about an issue is determined by his or her involvement with the issue.[61] Individuals who are highly involved with an issue or who have a strong or definite opinion will accept very few alternative opinions (i.e., they have a *narrow latitude of acceptance* and a *wide latitude of rejection*). Highly involved individuals will interpret a message that is congruent with their positions as more positive than it actually is (the **assimilation** effect), and one that is not congruent as more negative than it actually is (the **contrast** effect). Chapter 9 discusses the *assimilation contrast* theory in greater detail.

Persons who are uninvolved with an issue will be more receptive to arguments both for and against (they will have a *wide latitude of acceptance*) or they will take no position at all (they will have a *wide latitude of noncommitment*).

Thus, social judgment theory suggests that highly involved consumers find fewer brands acceptable (they are *narrow categorizers*) and are likely to interpret advertisements about these brands in a manner that is congruent with their previous experiences and opinions about the product. The uninvolved consumer is likely to be receptive to a greater number of messages regarding the purchase and will consider more brands (be a *broad categorizer*).[62] This type of person is less likely to be brand loyal and is a likely target for brand switching.

▲ **Evaluation of Involvement Theory** As the previous sections describe, involvement theory has evolved from the notion of high- and low-involvement *media,* to high- and low-involvement *consumers,* to high- and low-involvement *products* and *purchases,* to appropriate *methods of persuasion* in situations of high and low involvement. Although the theories themselves appear to be straightforward, it is difficult to operationalize them for marketing strategy applications because of the great variation in the conceptualization and measurement of *involvement* itself. There is no single, widely accepted meaning of involvement, because the term has been neither carefully defined nor conceptualized.[63] For example, one review identified five types of involvement: ego involvement, commitment, communication involvement, purchase importance, and extent of information search.[64] Another review identified involvement theory with advertising, with products, and with purchase decisions.[65] Some researchers see the person, product, and situation as the major components of involvement.[66] Others define low involvement as purchase situations in which there is little information search and no attitude formation regarding the product prior to purchase.[67] Some studies have tried to differentiate between brand involvement and product involvement.[68] Others differentiate between situational, enduring, and response involvement.[69]

Despite the lack of agreement about the definition of involvement, it generally is regarded as an important consumer behavior construct and receives a great deal of research attention. However, definition is not the only problem; there are also problems of measurement. Researchers who regard involvement as a cognitive state are concerned with the measurement of ego involvement, risk perception, and purchase importance. Researchers who focus on the behavioral aspects of involvement measure such factors as the search for and evaluation of product information.[70] Some researchers consider decision time an effective measure of involvement.[71] Others argue that involvement should be measured by the degree of importance the product has to the buyer.[72] One study concluded that since there really are so many different kinds of consumer involvement, researchers should measure an *involvement profile,* rather than a single involvement level.[73] The suggested profile would include interest in the product, the rewarding nature (e.g., perceived pleasure) of the product, its perceived ability to reflect the purchaser's personality, and the perceived risk associated with the purchase.[74] This view is consistent with the notion that involvement should be measured on a continuum, rather than as a dichotomy consisting of two mutually exclusive categories of "high" and "low" involvement.[75] Another study suggests three dimensions in the measurement of involvement: importance, pleasure, and risk.[76]

A new conceptualization of involvement proposes that involvement be defined as the *mobilization of behavioral resources* (physical, mental, and energy resources) for the achievement of a personally relevant goal to the extent that three conditions are met simultaneously: the goal is *subjectively relevant,* and the *perceived ability* and *perceived opportunity* to achieve that goal are viewed as favorable.[77] A college student may want to take a round-the-world trip after graduation (a subjectively relevant goal) and perceives his ability and opportunity to earn sufficient money to do so as favorable. Thus, he would engage in extensive problem solving to find a way to achieve his goal. Another student may have the same desire to travel around the world, but perceives her chances of earning enough money to do so as an impossible dream; thus, she is unlikely to spend much time in problem-solving. The extensive problem solver would be highly involved; the limited problem solver would have little involvement.

Despite the definitional and measurement problems described, involvement theory has a number of intuitively useful applications for the marketer. For example, the left-brain (cognitive processing)-right-brain (passive processing) paradigm seems to have strong implications for the content, length, and presentation of both print and television advertisements. There is evidence that people process information extensively when the purchase is of high personal relevance, and engage in limited information processing when the purchase is of low personal relevance. Uninvolved consumers appear to be susceptible to different kinds of persuasion than highly involved consumers.

Before the degree of involvement can be identified, the researcher must define exactly what it is that should be measured—ego, motivation, task involvement, situational variables, or what. It is clear that solid and widely accepted measures of product involvement (relevance) need to be developed.

BRAND LOYALTY

A major goal of marketers interested in how consumers learn is to encourage **brand loyalty**. Brand-loyal customers provide the basis for a stable and growing market share and can be a major intangible asset reflected in the purchase price of a company. A study of consumer purchase habits reported that brands with larger market shares have proportionately larger groups of loyal buyers.[78]

As straightforward as it may seem, brand loyalty is not a simple concept. A basic issue among researchers is whether to define the concept in terms of consumer *behavior* or consumer *attitudes*. To cognitive learning theorists, behavioral definitions (e.g., *frequency of purchase* or *proportion of total purchases*) lack precision, because they do not distinguish between the "real" brand-loyal buyer who is intentionally faithful, and the spurious brand-loyal buyer who repeats a brand purchase because it is the only one available at the store. Such theories say that brand loyalty must be measured by attitudes toward a brand, rather than by purchase consistency.

One study measured brand loyalty in three different ways: brand market share, the number of same-brand purchases in a 6-month period, and the average number of brands bought per buyer. Findings suggest that consumers buy from a mix of brands within their acceptable range (i.e., their *evoked set*, discussed in Chapter 19). Thus, the greater the number of acceptable brands in a specific product category, the less likely the consumer is to be brand loyal to one specific brand. Conversely, products having few competitors, as well as those purchased with great frequency, are likely to have greater brand loyalty.[79] Thus, a more favorable attitude toward a brand, service, or store, compared to potential alternatives, together with repeat patronage, are seen as the requisite components of customer loyalty.

An integrated conceptual framework views consumer loyalty as the relationship between an individual's *relative attitude* toward an entity (brand, service, store, or vendor) and *patronage behavior*.[80] The consumer's relative attitude consists of two dimensions: the strength of the attitude and the degree of attitudinal differentiation among competing brands. The consumer's relative attitude, and degree of repeat patronage, comprise his or her customer loyalty. As Figure 7-16 indicates, a consumer with a high relative attitude and high degree of repeat patronage would be defined as loyal; a consumer with a low relative attitude and high repeat patronage would be considered spuriously loyal. An example of

FIGURE 7-16

Brand Loyalty As a
Function of Relative
Attitude and Patronage
Behavior
Source: ALAN S. DICK and KUNAL
BASU, "Customer Loyalty: Toward
an Integrated Framework," *Journal
of the Academy of Marketing
Science* 22(2), 1994, 101.
Copyright © 1994 by Journal of
the Academy of Marketing
Science. Reprinted by permission
of Sage Publications.

		Repeat Patronage	
		High	Low
Relative Attitude	High	Loyalty	Latent Loyalty
	Low	Spurious Loyalty	No Loyalty

such spurious loyalty would be a consumer who perceives little differentiation among brands in a low involvement category and undertakes repeat brand purchases on the basis of situational cues, such as package familiarity, shelf positioning, or special prices.

Along these same lines, some theorists suggest that brand loyalty is correlated with the consumer's degree of involvement: high involvement leads to extensive information search and, ultimately, to brand loyalty, whereas low involvement leads to exposure and brand awareness, and then possibly to brand habits.[81] As a customer's satisfaction with and repeat purchases of a product increases, the search for information about alternative brands decreases.

Evidence suggests that loyal consumers—those who have a strong commitment to a brand, a service, or retail store—show strong resistance to counterpersuasion attempts. A syndicated research company reported that 74 percent of its respondents resist promotional efforts by rival brands once they find a brand with which they are satisfied.[82]

Food products found to have over 80 percent of brand-loyal users (defined as exclusive, one-brand users) include table salt, vinegar, nonstick cooking spray, dry milk, powdered breakfast drinks, and egg substitutes. Nonfood grocery products with over 80 percent brand-loyal users include waxed paper, oven cleaners, spot removers, and pet shampoos. One study concluded that brand loyalty tends to be time-dependent, that is, consumers can be brand loyal during one period of time and not another.[83]

Developing Brand Loyalty

Behavioral scientists who favor the theory of instrumental conditioning believe that brand loyalty results from an initial product trial that is reinforced through satisfaction, leading to repeat purchase. Cognitive researchers, on the other hand, emphasize the role of mental processes in building brand loyalty. They believe that consumers engage in extensive problem-solving behavior involving brand and attribute comparisons, leading to a strong brand preference and repeat purchase behavior.

Some studies have indicated that there is little difference in demographics between consumers who are brand loyal and those who are not.[84] Others have found that brand-loyal consumers are older, have higher incomes, and experience greater perceived risk.[85] Some ethnic groups are loyal to ethnic brands and to ethnic retailers; for example, Hispanics have been loyal to Goya products for generations, and Chinese-American consumers prefer shopping in Chinese-operated retail stores.

Marketers are interested not only in *how* brand loyalty develops, but also in *when* it develops. Research evidence suggests that a great deal of brand loyalty develops quite early, in the context of family life. Classic toys—Lego blocks, Barbie dolls, Lionel trains, GI Joes—enjoyed renewed popularity as baby boomers flocked to buy their children the toys they best remembered. Indeed, nostalgia has become an important advertising appeal for the baby boomer market.

Marketers must be careful not to impose unilateral changes on products that have a loyal following. The Coca-Cola Company discovered this in its classic marketing blunder in 1985, when it suffered an angry consumer backlash to its replacement of the original Coca-Cola formula with a newly formulated Coke. Procter & Gamble had to bring back its original green Prell shampoo after loyal consumers rebelled at a new blue formulation.[86]

▲ **Declining Brand Loyalty** Many marketing managers are concerned with a growing trend toward *brand switching*. Among the reasons given for the decline in brand loyalty are consumer boredom or dissatisfaction with a product, the constant availability of new product offerings, and an increased concern with price. In this era of lower-priced "value" brands, the market share of private label brands has increased in categories once considered the bastion of brand loyalty.[87] For this reason, many national brand marketers are upgrading their premium-priced national brands to distinguish them from private labels, and promoting them aggressively.

Declines in brand loyalty are also attributed to the increase in comparative advertising, increased targeting of specialty niches, and the increased diversity of supermarket shoppers. There also has been a tremendous increase in sales promotion "deals." In trying to increase market share, many companies have spent a greater proportion of their promotion budget on sales promotion (e.g., coupons, special price deals, sweepstakes, free samples, point-of-purchase displays) than on advertising. Yet advertising is a major source of information for consumers. Without advertising, it is unlikely that consumers would "learn" about new products and their attributes. Although promotional activities may boost sales in the short run, evidence suggests that brand-loyal consumers take advantage of such temporary price deals to increase their purchases (cannibalizing full-price sales), whereas deal-prone customers who succumb to a temporary inducement are quick to switch to another brand when the special offer ends or a better deal comes along. Thus, while sales promotion efforts do increase market share in the short run, they are unlikely to hold deal-prone consumers in the long run.

Many marketers believe it is more difficult to establish service brand loyalty than product brand loyalty. Some service organizations have started to promote consistency of operation and convenience in an effort to combat shifting loyalties. Others have adopted such sales promotion devices as frequent-user credits (e.g., frequent-flier programs, frequent-guest programs, even frequent-diner programs) to encourage brand loyalty.

Because of the importance of brand imagery to brand loyalty, many marketers develop a simple, descriptive promotional line (e.g., "The Friendly Skies") and, through heavy repetition, engrave it in consumers' memories. By using such everyday advertising tools as mnemonic devices, jingles, rhymes, and audience participation, marketers increase brand name rehearsal and enhance brand memory, even for low-involvement products.[88]

Despite the diversity of viewpoints among learning theorists, most marketers are interested in all measures of brand loyalty. They are concerned with actual consumer purchasing patterns, with consumer beliefs and opinions concerning their brand and competing brands, and with knowing how important the product is to the consumer. Developing a highly consistent market share of brand-loyal consumers is the ultimate goal of marketing strategy. Discovering how consumers learn about brands and become attached to certain brands assists marketers in achieving this goal.

Brand Equity

The term **brand equity** refers to the value inherent in a well-known brand name. From a consumer's perspective, brand equity is the *added value bestowed on the product by the brand name*.[89] Brand equity facilitates the acceptance of new products and the allocation of preferred shelf space, and enhances perceived value, perceived quality, and premium pricing options. For many companies, their most valuable assets are their brand names. Because of the escalation of new product costs and the high rate of new product failures, many companies prefer to leverage their brand equity through brand extensions, rather than risk launching a new brand.

Because a brand that has been promoted heavily in the past retains a cumulative level of name recognition, companies buy, sell, and rent (i.e., license) their brand names, knowing that it is easier to buy than to create a brand name with enduring strength. Table 7-1 presents the 20 most valuable brands of 1993, as compiled by *Financial World*.

Brand equity enables companies to charge a price premium—an additional amount over and above the price of an identical store brand. For example, researchers have estimated that, because of Colgate's brand equity, the Colgate-Palmolive Company is able to price the Colgate brand toothpaste about 37 cents higher than competitive store brands with objectively identical attributes.[90]

A relatively new strategy among some marketers is **co-branding** (also called *double branding*.) The basis of co-branding, in which two brand names are featured on a single product (e.g., Kellogg's Pop-Tarts with Smucker's fruit filling), is to use another product's brand equity to enhance the primary brand's equity. For example, Cranberry Newtons is a product of Nabisco and Ocean Spray, bearing both brand names. Some experts believe that using a second brand's equity may imply that the host brand can no longer stand on its own.[91] Others question whether a co-branded product causes consumer confusion as to who actually makes the product and whether the host brand can survive if the second brand endorsement is taken away.

table 7-1   The Twenty Most Valuable Brands of 1993

BRAND	BRAND VALUE (MILLIONS)	1993 RANK	1992 RANK
Coca-Cola	$35,950	1	2
Marlboro	33,045	2	1
Nescafe	11,549	3	4
Kodak	10,020	4	7
Microsoft	9,842	5	8
Budweiser	9,724	6	5
Kellogg's	9,372	7	6
Motorola	9,293	8	13
Gillette	8,218	9	11
Bacardi	7,163	10	14
Hewlett-Packard	6,996	11	16
Intel	6,480	12	21
Frito-Lay	5,907	13	18
Pampers	5,732	14	12
QE	5,710	15	17
Nintendo	5,224	16	23
Levi's	5,142	17	20
Pepsi	4,939	18	19
Campbell's	4,636	19	22
Newport	4,287	20	9

Source: ALEXANDRA OURUSOFF, "Brands: What's Hot. What's Not," *Financial World*, August 2, 1994, 44. Reprinted from Financial World. Copyright 1994. All rights reserved.

Well-known brand names are referred to as **mega-brands**. Among the best known brands are Campbell's Soup, Hallmark Cards, United Parcel Service, Hershey's, and McDonald's. Their names have become "cultural icons" and enjoy powerful advantages over the competition. To enhance the brand equity of their largest brands, some marketers are adopting a strategy of *brand consolidation*. For example, Procter & Gamble has folded its White Cloud bathroom tissue into its Charmin brand; it has also merged its Solo brand laundry detergent into Bold, and its Puritan cooking oil into the larger Crisco line.

Brand equity is important to marketers because it leads to brand loyalty, which in turn leads to increased market share and greater profits. To marketers, the major function of learning theory is to teach consumers that their product is best, to encourage repeat purchase, and, ultimately, to develop loyalty to the brand name.

summary

Consumer learning is the process by which individuals acquire the purchase and consumption knowledge and experience they apply to future related behavior. Although some learning is intentional, much learning is incidental. Basic elements that contribute to an understanding of learning are motivation, cues, response, and reinforcement.

There are two schools of thought as to how individuals learn: behavioral theories and cognitive theories. Both contribute to an understanding of consumer behavior. Behavioral theorists view learning as observable responses to stimuli, while cognitive theorists believe that learning is a function of mental processes.

Two types of behavioral learning theories are classical conditioning and instrumental conditioning. The principles of classical conditioning that provide theoretical underpinnings for many marketing applications include repetition, stimulus generalization, and stimulus discrimination. Neo-Pavlovian theories view traditional classical conditioning as associative learning rather than as reflexive action.

Instrumental learning theorists believe that learning occurs through a trial-and-error process in which positive outcomes (i.e., rewards) result in repeat behavior. Both positive and negative reinforcement can be used to encourage the desired behavior. The timing of learning schedules influences how long the learned material is retained. Massed learning produces more initial learning than distributed learning; however, learning usually persists longer with distributed (i.e., spread-out) reinforcement schedules.

Cognitive learning theory holds that the kind of learning most characteristic of humans is problem solving. Cognitive theorists are concerned with how information is processed by the human mind: how it is stored, retained, and retrieved. A simple model of the structure and operation of memory suggests the existence of three separate storage units: a sensory store, a short-term store (i.e., working memory), and a long-term store. The processes of memory include rehearsal, encoding, storage, and retrieval.

Involvement theory proposes that people engage in limited information processing in situations of low importance or relevance to them, and in extensive information processing in situations of high relevance. Hemispheral lateralization theory gave rise to the theory that TV is a low-involvement medium that results in passive learning, and that print, as a high-involvement medium, encourages more cognitive information processing.

A basic issue among researchers is whether to define brand loyalty in terms of consumers' behavior or consumers' attitudes toward the brand. Brand equity refers to the inherent value a brand name has in the marketplace. Marketers are consolidating their brands to enhance brand equity and to encourage brand loyalty in the face of a proliferation of private brands. For marketers, the purposes of understanding how consumers learn are to teach them that their brand is best, and to develop brand loyalty.

discussion questions

1. **a.** How can the principles of classical conditioning theory and neo-Pavlovian theory be applied to the development of marketing strategies?

   b. How is the classical conditioning concept of repetition applied to advertising?

2. Kraft Foods uses family branding, but Procter & Gamble (which makes Crest, Duncan Hines, Charmin, and Tide) does not. Yet, both companies are successful. Describe in learning terms the conditions under which family branding is a good policy and those under which it is not. What do you think are the reasons for the difference in family-branding policies between Kraft and P&G?

3. The Gillette Company, which produces the highly successful Sensor shaving blade, has recently introduced the Gillette Series consisting of shaving cream, skin conditioner, antiperspirant, and deodorant. How can the company use stimulus generalization to market these products? Is instrumental conditioning applicable to this marketing situation?

4. Which theory of learning (i.e., classical conditioning, instrumental conditioning, or cognitive learning) best explains the following consumption behaviors: (a) buying a pack of chewing gum, (b) preferring to fly on a particular airline, (c) buying a personal computer for the first time, and (d) buying a new car? Explain your choices.

5. **a.** Define the following memory structures: sensory store, working memory, and long-term store. Apply each of these concepts to the development of an advertising strategy.

   b. How does information overload affect the consumer's ability to comprehend an ad and store it in his or her memory?

6. Discuss the differences between low- and high-involvement media. How would you apply the knowledge of hemispheral lateralization to the design of TV commercials and print advertisements?

7. **a.** A cereal marketer is trying to use the concept of high- and low-involvement to target market segments. How should the marketer measure consumers' level of involvement with cereal?

   b. Can social judgment theory be used to market cereal more effectively? Explain your answer.

8. **a.** How can a marketer distinguish between real and spurious brand-loyal buyers? Is it important for marketers to measure and understand the differences between the two groups? Why or why not?

   b. Describe the marketing errors in advertising, pricing, and in-store promotions that might occur if a marketer fails to distinguish between the two groups.

exercises

1. Imagine you are the instructor in this course and that you are trying to increase students' participation in class discussions. How would you use reinforcement to achieve your objective?

2. Visit a supermarket. Can you identify any packages in which the marketer's knowledge of stimulus generalization and stimulus discrimination was incorporated into the package design? Note these examples and present them in class.

3. How many jingles for products and services can you recall? Make a list of them. Show the list to a friend. Can your friend recall these jingles? Can he or she recall more jingles or different jingles than you? How would you explain the differences between the two patterns of recall?

4. Compare and contrast limited and extensive problem solving. Relate the stages of one model described in Figure 7-11 to a recent purchase you have made.

5. Discuss a recent product purchase you regard as high involvement and another one you view as low involvement with three fellow classmates. Do they agree with your selections? Describe how their points of view may be related to their: (a) brand loyalty, (b) frequency of use, (c) price paid, (d) recollection of ads for the same products, (e) the product features they consider the most important, and (f) the risk associated with the purchase.

key words

- Activation
- Advertising wearout
- Assimilation-contrast theory
- Behavioral learning theory
- Brand equity
- Brand loyalty
- Broad categorizer
- Central and peripheral routes to persuasion
- Classical conditioning
- Cognitive associative learning
- Cognitive learning theory
- Conditioned response
- Conditioned stimulus
- Distributed learning
- Elaboration Likelihood Model (ELM)
- Encoding
- Episodically stored information
- Extensive information processing
- Family branding
- Hemispheral lateralization
- High- and low-involvement media
- Information overload
- Information processing
- Instrumental conditioning
- Involvement theory
- Licensing
- Limited information processing
- Massed learning
- Memory
- Modeling or observational learning
- Motivation, cues, response and reinforcement
- Narrow categorizer
- National brands
- Negative reinforcement
- Neo-Pavlovian theory
- Operant conditioning
- Positive reinforcement
- Product, line, form, and category extensions
- Rehearsal
- Retention
- Retrieval
- Schema
- Semantically stored information
- Sensory, short term, and long term stores
- Social judgment theory
- Split brain theory
- Stimulus discrimination
- Stimulus generalization
- Stimulus-Response theory
- Three-hit theory
- Unconditioned response
- Unconditioned stimulus
- Vicarious learning
- Working memory

end notes

1. TERENCE A. SHIMP, "Neo-Pavlovian Conditioning and Its Implications for Consumer Theory and Research," in Thomas S. Robertson and Harold H. Kassarjian, eds., *Handbook of Consumer Behavior* (New Jersey: Prentice-Hall, Inc., 1991), 162–87.
2. ROBERT A. RESCORLA, "Pavlovian Conditioning, It's Not What You Think It Is," *American Psychologist* 43(3), March 1988, 151–60.
3. N. J. MACKINTOSH, *Conditioning and Associative Learning* (New York: Oxford University Press, 1983), 10.
4. SHIMP, op. cit., p. 171.
5. Ibid.
6. CHRIS JANISZEWSKI and LUK WARLOP, "The Influence of Classical Conditioning Procedures on Subsequent Attention to the Conditioned Brand," *Journal of Consumer Research* 20, September 1993, 171–89.
7. DAVID W. SCHUMANN, RICHARD E. PETTY, and D. SCOTT CLEMONS, "Predicting the Effectiveness of Different Strategies of Advertising Variation: A Test of the Repetition-Variation Hypothesis," *Journal of Consumer Research* 17, September 1990, 192–202.
8. Ibid. See also H. RAO UNNAVA and ROBERT E. BURNKRANT, "Effects of Repeating Varied Ad Executions on Brand Name Memory," *Journal of Marketing Research* 28, November 1991, 406–16.
9. CURTIS P. HAUGTVEDT, DAVID W. SCHUMANN, WENDY L. SCHNEIER, and WENDY L. WARREN, "Advertising Repetition and Variation Strategies: Implications for Understanding Attitude Strength," *Journal of Consumer Research* 21, June 1994, 176–89.
10. Ibid.
11. PHIL GULLEN and HUGH JOHNSON, "Relating Product Purchasing and TV Viewing," *Journal of Advertising Research,* December 1986/January 1987, 9-19.

12. PETER A. DACIN and DANIEL C. SMITH, "The Effect of Brand Portfolio Characteristics on Consumer Evaluations of Brand Extensions," *Journal of Marketing Research* 31, May 1994, 229–242; SUSAN M. BRONIARCZYK and JOSEPH W. ALBA, "The Importance of the Brand in Brand Extension," *Journal of Marketing Research* 31, May 1994, 214–28.

13. Ibid.

14. FARA WARNER, "P&G is Promoting Products as a Category," *The Wall Street Journal,* April 25, 1995, B10.

15. STUART ELLIOTT, "Gump Sells, To Viacom's Surprise," *The New York Times,* October 7, 1994, D1.

16. STEVEN LEE MYERS, "City Hall's Going Retail in Wholesale Fashion," *The New York Times,* October 25, 1995, D2.

17. REBECCA QUICK, "Vatican Library Will Allow Companies to Use Its Name," *The Wall Street Journal,* April 19, 1995, B2.

18. CRAIG S. SMITH, "A Beer Tampering Scare in China Shows a Peril of Global Marketing," *The Wall Street Journal,* November 3, 1995, B1.

19. ANDREA ADELSON, "Retail Fact, Retail Fiction," *The New York Times,* September 16, 1995, 31.

20. GREGORY S. CARPENTER, RASHI GLAZER, and KENT NAKAMOTO, "Meaningful Brands from Meaningless Differentiation: The Dependence on Irrelevant Attributes," *Journal of Marketing Research* 31, August 1994, 339–50.

21. J. PAUL PETER and WALTER R. NORD, "A Classification and Extension of Operant Conditioning Principles in Marketing," *Journal of Marketing* 46, Summer 1982, 102–7.

22. S. RATNESHWAR, "New Directions in Exploring the Interface of Consumer Cognition and Motivation," *Advances in Consumer Research* 22, 1995, 271–72; JEROME B. KERNAN, "The Interface of Consumer Cognition and Motivation," *Advances in Consumer Research* 22, 1995, 273–74. See also CYNTHIA HUFFMAN and MICHAEL J. HOUSTON, "Goal-Oriented Experiences and the Development of Knowledge," *Journal of Consumer Research* 20, September 1993, 190–207.

23. KEREN A. JOHNSON, MARY R. ZIMMER, and LINDA L. GOLDEN, "Object Relations Theory: Male and Female Differences in Visual Information Processing," in M. Wallendorf and P. F. Anderson, eds., *Advances in Consumer Research* 14, 1987, 83–87.

24. MICHAEL D. JOHNSON and CLAES FORNELL, "The Nature and Methodological Implications of the Cognitive Representation of Products," *Journal of Consumer Research* 14, September 1987, 214–27.

25. JOSEPH W. ALBA and HOWARD MARMORSTEIN, "The Effects of Frequency Knowledge on Consumer Decision Making," *Journal of Consumer Research* 14, June 1987, 14–25.

26. SANDRA BLAKESLEE, "How the Brain Might Work: A New Theory of Consciousness," *The New York Times,* March 21, 1995, C1.

27. DANIEL GOLEMAN, "Brain May Tag All Perceptions with a Value," *The New York Times,* August 8, 1995, C1.

28. RUTH ANN SMITH, "The Effects of Visual and Verbal Advertising Information on Consumers' Inferences," *Journal of Advertising* 20(4), December 1991, 13–23.

29. H. RAO UNNAVA and ROBERT E. BURNKRANT, "An Imagery-Processing View of the Role of Pictures in Print Advertisements," *Journal of Marketing Research* 28, May 1991, 226–31.

30. KENNETH R. LORD and ROBERT E. BURNKRANT, "Television Program Elaboration Effects on Commercial Processing," in Michael Houston, ed., *Advances in Consumer Research* 15, 1988, 213–18.

31. JOAN MEYERS-LEVY and DURAIRAJ MAHESWASRAN, "Exploring Differences in Males' and Females' Processing Strategies," *Journal of Consumer Research* 18, June 1991, 63–70.

32. JOHNSON and FORNELL, op. cit.

33. ALBA and MARMORSTEIN, op. cit.

34. ROBERT J. KENT and CHRIS T. ALLEN, "Competitive Interference Effects in Consumer Memory for Advertising: The Role of Brand Familiarity," *Journal of Marketing* 58, July 1994, 97–105.

35. KEVIN LANE KELLER and RICHARD STAELIN, "Effects of Quality and Quantity of Information on Decision Effectiveness," *Journal of Consumer Research* 14, September 1987, 200–213.

36. See, for example, JACOB JACOBY, "Perspectives on Information Overload," *Journal of Consumer Research* 10, March 1984, 432–35; and THOMAS E. MULLER, "Buyer Response to Variations in Product Information Load," *Journal of Applied Psychology* 69, 1984, 300–306.

37. NARISH K. MALHOTRA, "Reflections on the Information Overload Paradigm in Consumer Decision Making," *Journal of Consumer Research* 10, March 1984, 436–40; and "Information Load and Consumer Decision Making," *Journal of Consumer Research* 8, March 1982, 419–30.

38. ITAMAR SIMONSON, JOEL HUBER, and JOHN PAYNE, "The Relationship Between Prior Brand Knowledge and Information Acquisition Order," *Journal of Consumer Research* 14, March 1988, 566–78.

39. JULIE L. OZANNE, MERRIE BRUCKS, and DHRUV GREWAL, "A Study of Information Search Behavior During the Categorization of New Products," *Journal of Consumer Research* 18, March 1992, 452–63.

40. KENT and ALLEN, op. cit.

41. FRANK R. KARDES and GURUMURTHY KALYA-NARAM, "Order-of-Entry Effects on Consumer Memory and Judgment: An Information Integration Perspective," *Journal of Marketing Research* 29, August 1992, 343–57.

42. LORNE BOZINOFF and VICTOR J. ROTH, "Recall and Recognition Memory for Product Attributes and Benefits," in Thomas C. Kinnear, ed., *Advances in Consumer Research* 11, 1984, 348–52.

43. KEVIN LANE KELLER, "Memory and Evaluation Effects in Competitive Advertising Environments," *Journal of Consumer Research* 17, March 1991, 463–76.

44. CAROLYN L. COSTLEY and MERRIE BRUCKS, "Selective Recall and Information Use in Consumer Preferences," *Journal of Consumer Research* 18, March 1992, 464–73.

45. RICHARD L. CELSI and JERRY C. OLSON, "The Role of Involvement in Attention and Comprehension Processes," *Journal of Consumer Research* 15, September 1988, 210–24.

46. JOSEPH W. ALBA, HOWARD MARMORSTEIN, and AMITAVA CHATTOPADHYAY, "Transitions in Preference Over Time: The Effects of Memory on Message Persuasiveness," *Journal of Marketing Research* 29, November 1992, 406–16.

47. JOHN H. LINGLE, JANET M. DUKERICH, and THOMAS M. OSTROM, "Accessing Information in Memory-Based Impression Judgments: Incongruity Versus Negativity in Retrieval Selectivity," *Journal of Personality and Social Psychology* 44, 1983, 262–72.

48. RAYMOND R. BURKE and THOMAS K. SRULL, "Competitive Interference and Consumer Memory for Advertising," *Journal of Consumer Research* 15, June 1988, 55–68.

49. SUSAN E. HECKLER and TERRY L. CHILDERS, "The Role of Expectancy and Relevancy in Memory for Verbal and Visual Information: What is Incongruency?" *Journal of Consumer Research* 18, March 1992, 475–92.

50. ALICE M. TYBOUT, BOBBY J. CALDER, and BRIAN STERNTHAL, "Using Information Processing Theory to Design Marketing Strategies," *Journal of Marketing Research* 18, February 1981, 73–79.

51. FLEMMING HANSEN, "Hemispheral Lateralization: Implications for Understanding Consumer Behavior," *Journal of Consumer Research* 8, June 1981, 23–36; PETER H. LINDZAY and DONALD NORMAN, *Human Information Processing* (New York: Academic Press, 1977); and MERLIN C. WITTROCK, *The Human Brain* (Englewood Cliffs, NJ: Prentice-Hall, 1977).

52. HERBERT E. KRUGMAN, "The Impact of Television Advertising: Learning Without Involvement," *Public Opinion Quarterly* 29, Fall 1965, 349–56; "Brain Wave Measures of Media Involvement," *Journal of Advertising Research* 11, February 1971, 3–10; and "Memory Without Recall, Exposure Without Perception," *Journal of Advertising Research, Classics* 1, September 1982, 80–85.

53. RAY ARORA, "Consumer Involvement and Advertising Strategy," *International Journal of Advertising* 4, 1985, 110–30.

54. See, for example, TERRY L. CHILDERS and MICHAEL J. HOUSTON, "Conditions for a Picture-Superiority Effect on Consumer Memory," *Journal of Consumer Research* 11, September 1984, 643–54; MORRIS B. HOLBROOK and WILLIAM L. MOORE, "Feature Interactions in Consumer Judgments of Verbal Versus Pictorial Presentations," *Journal of Consumer Research* 8, June 1981, 103–13; and RUTH ANN SMITH, MICHAEL J. HOUSTON, and TERRY L. CHILDERS, "Verbal Versus Visual Processing Modes: An Empirical Test of the Cyclical Processing Hypothesis," in Thomas C. Kinnear, ed., *Advances in Consumer Research* 11, 1984, 75–80.

55. SUSAN E. HECKLER and TERRY L. CHILDERS, "Hemispheric Lateralization: The Relationship of Processing Orientation with Judgment and Recall Measures for Print Advertisements," in M. Wallendorf and P. F. Anderson, eds., *Advances in Consumer Research* 14, 1987, 46–50.

56. BANWARI MITTAL, "A Framework for Relating Consumer Involvement to Lateral Brain Functioning," in M. Wallendorf and P. F. Anderson, eds., *Advances in Consumer Research* 14, 1987, 41–45.

57. JOHN T. CACIOPPO, RICHARD E. PETTY, CHUAN FENG KAO, and REGINA RODRIGUEZ, "Central and Peripheral Routes to Persuasion: An Individual Difference Perspective," *Journal of Personality and Social Psychology* 51(5), 1986, 1032–43.

58. See, for example, RICHARD E. PETTY and JOHN T. CACIOPPO, "Issues Involvement Can Increase or Decrease Persuasion by Enhancing Message-Relevant Cognitive Responses," *Journal of Personality and Social Psychology* 37, 1979, 1915–26; CACIOPPO and PETTY, "The Need for Cognition," *Journal of Personality and Social Psychology* 42, 1982, 116–31; and CACIOPPO, PETTY, and KATHERINE J. MORRIS, "Effects of Need for Cognition on Message Evaluation, Recall and Persuasion," *Journal of Personality and Social Psychology* 45, 1983, 805–18.

59. WAYNE D. HOYER, "An Examination of Consumer Decision Making for a Common Repeat Purchase Product," *Journal of Consumer Research* 11, December 1984, 822–29.

60. SANJAY PUTREVU and KENNETH R. LORD, "Comparative and Noncomparative Advertising: Attitudinal Effects Under Cognitive and Affective Involvement Conditions," *Journal of Advertising* 23(2), June 1994, 77–91.

61. MUZAFER SHERIF and CARL I. HOVLAND, *Social Judgment Assimilation and Contrast Effects in Communication and Attitude Change* (New Haven, CT: Yale University Press, 1961); and CAROLYN E. SHERIF, MUZAFER SHERIF, and R. W. NEBERGALL, *Attitude and Attitude Change: The Social Judgment-Involvement Approach* (Philadelphia: Saunders, 1965).

62. MARK B. TRAYLOR, "Product Involvement and Brand Commitment," *Journal of Advertising Research* 21, December 1981, 51–56.

63. THEO B. C. POIESZ and J. P. M. DE BONT, "Do We Need Involvement to Understand Consumer Behavior?" *Advances in Consumer Research* 22, 1995, 448–52. See also the following articles in Thomas C. Kinnear, ed., *Advances in Consumer Research* 11, 1984: JAMES A. MUNCY and SHELBY D. HUNT, "Consumer Involvement: Definitional Issues and Research Directions," 193–96; JOHN H. ANTIL, "Conceptualization and Operationalization of Involvement," 203–9; and MICHAEL L.

ROTHSCHILD, "Perspectives on Involvement: Current Problems and Future Directions," 216–17.

64. MUNCY and HUNT, in Thomas C. Kinnear, ed., *Advances in Consumer Research* 11, 1984, op. cit.

65. JUDITH L. ZAICHKOWSKY, "Conceptualizing Involvement," *Journal of Advertising* 15(2), 1986, 4–34.

66. JOHN H. ANTIL, in Thomas C. Kinnear, ed., *Advances in Consumer Research* 11, 1984, op. cit.

67. DAVID W. FINN, "The Integrated Information Response Model," *Journal of Advertising* 13, 1984, 24–33.

68. BANWARI MITTAL and MYUNG SOO LEE, "Separating Brand Choice Involvement from Product Involvement via Consumer Involvement Profiles," in Michael Houston, ed., *Advances in Consumer Research* 15, 1988, 43–49.

69. MARK E. SLAMA and ARMEN TASHCHIAN, "Validating the SOR Paradigm for Consumer Involvement with a Convenience Good," *Journal of the Academy of Marketing Science* 15(1), Spring 1987, 36–45.

70. JUDITH LYNNE ZAICHKOWSKY, "The Personal Involvement Inventory: Reduction, Revision, and Application to Advertising," *Journal of Advertising* 23(4), December 1994, 59–69; also ROBERT N. STONE, "The Marketing Characteristics of Involvement," in Thomas C. Kinnear, ed., *Advances in Consumer Research* 11, 1984, 210–15.

71. DANIEL L. SHERRELL and TERENCE A. SHIMP, "Consumer Involvement in a Laboratory Setting," in Bruce J. Walker, et al., eds., *An Assessment of Marketing Thought and Practice Proceedings of the American Marketing Association Educators Conference* 48 (Chicago: American Marketing Association, 1982), 104–8.

72. DAVID W. FINN, "The Integrated Information Response Model," op. cit.

73. GILLES LAURENT and JEAN-NOEL KAPFERER, "Measuring Consumer Involvement Profiles," *Journal of Marketing Research* 22, February 1985, 41–53.

74. JEAN NOEL KAPFERER and GILLES LAURENT, "Consumer Involvement Profiles: A New Practical Approach to Consumer Involvement," *Journal of Advertising Research* 25(6), December 1985/January 1986, 48–56.

75. JOHN H. ANTIL, in Thomas C. Kinnear, ed., *Advances in Consumer Research* 11, op. cit.

76. EDWARD F. MCQUARRIE and J. MICHAEL MUNSON, "The Zaichkowsky Personal Involvement Inventory: Modification and Extension," in M. Wallendorf and P. F. Anderson, eds., *Advances in Consumer Research* 14, 1987, 36–40.

77. POIESZ and CEES, op. cit.

78. S. P. RAJ, "Striking a Balance Between Brand 'Popularity' and Brand Loyalty," *Journal of Marketing* 49, Winter 1985, 53–59.

79. THOMAS EXTER, "Looking for Brand Loyalty," *American Demographics,* April 1986, 33.

80. ALAN S. DICK and KUNAL BASU, "Customer Loyalty: Toward an Integrated Conceptual Framework," *Journal of the Academy of Marketing Science* 22(2), 1994, 99–113.

81. See, for example, SHARON E. BEATTY, LYNN R. KAHLE, and PAMELA HOMER, "The Involvement-Commitment Model: Theory and Implications," *Journal of Business Research* 16, March 1988, 149–67.

82. DIANE CRISPELL and KATHLEEN BRANDENBURG, "What's in a Brand," *American Demographics,* May 1993, 28.

83. EXTER, op. cit.

84. Ibid.

85. ALSOP, op. cit.

86. STUART ELLIOTT, "P&G Discovers That a New Look to an Old Product Can Be Seen as Betraying Customers' Brand Loyalty," *The New York Times,* January 28, 1993, D20.

87. KATHLEEN DEVENY, "Private-Label Items Buffet Brand Loyalty," *The Wall Street Journal,* March 9, 1993, B11.

88. SCOTT A. HAWKINS and STEPHEN J. HOCH, "Low-Involvement Learning: Memory Without Evaluation," *Journal of Consumer Research* 19, September 1992, 212–25.

89. CHAN SU PARK and V. SRINIVASAN, "A Survey-Based Method for Measuring and Understanding Brand Equity and Its Extendibility," *Journal of Marketing Research* 31, May 1994, 271–288.

90. Ibid.

91. JOHN GRACE, "Double Branding," *Branding Issues 1990's* (New York: Gerstman+Meyers, Inc., 1990).

LEO BURNETT COMPANY, INC.
AS FILMED AND RECORDED   (9/94)   "Nap/ Football-Rev."   :30

FRUIT OF THE LOOM

FLCW2093

1. (MUSIC: UNDER THROUGHOUT)
(SFX: CROWD CHEERS THROUGOUT)

2. TV AVO: First 'n ten from the 37...

3. TJ throwing deep down the left side
Thomas is open. He's got it.

4. Hoover Thomas knocked out of
bounds and the clock is stopped.

5. It's pandemonium here in the
stadium. Down by 16 and now they're...

6. within a field goal to win it. 47-yard
attempt.
(CONTINUES UNDER)

7. (AVO): At Fruit of the Loom...our
sweats are roomy and soft.

8. Because before you can be...

9. comfortable...

10. you need to be...comfortable.

11. Fruit of the Loom. Clothes that
make you feel good.
TV AVO: And you saw it all!!

As consumers, each of us has a vast number of attitudes toward products, services, advertisements, direct mail, and retailers. Whenever we are asked whether we *like* or *dislike* a product (e.g., Windows 95), a service (e.g., H & R Block Tax—Return Preparation), a particular retailer (e.g., Old Navy Clothing Company), a specific direct marketer (e.g., Lands' End—Direct Merchants), or an advertising theme (e.g., "Rubbermaid, Nothing's better made"), we are being asked to express our **attitudes**.

Within the context of consumer behavior, an appreciation of prevailing attitudes has considerable strategic merit. For instance, there has been very rapid growth in the sales of natural ingredient bath, body, and cosmetic products throughout the world. This trend seems linked to the currently popular attitude that things "natural" are good and things "synthetic" are bad. Yet, in reality, the positive attitude favoring things natural is

> **G**ood and bad are but names very readily transferable to that or this.
>
> —Ralph Waldo Emerson
> "Self-Reliance," Essays,
> First Series, 1981

not based on any systematic evidence that natural cosmetic products are any safer or better for consumers.[1]

To get at the heart of what is driving consumers' behavior, *attitude research* has been used to study a wide range of strategic marketing questions. For example, attitude research is frequently undertaken to determine whether consumers will accept a proposed new-product idea, to gauge why a firm's target audience has not reacted more favorably to its new promotional theme, or to learn how target customers are likely to react to a proposed change in the firm's packaging. To illustrate, Fruit of the Loom frequently conducts research among male and female target consumers to determine their attitudes about size, fit, comfort, and fashion elements of its active wear clothing (e.g., T-shirts, sweatshirts, sweatpants, and sweatshorts), as well as testing reactions to potential active wear designs. The goal of this attitude research is to increase sales by better satisfying customer needs. Figures 8-1A and B present two ads for Fruit of the Loom active wear that have benefited from research into consumer attitudes and are consistent with Fruit of the Loom's commitment to providing consumers' with active wear that is both comfortable and fashionable.

Awareness of consumer attitudes is such a central concern of both product and service marketers that it is difficult to imagine any consumer research project that does not include the measurement of some aspect of consumer attitudes. An outgrowth of this widespread interest in consumer attitudes is a consistent stream of attitude research reported in the consumer behavior literature.

In this chapter we will discuss the reasons why attitude research has had such a pervasive impact on consumer behavior. We also will discuss the properties that have made attitudes so attractive to consumer researchers, as well as some of the common frustrations encountered in attitude research. Particular attention will be paid to a number of important models depicting the structure and composition of attitudes. In Chapter 9, we will continue our discussion of attitudes by focusing on the central topics of attitude formation, attitude change, and related issues.

WHAT ARE ATTITUDES?

As the opening paragraph of this chapter implies, attitudes are an expression of inner feelings that reflect whether a person is favorably or unfavorably predisposed to some "object" (e.g., a brand, a service, or a retail establishment). Because they are an outcome of psychological processes, attitudes are not directly observable but must be inferred from what people say or what they do.

Consumer researchers assess attitudes by asking questions or making inferences from behavior. For example, if a researcher determines from questioning a consumer that the individual consistently buys Suave products and recommends them to friends, the

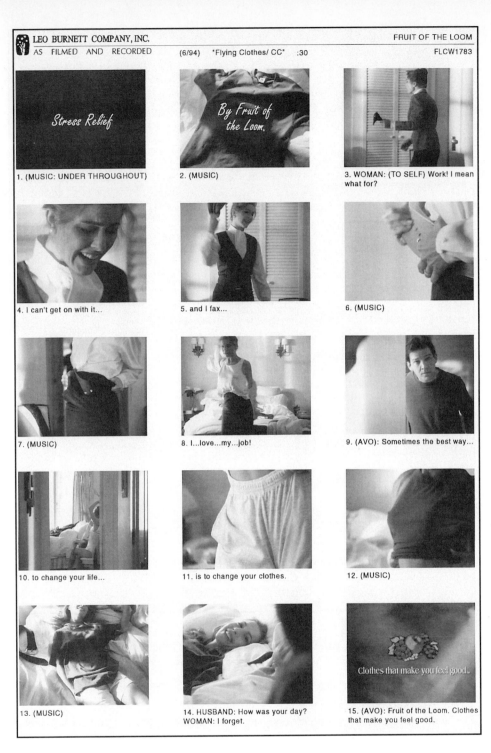

1. (MUSIC: UNDER THROUGHOUT)

2. (MUSIC)

3. WOMAN: (TO SELF) Work! I mean what for?

4. I can't get on with it...

5. and I fax...

6. (MUSIC)

7. (MUSIC)

8. I...love...my...job!

9. (AVO): Sometimes the best way...

10. to change your life...

11. is to change your clothes.

12. (MUSIC)

13. (MUSIC)

14. HUSBAND: How was your day? WOMAN: I forget.

15. (AVO): Fruit of the Loom. Clothes that make you feel good.

FIGURE 8-1A

Products Created to Reflect Consumers' Attitudes
Courtesy of Fruit of the Loom

researcher is likely to infer that the consumer possesses a positive attitude toward Suave products.

This illustration suggests that a whole universe of consumer behaviors—consistency of purchases, recommendations to others, top rankings, beliefs, evaluations, and intentions are related to attitudes. What, then, are attitudes? In a consumer behavior context, an attitude is *a learned predisposition to behave in a consistently favorable or unfavorable way*

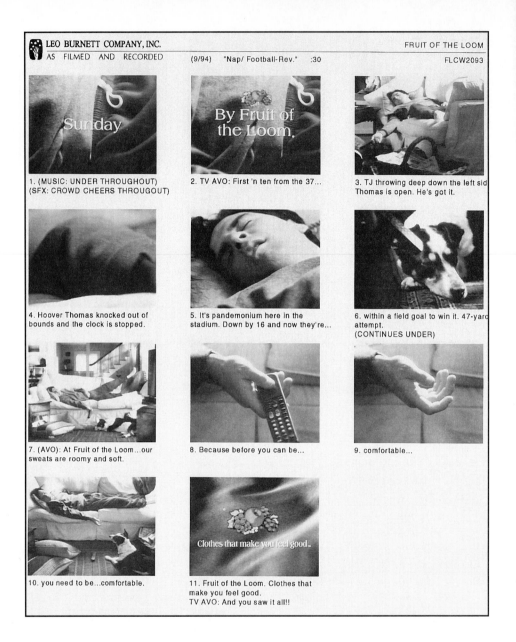

1. (MUSIC: UNDER THROUGHOUT)
(SFX: CROWD CHEERS THROUGOUT)

2. TV AVO: First 'n ten from the 37...

3. TJ throwing deep down the left sid
Thomas is open. He's got it.

4. Hoover Thomas knocked out of
bounds and the clock is stopped.

5. It's pandemonium here in the
stadium. Down by 16 and now they're...

6. within a field goal to win it. 47-yard
attempt.
(CONTINUES UNDER)

7. (AVO): At Fruit of the Loom...our
sweats are roomy and soft.

8. Because before you can be...

9. comfortable...

10. you need to be...comfortable.

11. Fruit of the Loom. Clothes that
make you feel good.
TV AVO: And you saw it all!!

FIGURE 8-1B

Products Created to
Reflect Consumers'
Attitudes
Courtesy of Fruit of the Loom

with respect to a given object. Each part of this definition describes an important property of an attitude and is critical to understanding the role of attitudes in consumer behavior.

The Attitude "Object"

The word *object* in our consumer-oriented definition of attitude should be interpreted broadly to include specific consumption- or marketing-related concepts, such as product, product category, brand, service, possessions, product use, causes or issues, people, advertisement, price, medium, or retailer.

In conducting attitude research, we tend to be object-specific. For example, if we were interested in learning shoppers' attitudes toward three major apparel retailers, our "object" might include The Gap, Limited Express, and Benetton; if we were examining consumer attitudes toward major brands of laptop computers, our "object" might include IBM, Toshiba, Compaq, Dell, and Gateway 2000.

Attitudes Are a Learned Predisposition

There is general agreement that attitudes are *learned*. This means that attitudes relevant to purchase behavior are formed as a result of direct experience with the product, information acquired from others, or exposure to mass media advertising and various forms of direct marketing (e.g., a retailer's catalog). It is important to remember that while attitudes may result from behavior, they are not synonymous with behavior. Instead, they reflect either a favorable or an unfavorable evaluation of the attitude object. As **learned predispositions**, attitudes have a motivational quality; that is, they might propel a consumer toward a particular behavior or repel the consumer *away* from a particular behavior.

Attitudes Have Consistency

Another characteristic of attitudes is that they are relatively consistent with the behavior they reflect. However, despite their *consistency*, attitudes are not necessarily permanent; they do change. (Attitude change is explored in the next chapter.)

It is important to illustrate what we mean by consistency. Normally, we expect consumers' behavior to correspond with their attitudes. For example, if a Dutch consumer reported preferring German over Japanese automobiles, we would expect that the individual would be more likely to buy a German car when next in the market for a new car. In other words, when consumers are free to act as they wish, we anticipate that their actions will be consistent with their attitudes. However, circumstances often preclude consistency between attitudes and behavior. For example, in the case of our Dutch consumer, the matter of affordability may intervene, and the consumer would find a particular Japanese car to be a more realistic choice than a German car. Therefore, we must consider possible *situational* influences on consumer attitudes and behavior.

Attitudes Occur Within a Situation

It is not immediately evident from our definition that attitudes occur within and are affected by the *situation*. By situation, we mean events or circumstances that, at a particular point in time, influence the relationship between an attitude and behavior. A specific situation can cause consumers to behave in ways seemingly inconsistent with their attitudes. For instance, let us assume that Marie purchases a different brand of shampoo each time the brand she is using runs low. Although her brand-switching behavior may seem to reflect a negative attitude or dissatisfaction with the brands she tries, it actually may be influenced by a specific situation, for example, her wish to economize. Although Marie may have a strong preference for Paul Mitchell shampoo, her tight budget may influence her often to purchase whatever brand is on "special."

The opposite can also be true. If Arthur rents a car from Alamo each time he goes on vacation, we may erroneously infer that he has a particularly favorable attitude toward Alamo. On the contrary, Arthur may find Alamo to be "just okay" (because more often than not they are inconveniently located off the airport). However, he may feel that Alamo is "good enough," given that he may be paying a little less than he would be paying if he rented from one of the major car rental companies located at the airport.

Indeed, individuals can have a variety of attitudes toward a particular behavior, each corresponding to a particular situation. Stan may feel it is alright to eat lunch at McDonald's but does not consider it appropriate for dinner. In this case, McDonald's has its "time and place," which functions as a boundary delineating the situations when Stan considers McDonald's acceptable. However, if Stan is coming home late from school one night, feels exhausted and hungry, and spots a McDonald's, he may just decide to have "dinner" there. Why? Because it is late, he is tired and hungry, and McDonald's is convenient. Has he changed his attitude? Probably not.

It is important to understand how consumer attitudes vary from situation to situation. For instance, it is useful to know whether consumer preferences for different burger chains (e.g., Burger King, McDonald's, Wendy's) vary in terms of eating situations (i.e., lunch or snack, evening meal when rushed for time, or evening meal with family when not rushed for time). Consumer preferences for the various burger restaurants might depend on the anticipated eating situation. Wendy's, for example, might be favored by some consumers as a good place to have dinner with their families. This suggests that its management might position Wendy's restaurants as a nice place to take the family for a leisurely (and inexpensive) dinner.

Clearly, when measuring attitudes, it is important to consider the situation in which the behavior takes place, or we can misinterpret the relationship between attitudes and behavior. Table 8-1 presents some additional examples of how specific situations might influence consumer attitudes toward specific brands of products or services.

STRUCTURAL MODELS OF ATTITUDES

Motivated by a desire to understand the relationship between attitudes and behavior, psychologists have sought to construct models that capture the underlying dimensions of an attitude.[2] To this end, the focus has been on specifying the composition of an attitude to better explain or predict behavior. The following section examines several important attitude models: the **tricomponent attitude model**, the **multiattribute attitude models**, the **trying-to-consume model**, and the **attitude-toward-the-ad model**. Each of these models

table 8-1   Examples of How Situations Might Influence Attitudes

PRODUCT/SERVICE	SITUATION	ATTITUDE
Timex wristwatch	Strap broke on my old watch	"I need a durable and inexpensive new watch."
Bose (Home sound system)	Big end-of-year bonus	"I worked hard this year; I earned this new sound system."
Northwestern Mutual Life	Newlyweds	"It's time for us to consider life insurance."
Saturn	Graduate from college	"I deserve a reliable new car."
First Alert (home smoke detector	New baby	"We need to make the baby's room really safe."
HBO	Moving into a new luxury apartment	"We should subscribe to HBO; with our high rent we will be staying home more."
Panasonic (telephone answering machine)	Gift for a new homeowner	"It's an affordable gift that's high in quality."
Samsonite	Vacation	"I need some strong and light-weight luggage now."

provides a somewhat different perspective on the number of component parts of an attitude and how those parts are arranged or interrelated.

Tricomponent Attitude Model

According to the tricomponent attitude model, attitudes consist of three major components: a *cognitive* component, an *affective* component, and a *conative* component (see Figure 8-2).

▲ **The Cognitive Component** The first component of the tricomponent attitude model consists of a person's *cognitions*, that is, the knowledge and perceptions that are acquired by a combination of direct experience with the **attitude object** and related information from various sources. This knowledge and resulting perceptions commonly take the form of *beliefs*, that is, the consumer believes that the attitude object possesses various attributes and that specific behavior will lead to specific outcomes.

Although it captures only a part of Ellen's belief system about two brands of underarm antiperspirants (e.g., Degree and Secret), Figure 8-3 illustrates just how complex a consumer's belief system can be. Ellen's belief system for both brands consists of the same basic four attributes: effectiveness, scent, strength, and formulation. However, Ellen has

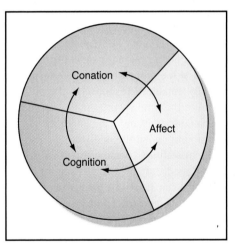

FIGURE 8-2

A Simple Representation of the Tricomponent Attitude Model

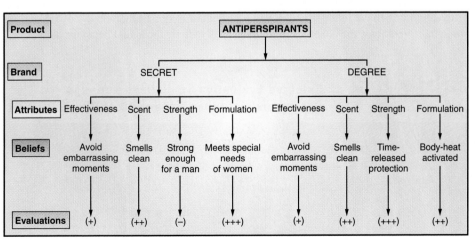

FIGURE 8-3

A Consumer's Belief System for Two Different Brands of Antiperspirants somewhat different beliefs about the two brands for several of the attributes. Specifically, when it comes to "formulation," Ellen regards the claim that Secret is "especially formulated for a woman's chemistry" as a real plus, whereas the claim that Degree is "body-heat activated" is somewhat less valued. When it comes to the attribute "strength," Ellen prefers Degree over Secret for being "a time-released product" (i.e., "It is like some headache remedies"). In contrast, she recalls ads for Secret that claim it is "strong enough for a man." She finds this thought to be a turnoff. In fact, Ellen is somewhat puzzled as to why Secret would claim to be strong enough for a man, yet especially formulated for a woman. She ponders, "What's the point, I'm a woman!" Research that reveals such consumer insights is useful in positioning a particular brand against competing brands (see the discussion of perceptual mapping in Chapter 6).

▲ **The Affective Component** A consumer's *emotions* or *feelings* about a particular product or brand constitute the **affective component** of an attitude. These emotions and feelings are frequently treated by consumer researchers as primarily *evaluative* in nature, that is, they capture an individual's direct or global assessment of the attitude-object (i.e., the extent to which the individual rates the attitude object as "favorable" or "unfavorable," "good" or "bad"). To illustrate, Table 8-2 shows a series of evaluative (affective) scale items that might be used to assess consumers' attitudes toward Oil of Olay Bath Bar.

Affect-laden experiences also manifest themselves as *emotionally charged states* (e.g., happiness, sadness, shame, disgust, anger, distress, guilt, or surprise). Research indicates that such emotional states may enhance or amplify positive or negative experiences and that later recollections of such experiences may impact what comes to mind and how the individual acts.[3] For instance, a person visiting an outlet mall is likely to be influenced by his or her emotional state at the time. If the an outlet mall shopper is feeling particularly joyous at the moment, a positive response to the outlet mall may be amplified. The emotionally enhanced response to the outlet mall may lead the shopper to recall with great pleasure the time spent at the outlet mall. It also may influence the individual shopper to persuade friends and acquaintances to visit the same outlet mall and to make the personal decision to revisit the mall.

In addition to using direct or global evaluative measures of an attitude-object (e.g., from "good to bad," or "pleasant to unpleasant," as depicted in Table 8-2), consumer researchers can also use a battery of affective response scales (e.g., that measure feelings and emotions) to construct a picture of consumers' overall feelings about a product, service, or ad. Table 8-3 gives an example of a five-point scale that measures affective responses.

▲ **The Conative Component** Conation, the final component of the tricomponent attitude model, is concerned with the *likelihood* or *tendency* that an individual will undertake a specific action or behave in a particular way with regard to the attitude object. According to some interpretations, the conative component may include the actual behavior itself.

table 8-2   Selected Evaluative Scale Used to Gauge Consumers' Attitudes Toward Oil of Olay Bath Bar

Compared to other moisturizer bath bars, Oil of Olay Bath Bar is:							
Good	[1]	[2]	[3]	[4]	[5]	[6]	[7]	Bad
Positive	[1]	[2]	[3]	[4]	[5]	[6]	[7]	Negative
Pleasant	[1]	[2]	[3]	[4]	[5]	[6]	[7]	Unpleasant
Appealing	[1]	[2]	[3]	[4]	[5]	[6]	[7]	Unappealing

table 8-3   Measuring Consumers' Feelings and Emotions with Regard to Using Oil of Olay Bath Bar

For the past 10 days you have had a chance to try the Oil of Olay Bath Bar. We would appreciate it if you would identify how your skin felt during this 10-day trial period.

For each of the words, below, we would appreciate it if you would mark with an "X" in the box corresponding to how your skin felt as a result of using the *Oil of Olay Bath Bar* during the past 10 days.

	VERY				NOT AT ALL
My skin felt — relaxed	[ ]	[ ]	[ ]	[ ]	[ ]
My skin felt — beautiful.............	[ ]	[ ]	[ ]	[ ]	[ ]
My skin felt — tight....................	[ ]	[ ]	[ ]	[ ]	[ ]
My skin felt — smooth	[ ]	[ ]	[ ]	[ ]	[ ]
My skin felt — supple.................	[ ]	[ ]	[ ]	[ ]	[ ]
My skin felt — clean	[ ]	[ ]	[ ]	[ ]	[ ]
My skin felt — refreshed	[ ]	[ ]	[ ]	[ ]	[ ]
My skin felt — oily.......................	[ ]	[ ]	[ ]	[ ]	[ ]
My skin felt — pampered............	[ ]	[ ]	[ ]	[ ]	[ ]
My skin felt — soft......................	[ ]	[ ]	[ ]	[ ]	[ ]

etc.

In marketing and consumer research, the conative component is frequently treated as an expression of the consumer's **intention to buy**. Buyer intention scales are used to assess the likelihood of a consumer purchasing a product or behaving in a certain way. Table 8-4 provides several examples of common intention-to-buy scales.

table 8-4   Two Examples of Intention-to-Buy Scales

Which of the following statements best describes the chance that you will buy a new camera during the next three months?

_____ I definitely will buy one.
_____ I probably will buy one.
_____ I am uncertain whether I will buy one.
_____ I probably will not buy one.
_____ I definitely will not buy one.

How likely are you to buy a new camera during the next three months?

_____ Very likely
_____ Likely
_____ Unlikely
_____ Very unlikely

Multiattribute Attitude Models

Multiattribute attitude models portray consumers' attitudes with regard to an attitude "object" (e.g., a product, a service, a direct mail catalog, or a cause or an issue) as a function of consumers' perception and assessment of the key attributes or beliefs held with regard to the particular attitude "object." While there are many variations of this type of attitude model, those proposed by Martin Fishbein and his associates have stimulated the greatest amount of research interest.[4] We have selected three Fishbein models to consider here: the **attitude-toward-object model**, the **attitude-toward-behavior model**, and the **theory-of-reasoned-action model**.

▲ **The Attitude-Toward-Object Model** The attitude-toward-object model is especially suitable for measuring attitudes toward a *product* (or *service*) category or specific *brands*.[5] According to this model, the consumer's attitude toward a product or specific brands of a product is a function of the presence (or absence) and evaluation of certain product-specific beliefs and/or attributes. In other words, consumers generally have favorable attitudes toward those brands that they believe have an adequate level of attributes that they evaluate as positive, and they have unfavorable attitudes toward those brands they feel do not have an adequate level of desired attributes or have too many negative attributes. Table 8-5 presents two hypothetical consumer belief systems for the IBM ThinkPad 701C "Butterfly" notebook PC (one favorable and the other unfavorable).

The Fishbein *attitude-toward-object* model is usually depicted in the form of the following equation:

$$\text{Attitude}_0 = \sum_{i=1}^{n} b_i e_i$$

table 8-5   Two Consumers' Hypothetical Belief Systems for the IBM ThinkPad 701C "Butterfly" (Expandable Full-sized Keyboard) Notebook PC

CONSUMER 1 (MAINLY FAVORABLE)

"IBM ThinkPad 701C is worth the extra money it costs."

"IBM ThinkPad 701C's small size and black case are really very professional looking."

"IBM ThinkPad 701C keyboard is a true innovation."

"The computer magazines have given the IBM ThinkPad 701C very high marks in comparison to its competition."

"The IBM ThinkPad 701C is really great for a road warrior like me."

CONSUMER 2 (MAINLY UNFAVORABLE)

"IBM ThinkPads have good keyboards."

"The IBM ThinkPad 701C is too rich for my purse."

"I travel too infrequently. I don't really need such a good subnotebook."

"Maybe that expandable keyboard will break down."

"I really could get a less expensive (and larger) laptop."

where **Attitude$_o$** is a separately assessed overall (or global) measure of *affect* for or against the attitude object (e.g., a product, brand, service, or retail establishment); b_i is the *strength* of the belief that the attitude object contains the *i*th attribute (e.g., the likelihood that Pizza Hut pizza is "crisp"); e_i is the evaluative dimension associated with the *i*th attribute (e.g., how "good" or "bad" is a "crisp pizza"); and Σ indicates that there are *n* salient attributes over which the b_i and e_i combinations are summated. Figure 8-4 shows examples of the type of questioning that might be used to measure the *attitude-toward-object* model.

▲ **The Attitude-Toward-Behavior Model** The focus of Fishbein's *attitude-toward-behavior* model is the individual's *attitude toward behaving* or *acting* with respect to an object, rather than the attitude toward the object itself.

The appeal of the attitude-toward-behavior model is that it seems to correspond more closely to actual behavior than does the attitude-toward-object model. For instance,

---

FIGURE 8-4

An Illustration of How Attitude-Toward-Object Is Measured and Calculated

$$\text{Attitude}_0 = \sum_{i=1}^{n} b_i e_i$$

1. Background

This exhibit is designed to demonstrate how the attitude-toward-object model might be used to measure and calculate consumers' attitudes with respect to three brand models of subnotebook computers (i.e., IBM ThinkPad 701C, Hewlett-Packard (HP) OmniBook 600CT and Digital HiNote Ultra CT475), each weighing less than 5 lbs. For some sense of realism, assume that a consumer research firm is conducting a study of target consumers' attitudes toward subnotebook computers.

Based upon a series of focus groups with target consumers ("road warriors"—business executives who travel much of the time), the research firm identified the following five major attributes that tend to be used by frequent business travelers to assess subnotebook computers:

(1) *Weight:*
    "Whether the subnotebook is lightweight"

(2) *Battery life:*
    "Whether the subnotebook's battery lasts a long time"

(3) *Keyboard quality:*
    "Whether the subnotebook has a comfortable keyboard"

(4) *Screen quality:*
    "Whether the subnotebook has a large and clear screen"

(5) *Price:*
    "Whether the subnotebook has a low street price"

2. Questions used to measure attitude-toward-the-watches (i.e., the "object")

The following are questions prepared by the consumer research firm to measure each of the component parts of the attitude-toward-object model, in terms of the identified five major attributes:

(1) *The evaluative (e_i) component might be measured as follows:*

    A subnotebook that is lightweight is:
        very good [+3] [+2] [+1] [0] [−1] [−2] [−3] very bad

    A subnotebook that has a long-lasting battery is:
        very good [+3] [+2] [+1] [0] [−1] [−2] [−3] very bad

The remaining three product attributes would also be measured on the same 7-point scale.

(Continued)

FIGURE 8-4

(Continued)

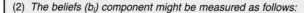

(2) *The beliefs (b$_i$) component might be measured as follows:*

How likely is the IBM ThinkPad 701C to be lightweight?
very likely [+3] [+2] [+1] [0] [−1] [−2] [−3] very unlikely

How likely is the IBM ThinkPad 701C to have a long-lasting battery?
very likely [+3] [+2] [+1] [0] [−1] [−2] [−3] very unlikely

How likely is the IBM ThinkPad 701C to have a comfortable keyboard?
very likely [+3] [+2] [+1] [0] [−1] [−2] [−3] very unlikely

How likely is the IBM ThinkPad 701C to have a large and clear screen?
very likely [+3] [+2] [+1] [0] [−1] [−2] [−3] very unlikely

How likely is the IBM ThinkPad 701C to have a low street price?
very likely[+3] [+2] [+1] [0] [−1] [−2] [−3] very unlikely

The same five belief-strength questions would be asked for the remaining two brands of sub-notebook computers. Given three brands of subnotebook computers and five major attributes, a total of fifteen belief-strength scales would be used.

3. Survey Research

The consumer research firm would next conduct airport intercept interviews with 350 target frequent business travelers who meet the client's demographic criteria (basically business executives who travel frequently on business, i.e., two or more times per month).

From the 350 completed questionnaires, an average response is determined for each (b$_i$) and (e$_i$) measure. A set of hypothetical summary results are:

Hypothetical Findings for the Attitude-Toward-Object Analysis for Subnotebook Computers (Average Results)

Attribute	Evaluation (e$_i$)	IBM ThinkPad		HP OmniBook		Digital HiNote Ultra	
	e	b	be	b	be	b	be
Weight	+3	+2	+6	+3	+9	+2	+6
Battery life	+2	−1	−2	+1	+2	+1	+2
Keyboard quality	+3	+3	+9	−2	−6	+1	+3
Screen quality	+3	+3	+9	+1	+3	+2	+6
Price	+2	−2	−4	+2	+4	−3	−6
Total Σ b$_i$e$_i$ score			+18		+12		+11

4. Comments

Three attributes are very important to frequent business travelers (e.g., "weight, keyboard quality, and screen quality), each is given a +3 value. Two remaining attributes (e.g., battery life and price) are also important, each is given a +2 value.

All three brand models of subnotebook computers were assessed positively, with the IBM ThinkPad 701C receiving the overall best score of +18. The HP OmniBook and the Digital HiNote Ultra each received almost the same scores (i.e., +12 and +11).

While the IBM ThinkPad 701C did best (+18 out of a possible +39), the two areas where there is room for improvement are battery life and its price. In a similar fashion the two other subnotebook brand models can use the information to improve their strategies.

The above comments represent just the strategic marketing thoughts that flow from the hypothetical findings. Its purpose is to illustrate the types of insights possible from such analysis.

knowing Steven's attitude about the act of purchasing a top–of–the–line Range Rover vehicle (i.e., his attitude toward the *behavior*) reveals more about the potential act of purchasing than does simply knowing his attitude toward sport utility vehicles (i.e., the attitude toward the *object*). This seems logical, for Steven might have a positive attitude toward the Range Rover but a negative attitude as to his prospects for purchasing such an expensive vehicle.

The attitude-toward-behavior model is depicted by the following equation:[6]

$$\text{Attitude(beh)} = \sum_{i=1}^{n} b_i e_i$$

where **Attitude(beh)** is a separately assessed overall measure of affect for or against carrying out a specific action or behavior (e.g., buying and using an IBM ThinkPad 701C subnotebook computer); b_i is the strength of the belief that an *i*th specific action will lead to a specific outcome (e.g., that an IBM ThinkPad 701C subnotebook will have a comfortable keyboard); e_i is an evaluation of the *i*th outcome (e.g., the "favorableness" of a comfortable keyboard); and Σ indicates that there are *n* salient outcomes over which the *b* and *e* combinations are summated. Figure 8-5 on page 246 presents sample questions that might be used to measure the *attitude-toward-behavior* model.

▲ **Theory-of-Reasoned-Action Model** The *theory of reasoned action* builds on other research conducted by Fishbein and his associates. It represents a comprehensive integration of attitude components into a structure that is designed to lead to both better explanation and better predictions of behavior. Like the basic tricomponent attitude model, the theory-of-reasoned-action model incorporates a *cognitive* component, an *affective* component, and a *conative* component; however, these are arranged in a pattern different from that of the tricomponent model.

Figure 8-6 on page 247 is a depiction of the theory of reasoned action. Examine it carefully. Working backward from *behavior* (e.g., the act of purchasing a particular service, product, or brand), the model suggests that the best predictor of behavior is the *intention to act*. Thus, if consumer researchers were solely interested in predicting behavior, they would directly measure intention (i.e., using an intention-to-act scale). However, if they were also interested in understanding the underlying factors that contribute to a consumer's intention to act in a particular situation, they would look behind intention and consider the factors that led to *intention*, that is, the consumer's *attitude toward behavior* and the *subjective norm*.

The consumer's *attitude toward behavior* can be directly measured as *affect* (i.e., a measure of overall favorability toward the purchase). Furthermore, as with *intention*, we can look behind the *attitude* to its underlying dimensions (see the discussion of the attitude-toward-behavior model).

In accordance with this expanded model, to understand *intention* we also need to measure the **subjective norms** that influence an individual's intention to act. A subjective norm can be measured directly by assessing a consumer's feelings as to what relevant others (family, friends, roommates, co-workers) would think of the action being contemplated; that is, would they look favorably or unfavorably on the anticipated action? For example, if a college student were considering purchasing the Pioneer 100 CD Changer and stopped to ask himself what his parents or girlfriend would think of such behavior (i.e., approve or disapprove), such a reflection would constitute his subjective norm.

As with *attitude*, consumer researchers can get behind the *subjective norm* to the underlying factors that are likely to produce it. They accomplish this by assessing the **normative beliefs** that the individual attributes to relevant others, as well as the individual's *motivation to comply* with each of the relevant others. For instance, consider the student

1. Direct Measure of Attitude-Toward-Behavior(beh)

Buying an HP OmniBook subnotebook is

good	[ ]	[ ]	[ ]	[ ]	[ ]	[ ]	[ ]	bad
positive	[ ]	[ ]	[ ]	[ ]	[ ]	[ ]	[ ]	negative
foolish	[ ]	[ ]	[ ]	[ ]	[ ]	[ ]	[ ]	wise
pleasant	[ ]	[ ]	[ ]	[ ]	[ ]	[ ]	[ ]	unpleasant
appealing	[ ]	[ ]	[ ]	[ ]	[ ]	[ ]	[ ]	unappealing

2. Indirect Measure of Attitude-Toward-Behavior(beh)

(1) Examples of behavioral beliefs (b_i):

Buying an HP OmniBook subnotebook is
very likely [ ] [ ] [ ] [ ] [ ] [ ] [ ] very unlikely
to give me a subnotebook computer that is lightweight.

Buying an HP OmniBook subnotebook is
very likely [ ] [ ] [ ] [ ] [ ] [ ] [ ] very unlikely
to give me a subnotebook computer that has a long-lasting battery.

Buying an HP OmniBook subnotebook is
very likely [ ] [ ] [ ] [ ] [ ] [ ] [ ] very unlikely
to give me a subnotebook computer that has a comfortable keyboard.

Buying an HP OmniBook subnotebook is
very likely [ ] [ ] [ ] [ ] [ ] [ ] [ ] very unlikely
to give me a subnotebook computer that has a large and clear screen.

Buying an HP OmniBook subnotebook is
very likely [ ] [ ] [ ] [ ] [ ] [ ] [ ] very unlikely
to give me a subnotebook computer that has a low street price.

The same five behavioral belief questions would be asked for the other two brands of subnotebook computers. Given three brand models of subnotebooks and five major attributes, a total of fifteen behavioral belief scales would be used.

(2) The evaluative (e_i) component might be measured as:

Buying a subnotebook computer that is lightweight is:
very good [ ] [ ] [ ] [ ] [ ] [ ] [ ] very bad

Buying a subnotebook computer that has a long-lasting battery is:
very good [ ] [ ] [ ] [ ] [ ] [ ] [ ] very bad

Buying a subnotebook computer that has a comfortable keyboard is:
very good [ ] [ ] [ ] [ ] [ ] [ ] [ ] very bad

Buying a subnotebook computer that has a large and clear screen is:
very good [ ] [ ] [ ] [ ] [ ] [ ] [ ] very bad

Buying a subnotebook computer that has low street price is:
very good [ ] [ ] [ ] [ ] [ ] [ ] [ ] very bad

FIGURE 8-5

An Illustration of How Attitude-Toward-Behavior Is Measured

contemplating the purchase of a 100 CD Changer. To understand his subjective norm about the desired purchase, we would have to identify his relevant others (parents and girlfriend); his beliefs about how each would respond to his purchase of the 100 CD Changer (e.g., "Mom and Dad would consider the 100 CD Changer an unnecessary luxury, but my girlfriend would love it"); and finally, his motivation to comply with his parents and/or his girlfriend.

The above discussion and examples suggest that the theory of reasoned action is a series of interrelated attitude components (i.e., *beliefs* precede *attitude* and *normative beliefs* precede *subjective norms*; *attitudes* and *subjective norms* precede *intention*; and *intention* precedes *actual behavior*).[7]

Consistent with the theory of reasoned action, an *attitude* is not linked to behavior as strongly or as directly as *intention* is linked to *behavior*.

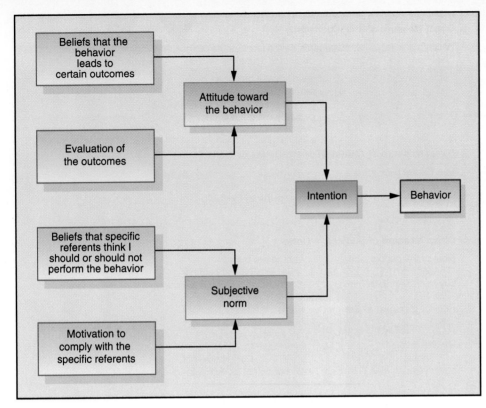

FIGURE 8-6

A Simplified Version of the Theory of Reasoned Action
Source: Adapted from IcEK AJZEN and MARTIN FISHBEIN, *Understanding Attitudes and Predicting Social Behavior* (Englewood Cliffs, NJ: Prentice Hall, 1980), 84. © 1980. Adapted by permission of Prentice-Hall, Inc.

Why study attitudes at all, if intention is ultimately a better predictor of behavior? The answer is simple: *intention* may be a better predictor, but it does not provide an adequate explanation of behavior. When marketers want to understand *why* consumers act as they do, they require something more than a basically mechanical measure of what consumers expect to do (e.g., their buying intentions). Similarly, a measure of *affect* may be equivalent to an attitude; however, marketers usually want to know the underlying or salient attributes or beliefs that produce the specific affect (attitude). Figure 8-7 on page 248 illustrates the type of questions that might be used in applying the *theory-of-reasoned-action* model.

Theory of Trying to Consume

There has been an effort underway to extend Fishbein's theory of reasoned action so that it might better accommodate consumers' goals as expressed by their "trying" to consume. It appears that the theory of reasoned action operates fairly well when an outcome (e.g., the actual purchase of a product) is closely preceded by deliberation leading up to the purchase and there is nothing to stop or block the behavior (e.g., shopping for a television set and buying one). However, Fishbein's model does not specifically account for those circumstances when a particular action or behavior is directed towards a **goal** (i.e., something the consumer is *trying* or planning to accomplish).[8]

The theory of trying to consume is designed to account for the many cases where the action or outcome is not certain but instead reflects the consumer's attempts to consume (i.e., purchase). In such cases, there are often *personal impediments* (a consumer is trying to find just the right eyeglass frames for under $200 or trying to lose weight but loves desserts) and/or *environmental impediments* (only the first 500 in line will be able to purchase tickets for the rock concert) that might prevent the desired action or outcome from

1. **Direct Measure of Intention to Buy**

   Which of the following statements best describes the chance that you will buy an IBM ThinkPad 701C* subnotebook computer during the next six months?

   _____ I definitely will buy one.
   _____ I probably will buy one.
   _____ I am uncertain whether I will buy one.
   _____ I probably will not buy one.
   _____ I definitely will not buy one.

2. **Direct Measure of Attitude-Toward-Behavior (beh)**

   See Exhibit 8–5, #1

3. **Indirect Measure of Attitude-Toward-Behavior (beh)**

   See Exhibit 8–5, #2

4. **Direct Measure of Subjective Norm**

   Most of the people who are important to me think I
       should [ ] [ ] [ ] [ ] [ ] [ ] [ ] should not
   buy myself an IBM ThinkPad 701C* subnotebook computer during the next six months.

5. **Indirect Measure of Subjective Norm**

   (1) *Normative belief:*

   My wife thinks I
       should [ ] [ ] [ ] [ ] [ ] [ ] [ ] should not
   buy myself an IBM ThinkPad 701C* subnotebook computer during the next six months.

   My friends think I
       should [ ] [ ] [ ] [ ] [ ] [ ] [ ] should not
   buy myself an IBM ThinkPad 701C* subnotebook computer during the next six months.

   (2) *Motivation to comply:*

   Typically, I like to do what my wife suggests that I
       should do [ ] [ ] [ ] [ ] [ ] [ ] [ ] should not do.

   Typically, I like to do what my friends suggest that I
       should do [ ] [ ] [ ] [ ] [ ] [ ] [ ] should not do.

   *Would also be measured for the two other brand models of subnotebook computers (i.e., HP OmniBook 600CT and Digital HiNote Ultra CT475).

FIGURE 8-7

An Illustration of How the Theory of Reasoned Action Is Measured

occurring. Again, the key point is that in these cases of trying, the outcome (e.g., purchase, possession, use, or action) is not, and cannot be assumed to be, certain. Table 8-6 lists a few examples of possible personal and environmental impediments that might negatively impact the outcome for a consumer trying to consume.

The theory of trying (see Figure 8-8) recasts Fishbein's theory-of-reasoned-action model by replacing *behavior* with *trying* to behave (consume) as the variable to be explained and/or predicted. Also, following the progression of thinking established by the theory-of-reasoned-action model, *trying* to accomplish a particular goal is preceded by *intention to try*, which in turn is determined by *attitude toward trying* and *social norms toward trying*. Still further, *attitude toward trying* is impacted by the individual consumer's (1) *attitude toward success* and **expectations of success**, (2) *attitude toward failure* and **expectations of failure**, and (3) *attitude toward process* (e.g., the consumer's assessment of how the "act" of trying to do something makes him or her feel, regardless of the outcome). Finally, each of the three attitudes (i.e., toward success, toward failure, and toward process) are determined by the summation of the "product" of the *consequence likelihoods* (e.g., the chance that a person anticipates "looking better from dieting") and *consequence evaluations* (e.g., how pleasant it would be for the person to "look better").

table 8-6

Selected Examples of Potential Impediments That Might Impact on Trying

POTENTIAL PERSONAL IMPEDIMENTS

"I wonder whether my fingernails will be longer by the time of my wedding."

"I want to try to lose fifteen pounds by next summer."

"I'm going to try to get tickets for a Broadway show for your birthday."

"I'm going to attempt to give up smoking by my birthday."

"I am going to increase how often I go to the gym from two to four times a week."

"Tonight, I'm not going to have dessert at the restaurant."

POTENTIAL ENVIRONMENTAL IMPEDIMENTS

"The first ten people to call in will receive a free T-shirt."

"Sorry, the shoes didn't come in this shipment from Italy."

"There are only three bottles of champagne in our stockroom. You better come in sometime today."

"I am sorry. We cannot serve you. We are closing the restaurant because of a problem with the oven."

Unique to the theory of trying to consume, the model proposes that the *frequency of past trying* (i.e., the consumer's prior experience with trying) impacts on both intention-to-try and the act of trying, and that *recency of past trying* (i.e., the consumer's most recent

FIGURE 8-8 The Theory of Trying

Source: RICHARD P. BAGOZZI and PAUL R. WARSHAW, "Trying to Consume," *Journal of Consumer Research* 17 (September 1990), 131. Reprinted by permission of The University of Chicago Press as publisher.

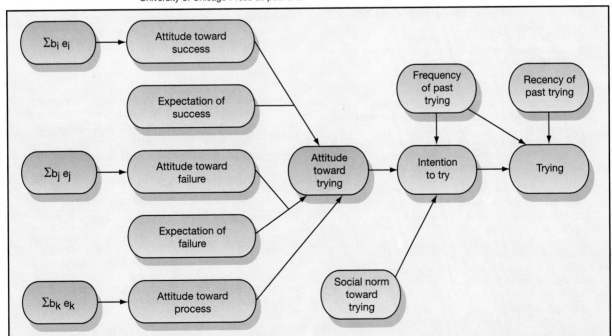

Note: Regarding the Σbe terms, the **b**'s are consequence likelihoods, the **e**'s are consequence evaluations; subscript **i** refers to consequences contingent on success, subscript **j** refers to consequences contingent on failure, and subscript **k** refers to consequences associated with the process of trying, independent of success or failure considerations.

experience with trying) impacts solely on trying. The results of initial research support the importance of these two factors in providing understanding and predictive accuracy of trying to consume. Figure 8-9 provides examples of the questions that might be used to measure the variables that make up the theory of trying (as depicted in Figure 8-8).

FIGURE 8-9 How the Theory of Trying Is Measured

Source: Based on RICHARD P. BAGOZZI and PAUL R. WARSHAW. "Trying to Consume," *Journal of Consumer Research* 17 (September 1990), 134. Reprinted by permission of The University of Chicago Press as publisher.

Trying is assessed by a self-report measure in terms of *past frequency*, *recency*, *beliefs*, and *evaluations of consequences*. Example: Trying to buy a house.

A. Past Frequency
During the past two years, I have looked for a house to buy

[1]	[2]	[3]	[4]	[5]	[6]
very many times	many times	several times	a couple of times	once	not at all

B. Recency
During the past six months, I have looked for a house to buy. _____ yes _____ no

C. Beliefs about consequent likelihoods are measured on a series of 7-point scales, using *extremely likely/extremely unlikely* as end-points.

1. Beliefs about **trying and succeeding:**
   a. I would feel very good about myself.
   b. My family would be very proud.
   c. My children would grow up in a better environment.
   d. My wife would be happier.
   e. My home life would be more enjoyable.

2. Beliefs about **trying but failing:**
   a. If I lose my job I won't have to worry about mortgage payments.
   b. No bank would give me a mortgage.
   c. I won't have to worry about gardening chores.
   d. I would have more free time.
   e. My family would be disappointed in me.

3. Beliefs about **the process itself:**
   a. It's fun going through other people's houses.
   b. Looking gives my wife and me something to do on weekends.
   c. Looking at houses I can't afford depresses me.
   d. It's hard to know how firm an asking price is.
   e. The broker is really working for the seller.

D. Evaluations of Consequences are assessed on the same series of 7-point scales as **beliefs**, using *very satisfying/very unsatisfying* as end points.

1. **Trying and succeeding:**
   a. I would feel very good about myself.
   b. My family would be very proud.
   c. My children would grow up in a better environment.
   d. My wife would be happier.
   e. My home life would be more enjoyable.

2. **Trying but failing:**
   a. I won't have to worry about mortgage payments.
   b. No bank would give me a mortgage.
   c. I won't have to worry about gardening chores.
   d. I would have more free time.
   e. My family would be disappointed in me.

3. **The process itself:**
   a. It's fun going through other people's houses.
   b. Looking gives my wife and me something to do on weekends.
   c. Looking at houses I can't afford depresses me.
   d. It's hard to know how firm an asking price is.
   e. The broker is really working for the seller.

Attitude Toward Trying is measured on a series of 7-point scales.

All things considered, looking for a house this past spring made me feel:

good	[1]	[2]	[3]	[4]	[5]	[6]	[7]	bad
frustrated	[1]	[2]	[3]	[4]	[5]	[6]	[7]	hopeful
happy	[1]	[2]	[3]	[4]	[5]	[6]	[7]	unhappy
satisfied	[1]	[2]	[3]	[4]	[5]	[6]	[7]	dissatisfied

1. Attitude toward **trying and succeeding:**
   a. Finding a house I can afford to buy would make me feel:

lucky	[1]	[2]	[3]	[4]	[5]	[6]	[7]	unlucky
richer	[1]	[2]	[3]	[4]	[5]	[6]	[7]	poorer

2. Attitude toward **trying but failing:**
   a. Not being able to find a house I can afford to buy would make me feel:

lucky	[1]	[2]	[3]	[4]	[5]	[6]	[7]	unlucky
richer	[1]	[2]	[3]	[4]	[5]	[6]	[7]	poorer

Expectations of Success and Failure are measured on a 7-point scale, using *extremely likely/extremely unlikely* as end points. (Expectations represent the individual's perceived control over his or her lifestyle and/or environment.)

1. a. Assuming I *try* to find a house next fall, it is:

extremely likely	[1]	[2]	[3]	[4]	[5]	[6]	[7]	extremely unlikely

that I will actually find a house I can afford.

2. b. Assuming I *try* to find a house next fall, it is:

extremely likely	[1]	[2]	[3]	[4]	[5]	[6]	[7]	extremely unlikely

that I can get a mortgage at a rate I can afford.

Subjective Norms Toward Trying are measured on a 7-point scale, using *extremely likely/extremely unlikely* as end points.

Most people who are important to me think that I should try to buy a house during the next year.

extremely likely	[1]	[2]	[3]	[4]	[5]	[6]	[7]	extremely unlikely

Attitude-Toward-the-Ad Models

In an effort to understand the impact of advertising or some other promotional vehicle (e.g., a catalog) on consumer attitudes toward particular products or brands, considerable attention has been paid to developing what has been referred to as **attitude-toward-the-ad models**.

Figure 8-10 presents a schematic of some of the basic relationships described by an attitude-toward-the-ad model. As the model depicts, the consumer forms various feelings (affects) and judgments (cognitions) as the result of exposure to an ad. These feelings and judgments in turn affect the consumer's *attitude toward the ad* and *beliefs about the brand* acquired from exposure to the ad. Finally, the consumer's attitude toward the ad and beliefs about the brand influence his or her *attitude toward the brand*.[9]

In assessing consumer attitudes toward an ad, researchers maintain that it is critical to distinguish between and separately measure *cognitive evaluations of the ad* (i.e., judgments about the ad, such as whether it is "humorous" or "informative") and *affective responses toward the ad* (i.e., feelings experienced from exposure to the ad, including "a sense of fear" or "a smile" or "laughter").[10] Table 8-7 on page 252 presents an example of how feelings or emotions (affective responses) and cognitive evaluations (judgments) have been measured within the context of studying attitudes toward an ad.

Drawing upon the Elaboration Likelihood Model (see Chapters 5, 7, 9, and 10), researchers have also examined various underlying elements of attitude toward the ad model. Specifically, they have suggested that in high-involvement situations it is more "central" factors (e.g., the message's argument or the informational content of the ad) that will influence consumers, whereas in low-involvement situations it is more "peripheral" factors (e.g., the use of celebrities or the visual mood) that impacts consumers' responses.[11] However, recent research shows that both central (the message argument, itself) *and* peripheral (the background music in a TV commercial) factors significantly influence the formation of the attitude toward the ad across various levels of consumer involvement.[12] These research findings imply that marketers need to ensure that even in low-involvement situations, their messages create favorable perceptions based on the argument's quality and credibility. Likewise, even in high-involvement situations, the marketers' message should also not neglect peripheral or context message elements.

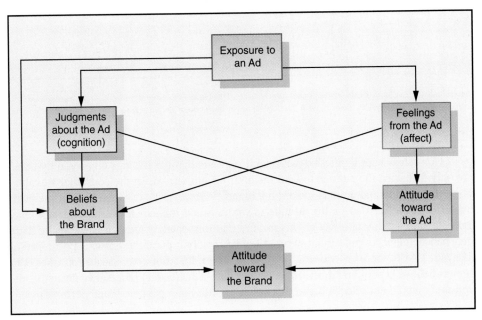

FIGURE 8-10

A Conception of the Relationship Among Elements in an Attitude-Toward-the-Ad Model
Source: Inspired by and based in part on JULIE A. EDELL and MARIAN CHAPMAN BURKE, "The Power of Feelings in Understanding Advertising Effects," *Journal of Consumer Research* 14 (December 1987), 431. Reprinted by permission of The University of Chicago Press as publisher.

table 8-7   Examples of How Feelings and Judgments Are Assessed in Studies of Attitudes Toward Advertisements

A. Gauging affective responses (feelings) to the ad:

Instructions:

We would like you to tell us how the ad you just saw made you *feel*. We are interested in your reactions to the ad, *not* how you would describe it.

The following are sample *feeling-items* that consumers would rank on a five-point scale in terms of how well the word describes the consumer's feelings ("very strongly" = 5; "not at all" = 1):

Active	[1]	[2]	[3]	[4]	[5]
Amused	[1]	[2]	[3]	[4]	[5]
Carefree	[1]	[2]	[3]	[4]	[5]
Creative	[1]	[2]	[3]	[4]	[5]
Elated	[1]	[2]	[3]	[4]	[5]
Joyous	[1]	[2]	[3]	[4]	[5]
Inspired	[1]	[2]	[3]	[4]	[5]
Sad	[1]	[2]	[3]	[4]	[5]
Suspicious	[1]	[2]	[3]	[4]	[5]

B. Gauging cognitive evaluations (judgments) of the ad:

Instructions:

Now please tell us how well you think each of the words listed below describes the ad you have just seen. Here we are interested in your thoughts about the ad, not about the brand or the product class.

The following are samples of judgment items that consumers would rank on a five-point scale in terms of how well the word describes the ad ("extremely well" = 5; "not at all well" = 1):

Believable	[1]	[2]	[3]	[4]	[5]
Exciting	[1]	[2]	[3]	[4]	[5]
Humorous	[1]	[2]	[3]	[4]	[5]
Interesting	[1]	[2]	[3]	[4]	[5]
Phony	[1]	[2]	[3]	[4]	[5]
Tender	[1]	[2]	[3]	[4]	[5]
Terrible	[1]	[2]	[3]	[4]	[5]
Valuable	[1]	[2]	[3]	[4]	[5]

Source: Adapted from MARIAN CHAPMAN BURKE and JULIE A. EDELL, "The Impact of Feelings on Ad-Based Affect and Cognition," *Journal of Marketing Research* 26 (February 1989), 73–74, published by the American Marketing Association. Reprinted by permission.

Consistent with Figure 8-10, research suggests that the feelings conveyed by an ad not only influence the attitude toward the ad itself but also affect the consumer's evaluations of the brand and attitude toward the brand.[13] However, it also appears that the positive effect of a liked ad on the attitude toward a brand immediately after exposure may dwindle after a delay of a week. This implies that immediately after an ad exposure there may be a heightened impact that wears off quite rapidly if purchase action is postponed or delayed.[14] Also, there is evidence that liking an ad does not compensate for what consumers believe is poor brand performance, nor does a disliked ad necessarily mean that the consumer would not select a brand that is felt to offer more positive brand performance.[15]

Such research is helping to create a better understanding of how the consumer's attitude toward specific ads influences the consumer's attitudes toward particular brands.

A number of other interesting observations can be drawn from attitude-toward-the-ad research. Specifically, it appears that for a novel product (e.g., "contact lens for pets"), the consumer's attitude toward the ad has a *stronger* impact on brand attitude and purchase intention than for a familiar product (e.g., pet food).[16] This same research found that beliefs about a brand (brand cognition) that result from ad exposure play a much stronger role in determining attitudes toward the brand for a familiar product. This research points up the importance of considering the nature of the attitude object in assessing the potential impact of advertising exposure.

Still other research indicates that both negative and positive feelings toward ads tend to exist side by side, with both uniquely influencing an attitude.[17] This suggests the importance of assessing a wide variety of feelings (both positive and negative) when one is studying the influence of ad exposure.

Finally, research reveals that attitudes toward ads in general seem to have little impact on the attitude toward a specific ad. However, the attitude toward a specific *type* of advertising (e.g., comparative advertising) may have some impact on the attitude toward a specific ad.[18] If corroborated, these findings would establish that individuals who profess to "hate" ads in general (or to "love" advertising) would still be likely to form a unique attitude toward a specific ad (e.g., liking or disliking it). In the case of responses to a specific *type* of advertising, the implications are different. It appears, for instance, that if a consumer dislikes comparative advertising, a specific comparative ad (e.g., Clairol Men's Choice versus Combé's Just for Men hair-coloring products) would be negatively influenced by the attitude toward comparative advertising in general.

summary

An attitude is a learned predisposition to behave in a consistently favorable or unfavorable way with respect to a given object (e.g., a product category, a brand, a service, an advertisement, or a retail establishment). Each property of this definition is critical to understanding why and how attitudes are relevant in consumer behavior and marketing.

Of considerable importance in understanding the role of attitudes in consumer behavior is an appreciation of the structure and composition of an attitude. Four broad categories of attitude models have received attention: the tricomponent attitude model, multiattribute attitude models, trying-to-consume attitude models, and attitude-toward-the-ad models.

The tricomponent model of attitudes consists of three parts: a cognitive component, an affective component, and a conative component. The cognitive component captures a consumer's knowledge and perceptions (i.e., beliefs) about products and services. The affective component focuses on a consumer's emotions or feelings with respect to a particular product or service. Evaluative in nature, the affective component determines an individual's overall assessment of the attitude object in terms of some kind of favorableness rating. The conative component is concerned with the likelihood that a consumer will act in a specific fashion with respect to the attitude object. In marketing and consumer behavior, the conative component is frequently treated as an expression of the consumer's intention to buy.

Multiattribute attitude models (i.e., attitude-toward-object, attitude-toward-behavior, and the theory of reasoned action) have received much attention from consumer researchers. As a group, these models examine consumer beliefs about specific-product attributes (e.g., product or brand features or benefits). Recently, there has been an effort underway to extend Fishbein's theory of reasoned action so that it might better accommodate consumers' goals as expressed by their "trying to consume" (i.e., a goal the consumer is trying or planning to accomplish). The theory of trying is designed to account for the many cases in which the action or outcome is not certain. The attitude-toward-the-ad models examine the influence of advertisements on the consumer's attitudes toward the brand.

discussion questions

1. Explain how situational factors are likely to influence the degree of consistency between attitudes and behavior.

2. Because attitudes are learned predispositions to respond, why don't marketers and consumer researchers just measure purchase behavior and forget attitudes?

3. Explain a person's attitude toward visiting Disney World in terms of the tricomponent attitude model.

4. Multiattribute models examine attitudes in terms of selected product attributes. What are the attributes on which you would like to evaluate your professor at the end of the semester? On which attributes would you evaluate this textbook?

5. In designing a new version of its Trinitron 27-inch color television, Sony conducted research into consumers attitudes toward the existing 27-inch model. Which attitude model would be more appropriate for this task: the tricomponent attitude model, attitude-toward-object model, or the attitude-toward-behavior model? Explain your choice and discuss the strategic marketing implications of the model you selected.

6. Assume that a VCR manufacturer conducted a consumer survey using the Fishbein attitude-toward-object model (see Figure 8-4) with the following results (average scores):

Attribute	Attribute Evaluations	Brand Beliefs
Clear picture	+3	+2
Cable-ready	+3	−1
Low price	+1	+1
Durable	+2	+3
Modern-looking	+1	+3

a. Calculate the overall score for the brand.

b. Calculate the maximum total score the brand could have received, given the attribute evaluations.

c. Discuss consumer perceptions of the strengths and weaknesses of this brand and their implications for marketing the brand.

7. Should a marketer of luxury cars use the attitude-toward-object model, the attitude-toward-behavior model, or the theory-of-reasoned-action model in assessing consumers' attitudes toward the company's cars? Explain your answer.

8. How can the marketer of a "nicotine patch" (a device which assists individuals to quit smoking) use the *theory of trying* to segment its market? Using this theory, identify two segments that the marketer should target and propose product positioning approaches to be directed at each of the two segments.

exercises

1. Find two print ads, one illustrating the use of the affective component and the other illustrating the cognitive component. Discuss each ad in the context of the tricomponent model. In your view, why has each marketer taken the approach it did in each of these ads?

2. Identify five attributes that you seek in a soft drink and two soft drink brands that you consumed over the past month. Using the format in Figure 8-4, (a) calculate your evaluative component regarding soft-drinks, (b) calculate your beliefs regarding each brand separately, and (c) compose an attitude-toward-object analysis for each of the two brands. What implications do your findings have for the marketer of the brand that received the lower total score in your analysis?

3. Watch a television commercial for a *product category you frequently use* that advertises a brand you have never tried. Using the dimensions and attributes presented in Table 8-7, evaluate your attitude toward the commercial. Discuss the relationship between your evaluation of the commercial and your attitude toward your regular brand.

key words

- Affective component
- Attitude consistency
- Attitude "object"
- Attitudes
- Attitude-toward-behavior model
- Attitude-toward-object model
- Attitude-toward-the-ad model
- Cognitions and beliefs
- Expectations of success and failure
- Goal
- Intention-to-buy scales
- Learned predispositions
- Multiattribute attitude models
- Normative beliefs
- Personal and environmental impediments to action
- Subjective norms
- Theory of trying
- Theory-of-reasoned-action model
- Tricomponent attitude model
- Trying-to-consume model

1. PATRICK M. REILLY, "Shoppers Buy Up a Bounty of Natural Beauty Products," *The Wall Street Journal*, June 8, 1994, B1.

2. RICHARD J. LUTZ, "The Role of Attitude Theory in Marketing," in Harold H. Kassarjian and Thomas S. Robertson, eds., *Perspectives in Consumer Behavior*, 4th edition (Englewood Cliffs, NJ: Prentice-Hall, 1991), 317–39.

3. JOEL B. COHEN and CHARLES S. ARENI, "Affect and Consumer Behavior," in Harold H. Kassarjian and Thomas S. Robertson, eds., op. cit, 188–240; and MADELINE JOHNSON and GEORGE M. ZINKHAN, "Emotional Responses to a Professional Service Encounter," *Journal of Service Marketing* 5, Spring 1991, 5–16.

4. ICEK AJZEN and MARTIN FISHBEIN, *Understanding Attitudes and Predicting Social Behavior* (Englewood Cliffs, NJ: Prentice-Hall, 1980); and MARTIN FISHBEIN and ICEK AJZEN, *Belief, Attitude, Intentions, and Behavior* (Reading, MA: Addison-Wesley, 1975).

5. MARTIN FISHBEIN, "An Investigation of the Relationships Between Beliefs About an Object and the Attitude Toward the Object," *Human Relations* 16, 1963, 233–40; and MARTIN FISHBEIN, "A Behavioral Theory Approach to the Relations Between Beliefs About an Object and the Attitude Toward the Object," in Martin Fishbein, ed., *Readings in Attitude Theory and Measurement* (New York: Wiley, 1967), 389–400.

6. AJZEN and FISHBEIN, op. cit., 62–63. Also, see: ROBERT E. BURNKRANT, H. RAO UNNAVA, and THOMAS J. PAGE, JR., "Effects of Experience on Attitude Structure," in Rebecca H. Holman and Michael R. Solomon, eds., *Advances in Consumer Research* 18 (Provo, UT: Association for Consumer Research, 1991), 28–29.

7. TERENCE A. SHIMP and ALICAN KAVAS, "The Theory of Reasoned Action Applied to Coupon Usage," *Journal of Consumer Research* 11, December 1984, 795–809; BLAIR H. SHEPPARD, JON HARTWICK, and PAUL R. WARSHAW, "The Theory of Reasoned Action: A Meta-Analysis of Past Research with Recommendations for Modifications and Future Research," *Journal of Consumer Research* 15, September 1986, 325–43; SHARON E. BEATLY and LYNN R. KAHLE, "Alternative Hierarchies of the Attitude-Behavior Relationship: The Impact of Brand Commitment and Habit," *Journal of the Academy of Marketing Science* 16, Summer 1988, 1–10; and RICHARD P. BAGOZZI, HANS BAUMGARTNER, and YOUJAE YI, "Coupon Usage and the Theory of Reasoned Action," in Rebecca H. Holman and Michael R. Solomon, eds., *Advances in Consumer Research* 18 (Provo, UT: Association for Consumer Research, 1991), 24–27.

8. RICHARD P. BAGOZZI and PAUL R. WARSHAW, "Trying to Consume," *Journal of Consumer Research* 17, September 1990, 127–40; RICHARD P. BAGOZZI, FRED D. DAVIS, and PAUL R. WARSHAW, "Development and Test of a Theory of Technological Learning and Usage," *Human Relations* 45(7), July 1992, 659–86; and ANIL MATHUR, "From Intentions to Behavior: The Role of Trying and Control," in Barbara B. Stern and George M. Zinkan, eds., *1995 AMA Educators' Proceedings* (Chicago: American Marketing Association, 1995), 374–75.

9. RAJEEV BATRA and MICHAEL L. RAY, "Affective Responses Mediating Acceptance of Advertising," *Journal of Consumer Research* 13, September 1986, 236–39; JULIE A. EDELL and MARIAN CHAPMAN BURKE, "The Power of Feelings in Understanding Advertising Effects," *Journal of Consumer Research* 14, December 1987, 421–33; and MARIAN CHAPMAN BURKE and JULIE A. EDELL, "The Impact of Feelings on Ad-Based Affect and Cognition," *Journal of Marketing Research* 26, February 1989, 69–83.

10. THOMAS J. MADDEN, CHRIS T. ALLEN, and JACQUELYN L. TWIBLE, "Attitude Toward the Ad: An Assessment of Diverse Measurement Indices Under Different Processing Sets," *Journal of Marketing Research* 25, August 1988, 242–52; and SCOT BURTON and DONALD R. LICTENSTEIN, "The Effect of Ad Claims and Ad Context on Attitude Toward the Advertisement," *Journal of Advertising* 17, 1988, 3–11. Also, see: SRINIVAS DURVASULA, J. CRAIG ANDREWS, STEVEN LYSONSKI, and RICHARD G. NETEMEYER, "Assessing the Cross–National Applicability of Consumer Behavior Models: A Model of Attitude Toward Advertising in General," *Journal of Consumer Research* 19, March 1993, 626–36.

11. SCOTT B. MACKENZIE, RICHARD LUTZ, and GEORGE E. BELCH, "The Role of Attitude Toward the Ad as a Mediator of Advertising Effectiveness: A Test of Competing Explanations," *Journal of Marketing Research*, May 1986, 130–43; and SCOTT B. MACKENZIE and RICHARD J. LUTZ, "An Empirical Examination of the Structural Antecedents of Attitude Toward the Ad in an Advertising Pretesting Context," *Journal of Marketing Research*, April 1989, 48–65.

12. KENNETH R. LORD, MYUNG-SOO LEE, and PAUL L. SAUER, "The Combined Influence Hypothesis: Central and Peripheral Antecedents of Attitude Toward the Ad," *Journal of Advertising* 24, Spring 1995, 73–85.

13. BURKE and EDELL, op. cit., 82–83.

14. AMITAVA CHATTOPADHYAY and PRAKASH NEDUNGADI, "Does Attitude Toward the Ad Endure? The Moderating Effects of Attention and Delay," *Journal of Consumer Research* 19, June 1992, 26–33.

15. GABRIEL BIEHAL, DEBRA STEPHENS, and ELEONORA CURLO, "Attitude Toward the Ad and Brand Choice," *Journal of Advertising* 21, September 1992, 19–39.

16. DENA SALIAGAS COX and WILLIAM B. LOCANDER, "Product Novelty: Does It Moderate the Relationship Between Ad Attitudes and Brand Attitudes?" *Journal of Advertising* 16, 1987, 39–44. Also, see: CYNTHIA B. HANSON and GABRIEL J. BIEHAL, "Accessibility Effects on the Relationship Between Attitude Toward the Ad and Brand Choice," in Frank R. Kardes and Mita Sujan, eds., *Advances in Consumer Research* 22 (Provo, UT: Association for Consumer Research, 1995), 152–58.

17. EDELL and BURKE, op. cit., 430–33.

18. DARREL D. MUEHLING, "Comparative Advertising: The Influence of Attitude-toward-the-Ad on Brand Evaluation," *Journal of Advertising* 16, 1987, 43–49; and DARREL D. MUEHLING, "The Influence of Attitudes-toward-Advertising-in-General on Attitudes-toward-an-Ad," in Terence A. Shimp et al., eds., *1986 AMA Educators' Proceedings* (Chicago: American Marketing Association, 1986), 29–34.

Now all **we** need is **a refrigerator** and a **sink.**

Blue is her favorite color. This week. Her latest work of art is just what the fridge door needed. Spending a rainy afternoon with her is just what I needed.

 For hands that love every color in the rainbow, there's new Ivory Liqui-Gel. It washes away dirt and germs, but retains skin's natural moisture better than soap can, helping your family's hands stay clean, soft and smooth

Ivory Skin Cleansing Liqui-Gel
A gentle kind of clean.

White liquid Ivory is still available in the refill size.

This chapter continues the discussion of attitudes begun in Chapter 8. The preceding chapter defined what we mean by *attitudes*, explored their various properties, and examined a number of attitude models and attitude measurement techniques. This chapter focuses on the important topics of **attitude formation** and **attitude change**. Particular attention is given to showing how marketers and advertisers create messages aimed at influencing consumers' attitudes. Building on this discussion, the chapter concludes with a brief examination of **cognitive dissonance theory** and **attribution theory**.

M ost of the change we see in life is due to truths being in and out of favor.

—Robert Frost 1875–1963
The Black Cottage

ATTITUDE FORMATION

How do people, especially young people, form their initial *general* attitudes toward "things"? Consider their attitudes toward clothing they wear, for example: underwear, casual wear, and business attire. On a more specific level, how do they form attitudes toward Fruit of the Loom or Calvin Klein underwear, or Levi's or the Gap casual wear, or Anne Klein or Emporium Armani business clothing? Also, what about where such clothing is purchased? Would they buy their underwear, casual wear, and business clothing at K-Mart, Sears, JC Penney, or Macy's? How do family members and friends, admired celebrities, mass media advertisements, even cultural memberships, influence the formation of their attitudes concerning consuming or not consuming each of these types of apparel items? Why do some attitudes seem to persist indefinitely, while others change fairly often? The answers to such questions are of vital importance to marketers, for without knowing how attitudes are formed, they are unable to understand or to influence consumer attitudes or behavior.

Our examination of attitude formation is divided into three areas: how attitudes are *learned*, the *sources of influence* on attitude formation, and the impact of *personality* on attitude formation.

How Attitudes are Learned

When we speak of the formation of an attitude, we refer to the shift from having no attitude toward a given object (e.g., a notebook computer) to having *some* attitude toward it (e.g., a notebook computer is useful when traveling). The shift from no attitude to an attitude (i.e., the *attitude formation*) is a result of learning. In this section we will briefly discuss how the learning theories discussed in Chapter 7 relate to attitude formation.

▲ **Classical Conditioning** Consumers often purchase new products that are associated with a favorably viewed brand name. Their favorable attitude toward the brand name is frequently the result of repeated satisfaction with other products produced by the same company. Using the classical conditioning terms and ideas introduced in Chapter 7, the brand name is the *unconditioned* stimulus that, through *repetition* and positive reinforcement, results in a favorable attitude (the unconditioned response). The idea of family branding is based on this form of attitude learning. For example, by giving a new skin cleaning gel the benefit of its well-known and respected family name, Ivory® is counting on an extension of the favorable attitudes already associated with the brand name to the Ivory® product. They are counting on *stimulus generalization* from the brand name to the new product (see Figure 9-1).

Similarly, marketers who associate their new products with admired celebrities are trying to create a positive association between the celebrity, who already enjoys a positive attitude, and the "neutral" new product. They hope the recognition and goodwill (the positive attitude) the celebrity enjoys is transferred to their product, so that potential consumers will quickly form positive attitudes toward the new product. In consumer goods marketing—like sneakers and soft drinks—it is commonplace to use celebrities to help launch new products (see Chapter 11 for examples of the power of celebrities).

▲ **Instrumental Conditioning** Sometimes, attitudes *follow* the purchase and consumption of a product. For example, a consumer may purchase a brand name product *without* having a prior attitude toward it, because it is the only product of its kind available (e.g., the last tube of toothpaste in a hotel drugstore). Consumers also make trial purchases of new brands from product categories in which they have little personal involvement (see Chap-

ter 7). If they find the purchased brand to be satisfactory, then they are likely to develop a favorable attitude toward it.

▲ **Cognitive Learning Theory** In situations in which consumers seek to solve a problem or satisfy a need, they are likely to form attitudes (either positive or negative) about products on the basis of information exposure and their own cognition (knowledge and beliefs). For instance, given a snowy winter, Ross has been looking for a pair of dress shoes to wear to work that are "weatherproof." When Ross learns that Florsheim has a line of men's waterproof shoes that are appropriate to wear with a business suit, he is likely to form a positive attitude toward Florsheim's Dri-Treds, especially if he has had positive experience with other types of Florsheim shoes (see Figure 9-2 on page 260).

In general, the more information consumers have about a product or service, the more likely they are to form attitudes about it, either positive or negative. However, regardless of available information, consumers are not always ready or willing to process product-related information. Furthermore, consumers often use only a limited amount of the information available to them. As Chapter 10 (Communication and Persuasion) points out, consumers usually absorb only three or four bits of information at one time. Research suggests that only two or three important beliefs about a product dominate in the formation of attitudes and that less important beliefs provide little additional input.[1] This finding suggests that marketers should fight off the impulse to include *all* the features of their products and services in their ads; rather, they should focus on the few key points that are at the heart of what distinguishes their product from the competition.

FIGURE 9-2

Linking the Satisfaction
of a Need and Attitude
Formation
Courtesy of Florsheim

Sources of Influence on Attitude Formation

The formation of consumer attitudes is strongly influenced by *personal experience*, the *influence* of family and friends, *direct marketing*, and *mass media*.

▲ **Direct Experience** The primary means by which attitudes toward goods and services are formed is through the consumer's direct experience in trying and evaluating them.[2] Recognizing the importance of direct experience, marketers frequently attempt to stimulate trial of new products by offering cents-off coupons or even free samples.

Figure 9-3 illustrates this strategy; the ad for Clairol's Natural Instincts includes a coupon for a full refund to encourage trial. To further create a positive attitude and to promote trial, Clairol also includes a toll-free 800 number that provides potential consumers with an opportunity to get their questions answered. In such cases, the marketer's objective is to get consumers to try the new product and then to evaluate it. If a product proves satisfactory, then it is likely that consumers will form positive attitudes and repurchase the product.

▲ **Influence of Family and Friends** As we come into contact with others, especially family, close friends, and admired individuals (e.g., a respected teacher), we form attitudes that influence our lives. The family is an extremely important source of influence on the formation of attitudes, for it is the family that provides us with many of our basic values and a wide range of less central beliefs. For instance, young children who are "rewarded" for good behavior with sweet foods and candy often retain a taste for (and positive attitude toward) sweets as adults.

FIGURE 9-3

A New Product with a Cents-Off Coupon Encouraging Trial
Courtesy of Clairol

▲ **Direct Marketing** Marketers are increasingly using highly focused direct marketing programs to target small consumer niches with products and services that fit their interests and lifestyles. (Niche marketing is sometimes called _micromarketing_.) Marketers very carefully target customers on the basis of their demographic, psychographic, or geodemographic profiles with highly personalized product offerings (e.g., golf clubs for left-handed people) and messages that show they understand their special needs and desires. Direct marketing efforts have an excellent chance of favorably influencing target consumers' attitudes, because the products and services offered, and the promotional messages conveyed, are very carefully designed to address the individual segment's needs and concerns and, thus, are able to achieve a higher "hit rate" than mass marketing.

▲ **Exposure to Mass Media** In countries where people have easy access to newspapers and a variety of general and special-interest magazines and television channels, consumers are constantly exposed to new ideas, products, opinions, and advertisements. These mass media communications provide an important source of information that influences the formation of consumer attitudes.

Personality Factors

Personality also plays a critical role in attitude formation. For example, individuals with a high *need for cognition* (i.e., those who crave information and enjoy thinking) are likely to form positive attitudes in response to ads or direct mail that are rich in product-related information. On the other hand, consumers who are relatively *low in need for cognition* are more likely to form positive attitudes in response to ads that feature an attractive model or well-known celebrity. (See Chapters 5, 7, 8, and 10 for relevant applications of the *central-and-peripheral-routes-to-persuasion theory*.) In a similar fashion, attitudes toward new products and new consumption situations are strongly influenced by specific personality characteristics of consumers.

ATTITUDE CHANGE

It is important to recognize that much that has been said about *attitude formation* is also basically true of attitude change. That is, attitude changes are *learned*; they are influenced by *personal experience* and other *sources of information*, and *personality* affects both the receptivity and the speed with which attitudes are likely to be altered.

Strategies of Attitude Change

Altering consumer attitudes is a key strategy consideration for most marketers. For marketers who are fortunate enough to be market leaders and to enjoy a significant amount of customer goodwill and loyalty, the overriding goal is to fortify the existing positive attitudes of customers so that they will not succumb to competitors' special offers and other enticements designed to win them over. For instance, in many product categories (e.g., greeting cards, in which Hallmark has been the leader, or wet shaving systems, in which Gillette has dominated), most competitors take aim at the market leaders when developing their marketing strategies. Their objective is to change the attitudes of the market leaders' customers and win them over. Among the **attitude-change strategies** that are available to them are: (1) changing the consumer's basic motivational function, (2) associating the product with an admired group or event, (3) resolving two conflicting attitudes, (4) altering components of the multiattribute model, and (5) changing consumer beliefs about competitors brands.

▲ **Changing the Basic Motivational Function** An effective strategy for changing consumer attitudes toward a product or brand is to make new needs prominent. One method for changing motivation is known as the **functional approach**.[3] According to this approach, attitudes can be classified in terms of four functions: the **utilitarian function**, the **ego-defensive function**, the **value-expressive function**, and the **knowledge function**.

THE UTILITARIAN FUNCTION We hold certain brand attitudes partly because of a brand's utility. When a product has helped us in the past, even in a small way, our attitude toward it tends to be favorable. One way of changing attitudes in favor of a product is by showing people that it can serve a utilitarian purpose that they may not have considered. For example, as its consistent market positioning, Malt-O-Meal cereals feature their utilitarian benefit in terms of costing less than the market leaders. Similarly, in Figure 9-4 Comet cleaner with bleach also stresses its superior cleaning ability (a utilitarian benefit).

THE EGO-DEFENSIVE FUNCTION Most people want to protect their self-images from inner feelings of uncertainty or doubt. Ads for cosmetics and personal care products, by acknowledging this need, increase both their relevance to the consumer and the likelihood of a favorable attitude change by offering reassurance to the consumer's self-concept. For example, the ad in Figure 9-5 for Ortho's Retin-A counter argues a number of common parental statements about teenage acne (e.g., "There's nothing you can do about it") with the statement "No matter what anybody says, it's your face and you can take action." Ortho's response shows understanding and is reassuring to potential consumers.

FIGURE 9-5

Appeal to the Ego-Defensive Function
Reprinted with permission of copyright owner, Ortho-McNeil Pharmaceutical Company

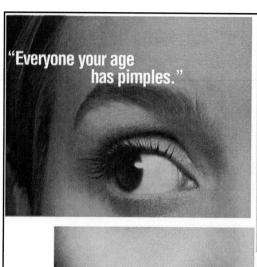

"Everyone your age has pimples."

"You'll grow out of it."

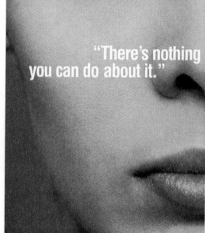

"There's nothing you can do about it."

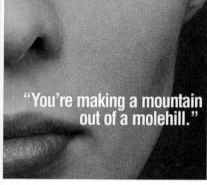

"You're making a mountain out of a molehill."

No matter what anybody says, it's your face and you can take action.

You can make it clearer. You can make it more healthy-looking. You can even make it blemish-free. Whether you have five pimples or fifteen.

Retin-A is a proven prescription treatment you can only get from your healthcare provider. Unlike other products that simply cover up or dry out pimples, Retin-A works at the source where blemishes begin.

It contains tretinoin, a vitamin A derivative much like the naturally occurring one in your body. Retin-A is thought to help lift excess oil and pore-clogging skin cells to the surface. It also helps prevent this cell build-up from recurring, so you can maintain the improvement in your skin.

Retin-A doesn't work overnight. However, with continued use you may start to notice an overall improvement. So be patient.

During the first few weeks, some irritation, including redness and peeling, will be experienced by most patients. Generally, these effects are manageable and diminish over time. However, some people with sensitive skin may experience excessive irritation. Since Retin-A may make your skin more sensitive to the sun's rays, be sure to protect your skin from natural or artificial sunlight. For more information, ask your healthcare provider about Retin-A or call: **1-800-99RETIN-A**.

ORTHO

a Johnson & Johnson company

Retin-A (tretinoin)

Retin-A for the skin you want to have.
See additional important information on the following page.

THE VALUE-EXPRESSIVE FUNCTION Attitudes are an expression or reflection of the consumer's general values, lifestyle, and outlook. If a consumer segment generally holds a positive attitude toward owning the latest electronic devices (being "high-tech"), then their attitudes toward new electronic devices are likely to reflect that orientation. Similarly, if a segment of consumers has a positive attitude toward being "in fashion," then their attitudes toward high-fashion clothing are likely to reflect this viewpoint. Thus, by knowing target consumers' attitudes, marketers can better anticipate their values, lifestyle, or outlook and can reflect these characteristics in their ads and direct marketing efforts. The advertisement for Suncloud sunglasses in Figure 9-6 is targeted to individuals who pursue an outdoors and athletic lifestyle. The firm claims it is dedicated to product innovation when it comes to "Working with the sun for the best vision possible."

THE KNOWLEDGE FUNCTION Individuals generally have a strong need to know and understand the people and things with whom they come in contact. The consumer's "need to know," a cognitive need, is important to marketers concerned with product positioning. Indeed, most product and brand positionings are attempts to satisfy the consumer's *need to know* and to improve the consumer's attitudes toward the brand by emphasizing its advantages over competitive brands. For instance, a message for an advanced design toothbrush might point out that it is superior to other toothbrushes in controlling gum disease by removing more plaque. The message might even use a bar graph to contrast its plaque removal abilities to other leading toothbrushes.

FIGURE 9-6

Appeal to Value-Expressive Function
Courtesy of Bausch & Lomb

COMBINING SEVERAL FUNCTIONS Because different consumers may like or dislike the same product or service for different reasons, a functional framework for examining attitudes can be very useful. For instance, three consumers may all have positive attitudes toward Suave hair care products. However, one may be responding solely to the fact that the products work well (the utilitarian function); the second may have the inner confidence to agree with the point "When you know beautiful hair doesn't have to cost a fortune" (an ego-defensive function). The third consumer's favorable attitudes might reflect the realization that Suave has for many years stressed "value" (equal or better products for less)—the **knowledge function**.

▲ **Associating the Product with a Special Group, Event, or Cause** Attitudes are related, at least in part, to certain groups, social events, or causes. It is possible to alter attitudes toward products, services, and brands by pointing out their relationships to particular social groups, events, or causes. For instance, the A.T. Cross advertisement in Figure 9-7

FIGURE 9-7 ▼

Linking a Company and Its Products to a Special Cause
Courtesy of A.T. Cross

describes the company's financial support of Literacy Volunteers of America, and the tie-in between the amount of support and consumers' purchasing their fine writing instruments. (Chapter 20 gives additional examples of cause-related marketing.)

▲ **Resolving Two Conflicting Attitudes** Attitude-change strategies can also take advantage of actual or potential conflict between attitudes. Specifically, if consumers can be made to see that their attitude toward a brand is in conflict with another attitude, they may be induced to change their evaluation of the brand.

For example, Allen, a young accountant who enjoys cooking, has generally believed that canola oil, touted as a "healthy" oil, is not particularly good tasting when used in food preparation. His view is consistent with the more general belief that foods that are good for you taste "bad," and foods that are bad for you taste "good." When Allen is introduced to the Wesson Best Blend oil by one of his friends, he becomes eager to try the new product because of his high regard for Wesson products (positive attitude) and the friend's claim that Wesson's Best Blend is both healthy and good tasting (two potentially conflicting beliefs). If Allen likes the product, then this may help him alter his conflicting beliefs about a food being both healthy *and* tasting good.

Similarly, if Lisa loves full-tasting cheeses (belief #1) but believes that there is too much fat in such cheeses (belief #2), her conflict between these two beliefs may keep her from frequently buying any cheeses. However, if Lisa learns that Healthy Choice has a line of fat-free cheeses, she may resolve her conflict between liking cheese and perceiving it to be high in fat (Figure 9-8 on page 268).

▲ **Altering Components of the Multiattribute Model** In Chapter 8 we discussed a number of multiattribute attitude models. These models have implications for attitude-change strategies. Using the Fishbein *attitude-toward-object* model as a framework, we will consider the following strategies for bringing about attitude change: (1) changing the *relative evaluation of attributes* (e_i), (2) changing *brand beliefs* (b_i), (3) *adding an attribute* (combined $b_i e_i$), and (4) changing the *overall brand rating* (A_o).

CHANGING THE RELATIVE EVALUATION OF ATTRIBUTES (e_i) The market for many product categories is structured so that different consumer segments are attracted to brands that offer different features or beliefs. For instance, within a product category such as headache remedies, there are brands like Extra-Strength Anacin that stress potency and brands like Tylenol that stress gentleness (i.e., contain no aspirin). These two brands of headache remedy historically have appealed to different segments of the overall headache remedy market. Similarly, when it comes to chewing gum, the market can be divided into regular gum and sugar-free gum or into regular gum and bubble gum.

In general, when a product category is naturally divided according to distinct product features or benefits that appeal to a particular segment of consumers, marketers usually have an opportunity to persuade consumers to "crossover," that is, to persuade consumers who prefer one version of the product (e.g., a 35-mm single-lens reflex camera) to shift their favorable attitudes toward another version of the product (e.g., a highly automatic point-and-shoot camera), and possibly vice versa.

Such a strategy is tantamount to *altering the relative evaluation of conflicting product attributes*. In other words, it serves to upgrade consumer beliefs about one product attribute, and either downgrade some other (i.e., parallel) attribute or convince consumers that it is not in conflict with the upgraded attribute. Because the attributes to be changed usually are important and distinctive, if a consumer's evaluation of one attribute can be upgraded, then there may well be a shift in the consumer's overall attitude or even in the intention to buy. If Paula's switch to decaffeinated coffee helps her sleep at night, she may switch to decaffeinated tea because she associates "decaffeination" with relaxation.

FIGURE 9-8

Resolving Two
Conflicting Attitudes
Courtesy of ConAgra

CHANGING BRAND BELIEFS (b$_i$) A second cognitive-oriented strategy for changing attitudes concentrates on changing beliefs or perceptions about the brand itself. This is by far the most common form of advertising appeal. Advertisers constantly are reminding us that their product has "more" or is "better" or "best" in terms of some important product attribute. As a variation on this theme of "more," ads for Palmolive *dishwashing liquid* are designed to *extend* consumers' brand attitudes with regard to the product's gentleness by suggesting that it be used for hand washing of fine clothing items. The WD-40 ad campaign (see Figure 9-9) presents an ongoing series of new and expanded applications for the product.

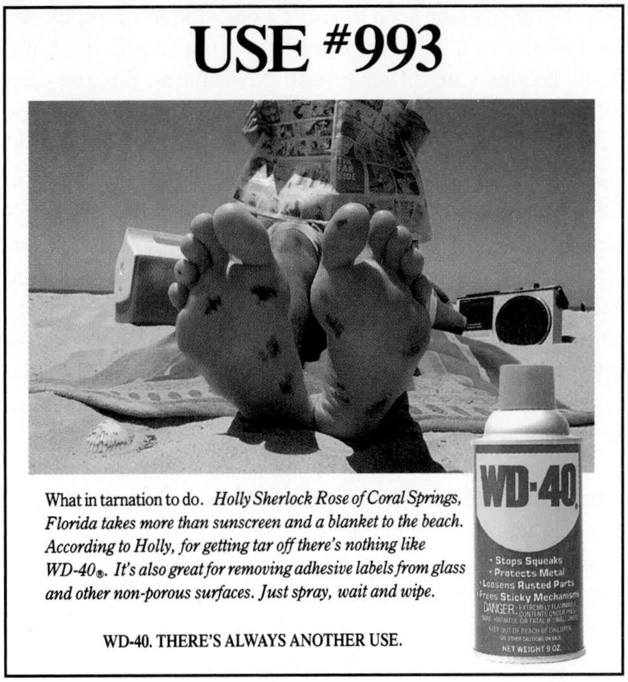
USE #993
What in tarnation to do. Holly Sherlock Rose of Coral Springs, Florida takes more than sunscreen and a blanket to the beach. According to Holly, for getting tar off there's nothing like WD-40®. It's also great for removing adhesive labels from glass and other non-porous surfaces. Just spray, wait and wipe.
WD-40. THERE'S ALWAYS ANOTHER USE.
WD-40
• Stops Squeaks
• Protects Metal
• Loosens Rusted Parts
• Frees Sticky Mechanisms
DANGER:
NET WEIGHT 9 OZ.

FIGURE 9-9

Changing Attitudes by Altering Beliefs About a Brand

Courtesy of WD-40

Three caveats are necessary here. First, in the long run, attempts to change consumer perceptions about a brand attribute will not work if the brand does not actually have the attribute in question. Second, marketers can encourage consumers (e.g., through advertising, a cents-off coupon, or some other marketing tool) to expand use of a brand to situations in which it would not normally be used if consumers' attitudes toward the brand are neither too similar nor too dissimilar from the brands usually used in the situation.[4] To accomplish this, a marketer would have to stress shared or common attributes between the two brands if they are really quite dissimilar or promote unique attributes between the brands if they are really quite similar.

Third, changes in the relative evaluations of both the attribute and the brand-attribute beliefs must not be too drastic, because too extreme an advertising position is likely to result in rejection of the whole message. This caution is based on the **assimilation-contrast** theory.[5] This theory warns that marketers trying to change attitudes by altering the relative evaluations of either attributes or brand-attribute beliefs must be careful to avoid "overkill" or overselling their case. According to this theory, consumers will *assimilate* (or accept) only moderate changes. When the change suggested by a message is too extreme, the contrast likely will result in distortion of the whole message and rejection of the message as being too extreme. For example, many people reject the notion of high cholesterol contributing to heart disease and strokes, because they cannot envision denying themselves butter, or red meat, or rich desserts.

ADDING AN ATTRIBUTE (COMBINED b_ie_i) Another cognitive strategy consists of *adding an attribute*. This can be accomplished either by adding an attribute that previously has been ignored or one that represents an improvement or technological innovation.

The first route, adding a previously ignored attribute is illustrated by the ad in Figure 9-10, which notes that yogurt has more potassium than a banana (a fruit associated with a high quantity of potassium). For consumers interested in increasing their intake of potassium, the comparison of yogurt and bananas has the power of enhancing their attitudes toward yogurt.

The second route adding an attribute that reflects an actual product change or technological innovation is easier to accomplish than stressing a previously ignored attribute.

An example can be seen in Dove's decision to introduce an unscented version of its popular moisturizing bar. For instance, a woman with a strong preference for unscented cosmetic products might have been unwilling to buy the original Dove soap. However, her attitude toward Dove may change when she learns that now it is available in an unscented version. In a similar fashion, Cat Chow Special Care formula for cats adds ingredients that helps cat owners maintain their cat's urinary tract health.

CHANGING THE OVERALL BRAND RATING (A_o) Still another cognitive-oriented strategy consists of attempting to alter consumers' *overall assessment of the brand* directly, without attempting to improve or change their evaluation of any single brand attribute. Such a strategy frequently relies on some form of global statement that "this is the largest-selling brand" or "the one all others try to imitate," or a similar claim that sets the brand apart from all its competitors. This strategy has regularly been part of Honda's advertising approach of affirming that its cars are used by other auto manufacturers as the "standard" to live up to.

▲ **Changing Beliefs About Competitors' Brands** Another approach to attitude change strategy involves changing consumer beliefs about the *attributes of competitive* brands or product categories. For instance, an ad for Advil makes a dramatic assertion of product superiority over aspirin and Tylenol: the ad claims that Advil lasts longer and is gentler than aspirin and that two Advil work better than Extra Strength Tylenol. In general, this strategy must be used with caution. Comparative advertising can boomerang by giving

FIGURE 9-10

Changing Attitudes by
Adding an Attribute
Courtesy of American Dairy
Farmers, National Dairy Board

visibility to competing brands and claims. (Chapter 10 discusses comparative advertising in greater depth.)

▲ **The Elaboration Likelihood Model (ELM)** Compared to the various specific strategies of attitude change that we have reviewed, the **elaboration likelihood model (ELM)** proposes the more global view that consumer attitudes are changed by two distinctly different "routes to persuasion": a central route or a peripheral route (see also Chapters 5, 7, and 10).[6] The *central route* is particularly relevant to attitude change when a consumer's motivation or ability to assess the attitude object is high; that is, attitude change occurs because the consumer seeks information relevant to the attitude object itself. When consumers are willing to exert the effort to comprehend, learn, or evaluate the available information about the attitude object, learning and attitude change occur via the central route.

In contrast, when a consumer's motivation or assessment skills are low, learning and attitude change occur via the peripheral route without the consumer focusing on information relevant to the attitude object itself. In such cases, attitude change often is an outcome of secondary inducements (e.g., cents-off coupons, free samples, beautiful background scenery, great package, or the encouragement of a celebrity endorsement).

BEHAVIOR CAN PRECEDE OR FOLLOW ATTITUDE FORMATION

Our discussion of attitude formation and attitude change has stressed the traditional "rational" view that consumers develop their attitudes before taking action (e.g., "Know what you are doing before you do it"). There are alternatives to this "attitude precedes behavior" perspective, alternatives that, on careful analysis, are likely to be just as logical and rational. For example, **cognitive dissonance theory** and **attribution theory** each provide a different explanation as to why behavior might precede attitude formation.

Cognitive Dissonance Theory

According to *cognitive dissonance theory*, discomfort or dissonance occurs when a consumer holds conflicting thoughts about a belief or an attitude object. For instance, when consumers have made a commitment—made a downpayment or placed an order for a product, particularly an expensive one such as an automobile or a personal computer—they often begin to feel cognitive dissonance when they think of the unique, positive qualities of the brands not selected ("left behind"). When cognitive dissonance occurs after a purchase, it is called **postpurchase dissonance**. Because purchase decisions often require some amount of compromise, postpurchase dissonance is quite normal. Nevertheless, it is likely to leave consumers with an uneasy feeling about their prior beliefs or actions—a feeling that they tend to resolve by changing their attitudes to conform with their behavior.

Thus, in the case of postpurchase dissonance, attitude change is frequently an *outcome* of an action or behavior. The conflicting thoughts or dissonant information that follow a purchase are prime factors that induce consumers to change their attitudes so that they will be consonant with their actual purchase behavior.

To illustrate how attitude change occurs in the context of postpurchase dissonance, let us consider Roger and his newly delivered Honda Civic coupe. The thought (i.e., the belief) initially raised by his mother that "You will never be able to get the family into a two-door car" still makes Roger have second thoughts as to whether he did the right thing by buying a "cute, little sports car." (Uneasiness about the car's size is now dissonant with the behavior of purchasing and owning the coupe.) To reduce the dissonance arising from this conflict, Roger can elect one or both of the following basic strategies: (1) adopt new cognitive beliefs supporting the original attitude or behavior (i.e., buying the coupe) or (2) reevaluate the conflicting beliefs to create consonance. To make owning the Honda Civic coupe consonant with the negative concern about accommodating his family, Roger can introduce a new supportive belief, for example, "The reason why I really need a smaller car is so it can fit into those 'small car' parking spaces at work." Alternatively, Roger may reevaluate the dissonant belief and reject it, for example, "The whole family is never likely to ride together, anyhow!"

What makes postpurchase dissonance relevant to marketing strategists is the premise that *dissonance* propels consumers to reduce the unpleasant feelings created by the rival thoughts. A variety of tactics are open to consumers to reduce postpurchase dissonance. The consumer can rationalize the decision as being wise, seek out advertisements that support the choice (while avoiding dissonance-creating competitive ads), try to "sell" friends on the positive features of the brand, or look to known satisfied owners for reassurance.

In addition to such consumer-initiated tactics to reduce postpurchase uncertainty, a marketer can relieve consumer dissonance by including messages in its advertising specifically aimed at reinforcing consumer decisions, offering stronger guarantees or warranties, increasing the number and effectiveness of its services, or providing detailed brochures on how to use its products correctly. Beyond these dissonance-reducing tactics, marketers increasingly are developing *affinity* or *relationship programs* (see Chapter 19) designed to reward good customers and to build customer loyalty and satisfaction. As noted earlier, the airlines, hotel chains, and major car rental companies have all developed such programs for their best customers.

Attribution Theory

As a group of loosely interrelated social psychological principles, *attribution theory* attempts to explain how people assign causality (e.g., blame or credit) to events on the basis of either their own behavior or the behavior of others.[7] In other words, a person might say, "I contributed to Care, Inc. because it really helps people in need," or "She tried to persuade me to buy that unknown autofocus camera because she'd make a bigger commission." In attribution theory, the underlying question is why: "Why did I do this," "Why did she try to get me to switch brands?" This process of making inferences about one's own or another's behavior is a major component of attitude formation and change.

Attribution theory describes attitude formation and change as an outgrowth of people's speculations as to their own behavior (self-perception) and experiences.

▲ **Self-Perception Theory** Of the various perspectives on attribution theory that have been proposed, **self-perception** theory—individuals' inferences or judgments as to the causes of their own behavior—is a good beginning point for a discussion of attribution.

INTERNAL AND EXTERNAL ATTRIBUTIONS In terms of consumer behavior, self-perception theory suggests that attitudes develop as consumers *look at and make judgments about their own behavior*. Simply stated, if a woman observes that she routinely purchases the *Wall Street Journal* on her way to work, she is apt to conclude that she likes the *Wall Street Journal* (i.e., she has a positive attitude toward this newspaper).[8] Drawing inferences from one's own behavior is not always as simple or as clear-cut as the newspaper example might suggest. To appreciate the complexity of self-perception theory, it is useful to distinguish between **internal** and **external attributions**. Let us assume that Joe has just finished using a popular computer graphics program (e.g., Harvard Graphics) for the first time and that his overhead transparency has come out spectacularly well. If, after reviewing the "masterpiece," he says to himself, "I'm really a natural at making great presentations," this statement would be an example of an *internal attribution*. It is an internal attribution because he is giving himself credit for the outcome (e.g., his ability, his skill, or his effort). That is, he is saying, "This graphic presentation is good because of me." On the other hand, if Joe concluded that the successful graphic presentation was due to factors beyond his control (e.g., a user-friendly program, the assistance of a friend, or just "luck"), this would be an example of an external attribution. In this case, he might be saying, "My great graphic presentation is beginner's luck."

This distinction between internal and external attributions can be of strategic marketing importance. For instance, it would generally be in the best interests of the firm that produces Harvard Graphics if PC users, especially inexperienced PC users, *internalized* their successful use of the graphics package. If they internalized such a positive experience, it is more likely that they will repeat the behavior and become a "satisfied" regular user. Alternatively, however, if they were to *externalize* their success, it would be preferable that they attribute it to the Harvard Graphics program, rather than to an incidental environmental factor such as "beginner's luck" or a friend's "foolproof" instructions.

According to the principle of **defensive attribution**, consumers are likely to accept credit personally for success (internal attribution) and to credit failure to others or to outside events (external attribution). For this reason, it is crucial that marketers offer uniformly high-quality products that allow consumers to perceive themselves as the reason for the success, that is, "I'm competent." Moreover, a company's advertising should serve to reassure consumers, particularly inexperienced ones, that its products will not let them down but will make them "heroes" instead.

FOOT-IN-THE-DOOR TECHNIQUE Self-perception theorists have explored situations in which consumer compliance with a minor request affects subsequent compliance with a more substantial request. This strategy, which is commonly referred to as the **foot-in-the-door technique**, is based on the premise that individuals look at their prior behavior (e.g., compliance with a minor request) and conclude that they are the kind of person who says "Yes" to such requests (i.e., an internal attribution). Such self-attribution serves to increase the likelihood that they will agree to a similar, more substantial request. Someone who donates five dollars to cancer research might be persuaded to donate a much larger amount, when properly approached. The initial donation is, in effect, the *foot-in-the-door*.

Research into the foot-in-the-door technique has concentrated on understanding how specific incentives (e.g., cents-off coupons of varying amounts) ultimately influence consumer attitudes and subsequent purchase behavior. It appears that different-size incentives create different degrees of internal attribution which, in turn, lead to different amounts of attitude change. For instance, individuals who try a brand without any inducements or individuals who buy a brand repeatedly are more likely to infer increasingly positive attitudes toward the brand from their respective behaviors (e.g., "I buy this brand because I like it"). In contrast, individuals who try a free sample are less committed to changing their attitudes toward the brand ("I tried this brand because it was free").

Thus, contrary to what might be expected, it is not the biggest incentive that is most likely to lead to positive attitude change. If an incentive is too big, marketers run the risk that consumers might externalize the cause of their behavior to the incentive and be *less* likely to change their attitudes and *less* likely to make future purchases of the brand. Instead, what seems most effective is a *moderate* incentive, one that is just big enough to stimulate initial purchase of the brand but still small enough to encourage consumers to internalize their positive usage experience and allow a positive attitude change to occur.[9]

▲ **Attributions Toward Others** In addition to understanding self-perception theory, it is important to understand **attributions toward others** because of the variety of potential applications to consumer behavior and marketing. As suggested earlier in this section, every time a person asks "Why?" about a statement or action of another person—a family member, a friend, a salesperson—attribution theory is relevant. For example, if Tobee and Chuck were in an electronics store contemplating the purchase of a digital cellular telephone, a salesperson's recommendation that they buy a Motorola phone that cost $220 more than the one they were initially considering would logically lead to the question "Why?" If the couple concluded that the salesperson suggested the Motorola phone because of its superior features (e.g., size, battery life, clarity), then they would be likely to judge the salesperson's motives as "sincere" and would possibly purchase the more expensive model. However, if they concluded that the salesperson was interested only in the greater commission, he or she would earn from selling the more expensive model, then they might judge the salesperson as "insincere" and not buy the more expensive model. Indeed, they might leave and go elsewhere, because they no longer trusted the salesperson or the store. They would be asking themselves, "Is the salesperson trying to sell us the more expensive model because of the superiority of the model or because of the higher commission?"

This example suggests that in evaluating the words or deeds of others, the consumer tries to determine if the other person's motives or skills are consistent with the consumer's best interests. If these motives or skills are judged congruent, the consumer is likely to respond favorably. Otherwise, the consumer is likely to reject the other person's words and make the purchase elsewhere.

▲ **Attributions Toward Things** Consumer researchers also are interested in consumers' *attributions toward things*, because products (or services) can readily be thought of as "things." It is in the area of judging product performance that consumers are most likely to form product attributions. Specifically, they want to find out why a product meets or does not meet their expectations. In this regard, they could attribute the product's successful performance (or failure) to the product itself, to themselves, to other people or situations, or to some combination of these factors.[10] To recap an earlier example, when Joe developed an excellent overhead transparency, he could attribute his success to the Harvard Graphics software program (product attribution), to his own skill (self- or internal-attribution), or to his friend who helped him (external attribution).

▲ **How We Test Our Attributions** After making initial attributions about a product's performance or a person's words or actions, we often attempt to determine whether the inference we made is correct. According to a leading attribution theorist, individuals acquire conviction about particular observations by acting like "naive scientists," that is, by collecting additional information in an attempt to confirm (or disconfirm) prior inferences. In collecting such information, consumers often use the following criteria:[11]

1. *Distinctiveness*—The consumer attributes an action to a particular product or person if the action occurs when the product (or person) is present and does not occur in its absence.

2. *Consistency over time*—Whenever the person or product is present, the consumer's inference or reaction must be the same, or nearly so.

3. *Consistency over modality*—The inference or reaction must be the same, even when the situation in which it occurs varies.

4. *Consensus*—The action is perceived in the same way by other consumers.

The following example illustrates how each of these criteria might be used to make inferences about product performance and people's actions.

If Jim, a homeowner who takes pride in his lawn, observes that his grass seems to be cut more evenly with his new Lawn-Boy mower than with his former lawnmower, he is likely to credit the new Lawn-Boy with the improved appearance of his lawn (i.e., *distinctiveness*). Furthermore, if

Jim finds that his new Lawn-Boy produces the same high-quality results each time he uses it, he will tend to be more confident about his initial observation (i.e., the inference has *consistency over time*). Similarly, he will also be more confident if he finds that his satisfaction with the Lawn-Boy extends across a wide range of other related tasks, such as mulching grass and picking up leaves (i.e., *consistency over modality*). Finally, Jim will have still more confidence in his inferences to the extent that his friends who own Lawn-Boys also have similar experiences (i.e., *consensus*).

Much like Jim, we go about gathering additional information from our experiences with people and things, and we use this information to test our initial inferences.

summary

How consumer attitudes are formed and how they are changed are two closely related issues of considerable concern to marketing practitioners.

When it comes to attitude formation, it is useful to remember that attitudes are learned and that different learning theories provide unique insights as to how attitudes initially may be formed. Attitude formation is facilitated by direct personal experience and influenced by the ideas and experiences of friends and family members and exposure to mass media. In addition, it is likely that an individual's personality plays a major role in attitude formation.

These same factors also have an impact on attitude change; that is, attitude changes are learned, and they are influenced by personal experiences and the information gained from various personal and impersonal sources. The consumer's own personality affects both the acceptance and the speed with which attitudes are likely to be altered.

Strategies of attitude change can be classified into six distinct categories: (1) changing the basic motivational function,

(2) associating the attitude object with a specific group or event, (3) relating the attitude object to conflicting attitudes, (4) altering components of the multiattribute model, (5) changing beliefs about competitors' brands, and (6) the elaboration likelihood model. Each of these strategies provides the marketer with alternative ways of changing consumers existing attitudes.

Most discussions of attitude formation and attitude change stress the traditional view that consumers develop attitudes before they act. However, this may not always, or even usually, be true. Both cognitive dissonance theory and attribution theory provide alternative explanations of attitude formation and change that suggest that behavior might precede attitudes. Cognitive dissonance theory suggests that the conflicting thoughts, or dissonant information, that follow a purchase decision might propel consumers to change their attitudes to make them consonant with their actions. Attribution theory focuses on how people assign causality to events and how they form or alter attitudes as an outcome of assessing their own behavior, or the behavior of other people or things.

discussion questions

1. Explain an attitude you recently formed toward a product or service in terms of both instrumental conditioning and cognitive learning theory.

2. Explain how the product manager of a breakfast cereal might change consumer attitudes toward the company's brand by: (a) changing beliefs about the brand, (b) changing beliefs about competing brands, (c) changing the relative evaluation of attributes, and (d) adding an attribute.

3. The Department of Transportation of a large city is planning an advertising campaign that encourages people to switch from private cars to mass transit. Give examples of how the department can use the following strategies to change commuters' attitudes: (a) changing the basic motivational function, (b) changing beliefs about public transportation, (c) using self-perception theory, and (d) using cognitive dissonance.

4. The Saturn Corporation is faced with the problem that many consumers perceive compact and mid-size American cars to be of poorer quality than comparable Japanese cars. Assuming that Saturn produces cars which are of equal or better quality than Japanese cars, how can the company persuade consumers of this fact?

5. What are the two routes to persuasion according to the Elaboration Likelihood Model? Under what conditions should a marketer select one route rather than another in trying to change consumer attitudes?

6. Should the marketer of a popular computer graphics program prefer consumers to make internal or external attributions? Explain your answer.

7. A college student has just purchased a new personal computer. What factors might cause the student to experience postpurchase dissonance? How might the student try to overcome it? How can the retailer who sold the computer help reduce the student's dissonance? How can the computer's manufacturer help?

exercises

1. What sources influenced your attitude about this course before classes started? Has your initial attitude changed since the course started? If so, how?

2. Describe a situation in which you acquired an attitude toward a new product through exposure to an advertisement for that product. Describe a situation where you formed an attitude toward a product or brand on the basis of personal influence.

3. Find advertisements that illustrate each of the four motivational functions of attitudes. Distinguish between ads that are designed to reinforce an existing attitude and those aimed at changing an attitude.

4. You are the product manager of Health Valley Foods, Inc. Develop a print advertisement for a new, fat-free canned soup designed to influence consumer beliefs about three attributes of the new product.

5. Think back to the time when you were selecting a college. Did you experience dissonance immediately after you made a decision? Why or why not? If you did experience dissonance, how did you resolve it?

key words

- Affinity marketing
- Assimilation-contrast theory
- Attitude-change strategies
- Attitude formation
- Attribution theory
- Attributions toward others
- Attributions toward things
- Cognitive dissonance theory
- Conflicting attitudes
- Defensive attribution
- Ego-defensive function
- Elaboration Likelihood Model
- Foot-in-the-door technique
- Functional approach
- Internal and external attributions
- Knowledge function
- Learning of attitudes
- Postpurchase dissonance
- Self-perception theory
- Sources of influence on attitude formation
- Utilitarian function
- Value-expressive function

end notes

1. MORRIS B. HOLBROOK, DAVID A. VELEZ, and GERARD J. TABOURET, "Attitude Structure and Search: An Integrative Model of Importance-Directed Information Processing," in Kent B. Monroe, ed., *Advances in Consumer Research* 8 (Ann Arbor: Association for Consumer Research, 1981), 35–41.

2. RICHARD P. BAGOZZI, HANS BAUMGARTNER, and YOUGAE YI, "Coupon Usage and the Theory of Reasoned Action," in Rebecca H. Holman and Michael R. Solomon, eds., *Advances in Consumer Research* 18 (Provo, UT: Association for Consumer Research, 1991), 24–27.

3. DANIEL KATZ, "The Functional Approach to the Study of Attitudes," *Public Opinion Quarterly* 24, Summer 1960, 163-91; SHARON SHAVITT, "Products, Personality and Situations in Attitude Functions: Implications for Consumer Behavior," in Thomas K. Srull, ed., *Advances in Consumer Research* 16 (Provo, UT: Association for Consumer Research, 1989), 300–305; and RICHARD ENNIS and MARK P. ZANNA, "Attitudes, Advertising, and Automobiles: A Functional Approach," in Leigh McAlister and Michael L. Rothschild, eds., *Advances in Consumer Research* 20 (Provo, UT: Association for Consumer Research 1992), 662–66.

4. BRIAN WANSINK, "Advertising's Impact on Category Substitution," *Journal of Marketing Research* 31, November 1994, 505–15.

5. CARL I. HOVLAND, O. J. HARVEY, and MUZAFER SHERIF, "Assimilation and Contrast Effects in Reactions to Communication and Attitude Change," *Journal of Abnormal and Social Psychology* 55, July 1957, 244–52.

6. RICHARD E. PETTY, et al., "Theories of Attitude Change," in Harold Kassarjian and Thomas Robertson, eds., *Handbook of Consumer Theory and Research* (Englewood Cliffs, NJ: Prentice Hall, 1991); and RICHARD E. PETTY, JOHN T. CACIOPPO, and DAVID SCHUMANN, "Central and Peripheral Routes to Advertising Effectiveness: The

Moderating Role of Involvement," *Journal of Consumer Research* 10, September 1983, 135–46. Also see CURTUS P. HAUGTVEDT and ALAN J. STRATHMAN, "Situational Product Relevance and Attitude Persistence," in Marvin E. Goldberg, Gerald Gorn, and Richard W. Pollay, eds., *Advances in Consumer Research* 17 (Provo, UT: Association for Consumer Research, 1990), 766–69; and SCOTT B. MACKENZIE and RICHARD A. SPRENG, "How Does Motivation Moderate the Impact of Central and Peripheral Processing on Brand Attitudes and Intentions?" *Journal of Consumer Research* 18, March 1992, 519–29.

7. EDWARD E. JONES, et al., "Attribution: Perceiving the Causes of Behavior" (Morristown, NJ: General Learning Press, 1972).

8. CHRIS T. ALLEN and WILLIAM R. DILLON, "Self-Perception Development and Consumer Choice Criteria: Is There a Linkage?" in Richard P. Bagozzi and Alice M. Tybout, eds., *Advances in Consumer Research* 10 (Ann Arbor: Association for Consumer Research, 1983), 45–50.

9. See, for example, LESLIE LAZAR KANUK, *Mail Questionnaire Response Behavior as a Function of Motivational Treatment* (New York: CUNY, 1974).

10. VALERIE S. FOLKES, "Consumer Reactions to Product Failure: Attributional Approach," *Journal of Consumer Research* 10, March 1984, 398–409; and "Recent Attribution Research in Consumer Behavior: A Review and New Dimensions," *Journal of Consumer Research* 14, March 1988, 548–65.

11. HAROLD H. KELLEY, "Attribution Theory in Social Psychology," in David Levine, ed., *Nebraska Symposium on Motivation* 15 (Lincoln: University of Nebraska Press, 1967), 197.

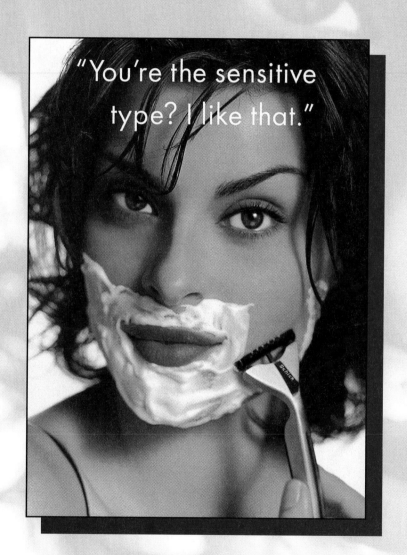

©1998

Communication is the unique tool that marketers use to persuade consumers to act in a desired way (e.g., to vote, to make a purchase, to make a donation, to patronize a retail store). Communication takes many forms: it can be verbal (either written or spoken), it can be visual (an illustration, a picture, a product demonstration, a frown), or a combination of the two. It can also be symbolic—represented, say, by a high price, or premium packaging, or a memorable logo—and convey special meaning that the marketer wants to impart. Communication can evoke emotions that put consumers in a more receptive frame of mind, and it can encourage purchases to solve problems or to avoid negative outcomes. In short, communication is the bridge between marketers and consumers, and between consumers and their sociocultural environments.

Although there are many ways to define communication, most writers would

G*ood communication is stimulating as black coffee, and just as hard to sleep after.*

—Anne Morrow Lindbergh
"Argonauta," *Gift from the Sea*, 1955

agree that communication is the transmission of a message from a sender to a receiver via a medium of some sort. There are many people who believe that the fifth essential component of communication is feedback, which alerts the sender as to whether the intended message was, in fact, received. The following section examines the five basic components of communication from the perspective of marketing and consumer behavior. Figure 10-1 depicts this basic communication model.

COMPONENTS OF COMMUNICATION

The **sender**, as the initiator of the communication, can be a formal or an informal source. A *formal source* is likely to represent either a for-profit (commercial) or a not-for-profit organization; an *informal source* can be a parent or a friend who gives product information or advice. Consumers often rely on informal communications sources in making purchase decisions because, unlike formal sources, the sender apparently has nothing to gain from the receiver's subsequent actions. For that reason, informal *word-of-mouth* communication tends to be highly persuasive. Research shows that consumers prefer personal information sources when they buy services, because they have greater confidence in such sources.[1]

The **receiver** of formal communications is likely to be a targeted prospect or a customer (e.g., a member of the marketer's target audience). There are also many intermediary and even unintended audiences for marketing communications. Examples of **intermediary audiences** are wholesalers, distributors, and retailers, who are sent *trade advertising* designed to persuade them to order and stock merchandise, and relevant professionals (such as architects or physicians), who are sent *professional advertising* in the hopes that they will specify or prescribe the marketer's products. **Unintended audiences** include everyone who is exposed to the message, even though not specifically targeted by the source. These unintended audiences often include publics that are important to the marketer, such as shareholders, creditors, suppliers, employees, bankers, and the local community, in addition to the general public. It is important to remember that no matter how large the audience, it is composed of individual receivers, each of whom interprets the message in his or her own special way.

The **medium**, or communications channel, can be **interpersonal**—an informal conversation (face-to-face, by telephone, by mail, by e-mail, or an on-line computer chat group) between two or more friends, or it can be a formal conversation between a salesperson and a customer. In one recent marketing campaign, actors were hired to go into nightclubs and restaurants in New York City and order martinis made with Hennessy

FIGURE 10-1

Basic Communication
Model

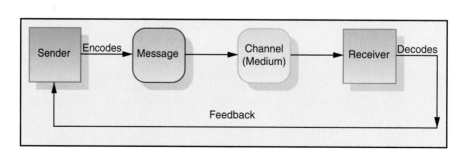

Cognac, rather than with gin or vodka. The intent of this promotion was to generate favorable word-of-mouth for the brand.[2]

Alternatively, the medium can be *impersonal*—a mass medium such as a newspaper, radio or television program, or even an Internet Web site. Many current print or television ads provide a World Wide Web address, and the computer-literate consumer can "visit" this Web site to find out more about the product or service being advertised.

Mass media are generally classified as *print* (newspapers, magazines, billboards) and *broadcast* (radio, television), although *electronic* media are becoming more important daily (e.g., fax, computers). New modes of *interactive communication* that permit the audiences of mass media to provide direct feedback are beginning to blur the distinction between interpersonal and impersonal communication. For example, in some communities consumers can do their grocery shopping electronically as the TV camera scans the grocery shelves. Home shopping networks are expanding dramatically, as consumers demonstrate their enthusiasm for TV shopping.[3] Direct marketers—also called *data-base marketers*—seek individual responses from advertisements placed in all the mass media: broadcast, print, and electronic, as well as from direct mail. (Direct marketing is discussed in greater detail later in the chapter.)

Despite the general use of the term *mass media* to describe impersonal media, there is a growing trend toward media demassification as publishers shift their focuses from large, general interest audiences to smaller, more specialized audiences. Some media try to create "captive" audiences. For example, as discussed elsewhere in the book, one communications company is providing free television equipment and programming to school districts that agree to run the company's special "school" channel (which includes two minutes of paid commercials) during class time.

The **message**, as was pointed out earlier, can be *verbal* or *nonverbal*, or a combination of the two. A verbal message, whether it is spoken or written, can usually contain more specific product (or service) information than a nonverbal message. Sometimes a verbal message is combined with an illustration or a demonstration, and together they may provide more information to the receiver than either would alone.

Nonverbal information often takes the form of *symbolic communication*. The study of **semiotics**, discussed in Chapter 2, is the study of the meanings implied by signs and symbols. Marketers often try to develop logos or symbols that are associated exclusively with their products. The Coca-Cola Company, for example, has trademarked both the word "Coke" in a specific typographic style and the shape of the traditional Coke bottle, and both are instantly recognizable to consumers as symbols of the company's best-selling soft drink. In 1994, the Supreme Court ruled that even a color that distinguishes a product (and serves no other function) can be registered as a trademark.[4]

Nonverbal communications take place in both interpersonal channels and in impersonal channels. For example, a good salesperson usually is alert to nonverbal feedback provided by consumer prospects. Such feedback may take the form of facial expressions (a smile, a frown, a look of total boredom, an expression of disbelief) or bodily movements (finger tapping, head nodding, head shaking, or clenched hands). Because *senders* often can "read" meaning into such bodily reactions, these nonverbal actions sometimes are referred to as "body language."

Feedback is an essential component of both interpersonal and impersonal communications. Prompt feedback permits the sender to reinforce, to change, or to modify the message to ensure that it is understood in the intended way. Clearly, it is easier to obtain feedback (both verbal and nonverbal) in interpersonal situations, but it is even more important for sponsors of impersonal communications to obtain feedback as promptly as possible. (Methods of obtaining feedback to impersonal communications are discussed in greater detail later in the chapter.)

Figure 10-2 presents a more detailed model of the communications process. It notes that the *sender* selects the *message, encodes* the message, and selects an appropriate *channel* through which to send it. The *receiver decodes* (interprets) the message and then responds or does not respond, depending on the accuracy of interpretation and the persuasiveness of the message. The receiver's response constitutes *feedback* to the sender. The following section describes how the communications process works.

THE COMMUNICATIONS PROCESS

In general, a company's marketing communications are designed to induce purchase, create a positive attitude toward the product, give the product a symbolic meaning, or show that it can solve the consumer's problem better than a competitive product (or service) can.

The Message Initiator (The Source)

The sponsor, or initiator, of the message first must decide what the message should convey and to whom it should be sent and then must **encode** the message in such a way that its meaning is interpreted by the targeted audience in precisely the intended way. The sources

FIGURE 10-2 Comprehensive Communication Model

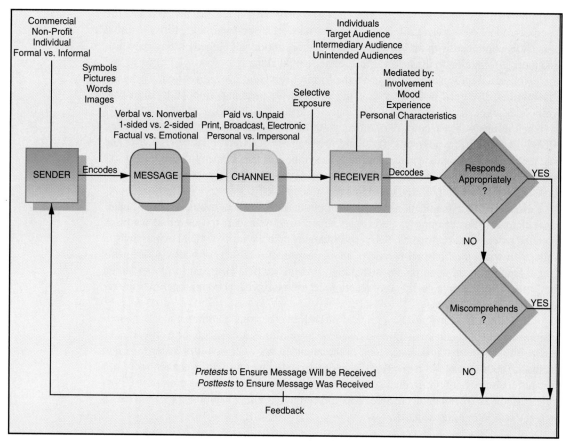

of impersonal communications usually are organizations that develop and transmit appropriate messages through special departments (e.g., advertising or public relations departments) or spokespersons. The destinations, or receivers, of such messages usually are a specific audience or several audiences that the organization is trying to inform, influence, or persuade. For example, an office supply chain may want to convince businesspeople to shop in its stores; a car rental company may want to persuade consumers planning vacations to use its services; a mail-order retailer may want to persuade consumers to call a toll-free telephone number for a copy of its catalog.

Senders have a large arsenal from which to draw in encoding their messages: they can use words, pictures, symbols, spokespersons, and special channels. They can buy space or time in carefully selected media to advertise or broadcast their message, or they can try to have their message published (or broadcast) in space or time usually reserved for editorial messages. (The latter usually is the result of public relations or publicity efforts and tends to be more believable because its commercial origins or intent are not readily apparent.)

▲ **Credibility of the Source** The *credibility of the source* affects the decoding of the message. The source of the communication—his or her perceived honesty and objectivity—has an enormous influence on how the communication is accepted by the receiver. When the source is well respected and highly thought of by the intended audience, the message is much more likely to be believed. Conversely, a message from a source considered unreliable or untrustworthy will be received with skepticism and may be rejected.

Credibility is built on a number of factors, the most important being the perceived intentions of the source. Receivers ask themselves, "Just what does he (or she) stand to gain if I do what is suggested?" If the receiver perceives any type of personal gain for the message sponsor as a result of the proposed action or advice, the message itself becomes suspect: "He wants me to buy that product just to earn a commission."

CREDIBILITY OF INFORMAL SOURCES One of the major reasons that informal sources such as friends, neighbors, and relatives have such a strong influence on a receiver's behavior is simply that they are perceived as having nothing to gain from a product transaction that they recommend.

Interestingly enough, informal communications sources, called *opinion leaders*, often do profit psychologically, if not tangibly, by providing product information to others. A person may obtain a great deal of ego satisfaction by providing solicited as well as unsolicited information and advice to friends. As Chapter 17 points out, this ego gratification may actually improve the quality of the information provided, because the opinion leader often deliberately seeks out impartial information in order to enhance his or her position as "expert" in a particular product category. The fact that the opinion leader does not receive material gain from the action recommended increases the likelihood that the advice will be seriously considered.

Even with informal sources, however, intentions are not always what they appear to be. Individuals who experience *postpurchase dissonance* often try to alleviate their uncertainty by convincing others to make a similar purchase. Each time they persuade a friend or an acquaintance to make the same brand selection, they are somewhat reassured that their own product choice was a wise one. The receiver, on the other hand, regards product advice from "the person who owns one" as totally objective, because the source is able to speak from actual experience. Thus, the increased credibility accorded the informal source may not really be warranted, despite the aura of perceived objectivity.

CREDIBILITY OF FORMAL SOURCES Formal sources such as neutral rating services or newspaper articles have greater credibility than advertisers because of the perception that they are more objective in their product assessments. That is why publicity is so valuable to a manufacturer: citations of a product in an editorial context, rather than in a paid advertisement, give the reader much more confidence in the message.

When the intentions of a source are clearly profit making, then *reputation, expertise,* and *knowledge* become important factors in message credibility. The credibility of commercial messages is often based on the composite evaluation of the reputations of the sender (the organization that approves and pays for the advertising message), the retail outlet that carries the product, the medium that carries the message, and the company spokesperson (the actor or sales representative who delivers the message).

Because consumers recognize that the intentions of *commercial sources* (manufacturers, service companies, commercial institutions, retailers) are clearly to make a profit, they judge commercial source credibility on such factors as past performance, the kind and quality of service they are known to render, the quality and image of other products they manufacturer, the type of retail outlets through which they sell, and their position in the community (e.g., evidence of their commitment to such issues as social responsibility or equal employment).

Firms with well-established reputations generally have an easier time selling their products than do firms with lesser reputations. The ability of a quality image to invoke credibility is one of the reasons for the growth of family brands. Manufacturers with favorable brand images prefer to give their new products the existing brand name in order to obtain ready acceptance from consumers.

Besides allowing a company to market new products with less risk, a quality image permits a company to experiment more freely in many more areas of marketing than would otherwise be considered prudent. The long-established manufacturer can open new retail outlets, try new price levels, or experiment with innovative promotional techniques with confidence that the company's good image will carry over. Because a manufacturer with a good reputation generally has high credibility among consumers, many companies spend a sizable part of their advertising budget on **institutional advertising**, which is designed to promote a favorable company image rather than to promote specific products.

The reputation of the *retailer* who sells the product has a major influence on message credibility. Products sold by well-known quality stores seem to carry the added endorsement (and implicit guarantee) of the store itself: "If Macy's carries it, it must be good." The aura of credibility generated by reputable retail advertising reinforces the manufacturer's message as well. A product carried in a traditional department store usually is perceived as being of better quality than one carried by a mass merchandiser (e.g., Wal-Mart), and a message concerning the product's attributes is more readily believed. That is why so many *national ads* (i.e., manufacturer-initiated ads) carry the line, "Sold at better stores everywhere."

The reputation of the *medium* that carries the advertisement affects the credibility of the message. The image of a prestige magazine like *Conde Nast Traveler* confers added status on the products advertised therein. The reputation of the medium as to its honesty or objectivity also affects the credibility of the advertising. Consumers often think that a medium they respect would not accept advertising for products it did not "know" were good. For example, the *Good Housekeeping* Seal of Approval carries a great deal of weight with many consumers. Because of the credibility of some media, manufacturers are often happy to avail themselves of the merchandising services they offer, such as counter cards and product hangtags that say, for example, "As Advertised in *Good Housekeeping* Magazine."

Because specialization in an area implies knowledge and expertise, special-interest magazines tend to be regarded with more credibility than general-interest magazines. This accounts for the increasing number of highly specialized magazines introduced each year.

People sometimes regard the *spokesperson* who gives the product message as the source (or initiator) of the message. Thus, the "pitchman"—whether he or she appears personally or in an advertisement—has a major influence on message credibility. In interpersonal communications, a salesperson who engenders confidence and who gives the impression of honesty and integrity generally is more successful in persuading a prospect than one who does not have these characteristics. Consumer confidence in a salesperson is created in diverse ways, whether warranted or not. A salesperson who "looks you in the eye" may appear more honest than one who evades direct eye contact. For many products, a sales representative who dresses well and drives an expensive, late-model car may have more credibility than one without such outward signs of success (and inferred representation of a best-selling product). For some products, however, a salesperson may achieve more credibility by dressing in the role of expert. For example, a man selling home improvements may achieve more credibility by looking like someone who just climbed off a roof or out of a basement than by looking like a stockbroker.

Interaction between the spokesperson and the medium affects the overall credibility of the presentation. Thus, in two experiments, a "likable" communicator's message was more persuasive in videotaped and audiotaped form, while the "unlikable" communicator was more persuasive in written format.[5]

In impersonal communication, the *reputation* or *expertise* of the advertising spokesperson may strongly influence the credibility of the message. This accounts for the popularity and effectiveness of **testimonials** as a promotional technique.

When an audience perceives a message to be incompatible with its source, a high-credibility source will be no more believable than a low-credibility source. Marketers who use testimonials must be sure that the specific wording of the endorsement lies within the recognized competence of the spokesperson. A football star can believably endorse an analgesic product with comments about how it relieves sore muscle pain; however, a recitation of its chemical properties is beyond his expected knowledge and expertise and thus reduces, rather than enhances, message credibility.

Researchers have studied the relationship between message comprehension and persuasion, and have found that when comprehension is low, receivers rely on the spokesperson's credibility in forming attitudes towards the product, but when comprehension (and thus systematic information processing) is high, the expertise of the source has far less impact on a receiver's attitudes.[6]

AUDIENCE ATTITUDES AFFECT CREDIBILITY The initial opinion that an audience holds prior to receiving the message can affect the persuasiveness of both high- and low-credibility sources. When the audience is favorably disposed to the message before its presentation, moderately credible sources produce more attitude change than highly credible sources. However, when the audience is opposed to the communicator's position, the high-credibility source is likely to be more effective than the less credible source.[7]

The consumer's own experience with the product or the retailer also affects the credibility of the message. Fulfilled product expectations tend to increase the credibility accorded future messages by the same advertiser, whereas unfulfilled product claims or disappointing products tend to reduce the credibility of future messages. The significant increase in mail-order sales in the last decade has been attributed to the fact that reputable catalog houses have lived up to their advertised claims of providing full and prompt refunds on all merchandise returns.

Many companies sponsor special entertainment and sports events to enhance their image and credibility with their target audiences. The nature and quality of these sponsorships constitute a subtle message to the consumer: "We're a great (kind, good-natured, socially-responsible) company; we deserve your business." For example, such firms as the American Express Company, Chase Manhattan Bank, The Hearst Corporation, Louis Vuitton, and Morgan Stanley sponsor concerts in public parks; Downy Fabric Softener and Purina Dog Chow together sponsored a Wizard of Oz stage show. The Tournament of Roses parade includes floats by such companies as Baskin-Robbins, Carnation, Kodak, Doctor Pepper, GTE, GM, and Hilton; the Puerto Rican Day Parade includes floats by such companies as Colgate-Palmolive, Pepsi, Canada Dry, Budweiser, and AT&T. Other kinds of corporate-sponsored special events include marching bands, fireworks displays, computerized skywriting, laser shows and, of course, athletic events. United States companies are reported to have spent in excess of $23.5 billion in sponsoring sports events in 1992. For the 1996 Atlanta Olympic Games, it has been estimated that 45 companies paid anywhere from $5 million to $45 million each for the right to use the Olympic logo in their advertising.[8]

THE EFFECTS OF TIME ON SOURCE CREDIBILITY The persuasive effects of high-credibility sources do not endure over time. Although a high-credibility source is initially more influential than a low-credibility source, research suggests that both positive and negative credibility effects tend to disappear after 6 weeks or so. This phenomenon has been termed the **sleeper effect**.[9] Consumers simply forget the source of the message faster than they forget the message itself. However, reintroduction of the message by the source serves to jog the audience's memory, and the original effect remanifests itself—that is, the high-credibility source remains more persuasive than the low-credibility source.[10] The implication for marketers who use high-credibility spokespersons is that they must rerun the ad or commercial regularly in order to maintain its persuasiveness.

Studies attribute the sleeper effect to *disassociation* (i.e., the consumer disassociates the message from its source) over time, leaving just the message content. The *differential decay* interpretation of the sleeper effect suggests that memory of a negative cue (e.g., a low-credibility source) simply decays faster than the message itself, leaving behind the primary message content.[11] A study that examined the impact of product information on consumer attitudes over time found that advertising messages that encouraged consumers to process the information elaboratively (i.e., to "internalize" the information) were more likely to show increased effectiveness over time despite an initial negative cue.[12]

The Target Audience (The Receivers)

Receivers **decode** the messages they receive on the basis of their personal experience and personal characteristics. If Mrs. Mahoney signed a contract to have her apartment painted because she received a well-designed, convincing direct mail brochure and a follow-up call from a sincere-sounding, respectable-looking contractor, and then was dissatisfied with the quality of work done, she might end up distrusting all direct mail communications, all home contractors and, perhaps, all smooth-talking salesmen. She is likely to decode any subsequent communications received through the mail with great skepticism. At the same time, her neighbor, Mrs. Greene, ordered a jacket and gloves from the Lands' End catalog and was so pleased with the quality, the service, and the fit that she studies all subsequent direct mail catalogs with great care, and decides to do all her shopping by direct mail. The level of trust each neighbor displays toward direct mail communications is based on her prior experience.

▲ **Comprehension** The amount of meaning accurately derived from the message is a function of the *message characteristics*, the receiver's opportunity and ability to *process the message*, and the receiver's *motivation*.[13] In fact, all of the personal characteristics described in Part II influence the accuracy with which an individual decodes a message. A person's *demographics* (e.g., age, gender, marital status), *sociocultural memberships* (social class, race, religion), and *lifestyle* are all key determinants in how a message is interpreted. A bachelor may interpret a friendly comment from his unmarried neighbor as a "come-on"; a student may interpret a professor's comments as an indication of test content. *Personality, attitudes, prior learning*—all affect how a message is decoded. *Perception*, based as it is on expectations, motivation, and past experience, certainly influences message interpretation. Direct marketers must be aware of the fact that not everyone can read and understand their marketing communications as intended. For example, it has been estimated that when advertising copy is written for an eighth-grade reading level, fully one-third of the direct mail recipients may be unable to comprehend the intended message, resulting in low response rates and lost sales.[14]

A person's **level of involvement** plays a key role in how much attention is paid to the message and how carefully it is decoded. People who have little interest (e.g., a low level of involvement) in golf, for example, may not pay much attention to an ad for a specially designed putter; people who are very interested (e.g., highly involved) in golf may read every word of a highly technical advertisement describing the new golf club. Thus, a target audience's level of involvement is an important consideration in the design and content of persuasive communications.

▲ **Mood** Mood, or *affect*, plays a significant role in how a message is decoded. The term *mood* is used here to describe an individual's "subjectively perceived affective state."[15] For example, someone might be in a cheerful mood or in an unhappy or hostile mood. A consumer's mood affects the way in which an advertisement is perceived, recalled, and acted upon. Research indicates that the consumer's mood states often are influenced by the *context* in which the advertising message appears (e.g., the adjacent TV program or newspaper story) and the *content* of the ad itself, which in turn may affect the consumer's evaluation and recall of the message.[16] Positive feelings induced by a commercial that shows positive outcomes may enhance the likelihood that consumers will buy the advertised product (e.g., a large-screen TV), while depressing commercials may induce negative moods. (This may, at times, be congruent with the marketer's objectives: consumers may be persuaded that a negative outcome will occur if they do not buy the advertised product, e.g., accident insurance.) In addition to inducing positive or negative *cognitive* moods, marketers can also induce *noncognitive* moods through the use of advertising stimuli such as background music.[17] Ralph Lauren creates a mood of timeless elegance and tradition in multipage advertisements that serve to enhance consumer attitudes toward the company's merchandise, while Guess? jeans uses the same multipage advertising technique to induce a mood of total sensuality. Other extraneous factors that influence consumer moods and affect the decoding of marketing communications include the *retail store image*, the *climate*, even the *weather*.

▲ **Selective Exposure and Selective Attention** Chapter 6 pointed out that consumers selectively expose themselves to various media. Similarly, they selectively expose themselves to advertising messages. Consumers have long exercised their right to ignore print advertisements; they exercise this same right with television commercials. TV remote controls offer viewers the ability to "wander" among program offerings with ease (often referred to as *grazing*), and to *zap* commercials by muting the audio or by *channel surfing*—switching channels to check out other program offerings during the commercial break. Some marketers try to overcome channel surfing during commercials by *roadblocking*, i.e., playing the same commercial simultaneously on competing channels. Despite attempts at roadblocking, households with TV remote controls zap commercials on the average of once every three and a half minutes.[18] Because research has shown that 15 to 25 percent of viewers defect from the channel they are watching between programs, NBC has made a concerted effort to eliminate the commercial pauses that traditionally have been placed between TV programs.[19]

The VCR created problems for television advertisers by enabling viewers to fast-forward, or *zip* through commercials on prerecorded programs or rented videotapes. Researchers have found that a majority of subjects zip indiscriminately to avoid all commercials, without first evaluating the commercials they zap.[20] Some marketers make the mistake of playing theme music at the beginning and end of a commercial break, thus signaling viewers that they can attend to other needs without missing program content. A related issue for advertisers is *time shifting*, which occurs when a commercial intended to be viewed during a particular time of day by a particular audience (e.g., retirees or stay-at-home housewives) may actually be seen by a different audience during another time period because the program was recorded. For example, a commercial for a multivitamin tablet scheduled to run on an afternoon TV soap opera might actually be watched late at night by members of a college sorority, who may be in class when their favorite soaps are broadcast. Clearly, 20-year-old coeds are not the intended audience for this vitamin.

▲ **Psychological Noise** Just as telephone static can impair reception of a message, so too can **psychological noise** (e.g., competing advertising messages or distracting thoughts). A viewer faced with the clutter of nine successive commercial messages during a program break may actually receive and retain almost nothing of what he has seen. Similarly, an executive planning a department meeting while driving to work may be too engrossed in her thoughts to "hear" a radio commercial. On a more familiar level, a student daydreaming about a Saturday night date may simply not "hear" a question directed to him by his professor. He is just as much a victim of noise—albeit psychological noise—as the student who literally cannot hear a question because of hammering in the next room. The best way for a sender to overcome noise is simply to repeat the message several times, much as a sailor does when sending an SOS over and over again to make sure it is received. (The effects of repetition on learning were discussed in Chapter 7.) The principle of *redundancy* also is seen in advertisements that use both illustrations and copy to emphasize the same points. Repeated exposure to an advertising message (redundancy of the advertising appeal) helps surmount psychological noise and thus facilitates message reception.

In addition to redundancy, copywriters may use other "hooks" to break through the noise and clutter. Two general ways to do this are **subverting** and **forcing**. *Subverting* involves the presentation of something unexpected, either because it is disconcerting or charming. *Forcing* attempts to jolt the viewer into paying some initial notice to the advertisement, and sometimes involves a "teaser" element.[21]

Feedback–The Receiver's Response

Since marketing communications are usually designed to persuade a target audience to act in a desired way (e.g., to purchase a branded product, to vote for a presidential candidate, to pay income taxes early), the ultimate test of marketing communications is the receiver's response. For this reason, it is essential for the sender to obtain **feedback** as promptly and as accurately as possible. Only through feedback can the sender determine whether and how well the message has been received.

An important advantage of *interpersonal* communication is the ability to obtain immediate feedback through verbal as well as nonverbal cues. Experienced communicators are very attentive to feedback and constantly modify their messages based on what they see or hear from the audience. Immediate feedback is the factor that makes personal selling so effective. It enables the salesperson to tailor the sales pitch to the expressed needs and observed reactions of each prospect. Similarly, it enables a political candidate to stress specific aspects of his or her platform selectively in response to questions posed by prospective voters in face-to-face meetings. Immediate feedback in the form of inattention serves to alert the college professor to the need to awaken the interest of a dozing class; thus, the professor may make a deliberately provocative statement such as: "This material will probably appear on your final exam."

Feedback is just as important a concept in *impersonal* (mass) communications as it is in interpersonal communications. Indeed, because of the high costs of advertising space and time in mass media, many people consider such feedback even more essential than interpersonal feedback. The organization that initiates the message must develop some method for determining whether its mass communications are, in fact, received by the intended audience, understood in the intended way, and successful in achieving the intended objectives.

Unlike interpersonal communication, mass communications feedback is rarely direct; instead, it is usually inferred. Receivers buy (or do not buy) the advertised product; they renew (or do not renew) their magazine subscriptions; and they vote (or do not vote) for the political candidate. Senders infer how persuasive their messages are from the resulting action (or inaction) of the targeted audience.

Advertisers often try to gauge the effectiveness of their messages by conducting audience research to find out which media are read, which television programs are viewed, and which advertisements are remembered by their target audience. When feedback indicates that the audience does not note or miscomprehends the ad, the sponsor has the opportunity to modify or revise the message so that the intended communication does, in fact, take place.

Mass communications feedback does not have the timeliness of interpersonal feedback (although retailers usually can assess the effectiveness of their morning newspaper ads by midday on the basis of sales activity for the advertised product). Other commercial sources (e.g., manufacturers) are constantly seeking innovative methods of finding out quickly how effective their consumer advertising is. For example, an important feedback mechanism for food and other packaged goods is based on the Universal Product Code (UPC) and tied to computerized cash registers. Supermarket scanner data can be combined with data from other sources (e.g., media and promotion information) to measure the correlation between advertisements, special promotions, and sales.

The Nielsen SCANTRACK household panel service is an integrated tracking system that pulls together all the causal factors of consumer purchasing—advertising, promotion, and retailer activity—in an effort to track the specific cues that induce people to buy certain products. Nielsen has provided household panel members with hand-held scanners that they use to scan (either at home or in the store) the UPC code of each item they buy and the coupons they redeem. By equipping the households with TV meters as well, Nielsen can report to a subscriber how often each family views its commercials (and its competitors' commercials), as well as which newspapers, magazines, and coupon mailings the family receives. The data input records price increases and in-store specials, and provides information as to brand switching, the level of product usage, and repeat purchases. Most importantly, it provides the feedback necessary to evaluate the effectiveness of a marketing communications strategy, and indicates precisely which part of the marketing campaign, if any, needs revision.[22]

Another type of feedback that companies seek from mass audiences is the degree of customer satisfaction or dissatisfaction with a product purchase. They try to discover—and correct as swiftly as possible—any problems that occur in order to retain the brand's image of reliability. Many companies have established 24-hour hotlines to encourage comments and questions from their consumers. Federal Express conducts a quarterly customer satisfaction survey by telephoning 2100 customers chosen at random.

Advertising effectiveness research, called **copy testing**, can be done *before* the advertising is actually run in media (pretesting), or *after* it appears (posttesting). **Pretests** are used to determine which, if any, elements of an advertising message should be revised before major media expenses are incurred. **Posttests** are used to evaluate the effectiveness of an ad that has already run and to see which elements, if any, should be changed to improve the impact of future ads.

One popular method for evaluating the effectiveness of magazine advertisements is through a syndicated service called the Starch Readership Service. Readers of a given issue of a magazine are asked to point out which ads they *noted*, which they *associated* with the sponsor, and which they *read most*. The resulting readership score is meaningful when compared

to similar-sized ads, to competitive ads, and to the marketer's own prior ads. Figure 10-3 presents an example of a "Starched" advertisement. There is evidence that high *noted* Starch scores are correlated with a favorable attitude toward the advertised brand and a positive brand purchase intention.[23] Thus, Starch scores may have validity beyond immediate processing of the ad and may indicate more lasting communications effects for the brand.

Syndicated services such as the A.C. Nielsen Company collect data on the size and characteristics of television audiences through electronic means, supplemented by diaries kept by a national sample of viewers. **Recall** and **recognition** posttests are conducted to determine whether consumers remember seeing a commercial, whether they can recall its content, and to assess the commercial's influence on consumers' attitudes toward the product and their buying intentions.

DESIGNING PERSUASIVE COMMUNICATIONS

In order to create persuasive communications, the sponsor (who may be an individual, a for-profit company, or a not-for-profit organization) must first establish the *objectives* of the communication, then select the appropriate *audience* for the message and the appropriate *media* through which to reach them, and then design (i.e., encode) the *message* in a manner that is appropriate to the medium and to the audience. The communications strategy should also include an *a priori* control plan that provides for prompt *feedback*, to enable the sponsor to make modifications and adjustments to the media and the message if and as needed.

Communications Strategy

In developing its communications strategy, the sponsor must establish the primary **communications objectives**. These might consist of creating awareness of a service, promoting sales of a product, encouraging (or discouraging) certain practices, attracting retail patronage, reducing postpurchase dissonance, creating goodwill or a favorable image, or any combination of these and other communications objectives.

An essential component of a communications strategy is selecting the appropriate **audience**. It is important to remember that an audience is made up of individuals—in many cases, great numbers of individuals. Because each individual has his or her own traits, characteristics, interests, needs, experience, and knowledge, it is essential for the sender to segment the audience into groups that are homogeneous in terms of some relevant characteristic. Segmentation enables the sender to create specific messages for each target group, and to run them in specific media that are seen (or heard) by each target group. It is unlikely that a marketer could develop a single message that would appeal simultaneously to a total audience. Efforts to use "universal" appeals phrased in simple language that everyone can understand invariably result in unsuccessful advertisements to which few people relate.

Because it enables marketers to tailor marketing communications to the specific needs of similar groups of people, market segmentation overcomes some of the problems inherent in trying to communicate with mass audiences. Take, for example, the problem of hostile audiences. Even though people tend to avoid viewpoints opposite to their own, there are times when it makes sense to advertise to hostile audiences. Although it may not change the beliefs of those fully persuaded, an ad can prevent others from being infected with the same degree of hostility. Research findings of a Chevron campaign directed at hostile audiences indicated that the company's promotional efforts resulted in more positive consumer attitudes as well as increased sales of the firm's gasoline. The campaign's greatest impact in terms of attitude change and increased purchase behavior was observed among a market segment described as *inner directed*—those consumers who "think for themselves."[24]

Companies that have many diverse audiences sometimes find it useful to develop a communications strategy that consists of an overall (i.e., *umbrella*) communications message to all their audiences, from which they spin off a series of related messages targeted directly to the specific interests of each individual segment.

To maintain positive communications with all of their publics, most large organizations employ public relations counselors, or establish their own public relations departments, to provide favorable information about the company and to suppress unfavorable information. A good public relations person will develop a close working relationship with editors and program directors of all of the relevant media in order to facilitate editorial placement of desired messages. Publicity campaigns designed to promote the image of the company are becoming increasingly popular, and marketers have developed methods to monitor and increase their effectiveness.

Media Strategy

Media strategy is an essential component of a communications plan. It calls for the placement of ads in the specific media read, viewed, or heard by selected target markets. To accomplish this, advertisers develop, through research, a **consumer profile** of their target customers that includes the specific media they read or watch. Media also research their own audiences in order to develop descriptive **audience profiles**. A cost-effective media choice is one that closely matches the advertiser's *consumer profile* to a medium's *audience profile*.

Before selecting specific media vehicles, advertisers must select a general media *category* that will enhance the message they want to convey. Which category the marketer selects depends on the product or service to be advertised, the market segments to be reached, and the marketer's advertising objectives. Rather than select one media category to the exclusion of others, many advertisers use a multimedia campaign strategy, with one primary category carrying the major burden of the campaign and other categories providing supplemental support.

Numerous research studies have compared the effectiveness of each medium over others for various products, audiences, and advertising objectives. In general, the findings have been inconclusive. Each media category has certain advantages and certain disadvantages that the marketer must consider in developing a media strategy for a specific campaign. Some media categories are more appropriate vehicles for certain products or messages than others. For example, a retailer who wants to advertise a Memorial Day bathing suit sale is likely to advertise in local newspapers, because that is where consumers are accustomed to looking for sales announcements. A manufacturer who wants to present a detailed argument in favor of its refrigerators is likely to advertise in household magazines, where readers are accustomed to reading detailed articles and stories. A marketer who wants to promote a snow blower with unique features would be wise to use a medium like television, on which the machine can be demonstrated in action.

Once marketers have identified the appropriate media category, they can then choose the specific medium in that category that reaches their intended audiences. Some evidence suggests that the magazines that people read provide a more accurate indication of their behavior as consumers than demographics such as age and marital status.[25] Table 10-1 presents the results of a recent study that judges consumers by the magazines that they read.

table 10-1   Judging Consumers by the Magazines They Read

A new research survey suggests that what people read, particularly which magazines they choose, can accurately predict their behavior as shoppers and consumers. The survey divides readers into five categories, or media communes.

	"HOME ENGINEERS"	"REAL GUYS"	"ETHNIC PEWNEPS*"	"INFORMATION GRAZERS"	"ARMCHAIR ADVENTURERS"
TYPICAL MAGAZINES READ	Family Circle Good Housekeeping Woman's Day	Guns & Ammo Popular Mechanics Mechanix Illustrated	Ebony Essence Jet	People Time Bon Appétit	Reader's Digest Modern Maturity Travel & Leisure
PRIMARY SEX	Female	Male	Both	Male	Both
INCOME†	$33,000	$39,000	$26,000	$44,000	$35,000
POLITICS	Mixed	Mixed	Democrats	Democrats	Republicans
FAVORITE TELEVISION PROGRAMS	"Oprah" "60 Minutes" "Donahue"	"Cheers" "America's Most Wanted" "N.F.L. Live"	"Arsenio Hall" "Oprah" "Fresh Prince of Bel Air"	"L.A. Law" "Roseanne" "A Current Affair"	"Matlock" "60 Minutes" "Wheel of Fortune"
MOST FREQUENTLY USED PRODUCTS	Eye shadow Face powder Foundation, makeup	Disposable diapers Bottled water Contact lens products	Nail polish Contact lens products Instant coffee	Disposable diapers Powdered drink mixes Frozen deserts	Antacids Decaffeinated coffee Instant coffee

*Shorthand for "people who need people."   †Average annual household income.

Source: STUART ELLIOTT, "Determining Demographics by What's on the Coffee Table," *The New York Times*, January 7, 1993, D18. Copyright © 1993 by The New York Times. Reprinted by permission.

The major issues that marketers must consider when selecting specific media are overlapping audiences, the characteristics of the audience, and the effectiveness of their advertisements (commercials).

▲ **The World Wide Web** According to a recent newspaper article, "If the medium is the message, then the message these days is the World Wide Web." No discussion of communications media today would be complete without some mention of the Web's increasingly important role as an advertising medium. For example, several years ago a Schick razor advertisement similar to the one presented in Figure 10-4 would most probably have asked readers to call a toll-free number for more product information. Instead, this ad provides

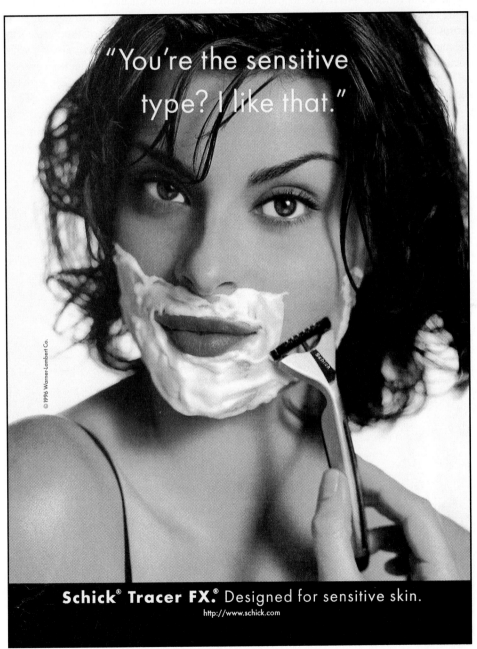

FIGURE 10-4 ▼

Print Ad Providing Internet "Address"
Courtesy of Warner-Lambert Company

the Internet address of Schick's Home Page. Currently, radio and TV stations have Web sites that promote their programs and stars, and most new movies have Web sites that promote the movie, contain clips from the film, and offer information about the film's major stars. A number of newspapers and magazines have also started offering cyberspace editions. More and more product and service advertisers today are including Web addresses, and the Net "surfer" can visit "sites" to purchase clothing, rent a car, make airline reservations, receive worldwide weather information, and so on. A number of Internet-based providers are offering marketers and retailers the chance to sell their products to millions of Internet users through "cyber-malls."[26]

 Overlapping Audiences Because many media—especially those with similar editorial features and formats—have overlapping audiences, advertisers usually place their advertising messages simultaneously or sequentially in a number of media with similar audience profiles. This enables them to achieve both **reach** and **frequency**. The term *reach* refers to the number of different people or households that are exposed to the advertisement (either because they hear or watch the program or read the newspaper or magazine); *frequency* refers to how often they are exposed to the ad during a specific period of time. The term **effective reach** combines both concepts and has been defined as a *minimum of three confirmed exposures to an individual member of a target group over an agreed-upon time period.*[27] The **effective reach threshold** suggests that 45 percent of the target group should be reached over the agreed-upon time period. Figure 10-5 illustrates how an ad in two similar media vehicles is likely to reach a unique audience in each medium, as well as an overlapping segment that reads both magazines and thus receives two exposures.

 Audience Characteristics Marketers use various syndicated marketing research services to obtain data on media audiences—their demographics, product purchases, brand preferences. Many marketers have adopted a media strategy called **precision targeting**. This strategy has been facilitated by media that seek a specific niche for themselves in the marketplace by catering to the needs and interests of a highly specific target segment.

FIGURE 10-5

Unique and Overlapping Readership of Magazines with Similar Audience Profiles

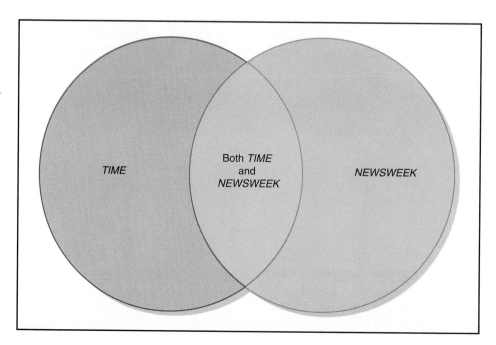

Magazine publishers are constantly looking for ways to refine their audiences. **Selective binding** is a new technique that enables publishers to narrowly segment their subscription bases. When readers subscribe, they are asked to provide demographic information, which the publisher enters into a data base. Through a sophisticated computerized system, the publisher is able to select specific subscribers, based on reader demographic profiles, to receive special sections that are bound into a limited number of magazines. Selective binding not only enables magazines to target subscribers more precisely, but also enables them to offer advertisers a more specialized audience. *Child Magazine* has a data base containing the birth dates of subscribers' children. Each month, subscribers receive an insert in their issue that is pegged to the ages of their children. A questionnaire sent to *Sports Illustrated* subscribers identified 400,000 serious golfers. From January to September, these readers receive a sixteen-page *Golf Plus* insert with their copy of the magazine.[28]

Direct mail and direct marketing are excellent examples of *precision targeting*. **Direct mail** is advertising that is sent directly to the mailing address of a target customer. **Direct marketing** is not a medium, but a marketing technique that uses various media (mail, print, broadcast, telephone, cyberspace) for the purpose of soliciting a direct response from a consumer. A major advantage of direct marketing is its ability to generate measurable responses. This capability enables direct marketers to measure the profitability of their efforts directly through such variables as cost-per-inquiry, cost-per-sale, and income-per-advertisement, and to evaluate the timing and frequency of campaigns.

A prime objective in direct marketing is to build and constantly refine an electronic data base of qualified buyers. This is done by soliciting both inquiries and direct orders. Computer analysis of the data base can yield highly selective customer segments. For example, by joining with MasterCard to create the GM Card, General Motors currently has a data base of over 12 million GM drivers. By surveying these cardholders, GM finds out what they currently drive and what they would like for their next vehicle. Thus, for example, if a cardholder expresses an interest in a sports-utility vehicle, GM can mail the appropriate brochure (e.g., Chevy Blazer) to the cardholder's home.[29]

Many people are concerned that the direct marketing practice of preserving and building the shopping histories of customers in their data bases is an invasion of privacy. In an effort to counter this concern, Equifax, one of the nation's largest credit bureaus, has set up a consensual data base that contains only the names of people who agree to be listed and who specify the types of information they would like to receive by mail. To induce participation, consumers are given up to $250 a year in discounts on products they want.[30] The privacy issue notwithstanding, a recent annual survey of promotional practices conducted by Donnelley Marketing Inc. found that 85 percent of retailers and manufacturers believe that, in order to be competitive beyond the year 2000, they will need to use data base marketing.[31] New technology, such as electronic transfer systems using computers, interactive television, and the electronic superhighway (i.e., the Internet), seem to be pushing the effort. As one university business school professor recently commented, "Once the superhighway is fully paved, everything you do will be recorded."[32]

Mail-order catalogs are a prime example of direct marketing sent through the mails to carefully-honed data bases. A number of companies have experienced dramatic success in catalog selling, including L.L. Bean, Sharper Image, and Lands' End. According to the Direct Marketing Association, in a recent year over 10,000 companies distributed 13.5 billion catalogs. Such mailings reached approximately 55 percent of the United States adult population and resulted in $51.5 billion in mail-order catalog sales.[33] Given the huge amount of competition in the field, some catalog retailers are trying to engage in **relationship marketing** by including in their catalogs editorial content that they think will make them more "human" to their customers. For example, some cookware catalogs include recipes and menus; some clothing catalogs include such information as how silk fabric is produced or how cashmere sweaters are made. There is also some evidence that relationship marketing is helping catalog retailers overcome the perception that catalog prices are higher than store prices.[34]

Relationship marketing is also being practiced by manufacturers and service providers. Harley Davidson enhances its "customer bonding" efforts by mailing a bimonthly magazine to each of the more than 250,000 members of its Harley Owners Group; the Claridge Hotel and Casino in Atlantic City continually makes special offers to the frequent gamblers who hold their Gold Claridge Comp Cards. IBM offers 24-hour a day, 7-day a week toll-free support to consumers who purchase its PCs—typically responding to 8,000 to 10,000 calls a day.[35]

Electronic shopping (through home-shopping TV channels, interactive cable, home computers, and stand-alone shopping kiosks) is also considered *direct marketing* because it generates an electronic data base of buyers. The popularity of electronic shopping stems from a shortage of free time among working women and the dislike of crowded shopping malls. In some cases, consumers simply find home shopping an entertaining way to relax in the comfort of their homes. Some advertisers are using fax machines to reach an upscale, educated market segment through numbers listed in fax phone books.

Clearly, marketers must be familiar with the characteristics of their audiences, the characteristics of their products, and the characteristics of media in order to make effective media choices.

Message Strategies

The *message* is the thought, idea, attitude, image, or other information that the sender wishes to convey to the intended audience. In trying to encode the message in a form that will enable the audience to understand its precise meaning, the sender must recognize exactly what he or she is trying to say and why (what the objectives are and what the message is supposed to accomplish). Senders must also know their audiences' characteristics in terms of education, interests, needs, and realms of experience. They must then try to phrase or encode their messages in ways that fall within their target audiences' zones of understanding and familiarity. For example, one marketer categorizes buyers as *Righteous, Social*, or *Pragmatic*.[36] According to this categorization, the Righteous Buyer responds to recommendations from independent sources such as *Consumer Reports*, while the Social Buyer relies on the recommendations of friends, on celebrity endorsements, and on testimonials. In contrast, the Pragmatic Buyer is interested in receiving the best value for the money (although not necessarily choosing the least expensive brand). Table 10-2 presents a comparative analysis of these three types of buyers.

Persuasive messages should begin with an appeal to the needs and interests of the audience and end with an appeal relevant to the marketer's own needs. Marketers have found that the most effective ads conclude by telling the audience exactly what it is they want them to do: "Visit your Buick showroom today"; "Ask for it at your favorite cosmetics counter"; "Send us your order by return mail"; "Call our toll-free number for the dealer nearest you." Advertisements that do *not* conclude with an *action closing* tend to elicit fewer consumer responses than those that do.

Nonverbal stimuli such as photographs or illustrations are commonly used in advertising to add meaning or to reinforce message arguments. One study showed that when verbal information was *low* in imagery, the inclusion of pictures that provided examples increased recall of the verbal information in both an immediate posttest and a delayed posttest. However, when the verbal information was *high* in imagery, the addition of pictures did not increase the subjects' ability to recall the verbal information contained in the ad.[37]

A number of studies have tried to manipulate the proportions of illustration and body copy used in print ads to determine the impact on recall and persuasion, but the findings

table 10-2 The *Righteous, Social,* and *Pragmatic* Buyer: A Comparative Analysis

	RIGHTEOUS	SOCIAL	PRAGMATIC
COPY APPEALS	Describe quality. Note achievements, awards, community and environmental positions.	Offer quality-of-life enhancements, exclusivity.	Benefit-driven. Focus on bottom line.
COPY LENGTH	Wants information. Detailed copy facilitates decisions.	Provide short, lively copy.	Repeat benefits and price. Keep it to the point. Bottom line-oriented.
ENDORSEMENTS	Highly important when from an independent source.	Impressed with credible celebrity endorsements.	Not important.
VISUALS	Show the product fully. Use detail in comparison charts.	Show people having fun. Whimsical!	Include charts for comparison. Show practical use of product.
PRICING	Emphasize fair price, value.	Full retail price easily accepted.	Offer a discount or a special deal.
GUARANTEES	Provide strongly worded guarantees.	Important, and a decision tie-breaker.	Provide strongly worded guarantees.
FREE TRIAL	"I can test it myself!"	"I can show it off!"	"I can use it and return it if I don't like it!"
SHIPPING AND HANDLING	Show fairness. Wants costs itemized.	Include in price.	Ship it free.
PREMIUMS	Relate to purchase.	Appeal to the Ego. Fun.	Emphasize giving something free.
TIME LIMITS OF OFFER	Don't ever break your word.	Helps incite action now.	There's always another deal.
SWEEPSTAKES/ CONTESTS	No great appeal.	Dreams of winning and impressing others.	Wants something for nothing.
CHARTER MEMBERSHIP	Provides some appeal.	"I'm the first to have it!"	Appeals if there's a special deal.

Source: Adapted from GARY HENNERBERG, "The Righteous, Social, and Pragmatic Buyer," *Direct Marketing*, May 1993, 31–32. Reprinted with permission from Direct Marketing magazine, 224 Seventh Street, Garden City, NY 11530, 516-746-6700.

have been fragmented and inconclusive. For example, one study showed that in some instances, body copy alone induced more favorable consumer evaluations than body copy used in conjunction with a visual; in other instances the reverse was true.[38] Another study found that all-copy print ads were rated as more utilitarian/rational, and all-visual print ads were rated as more familiar.[39] Other researchers found that the attractiveness of the illustration in a print ad influenced brand attitudes.[40] Although the evidence is somewhat inconclusive as to what makes a print ad memorable or persuasive, it is generally agreed that creativity and successful positioning are essential components in persuasive communications. Marketers also are beginning to use creative typography to evoke favorable moods (see Figure 10-6 on page 298).

▲ **Method of Presentation** The manner in which a message is presented strongly influences its persuasiveness. For example, people are much more influenced by word-of-mouth communications than they are by a printed format. However, research indicates that

FIGURE 10-6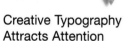

Creative Typography
Attracts Attention
Courtesy of Young and Rubicam
and the Idaho Potato Commission

this effect is reduced or eliminated when a prior impression of the target brand is available from memory.[41]

Researchers study not only the *semantics* of ad messages (i.e., the meanings of the words used and resulting inferences) but also the *syntax* (the sentence structure). One study found that ads using simple syntax produced greater levels of recall, regardless of the strength of the argument, than ads of greater complexity.[42] A study designed to explore the differences between persuasive and nonpersuasive TV commercials found that highly persuasive commercials tended to have stronger linkages between the visuals in the advertising.[43] The findings concluded that this "wholeness" provided a more complete or unified experience for the consumer.

The following discussion examines the influence of involvement theory, one-sided versus two-sided messages, comparative advertising, and order effects on message presentation. Table 10-3 lists twelve techniques summarized from the literature on communications to make a message more memorable and persuasive.[44]

INVOLVEMENT THEORY AND MESSAGE PRESENTATION The central-and-peripheral-routes-to-persuasion theory suggests that individuals are more likely to devote active cognitive effort to evaluating the pros and cons of a product in a high-involvement purchase situation and more likely to focus on peripheral message cues in a low-involvement situation. Thus, for *high-involvement* products, marketers should follow the **central route to persuasion**; that is, they should present advertisements with strong, well-documented, issue-relevant arguments that encourage cognitive processing (see Figure 10-7 on page 300). When involvement is *low*, marketers should follow the **peripheral route to persuasion** by emphasizing such noncontent message elements as background scenery, music, or celebrity spokespersons. Such highly visual or symbolic cues provide the consumer with pleasant, indirect associations with the product and provoke favorable inferences about its merits.

Despite the fact that *action closings* tend to be more effective in encouraging consumer response, researchers have found that, for high-involvement audiences, open-ended advertisements (that is, ads that do not draw explicit conclusions) are very effective in terms of creating positive brand attitudes and purchase intentions.[45] The results from one study found that, while peripheral advertising cues can affect brand choice, the extent of this influence depends on the particular brand-relevant information available at the time of choice.[46]

table 10-3 Communication Techniques for Persuasive Advertising

1. Get the audience aroused.
2. Give the audience a reason for listening.
3. Use questions to generate involvement.
4. Cast the message in terms familiar to your audience and build on points of interest.
5. Use thematic organization—tie material together by a theme and present in a logical, irreversible sequence.
6. Use subordinate category words—that is, more concrete, specific terms. (Example: *duck* rather than *bird*, *duck* being a subordinate word to *bird*.)
7. Repeat key points.
8. Use rhythm and rhyme.
9. Use concrete rather than abstract terms.
10. Use the *Zeigarnik* effect—leave the audience with an incomplete message, something to ponder so that they have to make an effort to achieve *closure*.
11. Ask your audience for a conclusion.
12. Tell the audience the implications of their conclusion.

Source: JAMES MACLACHLAN, "Making a Message Memorable and Persuasive," *Journal of Advertising Research* 23 (December 1983-January 1984), 51–59. © Copyright 1983 by the Advertising Research Foundation. Reprinted by permission.

FIGURE 10-7

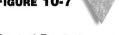

Central Route to
Persuasion
Courtesy of Simple Technology

Studies that examined **message framing** effects on persuasion have had mixed results. Some studies show that *positively-framed messages* (those that specify benefits to be *gained* by using a product) are more persuasive than *negatively-framed messages* (which specify benefits *lost* by not using a product); other studies have found the reverse to be true. One study found a tentative explanation for these mixed results by factoring in the level of involvement (i.e., cognitive processing). It found that positively-framed messages are more persuasive when there is little emphasis on detailed processing (low-involvement situations) and negatively-framed messages more persuasive when detailed processing is required (high-involvement situations).[47] A recent study of a credit card company's customers who had not used their cards in the past three months found that *loss framing* (i.e., what the consumer might lose by not using the credit card) had a much stronger effect on usage behavior than *gain framing*, and a study that compared a fictitious to an established brand of VCR found that the influence of price on consumers' perceptions of performance (i.e., functional risk) was greater when the message was negatively framed and source credibility was low.[48]

Some researchers tend to oversimplify the two-route approach to persuasion by recommending the exclusive use of either emotional (i.e., right-brain, peripheral route) or rational (left-brain, central route) message appeals. The distinction between these two approaches is readily seen in advertisements that make heavy use of emotional, symbolic cues in their formats, as opposed to straightforward, factual presentations.

Some researchers argue that it is impossible to deliver either a completely rational or a completely emotional message and suggest that marketers incorporate both routes to persuasion in their advertisements. These researchers believe that ads incorporating both factual, objective product messages (the central route) and highly visual symbolic cues that support the product claim (the peripheral route) are likely to be more persuasive than ads that use either the central or peripheral route exclusively.

ONE-SIDED VERSUS TWO-SIDED MESSAGES Should marketers tell their audiences only the good points about their products, or should they also tell them the bad (or the commonplace)? Should they pretend that their product is the only one of its kind, or should they acknowledge competing products? These are very real strategy questions that marketers face every day, and the answers depend on the nature of the audience and the nature of the competition.

If the audience is friendly (e.g., if it uses the advertiser's products), if it initially favors the communicator's position, or if it is not likely to hear an opposing argument, then a **one-sided** (*supportive*) message that stresses only favorable information is most effective. However, if the audience is critical or unfriendly (e.g., if it uses competitive products), if it is well educated, or if it is likely to hear opposing claims, then a **two-sided** (*refutational*) message is likely to be more effective.

Two-sided advertising messages are more credible than one-sided advertising messages because they acknowledge that the advertised brand has shortcomings. Such messages tend to be effective when salespeople, in personal selling situations, must address customer concerns and in public relations campaigns that must address negative publicity. They can also be particularly effective when consumer attitudes toward the brand are already negative, or when they are likely to see competitors' negative counterclaims. For example, in its campaign to regain consumer confidence and to convince customers of its intensified commitment to quality, Continental Airlines admitted to a variety of problems, including flight delays and lost luggage.[49]

Some marketers stress only positive factors about their products, and pretend that competition does not exist. However, when competition does exist, and when it is likely to be vocal, such advertisers tend to lose credibility with the consumer. Claim credibility can sometimes be enhanced by actually disclaiming superiority of some product features in relation to a competing brand, or by not claiming that the product is a universal cure. For example, an ad for Rogaine indicates that at the conclusion of a 12-month clinical test, almost 50 percent of the men using the product experienced modest to dense hair regrowth, 36 percent experienced minimal hair regrowth, and 16 percent had no regrowth (see Figure 10-8 on page 302).

COMPARATIVE ADVERTISING **Comparative advertising**, a marketing strategy used by increasing numbers of marketers, can be defined as *advertising that claims product superiority over one or more explicitly named or implicitly identified competitors*, either on an overall basis or on selected product attributes: Figure 10-9 on page 303 shows a comparative ad which claims that, in a "blind" taste test, almost 50 percent of traditional vodka-and-tonic drinkers preferred rum and tonic.

John's losing his hair. His mission: get it back.

ASAP!
But how?
Weaving? No.
Transplant?
Not for him.
A hairpiece?
Never, never.
What John really
wants is his
own hair back.
And now he's learned,
**for male pattern
baldness, only**
Rogaine **has been
proven to regrow hair.**

Normal hair grows and rests in cycles. The exact mechanism by which *Rogaine* Topical Solution (minoxidil topical solution 2%) stimulates hair growth is unknown. But many scientists believe that *Rogaine* works, in part, by taking advantage of the existing hair's growth cycle. Prolong the growth cycle so that more hairs grow longer and thicker at the same time, and you may see improved scalp coverage.

Will *Rogaine* work for you?

Dermatologists conducted 12-month clinical tests. After 4 months, 26% of patients using *Rogaine* reported moderate to dense hair regrowth, compared with 11% of those using a placebo (a similar solution without minoxidil — the active ingredient in *Rogaine*). After 1 year of use, almost half of the men who continued using *Rogaine* in the study rated their regrowth as moderate (40%) to dense (8%). Thirty-six percent reported minimal regrowth. The rest (16%) had no regrowth.

Side effects were minimal: 7% of those who used *Rogaine* had itching of the scalp. (Roughly 5% of those using a placebo

reported the same minor irritations.) *Rogaine* should only be applied to a normal, healthy scalp (not sunburned or irritated).

Make a commitment to see results.

Studies indicate that *at least 4 months of twice-daily treatment with* Rogaine *are usually necessary before there is evidence of regrowth.* So why not make it part of your normal routine when you wake up and go to bed, like brushing your teeth.

As you'd expect, if you're younger, have been losing your hair for a shorter period of time, and have less initial hair loss, you're more likely to have a better response.

Rogaine is a treatment, not a cure. So further progress is only possible by using it continuously. If you stop using it, you will probably shed the newly regrown hair within a few months.

Get your free Information Kit, plus a $10 incentive to see a doctor.

Why wait? Find out whether *Rogaine* is for you. Call **1-800-965-1199** for a free Information Kit about the product and how to use it. **And because *Rogaine* requires a prescription,** we'll include a list of nearby dermatologists or other doctors experienced in treating hair loss, plus a $10 incentive to visit a doctor soon.

Call

1-800-965-1199

for your free Information Kit
on *Rogaine* and a $10
incentive to see a doctor.

Rogaine
TOPICAL SOLUTION minoxidil 2%

See next page for important additional information.

©1994 The Upjohn Company USJ 2659 00 January 1995

FIGURE 10-8

Two-sided Appeal
Courtesy, Pharmacia & Upjohn

Comparative advertising is useful for product positioning, for target market selection, and for brand positioning strategies that stress the differential advantage of the "underdog" product over leading brands. To reinforce credibility, some marketers cite an independent research organization as the supplier of data used for the comparison.

Although comparative advertising is used widely, some critics maintain that comparative ads may assist recall of the competitor's brand at the expense of the advertised brand. For example, while the "pink bunny" that just keeps on running may be one of the most memorable TV commercial animated figures, consumers often associate the commercials with Duracell batteries, rather than with their actual sponsor, Eveready's Ener-

FIGURE 10-9

Comparative Advertising
Courtesy of Rums of Puerto Rico

gizer battery. Indeed, a survey found that 40 percent of respondents citing the bunny commercial as the most outstanding ad were certain that it was for Duracell batteries.[50] In general, studies have found that comparative ads are capable of exerting more positive effects on brand attitudes, purchase intentions, and purchase than noncomparative advertisements; however, comparative ads have also been found to reduce persuasion.[51]

A study of comparative advertising using an information-processing perspective found that comparative ads elicited higher levels of processing activity (high involvement), had better recall, and were perceived as more relevant than noncomparative ads.[52] Comparative ads were also found to outperform noncomparative ads when the advertised brand had a low market share or was unknown.[53] Research evidence suggests that future studies of comparative versus noncomparative advertising should use *relative measures* (i.e., measures using the comparison brand as a reference point), rather than *nonrelative measures* to gauge the levels of persuasion.[54]

There has been a great deal of interest and research into the effects of comparative advertising.[55] Visa International, Inc. ran a comparative ad on TV that flaunted its sponsorship of the 1988 Summer Olympics in Seoul, Korea with the line: ". . . the Olympics don't take place every year, and this year the Olympics don't take American Express." American Express retaliated with one-sided commercials set against the Seoul Olympic Stadium stating that the city's hotels and restaurants were proud to welcome the American

Express Card. It was particularly irritating to Visa, which had paid $15 million for TV rights, to see its nonsponsor rival get "free" mileage out of the Olympic Games. The 1996 Olympic Committee in Atlanta attempted to prevent advertisers from trading on the Olympic Games without sponsorship (a practice called *ambush marketing*) by threatening to run full-page ads naming violators and crying "thief."

ORDER EFFECTS Is it best to present your commercial first or last? Should you give the bad news first or last? Communications researchers have found that the order in which a message is presented affects audience receptivity.[56] For this reason, politicians and other professional communicators often jockey for position when they address an audience sequentially; they are aware that the first and last speeches are more likely to be retained in the audience's memory than those in between. On TV, the position of a commercial in a commercial pod can be critical. The commercials shown first are recalled best, those in the middle the least, and the ones at the end slightly better than those in the middle.[57] There is also evidence to suggest that television commercials that interrupt an exciting or suspenseful part of a program tend to be less well remembered than those presented during a low-involvement point in the TV show.[58] A recent study examining order presentation and media differences found that presentation order affects recall and memory-based attitudes for audio messages (e.g., radio ads) but not for visual messages (e.g., print ads).[59]

When just two competing messages are presented, one after the other, the evidence as to which position is more effective is somewhat conflicting. Some researchers have found that the material presented first produces a greater effect (the **primacy effect**), while others have found that the material presented last is more effective (the **recency effect**).

Magazine publishers recognize the impact of order effects by assigning *preferred position* placement to front, back, and inside covers of magazines, which means they charge more for these positions than for inside magazine pages because of their greater visibility and recall.

Order is also important in listing product benefits within an ad. If audience interest is low, the most important point should be made first to attract attention. However, if interest is high, it is not necessary to pique curiosity, and so product benefits can be arranged in ascending order, with the most important point mentioned last.

When both favorable information and unfavorable information are to be presented (e.g., in an annual stockholders' report), placing the favorable material first often produces greater tolerance for the unfavorable news. It also produces greater acceptance and better understanding of the total message.

Before concluding our discussion of order effects, it is important to note the growing popularity of the television *infomercial*, where the commercial is the program content. This increasingly popular form of advertising was responsible for an estimated $1 billion in sales in 1995 and appears to be especially suitable for products and services for which consumers need or want more information to make a buying decision than a standard 30- or 60-second commercial provides.[60]

▲ **Advertising Appeals** Sometimes objective, factual appeals are more effective in persuading a target audience, sometimes emotional appeals are more effective. It depends on the kind of audience to be reached and their degree of involvement in the product category. In general, however, logical, reason-why appeals are more effective in persuading educated audiences, and emotional appeals are more effective in persuading less educated consumers. The following section examines the effectiveness of several frequently used emotional appeals.

FEAR APPEALS Fear is an effective advertising appeal often used in marketing communications. Some researchers have found a *negative* relationship between the intensity of fear appeals and their ability to persuade, so that strong fear appeals tend to be less effective than mild fear appeals. (See also the discussion of assimilation-contrast theory in Chapter 9.) A number of explanations have been offered for this phenomenon. Strong fear appeals concerning a highly relevant topic (e.g., cigarette smoking) cause the individual to experience cognitive dissonance, which is resolved either by rejecting the practice or by rejecting the unwelcome information. Because giving up a comfortable habit is difficult, consumers more readily reject the threat. This they do by a variety of techniques, including denial of its validity ("There still is no real proof that smoking causes cancer"), the belief that they are immune to personal disaster ("It can't happen to me"), and a diffusing process that robs the claim of its true significance ("I play it safe by smoking only filter cigarettes"). A recent study that focused on oven cleaner warning labels found that subjects were able to recall more information from the low fear appeal label than from the high fear appeal label.[61]

Some researchers have found a positive relationship between fear and persuasiveness. They believe that when individuals focus on controlling the danger (a cognitive response) rather than controlling their fear (an emotional response), there is a greater probability they will accept the message's recommendation.[62] According to the *Ordered Protection Motivation* (OPM) model, individuals cognitively appraise the available information regarding the severity of the threat, then they appraise the likelihood that the threat will occur; they evaluate whether coping behavior can eliminate the threat's danger, and if so, whether they have the ability to perform the coping behavior.[63]

There is some indication that the mention of possible harmful effects of a product category in a usage situation, in the context of showing the benefits of the advertised product, causes negative attitudes toward the product itself.[64] For example, when a luxury automobile company featured its 24-hour emergency hotline in a series of advertisements, some consumers were "turned off" by even the suggestion that a brand new, expensive car would experience roadside mechanical problems. In some cases, marketers found that ads for condoms that stressed protection against AIDS were not as effective as condom ads that did not mention the dreaded disease. For that reason, some condom marketers changed their advertising approach from fear appeals to humor, discount promotions, or appeals directed at particular ethnic and lifestyle segments.

Future studies on fear appeals should differentiate between physical and psychological fear approaches (e.g., health versus social disapproval) and should develop better measures of fear levels. For example, it would be useful to measure the difference in impact of a fear appeal that portrayed the product as a preventative against a crippling disease (e.g., osteoporosis) and one that portrayed the product as a preventative against social embarrassment (e.g., slipping dentures).

HUMOR IN ADVERTISING Many marketers use humorous appeals in the belief that humor will increase the acceptance and persuasiveness of their advertising communications. Indeed, some estimates claim that almost 25 percent of TV commercials and over 30 percent of radio commercials use some form of humor.[65] Some marketers avoid the use of humor because they fear their product will become an object of ridicule, that consumers will laugh at them rather than with them. A recent review of the impact of humor on advertising concluded that:

- Humor attracts attention.
- Humor does not harm comprehension. *(In some cases it may even aid comprehension.)*
- Humor is not more effective at increasing persuasion.
- Humor does not enhance source credibility.
- Humor enhances liking.
- Humor that is relevant to the product is superior to humor that is unrelated to the product.

- Audience demographic factors (e.g., gender, ethnicity, age) affect the response to humorous advertising appeals.
- The nature of the product affects the appropriateness of a humorous treatment.
- Humor is more effective with existing products than with new products.
- Humor is more appropriate for low-involvement products and feeling-oriented products than for high-involvement products.[66]

There is evidence that audience characteristics may confound the effects of humor. Younger, better-educated, upscale, and professional people are receptive audiences for humorous messages. The program or editorial matter that surrounds a humorous message also influences its effectiveness. Humorous commercials seem to work best when presented in an action-adventure environment, rather than in a situation-comedy environment. This is an illustration of the Gestalt principle of *contrast* (see Chapter 6).

Because of the many qualifying conditions on the effectiveness of humor, perhaps the wisest policy for marketers to follow is to use humor selectively for products and audiences that seem to lend themselves strongly to this approach. It is also advisable for marketers to pretest humorous advertising treatments to be certain of their appropriateness for the audience and the product. For example, it is possible that humor in an advertisement makes consumers less sensitive to the strength of the ad's claims.[67]

A study that examined the behavioral impact of humorous promotions within a field setting found that relevant humor increased patronage, but that humor not relevant to the object of the promotion either had no impact or it had a negative impact.[68] Additional research is needed in terms of relevance to the product, the context in which the humorous ad will appear, audience factors, types of humor used, and message intensity. Figure 10-10 presents an ad for McDonald's with a humorous appeal.

"AGONY" ADVERTISING All of us have at one time or another been repelled by so-called *agony* commercials, which depict in diagrammatic detail the internal and intestinal effects of heartburn, indigestion, clogged sinus cavities, hammer-induced headaches, and the like. Nevertheless, pharmaceutical companies continue to run such commercials with great success because they appeal to a certain segment of the population that suffers from ailments that are not visible, and which therefore elicit little sympathy from family and friends. Their complaints are legitimized by commercials with which they immediately identify. With the sponsor's credibility established ("They really understand the misery I'm going through"), the message itself tends to be highly persuasive in getting consumers to buy the advertised product.

ABRASIVE ADVERTISING How effective can unpleasant or annoying ads be? Studies of the *sleeper effect*, discussed earlier, indicate that the effectiveness of an advertising message increases over time, despite the initial presence of a negative cue. This has interesting implications for marketing and helps explain the old public relations dictum: "It matters not whether they think well of you or ill of you so long as they remember your name." It suggests that the memory of an unpleasant commercial that saturates the media and antagonizes listeners or viewers may dissipate in the end, leaving only the brand name and the persuasive message in the minds of consumers.

SEX IN ADVERTISING In our highly permissive society, sensual advertising seems to permeate the print media and the airwaves. Sex in advertising ranges from the blatancy of nudes and obvious double entendre to devices so subtle it takes a trained observer to recognize them.

The use of sex in advertising has been increasing at a significant rate for more than the past 20 years.[69] During the past few years, though, sex has become somewhat less explicit in advertising, as the public's fear of AIDS caused advertisers to turn to more romantic and less overtly sexual themes, and as sexual harassment became more of a public issue. Indeed, during 1995, Calvin Klein was pressured to withdraw advertisements that

FIGURE 10-10

Humorous Appeal
Courtesy of McDonald's
Corporation

some people labeled "kiddie porn"; much of the public was unwilling to accept what appeared to be young teenagers in sexual poses. In a recent survey among adult consumers, 38 percent of women and 23 percent of men felt that sexually charged ads can promote sexual harassment.[70] Sexual imagery is not likely to disappear from television commercials and print ads any time soon, but it is likely to be handled more subtly than in the previous decade. Some advertisers, in response to the increasingly controversial topics of sex and violence that have become staples on a number of daytime talk shows, have begun to pull their ads from the most contentious programs.[71]

There are many instances in which advertisers who have used sex as a thematic appeal have been very successful. In other instances, such advertising has proved either damaging or simply ineffective. Consumer reaction to advertisements with sexual appeals is difficult to predict. So why do advertisers continue to use sex in their advertising? The answer is simple. There are few appeals in advertising that equal its attention-getting value. Many psychologists believe that the skillful manipulation of sexual appeals in visual images, in copy, or in both may arouse subconscious desires that manifest themselves in the purchase of goods or services. Readership studies show that sex is one element that arouses the immediate interest of both men and women.

Although sexual themes may attract a reader's attention, they rarely encourage curiosity about the product. A study that examined the effects of sexual advertising appeals on cognitive processing and communication éffectiveness found that sexual appeals interfere with message comprehension, particularly when there is substantial information for processing.[72] It also found that more product-related thinking occurs in response to nonsexual appeals, and that visual sexual elements in the ad are more likely to be processed than the verbal content, drawing cognitive processing away from product or message evaluation.[73] These findings support the notion that sexual advertising appeals detract from the processing of message content.

Sex in an ad can also offend. Indeed, a recent survey of adult consumers found that nearly one-third of Americans find sexual references or images in advertising offensive. Seventy-five percent of a key consumer group, women aged 35 to 54, claimed to be "frequently" or "occasionally" offended by sex in advertising (while women aged 55+ reported being more frequently offended). Additionally, the study found that middle-aged consumers (both men and women) were more likely than other age categories to avoid buying products because of the sexual content of their advertising.[74]

There are strong indications that the type of interest that sex evokes often stops exactly where it started—with sex. If a sexually suggestive or explicit illustration is not relevant to the product advertised, it makes no selling impression on the reader. This highlights the potential risk of sexually oriented advertising: the advertiser may be trading persuasiveness for "stopping power." Researchers who investigated the impact of female nudity in advertisements concluded that nudity may negatively impact the product message.[75] Nudity in an advertisement often causes tension, and high levels of tension are associated with negative feelings toward the ad.[76]

The use of a sexual appeal in an advertisement does not necessarily imply that the model appears without clothing. For example, while the headline in Figure 10-11 implies sex, the ad is for Grey Poupon mustard.

Men and women respond differently to sex in advertising. For example, a recent study found that men viewing nude ads displayed the strongest positive attitudes toward both the ad and the brand—much more so than when they were presented with "demure" versions of the ads. In contrast, women in this study displayed the least positive attitudes to sexy or erotic ads.[77] Given such findings, it is surprising that many more ads with nudes and sensual themes can be found in women's magazines like *Vogue* and *Cosmopolitan* than in male magazines like *Playboy*.

One thread seems to run through all the research findings regarding sex in advertising: the advertiser must be sure that the product, the ad, the target audience, and the use of sexual themes and elements all work together. When sex is relevant to the product, it can be an extremely potent copy theme.

▲ **Audience Participation** Earlier, we spoke about the importance of feedback in the communications process. The provision of feedback changes the communications process from one-way to two-way communication. This is important to senders, because it enables them to determine whether and how well communication has taken place. But feedback also is important to receivers, because it enables them to participate, to be involved, to experience in some way the message itself. Participation by the receiver reinforces the message. An experienced communicator asks questions and opinions of an audience to draw them into the discussion. Many professors use the participative approach in classrooms rather than the more sterile lecture format because they recognize that student participation tends to facilitate internalization of the information discussed.

Although participation is easily accomplished in interpersonal situations, it takes a great deal of ingenuity in impersonal situations. Thus, it is a challenge for imaginative marketers to get consumers involved in their advertising. The *counterargumentation* pro-

voked by two-sided messages is one way of doing so. Incomplete messages, requiring *closure*, is another.

Examples of ads requiring **audience participation** include word games (where the reader fills in the missing letters) and identification games (where the receiver tries to guess the identity of the celebrity spokesperson). American Express has used this technique in a series of credit card ads headlined "Do You Know Me?" Radio and television commercials achieve this same effect as listeners try to identify the celebrity behind a familiar voice-over.

Crisis Communications Strategies

As a number of major companies have discovered in the past few years, unexpected disasters—fires, deaths, oil spills, poisonings—do occur, and these can have catastrophic effects on the company's business if not handled properly. Those companies that have emerged unscathed from such disasters unvariably have had a *crisis communications plan* in place: they knew precisely who should meet with the press, had press releases ready to go, provided hotlines for the public, gave the press telephone access and camera opportunities, provided constant updates on the situation, and in general reassured the public and eliminated antagonism from the press. Companies that do not have a crisis communications plan ready to go in times of disaster are totally unprepared for the press and the public and generally lose public confidence (and a great deal of business).

In 1982, when seven people died in Chicago after ingesting cyanide-laced Tylenol capsules, Johnson & Johnson spent $100 million on an immediate recall of its best-selling product, and another $30 million in replacing the product in tamper-resistant packaging and promoting the "new" Tylenol. The company chairman went on television as soon as the disaster occurred to answer all questions and to alleviate consumer concern. Most marketing professionals thought the company would have to drop the Tylenol brand, even though the cause was traced to limited product tampering, but because of the openness and frankness and rapidity of the company response, the product achieved even greater sales volume when it returned to the shelves.

On October 30, 1994, a college professor published a note on the Internet about a flaw in the Intel Pentium computer chip. Later it was learned that Intel had discovered these Pentium flaws the previous summer but had chosen not to disclose them to the public. For the next several weeks, Intel maintained that these defective chips did not need replacement, claiming that the odds of a chip causing a mathematical error were "9 billion to 1." Intel said it would consider replacement only in cases where users could prove that their computers were used for complex mathematical computations. It was only after receiving a great deal of negative publicity that Intel agreed, almost 2 months later, to offer Pentium computer owners a no-questions-asked return/exchange policy. By that time, the company's image had taken a severe beating. As *The New York Times* noted, "Intel officials were out of touch with the new consumer market they had cultivated," and Intel officials "had not prepared themselves for the new obligations and responsibilities" that come with being a consumer products company.[78]

Sophisticated companies now have crisis teams that try to identify every possible kind of disaster that could befall their company and to develop detailed communications plans for each type of crisis. Then, should disaster occur, they know exactly who should do what, who should speak to the press, and what to say to calm public fears and to retain public confidence.[79]

summary

This chapter has described how the consumer receives and is influenced by marketing communications. Communication is defined as the transmission of a message from a sender to a receiver through a channel or medium of some sort.

There are five basic components of communication: the sender, the receiver, the medium, the message, and some form of feedback (the receiver's response). In the communications process, the sender encodes the message using words, pictures, symbols, or spokespersons, and sends it through a selected channel of communication. The receiver decodes (interprets) the message based on personal characteristics and experience and responds (or does not respond) based on such factors as comprehension, psychological noise, selective exposure, and selective attention.

There are two types of communication: interpersonal and impersonal (or mass) communication. Interpersonal communication occurs on a personal level between two or more people and may be verbal or nonverbal. In mass communication, there is no direct contact between source and receiver. Interpersonal communications take place in person, by telephone, or by mail; mass communication uses such impersonal media as television, radio, newspapers, and magazines. In both types of communication, feedback is an essential component because it provides the sender with some notion as to whether and how well the message has been received.

The credibility of the source, a vital element in message persuasiveness, often is based on his or her perceived intentions. Informal sources and neutral or editorial sources generally are considered highly objective and, therefore, very credible. The credibility of a commercial source is more problematic, and usually is based on a composite evaluation of its reputation, expertise, and knowledge, and that of the medium, the retail channel, and the company spokespersons it uses.

Media selection depends on the product, the audience, and the advertising objectives of the campaign. In addition to consumers, a marketer's audiences include selling intermediaries and other publics that are relevant to the organization's success.

The manner in which a message is presented influences its impact. For example, one-sided messages are more effective in some situations and with some audiences; two-sided messages are more effective with others. High-involvement products (i.e., those with great relevance to a consumer segment) are best advertised through the central route to persuasion, which encourages active cognitive effort. Low-involvement products are best promoted through peripheral cues, such as background scenery, music, or celebrity spokespersons.

Emotional appeals frequently used in advertising include fear appeals, humorous appeals, "agony" appeals, and sexual appeals. When sexual themes are relevant to the product, they can be very effective; when used solely as attention-getters, they rarely achieve brand recall. Audience participation is a very effective communications strategy because it encourages internalization of the advertising message. Future research is needed to identify the many product, audience, and situational variables that mediate the effects of message order and presentation in persuading consumers to buy.

discussion questions

1. Explain the differences between feedback from interpersonal communications and feedback from impersonal communications. How can the marketer obtain and use each kind of feedback?

2. List and discuss the effects of psychological barriers on the communications process. How can a marketer overcome the communications barrier known as "noise"?

3. a. What factors influence the perceived credibility of an informal communications source? List and discuss factors that determine the credibility of formal communications sources of product information.

   b. What are the implications of the sleeper effect for the selection of spokespersons and the scheduling of advertising messages?

4. General Motors uses both magazines and television to promote its new model Cadillac Seville. (a) How would you measure the advertising effectiveness of a TV commercial promoting the new model and the extent to which it has reached the intended audience? (b) How would you measure the same factors for a magazine advertisement promoting the new car?

5. Explain the difference(s) between direct mail and direct marketing. Discuss the reasons for the continued growth of direct marketing and the objectives of direct marketing.

6. a. Should marketers use more body copy than artwork in print ads? Explain your answer.

   b. For what kinds of audiences would you consider using comparative advertising? Why?

7. You are the marketing manager for a headache remedy. Your advertising agency has just presented you with two different promotional strategies, one using a humorous approach and one taking an "agony" approach. Which approach would you adopt? Why?

8. In June 1993, several incidents in which syringes were purportedly found in Pepsi cans were widely reported throughout the country. Although it was found that most of these incidents were hoaxes, the Pepsi Company had to deal with the highly extensive media coverage that resulted. How would a crisis communications plan have helped the company handle the adverse publicity? Describe the components of such a plan.

exercises

1. Bring two advertisements to class: one illustrating a one-sided message and the other a two-sided message. Explain why each marketer may have chosen that specific message strategy and evaluate each ad's effectiveness.

2. Choose a television commercial that uses a humorous appeal. Interview members of your family who saw the same commercial and measure their (a) recall of the brand advertised, (b) recall of the information presented, (c) like or dislike of the commercial, and (d) preference for the brand advertised. How would you explain your findings in view of the research evidence on humor in advertising presented in this chapter?

3. Find three print ads, one using a fear appeal, the second a sex appeal, and the third an audience participation appeal and present them in class. For each ad, discuss whether you think the appeal used is effective and why.

4. Watch one hour of TV on a single channel during prime time and record the broadcast. List all the commercials you can recall seeing. For each commercial, identify (a) the message framing approach used and (b) whether the message was one-sided or two-sided. Compare your list with the actual taped broadcast. Explain any discrepancies between your recollections and the actual broadcast on the basis of concepts discussed in this chapter.

5. For three of the commercials you watched in the course of the above exercise, identify whether the marketer used the central or peripheral route to persuasion. Explain your answer and speculate on why each marketer chose the approach it used to advertise the product or service.

key words

- Audience profile
- Central route to persuasion
- Communications objectives
- Comparative advertising
- Consumer profile
- Copy appeals
- Copy pretests and posttests
- Crisis communications
- Direct mail
- Direct marketing
- Effective reach
- Encoding and decoding
- Endorsements
- Feedback
- Formal and informal communications sources

- Impersonal communications
- Impersonal (mass) media
- Institutional advertising
- Interactive communication
- Intermediary audiences
- Interpersonal communications
- Media demassification
- Media strategy
- Message framing
- Nonverbal communication
- One-sided vs. two-sided messages
- Peripheral route to persuasion
- Precision targeting

- Primacy and recency effects
- Psychological noise
- Reach and frequency
- Recall and recognition measures
- Selective binding
- Sleeper effect
- Source credibility
- Testimonials
- Unintended audiences
- Word-of-mouth communication
- Zipping and zapping

end notes

1. KEITH B. MURRAY, "A Test of Services Marketing Theory: Consumer Information Acquisition Activities," *Journal of Marketing* 55, January 1991, 10–25.

2. STUART ELLIOTT, "Determining Demographics by What's on the Coffee Table," *The New York Times*, January 7, 1993, D18.

3. For a discussion of nontraditional media, see SCOTT HUME, "Steady Diet of Basics," *Advertising Age*, August 19, 1991, 27–33.

4. See, for example, PAUL N. BLOOM and TORGER REVE, "Transmitting Signals to Consumers for Competitive Advantage," *Business Horizons*, July-August 1990, 58–66, and LINDA GREENHOUSE, "High Court Ruling Upholds Trademarking of a Color," *The New York Times*, March 29, 1994, D1.

5. SHELLY CHAIKEN and ALICE H. EAGL, "Communication Modality as a Determinant of Persuasion: The Role of Communicator Salience," *Journal of Personality and Social Psychology* 45, 1983, 241–56.

6. S. RATNESHWAR and SHELLY CHAIKEN, "Comprehension's Role in Persuasion: The Case of Its Moderating Effect on the Persuasive Impact of Source Cues," *Journal of Consumer Research* 18, June 1991, 52–62.

7. ROBERT R. HARMON and KENNETH A. CONEY, "The Persuasive Effects of Source Credibility in Buy and Lease Situations," *Journal of Marketing Research* 19, May 1982, 255–60; "Information: Implications for the Sleeper Effect," *Journal of Consumer Research* 15, June 1988, 24–36.

8. JEFF JENSEN, "Is Olympic Sponsor Pie Sliced Too Thin?," *Business Marketing* 80, December 1995, 1.

9. CARL I. HOVLAND, ARTHUR A. LUMSDAINE, and FRED D. SHEFFIELD, "Experiments on Mass Communication" (New York: Wiley, 1949), 182–200.

10. DARLENE B. HANNAH and BRIAN STERNTHAL, "Detecting and Explaining the Sleeper Effect," *Journal of Consumer Research* 11, September 1984, 632–42.

11. ANTHONY R. PRATKANIS et al., "In Search of Reliable Persuasion Effects: III. The Sleeper Effect is Dead. Long Live the Sleeper Effect," *Journal of Personality and Social Psychology* 34(2), 1988, 203–18. See also JOSEPH W. ALBA, HOWARD MARMORSTEIN, and AMITAVA CHATTOPADHYAY, "Transitions in Preference over Time: The Effects of Memory on Message Persuasiveness," *Journal of Marketing Research* 29, November 1992, 414.

12. DAVID MAZURSKY and YAACOV SCHUL, "The Effects of Advertisement Encoding on the Failure to Discount Information: Implications for the Sleeper Effect," *Journal of Consumer Research* 15, June 1988, 24–36.

13. DAVID GLEN MICK, "Levels of Subjective Comprehension in Advertising Processing and Their Relations to Ad Perceptions, Attitudes, and Memory," *Journal of Consumer Research* 18, March 1992, 411–24.

14. JEAN HARRISON-WALKER, "The Import of Illiteracy to Marketing Communication, *Journal of Consumer Marketing* 12(1), 1995, 50–64.

15. WILLIAM R. SWINYARD, "The Effects of Mood, Involvement, and Quality of Store Experience on Shopping Intentions," *Journal of Consumer Research* 20, September 1993, 271–80.

16. See MAHIMA MATHUR and AMITAVA CHATTOPADHYAY, "The Impact of Moods Generated by Television Programs on Responses to Advertising," *Psychology and Marketing* 8(1), Spring 1991, 59–77.

17. See GORDON C. BRUNER II, "Music, Mood, and Marketing," *Journal of Marketing*, October 1990, 94–104.

18. CAROL FELKER KAUFMAN and PAUL M. LANE, "In Pursuit of the Nomadic Viewer," *Journal of Consumer Marketing* 11(4), 1994, 4–17.

19. BILL CARTER, "NBC Cancels the Pause Between Shows," *The New York Times*, October 3, 1994, D6.

20. See, for example, JOHN J. CRONIN and NANCY E. MENELLY, "Discrimination vs. Avoidance: Zipping of Television Commercials," *Journal of Advertising* 21(2), June 1992, 1–7; and PATRICIA A. STOUT and BENEDICTA L. BURDA, "Zipped Commercials: Are They Effective?" *Journal of Advertising* 18(4), 1989, 23–32.

21. ARTHUR J. KOVER, "Copywriters' Implicit Theories of Communication: An Exploration," *Journal of Consumer Research* 21, March 1995, 596–611.

22. LAURENCE N. GOLD, "The Evolution of Television Advertising Sales Measurement: Past, Present, and Future," *Journal of Advertising Research*, June/July 1988, 19–24.

23. GEORGE M. ZINKHAN and BETSY D. GELB, "What Starch Scores Predict," *Journal of Advertising Research* 26(4), August 1986, 45–50.

24. LEWIS C. WINTERS, "Does It Pay to Advertise to Hostile Audiences with Corporate Advertising?" *Journal of Advertising Research*, June/July 1988, 11–18.

25. STUART ELLIOTT, "Advertising," *The New York Times*, January 14, 1994, D15.

26. See, for example, JOHN MARKOFF, "If Medium Is the Message, the Message Is the Web," *The New York Times*, November 20, 1995, A1 and D5; EDWARD BAIG, "Surfing for Safaris—Or Cruises, Beaches, B&Bs. . . ," *Business Week*, May 20, 1996, 106–7; and ELAINE SHERMAN and MARTIN T. TOPOL, "Anticipating the Impact of New Technologies on Retailing," *Journal of Retailing and Consumer Services* 3(2), 1996, 107–11.

27. GEORGE B. MURRAY and JOHN R. G. JENKINS, "The Concept of 'Effective Reach' in Advertising," *Journal of Advertising Research*, May/June 1992, 34–42.

28. DEIRDRE CARMODY, "Magazines Go Niche-Hunting with Custom-Made Selections," *The New York Times*, June 26, 1995, D7.

29. "A Potent New Tool for Selling: Database Marketing," *Business Week*, September 5, 1994, 56–62.

30. MARK D. UEHLING, "Here Comes the Perfect Mailing List," *American Demographics*, August 1991, 10–12.

31. *Business Week*, September 5, 1994, op. cit.

32. DEBORAH L. JACOBS, "They've Got Your Name. You've Got Their Junk," *The New York Times*, March 13, 1994, F5.

33. HOLLY BRUBACH, "Mail-Order America," *The New York Times Magazine*, November 21, 1993, 54–70.

34. MICHELLE A. MORGANOSKY, "Change in US Retail Market Structure: What Does It Mean to Advertisers?," *International Journal of Advertising* 12, 1993, 37–43.

35. *Business Week*, May 20, 1996, op. cit., and MATTHEW L. WALD, "Soothing the Panicky PC User," *The New York Times*, July 19, 1994, D1 and D5.

36. GARY HENNERBERG, "The Righteous, Social and Pragmatic Buyer," *Direct Marketing*, May 1993, 31–34.

37. H. RAO UNNAVA and ROBERT E. BURNKRANT, "An Imagery-Processing View of the Role of Pictures in Print Advertisements," *Journal of Marketing Research* 28, May 1991, 226–31.

38. JOLITA KISIELIUS and BRIAN STERNTHAL, "Detecting and Explaining Vividness Effects in Attitudinal Judgments," *Journal of Marketing Research* 21, February 1984, 54–64.

39. ELIZABETH C. HIRSCHMAN and MICHAEL R. SOLOMON, "Utilitarian, Aesthetic, and Familiarity Responses to Verbal Versus Visual Advertisements," in Thomas C. Kinear, ed., *Advances in Consumer Research* 11 (Provo, UT: Association for Consumer Research, 1983), 426–31.

40. YEHOSHUA TSAL, "Effects of Verbal and Visual Information on Brand Attitudes," in Elizabeth C. Hirschman and Morris B. Holbrook, eds., *Advances in Consumer Research* 12 (Provo, UT: Association for Consumer Research, 1984), 265–67.

41. PAUL M. HERR, FRANK R. KARDES, and JOHN KIM, "Effects of Word-of-Mouth and Product Attribute Information on Persuasion: An Accessibility-Diagnosticity Perspective," *Journal of Consumer Research* 17, March 1991, 454–62.

42. TINA M. LOWREY, "The Relation Between Syntactic Complexity and Advertising Persuasiveness," *Advances in Consumer Research* 19, 1992, 270–74.

43. CHARLES E. YOUNG and MICHAEL ROBINSON, "Visual Connectedness and Persuasion," *Journal of Advertising Research*, March/April 1992, 51–59.

44. JAMES MACLACHLAN, "Making a Message Memorable and Persuasive," *Journal of Advertising Research* 23, December 1983-January 1984, 51–59.

45. ALAN G. SAWYER and DANIEL J. HOWARD, "Effects of Omitting Conclusions in Advertisements to Involved and Uninvolved Audiences," *Journal of Marketing Research* 28, November 1991, 467–74.

46. PAUL W. MINIARD, DEEPAK SIRDESHMUKH, and DANIEL E. INNIS, "Peripheral Persuasion and Brand Choice," *Journal of Consumer Research* 19, September 1992, 226–39.

47. DURAIRAJ MAHESWARAN and JOAN MEYERS-LEVY, "The Influence of Message Framing and Issue Involvement," *Journal of Marketing Research* 27, August 1990, 361–67.

48. YOAV GANZACH and NILI KARSAHI, "Message Framing and Buying Behavior: A Field Experiment," *Journal of Business Research* 32, 1995, 11–17; and DHRUV GREWAL, JERRY GOTLIEB, and HOWARD MARMORSTEIN, "The Moderating Effects of Message Framing and Source Credibility on the Price-Perceived Risk Relationship," *Journal of Consumer Research* 21, June 1994, 145–53.

49. AYN E. CROWLEY and WAYNE D. HOYER, "An Integrative Framework for Understanding Two-Sided Persuasion," *Journal of Consumer Research* 20, March 1994, 561–74.

50. JOANNE LIPMAN, "Too Many Think the Bunny Is Duracell's, Not Eveready's," *The Wall Street Journal*, July 31, 1990, B1 and B7.

51. RANDALL L. ROSE, PAUL W. MINIARD, MICHAEL J. BARONE, KENNETH C. MANNING, and BRIAN D. TILL, "When Persuasion Goes Undetected: The Case of Comparative Advertising," *Journal of Marketing Research* 30, August 1993, 315–30.

52. DARREL D. MUEHLING, JEFFREY J. STOLTMAN, and SANFORD GROSSBART, "The Impact of Comparative Advertising on Levels of Message Involvement," *Journal of Advertising* 19(4), 1990, 41–50; see also JERRY B. GOTLIEB and DAN SAREL, "Comparative Advertising Effectiveness: The Role of Involvement and Source Credibility," *Journal of Advertising* 20(1), 1991, 38–45.

53. PAUL W. MINIARD, MICHAEL J. BARONE, RANDALL L. ROSE, and KENNETH C. MANNING, "A Re-Examination of the Relative Persuasiveness of Comparative and Noncomparative Advertising," *Advances in Consumer Behavior* 21, 1994, 299–302.

54. ROSE et al., op. cit.

55. For a review of recent research, see KAREN E. JAMES and PAUL J. HENSEL, "Negative Advertising: The Malicious Strain of Comparative Advertising," *Journal of Advertising* 20(2), June 1991, 53–69.

56. For basic readings in this area, see Carl I. Hovland, ed., *The Order of Presentation in Persuasion* (New Haven: Yale University Press, 1957).

57. PETER H. WEBB and MICHAEL L. RA, "Effects of TV Clutter," *Journal of Advertising Research* Classics II, September 1984, 19–24.

58. VALERIE STARR and CHARLES A. LOWE, "The Influence of Program Context and Order of Ad Presentation on Immediate and Delayed Responses to Television Advertisements," *Advances in Consumer Research* 22, 1995, 184–90.

59. H. RAO UNAVA, ROBERT E. BURNKRANT, and SUNIL EREVELLES, "Effects of Presentation Order and Communication Modality on Recall and Attitude," *Journal of Consumer Research* 21, December 1994, 481–90.

60. STUART ELLIOTT, "Advertising," *The New York Times*, November 9, 1995, D11.

61. MARK A. DETURCK, ROBERT A. RACHLINE, and MELISSA J. YOUNG, "Effects of a Role Model and Fear in Warning

Label on Perceptions of Safety and Safety Behavior," *Advances in Consumer Research* 21, 1994, 208–12.

62. KEN CHAPMAN, "Fear Appeal Research: Perspective and Application," *Proceedings of the American Marketing Association*, Summer 1992, 1–9; also JOHN F. TANNER, JR., JAMES B. HUNT, and DAVID R. EPPRIGHT, "The Protection Motivation Model: A Normative Model of Fear Appeals," *Journal of Marketing* 55, July 1991, 36–45.

63. JAMES B. HUNT, JOHN F. TANNER, JR., and DAVID R. EPPRIGHT, "Forty Years of Fear Appeal Research: Support for the Ordered Protection Motivation Model," *American Marketing Association* 6, Winter 1995, 147–53.

64. MERYL P. GARDNER and ROSALYN S. LEVIN, "Truth and Consequences: The Effects of Disclosing Possibly Harmful Results of Product Use," in Bruce J. Walker et al., *An Assessment of Marketing Thought and Practice, 1992 Educators' Conference Proceedings*, 39–42.

65. HYONGOH CHO, "Humor Mechanisms, Perceived Humor and Their Relationships to Various Executional Types in Advertising," *Advances in Consumer Research* 22, 1995, 191–97.

66. MARC G. WEINBERGER and CHARLES S. GULAS, "The Impact of Humor in Advertising: A Review," *Journal of Advertising* 21(4), December 1992, 35–59.

67. STEPHEN M. SMITH, "Does Humor in Advertising Enhance Systematic Processing?" *Advances in Consumer Behavior* 20, 1993, 155–58.

68. WEINBERGER and GULAS, op. cit.

69. MICHAEL S. LATOUR and TONY L. HENTHORNE, "Female Nudity: Attitudes Toward the Ad and the Brand and Implications for Advertising Strategy," *Journal of Consumer Marketing* 10(3), 1993, 25–32.

70. DORIS WALSH, "Safe Sex in Advertising," *American Demographics*, April 1994, 24–30; and STUART ELLIOTT, "Calvin Klein to Withdraw Child Jean Ads," *The New York Times*, August 28, 1995, D1 and D9.

71. SALLY GOLL BEATTY, "Are Daytime Shows Too Hot to Handle?" *The Wall Street Journal*, November 2, 1995, B10.

72. JESSICA SEVERN, GEORGE E. BELCH, and MICHAEL A. BELCH, "The Effects of Sexual and Non-Sexual Advertising Appeals and Information Level on Cognitive Processing and Communication Effectiveness," *Journal of Advertising* 19(1), 1990, 14–22.

73. Ibid.

74. WALSH, op. cit.

75. MICHAEL S. LATOUR, ROBERT E. PITTS, DAVID C. SNOOK-LUTHER, "Female Nudity, Arousal, and Ad Response: An Experimental Investigation," *Journal of Advertising* 19(4), 1990, 51–62.

76. LATOUR and HENTHORNE, op. cit.

77. Ibid.

78. JOHN MARKOFF, "Intel's Crash Course on Consumers," *The New York Times*, December 21, 1994, D6.

79. JOSEPH WISENBLIT, "Crisis Management Planning Among U.S. Corporations: Empirical Evidence and a Proposed Framework," *SAM Advanced Management Journal* 54(2), Spring 1989, 31–41.

PART THREE

Consumers in Their Social and Cultural Settings

THE SIX CHAPTERS THAT FOLLOW ARE designed to provide the

reader with a detailed picture of the social and cultural dimensions of

consumer behavior. Part III explains how social and cultural concepts

affect the attitudes and behavior of individuals in the United States and

the world beyond, and shows how these concepts are employed by

marketing practitioners to achieve their marketing objectives.

With the exception of those very few people who are classified as hermits, most individuals interact with other people on a daily basis. Like almost all human behavior, an individual's social behavior and social relationships often are motivated by expectations of satisfying specific needs. For example, a person might become a Boy Scout or Girl Scout leader to satisfy a need for community service and recognition. Another person might visit a local dance club to meet compatible people and satisfy social needs. A third person might join a warehouse membership club (such as the Costco-Price Club or Sam's Warehouse) to obtain the benefits of group buying power. These are just a few of the almost infinite number of reasons why people interact with others.

This chapter discusses the basic concepts of social interaction and group dynamics. It emphasizes, in particular, how reference groups both directly and indirectly

All economic movements, by their very nature, are motivated by crowd psychology.

—Bernard Baruch, 1932

influence consumer behavior. The five chapters that follow discuss other social and societal groupings that influence consumer buying processes: the family, socioeconomic class, culture, subculture, and cross-cultural exposure.

What is a Group?

A **group** may be defined as *two or more people who interact to accomplish either individual or mutual goals*. The broad scope of this definition includes an intimate "group" of two next-door neighbors who do their supermarket shopping together and a larger, more formal group, such as a neighborhood homeowners association, whose members are mutually concerned with the schools, roads, taxes, and types of businesses in their neighborhood. Included in this definition, too, are more remote, one-sided social relationships in which an individual consumer looks to others for help in deciding which products or services to own or use, even though these others are largely unaware that they are serving as consumption-related role models.

Types of Groups

There are many ways to classify groups, such as by regularity of contact, by structure and hierarchy, by membership, even by size. For example, it is often desirable to distinguish between groups in terms of size or complexity. However, it is difficult to offer a precise point at which a group is considered large or small. A large group might be one in which a single member knows only a few of the group's members personally or is aware of the specific roles or activities of only a few group members. In contrast, members of a small group are likely to know each member personally and are aware of every member's specific role or activities in the group. For instance, each member of the staff of a small community newspaper is likely to know all of the other members and be aware of their duties and interests within the group.

In the realm of consumer behavior, we are principally concerned with the study of small groups, because such groups are more likely to influence the consumption behavior of group members.

▲ **Primary Versus Secondary Groups** If a person interacts on a regular basis with other individuals (with members of his or her family, with neighbors, or with co-workers whose opinions are valued), then these individuals can be considered a **primary group** for that person. On the other hand, if a person interacts only occasionally with others, or does not consider their opinions particularly important, then these others constitute a **secondary group** for that person. The critical distinctions between primary and secondary groups, therefore, are the *perceived importance* of the groups to the individual and the *frequency* or *consistency* with which the individual interacts with them.

▲ **Formal Versus Informal Groups** Another useful way to classify groups is by their formality, that is, the extent to which the group structure, the members' roles, and the group's purpose are clearly defined. If a group has a highly defined structure (for example, a formal membership list), specific roles and authority levels (e.g., a president, treasurer, and secretary), and specific goals (e.g., to assist the elderly, dissuade people from smoking, or increase the knowledge or skills of members), then it would be classified as a **formal** group. The local chapter of one of the major American political parties, with elected officers and members who meet regularly to discuss topics of civic interest, would be classified as a formal group. On the other hand, if a group is more loosely defined—if it consists, for example, of three men who became friends while studying architecture and who meet for dinner once a month or of two couples who frequently go to a local movie together—then it is considered an **informal group**.

From the standpoint of consumer behavior, informal social or friendship groups are generally more important to the marketer, because their less clearly defined structures provide a more conducive environment for the exchange of information and influence about consumption-related topics.

▲ **Membership Versus Symbolic Groups** Sometimes, groups are classified by membership status. A group to which a person either belongs or would qualify for membership is called a **membership group**. For example, the group of women with whom a young actress plays tennis weekly would be considered, for her, a membership group. Another example of a membership group is your college's alumni association; still another, for marketing practitioners, is the American Marketing Association.

There are groups in which an individual is not likely to receive membership, despite acting like a member by adopting the group's values, attitudes, and behavior, is considered a **symbolic group**. For instance, professional golfers may constitute a symbolic group for an amateur golfer who identifies with certain players by imitating their behavior whenever possible (e.g., by purchasing a specific brand of golf clubs or golf balls). The amateur golfer does not, however (and probably never will), qualify for membership as a professional golfer, because he has neither the skills nor the opportunity to compete professionally.

In summary, small, informal, primary membership groups are of the greatest interest to marketers, because they exert the greatest potential influence on consumption decisions.

Consumer-Relevant Groups

To more fully comprehend the kind of impact that specific groups have on individuals, this chapter will examine six basic **consumer-relevant groups**: the family, friendship groups, formal social groups, shopping groups, consumer-action groups, and work groups.

▲ **Family** An individual's *family* often is in the best position to influence his or her consumption decisions. The family's importance in this regard is based on the frequency of contact that the individual has with other family members and or the extent of influence that the family has on establishing a wide range of values, attitudes, and behavior. (Chapter 12 examines the family's influence on purchase and consumption behavior.)

▲ **Friendship Groups** *Friendship groups* are typically classified as informal groups, because they are usually unstructured and lack specific authority levels. In terms of relative influence, after an individual's family, his or her friends are most likely to influence the individual's purchase decisions.

Seeking and maintaining friendships is a basic drive of most people. Friends fulfill a wide range of needs: they provide companionship, security, and opportunities to discuss problems that an individual may be reluctant to discuss with family members. Friendships are also a sign of maturity and independence, for they represent a breaking away from the family and the forming of social ties with the outside world.

The opinions and preferences of friends are an important influence in determining the products or brands a consumer ultimately selects. Recognizing the power of peer group influence, marketers of products such as brand-name clothing, fine jewelry, snack foods, and alcoholic beverages frequently depict friendship situations in their ads.

Consumers are more likely to seek information from those friends they believe have values or outlooks similar to their own. The greater the perceived similarity, the more likely they are to be influenced by their friends' judgments in arriving at a purchase decision.

▲ **Formal Social Groups** In contrast to the relative intimacy of friendship groups, *formal social groups* are more remote and serve a different function for the individual. A person joins a formal social group to fulfill such specific goals as making new friends, meeting "important" people (e.g., for career advancement), broadening perspectives, pursuing a special interest, or promoting a specific cause. Because members of a formal social group often consume certain products together, such groups are of interest to marketers. For example, the membership of a ski club would be of particular interest to tour operators, travel agents, sporting-goods retailers, ski-magazine publishers, and the manufacturers of ski equipment and clothing. The membership list of a townwide service organization (e.g., Lion's Club or Kiwanis) would be of interest to local luggage stores, insurance agents, automobile dealers, tax accountants, and special-interest publications.

Membership in a formal social group may influence a consumer's behavior in several ways. For example, members of such groups have frequent opportunities to informally discuss products, services, or stores. Some members may copy the consumption behavior of other members whom they admire.

▲ **Shopping Groups** Two or more people who shop together, whether for food, for clothing, or simply to pass the time, can be called a *shopping group*. Such groups are often offshoots of family or friendship groups, and therefore they function as what has been referred to as **purchase pals**.[1] The motivations for shopping with a purchase pal range from a primarily social motive (e.g., to share time together and enjoy lunch after shopping) to helping reduce the risk when making an important decision (e.g., have someone along whose expertise will reduce the chance of making an incorrect purchase). In instances where none of the members of the shopping group knows much about the product under consideration (e.g., an expensive home entertainment center), a shopping group may form for defensive reasons; members may feel more confident with a collective decision.

A special type of shopping group is the in-home shopping party, which typically consists of a group who gathers together in the home of a friend to attend a "party" devoted to demonstrating and evaluating a specific line of products. The in-home party approach provides marketers with an opportunity to demonstrate the features of their products simultaneously to a group of potential customers. Early purchasers tend to create a bandwagon effect: Undecided guests often overcome a reluctance to buy when they see their friends make positive purchase decisions. Furthermore, some of the guests may feel obliged to buy because they are in the home of the sponsoring host or hostess.

▲ **Consumer-Action Groups** A particular kind of consumer group—a **consumer-action group**—has emerged in response to the consumerist movement. Consumer-action groups can be divided into two broad categories: those that organize to correct a specific consumer abuse and then disband and those that organize to address broader, more pervasive problem areas and operate over an extended or indefinite period of time. A group of irate neighbors who band together to protest the opening of a topless bar in their neighborhood or a group of parents who attend a meeting of the local school board to question some of the decisions made by the high school principal are examples of temporary, cause-specific consumer-action groups. An example of a more enduring consumer-action group is Mothers Against Drunk Driving (MADD), a group founded in 1980, and operating today throughout the United States within local community groups. MADD representatives serve on numerous public advisory boards and help establish local task forces to combat drunk driving. Additionally, the organization supports actions to restrict alcoholic beverage advertising and is opposed in general to any advertising and products that may have a negative impact on youth.

The overriding objective of many consumer-action groups is to bring sufficient pressure to bear on selected members of the business community to make them correct perceived consumer abuses.[2]

▲ **Work Groups** The sheer amount of time that people spend at their jobs, frequently more than 35 hours per week, provides ample opportunity for *work groups* to serve as a major influence on the consumption behavior of members.

Both the formal work group and the informal friendship-work group can influence consumer behavior. The formal work group consists of those individuals who work together as a team. Their direct and sustained work relationship offers substantial opportunity for one or more members to influence the consumption-related attitudes and activities of other team members. Informal friendship-work groups consist of people who have become friends as a result of working for the same firm, whether or not they work together as a team. Members of informal work groups may influence the consumption behavior of other members during coffee or lunch breaks or at after-work meetings.

Recognizing that work groups influence consumers' brand choices and that most women now work outside of their homes, firms that in the past sold their products exclusively through direct calls on women in their homes now are redirecting their sales efforts to offices and plants during lunch hour visits. For instance, Avon and Tupperware, two leading direct-to-home marketers, encourage their sales representatives to reach working women at their places of employment.[3]

REFERENCE GROUPS

A **reference group** *is any person or group that serves as a point of comparison (or reference) for an individual in forming either general or specific values, attitudes, or behavior.* This basic concept provides a valuable perspective for understanding the impact of other people on an individual's consumption beliefs, attitudes, and behavior. It also provides some insight into the methods marketers sometime use to effect desired changes in consumer behavior.

What Is a Reference Group?

From a marketing perspective, *reference groups* are groups that serve as *frames of reference* for individuals in their purchase or consumption decisions. The usefulness of this concept is enhanced by the fact that it places no restrictions on group size or membership, nor does it require that consumers identify with a tangible group (i.e., the group can be symbolic: owners of successful small businesses, leading corporate chief executive officers, rock stars, or golf celebrities).

Reference groups that influence *general* or *broadly defined* values or behavior are called **normative reference groups**. An example of a child's normative reference group is the immediate family, which is likely to play an important role in molding the child's general consumer values and behavior (e.g., which foods to select for good nutrition, appropriate ways to dress for specific occasions, how and where to shop, or what constitutes "good" value).

Reference groups that serve as benchmarks for specific or narrowly defined attitudes or behavior are called **comparative reference groups**. A comparative reference group might be a neighboring family whose lifestyle appears to be admirable and worthy of imitation (the way they maintain their home, their choice of home furnishings and cars, their taste in clothing, or the number and types of vacations they take).

Both normative and comparative reference groups are important. Normative reference groups influence the development of a basic code of behavior; comparative reference groups influence the expression of specific consumer attitudes and behavior. It is likely that the specific influences of comparative reference groups to some measure depend on the basic values and behavior patterns established early in a person's development by normative reference groups.

▲ **Broadening the Reference Group Concept** Like many other concepts borrowed from the behavioral sciences, the meaning of "reference group" has changed over the years. As originally used, reference groups were narrowly defined to include only those groups with which a person interacted on a direct basis (e.g., family and close friends). However, the concept gradually has broadened to include both direct and indirect individual or group influences. **Indirect reference groups** consist of those individuals or groups with whom a person does not have direct face-to-face contact, such as movie stars, sports heroes, political leaders, or TV personalities.

Referents a person might use in evaluating his or her own general or specific attitudes or behavior vary from one individual, to several family members, to a broader kinship or from a voluntary association to a social class, a profession, an ethnic group, a community, an age category, or even a nation or culture. As Figure 11-1 indicates, the major societal groupings that influence an individual's consumer behavior are, in order: family, friends, social class, various subcultures, one's own culture, and even other cultures. For instance, within the scope of "selected subcultures" we would include various age categories (e.g., teenagers or baby boomers) that might serve as a reference group for their own or others' behavior. The advertisement in Figure 11-2 declares: "Popular

FIGURE 11-1

Major Consumer
Reference Groups

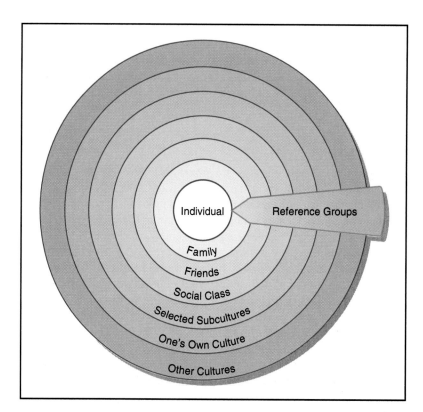

FIGURE 11-2 ▼

Ad Appealing to an Age
Category Grouping
© 1994 Creata Card, Inc.

teenagers everywhere are giving these keen, personalized holiday cards. Do they know something you don't?" In effect, the ad is suggesting to teenagers that members of their own age category reference group are giving such cards and that it is an "in" thing to do. (Age category and other important consumer reference groups are discussed in more detail in Chapters 12 through 16.)

▲ **Types of Reference Groups** Reference groups can be classified in terms of a person's membership or degree of involvement with the group, as well as in terms of the positive or negative influences they have on his or her values, attitudes, and behavior. Table 11-1 depicts the four types of reference groups that emerge from a cross-classification of these factors: contactual groups, aspirational groups, disclaimant groups, and avoidance groups.

A **contactual group** is one in which a person holds membership or has regular face-to-face contact and of whose values, attitudes, and standards he or she approves. Thus, a contactual group is likely to have a congruent influence on an individual's attitudes or behavior.

An **aspirational group** is a group in which a person does not hold membership and does not have face-to-face contact but wants to be a member. Thus, it often serves as a positive influence on that person's attitudes or behavior.

A **disclaimant group** is a group in which a person holds membership or has face-to-face contact but disapproves of the group's values, attitudes, and behavior. Thus, the person tends to adopt attitudes and behavior that are in opposition to the norms of the group.

An **avoidance group** is a group in which a person does not hold membership and does not have face-to-face contact and of whose values, attitudes, and behavior he or she disapproves. Thus, the person tends to adopt attitudes and behavior that are in opposition to those of the group.

To illustrate, consider Tom Fisk who recently finished a stint in the Navy and is now beginning his new career as a computer specialist for a local telephone company. The telephone company's experienced computer staff members serve as Tom's *contactual* groups. Tom believes that continuing his education to obtain an advanced degree in computers will enhance his career opportunities. It is clear that individuals who hold advanced degrees or training in computers serve as an *aspirational group* for him. In contrast, Tom views those high school friends who neither took advantage of available post-high school education, nor joined the armed forces, as he did, to be "losers"; these high school friends are a *disclaimant group*. Finally, because of personal growth and maturing occurring as a result of his Navy service, Tom now feels even more committed to his belief of the importance of wholesome family and religious values. Tom vocally rejects the actions of those peers who he perceives do not demonstrate adequate respect for their families and religion; thus, such individuals continue to serve as an *avoidance group*.

Factors That Affect Reference Group Influence

The degree of influence that a reference group exerts on an individual's behavior usually depends on the nature of the individual and the product and on specific social factors. This section discusses how and why some of these factors influence consumer behavior.

▲ **Information and Experience** An individual who has firsthand experience with a product or service, or can easily obtain full information about it, is less likely to be influenced

table 11-1 Types of Reference Groups

	MEMBERSHIP GROUP	NONMEMBERSHIP GROUP
POSITIVE INFLUENCE	Contactual group	Aspirational group
NEGATIVE INFLUENCE	Disclaimant group	Avoidance group

by the advice or example of others. On the other hand, a person who has little or no experience with a product or service and does not expect to have access to objective information about it (e.g., a person who believes that relevant advertising may be misleading or deceptive) is more likely to seek out the advice or example of others. For instance, when a recent college graduate wants to impress her boyfriend, she may take him to a restaurant that she knows from experience to be good or to one that has been highly recommended by the local newspaper's Dining Out Guide. If she has neither personal experience nor information she regards as valid, she may seek the advice of friends or imitate the behavior of others by taking him to a restaurant she knows is frequented by young business executives whom she admires.

▲ **Credibility, Attractiveness, and Power of the Reference Group** A reference group that is perceived as credible, attractive, or powerful can induce consumer attitude and behavior change. For example, when consumers are concerned with obtaining accurate information about the performance or quality of a product or service, they are likely to be persuaded by those whom they consider trustworthy and knowledgeable. That is, they are more likely to be persuaded by sources with *high credibility* (see Chapter 10).

When consumers are primarily concerned with the acceptance or approval of others they like, with whom they identify, or who offer them status or other benefits, they are likely to adopt their product, brand, or other behavioral characteristics. When consumers are primarily concerned with the power that a person or group can exert over them, they might choose products or services that conform to the norms of that person or group in order to avoid ridicule or punishment. However, unlike other reference groups that consumers follow because they are credible or because they are attractive, *power groups* are not as likely to cause attitude change. Individuals may conform to the behavior of a powerful person or group but are not as likely to experience a change in their own attitudes.

Different reference groups may influence the beliefs, attitudes, and behavior of an individual at different points in time or under different circumstances. For example, the dress habits of a young male executive may vary, depending on his place and role. He may conform to the dress code of his office by wearing dress shirts and conservative business suits by day and drastically alter his mode of dress after work by wearing more trendy, flamboyant styles.

▲ **Conspicuousness of the Product** The potential influence of a reference group on a purchase decision varies according to how visually or verbally conspicuous the product is to others. A visually conspicuous product is one that will stand out and be noticed (e.g., a luxury item or novelty product); a verbally conspicuous product may be highly interesting, or it may be easily described to others. Products that are especially conspicuous and status-revealing (a new automobile, fashion clothing, or home furniture) are most likely to be purchased with an eye to the reactions of relevant others. Privately consumed products that are less conspicuous (canned fruits or laundry soaps) are less likely to be purchased with a reference group in mind.

As Figure 11-3 on page 328 reveals, the success of status sport shoes such as FILA is aided by the fact that it is relatively easy to spot a person wearing them, given the distinctive logos strategically placed on the shoes themselves (e.g., on the tongue of the shoe, the heel, or even the sole). In a somewhat similar fashion, the market acceptance of the Sharp Zaurus—a keyboard enhanced Personal Digital Assistant—is aided by the fact that it is a conspicuous product. When an executive takes it out at a business meeting and starts to enter an appointment or looks up something; others at the meeting become interested

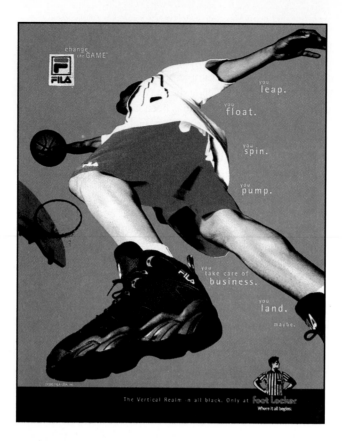

and ask questions about how it works and how good it is. The product also reflects on the user: it says that he or she is "high tech" (see Figure 11-4).

Reference Groups and Consumer Conformity

Marketers are traditionally interested in the ability of reference groups to change consumer attitudes and behavior (i.e., to encourage *conformity*). To be capable of such influence, a reference group must:

1. *Inform or make the individual aware of a specific product or brand;*
2. *Provide the individual with the opportunity to compare his or her own thinking with the attitudes and behavior of the group;*
3. *Influence the individual to adopt attitudes and behavior that are consistent with the norms of the group; and*
4. *Legitimize an individual's decision to use the same products as the group.*

How group membership affects brand choice often depends on the specific product (e.g., pizza versus toothpaste), the type of social relationship (roommates, friends, or dates), and the social structure of the group (extent of personal ties between group members). For example, research conducted among members of a college sorority concluded that members of close-knit groups were more likely to reveal a preference for the same brands.[4] The findings also suggest that product conspicuousness is unnecessary for similarity of brand choice to occur. Specifically, the evidence indicates that even for relatively "private" products (e.g., shampoo and toothpaste), strong brand congruence may occur

FIGURE 11-4

The Public Use of a Product Can Impact Acceptance
Courtesy of Sharp Electronics Corporation

when the particular social setting provides an opportunity for such products to be observed (e.g., when sorority sisters happen to share the same bathroom). This evidence underscores the fact that a consumer's selection of a product category, brand, style, or type of product often is influenced by the preferences and actions of others.

Realizing the power of reference groups and their influence on consumers' conformity, a new brand or a brand that is not the market leader may want to elect a strategy that asks consumers to strike out and be innovative and not just follow the crowd when making a purchase decision. An illustration of this type of marketing is the ad for Panasonic sound products. It dramatically challenges potential consumers to "Listen like a rebel" (i.e., be a "rebel") and "Don't be a sheep. Dare to compare Panasonic sound to the other guys" (see Figure 11-5).

Figure 11-5

Ad Suggesting "Don't Conform. Compare."
Courtesy of Panasonic

Applications of the Reference Group Concept

Reference group appeals are used very effectively by some advertisers to communicate with their markets. People or group situations with whom a target audience can *identify* are used to promote goods and services by subtly inducing the prospective consumer to identify with the pictured user of the product or service. This identification may be based on admiration (e.g., of an athlete), on aspiration (of a celebrity or a way of life), on empathy (with a person or a situation), or on recognition (of a person real or stereotypical or of a situation). In some cases, the prospective consumer may think, "If she uses it, it must be good. If I use it, I'll be like her." In other cases, the prospective consumer says to himself, "He has the same problems that I have. What worked for him will work for me."

Five major types of reference group appeals in common marketing usage are *celebrity appeals*, *expert appeals*, *common man appeals*, *executive appeals*, *trade or spokes-character appeals*. These appeals, as well as less frequently employed appeals, are often operationalized in the form of testimonials or endorsements. In the case of the common man, they may be presented as *slice-of-life* commercials.

Celebrities

Celebrities, particularly movie stars, TV personalities, popular entertainers, and sports icons, provide a very common type of reference group appeal. To their loyal followers and to much of the general public, celebrities represent an idealization of life that most people imagine that they would love to live. Advertisers spend enormous sums of money to have celebrities promote their products, with the expectation that the reading or viewing audience will react positively to the celebrity's association with their product.[5]

Research comparing the impact of advertisements with and without celebrity endorsers found that those featuring celebrities were rated more positively. This was especially true among teenagers, who were more likely to project the celebrity's credibility to the advertising message and the endorsed product.[6]

▲ **How Celebrities Are Used** A firm that decides to employ a celebrity to promote its product or service has a choice of using the celebrity to give a **testimonial**, to give an **endorsement**, as an **actor** in a commercial, or as a company **spokesperson**. These promotional roles differ as follows:

1. Testimonial. *If the celebrity has personally used the product or service and is in a position to attest to its quality, then he or she may give a testimonial citing its benefits. In an ad for 1-Day Acuvue® disposable contact lenses, Pat Riley (the well-known professional basketball coach) states: "Throw away your contact lenses. I do it everyday" (Figure 11-6 on page 332).*

2. Endorsement. *Celebrities often are asked to lend their names to ads for products or services with which they may or may not be experts. For example, Senior P.G.A. champion, Larry Laoretti, has endorsed TE-AMO cigars—a product he enjoys but one not related directly to his skills as a professional golfer (see Figure 11-7 on page 333).*

3. Actor. *A celebrity may be asked to present a product or service as part of a character enactment, rather than as a personal testimonial or endorsement. For instance, Jerry Stiller and Estelle Harris, two character actors, who play George's parents on the Jerry Seinfeld Show, have appeared in their roles in an AT&T TV commercial, and Jason Alexander, who plays George, has appeared in Rold Gold pretzels commercials.[7]*

4. Spokesperson. *A celebrity who represents a brand or company over an extended period of time, often in print and television ads, as well as in personal appearances, is usually called a company spokesperson. Eventually, the celebrity's appearance becomes closely associated with the brand or company. For many years Lee Trevino has represented Motorola as a spokesperson for its telecommunications products (see Figure 11-8 on page 334).*

Table 11-2 on page 334 lists some currently popular celebrity endorsers and the client products or services they have represented.

▲ **Credibility of the Celebrity** Of all the benefits that a celebrity might contribute to a firm's advertising program, fame, talent, credibility, or charisma, celebrity credibility with

FIGURE 11-6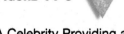

A Celebrity Providing a
Testimonial
Courtesy of Vista Con

the consumer audience is the most important. By **celebrity credibility** we mean the audience's perception of both the celebrity's expertise (how much the celebrity knows about the product area) and *trustworthiness* (how honest the celebrity is about what he or she says about the product).[8] To illustrate, when a celebrity endorses only one product, consumers are likely to perceive the product in a highly favorable light and indicate a greater intention to purchase it. In contrast, when a celebrity endorses a variety of products, his or her perceived credibility is reduced because of the apparent economic motivation underlying the celebrity's efforts.[9]

▲ **Does It Matter Who the Celebrity Is?** It is widely assumed that celebrity endorsers bring the benefit of their symbolic images (i.e., their personal "meaning") to the products and services to which they lend their name and person. Specifically, the cultural meaning that "resides" within a particular celebrity endorser is "passed on" to the product or service being endorsed.[10] Indeed, *prototypical bonding* is the term used to describe the process of associating a spokesperson's attributes, traits, or values with a particular service or product.[11] Research that compared the use of Christie Brinkley and Madonna as celebrity endorsers for bath towels—a particularly ordinary product category—found that compared to those endorsed by Madonna, the towels endorsed by Christie Brinkley were judged to be much more attractive, of higher quality, much softer, more feminine, and more sophisticated. In addition, Madonna's towels were considered almost unpleasant, low class, intense, and nasty, while Brinkley's towels were perceived as pleasant, higher class, and

FIGURE 11-7

A Celebrity
Endorsement
Courtesy of Consolidated Cigar

lower keyed.[12] These sharply contrasting profiles point up that not all celebrities succeed as product or service endorsers. Celebrities also appear to come into and fade out of favor as product endorsers. For instance, celebrity endorsers might be "in" for several years and then quickly find themselves "out" (i.e., less popular) as product endorsers. Examples of

FIGURE 11-8

A Celebrity as a Spokesperson
Courtesy of Motorola, Inc. © 1993 Motorola, Inc.

celebrity endorsers who lost some of their appeal include Cher, Ray Charles, and Sally Struthers.[13] The reasons why celebrities "ping-pong" back and forth in their popularity as endorsers seems to reflect that advertisers and their ad agencies are, now more than ever, assessing the benefits of the celebrities that they use. They appear to be trying to identify a

table 11-2 Popular Celebrity Stars (Not Sports Celebrities)

CELEBRITY	PRODUCT/SERVICE
Jason Alexander (George on Seinfeld)	Rold Gold Pretzels
June Allyson	Depend
Shari Belafonte	Ultra Slim-fast
Candice Bergen	Sprint
Chevy Chase	Doritos
Bill Cosby	Jell-O
Cindy Crawford	AT&T; Revlon
Kathie Lee Gifford	Carnival Cruise Line
Whitney Houston	AT&T
Julia Louis-Dreyfuss (Elaine on Seinfeld)	Clairol Nice 'n Easy
Jerry Seinfeld	American Express
Cybill Shepard	L'Oreal
Jaclyn Smith	Kmart
Elizabeth Taylor	White Diamonds (her) perfume

better celebrity *match* for their products and to avoid celebrities that have become over-exposed because of too many endorsements.

Sometimes, there can be undesirable confusion regarding for whom a celebrity endorser or spokesperson is working. For instance, while Candice Bergen has a long track record as a spokesperson for the long distance telephone company, Sprint, one in three consumers surveyed nevertheless associated her with arch rivals AT&T or MCI.[14] Clearly, such confusion is not what an advertiser is seeking when selecting a celebrity endorser.

Not all companies feel that using celebrity endorsers is the best way to advertise. For example, Gap, Inc., used celebrities throughout the 1980s in its "Individuals of Style campaign"; however, its current ads focus more heavily on the clothes. Some companies avoid celebrities because they fear that if the celebrity gets involved in some undesirable act or event (e.g., an ugly matrimonial problem, a scandal, or a criminal case), that the negative news or press coverage will negatively impact on the sale of the endorsed brand.[15]

The Expert

A second type of reference group appeal used by marketers is the expert, a person who, because of his or her occupation, special training, or experience, is in a unique position to help the prospective consumer evaluate the product or service that the advertisement promotes. For example, an advertisement for a quality frying pan may feature the endorsement of a chef; an ad for fishing tackle may contain the endorsement of a professional fishing guide; or an ad for volleyball shoes might feature the endorsement of a champion volleyball team (see Figure 11-9 on page 336).

The "Common Man"

A reference group appeal that uses the testimonials of satisfied customers is known as the *common-man* approach. The advantage of the common-man appeal is that it demonstrates to prospective customers that someone just like them uses and is satisfied with the product or service being advertised. The common-man appeal is especially effective in public-health announcements (e.g., antismoking or high-blood pressure messages), for most people seem to identify with people like themselves when it comes to such messages.[16]

The Saturn Corporation consistently has used a variation of the common-man approach, when it tells of the interesting experiences of satisfied Saturn customers—often showing the consumers in a dramatization of the customer's unique experience. In one example, Darlene and Tom Robison were "run off the highway, rolled their car," and yet were able to walk away from the accident. In a similar fashion, Figure 11-10 on page 337 presents a portion of a letter (in script format) from a Navy man's wife commending the functionality of her husband's Timex Indiglo wristwatch.

Many television commercials show a typical person or family solving a problem by using the advertised product or service. These commercials are known as **slice-of-life commercials** because they focus on "real-life" situations with which the viewer can identify. For example, one commercial focuses on how a laundry detergent can deodorize clothes; another talks about how a certain breakfast cereal provides enough energy to get an individual through a hectic morning. When viewers identify with the situation, they are likely to adopt the solution that worked in the TV commercial.

The Executive and Employee Spokesperson

During the past two decades, an increasing number of firms have used their top executives as spokespersons in consumer ads. The popularity of this type of advertising probably is due to the success and publicity received by a number of innovative executive spokespersons. For instance, Lee Iacocca was highly effective in persuading consumers that

We put a lot into our new volleyball shoes. A whole team, in fact.

The USA National Volleyball Team

All the new Kaepa volleyball shoes are loaded with features. Like Infinity° Snapper° Rubber, for unparalleled traction on the court. Forefoot shock-absorption. And a lightweight molded EVA midsole. We even designed one with a built-in ankle brace for maximum support and flexibility. So no matter who you are, or at what level you compete, you'll really get into our shoes. Just like the USA National Volleyball Team.

Kaepa.

USA Volleyball Team

Shoes pictured above: the Women's Volo Mid, the Women's Brace, the Men's Brace, and the Men's Volo Low.
Kaepa is the official shoe of the USA National Volleyball Team. Available at The Athlete's Foot and Just For Feet or call 1-800-707-1189.

FIGURE 11-9

An Expert Appeal
Courtesy of Kaepa

Chrysler automobiles were worthy of their purchase consideration. Similarly, Frank Perdue spoke about the superiority of his Perdue chickens; Victor Kiam, the president of Remington Products, spoke about the benefits of his made-in-America shavers; and Bill Marriott, the president of the Marriott Corporation, promoted the chain's hotels. Figure 11-11 on page 338 presents an advertisement from Wendy's ongoing campaign, featuring its founder Dave Thomas.

Like the celebrity spokesperson, executive spokespersons seem to be admired by the general population because of their achievements and the status implicitly conferred on

FIGURE 11-10

A "Common-Man"
Appeal
Courtesy of Timex

business leaders in the United States. The appearance of a company's chief executive in its advertising seems to imply that someone at the top is watching over the consumers' best interests, and it encourages consumers to have more confidence in the firm's products or services.

A variation on the top executive spokesperson is the lower level manager or frontline employee who "speaks" directly to the consuming public. This type of spokesperson may be a factory worker who tells the consumer how he or she is working to build the best products, or it may even be an engineer or scientist who was responsible for creating, discovering, or developing a particular product. The power of such advertising is that it appears to be, in an "eye-to-eye" manner, the employee talking directly to the consumer (see Figure 11-12 on page 339).

Trade or Spokes-Characters

Trade or spokes-characters (e.g., Mr. Peanut, Tony the Tiger, or Cap 'n Crunch), as well as familiar cartoon characters (Ninja Turtles, Mr. Magoo, Bart Simpson), serve as quasi-celebrity endorsers. These trade spokes-characters present an idealized image and dispense information that can be very important for the product or service that they "work for."[17] A sample of some of the many different varieties of trade spokes-characters, as well the products or services that they promote, is shown in Table 11-3 on page 340.

According to a *People* magazine poll, Mr. Clean (see Figure 11-13 on page 341), a trade character that had not been seen on TV for 10 years, was better known than the vice

president of the United States.[18] With few exceptions, trade characters serve as an exclusive spokesperson for a particular product or service. They sometimes provide a kind of personality for the product or service and make the product appear more friendly (Ronald McDonald) or less complex (when IBM PC's used the little tramp).

Other Reference Group Appeals

A variety of other promotional strategies can function creatively as frames of reference for consumers. Respected retailers and the editorial content of selected special-interest magazines can also function as frames of reference that influence consumer attitudes and behavior. For instance, a customer might feel that if a leading fashion specialty store such as Bergdorf Goodman depicts men's single-breasted suits with peaked lapels as "in," then the style must be acceptable and in good taste. Similarly, a regular reader of *GQ* might see unstructured and relaxed sport coats as appropriate to wear to work if the magazine were to feature them in office surroundings. In these two instances, the retailer and the magazine are functioning as frames of reference that influence consumer behavior.

Finally, **seals of approval** and even objective product ratings can serve as positive endorsements that encourage consumers to act favorably toward certain products. For instance, many parents of young children look for the American Dental Association's seal of approval before selecting a brand of toothpaste. A high rating by an objective rating magazine, such as *Consumer Reports*, can also serve as an endorsement for a brand.

TO KNOW WHAT CARS AND TRUCKS WILL BE LIKE IN *2005* TALK TO THE PEOPLE WHO *LIVE THERE.*

BUCKLE UP—TOGETHER WE CAN SAVE LIVES

AT Ford Motor Company, we give our young designers all the tools they need to help them INVENT THE FUTURE. We even link them electronically to other Ford design studios from Turin, Italy to Melbourne, Australia. In this "GLOBAL STUDIO" environment, these men and women of the computer age design vehicles for people living in a RAPIDLY CHANGING WORLD. In this way, our customers get what they want before they even know they want it. To us, that's part of what quality is all about.

FORD DESIGNERS FROM LEFT TO RIGHT: SUSAN K. WESTFALL, DAVID HILTON, GARY BRADDOCK, SOO KANG, PAUL ARNONE, AARON WALKER

· FORD · FORD TRUCKS ·  · LINCOLN · MERCURY ·

QUALITY IS JOB 1.

FIGURE 11-12

A Company's Employees Addressing Potential Consumers
Courtesy of Ford Motor Company

Benefits of the Reference Group Appeal

Reference group appeals have two principal benefits: they increase brand awareness, and they serve to reduce perceived risk.

▲ **Increased Brand Awareness** Reference group appeals provide the advertiser with the opportunity to gain and retain the attention of prospective consumers with greater ease and

table 11-3 A Sample of Popular Trade Spokes-Characters

TRADE SPOKES-CHARACTER	SPONSOR PRODUCT/SERVICE
Mr. Peanut	Planters Peanuts
Betty Crocker	General Mills
Mr. Clean	Detergent product (same name)
Tony the Tiger	Sugar Frosted Flakes
Tiger	Exxon
Pink Panther	Owens-Corning insulation
Morton Salt Girl	Morton salt
Campbell kids	Campbell soups and other products
Snoopy and other Schultz comic strip characters	MetLife
California Raisins	California Raisin Growers Association
Quaker Oats man	Quaker Oats products
Elsie the Cow	Selected Borden's products
Morris the cat	
Ronald McDonald	McDonald's
Mickey Mouse	A line of licensed Mickey products
Eveready bunny	Eveready Batteries
Buster Brown	Buster Brown Shoes
Speedy	Alka-Seltzer
Mr. Whipple	Charmin paper products
Zip-Lock Finger Puppets	Zip-Lock bags
Garfield the cat	Embassy Suites

Inspired by: MARGARET F. CALLCOTT and WEI-NA LEE, "Establishing the Spokes-Character in Academic Inquiry: Historical Overview and Framework for Definition," in Frank R. Kardes and Mita Sujan, eds., *Advances in Consumer Research* 22 (Provo, UT: Association for Consumer Research, 1995), 144–51.

effectiveness than is possible with many other types of promotional campaigns. This is particularly true of the *celebrity* form of reference group appeal, where the personality used is generally well known to the relevant target segment. Celebrities tend to draw attention to the product through their own popularity. This may be especially true when the various brands competing within the same product category, are perceived by potential consumers to be largely similar or "tied" in terms of the main benefits provided. In such cases the use of a celebrity might break the tie and attract consumers to the brand being endorsed.[19]

Even in the case of less known or unknown **spokesmodels** (those without celebrity status), it appears that a combination of their "good looks" (e.g., physical attractiveness) and consumers' perceptions of their personalities contribute to positive judgments about the product being promoted.[20]

These various benefits of the celebrity, or even an attractive spokesmodel, give the advertiser a competitive advantage in gaining audience attention, particularly on television, where there are so many brief and similar commercial announcements.

▲ **Reduced Perceived Risk** The use of a reference group appeal may also serve to lower the consumer's perceived risk in purchasing a specific product. The example set by the endorser or testimonial-giver may demonstrate to the consumer that uncertainty about the product purchase is unwarranted.

On the basis of very positive experiences in the marketplace, advertisers continue to use celebrities, experts, and common-man appeals, as well as other reference group appeals, to promote and to differentiate their products.

FIGURE 11-13

Trade Character as
Spokesperson
© The Proctor & Gamble
Company. Used by permission.

summary

Almost all individuals regularly interact with other people who directly or indirectly influence their purchase decisions. Thus, the study of groups and their impact on the individual is of great importance to marketers concerned with influencing consumer behavior. Groups may be classified according to regularity of contact (primary or secondary groups), structure and hierarchy (formal or informal groups), size or complexity (large or small groups), and membership or aspiration (membership or symbolic groups).

Six basic types of consumer-relevant groups influence the consumption behavior of individuals: family, friendship groups, formal social groups, shopping groups, consumer-action groups, and work groups.

Consumer reference groups are groups that serve as frames of reference for individuals in their purchase decisions. Reference groups that influence general values or behavior are called normative reference groups; those that influence specific attitudes are called comparative reference groups. The concept of consumer reference groups has been broadened to include groups with which consumers have no direct face-to-face contact, such as celebrities, political figures, and social classes.

Reference groups that are classified in terms of a person's membership and the positive or negative influences that they exert include contactual groups, aspirational groups, disclaimant groups, and avoidance groups. The credibility, attractiveness, and power of the reference group affect the degree of influence it has. Reference group appeals are used very effectively by some advertisers in promoting their goods and services, because they subtly induce the prospective consumer to identify with the pictured user of the product.

The five types of reference groups most commonly used in marketing are celebrities, experts, the common man, the executive and employee spokesperson, and the trade spokes-character. Celebrities are used to give testimonials or endorsements as actors or as company spokespersons. Experts may be recognized experts in the product category or actors playing the part of experts (e.g., an automobile mechanic). The common-man approach is designed to show that individuals, just like the prospect, are satisfied with the advertised product. Increasingly, firms are using their top executives as spokespersons, because their appearance in company advertisements seems to imply that someone at the top is watching over the consumer's interest.

Reference group appeals are effective promotional strategies because they increase brand awareness and reduce perceived risk among prospective consumers.

discussion questions

1. Describe one group that serves as an aspirational group for you and another that serves as an avoidance group. In what ways have they influenced your consumption patterns?

2. When is using an aspirational group likely to be a more effective advertising strategy than a contactual group?

3. As a marketing consultant, you have been asked to evaluate a new promotional campaign for a large retail chain. The campaign strategy is aimed at increasing group shopping. What recommendations would you make?

4. Virtually all groups develop norms and codes of behavior. Identify five norms that guide the behavior of students and professors in your university. Are your fellow students a normative or comparative reference group for you? Explain.

5. What reference group factors are likely to influence a smoker's decision as to whether or not to use a nicotine patch in the quest to quit smoking?

6. Many celebrities who are considered to be persuasive role models often appear in TV beer commercials. Does the use of such celebrities in beer advertising constitute an unethical marketing practice? Discuss.

7. You are the marketing vice president of a large soft drink company. Your company's advertising agency is in the process of negotiating a contract to employ a superstar female singer to promote your product. Discuss the reference group factors that you would raise before the celebrity is hired.

exercises

1. Prepare a list of formal and informal groups to which you belong and give examples of purchases for which each served as a reference group. In which of the groups you listed is the pressure to conform the greatest? Why?

2. With a paper and pencil, spend one hour watching a network television channel during prime time. Record the total number of commercials that aired. For each commercial using a celebrity endorser, record the celebrity's name, the product or service advertised, and whether the celebrity was used in a testimonial, as an endorser, an actor, or a spokesperson.

3. Find a magazine advertisement for a consumer product that uses an expert as a reference group appeal and another ad that features a top corporate executive. What impact do you feel each reference group has on consumers? Why?

4. Identify three print ads or TV commercials depicting slice-of-life situations. Evaluate the persuasiveness of each ad. Do the persons portrayed in these ads mirror consumer reality? How does this portrayal affect the persuasiveness of the ads?

key words

- **Aspirational group**
- **Avoidance group**
- **Celebrity credibility**
- **Common-man appeals**
- **Comparative reference groups**
- **Consumer-action group**
- **Consumer conformity**
- **Consumer-relevant groups**
- **Contactual group**
- **Corporate spokespersons**

- **Disclaimant group**
- **Endorsement**
- **Expert appeals**
- **Formal and informal groups**
- **Group**
- **Indirect reference groups**
- **Membership group**
- **Normative reference groups**
- **Primary group**
- **Product conspicuousness**
- **Purchase pals**

- **Reference group**
- **Referents**
- **Seals of approval**
- **Secondary group**
- **Shopping group**
- **Slice-of-life commercials**
- **Spokesmodels**
- **Spokesperson**
- **Symbolic group**
- **Testimonial**

end notes

1. PAMELA KIECKER and CATHY L. HARTMAN, "Purchase Pal Use: Why Buyers Choose to Shop with Others," in Rajan Varadarajan and Bernard Jaworski, eds., *1993 AMA Winter Educators' Proceedings* 4 (Chicago: American Marketing Association, 1993), 378–84.

2. ROBERT O. HERRMANN, "The Tactics of Consumer Resistance: Group Action and Marketplace Exist," in Leigh McAlister and Michael L. Rothschild, eds., *Advances in Consumer Research* 20 (Provo, UT: Association for Consumer Research 1993), 130–34.

3. LAURIE M. GROSSMAN, "Going Stale: Families Have Changed But Tupperware Keeps Holding Its Parties; Rivals Gained by Dropping Homey Sales Technique as More Women Worked," *The Wall Street Journal*, July 21, 1992, A1; JEFFREY A. TRACHTENBERG, "Advertising: Avon's New TV Campaign Says 'Call Us,'" *The Wall Street Journal*, December 28, 1992, B1; and BILL KELLEY, "Bucking the Snake Oil Syndrome," *Sales and Marketing Management* 143, September 1991, 87–92.

4. PETER H. REINGEN, BRIAN L. FOSTER, JACQUELINE JOHNSON BROWN, and STEPHEN B. SEIDMAN, "Brand Congruence in Interpersonal Relations: A Social Network Analysis," *Journal of Consumer Research* 11, December 1984, 771–83.

5. For some interesting reflections on the use of celebrities, see: LINDA M. SCOTT, "The Troupe: Celebrities as Dramatis Personae in Advertisements," in Rebecca H. Holman and Michael R. Solomon, eds., *Advances in Consumer Research* 18 (Provo, UT: Association for Consumer Research, 1991), 355–62.

6. CHARLES ATKIN and MARTIN BLOCK, "Effectiveness of Celebrity Endorsers," *Journal of Advertising Research* 23, February-March, 1983, 57–61.

7. STUART ELLIOTT, "Want to Break into Commercials?" *The New York Times*, March 8, 1995, D18.

8. ROOBINA OHANIAN, "The Impact of Celebrity Spokespersons Perceived Image on Consumers' Intention to Purchase," *Journal of Advertising Research*, February-March, 1991, 46–54.

9. CAROLYN TRIPP, THOMAS D. JENSEN, and LES CARLSON, "The Effects of Multiple Product Endorsements by Celebrities on Consumers' Attitudes and Intentions," *Journal of Consumer Research* 20, March 1994, 535–47; and DAVID C. BOJANIC, PATRICIA K. VOLI, and JAMES B. HUNT, "Can Consumers Match Celebrity Endorsers with Products?" in Robert L. King, ed., *Developments in Marketing Science* (Richmond, VA: Academy of Marketing Science, 1991), 303–7.

10. GRANT MCCRACKEN, "Who Is the Celebrity Endorser? Cultural Foundations of the Endorsement Process," *Journal of Consumer Research* 16, December 1989, 310–22;

LYNN LANGMEYER and MARY WALKER, "A First Step to Identify the Meaning in Celebrity Endorsers," in Holman and Solomon, eds., *Advances in Consumer Research* 18 (op. cit.), 364–71; W. JEFFREY BURROUGHS, MARY-ANN HOOTEN, and PATRICIA KNOWLES, "Celebrity-Product Congruence and Endorser Effectiveness," in Ravi Achrol and Andrew Mitchell, eds., *1994 AMA Educators' Proceedings* 5 (Chicago: American Marketing Association, 1994), 395–6.

11. MARTIN R. LAUTMAN," End-Benefit Segmentation and Prototypical Bonding," *Journal of Advertising Research*, June-July 1991, 9–18.

12. MARY WALKER, LYNN LANGMEYER, and DANIEL LANGMEYER, "Celebrity Endorsers: Do You Get What You Pay For?" *Journal of Consumer Marketing* 9, Spring 1992, 69–76.

13. KERVIN GOLDMAN, "Catch a Falling Star: Big Names Plummet from List of Top 10 Celebrity Endorsers," *The Wall Street Journal*, October 19, 1994, B1; and KEVIN GOLDMAN "Women Endorsers More Credible Than Men, A Survey Suggests," *The Wall Street Journal*, October 12, 1995, B5.

14. Ibid.

15. BRIAN D. TILL and TERENCE A. SHIMP, "Can Negative Celebrity Information Hurt the Endorsed Brand?" in Barbara B. Stern and George M. Zinkan, eds., *1995 AMA Educators' Proceedings* 5 (Chicago: American Marketing Association, 1995), 154–55.

16. "Study Identifies Qualities of Effective Public Health Service Announcements," *Marketing News*, April 1981, 7.

17. MARGARET F. CALLCOTT and WEI-NA LEE, "Establishing the Spokes–Character in Academic Inquiry: Historical Overview and Framework for Definition," in Frank R. Kardes and Mita Sujan, eds., *Advances in Consumer Research* 22 (Provo, UT: Association for Consumer Research, 1995), 144–51.

18. "New Life for Madison Avenue's Old-Time Start," *Business Week*, April 1, 1985, 94; and see also, "Good Grief! Charlie Brown Is Selling Insurance," *Adweek's Marketing Week* 23, November 1987, 17.

19. TIMOTHY B. HEATH, DAVID L. MOTHERSBAUGH, and MICHAEL S. MCCARTHY, "Spokesperson Effects in High Involvement Markets," in Leigh McAlister and Michael L. Rothschild, eds., *Advances in Consumer Research* 20 (Provo, UT: Association for Consumer Research 1993), 704–8.

20. ANNE M. BRUMBAUGH, "Physical Attractiveness and Personality in Advertising: More than Just a Pretty Face?" in Leigh McAlister and Michael L. Rothschild, eds., *Advances in Consumer Research* 20 (Provo, UT: Association for Consumer Research 1993), 159–64.

Before

There's something you should do before life hits you in the knees with ten bags of

the spouse,

groceries and the need for a garden hose. You should know how it feels to have the

the house,

sun on your head and a growl at your back as you flick through five gears with

the kids,

no more baggage than a friend. This has been known since the beginning of cars.

you get

Which is why roadsters were invented. The Mazda Miata. The roadster returned.

one chance.

mazda
IT JUST FEELS RIGHT.

The Mazda MX-5 Miata features a new, larger, 128-horsepower DOHC 16-valve engine. Standard dual air bags. And has been named to Automobile Magazine's "All Star" list for 5 consecutive years. The Miata is backed by a best-in-class, 36-month/50,000-mile, no-deductible, "bumper-to-bumper" limited basic warranty. See your Mazda Dealer for details. For a free brochure, call 1-800-639-1000. © 1994 Mazda Motor of America, Inc.

mazda
IT JUST FEELS RIGHT.

The family is a complex and ever-evolving core institution in many of the world's societies or nations. It is also a major influence on the consumer behavior of its members. There are many examples of how the family influences the consumption behavior of its members. A child learns how to enjoy candy by observing an older brother or sister and learns the use and value of money by listening to and watching his or her parents. Decisions about a new car, a vacation trip, or whether to go to a local or an out-of-town college are consumption decisions usually made within the context of a family setting. The family commonly provides the opportunity for product exposure and trial and imparts consumption values to its members. As a major consumption unit, the family is also a prime target for many products and services.

To determine how the family makes its purchase decisions and how the family affects the future purchase behavior of its

A consumer is born every ten seconds.

—Edwin Newman 1976

members, it is useful to understand the functions provided and the roles played by family members to fulfill their consumption needs. As background, we will first examine some basic family concepts; then we will discuss family consumer decision making and the marketing implications of the family life cycle.

THE FAMILY IS A CONCEPT IN FLUX

Although the term *family* is a basic concept, it is not easy to define because family composition and structure, as well as the roles played by family members are almost always in transition. To illustrate the diversity in types of families, Figure 12-1 presents an ad from a series of advertisements for Family Circle, a highly regarded consumer magazine dealing with family matters. The photographs dramatically captures the idea that a wide variety of family types and family values existing in contemporary society. Traditionally, however, **family** is defined as *two or more persons related by blood, marriage, or adoption who reside together*. In a more dynamic sense, the individuals who constitute a family might be described as members of the most basic social group who live together and interact to satisfy their personal and mutual needs.

Although families sometimes are referred to as *households*, not all households are families. For example, a household might include individuals who are not related by blood, marriage, or adoption, such as unmarried couples, family friends, roommates, or boarders. However, within the context of consumer behavior, households and families usually are treated as synonymous, and we will continue this convention.[1]

FIGURE 12-1

From a Series of Ads
Suggesting the
Diversity of the
Contemporary Family
Courtesy of Family Circle

In most Western societies, three types of families dominate: the married couple, the nuclear family, and the extended family. The simplest type of family, in number of members, is the *married couple*—a husband and a wife. As a household unit, the married couple generally is representative of new marrieds who have not yet started a family, and older couples who have already raised their children.

A husband and wife and one or more children constitute a **nuclear family**. This type of family is still commonplace but has been on the decline. The nuclear family, together with at least one grandparent living within the household, is called an **extended family**. The incidence of the extended family has suffered because of the geographic mobility that was commonplace among young people during the 1970s and 1980s. Indeed, the two-generation family and the extended three-generation family, which at one time were the norm, both have been declining as a variety of family lifestyles have been increasing. In contrast, because of divorce, separation, and out-of-wedlock births, there has been a rapid increase in the number of **single-parent family** households consisting of one parent and at least one child.

Not surprisingly, which type of family is most "typical" can vary considerably from culture to culture. For instance, in an individualistic society such as that in Canada, the nuclear family is most common. In a kinship culture (with extended families) such as that in Thailand, a family would commonly include a head of household, married adult children, and grandchildren.[2]

Functions of the Family

Four basic functions provided by the family are particularly relevant to a discussion of consumer behavior. These include **economic well-being**, **emotional support**, **suitable family lifestyles**, and **socialization of family members**.

Economic Well-Being

Although families in affluent nations of North America, Europe, and Asia are no longer formed primarily for economic security, providing financial means to its dependents is unquestionably a basic family function. How the family divides its responsibilities for providing economic well-being has changed considerably during the past twenty-five years. No longer are the traditional roles of husband as economic provider and wife as homemaker and child rearer still valid. For instance, it is very common for married women with children in the United States and other industrial countries to be employed outside the home and for their husbands to share household responsibilities. The economic role of children also has changed. Today, despite the fact that many teenage children work, they rarely assist the family financially. Instead, many teenagers are expected to pay for their own amusements; others contribute to the costs of their formal education and prepare themselves to be financially independent.

Emotional Support

The provision of emotional nourishment (including love, affection, and intimacy) to its members is an important basic function of the contemporary family. In fulfilling this function, the family provides support and encouragement and assists its members in coping with decision making and personal or social problems.[3] To make it easier for working parents to show their love, affection, and support to their children, greeting card companies have been increasingly creating cards for parents to give to their children.

If the family cannot provide adequate assistance when it is needed, it may turn to a professional counselor or psychologist as an alternative. For instance, in most communities, educational and psychological centers are available that are designed to assist parents who want to help their children improve their learning and communication skills or, generally, better adjust to their environments.

Suitable Family Lifestyles

Another important family function in terms of consumer behavior is the establishment of a suitable *lifestyle* for the family. Upbringing, experience, and the personal and jointly held goals of the spouses determine the importance placed on education or career, on reading, on television viewing, on the learning of computer skills, on the frequency and quality of dining out, and on the selection of other entertainment and recreational activities. Researchers have identified a shift in the nature of family "togetherness." Whereas a family being together once meant doing things together, today it means being in the same household and each person doing his or her own thing.[4] Figure 12-2 shows the range of reasons why families are staying home more. Family lifestyle commitments, including the allocation of time is greatly influencing consumption patterns. For example, the increase in the number of married women working outside the home has reduced the time that they have available for household chores and has created a market for convenience products and fast-food restaurants. Also, with both parents working, an increased emphasis is being placed on the notion of "quality time," rather than on the "quantity of time" spent with children

FIGURE 12-2

Reasons Why Families
Are Staying Home More
Source: AMERICA'S RESEARCH
GROUP and LEAH HARAN, "Families
Together Differently Today,"
Advertising Age, October 23,
1995, 12. Reprinted with permission. Copyright 1995 by Crain
Communications.

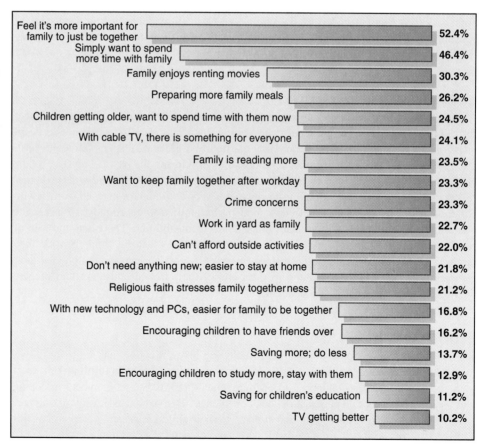

and other family members. Realizing the scarcity of quality family time, Hilton hotels feature a variety of vacation and weekend packages targeted to couples and their children (see Figure 12-3).

Socialization of Family Members

The socialization of family members, ranging from young children to adults, is a central family function. In the case of young children, this process includes imparting to children the basic values and modes of behavior consistent with the culture. These generally include moral and religious principles, interpersonal skills, dress and grooming standards, appropriate manners and speech, and the selection of suitable educational and occupational or career goals. To illustrate how this socialization responsibility is expanding, parents are increasingly anxious to see their young children possess adequate computer skills,

FIGURE 12-3

An Offer of a Special
Family Vacation
Package
Courtesy of Hilton Hotels
Corporation

almost before they are able to talk or walk—as early as twelve months after their birth. Because parents seem to be so intensively interested in their young children learning about using a computer, hardware and software developers are rapidly creating products targeted at parents seeking to buy such items for their very young children.[5]

Socialization skills (manners, goals, values, and other qualities) are imparted to a child *directly* through instruction and *indirectly* through observation of the behavior of parents and older siblings. The birthday party for a young child is an example of a social event designed to help children acquire social skills. According to mothers of 2- to 5-year-old children, encouraging the child to assist in the planning and conducting of a birthday party is part of the overall process of socialization and is a means of teaching important social skills.[6] Figure 12-4 presents the findings of a poll of adult Americans as to those qualities they feel are most important for children to possess. As the results reveal, *responsibility* is considered the most important quality.

Marketers frequently target parents looking for assistance in the task of socializing their children. To this end, marketers are sensitive to the fact that the socialization of young children provides an opportunity to establish a foundation on which later experiences continue to build throughout life. These experiences are reinforced and/or modified as the child grows into adolescence, the teenage years, and eventually into adulthood.

▲ **Consumer Socialization of Children** The aspect of childhood socialization that is particularly relevant to the study of consumer behavior is **consumer socialization**, which is defined as *the process by which children acquire the skills, knowledge, and attitudes necessary to function as consumers.* A variety of studies have focused on how children develop consumption skills. Many children acquire their consumer behavior norms through observation of their parents, who function as role models. Although preadolescent children tend to rely on their parents and older siblings as the major sources of cues for basic consumption learning, adolescents and teenagers are likely to look to their friends for models of acceptable behavior.[7]

Shared shopping experiences (i.e., coshopping when mother and child shop together) also give children the opportunity to acquire in-store shopping skills. Possibly because of their more harried lifestyles, working mothers are more likely to undertake coshopping with their children than are nonworking mothers. Coshopping is a way of spending time with one's children while at the same time accomplishing a necessary task. Also, because of the frequent extreme time pressure faced by working mothers, there is evidence that children have more of a say on what they get simply because an exhausted mother is more likely to yield and say "Yes."[8]

Consumer socialization also serves as a tool by which parents influence other aspects of the socialization process. For instance, parents frequently use the promise or re-

FIGURE 12-4

Adult Opinions as to Important Qualities for Children to Have
Source: "Roper's America: Important Qualities for Our Children to Have," *Adweek's Marketing Week* (November 11, 1991), 10. Reprinted by permission of Roper Starch Worldwide.

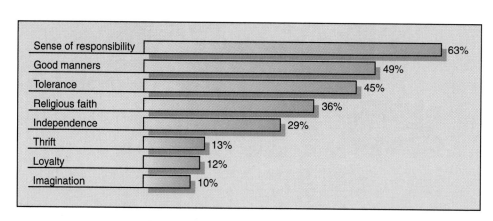

Sense of responsibility	63%
Good manners	49%
Tolerance	45%
Religious faith	36%
Independence	29%
Thrift	13%
Loyalty	12%
Imagination	10%

ward of material goods as a device to modify or control a child's behavior. A mother may reward her child with a gift when the child does something to please her, or she may withhold or remove it when the child disobeys. Research conducted by one of the authors supports this behavior-controlling function. Specifically, adolescents reported that their parents frequently used the promise of chocolate candy as a means of controlling their behavior (e.g., getting them to complete homework or to clean their rooms).

Consumer socialization has two distinct components: socialization *directly related* to consumption, such as the acquisition of skills and knowledge concerned with budgeting, pricing, brand attitudes, and actual product usage (see Figure 12-5), and socialization *indi-*

FIGURE 12-5

Assisting Children to Learn to Use a Product for Themselves
Courtesy of 3M Corporation

rectly related to consumption, such as the underlying motivations that spur a young man to purchase his first razor or a young girl to want her first bra. Both types of socialization are significant. The indirect component of consumer socialization is often of most interest to marketers, who want to understand why people buy their products. The direct component of consumer socialization is often of greatest interest to academic consumer researchers, who have broader goals of understanding all aspects of consumer behavior.

▲ **Adult Consumer Socialization** The socialization process is not confined to childhood; rather, it is an ongoing process. It is now accepted that socialization begins in early childhood and extends throughout a person's entire life. For example, when a newly married couple establishes a separate household, their adjustment to living and consuming together is part of this continuing process. Similarly, the adjustment of a retired couple who decide to move to Florida is also part of the ongoing socialization process. Even a family that is welcoming a pet into their home, as a new family member, must face the challenge of socializing the pet so that it fits into the family environment.[9]

▲ **Intergenerational Socialization** It appears that it is quite common for selected product loyalty or brand preferences to be *transferred* from one generation to another—*intergeneration brand transfer*—maybe even three or four generations within the same family. For instance, specific brand preferences for products like peanut butter, mayonnaise, ketchup, coffee, and canned soup are all product categories that are frequently "passed-on" from one generation to another generation. The following are several verbatims from research with college-aged consumers as to how they feel about product usage extending over several generations:[10]

> *My mother stills buys almost every brand that her mother did. She is scared to try anything else, for it will not meet the standards, and (she) would feel bad not buying something that has been with her so long. (Respondent is an Italian-American male in his early twenties)*

> *I find it hard to break away from the things I've been using since I was little; like Vaseline products, Ivory soap, Lipton tea, and corn flakes. I live on campus so I have to do my own shopping, and when I do I see a lot of my mother in myself. I buy things I'm accustomed to using . . . products my mother buys for the house. (Respondent is West Indian-American female)*

Another type of transfer between family members is the giving or loaning of "things."[11] When one family member gives or loans another family member some hand-me-down clothing, an old car or TV, a set of dishes or flatware, a sofa, or a ten-year-old baseball glove, these transfers serve as substitutes for the purchase of such items in the marketplace.

Figure 12-6 presents a simple model of the socialization process that focuses on the socialization of young children but that can be extended to family members of all ages. Note that the arrows run both ways between the young person and other family members and between the young person and his or her friends. This two-directional arrow signifies that socialization is really a two-way street, in which the young person is both socialized and influences those who are doing the socializing. Supporting this view is the reality that children of all ages often influence the opinions and behavior of their parents.[12]

FAMILY DECISION MAKING

Although many marketers recognize the family as the basic decision-making unit, they most frequently examine the attitudes and behavior of the one family member whom they believe to be the major decision maker. In some cases, they also examine the attitudes and

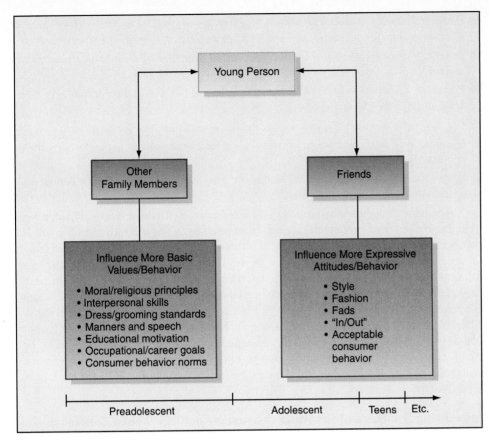

FIGURE 12-6

A Simple Model of the
Socialization Process

behavior of the person most likely to be the primary user of the product or service. For instance, in the case of men's underwear, which is frequently purchased by women for their husbands and unmarried sons, it is commonplace to seek the views of both the men who wear the underwear and the women who buy it. By considering both the likely user and the likely purchaser, the marketer obtains a richer picture of the consumption process.

Family Roles

For a family to function as a cohesive unit, roles or tasks such as doing the laundry, preparing meals, setting the dinner table, taking out the garbage, and walking the dog must be carried out by one or more family members. In a dynamic society, family-related roles are constantly changing. For instance, given the substantial number of married women working outside the home, and the greater assumption of household tasks by men, marketers must be particularly sensitive to how shifting family roles may affect the composition of their target markets. In addition, they must be careful to phrase their ads in ways that are appropriate and acceptable to their target markets.

▲ **Key Family Consumption Roles** There are eight distinct roles in the family decision-making process. A look at these roles provides further insight into how family members interact in their various consumption-related roles:

■ Influencers. *Family member(s) who provide information to other members about a product or service.*

■ Gatekeepers. *Family member(s) who control the flow of information about a product or service into the family.*

- Deciders. *Family member(s) with the power to determine unilaterally or jointly whether to shop for, purchase, use, consume, or dispose of a specific product or service.*
- Buyers. *Family member(s) who make the actual purchase of a particular product or service.*
- Preparers. *Family member(s) who transform the product into a form suitable for consumption by other family members.*
- Users. *Family member(s) who use or consume a particular product or service.*
- Maintainers. *Family member(s) who service or repair the product so that it will provide continued satisfaction.*
- Disposers. *Family member(s) who initiate or carry out the disposal or discontinuation of a particular product or service.*

The number and identity of the family members who fill these roles vary from family to family and from product to product. In some cases, a single family member will independently assume a number of roles; in other cases, a single role will be performed jointly by two or more family members. In still other cases, one or more of these basic roles may not be required. For example, a family member may be walking down the snack food aisle at a local supermarket when he picks out an interesting new chocolate candy. His selection does not directly involve the influence of other family members. He is the *decider*, the *buyer* and, in a sense, the *gatekeeper*; however, he may or may not be the sole consumer (i.e., user). Products may be consumed by a single family member (beer, lipstick), consumed or used directly by two or more family members (frozen vegetables, shampoo), or consumed indirectly by the entire family (central air conditioning, a home security alarm system, or an art glass collection).

▲ **Influencing Spouses and Resolving Consumer Conflicts** When it comes to making purchasing decisions, husbands and wives frequently find themselves in disagreement about when to spend or save, how much to spend on some item, what color fits best, or where to buy something. These are just a few of the many consumer behavior decisions where there might be disagreement. To avoid or resolve potential disagreements, husbands and wives commonly attempt to influence each other to arrive at what they feel to be the best outcome. Six *influence strategies* for resolving husband-wife consumption-related conflicts have been identified:[13]

- Expert. *An attempt by a spouse to use his or her superior information about decision alternatives to influence the other spouse.*
- Legitimacy. *An attempt by a spouse to influence the other spouse on the basis of position in the household.*
- Bargaining. *An attempt by a spouse to secure influence now that will be exchanged with the other spouse at some future date.*
- Reward. *An attempt by a spouse to influence the behavior of the other spouse by offering a reward.*
- Emotional. *An attempt by a spouse to use an emotion-laden reaction to influence the other spouse's behavior.*
- Impression. *Any persuasive attempts by one spouse to influence the behavior of the other.*

These influence strategies tend to be used by either husbands or wives when they find themselves in disagreement or in conflict with the other spouse regarding a specific consumer decision. For instance, we all have experienced occasions on which different family members want to eat at different types of restaurants, see different movies, or go on a different type of family vacation. These are only a few examples of the almost endless possibilities of potential family consumption conflicts that might need to be resolved. (Figure 12-7 presents examples of other issues on which married couples tend to disagree.)

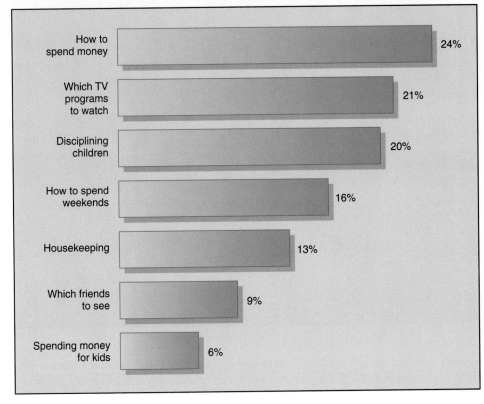

FIGURE 12-7

Some Common Issues on Which Married Couples Disagree
Source: "Roper's America: Money Is the Root of Most Arguments," *Adweek's Marketing Week* (April 2, 1990), 10. Reprinted by permission of Roper Starch Worldwide.

In a consumer behavior context, advertising or an in-store shopping experience (e.g., a point-of-purchase display or handling a product) might provide enough additional information to enable a husband or wife to effectively change the other spouse's views.

Dynamics of Husband-Wife Decision Making

Marketers are interested in the relative amount of influence that a husband and a wife have when it comes to family consumption choices. Most husband-wife influence studies classify family consumption decisions as **husband-dominated**, **wife-dominated**, **joint** (i.e., *equal* or *syncratic*), and **autonomic** (i.e., *solitary* or *unilateral*).[14]

Studies that have examined both the extent and nature of husband-wife influence in family decisions have found that such influence is fluid and likely to shift, depending on the specific product or service, the family role structure orientation, and the specific stage in the decision-making process. These factors also are influenced by changing lifestyles, particularly the changes in family lifestyle options associated with women working outside of the home and the increased occurrence of dual-income households. The Lands' End ad in Figure 12-8 on page 356 acknowledges the changing priorities of the household and how shopping by catalog is in line with these lifestyle shifts.

▲ **Variations by Product or Service** The relative influence of a husband and wife on a particular consumer decision depends in part on the product and service category. For instance, during the 1950s, the purchase of a new automobile was strongly husband-dominated, while food and financial-banking decisions more often were wife-dominated. Forty years later, the purchase of the family's principal automobile is still often husband-dominated. However, in other contexts or situations (e.g., a second car or a car for a single or

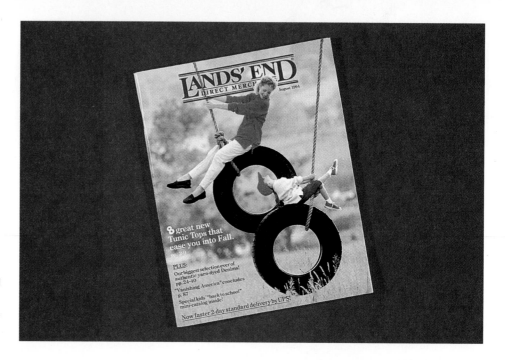

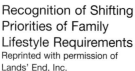
working woman), female car buyers are a rapidly expanding segment of the automobile market, a segment to which many car manufacturers are currently paying separate marketing attention. Also, in case of financial decision making, there has been a trend away from wife-dominated decisions to joint decisions (see Figure 12-9).[15]

▲ **Variations by Family Role Structure Orientation** A family's orientation regarding sex roles is a key factor when it comes to consumption decisions. In families with a modern sex role orientation (i.e., a commitment to husband-wife equality), consumption decisions are likely to be evenly distributed between the two spouses, and there is less disagreement between husband and wife as to the purchase decision.[16]

Role structure and decision making within the family appear to be related to *culture* and *subculture*. Recent research comparing husband-wife decision making patterns in the People's Republic of China and the United States reveals that among the Chinese there were substantially fewer "joint" decisions and more "husband-dominated" decisions for many household purchases.[17] However, when limiting the comparison to urban and rural Chinese households (i.e., a "within-China" comparison), the research showed that in a larger city like Beijing, married couples were more likely than rural couples to share equally in purchase decisions. Other research shows that Mexican-American families tend to be more husband-dominant than Anglo families and that Anglo families engage in more joint purchase decisions.[18] However, these findings may be influenced by the extent to which Hispanic-American couples have assimilated general American values and attitudes. Hispanic-American couples who are more assimilated were found to have husbands and wives who shared equally in decision making, whereas in more traditional households the husband more often dominated in arriving at a decision.[19]

The subcultural factor of religion, and the related dimension of religious orientation, also have been found to be associated with family decision making.[20] Specifically, in exploring the consumer-related marital roles of Catholic and Jewish families and proreligious and nonreligious families, research suggests that, in both Catholic and proreligious families, husbands have the major influence on specific purchase decisions. In contrast, in both Jewish and nonreligious families, husbands and wives share equally in most decision

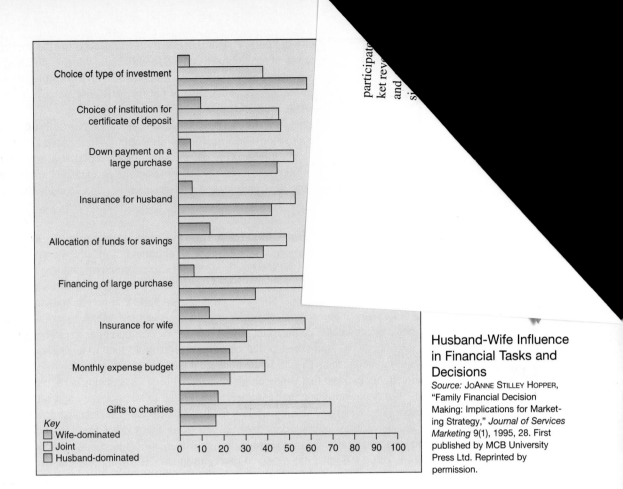

Choice of type of investment

Choice of institution for
certificate of deposit

Down payment on a
large purchase

Insurance for husband

Allocation of funds for savings

Financing of large purchase

Insurance for wife

Monthly expense budget

Gifts to charities

Key
☐ Wife-dominated
☐ Joint
☐ Husband-dominated

0   10   20   30   40   50   60   70   80   90   100

**Husband-Wife Influence
in Financial Tasks and
Decisions**
Source: JoANNE STILLEY HOPPER,
"Family Financial Decision
Making: Implications for Market-
ing Strategy," *Journal of Services
Marketing* 9(1), 1995, 28. First
published by MCB University
Press Ltd. Reprinted by
permission.

making. For instance, in the majority of Jewish families, husbands and wives jointly decided how much to spend on an automobile, while in Catholic families, husbands played a
more dominant role in deciding how much to spend. Similarly, compared to the proreligious families, more of the nonreligious families (regardless of which of the two religions
was involved in the comparison) jointly decided what model automobile to purchase. In
the case of proreligious families, husbands exercised more control.

▲ **Variations by Stage in the Decision-Making Process** The roles of husbands and
wives may differ at various points throughout the decision-making process. A simple,
three-stage, family decision-making model includes *problem recognition, search for information,* and *final decision.* The initial decision-making role pattern established in stage
one (problem recognition) usually continues during the two remaining stages (search for
information and final decision). However, for some decisions, there are stage-to-stage
shifts. For instance, recognition of the need for a new washing machine may be wife-dominant, the search for information concerning the potential purchase might be largely autonomic (usually performed by the wife), and the final decision might be made jointly by
both spouses.

Children

As any parent knows, young children attempt to influence family decisions as soon as they
possess the basic communication skills needed to interact with other family members
("Buy me this. . . . ," "I want this. . . . ," "Let's eat at. . . . ,"). Older children are likely to

more directly in family consumption activities. Research on the children's market reveals that children aged 5 to 14 have some $165 billion in "direct" purchasing power and that they influence about $400 billion of their household's overall purchase decisions.[21] These children influence a wide range of family decisions, such as choice of vacations, stereo equipment, and home computers.

The parent-child relationship, as it relates to consumer behavior, can be viewed as an *influence*-versus-*yield* situation. Specifically, children attempt to influence their parents to make a purchase (to yield). In observing shoppers in a supermarket, it is quite evident that children not only attempt to influence their parents to make purchases of special interest to them (cereal, candy) but also products of remote interest (e.g., laundry detergents) for which they see ads on TV.[22]

▲ **Children and Television** Older children and those with greater media exposure tend to recall more advertising slogans. (Interestingly, as children get older, they tend to watch less television.) The impact of TV advertising appears to vary among children of different age groups. For years, it was believed that preschoolers were not able to distinguish between programs and commercials. However, research suggests that preschoolers as young as one to three years of age do understand TV commercials and are able to discern between the program content and the commercial.[23] This new evidence emerges as a result of changes in research methods. Traditional verbal measurement methods tend to *underestimate* the child's ability to understand TV ads, while nonverbal measures, such as asking the child to point to something, indicate that young children are capable of understanding TV commercials.

It was also found that commercials targeted to adults have great influence on children. For example, TV commercials for lipstick favorably influenced 9- and 10-year-old girls' perceptions of the product and brand, because they associated the product with being an adult.[24] Older children recognize more *symbolism* in advertising than do younger children. Those who had experience with the product held strong consumption-based stereotypes, suggesting that personal experience is more important than media exposure.[25]

▲ **Latchkey Kids** Many consumer-goods firms target special marketing efforts at preteen **"latchkey" children** (those who are home alone for at least part of each school day while their parents work). These children receive special attention from such companies as Whirlpool, General Foods, Lipton, American Home Products, and Hasbro. One program is *Kidsmarts*, a magazine that is being distributed by Lipton to approximately 150,000 households to help working parents and their children make after-school hours more productive and secure until parents come home. Not surprisingly, the magazine contains ads and cents-off coupons for Lipton products that are consumed by children in this age group.

In a survey of parents with children under 14 years of age, Whirlpool found that more than 70 percent of latchkey children help their parents with housework. Specifically, about 55 percent of these children wash dishes, 52 percent prepare meals, and 48 percent do the laundry.[26] These children use microwave ovens and other household appliances. Participating in such activities makes them a special market niche for many different products.

These examples also suggest that latchkey kids constitute a special market with distinctive needs. Marketers are attracted to these young consumers, because they realize that consumer loyalties established at such a young age have the potential to last a very long time. For this reason, AT&T Wireless and other cellular telephone and beeper companies are targeting parents of young children, especially latchkey kids, to give their children a beeper that the child must respond to when the parents call.

▲ **Teenagers** Experts on the teen market have identified a variety of factors as to why they are a particularly significant target market. According to one expert there are six key reasons why teenagers deserve a marketer's special attention:[27]

1. ***Teens spend a lot of money***. *The sheer buying power of teenagers make them a very attractive consumer audience. They spend more than $60 billion of their own money; more than 65 percent of them have a savings account; and about 20 percent of teenagers have a credit card.*

2. ***Teens also spend family money***. *Besides their own money, teens also spend a good portion of their family's money (estimated to be more than $35 billion). This is especially critical, because many households with teenagers have both parents working full-time and, therefore, more of the family's shopping responsibilities are being delegated to teen children.*

3. ***Teens influence what the family buys***. *Teens influence their parents purchases when shopping with their parents; when suggesting their preferred brands, even when they are not shopping with their parents, when their parents seek their advice, and when they are asking for a gift.*

4. ***Teens are trendsetters***. *Teens also influence fads and fashion in many different product categories. Examples are blue jeans and music.*

5. ***Teens are a growing market***. *Whereas there were an estimated 29 million teenagers in 1995, it is expected that by the year 2010 (as the baby boomer's children become teenagers), the number of teens will increase to almost 35 million American teenagers.*

6. ***Teens are future consumers***. *Finally, beyond their current spending levels, teens are the future consumers for many products and brands. Marketers of branded products and services are increasingly working hard to secure early brand awareness and preferences with teenagers. This is a strategically important move, because teens represent the future lifeblood for many brands.*

In addition to these important reasons for paying attention to teens, teens enjoy shopping. The income of both teenage boys and girls is mostly earned by working after school (some teens are "dual-income teenagers," receiving income as part allowance and part earnings). A significant number of teenagers work at least part-time, and most of their income is discretionary. In terms of spending patterns, high school students (those in grades 7 through 12) are most interested in sports and fitness. Boys between the ages of 16 and 19 spend most of their money on movies, dating, entertainment, car expenses, and clothing, while girls of that age spend most of their money on clothing, cosmetics, and fragrances.

When communicating with teens, it is worthwhile to remember that younger teens (i.e., those from ages 13 to 15) look forward to being called "teens," whereas older teens (e.g., those 17 to 19) dislike being referred to as "teens" (or even as "teenagers").[28]

The teen market can also be segmented in terms of lifestyle groups. Table 12-1 on page 360 presents a four-category segmentation schema of the teenage market. Such a segmentation framework has value for marketers who wish to focus their marketing efforts on a particular subgroup of teens.

▲ **College-Age Children** College students are another important family subgroup. It is estimated that 12.5 million college students represent a $33 to $60 billion market, (with some $13 billion of discretionary income).[29] This market consumes a wide range of necessities (books, personal clothing, and gasoline), as well as elective purchases of goods and services (rock concerts and spring vacations). In many cases, college students also exert influence on the purchase decisions of their families.

Like preteens and teenagers, college students are still in the process of establishing many of their brand preferences and shopping habits. According to MasterCard, about three-fourths of college students maintain their first credit card for 15 years, and 60 percent keep it for life.[30] One interesting study found that female college students and their mothers tended to share specific brand preferences (e.g., aspirin and pain relievers) and shopping

table 12-1   Lifestyle Segments of the Teen Market

SEGMENT NAME	KEY CHARACTERISTICS
• Socially Driven	Primarily female; active and extroverted. They are optimistic and plan to attend college.
• Versatile Participant	Slightly more females than males; responsible teens but less optimistic and less likely to plan to attend college than the Socially Driven. They are comfortable in social and solitary situations.
• Passive Introverts	Slightly more males than females; withdrawn, self-conscious, and the least comfortable in social situations. They are less optimistic about the future, and they spend the least.
• Sports Oriented	Primarily males; outgoing, active, and greatly interested in participating in and watching sports. Sports influence their self-image and what they buy.

Source: Drawn from GRADY HAUSER, "How Teenagers Spend the Family Dollar," *American Demographics* (December 1986), 41.

strategies (e.g., prepurchase planning and willingness to try new products). However, when it came to more remote and broad-ranging beliefs about the nature of the marketplace (e.g., perceptions of the price-quality relationship or distrust of marketing practices), college girls and their mothers were less likely to have the same outlook.[31]

Marketers frequently attempt to gain the attention and loyalty of college students because of their current and future prospects as consumers. College newspapers and college radio stations are important media to use in reaching these students. Many consumer goods firms are eager to obtain shelf space in college bookstores and even to establish networks of students to represent them and their products on campus (e.g., AT&T has on-campus representatives to promote its long-distance services).

THE FAMILY LIFE CYCLE

Sociologists and consumer researchers have long been attracted to the concept of the **family life cycle** (FLC) as a means of depicting what was once a rather steady and predictable series of stages that most families progressed through. However, with the advent of many diverse family and lifestyle arrangements, what was the rule has been on the decline. This decline in the percentage of families that progress through a traditional FLC (to be explored shortly) seems to be caused by a host of societal factors, including an increasing divorce rate, the explosive number of out-of-wedlock births, and the 30-year (1950s to 1970s) decline in the number of extended families that transpired as many young families moved to advance their job and career opportunities.

Despite the decline in its predictive precision, the FLC remains a useful marketing tool when one keeps in mind that there are family and lifestyle arrangements that are not fully accounted for by the traditional representation. FLC analysis enables marketers to segment families in terms of a series of stages spanning the life course of a family unit. The FLC is a composite variable created by systematically combining such commonly used demographic variables as *marital status*, *size of family*, *age of family members* (focusing on the age of the oldest or youngest child), and *employment status* of the head of household. The ages of the parents and the relative amount of disposable income usually are inferred from the stage in the family life cycle.

To reflect the current realities of a wide range of family and lifestyle arrangements, our treatment of the FLC concept is divided into two sections. The first section considers the traditional FLC schema. This depiction has dominated most of the thinking about the FLC, yet it is increasingly being challenged, because it fails to account for various important family living arrangements. To rectify these limitations, the second section focuses on alternative FLC stages, including increasingly important nontraditional family structures.

Traditional Family Life Cycle

The traditional FLC is a progression of stages through which many families pass, starting with bachelorhood, moving on to marriage (and the creation of the basic family unit), then to family growth (with the birth of children), to family contraction (as grown children leave the household), and ending with the dissolution of the basic unit (due to the death of one spouse). Although different researchers have expressed various preferences in terms of the number of FLC stages, the traditional FLC models proposed over the years can be synthesized into just five basic stages, as follows:

- *Stage I: **Bachelorhood**   Young single adult living apart from parents*
- *Stage II: **Honeymooners**   Young married couple*
- *Stage III: **Parenthood**   Married couple with at least one child living at home*
- *Stage IV: **Postparenthood**   An older married couple with no children living at home*
- *Stage V: **Dissolution**   One surviving spouse*

The following discussion examines the five stages in detail and shows how they lend themselves to market segmentation strategies.

▲ **Stage I: Bachelorhood** The first FLC stage consists of young single men and women who have established households apart from their parents. Although most members of this FLC stage are fully employed, many are college or graduate students who have left their parents' homes. Young single adults are apt to spend their incomes on rent, basic home furnishings, the purchase and maintenance of automobiles, travel and entertainment, and clothing and accessories. Members of the **bachelorhood** stage frequently have sufficient disposable income to indulge themselves. Marketers target singles for a wide variety of products and services. For instance, Figure 12-10 on page 362 shows how Mazda is targeting its sporty Miata at the young singles market with the thought ". . . You get one chance."

In most large cities, there are travel agents, housing developments, health clubs, sports clubs, and other service and product marketers that find this FLC stage a lucrative target niche. *Meeting*, *dating*, and *mating* are prominent concerns of many young adults who typically are beginning their working lives after recently completing college or some other form of career or job training.[32] It is relatively easy to reach this segment, because many special-interest publications target singles. For example, *GQ* and *Playboy* are directed to a young, sophisticated, single male audience, whereas *Cosmopolitan* and *Glamour* are directed to young single females.

Marriage marks the transition from the bachelorhood stage to the honeymooner stage. Engaged and soon-to-be-married couples have a combined income of more than $48,000 (30 percent greater than the average United States household); therefore, they are the target for many products and services (the bridal industry is a $32-billion-a-year market).[33]

▲ **Stage II: Honeymooners** The *honeymoon* stage starts immediately after the marriage vows are taken and generally continues until the arrival of the couple's first child. This

FIGURE 12-10

Targeting Bachelorhood
Market
Courtesy of Mazda

FLC stage serves as a period of adjustment to married life. Because many young husbands and wives both work, these couples have available a combined income that often permits a lifestyle that provides them with the opportunities of more indulgent purchasing of possessions or allows them to save or invest their extra income. Figure 12-11 is a TIAA-CREF ad targeted to honeymooners, suggesting the wisdom of investing and insurance programs.

Honeymooners have considerable start-up expenses when establishing a new home (major and minor appliances, bedroom and living room furniture, carpeting, drapes, dishes, and a host of utensils and accessory items). During this stage, the advice and experience of other married couples are likely to be important to newlyweds. Also important as sources of new product information are the so-called shelter magazines, such as *Better Homes and Gardens* and *Metropolitan Home*.

▲ **Stage III: Parenthood** When a couple has its first child, the honeymoon is considered over. The *parenthood* stage (sometimes called the full-nest stage) usually extends over more than a 20-year period. Because of its long duration, this stage can be divided into shorter phases: the preschool phase, the elementary school phase, the high school phase, and the college phase. Throughout these parenthood phases, the interrelationships of fam-

TIAA-CREF.
Proven
Solutions
To Last
a Lifetime.

A great relationship may do a lot for you emotionally. But it's not going to help the two of you much financially. For a comfortable, worry-free future, you need sound advice and solid thinking. That's why over 1.7 million people depend on TIAA-CREF. We offer investment, insurance, and personal savings plans that can help you reach your financial goals. To find out more, call 1 800 226-0147 for a free Personal Investing Kit, including a current CREF Prospectus. It's your first step towards developing a lasting relationship—with your money. TIAA-CREF. Financial services exclusively for people in education and research.

For more complete information, including fees and expenses, please read the CREF Prospectus offered above. Read it carefully before investing.

Ensuring the future for those who shape it.™

You may be able to

live on love.

But you definitely

can't retire on it.

FIGURE 12-11

Targeting Honeymooner Market
Reprinted with permission of TIIA-CREF. Photo courtesy of Ron Chapple/FPG International.

ily members and the structure of the family gradually change (see Figure 12-12 on page 364). Furthermore, the financial resources of the family change significantly, as one (or both) parents progress in a career and as childrearing and educational responsibilities gradually increase and finally decrease as children become self-supporting.

An increase in the number of births among baby boomers (born between 1946 and 1964) has resulted in a "baby boomlet." These parents are older (34 to 52), better educated, more affluent, and more socially aware. Many (44 percent) also feel that they are better parents to their children than their parents were to them. Their children often become the focus of their lives, and they spend money accordingly.[34] "Boomer" parents have become an important target for companies that serve the baby market. They also are an important market for many investment and insurance services.

FIGURE 12-12

Targeting a Subgroup
of the Parenthood
Stage
Courtesy of Sub-Zero

Many magazines cater to the information and entertainment needs of parents and children. For example, there are many other special-interest publications, such as *Humpty Dumpty*, designed for the young child just learning to read; *Scholastic Magazine*, for the elementary school pupil; *Boy's Life*, for young boys; and *American Girl*, *Seventeen*, *Glamour*, and *Mademoiselle*, for teen and postteen girls interested in fashion.

▲ **Stage IV: Postparenthood** Because parenthood extends over many years, it is only natural to find that *postparenthood*, when all the children have left home, is traumatic for some parents and liberating for others. This so-called *empty-nest stage* signifies for many parents almost a "rebirth," a time for doing all the things they could not do while the children were at home and they had to worry about soaring educational expenses. For the mother, it is a time to further her education, to enter or reenter the job market, to seek new interests. For the father, it is a time to indulge in new hobbies. For both, it is the time to travel, to entertain, perhaps to refurnish their home or to sell it in favor of a new home or condominium (see Figure 12-13).

It is during this stage that married couples tend to be most comfortable financially. Today's empty nesters have more leisure time. They travel more frequently, take extended vacations, and are likely to purchase a second home in a warmer climate. They have higher disposable incomes because of savings and investments, and they have fewer expenses (no mortgage or college tuition bills). For this reason, families in the postparenthood stage are an important market for luxury goods, new automobiles, expensive furniture, and vacations to faraway places.

Many empty nesters retire while they are still in good health. Retirement provides the opportunity to pursue new interests, to travel, and to fulfill unsatisfied needs. Hotels, airlines, and car-leasing companies have responded to this market with discounts to consumers over 60; some airlines have established special travel clubs with unlimited mileage for a flat fee. Adult communities have sprung up in many parts of the nation. Of course, for older retired couples who do not have adequate savings or income, retirement is far different and very restrictive.

FIGURE 12-13

Targeting the Post-parenthood Stage
Reprinted with permission of Del Webb Corporation

Older consumers tend to use television as an important source of information and entertainment. They favor programs that provide the opportunity to "keep up with what's happening," especially news and public affairs programs. In addition, a number of special-interest magazines cater exclusively to this market, such as *Modern Maturity*. (Chapter 15 contains a more detailed discussion of the older consumer as a subcultural market segment.)

▲ **Stage V: Dissolution** *Dissolution* of the basic family unit occurs with the death of one spouse. When the surviving spouse is in good health, is working or has adequate savings, and has a supportive family and friends, the adjustment is easier. The surviving spouse (usually, the wife) often tends to follow a more economical lifestyle. Many surviving spouses seek each other out for companionship; others enter into second (or third and even fourth) marriages.

To complete the discussion of the traditional FLC stages, Table 12-2 presents the most popular ("Top 10") grocery items for each of seven different life stages that correspond quite closely to the FLC stages that were just examined. For example, the table reveals that *young singles* are particularly heavy purchasers of audiocassettes and frozen pizza, while *childless younger couples* buy lots of dog food. *Maturing families* are heavy consumers of many items, including cereals, fruit drinks, and potato chips, and *older singles* purchase a lot of frozen dinners.

Modifications to the FLC

As we already noted, the traditional FLC model has lost it ability to fully represent the progression of stages through which current family and lifestyle arrangement move. To compensate for these limitations, consumer researchers have been attempting to search out expanded FLC models that better reflect diversity of family and lifestyle arrangements.[35] Figure 12-14 on page 368 presents an FLC model that depicts along the main horizontal the stages of the traditional FLC and above and below the main horizontal selected alternative FLC stages that account for some important nontraditional family households that marketers are increasingly targeting. The underlying sociodemographic forces that drive this expanded FLC model include divorce and later marriages, with and without the presence of children. Although somewhat greater reality is provided by this modified FLC model, it only recognizes families that started in marriage, ignoring such single-parent households as unwed mothers and families formed because a single person or single persons adopt a child.

▲ **Nontraditional FLC Stages** Table 12-3 on page 368 presents an extensive categorization of nontraditional FLC stages that are derived from the dynamic sociodemographic forces operating during the past 25 years. These nontraditional stages include not only family households but also nonfamily households: those consisting of a single individual and those consisting of two or more unrelated individuals. At one time, nonfamily households were so uncommon that it was not really important whether they were considered or not. However, as Table 12-4 on page 369 reveals, nearly 30 percent of all households are currently nonfamily households (i.e., men or women living alone or with another person as an unmarried couple). The table points out how FLC stages have shifted and shows that nonfamily households actually outnumber married couples with children, the once stereotypical family.

▲ **Consumption in Nontraditional Families** When households undergo status changes (e.g., divorce, temporary retirement, a new person moving into the household, or the death of a spouse), they often undergo spontaneous changes in brand preferences and, thus, become attractive targets for many marketers.[36] For example, divorce often requires that one (or both) former spouses find a new residence, get new telephones (with new telephone numbers), buy new furniture, and perhaps find a job. These requirements mean that a di-

table 12-2   Top 10 Product Categories by Selected Life Stages

LIFE STAGE GROUP	PERCENT OF POP-ULATION	CATEGORY	DOLLAR INDEX*	LIFE STAGE GROUP	PERCENT OF POP-ULATION	CATEGORY	DOLLAR INDEX*
YOUNG SINGLES	3.5	Carbonated soft drinks.........69				Potato chips 160	
		Cigarettes 28				Toilet tissue.........................121	
		Ready-to-eat cereal 47				Packaged detergents...........154	
		Low-calorie carbonated				Disposable diapers...............161	
		soft drinks.........................72		ESTABLISHED FAMILIES	7.1	Cigarettes............................108	
		Audiocassettes/records.....224				Carbonated soft drinks 160	
		Magazines 96				Ready-to-eat cereal 132	
		Beer.......................................82				Low-calorie carbonated	
		Videocassettes 89				soft drinks......................135	
		Frozen pizza 141				Cookies 136	
		Cookies 51				Toilet tissue........................133	
CHILDLESS YOUNGER COUPLES	7.6	Cigarettes 64				Packaged detergents...........155	
		Carbonated soft drinks.........94				Potato chips.........................140	
		Ready-to-eat cereal 71				Ice cream.............................137	
		Low-calorie carbonated				Fruit drinks—other	
		soft drinks.........................90				container........................144	
		Videocassettes 107		EMPTY NESTERS	21.5	Cigarettes 120	
		Beer.......................................91				Carbonated soft drinks.........84	
		Dry dog food 135				Ready-to-eat cereal...............94	
		Toilet tissue...........................80				Low-calorie carbonated	
		Cookies 60				soft drinks.........................111	
		Magazines 86				Cookies 113	
NEW FAMILIES	6.7	Disposable diapers...............736				Ground coffee 160	
		Cigarettes 59				Toilet tissue 118	
		Ready-to-eat cereal 124				Beer.....................................107	
		Carbonated soft drinks.......104				Greeting cards 135	
		Modified milk 765				Magazines 118	
		Low-calorie carbonated		OLDER SINGLES	14.0	Cigarettes..............................92	
		soft drinks.........................90				Ready-to-eat cereal...............53	
		Cookies 106				Carbonated soft drinks 42	
		Videocassettes 141				Low-calorie carbonated	
		Beer.....................................101				soft drinks.........................65	
		Toilet tissue...........................95				Magazines 106	
MATURING FAMILIES	21.3	Cigarettes 64				Beer.......................................86	
		Ready-to-eat cereal..............168				Cookies 67	
		Carbonated soft drinks.........141				Greeting cards......................105	
		Cookies................................134				Frozen dinners.....................124	
		Low-calorie carbonated				Books....................................111	
		soft drinks........................106					
		Fruit drinks—other					
		container........................204					

*A dollar index of 100 indicates average purchasing levels, whereas an index of 150 means a given life stage group spends 90% more than one would expect given its percentage of the population.

Source: Adapted from SCOTTY DUPREE, "A Snapshot of Mature Life Stage Group Purchases," *Brandweek* (November 2, 1992), 18; "A Snapshot of Younger Life Stage Group Purchases," *Brandweek* (November 9, 1992), 28.

vorced person might need to contact real estate agents, call the local and long-distance telephone companies, visit furniture stores, and possibly contact a personnel agency or career consultant.[37] For divorced parents, especially fathers, it many mean spending most of their free time with children. Recognizing such needs, McDonald's has used a TV ad in the

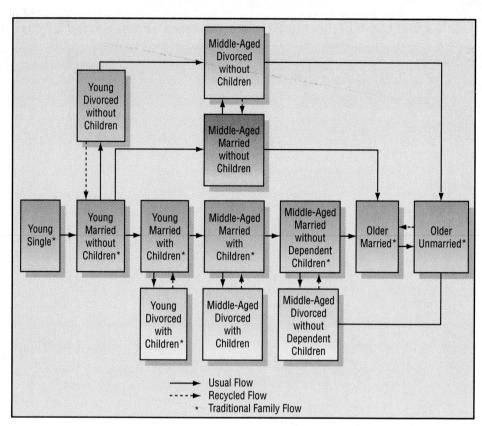

FIGURE 12-14

An Extended Family Life Cycle Schema Accounts for Alternative Consumer Lifestyle Realities

Source: PATRICK E. MURPHY and WILLIAM A. STAPLES, "A Modernized Family Life Cycle," *Journal of Consumer Research* 6 (June 1979), 17. Reprinted by permission of The University of Chicago Press as publisher.

Young Divorced without Children

Middle-Aged Divorced without Children

Middle-Aged Married without Children

Young Single*

Young Married without Children*

Young Married with Children*

Middle-Aged Married with Children*

Middle-Aged Married without Dependent Children*

Older Married*

Older Unmarried*

Young Divorced with Children*

Middle-Aged Divorced with Children

Middle-Aged Divorced without Dependent Children

→ Usual Flow
- - -▶ Recycled Flow
* Traditional Family Flow

table 12-3   Noteworthy Nontraditional FLC Stages

ALTERNATIVE FLC STAGES	DEFINITION/COMMENTARY
FAMILY HOUSEHOLDS	
• Childless couples	It is increasingly acceptable for married couples to elect not to have children. Contributing forces are more career-oriented married women and delayed marriages.
• Couples who marry later in life in their late 30s	More career-oriented men and women and greater occurrence of couples living together. Likely to have fewer or even no children.
• Couples who have first child	Likely to have fewer children. Stress quality lifestyle: "Only the best is good enough."
• Single parents I	High divorce rates (about 50 percent) contribute to a portion of single-parent households.
• Single parents II	Young man or woman who has one or more children out of wedlock.
• Single parents III	A single person who adopts one or more children.
• Extended family	Young single-adult children who return home to avoid the expenses of living alone while establishing their careers. Divorced daughter or son and grandchild(ren) return home to parents. Frail elderly parents who move in with children. Newlyweds living with in-laws.
NONFAMILY HOUSEHOLDS	
• Unmarried couples	Increased tolerance of heterosexual and homosexual couples.
• Divorced persons (no children)	High divorce rate contributes to dissolution of households before children are born.
• Single persons (most are young)	Primarily a result of delaying first marriage; also, men and women who never marry.
• Widowed persons (most are elderly)	Longer life expectancy, especially for women, means more over-75 single-person households.

table 12-4 Selected Sociodemographic Characteristics of Family and Nonfamily Households

	NUMBER OF HOUSEHOLDS BY TYPE IN 1990 (IN 000s)	MEDIAN INCOME (IN 1990)	DISTRIBUTION OF HOUSEHOLDS BY TYPE		
ALL HOUSEHOLDS	94,312	29,943			100.1%*
Family households	66,322	35,707			
Married couples	52,147	39,996			
with children	25,410	41,260	27.0		
without children	26,737	38,254	28.3	55.3	
Female-headed families	11,268	16,932			
with children	7,707	13,000	8.2		
without children	3,561	27,020	3.7	11.9	
Male-headed families	2,907	29,046			
with children	1,386	25,211	1.5		
without children	1,521	31,475	1.6	3.1	70.3
Nonfamily households	27,990	17,690			
Living alone	23,591	15,344			
Women	14,141	12,548	15.0		
Men	9,450	19,964	10.1	25.1	
Living with others	4,399	34,826			
Female headed	1,699	32,832	1.8		
Male headed	2,700	37,035	2.9	4.7	29.8

*Rounding Error

Source: U.S. Bureau of the Census, *Statistical Abstract of the United States:* 1992 (112th edition), Washington, D.C. 1992.

United Kingdom that features a young child orchestrating a meeting between his separated parents at McDonald's.[38]

In another sphere, the substantial increase in dual-income households (i.e., working wives and the subset of working mothers) has also tended to muddy the lifestyle assumptions implicit in the traditional FLC.[39] Most dual-income families have children (the majority of those children are between 6 and 17 years of age). The most affluent dual-income segment is, not surprisingly, the "crowded nesters." This dual-income couple, with an adult child living at home, has the advantage of an additional potential source of income to contribute to the general well-being of the household.

The portrayal of nontraditional FLC stages in contemporary advertising of products and services is evidence that marketers are eager to make their products and services more relevant to varying family lifestyles and, thus, to expand their markets.

summary

The family is a major influence on the consumption behavior of its members; it is also the prime target market for most products and product categories. As the most basic membership group, families are defined as two or more persons related by blood, marriage, or adoption who reside together. There are three types of families: married couples, nuclear families, and extended families. The basic functions of the family are the provision of economic and emotional support, childhood socialization, and a suitable lifestyle for its members.

The members of a family assume specific roles and tasks in their everyday functioning; such roles or tasks extend to the realm of consumer purchase decisions. Key consumer-related roles of family members include influencers, gatekeepers, deciders, buyers, preparers, users, maintainers, and disposers. A family's decision-making style often is influenced by its social class, lifestyle, role orientation, and stage in the family life cycle, as well as by the product's importance, perceived risk, and time constraints of the purchase itself.

The majority of consumer studies classify family consumption decisions as husband-dominated, wife-dominated, joint, or autonomic decisions. The extent and nature of husband-wife influence in family decisions depends on the specific product or service, the stage in the decision-making process (problem recognition, information search, or final decision), and the specific product features under consideration.

Consumer socialization is an important component of the socialization process of children. It is the vehicle through which the family imparts consumer-relevant knowledge, attitudes, and skills. Children are not only influenced by their families; they also influence their family consumption decisions.

Classification of families by stage in the family life cycle (FLC) provides valuable insights into family consumption-related behavior. The traditional FLC begins with bachelorhood, moves on to marriage, then to an expanding family, to a contracting family, and to an end with the death of a spouse. Dynamic sociodemographic changes in society have resulted in many nontraditional stages that a family or nonfamily household might pass through (e.g., childless couples, couples marrying later in life, single parents, unmarried couples, or single-person households). These nontraditional stages are becoming increasingly important to marketers in terms of specific market niches.

discussion questions

1. Some consumer behavior researchers maintain that the family, rather than the individual, should be the unit of analysis in consumer behavior. What are the advantages and disadvantages of using the family as the unit of analysis?

2. How does the family influence the consumer socialization of children? What role does television advertising play in consumer socialization?

3. As a marketing consultant, you were retained by the Walt Disney Company to design a study investigating how families make vacation decisions. Whom, within the family, would you interview? What kind of questions would you ask? How would you assess the relative "power" of each family member in making vacation-related decisions?

4. The Walt Disney Company is planning a TV campaign promoting Disney World. Does the company need to know which consumption role is played by each family member regarding vacation decisions? How would such knowledge enable the company to create more effective TV commercials?

5. Using the influence strategies for resolving husband-wife consumer-related conflicts discussed in this chapter, cite the strategies that are most likely to be used in the following cases:

   a. An older, retired couple, in which the wife wants to move to an apartment in an urban area but the husband wants to remain in their large suburban house.

   b. A teenage son wants a TV set in his own room. The parents object because they believe he will give less attention to schoolwork if he has his own TV.

   c. A teenage son was selected for a special program for gifted students that takes place at a rather costly summer camp. The teenage daughter wants to go on a European summer vacation with friends. The parents cannot afford both.

6. In purchasing a new television set, how would you expect the following factors to influence the dynamics of husband-wife decision making: (a) The features of the product; (b) the family's role structure orientation; and (c) the stage of the decision-making process. How would you use the assessments you listed above in advertising a new model TV set?

7. a. Describe the role of young children in the family consumption process.

   b. What role do teenagers play in family decision making?

   c. What is the marketing significance of the increase in the number of latchkey kids and their distinctive lifestyle?

8. Which of the five stages of the traditional family life cycle constitute the most lucrative segment(s) for the following products and services: (a) telephone party lines, (b) a Club Med vacation, (c) Domino's pizza, (d) compact disc players, (e) mutual funds, and (f) motor homes? Explain your answers.

9. You are the marketing manager of a furniture company. Discuss how you would segment your market and develop a product line for the nontraditional family households listed in Table 12-3.

10. As the marketing manager of a high-quality, fairly expensive line of frozen dinners, how would you use the nonfamily household information listed in Table 12-3 to segment the market and position your product?

11. A domestic airline's frequent-flyer program states that award tickets are transferable only to family members. As the airline executive charged with reevaluating this policy, how would you use the census data listed in Table 12-4 to decide whether or not to change the present policy?

1. Think of a recent major purchase your family has made. Analyze the roles performed by the various family members in terms of the following consumption roles: influencers, gatekeepers, deciders, buyers, preparers, users, maintainers, and disposers.

2. Select three product categories and compare the brands you prefer to those your parents prefer. To what extent are the preferences similar? Discuss the similarities in the context of consumer socialization.

3. Watch one hour of children's programming on commercial television and prepare a list of the commercials shown. For each ad, identify the persuasive appeal used, the approximate age of the child targeted, and your opinion as to whether or not the child is likely to differentiate between the program content and the commercial. Are your opinions on this issue consistent with the information presented in this book? Explain.

4. Identify one traditional family and one nontraditional family (or household) featured in a TV sitcom or series (the two families-households can be featured in the same or in different TV shows). Classify the traditional group into one stage of the traditional FLC. Classify the nontraditional group into one of the categories described in Table 12-3. Select two characters of the same gender and approximate age, one from each group, and compare their consumption behavior (e.g., clothes, furniture, or stated or implied attitudes toward spending money).

- Autonomic (unilateral) decisions
- Consumer socialization
- Economic well-being
- Emotional support
- Extended family
- Families versus households
- Family
- Family consumption roles
- Family decision making

- Family life cycle
- Family role structure orientation
- Functions of the family
- Husband-dominated decisions
- Husband-wife consumption-related conflict resolutions
- Joint (syncratic) decisions
- Latchkey children

- Nontraditional FLC stages
- Nuclear family
- Single-parent family
- Socialization of family members
- Stages in the decision-making process
- Suitable family lifestyles
- Traditional family life cycle
- Wife-dominated decisions

1. DIANE CRISPELL, "How to Avoid Big Mistakes," *American Demographics*, March 1991, 48–50.
2. TERRY L. CHILDERS and AKSHAY R. RAO, "The Influence of Familial and Peer-Based Reference Groups on Consumer Decisions," *Journal of Consumer Research* 19, September 1992, 198–211.
3. JONGHEE PARK, PATRIYA TANSHUHAJ, ERIC R. SPANGENBERG and JIM McCULLOUGH, "An Emotion-Based Perspective of Family Purchase Decisions," in Frank R. Kardes and Mita Sujan, eds., *Advances in Consumer Research* 22 (Provo, UT: Association for Consumer Research 1995), 723–28.
4. LEAH HARAN, "Families Together Differently Today," *Advertising Age*, October 23, 1995, 1 and 12.
5. LAURIE FLYNN, "A Head Start for Children in Computing," *The New York Times*, September 25, 1995, D5; and KIM CLELAND, "Online Services Offer Community to Young Hackers," *Advertising Age*, February 13, 1995, S-4 and S-8.
6. CELE OTNES, MICHELLE NELSON and MARY ANN McGRATH, "The Children's Birthday Party: A Study of Mothers as Socialization Agents," in Frank R. Kardes and Mita Sujan, eds., *Advances in Consumer Research* 22 (Provo, UT: Association for Consumer Research 1995), 622–27.

7. GEORGE P. MOSCHIS, ROY L. MOORE, and RUTH B. SMITH, "The Impact of Family Communication on Adolescent Consumer Socialization," in Thomas C. Kinnear, ed., *Advances in Consumer Research* 11 (Provo, UT: Association for Consumer Research, 1983), 314–19; LES CARLSON and SANFORD GROSSBART, "Parental Style and Consumer Socialization of Children," *Journal of Consumer Research* 15, June 1988, 77-94; and SCOTT WARD, "Consumer Socialization," *Journal of Consumer Research* 1, September 1974, 9.

8. STEVEN A. HOLMES, "Shoppers! Deciding? Just Your Child," *The New York Times*, January 8, 1995, 4.

9. ELIZABETH C. HIRSCHMAN, "Consumers and Their Animal Companions," *Journal of Consumer Research* 20, March 1994, 616–32.

10. BARBARA OLSEN, "Brand Loyalty and Lineage: Exploring New Dimensions for Research," in Leigh McAlister and Michael L. Rothschild, eds., *Advances in Consumer Research* 20 (Provo, UT: Association for Consumer Research, 1993) 575–79; and MARILYN LAVIN, "Husband-Dominant, Wife-Dominant, Joint," *Journal of Consumer Marketing* 10, 1993, 33–42.

11. RITHA FELLERMAN and KATHLEEN DEBEVEC, "Kinship Exchange Networks and Family Consumption," in Leigh McAlister and Michael L. Rothschild, eds., *Advances in Consumer Research* 20 (Provo, UT: Association for Consumer Research 1993) 458–62.

12. SHARON E. BEATTY and SALIL TALPADE, "Adolescent Influence in Family Decision Making: A Replication with Extension," *Journal of Consumer Research* 21, September 1994, 332–41; and PETER ZOLLO, "Talking to Teens," *American Demographics*, November 1995, 22–28.

13. See WILLIAM J. QUALLS, "Toward Understanding the Dynamics of Household Decision Conflict Behavior," in Michael Houston, ed., *Advances in Consumer Research* 15 (Provo, UT: Association for Consumer Research, 1988), 442-48; and WILLIAM J. QUALLS, "Household Decision Behavior: The Impact of Husbands' and Wives' Sex Role Orientation," *Journal of Consumer Research* 14, September 1987, 264-78. See also ERICH KIRCHLER, "Spouses' Influence Strategies in Purchase Decisions as Dependent on Conflict Type and Relationship Characteristics," *Journal of Economic Psychology* 11, March 1990, 101–18.

14. KIM P. CORFMAN, "Perceptions of Relative Influence: Formation and Measurement," *Journal of Marketing Research* 28, May 1991, 125-36. Also, for additional articles on family decision-making roles and structures, see CHRISTINA KWAI-CHOI and ROGER MARSHALL, "Who Do We Ask and When: A Pilot Study about Research in Family Decision Making," in Michael Levy and Dhruv Grewal, eds., *Developments in Marketing Science* 16 (Coral Gables, Florida: Academy of Marketing Science, 1993), 30–5.

15. JOANNE STILLEY HOPPER, "Family Financial Decision Making: Implications for Marketing Strategy," *Journal of Services Marketing* 9(1), 1995, 24–32.

16. AMARDEEP ASSAR and GEORGE S. BOBINSKI, "Financial Decision Making of Baby Boomer Couples," in Rebecca Holman and Michael R. Solomon, eds., *Advances in Consumer Research* 18 (Provo, UT: Association for Consumer Research, 1991), 657–65.

17. JOHN B. FORD, MICHAEL S. LATOUR, and TONY L. HENTHORNE, "Perception of Marital Roles in Purchase Decision Processes: A Cross-Cultural Study," *Journal of the Academy of Marketing Science* 23(2), 1995, 120–31; and TONY L. HENTHORNE, MICHAEL S. LATOUR, and ROBERT MATTHEWS, "Perception of Marital Roles in Purchase Decision Making: A Study of Japanese Couples," *American Marketing Association*, Winter 1995, 321–22.

18. GIOVANNA IMPERIA, THOMAS C. O'GUINN, and ELIZABETH A. MACADAMS, "Family Decision Making Role Perceptions among Mexican-American and Anglo Wives: A Cross-Cultural Comparison," in Holman and Solomon, eds., *Advances in Consumer Research* 18, 71–74.

19. CYNTHIA WEBSTER, "Effects of Hispanic Ethnic Identification on Marital Roles in the Purchase Decision Process," *Journal of Consumer Research* 21, September 1994, 319–31.

20. NEJDET DELENER and LEON G. SCHIFFMAN, "Family Decision Making: The Impact of Religious Factors," in Gary Frazier et al., eds., *1988 AMA Educators' Proceedings* (Chicago: American Marketing Association, 1988), 80–83.

21. "Kids Market Keeps Growing Up," *Advertising Age*, May 15, 1995, 1.

22. PACO UNDERHILL, "Kids in Stores," *American Demographics*, June 1994, 22–27; JAMES U. MCNEAL, "The Littlest Shoppers," *American Demographics*, February 1992, 48–53; and JAMES U. MCNEAL, "Planning Priorities for Marketing to Children," *The Journal of Business Strategy*, May/June 1991, 12–15.

23. M. CAROLE MACKLIN, "Preschoolers' Understanding of the Informational Function of Television Advertising," *Journal of Consumer Research* 14, September 1987, 229–39; MARY ANN STUTTS and GARLAND G. HUNNICUTT, "Can Young Children Understand Disclaimers in Television Commercials?" *Journal of Advertising* 16, 1987, 41–46; and MARIEA GRUBBS HOY, "The Toddler Years: The Missing Sample in Marketing Research with Children," in A. Parasuraman and William Bearden, et al., eds., *1990 AMA Educators' Proceedings* (Chicago: American Marketing Association, 1990), 112–17.

24. GERALD J. GORN and RENEE FLORSHEIM, "The Effects of Commercials for Adult Products on Children," *Journal of Consumer Research* 11, March 1985, 962–67.

25. RUSSELL BELK, ROBERT MAYER, and AMY DRISCOLL, "Children's Recognition of Consumption Symbolism in Children's Products," *Journal of Consumer Research* 10, March 1984, 386–97.

26. PAMELA SEBASTIAN, "Business Bulletin: A Special Background Report on Industry and Finance," *The Wall Street Journal* 12, September 1991, A1; and MARY LU

CARNEVALE, "Technology and Medicine: Bell South Unit and Swatch to Wristwatch Pager," *The Wall Street Journal*, March 4, 1992, B7.

27. PETER ZOLLO, "Talking to Teens," 22–28.

28. Ibid., 26.

29. CARRIE GOERNE, "Corporate Sponsors Embark on Campus Tours," *Marketing News*, September 28, 1992, 12; and LINDA PUNCH, "Better Marks for College Cards," *Credit Card Management*, September 1991, 64–67.

30. TERRY LEFTON, "Credit Cards Go to High School," *Adweek's Marketing Week*, May 11, 1992,

31. ELIZABETH S. MOORE-SHAY and RICHARD J. LUTZ, "Intergenerational Influences on the Formation of Consumer Attitudes and Beliefs about the Marketplace: Mothers and Daughters," in Michael Houston, ed., *Advances in Consumer Research* 15, op. cit., 461–67.

32. AARON BARNARD, MARA B. ADELMAN, and JONATHAN E. SCHROEDDER, "Two Views of Consumption in Mating and Dating," in Holman and Solomon, eds., *Advances in Consumer Research* 18, 532–37.

33. CYNDEE MILLER, "'Til Death Do They Part," *Marketing News*, March 27, 1995, 1–2; and NELLIE S. HUANG, "No More Toasters, Please," *Smart Money*, April 1993, 133–35.

34. JENNIFER FULKERSON, "Rating Mom and Pop," *American Demographics*, June 1995, 19–22.

35. CHARLES M. SCHANINGER and WILLIAM D. DANKO, "A Conceptual and Empirical Comparison of Alternative Household Life Cycle Models," *Journal of Consumer Research* 19, March 1993, 580–94.

36. ROSHAN "BOB" D. AHUJA and KANDI M. STINSON, "Female-Headed Single Parent Families: An Exploratory Study of Children's Influence in Family Decision Making," in Leigh McAlister and Michael L. Rothschild, eds., *Advances in Consumer Research* 20 (Provo, UT: Association for Consumer Research, 1993), 469–74.

37. MYRA JO BATES and JAMES W. GENTRY, "Keeping the Family Together: How We Survived the Divorce," in Chris T. Allen and Deborah Roedder John, eds., *Advances in Consumer Research* 21 (Provo, UT: Association for Consumer Research, 1994), 30–34.; and ROBERT E. WILKES, "Redefining Family in America: Characteristics and Expenditures of Single-Parent Families," *American Marketing Association*, Winter 1995, 270–76.

38. JULIANA KORANTENG, "No Ad Ban for McDonald's," *Advertising Age*, May 15, 1995, 12.

39. JUDITH J. MADILL-MARSHALL, LOUISE HESLOP, and LINDA DUXBURY, "Coping with Household Stress in the 1990s: Who Uses 'Convenience Foods' and Do They Help?" in Frank R. Kardes and Mita Sujan, eds., *Advances in Consumer Research* 22 (Provo, UT: Association for Consumer Research, 1995), 729–34.

Sometimes more is more.

Introducing an exceptional argument against the age-old rule that less is more.

The new Range Rover 4.0 SE, a vehicle unlike any other.

Because while its performance rivals the worthiest European road sedans, the Range Rover leaves them behind in a host of other areas.

Like passenger room, cargo space, and the mountains of Chile.

As if that weren't enough, it's been polished, plushed, and primped with every amenity from burl walnut trim to dual electronic climate controls—with pollen filters. There are even individually heated front seats.

What's more, it comes complete with electronic traction control. Dual airbags. All-terrain ABS. And electronic air suspension.

So why not call 1-800-FINE 4WD for the dealer nearest you?

Of course, $54,000* isn't inexpensive. But then again, no other vehicle has everything you'd ever want.

And more.

RANGE ROVER

Always use your seatbelts. SRS/airbags alone do not provide sufficient protection.

Some form of class structure or social stratification has existed in all societies throughout the history of human existence. In contemporary societies, an indication of the presence of social classes is the common reality that people who are better educated or have more prestigious occupations of physician and lawyer often are more highly valued than those of truckdriver and farmhand. All four occupations, however, are necessary for our society's well-being. Moreover, as will be discussed later, a wide range of differences in values, attitudes, and behavior exists among members of different social classes.

The major questions that will be explored in this chapter are these: What is social class? What are its determinants? How is social class measured? How do members of specific social-class groups behave? How do social-class-linked attitudes and behavior influence consumer behavior?

All the people like us are We, and everyone else is They.

—Rudyard Kipling
"We Are They" (1926)

WHAT IS SOCIAL CLASS?

Although **social class** can be thought of as a continuum—a range of social positions—on which each member of society can be placed, researchers have preferred to divide the continuum into a small number of specific social classes, or **strata**. Within this framework, the concept of social class is used to assign individuals or families to a **social-class category**. Consistent with this practice, social class is defined as *the division of members of a society into a hierarchy of distinct status classes, so that members of each class have relatively the same status and members of all other classes have either more or less status.*

To appreciate more fully the complexity of social class, we will briefly consider several underlying concepts pertinent to this definition.

Social Class and Social Status

Researchers often measure social class in terms of **social status**; that is, they define each social class by the amount of status the members of that class have in comparison with members of other social classes. In social-class research (sometimes called "social stratification"), *status* is frequently thought of as the relative rankings of members of each social class in terms of specific status factors. For example, relative *wealth* (amount of economic assets), *power* (the degree of personal choice or influence over others), and *prestige* (the degree of recognition received from others) are three factors frequently used when estimating social class. When considering consumer behavior and marketing research, status is most often defined in terms of one or more of the following convenient demographic (more precisely, socioeconomic) variables: *family income*, *occupational status*, and *educational attainment*. These socioeconomic variables, as expressions of status, are used by marketing practitioners on a daily basis to measure social class.

▲ **Social Class Is Hierarchical** Social-class categories usually are ranked in a hierarchy, ranging from low to high status. Thus, members of a specific social class perceive members of other social classes as having either more or less status than they do. To many people, therefore, social-class categories suggest that others are either *equal* to them (about the same social class), *superior* to them (higher social class), or *inferior* to them (lower social class).

This hierarchical aspect of social class is important to marketers. Consumers may purchase certain products because these products are favored by members of their own or a higher social class (e.g., a fine French Champagne), and consumers may avoid other products because they perceive the products to be "lower-class" products (e.g., a digital readout wristwatch as a dress watch).

▲ **Social Class and Market Segmentation** The various social-class strata provide a natural basis for market segmentation for many products and services. In many instances, consumer researchers have been able to relate product usage to social-class membership. For instance, Figure 13-1 presents sample covers of a new magazine, *City Family*, which is targeted to lower-income families residing in large cities like New York. The magazine serves a valuable service by providing practical information on a variety of topics and issues of particular relevance to low-income city dwellers. It also provides an opportunity for marketers, health-care providers, and public agencies to communicate with this specific socioeconomic group.[1] The existence of both downscale and upscale publications provides all types of organizations with a chance to effectively market to households in terms of the needs and interests of specific social strata.

FIGURE 13-1

▲ **Social Class and Behavioral Factors** The classification of society's members into a small number of social classes has enabled researchers to note the existence of shared values, attitudes, and behavioral patterns among members *within* each social class and differing values, attitudes, and behavior *between* social classes. Consumer researchers have been able to relate social-class standing to consumer attitudes concerning specific products and to examine social-class influences on the actual consumption of products.

▲ **Social Class as a Frame of Reference** Social-class membership serves consumers as a frame of reference (i.e., a reference group) for the development of their attitudes and behavior. In the context of reference groups, members of a specific social class may be expected to turn most often to other members of the same class for cues (or clues) regarding appropriate behavior. In other cases, members of a particular social class (e.g., upper-lower class) may aspire to advance their social-class standing by emulating the behavior of members of the middle class. To accomplish this goal, they might read middle-class magazines, do "middle-class things" (e.g., visit museums and advance their education), and hang out at middle-class restaurants so that they can observe middle-class behavior. (For a detailed discussion of reference groups, see Chapter 11.)

Social-Class Categories

Little agreement exists among sociologists on how many distinct class divisions are necessary to adequately describe the class structure of the United States. Most early studies divided the organization of specific communities into five- or six-class social structures. However, other researchers have found nine-, four-, three-, and even two-class schemas suitable for their purposes. The choice of how many separate classes to use depends on the amount of detail that the researcher believes is necessary to explain adequately the attitudes or behavior under study. Marketers are interested in the social-class structures of communities that are potential markets for their products and in the specific social-class level of their potential customers. Tables 13-1 and 13-2 illustrate the number and diversity of social-class schemas and show the distribution of the United States population in terms of several different subdivisions (five-, six-, and seven-category subdivisions).

As Table 13-2 shows, the percentage of the population accounted for in each social class appears to fluctuate, depending on the number of categories used and the composition of each category. It also reveals the small size of the upper-upper class, which is the reason why most mass marketers simply ignore them. On the other hand, its small size and highly cultivated tastes make the upper class a particularly desirable target market for spe-

table 13-1   Variations in the Number and Types of Social-Class Categories

TWO-CATEGORY-SOCIAL CLASS SCHEMAS

- Blue-collar, white-collar
- Lower, upper
- Lower, middle

THREE-CATEGORY SOCIAL-CLASS SCHEMAS

- Blue collar, gray collar, white collar
- Lower, middle, upper

FOUR-CATEGORY SOCIAL-CLASS SCHEMA

- Lower, lower-middle, upper-middle, upper

FIVE-CATEGORY SOCIAL-CLASS SCHEMAS

- Lower, working-class, lower-middle, upper-middle, upper
- Lower, lower-middle, middle, upper-middle, upper

SIX-CATEGORY SOCIAL-CLASS SCHEMA

- Lower-lower, upper-lower, lower-middle, upper-middle, lower-upper, upper-upper

SEVEN-CATEGORY SOCIAL-CLASS SCHEMA

- Real lower-lower, a lower group of people but not the lowest, working class, middle class, upper-middle, lower-upper, upper-upper

NINE-CATEGORY SOCIAL-CLASS SCHEMA

- Lower-lower, middle-lower, upper-lower, lower-middle, middle-middle, upper-middle, lower-upper, middle-upper, upper-upper

table 13-2   Selected Social-Class Distribution in Population

NUMBER OF CLASSES	PERCENT OF POPULATION
FIVE CATEGORY[a]	
Upper	11.4%
Upper-middle	12.7
Middle	20.6
Lower-middle	16.6
Lower	28.0
	89.3%*
SIX CATEGORY[b]	
Upper-upper	0.9%
Lower-upper	12.7
Upper-middle	7.2
Lower-middle	28.4
Upper-lower	44.0
Lower-lower	19.5
	100.0%
SEVEN CATEGORY[c]	
Upper-upper	0.3
Lower-upper	1.2
Upper-middle	12.5
Middle	32.0
Working class	38.0
A lower group but not the lowest	9.0
Real lower-lower	7.0
	100.0%

*Rounding errors

Sources: Adapted from
[a]McKinley L. Blackburn and David E. Bloom. "What's Happening to the Middle Class?" *American Demographics* (January 1985), 21.
[b]Pierre Martineau, *Motivation in Advertising*, New York: McGraw-Hill Book Company, 1957.
[c]Richard P. Coleman, "The Continuing Significance of Social Class to Marketing," *Journal of Consumer Research* 11 (December 1983), 267.

cialty firms with a particular expertise and the ability to cater to the small number of particularly affluent consumers (see Figure 13-2 on page 380).

THE MEASUREMENT OF SOCIAL CLASS

Although most behavioral scientists tend to agree that social class is a valid and useful concept, no general agreement exists on how to measure it. To a great extent, researchers are uncertain about the underlying dimensions of social-class structure. To attempt to resolve this dilemma, researchers have used a wide range of measurement techniques that they believe give a "fair" approximation of social class.

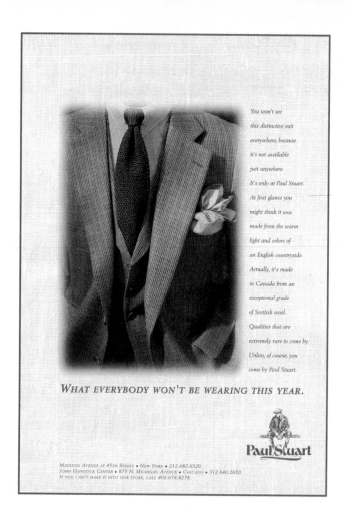

FIGURE 13-2

Retailer Targeting Its
Upscale Customers
Courtesy of Paul Stuart

Systematic approaches for measuring social class fall into the following broad categories: **subjective measures**, **reputational measures**, and **objective measures** of social class.

Subjective Measures

In the *subjective* approach to measuring social class, individuals are asked to estimate their own social-class positions. Typical of this approach is the following question:

Which one of the following four categories best describes your social class: the lower class, the lower-middle class, the upper-middle class, or the upper class?

Lower class	[ ]
Lower-middle class	[ ]
Upper-middle class	[ ]
Upper class	[ ]
Do not know/refuse to answer	[ ]

The resulting classification of social-class membership is based on the participants' self-perceptions or self-images. Social class is treated as a "personal" phenomenon, one that reflects an individual's sense of belonging or identification with others. This feeling of social-group membership is often referred to as *class consciousness*.

Subjective measures of social-class membership tend to produce an overabundance of people who classify themselves as *middle class* (thus understating the number of people—the "fringe" people—who would, perhaps, be more correctly classified as either *lower* or *upper class*). Moreover, it is likely that the subjective perception of one's social-class membership, as a reflection of one's self-image, is related to product usage and consumption preferences (see Chapter 5).

Reputational Measures

The *reputational* approach for measuring social class requires selected community informants to make initial judgments concerning the social-class membership of *others* within the community. The final task of assigning community members to social-class positions, however, belongs to the trained researcher.

Sociologists have used the reputational approach to obtain a better understanding of the specific class structures of communities under study. Consumer researchers, however, are concerned with the measurement of social class to understand markets and consumption behavior better, not social structure. In keeping with this more focused goal, the reputational approach has proved to be impractical.

Objective Measures

In contrast to the subjective and reputational methods, which require people to envision their own class standing or that of other community members, *objective* measures consist of selected demographic or socioeconomic variables concerning the individual(s) under study. These variables are measured through questionnaires that ask respondents several factual questions about themselves, their families, or their places of residence. When selecting objective measures of social class, most researchers favor *one* or *more* of the following variables: **occupation**, **amount of income**, and **education**. To these socio-economic factors, they sometimes add **geodemographic clustering** data in the form of zip-code and residence-neighborhood information. These socioeconomic indicators are especially important as a means of locating concentrations of consumers with specific social-class membership.

Socioeconomic measures of social class are of considerable value to marketers concerned with segmenting markets. Marketing managers who have developed socioeconomic profiles of their target markets can locate these markets (i.e., identify and measure them) by studying the socioeconomic data periodically issued by the United States Bureau of the Census and numerous commercial geodemographic data services. To reach a desired target market, marketers match the *socioeconomic profiles* of their target audiences to the *audience profiles* of selected advertising media (see Chapter 10). Socioeconomic audience profiles are regularly developed and routinely made available to potential advertisers by most of the mass media (see Table 13-3 on page 382). Readers' median income data for a selection of print media are presented in Table 13-4.

Objective measures of social class fall into two basic categories: **single-variable indexes** and **composite-variable indexes**.

▲ **Single-Variable Indexes** A **single-variable index** uses just one socioeconomic variable to evaluate social-class membership. Some of the variables that are used for this purpose are discussed next.

OCCUPATION **Occupation** is a widely accepted and probably the best documented measure of social class, because it implies occupational status. The importance of occupation as a social-class indicator is dramatized by the frequency with which people ask others they meet for the first time, "What do you do for a living?" The response to this question serves as a guide in "sizing up" (i.e., evaluating and forming opinions of) others.

table 13-3
Socioeconomic Profile of *Vanity Fair* Readers

	TOTAL READERS (000)	PERCENT	INDEX (UNITED STATES AVERAGE = 100)
Total women	3,698	78%	150
Professional/managerial	1,484	31	184
Household income			
$40,000+	2,987	63	140
$60,000+	1,880	40	164
$80,000+	1,443	30	210
Median Income $49,211			
Attended/graduated College+	3,064	65	140
Live in metropolitan area	4,421	93	116

Source: From *Vanity Fair* Demographic Profile, derived from 1995 MRI data. Reprinted by permission.

table 13-4
Readers Median Household Income for Selected Publications

NEWSPAPER/MAGAZINE	MEDIAN HOUSEHOLD INCOME
Wall Street Journal	$82,167.8
New York Times Daily	74,654.0
Barron's	57,008.5
Forbes	64,994.6
PC World	60,345.5
Architectural Digest	61,734.8
Money	59,109.1
Smithsonian	48,569.8
New Yorker	53,066.6
National Geographic	43,431.9
Newsweek	51,768.3
Time	47,819.5
Car & Driver	51,924.6
People	44,141.5
Esquire	42,041.9
Town & Country	41,772.4
Cosmopolitan	43,591.3
Outdoor Life	37,384.8
Playboy	41,036.3
Field & Stream	37,178.0
Hunting	34,064.1
Family Circle	36,442.8
Soap Opera Weekly	28,868.1
Ebony	25,952.0
True Story	18,489.8

Source: From *1995 Magazine Audience Estimates* (New York: Mediamark Research, Inc.). Reprinted by permission.

More important, marketers frequently think in terms of specific occupations when defining a target market for their products (e.g., "Physicians and lawyers are our best customers for limited edition fountain pens"), or broader occupational categories ("We target our vacation resort club to executives and professionals"). Still further, the likelihood that particular occupations would be receptive to certain products or services often provides the basis for an occupational screener requirement for participation in focus groups or survey research (see Chapter 2) and for marketers to select occupational databases to target with direct marketing campaigns (e.g., a list of female medical doctors practicing in Dallas, Texas).[2]

Table 13-5 presents findings from a continuing survey that estimates the relative *honesty* and perceived *ethical standards* that people assign to many basic occupational titles. Because this ranking is based more on *respect* or *societal prestige* than on status or wealth, it is not surprising that the rankings only vaguely suggest that occupations toward the top half of the table earn greater incomes and/or require more formal education than those toward the bottom half. In reality, however, a close association exists between occupational status, income, and education.

EDUCATION The level of a person's formal education is another commonly accepted approximation of social-class standing. Generally speaking, the more education a person has, the more likely it is that the person is well-paid (i.e., has a higher income) and has an

table 13-5   Occupational Rankings in Terms of Honesty and Ethical Standards

OCCUPATIONAL	1994 RANK	COMBINED PERCENT*
Druggists/pharmacist	1	61%
Clergy	2	54
Dentists	3	51
College teachers	4	50
Engineers	5	49
Medical doctors	6	47
Policemen	7	46
Funeral directors	8	31
Public opinion pollsters	9	27
Bankers	10	27
Business executives	11	22
TV reporters, commentators	12	22
Journalists	13	20
Local officeholders	14	18
Building contractors	15	17
Newspaper reporters	16	17
Lawyers	17	17
Stockbrokers	18	15
Real estate agents	19	14
Labor union leaders	20	14
State officeholders	21	12
Advertising practitioners	22	12
Senators	23	12
Insurance salesmen	24	9
Congressmen	25	10
Car salesmen	26	6

*Rank is based on the combination of "very high" and "high" rating.

Source: From *The Gallup Poll*, October 1994. Reprinted by permission.

admired or respected position (i.e., high occupational status).[3] Using United States Census data, Table 13-6 supports the close relationship between educational attainment and amount of household income.

INCOME Individual or family income is another socioeconomic variable frequently used to approximate social-class standing. Researchers who favor income as a measure of social class use either *amount* or *source* of income. Table 13-7 illustrates the types of categories used for each of these income variables.

Although income is a popular estimate of social-class standing, not all consumer researchers agree that it is an appropriate index of social class. Some argue that a blue-collar automobile mechanic and a white-collar assistant bank manager may both earn $42,000 a year, yet because of (or as a reflection of) social-class differences, each will spend that income in a different way. How they decide to spend their incomes reflects different *values*. Within this context, it is the difference in values that is an important discriminant of social class between people, not the *amount of income* they earn.

Supporting this viewpoint is the marketplace behavior of "underprivileged" upper-class and "overprivileged" middle-class American families *with the same basic annual incomes*. Specifically, overprivileged middle-class consumers can be differentiated from underprivileged upper-class consumers by their more likely ownership of such products as campers, motorboats, pickup trucks, tractor lawnmowers, and backyard swimming pools. In contrast, underprivileged upper-class consumers with the same income spend relatively greater amounts on private club memberships, special educational experiences for their children, and cultural objects and events.[4]

Further substantiating the importance of consumers' personal values, rather than amount of income, is the observation that affluence may be more a function of *attitude* or *behavior* than of income level.[5] These "attitudinally affluent" consumers represent a broad segment who do *not* have the income needed to be considered affluent in today's society, yet desire to have the best. They buy less but buy better quality, assigning priorities and gradually working their way toward having everything they want.

OTHER VARIABLES *Quality of neighborhood and dollar value of residence* are rarely used as sole measures of social class. However, they are frequently used informally to sup-

table 13-6   The Relationship Between Formal Education and Household Income

	TOTAL	NO MORE THAN ELEMENTARY SCHOOL	SOME HIGH SCHOOL	HIGH SCHOOL GRADUATE	1 TO 3 YEARS OF COLLEGE	AT LEAST 4 YEARS OF COLLEGE
ALL HOUSEHOLDS	100%	100%	100%	100%	100%	100%
Under $5,000	4.6	9.4	8.7	4.0	3.1	1.4
$5,000 to $9,999	10.0	27.7	20.1	9.3	6.4	1.9
$10,000 to $14,999	9.5	13.2	15.6	10.1	7.4	3.1
$15,000 to $24,999	16.8	21.8	22.0	19.0	16.0	8.3
$25,000 to $34,999	14.8	10.9	13.5	17.5	16.7	11.7
$35,000 to $49,000	17.1	7.5	11.6	19.0	20.5	18.4
$50,000 to $74,999	16.1	3.2	6.4	15.5	20.1	25.2
$75,000 and Over	11.0	1.3	2.1	5.6	4.9	29.9
Number of households (000's)	96,391	9,060	9,933	30,103	15,387	21,382
Median income	$30,796	$13,383	$17,375	$29,006	$35,327	$54,117

Source: U.S. Bureau of the Census, *Statistical Abstract of the United States:* 1994 (114 edition), Washington, D.C., 1994, 465.

table 13-7 Typical Categories Used for Assessing Amount or Source of Income

AMOUNT OF INCOME

Under $15,000 per year
$15,000–$24,999
$25,000–$39,999
$40,000–$49,999
$50,000–$74,999
$75,000–$99,999
$100,000–$149,999
$150,000 and over

SOURCE OF INCOME

Public welfare
Private financial assistance
Wages (hourly)
Salary (yearly)
Profits or fees
Earned wealth
Inherited wealth, interest, dividends, royalties

port or verify social-class membership assigned on the basis of occupational status or income.

Finally, *possessions* have been used by sociologists as an index of social class.[6] The best-known and most elaborate rating scheme for evaluating possessions is **Chapin's Social Status Scale**, which focuses on the presence of certain items of furniture and accessories in the living room (types of floor or floor covering, drapes, fireplace, library table, telephone, or bookcases) and the condition of the room (cleanliness, organization, or general atmosphere).[7] Conclusions are drawn about a family's social class on the basis of such observations. To illustrate how home decorations reflect social-class standing, studies reveal that lower-class families are likely to place their television sets in the living room, while middle- and upper-class families usually place their television sets in the bedroom or family room.[8] The marketing implications of such insights suggest that advertisements for television sets targeted at lower-class consumers should show the set in a living room, whereas advertisements directed to middle- or upper-class consumers should show the set in a bedroom, a family room, or a media room. Figure 13-3 on page 386 presents an ad for Bose® Acoustimass® Home Theater speakers that is aimed at upper-class consumers seeking to have a home theater system.

▲ **Composite-Variable Indexes** Composite indexes systematically combine a number of socioeconomic factors to form *one* overall measure of social-class standing. Such indexes are of interest to consumer researchers because they may better reflect the complexity of social class than single-variable indexes. For instance, research exploring consumers' perceptions of mail and phone order shopping reveals that the *higher* the socioeconomic status (in terms of a composite of income, occupational status, and education), the *more* positive the consumers' ratings of mail and phone order buying, relative to in-store shopping.[9] The research also found that downscale consumers (a low composite of three variables) were *less* positive toward magazine and catalog shopping and more positive toward

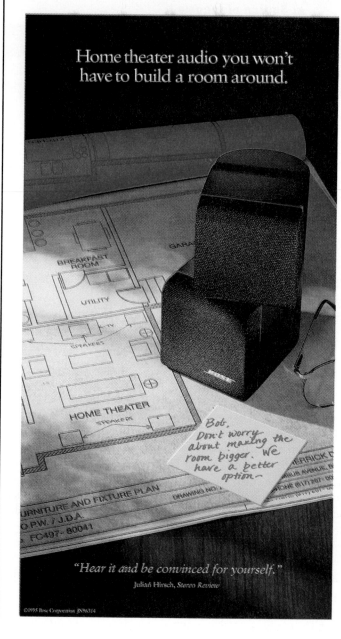

FIGURE 13-3

Targeting the Upper-Class Consumer
Courtesy of Bose Corporation

in-store shopping than more upscale socioeconomic groupings.[10] Armed with such information, retailers like K-mart, Wal-Mart, and Target that especially target their stores merchandise to working class (more downscale) consumers would have a real challenge using direct marketing catalogs and telephone selling approaches. In contrast, retailers concentrating on upscale consumers, such as Saks, have been especially effective in developing catalog programs targeted to specific segments of affluent or upscale consumers.

Several of the more important composite indexes are the **Index of Status Characteristics** and the **Socioeconomic Status Score**.

INDEX OF STATUS CHARACTERISTICS A classic composite measure of social class is Warner's Index of Status Characteristics (ISC).[11] The ISC is a weighted measure of the following socioeconomic variables: occupation, source of income (not amount of income), house type, and dwelling area (quality of neighborhood).

SOCIOECONOMIC STATUS SCORES The United States Bureau of the Census developed the Socioeconomic Status Score (SES), which combines three basic socioeconomic variables: occupation, family income, and educational attainment.[12]

Table 13-8 summarizes the variables included in the Index of Status Characteristics and the SES.

Lifestyle Profiles of the Social Classes

Consumer research has found evidence that within each of the social classes, there is a constellation of specific **lifestyle factors** (shared beliefs, attitudes, activities, and behaviors) that tend to distinguish the members of each class from the members of all other social classes.

To capture the lifestyle composition of the various social-class groupings, Table 13-9 on page 388 presents a consolidated portrait, pieced together from numerous sources, of the members of the following six social classes: upper-upper class, lower-upper class, upper-middle class, lower-middle class, upper-lower class, and lower-lower class. Each of these profiles is only a *generalized* picture of the class. People in any class may possess values, attitudes, and behavioral patterns that are a hybrid of two or more classes.

Lifestyle differences should be considered when choosing appropriate appeals to communicate with the core members of any social-class group. For example, Table 13-10 on page 389 provides lifestyle information regarding consumers 65 years and over, with annual incomes of at least $75,000. It shows that, compared with national averages, these affluent older consumers are three times more likely to own a vacation home, take more than three times as many foreign trips, are nearly twice as involved in news and current

table 13-8 Two Composite Measures of Social Class

COMPOSITE INDEX	VARIABLES	WEIGHT
Index of Status Characteristics (ISC)[a]	Occupation Source of income House type Dwelling area	.4 .3 .2 .1
Socioeconomic Status Score (SES)[b]	Occupation Family income Education	

Sources:

[a] W. LLOYD WARNER et al., *Social Class in America: A Manual of Procedure for the Measurement of Social Status* (New York: Harper & Row, 1960), 123.

[b] *Methodology and Scores of Socioeconomic Status*, Working Paper No. 15 (Washington, DC: U.S. Bureau of the Census, 1963).

table 13-9   Social Class Profiles

THE UPPER-UPPER CLASS—COUNTRY CLUB ESTABLISHMENT

- Small number of well-established families
- Belong to best country clubs and sponsor major charity events
- Serve as trustees for local colleges and hospitals
- Prominent physicians and lawyers
- May be heads of major financial institutions, owners of major long-established firms
- Accustomed to wealth, so do not spend money conspicuously

THE LOWER-UPPER CLASS—NEW WEALTH

- Not quite accepted by the upper crust of society
- Represent "new money"
- Successful business executives
- Conspicuous users of their new wealth

THE UPPER-MIDDLE CLASS—ACHIEVING PROFESSIONALS

- Have neither family status nor unusual wealth
- Career-oriented
- Young successful professionals, corporate managers, and business owners
- Most are college graduates, many with advanced degrees
- Active in professional, community, and social activities
- Have a keen interest in obtaining the "better things in life"
- Their homes serve as symbols of their achievements
- Consumption is often conspicuous
- Very child-oriented

THE LOWER-MIDDLE CLASS—FAITHFUL FOLLOWERS

- Primarily nonmanagerial white-collar workers and highly paid blue-collar workers
- Want to achieve "respectability" and be accepted as good citizens
- Want their children to be well-behaved
- Tend to be churchgoers and are often involved in church-sponsored activities
- Prefer a neat and clean appearance and tend to avoid faddish or highly-styled clothing
- Constitute a major market for do-it-yourself products

THE UPPER-LOWER CLASS—SECURITY-MINDED MAJORITY

- The largest social class segment
- Solidly blue collar
- Strive for security (sometimes gained from union membership)
- View work as a means to "buy" enjoyment
- Want children to behave properly
- High wage earners in this group may spend impulsively
- Interested in items that enhance their leisure time (e.g., TV sets, hunting equipment)
- Husbands typically have a strong "macho" self-image
- Males are sports fans, heavy smokers, beer drinkers

THE LOWER-LOWER CLASS—ROCK BOTTOM

- Poorly educated, unskilled laborers
- Often out of work
- Children are often poorly treated
- Tend to live a day-to-day existence

table 13-10   Segment Profile: 65 Years and Over, Income $75,000 Plus

THE TOP TEN LIFESTYLES RANKED BY INDEX

Stock/Bond Investments	317
Supports Health Charities	235
Own a Vacation Home/Property	313
Grandchildren	220
Real Estate Investments	313
Military Veteran in Household	210
Foreign Travel	308
Current Affairs/Politics	196
Frequent Flyer	237
Attend Cultural/Arts Events	186

HOMELIFE

	HOUSEHOLDS	%	INDEX
Avid Book Reading	578,931	49.5	131
Bible/Devotional Reading	166,083	14.2	73
Gardening	472,518	40.4	124
Grandchildren	598,834	51.2	220
Home Furnishing/Decorating	208,188	17.8	88
House Plants	402,342	34.4	106
Own a Cat	182,457	15.6	59
Own a Dog	258,481	22.1	65
Subscribe to Cable TV	866,672	74.1	115
Vegetable Gardening	236,259	20.2	91

GOOD LIFE

	HOUSEHOLDS	%	INDEX
Attend Cultural/Arts Events	302,926	25.9	186
Fashion Clothing	134,504	11.5	89
Fine Art/Antiques	191,814	16.4	159
Foreign Travel	504,097	43.1	308
Frequent Flyer	592,986	50.7	237
Gourmet Cooking/Fine Foods	264,329	22.5	135
Own a Vacation Home/Property	391,815	33.5	313
Travel for Business	294,739	25.2	127
Travel for Pleasure/Vacation	642,109	54.9	146
Travel in USA	533,922	54.2	157
Wines	237,428	20.3	168

INVESTING & MONEY

	HOUSEHOLDS	%	INDEX
Casino Gambling	125,147	10.7	88
Entering Sweepstakes	123,977	10.6	78
Moneymaking Opportunities	147,389	12.6	109
Real Estate Investments	223,393	19.1	313
Stock/Bond Investments	587,665	51.1	317

GREAT OUTDOORS

	HOUSEHOLDS	%	INDEX
Boating/Sailing	171,931	14.7	141
Camping/Hiking	91,229	7.8	34
Fishing Frequently	189,475	16.2	70
Hunting/Shooting	99,416	8.5	56
Motorcycles	24,562	2.1	28
Recreational Vehicles	79,533	6.8	82
Wildlife/Environmental	187,136	16.0	99

SPORTS, FITNESS & HEALTH

	HOUSEHOLDS	%	INDEX
Bicycling Frequently	130,995	11.2	67
Dieting/Weight Control	246,785	21.1	103
Golf	419,886	35.9	183
Health/Natural Foods	164,913	14.1	82
Improving Your Health	295,908	25.3	105
Physical Fitness/Exercise	439,769	37.6	110
Running/Jogging	85,381	7.3	65
Snow Skiing Frequently	60,819	3.2	73
Tennis Frequently	114,821	9.8	181
Walking for Health	549,711	47.0	138
Watching Sports on TV	501,758	42.9	113

HOBBIES & INTERESTS

	HOUSEHOLDS	%	INDEX
Automotive Work	66,667	5.7	38
Buy Prerecoded Videos	134,504	11.5	64
Career-Oriented Activities	71,345	6.1	66
Coin/Stamp Collecting	94,737	8.1	119
Collectibles/Collections	115,790	9.9	87
Crafts	181,288	15.5	87
Current Affairs/Politics	364,915	31.2	196
Home Workshop	275,025	23.6	93
Military Veteran in Household	508,191	52.0	210
Needlework/Knitting	185,966	15.9	97
Our Nation's Heritage	87,720	7.5	150
Self-Improvement	163,744	14.0	75
Sewing	164,913	14.1	77
Supports Health Charities	425,734	36.4	235

HIGH-TECH ACTIVITIES

	HOUSEHOLDS	%	INDEX
Electronics	93,568	8.0	71
Home Video Games	31,579	2.7	23
Listen to Records/Tapes/CDs	494,740	2.3	84
Own a CD Player	704,088	80.2	107
Photography	261,990	22.4	125
Science Fiction	43,275	3.7	40
Science/New Technology	108,773	9.3	104
Use a Personal Computer	479,535	41.0	103
Use an Apple/Macintosh	118,129	10.1	111
Use an IBM Compatible	389,476	33.3	99
VCR Recording	150,878	12.9	70

Source: From the *Lifestyle Market Analyst* 1996. Data provided by National Demographics and Lifestyles. Published by SRDS. Copyright © 1996 by SRDS. Reprinted with permission.

affairs, and are wine, tennis, and golf enthusiasts. The table also indicates other types of lifestyle activities valued by these older affluent consumers.

Social Class Mobility

Social class membership in the United States is not so hard and fixed as it is in some other countries and cultures. While individuals can move either up or down in social-class standing from the class position held by their parents, American's have primarily thought in terms of *upward mobility* because of the availability of free education and opportunities for self-development and self-advancement. Indeed, the classic Horatio Alger tale of a penniless young orphan who managed to achieve great success in business and in life is depicted over and over again in American novels, movies, and television shows. Today, many young men and women with ambition to get ahead dream of going to college and eventually starting their own successful businesses.

Because upward mobility has commonly been attainable in American society, the higher social classes often become reference groups for ambitious men and women of lower social status. Familiar examples of upward mobility are: the new management trainee who strives to dress like the boss; the middle manager who aspires to belong to the status country club; the graduate of a municipal college who wants to send his daughter to Princeton. The ad for Ranger Rover in Figure 13-4 is targeted to upwardly mobile individuals striving to express their status attainment. The appeal of the headline "Sometimes more is more" and the beautiful home and outdoors surroundings are additional clues to the status appeal.

Recognizing that individuals often aspire to the lifestyle and possessions enjoyed by members of a higher social class, marketers frequently incorporate the symbols of higher-class membership, both as products and props in advertisements targeted to lower social-class audiences. For example, ads often present or display marketers' products within an upper-class setting: the products are displayed in front of a fireplace with a beautiful mantle (a board game), being shown on the desk of an elegantly appointed executive office (a new desktop computer), shown being consumed by fashionably (European) dressed models (a domestic wine), shown appearing on an exquisitely set dining-room table (a bottle of jam), and shown parked outside of a famous restaurant (a new model automobile).

Another characteristic of social-class mobility is that products and services traditionally within the realm of one social class may filter down to lower social classes. For instance, plastic surgery was once affordable only for movie stars and other wealthy consumers. Today, however, consumers of all economic strata undergo cosmetic procedures.

Signs of Downward Mobility

All is not bright with regard to social mobility. Although the United States is frequently associated with **upward mobility**, because it was the rule for much of its history, there now are strong signs of some **downward mobility**. Social commentators have suggested that *some* young adults (e.g., members of the X-Generation described in Chapter 15) are not only likely to find it very difficult to "do better" than their parents (better jobs, own homes, more disposable income, more savings) but may not even do as well as their parents. For instance, many recent college graduates are finding it painfully difficult to secure good-paying, entry-level jobs in their chosen areas of study.

There is further evidence of a slide in social class mobility. Defining middle-class as households having an after-tax income between $24,000 and $72,000, researchers found

FIGURE 13-4 ▼ Appeal to Upward Mobility
Courtesy of Range Rover

Sometimes more is more.

Introducing an exceptional argument against the age-old rule that less is more.

The new Range Rover 4.0 SE, a vehicle unlike any other.

Because while its performance rivals the worthiest European road sedans', the Range Rover leaves them behind in a host of other areas.

Like passenger room, cargo space, and the mountains of Chile.

As if that weren't enough, it's been polished, plushed, and primped with every amenity from burl walnut trim to dual electronic climate controls–with pollen filters. There are even

 **RANGE ROVER**

individually heated front seats.

What's more, it comes complete with electronic traction control. Dual airbags. All-terrain ABS. And electronic air suspension.

So why not call 1-800-FINE 4WD for the dealer nearest you?

Of course, $54,000* isn't inexpensive.

But then again, no other vehicle has everything you'd ever want.

And more.

Always use your seatbelts. SRS/airbags alone do not provide sufficient protection.

that the chance of becoming either affluent or poor has increased, whereas the chance of staying middle-class has been declining.[13] Moreover, the same research indicates that the odds that young men's income will reach middle-class levels by the time they reach their thirtieth birthday has also been declining. Somewhat unexpectedly, this regressive pattern holds true, regardless of race, parents' income, and young persons' educational level.

GEODEMOGRAPHIC CLUSTERING

In recent years, traditional social-class measures have been enhanced by the linkage of geographic and socioeconomic consumer data to create more powerful geodemographic clusters. The underlying rationale for **geodemographic clustering** is that "birds of a feather flock together."

One of the most popular clustering services is **PRIZM**, which identifies a variety of socioeconomic and demographic factors (education, income, occupation, family life cycle, ethnicity, housing, and urbanization) drawn from United States Census data. This material is combined with survey and panel data on actual consumer behavior (e.g., product purchase and usage, mail-order buying, and media-exposure habits) to locate concentrations of consumers with similar characteristics.

PRIZM assigns every one of the United States micro-neighborhoods (zip code + 4 areas) to one of 62 PRIZM clusters (see Table 13-11). To make its clusters simpler to deal with, PRIZM has collapsed 62 clusters into 15 groups (S1 through R3, as shown in Table 13-11). Marketers can superimpose these geodemographic clusters onto a host of product and service usage data, media-exposure data, and lifestyle data (such as VALS, discussed in Chapter 5) to create a sharp, refined picture of their target markets. To illustrate, Table 13-12 on page 395 presents a lifestyle comparison of two PRIZM clusters, *Young Literati* and *Boomer & Babies*. Although their age ranges are very similar (concentrated in 25 to 34 and 35 to 44 age groupings), these two clusters appear quite different. For example, while *Young Literati* are more likely to be single, rent foreign videos, attend live theater, drive an Audi, and eat Quaker Puffed Rice, *Boomers & Babies* are more likely to be married, own tropical fish, visit Sea World, drive a Volvo, and eat Kellogg's Fruit Loops.

THE AFFLUENT CONSUMER

Affluent households constitute an especially attractive target segment because its members have incomes that provide them with a disproportionately larger share of all discretionary income—the "extras" that allow the purchase of luxury cruises, foreign sports cars, time-sharing ski-resort condos, fine jewelry, and surfing on the Internet. For instance, the average income of all American households is $42,000, whereas the average income of Internet using households is $67,000.[14]

For almost 20 years, Mendelsohn Media Research has conducted an annual study of the *affluent* market (currently defined as $70,000-plus in household income). While it consists of only 23 percent of all households, this upscale market segment consumed more wine (i.e., 6.1 drinks per adult), more domestic airline flights (i.e., 6.4 roundtrip per adult), and more car rentals (i.e., 4.8 car rentals per adult) than nonaffluent households. The average household income for these consumers is $113,300, and 68 percent are employed in either a professional or managerial capacity.[15] Table 13-13 on page 396 presents additional information about the total and per-household expenditures for various items by *affluent* consumers. Table 13-14 presents several other consumption-related comparisons between

table 13-11 An Overview of the 62 PRIZM Clusters

GROUP CODES	NUMBER	NICKNAMES	PERCENT OF UNITED STATES HOUSEHOLDS	MEDIAN HOUSEHOLD INCOME
S1 Elite Suburbs	01	Blue Blood Estates	0.8	$113,000
	02	Winner's Circle	1.9	80,600
	03	Executive Suites	1.2	58,000
	04	Pools & Patios	1.9	57,800
	05	Kids & Cul-de-Sacs	3.0	61,600
U1 Urban Uptown	06	Urban Gold Coast	0.5	59,300
	07	Money & Brains	1.1	59,000
	08	Young Literati	1.0	52,100
	09	American Dreams	1.4	51,700
	10	Bohemian Mix	1.7	33,700
C1 2nd City	11	Second City Elite	1.7	58,800
	12	Upward Bound	2.0	54,500
	13	Gray Power	2.0	36,000
T1 Landed Gentry	14	Country Squires	1.0	75,600
	15	God's Country	2.7	57,500
	16	Big Fish, Small Pond	1.9	46,000
	17	Greenbelt Families	0.9	46,700
S2 The Affluentials	18	Young Influentials	1.1	44,100
	19	New Empty Nests	1.8	45,100
	20	Boomers & Babies	1.3	46,000
	21	Suburban Sprawl	1.8	41,000
	22	Blue-Chip Blues	2.2	41,700
S3 Inner Suburbs	23	Upstarts & Seniors	1.2	31,800
	24	New Beginnings	1.4	31,400
	25	Mobility Blues	1.6	30,900
	26	Gray Collars	2.1	31,400
U2 Urban Midscale	27	Urban Achievers	1.6	35,600
	28	Big City Blend	1.0	35,500
	29	Old Yankee Rows	1.4	31,500
	30	Mid-City Mix	1.3	31,400
	31	Latino America	1.3	30,100
C2 2nd City Centers	32	Middleburg Managers	1.5	37,800
	33	Boomtown Singles	1.2	32,000
	34	Starter Families	1.6	32,200
	35	Sunset City Blues	1.8	31,400
	36	Towns & Gowns	1.4	18,600
T2 Exurban Blues	37	New Homesteaders	2.0	36,800
	38	Middle America	1.3	37,300
	39	Red, White, & Blues	2.3	34,000
	40	Military Quarters	0.5	29,200

(Continued)

table 13-11 (Continued)

GROUP CODES	NUMBER	NICKNAMES	PERCENT OF UNITED STATES HOUSEHOLDS	MEDIAN HOUSEHOLD INCOME
R1 Country Families	41	Big Sky Families	1.5	45,200
	42	New Eco-topia	1.0	35,300
	43	River City, USA	2.0	35,700
	44	Shotguns & Pickups	1.6	33,300
U3 Urban Cores	45	Single City Blues	1.7	19,600
	46	Hispanic Mix	1.4	17,600
	47	Inner Cities	2.1	15,000
C3 2nd City Blues	48	Smalltown Downtown	1.9	21,500
	49	Hometown Retired	1.3	18,000
	50	Family Scramble	2.0	19,400
	51	Southside City	2.0	15,800
T3 Working Towns	52	Golden Ponds	2.0	26,000
	53	Rural Industria	1.6	26,000
	54	Norma Rae-ville	1.4	19,400
	55	Mines & Mills	2.0	19,600
R2 The Heartlanders	56	Agri-Business	1.7	32,300
	57	Grain Belt	2.0	22,600
R3 Rustic Living	58	Blue Highways	2.2	27,000
	59	Rustic Elders	1.9	25,200
	60	Back Country Folks	1.8	25,600
	61	Scrub Pine Flats	1.5	21,600
	62	Hard Scrabble	2.0	17,400

Source: Courtesy of Claritas Inc. (PRIZM and 62 Cluster nicknames are registered trademark of Claritas Inc.) Reprinted by permission.

affluent and average United States households. An examination of these tables explains why marketers are eager to target affluent consumers.

The Media Exposure of the Affluent Consumer

As might be expected, the media habits of the affluent differ from those of the general population.[16] For example, those households earning more than $70,000 a year view less TV per day than less affluent households. A profile of the media habits of $70,000-plus affluent adult householders shows they read 7.2 magazines; they listen to 85.0 hours of radio and watch 23.4 hours of TV per week; and 78.6 percent subscribe to cable TV. Magazines that cater to the tastes and interests of the affluent include *Architectural Digest*, *Avenue*, *Gourmet*, *Southern Accents*, and *Town & Country*.

Segmenting the Affluent Market

The affluent market is not one single market. Contrary to popular stereotypes, the wealth in America is not found only behind "the tall, cloistered walls of suburban country clubs."[17]

table 13-12
A Comparison of TWO PRIZM Clusters: "Young Literati" (Cluster 08) and "Boomers & Babies" (Cluster 20)

"YOUNG LITERATI" (CLUSTER 08)		"BOOMERS & BABIES" (CLUSTER 20)	
1.0% OF U.S. HOUSEHOLDS		**1.3% OF U.S. HOUSEHOLDS**	
Predominant age range	25–34, 35–44	Predominant age range	25–34, 35–44
Median household income	$52,100	Median household income	$46,000
Housing type	Owner and renter apartment	Housing type	Owner/single unit
Median home value	$245,200	Median home value	$97,200
Family type: single	56.8%	Family type: married couples w/child	24%
College/graduate education	45.6%	College/graduate education	22%
Professional/manager	45.6%	Professional/manager	28%

LIFESTYLE	**LIFESTYLE**
Rent foreign videos	Visit Sea World
Travel to Japan, Asia	Join a health club/gym
Go jogging	Own tropical fish
Spend $60-plus dry cleaning	Go roller skating
Attend live theater	Go jogging

PRODUCTS AND SERVICES	**PRODUCTS AND SERVICES**
Have travel insurance	Have a first mortgage loan
Own state/local government bonds	Have a noninterest checking account
Own tax exempt funds	Have a personal education loan
Use an ATM card	Use an ATM card
Own stocks valued $10,000-plus	Own stock valued less than $10,000
Own an Audi/Volkswagen	Own a Volkswagen/Volvo
Use olive oil	Use Polaroid instant film
Buy Quaker Puffed Rice	Eat Kelloggs Fruit Loops

RADIO/TV	**RADIO/TV**
Listen to progressive rock radio	Listen to variety radio
Watch The Travel Channel	Watch Nickleodeon
Listen to soft contemporary radio	Listen to jazz radio
Watch BET	Watch Married With Children
Watch Lehrer News Hour	Watch MTV

PRINT	**PRINT**
Read newspaper business section	Read Sunset
Read Self	Read newspaper home and garden section
Read Metropolitan Home	Read Seventeen Magazine
Read newspaper style/fashion section	Read Parent's Magazine
Read Rolling Stone	Read Working Mother
Read Elle	Read Baby Talk
Read GQ	Read Personal Computing

Source: Courtesy of Claritas Inc. (PRIZM and 62 Cluster nicknames are registered trademark of Claritas Inc.) Reprinted by permission.

Wealth is spread among niches, including Asian immigrants, single women, and young Cuban-Americans, to name a few.

Because not all affluent consumers share the same lifestyles (i.e., activities, interests, and opinions), various marketers have tried to isolate meaningful segments of the affluent

table 13-13 — Total Affluent Household Expenditures 1995

	TOTAL AFFLUENT HOUSEHOLD EXPENDITURES (IN MILLIONS)	EXPENDITURES PER PURCHASING AFFLUENT HOUSEHOLDS
Home furnishings	$36,453	$2,841
Personal computers for (non-laptop) business or personal home use, excluding software	11,916	2,416
Household or kitchen appliances	7,440	919
Jewelry	8,661	960
Photographic equipment	2,358	186
Cosmetics and fragrances	3,427	245
Women's apparel	17,082	1,208
Men's apparel	14,606	1,030
Children's apparel	4,467	487
Sports/athletic equipment/home fitness equipment	4,530	466
Artwork and collectibles	7,046	1,274

Source: 1995 *Mendelsohn Affluent Survey* (New York: Mendelsohn Media Research, Inc., 1995).

table 13-14 — The Attractiveness of the Affluent Market

	TOTAL (000'S)			UNDER $40,000 INCOME (000'S)			$40,000–$59,999 INCOME (000'S)			$60,000–$74,999 INCOME (000'S)			$75,000+ INCOME (000'S)		
	HOUSE	%	INDEX	HOUSE	%	INDEX	HOUSE	%	INDEX	HOUSE	%	INDEX	HOUSE	%	INDEX
	190,553	100.00		102,765			39,243			18,256			30,289		
Drink imported wines	27,034	100.00	100	8,750	32.37	60	5,704	21.10	102	3,788	14.01	146	8,792	32.52	205
Stereo/radio equipment/ systems (ever bought)	139,513	100.00	100	67,722	48.54	90	31,829	22.81	111	15,060	10.79	113	24,902	17.85	112
Currently enrolled in frequent-flyer program	29,852	100.00	100	7,009	23.48	44	5,924	19.84	96	4,274	14.32	149	12,644	42.36	266
Total rent cars	33,786	100.00	100	9,568	28.32	53	7,848	23.23	113	4,817	14.26	149	11,554	34.20	215
Own electric	60,497	100.00	100	23,906	39.52	73	14,622	24.17	117	7,784	12.87	134	14,185	23.45	148
Own VCR (one or more)	168,258	100.00	100	85,823	51.01	95	36,129	21.47	104	17,422	10.35	108	28,884	17.17	108
Own a video camera/ camcorder	48,968	100.00	100	16,390	33.47	62	12,485	25.50	124	7,256	14.82	155	12,837	26.22	165

Source: Based on Simmons Choices Systems, Simmons Market Research Bureau. Reprinted by permission of Simmons Study of Media and Market, 1995.

market. To assist the many marketers interested in reaching subsegments of the affluent market, Mediamark Research, Inc. (MRI), has developed the following affluent market-segmentation schema (defined as the top 10 percent of households in terms of income).[18]

1. Well-feathered nests. *Households that have at least one high-income earner and children present.*

2. No strings attached. *Households that have at least one high-income earner and no children.*

3. Nanny's in charge. *Households that have two or more earners, none earning high incomes, and children present.*

4. Two careers. *Households that have two or more earners, neither earning high incomes, and no children present.*

5. The good life. *Households that have a high degree of affluence with no person employed or with the head of household not employed.*

Armed with such **affluent lifestyle** segments, MRI provides subscribing firms with profiles of users of a variety of goods and services frequently targeted to the affluent consumer (e.g., domestic and foreign travel, leisure clothing, lawn-care services, rental cars, and various types of recreational activities). For instance, in terms of recreation, the *well-feathered nester* can be found on the tennis court, the *good lifer* may be playing golf, while the *two-career* couple may be off sailing.[19]

With few local marketers vying for their business, **the rural affluent** represent an untapped (and somewhat difficult to pinpoint) subsegment of the affluent market. The rural affluent fall into four categories:[20]

1. Suburban transplants. *Those who move to the country but still commute to a high-paying urban job.*

2. Equity-rich suburban expatriates. *Urbanites who sell their homes for a huge profit, buy a far less expensive home in a small town, and live off the difference.*

3. City folks with country homes. *Wealthy snowbirds and vacationers who spend winters or summers in scenic rural areas, especially mountainous and coastal areas.*

4. Wealthy landowners. *Wealthy farmers and other natives who make a comfortable living off the land.*

THE NONAFFLUENT CONSUMER

Although many advertisers would prefer to show their products as part of an affluent lifestyle, blue-collar and other nonprofessional people represent a vast group of consumers that marketers cannot ignore. In fact, households earning $34,000 or less control more than 30 percent of the total income in the United States. Lower-income or **"downscale" consumers** (frequently defined as having household incomes of $30,000 or less) may actually be more brand loyal than wealthier consumers, because they can ill afford to make mistakes by switching to unfamiliar brands. They also are more likely to be either younger or older than upscale consumers, as well as single or divorced.[21]

Understanding the importance of speaking *to* (not *at*) the downscale consumers, companies such as MasterCard and McDonald's target "average Joes" (and Janes), with ads reflecting the modest lifestyles of some of their customers.[22]

Selected Consumer Behavior Applications of Social Class

Social class profiles provide a broad picture of the values, attitudes, and behavior that distinguish the members of various social classes. This section focuses on specific consumer research that relates social class to the development of marketing strategy.

Clothing, Fashion, and Shopping

A Greek philosopher once said, "Know, first, who you are; and then adorn yourself accordingly."[23] This bit of wisdom is relevant to clothing marketers today, because most people dress to fit their self-images, which include their perceptions of their own social-class membership.

Members of specific social classes differ in terms of what they consider fashionable or in good taste. For instance, lower middle-class consumers have a strong preference for T-shirts, caps, and other clothing that offer an external point of identification, such as the name of an admired person or group (e.g., Elizabeth Taylor), a respected company or brand name (Heineken), or a valued trademark (Nike). These consumers are prime targets for licensed goods. In contrast, upper-class consumers are likely to buy clothing that is free from such supporting associations. Upper-class consumers also seek clothing with a more subtle look, such as the kind of sportswear found in an L.L. Bean catalog, rather than designer jeans. More research is needed to examine the relationship between various appearance-related purchase behaviors and social-class membership.

Social class is also an important variable in determining where a consumer shops. People tend to avoid stores that have the image of appealing to a social class very different from their own. In the past, some mass merchandisers who tried to appeal to a higher class of consumers found themselves alienating their traditional customers. This implies that retailers should pay attention to the social class of their customer base and the social class of their store appeal to ensure that they send the appropriate message through advertising. For instance, the Gap has rapidly rolling-out the Old Navy Clothing stores in an effort to attract working class families who normally purchase their casual and active wear clothing from general merchandise retailers like Kmart, Wal-Mart, or Target.

The Pursuit of Leisure

Social-class membership is also closely related to the choice of recreational and leisure-time activities. For instance, upper-class consumers are likely to attend the theater and concerts, to play bridge, and to attend college football games. Lower-class consumers tend to be avid television watchers and fishing enthusiasts, and they enjoy drive-in movies and baseball games. Furthermore, the lower-class consumer spends more time on commercial types of activities (bowling, playing pool or billiards, or visiting taverns) and craft activities (model building, painting, and woodworking projects), rather than cerebral activities (e.g., reading, visiting museums).

Saving, Spending, and Credit

Saving, spending, and credit-card usage all seem to be related to social-class standing. Upper-class consumers are more future-oriented and confident of their financial acumen;

they are more willing to invest in insurance, stocks, and real estate. In comparison, lower-class consumers are generally more concerned with immediate gratification; when they do save, they are primarily interested in safety and security. Therefore, it is not surprising that when it comes to bank credit-card usage, members of the lower social classes tend to use their bank credit cards for installment purchases, while members of the upper social classes pay their credit card bills in full each month. In other words, lower-class purchasers tend to use their credit cards to "buy now and pay later" for things they might not otherwise be able to afford, while upper-class purchasers use their credit cards as a convenient substitute for cash.

Social Class and Communication

Social class groupings differ in terms of their *media* habits and in how they transmit and receive communications. Knowledge of these differences is invaluable to marketers who segment their markets on the basis of social class.

When it comes to describing their world, lower-class consumers tend to portray it in rather personal and concrete terms, while middle-class consumers are able to describe their experiences from a number of different perspectives. A simple example illustrates that members of different social classes tend to see the world differently. The following responses to a question asking where the respondent usually purchases gasoline were received:

Upper-middle-class answer: At Mobil or Shell.

Lower-middle-class answer: At the station on Main and Fifth Street.

Lower-class answer: At Ed's.

Such variations in response indicate that middle-class consumers have a broader or more general view of the world, while lower-class consumers tend to see the world through their own immediate experiences.

Regional differences in terminology, choice of words and phrases, and patterns of usage also tend to increase as we move down the social-class ladder. Therefore, in creating messages targeted to the lower classes, marketers try to word advertisements to reflect particular regional preferences that exist (e.g., "soda" is "pop" in the Midwest).

Selective exposure to various types of mass media differs by social class. In the selection of specific television programs and program types, higher-social-class members tend to prefer current events and drama, while lower-class individuals tend to prefer soap operas, quiz shows, and situation comedies. Higher-class consumers tend to have greater exposure to magazines and newspapers than do their lower-class counterparts. Lower-class consumers are likely to have greater exposure to publications that dramatize romance and the lifestyles of movie and television celebrities. For example, magazines such as *True Story* appeal heavily to blue-collar or working-class women ("Middle America") who enjoy reading about the problems, fame, and fortunes of others. Notice that in Table 13-4, *True Story* readers had the lowest median household income of all the publications listed. Figure 13-5 on page 400 presents an ad offering marketers the opportunity to rent lists of subscribers to *True Story*. Many magazines appealing to both upscale and downscale audiences rent lists of their subscribers to marketers of products and services interested in reaching specific demographic-lifestyle audiences.

A Woman's Audience *with* Unlimited Money Making Potential!

TRUE STORY

525,524 Current Active Subscribers
40,339 (30-Day) HOT LINE Subscribers
110,959 (60-Day) HOT LINE Subscribers
151,636 (90-Day) HOT LINE Subscribers
5,158 Canadian Subscribers
5,633 Monthly Changes of Address

COMPLETE WITH DEMOGRAPHIC ENHANCEMENTS

True Story magazine is a favorite of aware home and family minded women from coast-to-coast. If your offer is designed for home makers with children—here's *your* list!

Published monthly, *True Story* is a full-service periodical written with the active homemaker in mind. Each information-packed issue is brimming with articles on children...cooking...household hints...crafts...and much more. A one-year subscription is invoiced at $14.95.

A Classic "Middle America" Audience!

Eighty-five percent women, the typical *True Story* subscriber has a median age of 33, 56.1% are married, 54.8% have two or more children, an average household income of $23,000 and 82.3% are homemakers.

Selects To Zero-In On Your Precise Market Segment!

You can reach your best prospects with some very valuable demographic overlays. For instance, you can break-out these choice responders by such data elements as Age... Income...Marital Status...Presence of Children...Home Ownership...Length of Residence...Credit Card Users... Telephone Numbers...and more.

The List Synonymous with Mail Order Buying Women!

Books and magazines, continuity programs, apparel, domestics, kitchen conveniences, recipes, jewelry, cosmetics, diet aids, children's indulgences, credit cards, insurance, housewares, collectibles, mid-ticket gift and general merchandise catalogs, cards and stationery, and the full range of home and family goods and services are just few of the offers for which *True Story* is a must.

HE CALLS IT LOVEMAKING—I CALL IT RAPE!

TRUE STORY
For Today's Woman

Truth Is Stranger Than Fiction
THE LITTLE GIRL WHO WAS BORN A BOY!

I SLEEP WITH MY HUSBAND, BUT HAVE SEX WITH HIS BROTHER!

MY SON WAS SHOT ON HALLOWEEN!
Trick-or-Treat Nightmare

Birth Mother:
WHY WON'T SHE LOVE ME?

My Ex-lover's Chilling Confession:
"I HAVE AIDS!"

Beauty Exclusive!
PUT ON A PRETTY FALL FACE
Our Easy Tips Show You How!

Without question *True Story* is one of the best all-around women's mailing lists available. Here's the eager responders you've looking for...so order your tests today!

IMMEDIATE GRATIFICATION INFORMATION REQUEST
Simply **FAX** this form to **212-388-8890**

SK **STEVENS·KNOX** LIST MANAGEMENT
304 Park Avenue South
New York, NY 10010
Phone (212) 388-8800 • Fax (212) 388-8890

☐ Yes! I want to know more about these mail responsive homemakers. Please rush me the latest **True Story** data card.

☐ I have an IBM-compatible PC with Windows†. Please send me a copy of the **Listkette™ Recco System**...A quick, easy-to-use computerized reference guide to America's most useful & responsive mailing lists.

Name_____
Title _____
Firm _____
Address _____
City _____ State _____ Zip_____
Phone (_____) _____

summary

Social stratification, the division of members of a society into a hierarchy of distinct social classes, exists in all societies and cultures. Social class usually is defined by the amount of status that members of a specific class possess in relation to members of other classes. Social-class membership often serves as a frame of reference (a reference group) for the development of consumer attitudes and behavior.

The measurement of social class is concerned with classifying individuals into social-class groupings. These groupings are of particular value to marketers, who use social classification as an effective means of identifying and segmenting target markets. There are three basic methods for measuring social class: subjective measurement, reputational measurement, and objective measurement. Subjective measures rely on an individual's self-perception; reputational measures rely on an individual's perceptions of others; and objective measures use specific socioeconomic measures, either alone (as a single-variable index) or in combination with others (as a composite-variable index). Composite-variable indexes, such as the Index of Status Characteristics and the Socioeconomic Status Score, combine a number of socioeconomic factors to form one overall measure of social-class standing.

Class structures range from two-class to nine-class systems. A frequently used classification system consists of six classes: upper-upper, lower-upper, upper-middle, lower-middle, upper-lower, and lower-lower. Profiles of these classes indicate that the socioeconomic differences between classes are reflected in differences in attitudes, in leisure activities, and in consumption habits. This is why segmentation by social class is of special interest to marketers.

In recent years, some marketers have turned to geodemographic clustering as an alternative to a strict social-class typology. Geodemographic clustering is a technique that combines geographic and socioeconomic factors to locate concentrations of consumers with particular characteristics. Particular attention currently is being directed to affluent consumers, who represent the fastest-growing segment in our population.

Research has revealed social-class differences in clothing habits, home decoration, and leisure activities, as well as saving, spending, and credit habits. Thus, astute marketers tailor specific product and promotional strategies to each social-class target segment.

discussion questions

1. Marketing researchers generally use the objective method to measure social class, rather than the subjective or reputational methods. Why is the objective method preferred by researchers?

2. Under what circumstances would you expect income to be a better predictor of consumer behavior than a composite measure of social class (e.g., based on income, education, and occupation)? When would you expect the composite social-class measure to be superior?

3. Describe the correlation between social status (or prestige) and income. Which is a more useful segmentation variable? Discuss.

4. Which status-related variable, occupation, education or income, is the most appropriate segmentation base for: (a) expensive vacations, (b) opera subscriptions, (c) *People* magazine subscriptions, (d) fat-free foods, (e) personal computers, (f) pocket-size cellular telephones, and (g) health clubs?

5. Consider the Rolex watch, which has a retail price range starting at about $2000 for a stainless-steel model to thousands of dollars for a solid-gold model. How might the Rolex company use geodemographic clustering in its marketing efforts?

6. How would you use the research evidence on affluent households presented in this chapter to segment the market for: (a) home exercise equipment, (b) vacations, and (c) banking services?

7. How can a marketer use knowledge of consumer behavior to develop financial services for affluent consumers? For "downscale" consumers?

8. You are the owner of two furniture stores, one catering to upper-middle-class consumers and the other to lower-class consumers. How do social-class differences influence each store's: (a) product lines and styles, (b) advertising media selection, (c) the copy and communications style used in the ads, and (d) payment policies?

exercises

1. Copy the list of occupations in Table 13-5 and ask students majoring in areas other than marketing (both business and nonbusiness) to rank the relative prestige of these occupations. Are any differences in the rankings related to the students' majors? Explain.

2. At this point in the semester, you probably know your professors quite well. Using the Index of Status Characteristics (Table 13-8) and the information in Tables 13-5 and 13-6, compute social-class scores for your professor in this class and another professor whose course you are presently taking. Ask several classmates to do so as well.

Compare your scores with the other students' scores and explain any differences you found.

3. Find three print ads in one of the publications listed in Table 13-4. Using the social-class characteristics listed in Table 13-9, identify the social class targeted by each ad and evaluate the effectiveness of the advertising appeals used.

4. Select two households featured in two different TV series or sitcoms. Classify each household into one of the social classes discussed in the text and analyze its lifestyle and consumption behavior.

key words

- Affluent consumers
- Chapin's Social Status Scale
- Composite-variable indexes
- Downscale consumers
- Downward mobility
- Geodemographic clustering
- Index of Status Characteristics
- Lifestyle profiles of social classes
- Objective measures
- Occupational status
- PRIZM
- Reputational measures
- Single-variable index
- Social class
- Social-class category
- Social prestige
- Social status
- Socioeconomic profiles of target markets
- Socioeconomic Status Score
- Subjective measures of social class
- Upward mobility

end notes

1. STEVE LONDON, "A City Magazine for the Poor," *American Demographics*, May 1994, 14–15; and JEFFREY A. TANNENBAUM, "New Magazines Targeting Poor Instead of Wealthy," *The Wall Street Journal*, November 7, 1994, B1–B2.

2. For an interesting article that relates occupations to possessing goods, see: CECELIA WITTMANYER, STEVE SCHULZ, and ROBERT MITTELSTAEDT, "A Cross–Cultural Look at the 'Supposed to Have It' Phenomenon: The Existence of a Standard Package Based on Occupation," in CHRIS T. ALLEN and DEBORAH ROEDDER JOHN, eds., *Advances in Consumer Research* 21 (Provo, UT: Association for Consumer Research, 1994), 427–33.

3. DIANE CRISPELL, "The Real Middle Americans," *American Demographics*, October 1994, 28–35.

4. RICHARD P. COLEMAN, "The Continuing Significance of Social Class to Marketing," *Journal of Consumer Research* 10, December 1983, 274.

5. DENNIS RODKIN, "Wealthy Attitude Wins over Healthy Wallet: Consumers Prove Affluence Is a State of Mind," *Advertising Age*, July 9, 1990, S4, S6.

6. JANEEN ARNOLD COSTA and RUSSELL W. BELK, "Nouveaux Riches as Quintessential Americans: Case Studies of Consumption in an Extended Family," *Advances in Nonprofit Marketing* 3 (Greenwich, CT: JAI Press, 1990), 83–140.

7. F. STUART CHAPIN, *Contemporary American Institutions* (New York: Harper, 1935), 373–97.

8. JOAN KRON, *Home-Psych* (New York: Potter, 1983), 90–102.

9. ROBERT B. SETTLE, PAMELA L. ALRECK, and DENNY E.

McCORKLE, "Consumer Perceptions of Mail/Phone Order Shopping Media," *Journal of Direct Marketing* 8, Summer 1994, 30–45.

10. Ibid.

11. W. LLOYD WARNER, MARCHIA MEEKER, and KENNETH EELLS, *Social Class in America: Manual of Procedure for the Measurement of Social Status* (New York: Harper & Brothers, 1960).

12. *Methodology and Scores of Socioeconomic Status*, Working Paper No. 15 (Washington, DC: U.S. Bureau of the Census, 1963).

13. KEITH BRADSHER, "America's Opportunity Gap," *The New York Times*, June 4, 1995, 4.

14. JOAN BRIGHTMAN, "Mystery Guests," *American Demographics*, August 1995, 14–16.

15. *Affluence: The Mendelsohn Affluent Survey 1995* (New York: Mendelsohn Media Research, Inc., 1995).

16. Ibid.

17. "Marketing to Affluents: Hidden Pockets of Wealth," *Advertising Age*, July 9, 1990, S1.

18. *How to Get to the Rich Quick* (brochure) (Mediamark Research, Inc., 1985).

19. For some further insights about the affluence of dual-income households, see: DIANE CRISPELL, "The Very Rich Are Sort of Different," *American Demographics*, March 1994, 11–13.

20. SHARON O'MALLEY, "Country Gold," *American Demographics*, July 1992, 26–34.

21. KATHLEEN DEVENY, "Downscale Consumers, Long Neglected, Start to Get Some Respect from Marketers," *The Wall Street Journal*, May 31, 1990, B1, B6; and JAN LARSON, "Reaching Downscale Markets," *American Demographics*, November 1991, 38–41. For interesting related reading, see RONALD PAUL HILL, "Homeless Women, Special Possessions, and the Meaning of 'Home': An Ethnographic Case Study," *Journal of Consumer Research* 18, December 1991, 298–310.

22. JUDITH GRAHAM, "MasterCard Ads Seek Middle-Class Appeal," *Advertising Age*, February 26, 1990, 22.

23. Epictetus, Discourses (second century) in Thomas Higginson, trans., *The Enchiridon*, 2nd edition (Indianapolis: Bobbs-Merrill, 1955).

The study of culture is a challenging undertaking, because its primary focus is on the broadest component of social behavior—an entire society. In contrast to the psychologist, who is principally concerned with the study of individual behavior, or the sociologist, who is concerned with the study of groups, the anthropologist is primarily interested in identifying the very fabric of society itself.

This chapter explores the basic concepts of culture, with particular emphasis on the role that culture plays in influencing consumer behavior. We first consider the specific dimensions of culture that make it a powerful force in regulating human behavior. After reviewing several measurement approaches that researchers use in their efforts to understand the impact of culture on consumption behavior, we show how a variety of core American cultural values influence consumer behavior.

Culture is not an exotic notion studied by a select group of anthropologists in the South Seas. It is a mold in which we are all cast, and it controls our daily lives in many unsuspected ways.

—Edward T. Hall

This chapter is concerned with the general aspects of culture; the following two chapters focus on subculture and on cross-culture and show how marketers can use such knowledge to shape and modify their marketing strategies.

Wʜᴀᴛ ɪꜱ Cᴜʟᴛᴜʀᴇ?

Given the broad and pervasive nature of culture, its study generally requires a detailed examination of the character of the total society, including such factors as language, knowledge, laws, religions, food customs, music, art, technology, work patterns, products, and other artifacts that give a society its distinctive flavor. In a sense, culture is a society's personality. For this reason, it is not easy to define its boundaries.

Because our objective is to understand the influence of culture on consumer behavior, we define culture as the *sum total of learned beliefs, values, and customs that serve to direct the consumer behavior of members of a particular society.*

The *belief* and *value* components of our definition refer to the accumulated feelings and priorities that individuals have about "things" and possessions. More precisely, **beliefs** consist of the very large number of mental or verbal statements (i.e., "I believe . . .") that reflect a person's particular knowledge and assessment of something (another person, a store, a product, a brand). **Values** also are beliefs. Values differ from other beliefs, however, because they meet the following criteria: (1) they are *relatively few* in number; (2) they serve as a guide for *culturally appropriate* behavior; (3) they are *enduring* or difficult to change; (4) they are *not tied to specific objects* or situations; and (5) they are *widely accepted* by the members of a society.

Therefore, in a broad sense, both values and beliefs are *mental images* that affect a wide range of specific attitudes which, in turn, influence the way a person is likely to respond in a specific situation. For example, the criteria a person uses to evaluate alternative brands in a product category (e.g., Kodak versus Fuji 35-mm film), or his or her eventual preference for one of these brands over the other, are influenced by both a person's general *values* (e.g., perceptions as to what constitutes quality and the meaning of country of origin) and specific *beliefs* (e.g., particular perceptions about the quality of American-made versus Japanese-made film).

In contrast to beliefs and values, **customs** are *overt modes of behavior that constitute culturally approved or acceptable ways of behaving in specific situations.* Customs consist of everyday or routine behavior. For example, a consumer's routine behavior, such as adding sugar and milk to coffee, or putting ketchup on hamburgers and mustard on frankfurters, are *customs*. Thus, while beliefs and values are *guides* for behavior, customs are *usual and acceptable ways of behaving.*

By our definition, it is easy to see how an understanding of various cultures of a society helps marketers predict consumer acceptance of their products.

Cʜᴀʀᴀᴄᴛᴇʀɪꜱᴛɪᴄꜱ ᴏꜰ Cᴜʟᴛᴜʀᴇ

To comprehend the scope and complexity of culture more fully, it is useful to examine a number of its underlying characteristics.

The Invisible Hand of Culture

The impact of culture is so natural and automatic that its influence on behavior is usually taken for granted. For instance, when consumer researchers ask people why they do certain things, they frequently answer, "Because it's the right thing to do." This seemingly superficial response partially reflects the ingrained influence of culture on our behavior. Often, it is only when we are exposed to people with different cultural values or customs (e.g., when visiting a different region or a different country) that we become aware of how culture has molded our own behavior. Thus, a true appreciation of the influence culture has on our daily life requires some knowledge of at least one other society with different cultural characteristics. For example, to understand that brushing our teeth twice a day with flavored toothpaste is a cultural phenomenon requires some awareness that members of another society either do not brush their teeth at all or do so in a manner distinctly different from that our own society.

Culture Satisfies Needs

Culture exists to satisfy the needs of the people within a society. It offers *order*, *direction*, and *guidance* in all phases of human problem solving by providing "tried-and-true" methods of satisfying physiological, personal, and social needs. For example, culture provides standards and "rules" about when to eat (e.g., "not between meals"), where to eat (e.g., "in a busy restaurant, because the food is likely to be good"), and what is appropriate to eat for breakfast (e.g., juice and cereal), lunch (e.g., a sandwich), dinner (e.g., "something hot and good and healthy"), and snacks (e.g., "something with quick energy"), and what to serve to guests at a dinner party (e.g., "a formal sitdown meal"), at a picnic (e.g., barbecued "franks and hamburgers), or at a wedding (e.g., champagne). Similarly, culture also provides insights as to suitable dress for specific occasions (e.g., what to wear around the house, what to wear to school, what to wear to work, what to wear to church, what to wear at a fast food restaurant or a movie theater). Dress codes are shifting dramatically; people are dressing more casual all the time and in most situations. Today, only a few big-city restaurants and clubs have business dress requirements. With the relaxed dress code in the corporate work environment, fewer men are wearing dress shirts, ties, and business suits, and fewer women are wearing dresses, suits, and pantyhose.[1] In their place casual slacks, sports shirts and blouses, jeans, and the emerging category of "dress casual" have been increasing in sales.

Soft-drink companies would prefer that consumers received their morning "jolt" of caffeine from one of their products, rather than from coffee. Because most Americans do not consider soda a suitable breakfast beverage, the real challenge for soft-drink companies is to overcome culture, not competition. In fact, coffee accounts for more than 45 percent of the morning beverage market. However, it has been challenged on all fronts by juices, milk, teas (hot and iced), and a host of different types of soft drinks.[2]

Cultural beliefs, values, and customs continue to be followed as long as they yield satisfaction. When a specific standard no longer satisfies the members of a society, however, it is modified or replaced, so that the resulting standard is more in line with current needs and desires. For instance, it was once considered a sign of a fine hotel that they provide down or goose feather pillows in rooms; today, with so many guests allergic to such materials, synthetic polyfill pillows are becoming the rule. Thus, culture gradually but continually evolves to meet the needs of society.

In a cultural context, if a product is no longer acceptable because a value or custom that is related to its use does not adequately satisfy human needs, then the firm producing the product must be ready to revise its product offering. Marketers also must be alert to newly embraced customs and values. For example, as Americans have become more health- and fitness-conscious, there has been an increase in the number of walkers, joggers, and runners on the nation's streets and roads. Astute shoe manufacturers who responded by offering an increased variety of appropriate footwear have been able to improve their market positions. In contrast, marketers who were not perceptive enough to note the opportunities created by changing values and lifestyles lost market share and, in some cases, were squeezed out of the market.

Culture Is Learned

Unlike innate biological characteristics (e.g., sex, skin, hair color, or intelligence), culture is *learned*. At an early age, we begin to acquire from our social environment a set of beliefs, values, and customs that make up our culture. For children, the learning of these acceptable cultural values and customs is reinforced by the process of playing with their toys.[3] As children play, they act out and rehearse important cultural lessons and situations. This cultural learning prepares them for later real-life circumstance.

▲ **How Culture Is Learned** Anthropologists have identified three distinct forms of cultural learning: **formal learning**, in which adults and older siblings teach a young family member "how to behave"; **informal learning**, in which a child learns primarily by imitating the behavior of selected others, such as family, friends, or TV heroes (see Figure 14-1); and **technical learning**, in which teachers instruct the child in an educational environment about *what* should be done, *how* it should be done, and *why* it should be done.

A young girl who is told by her mother to stop climbing trees because "girls don't do that" is *formally* learning a value that her mother feels is right. When she watches her mother preparing food, she is *informally* learning certain cooking habits. When she takes ballet lessons, she is experiencing *technical* learning.

Although a firm's advertising can influence all three types of cultural learning, it is likely that many product advertisements enhance informal cultural learning by providing the audience with a model of behavior to imitate. This is especially true for visible or conspicuous products and products that are evaluated in public settings (e.g., clothing, or beepers, portable cellular telephones), where peer influence is likely to play an important role.[4]

The repetition of advertising messages creates and reinforces cultural beliefs and values. For example, many advertisers continually stress the same selected benefits of their products or services. Ads for portable cellular telephone service often stress the convenience of scheduling and rescheduling appointments, as well as the security of having a phone at all times in case of some emergency. It is difficult to say whether cellular phone subscribers *inherently* desire these benefits from their cellular telephone service or whether, after several years of cumulative exposure to advertising appeals, they have been *taught* by marketers to desire them. In a sense, although specific product advertising may reinforce the benefits that consumers want from the product (as determined by consumer behavior research), such advertising also "teaches" future generations of consumers to expect the same benefits from the product category.

Figure 14-2 on page 410 shows that cultural meaning moves from the culturally constituted world to consumer goods and from there to the individual consumer by means of various consumption-related vehicles. To illustrate this process, Table 14-1 shows how the ever-popular T-shirt can furnish cultural meaning for wearers. Specifically, T-shirts can function as *trophies* (e.g., as proof of participation in sports or travel) or as self-proclaimed labels of *belonging to a cultural category* (e.g., "49er," "native Floridian"). T-shirts can also be used as a means of *self-expression*, which may provide wearers with the additional benefit of serving as a "topic" initiating social dialogue with others.[5]

▲ **Enculturation and Acculturation** When discussing the acquisition of culture, anthropologists often distinguish between the learning of one's own, or *native*, culture and the

America's favorite baby can be your baby's first doll.

Who wouldn't love the Gerber® Nursery™ dolls! But there's more to our dolls than just a pretty face to love: each one helps your baby learn.
TUB TIME™ BABY DOLL. Your child can be washing her baby while you wash her! This doll even has a soft cuddly hooded terry robe to snuggle into after her bath.
FEEL BETTER™ BABY DOLL. Comes with a stethoscope to hear the doll's heartbeat. Teaches that seeing the doctor is nothing to be afraid of.

LOVING TEARS™ BABY DOLL. She takes her bottle and then cries real tears after she's fed! Your baby will love comforting her baby-just the way her mother does!
POTTY TIME™ BABY DOLL. She has training pants, a bottle and a potty. She drinks, wets and helps your baby get a head start on toilet training.

GERBER and BABY HEAD trademarks and slogan owned by Gerber Products Company and used under license by Toy Biz, Inc. © 1994 Toy Biz, Inc.

 Gerber
Babies are our business... ™

FIGURE 14-1

Informal Learning of Culture
Courtesy of Toy Biz, Inc.

learning of some other culture. The learning of one's own culture is known as **enculturation**. The learning of a new or foreign culture is known as **acculturation**. In Chapter 16, we will see that acculturation is an important concept for marketers who plan to sell their products in foreign or multinational markets. In such cases, marketers must study the specific culture(s) of their potential target markets to determine whether their products will be acceptable to its members and, if so, how they can best communicate the characteristics of their products to persuade the target market to buy.

▲ **Language and Symbols** To acquire a common culture, the members of a society must be able to communicate with each other through a common language. Without a common

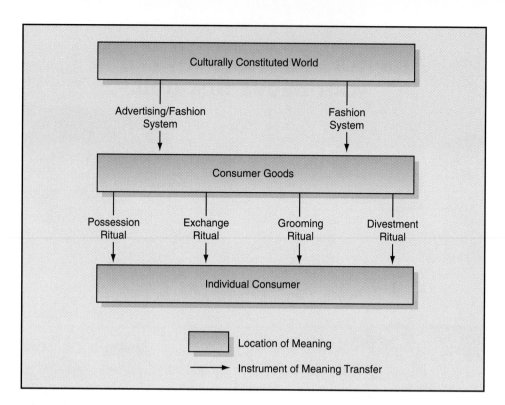

FIGURE 14-2

The Movement of
Cultural Meaning
Source: GRANT MCCRACKEN,
"Culture and Consumption: A
Theoretical Account of the
Structure and Movement of the
Cultural Meaning of Consumer
Goods," *Journal of Consumer
Research* 13 (June 1986), 72.
Reprinted by permission of The
University of Chicago Press as
publisher.

table 14-1 What's on the T-Shirts—Consumer Diaries

CONSUMER* GENDER AGE	#1 FEMALE 29	#2 FEMALE 34	#3 FEMALE 39	#4 MALE 26	#5 MALE 25
T-SHIRT CATEGORIES	**NUMBER OF T-SHIRTS**				
Affiliations and loyalties					
Work	1	0	1	1	3
Teams/organizations	6	0	2	5	4
Activities					
Sports Participation	6	18	4	6	0
Event attendance	5	0	2	5	3
Travel/vacation	7	6	7	2	8
Special/other	0	6	0	0	0
Personal Meanings					
Self-expression	1	0	1	2	7
Gifts	0	5	5	0	0
Impersonal					
Company/product	4	0	0	1	4
Fashion	0	2	0	0	0
Totals	30	37	22	22	29

*The first consumer was the author of the article—T. Bettina Cornwell.

Sources: Adapted from T. BETTINA CORNWELL, "T-Shirts as Wearable Diary: An Examination of Artifact Consumption and Garnering Related to Life Events," in Marvin E. Goldberg, Gerald Gorn, and Richard W. Pollay, eds., *Advances in Consumer Research* 17 (Provo, UT: Association for Consumer Research, 1990), 377. Reprinted by permission.

language, shared meaning could not exist, and true communication would not take place (see Chapter 10).

To communicate effectively with their audiences, marketers must use appropriate **symbols** to convey desired product images or characteristics. These symbols can be *verbal* or *nonverbal*. Verbal symbols may include a television announcement or an advertisement in a magazine. Nonverbal communication includes the use of such symbols as figures, colors, shapes, and even textures to lend additional meaning to print or broadcast advertisements, to trademarks, and to packaging or product designs.

Basically, the symbolic nature of human language sets it apart from all other animal communication. A symbol is anything that stands for something else. Any word is a symbol. The word "razor" calls forth a specific image related to an individual's own knowledge and experience. The word "hurricane" calls forth the notion of wind and rain and also has the power to stir us emotionally, arousing feelings of danger and the need for protection and safety. Similarly, the word "jaguar" has symbolic meaning: to some it suggests a fine luxury automobile, to others it implies wealth and status; to still others it suggests a sleek, wild animal to be seen at the zoo.

Because the human mind can process symbols, it is possible for a person, for example, to "experience" cognitively a visualization for a product like the advertisement for Edge skin moisturizing gel by contrasting two scenes—one of a parched desert without the gel and one of a rich green landscape with the gel. Such a comparison presents the idea that a skin-moisturizing gel will transform a person's dry skin to a comfortable moist state. The capacity to learn symbolically is primarily a human phenomenon; most other animals learn by direct experience. Clearly, the ability of humans to understand symbolically how a product, service, or idea can satisfy their needs makes it easier for marketers to "sell" the features and benefits of their offerings. Through a shared language and culture, individuals already know what the image means; thus, an association can be made without actively thinking about it. Table 14-2 on page 412 illustrates how beer advertisers use common "symbols" (i.e., images and themes) drawn from a shared culture to evoke particular meanings in consumers.

A symbol may have several, even contradictory, meanings, so the advertiser must ascertain exactly what the symbol is communicating to its intended audience. For example, the advertiser who uses a trademark depicting an old craftsman to symbolize careful workmanship may instead be communicating an image of outmoded methods and lack of style. The marketer who uses slang in an advertisement to attract a teenage audience must do so with great care; slang that is misused or outdated will symbolically date the marketer's firm and product.

Price and channels of distribution also are significant symbols of the marketer and the marketer's product. For example, price often implies quality to potential buyers (see Chapter 6). For certain products (e.g., clothing), the type of store in which the product is sold also is an important symbol of quality. In fact, all the elements of the marketing mix the product, its promotion, price, and the stores at which it is available are symbols that communicate ranges of quality to potential buyers.

▲ **Ritual** In addition to language and symbols, culture includes various ritualized experiences and behaviors that until recently have been neglected by consumer researchers. A **ritual** is a type of symbolic activity consisting of a series of steps *(multiple behaviors)* occurring in a fixed sequence and repeated over time.[6]

In practice, rituals extend over the human life cycle from birth to death, including a host of intermediate events (e.g., confirmation, graduations, and marriage). These rituals can be very public, elaborate, religious, or civil ceremonies, or they can be as mundane as an individual's grooming behavior or flossing.[7] Ritualized behavior is typically rather formal and often is scripted behavior (e.g., a religious service requiring a prayer book or the

table 14-2　Some Examples of Symbols Found in Beer Advertisements

BRAND	SYMBOL	MEANING
Busch	Cowboy	Applies the myth of the frontier as pure, free from the corruption of civilization, yet full of sudden danger. The cowboy demonstrates mastery over nature; the cowboy is the archetypical man's man.
Busch, Rolling Rock, Heileman's Old Style, Molson's Golden	Stream water	Stress that beer is a form of bottled nature; that drinking beer is a safe way to face the challenge of nature.
Busch	Wild horses	Implies untamed nature; drinking beer is a substitute for taming wild horses.
Old Milwaukee	Wilderness (e.g., Florida Everglades and Glacier Bay, Alaska)	Special place untouched by civilization; allows men to engage in recreational activities not possible in the city or suburbs; drinking beer acts as a substitute for actually visiting the place.
Busch, Old Milwaukee, Budweiser	Laborers and athletes	Depicts physical challenge; beer presented as a reward for hard work or play; drinking beer is a way to symbolically reenact the feat.

Sources: Adapted from Lance Strate, "The Cultural Meaning of Beer Commercials," in Rebecca H. Holman and Michael R. Solomon, eds., *Advances in Consumer Research* 18 (Provo, UT: Association for Consumer Research, 1991), 115–119. Reprinted by permission.

code of proper conduct in a court of law). It is also likely to occur repeatedly over time (e.g., singing the national anthem before a baseball game).

Most important from the standpoint of marketers is the fact that rituals tend to be replete with ritual *artifacts* (products) that are associated with or somehow enhance the performance of the ritual. For instance, tree ornaments, stockings, and various food items are linked to the ritual of Christmas celebration; other rituals (such as a graduation, a wedding or wedding anniversary, a Thursday night card game, or a Saturday afternoon visit to the hair salon) have their own specific artifacts associated with them (see Table 14-3). For special occasions, such as wedding anniversaries, some types of artifacts are perceived as more appropriate and are appreciated more than others, such as jewelry versus household goods.[8]

In addition to a ritual, which is the way that something is traditionally done, there is also **ritualistic behavior**, which can be defined as *any behavior that is made into a ritual*. For example, a baseball player may swing his bat a certain number of times and kick the dirt near home plate before a pitch to ensure a good swing. Table 14-4 describes the shift in a young woman's ritualistic behavior, with respect to nightly beauty care, from the time she was a college student to her present position as a young marketing executive.

Culture Is Shared

To be considered a cultural characteristic, a particular belief, value, or practice must be shared by a significant portion of the society. Thus, culture frequently is viewed as *group customs* that link together the members of a society. Of course, common language is the

table 14-3   Selected Rituals and Associated Artifacts

SELECTED RITUALS	TYPICAL ARTIFACTS
Graduation	Pen, U.S. Savings Bond, card, wristwatch
Valentine's Day	Candy, card, flowers
Sunday football	Beer, potato chips, pretzels
Retirement	Company party, watch, plaque
Wedding	White gown, (something old, something new, something borrowed, something blue)
50th Wedding Anniversary	Catered party, card and gift, display of photos of the couple's life together
Starting a new job	Get a haircut, buy some new clothing
New Year's Eve	Champagne, party, fancy dress
Birth of child	U.S. Savings Bond, silver baby spoon
Going to the gym	Towel, exercise clothes, water, portable tape player
Get a job promotion	Taken out to lunch by coworkers, receive token gift

table 14-4   Nightly Facial Beauty Ritual—Then and Now

AS A COLLEGE STUDENT

1. I pull my hair back with a headband.
2. I remove all of my mascara with Almay Eye Make-up Remover Pads.
3. I then wash my face to remove all makeup with a facial cleanser like Neutrogena.
4. Next, I use a gentle facial scrub, such as Aapri, to remove all dead and dry skin and pat my skin dry with a towel.
5. Then I use an astringent, like Clinique, to remove any deep-down make-up residue and flaky skin and to tighten my pores.
6. I apply Clinique Dramatically Different moisturizer all over my face and throat to soften my skin.
7. Finally, if I have any blemishes, I dab some Clearasil on them so they will fade away.
8. Then once a week, I use a facial mask to remove all dirt and residue that has accumulated over the week's time.

5 YEARS LATER—AS A YOUNG MARKETING EXECUTIVE

1. I pull my hair back with a headband.*
2. I wash my face with tepid water using Dove facial cleanser to remove all makeup.**
3. Next, I use a Q-tip with some moisturizer around my eyes to make sure all eye makeup is removed.***
4. I apply Dermacil facial cream to my face to heavily moisturize and Clinique Dramatically Different Lotion on my neck and throat.**
5. If I have a blemish, I apply Clearasil Treatment to the area to dry it out.*
6. Twice weekly (or as necessary) I use Aapri Facial Scrub to remove dry and dead skin.**
7. Once a week I apply Clinique Clarifying Lotion 2 with a cotton ball to my face and throat to remove deep down dirt and oils.**
8. Once monthly I get a professional salon facial to deep clean my pores.***

*No change from five years ago.

**Slight variation

***New step

critical cultural component that makes it possible for people to share values, experiences, and customs.

Various social institutions within a society transmit the elements of culture and make the sharing of culture a reality. Chief among such institutions is the *family*, which serves as the primary agent for enculturation, the passing along of basic cultural beliefs, values, and customs to society's newest members. A vital part of the enculturation role of the family is the consumer socialization of the young (see Chapter 12). This includes teaching such basic consumer-related values and skills as the meaning of money; the relationship between price and quality, the establishment of product tastes, preferences, and habits, and appropriate methods of response to various promotional messages.

In addition to the family, two other institutions traditionally share much of the responsibility for the transfer of selected aspects of culture: *educational institutions* and *houses of worship*. Educational institutions specifically are charged with imparting basic learning skills, history, patriotism, citizenship, and the technical training needed to prepare people for significant roles within society. Religious institutions provide and perpetuate religious consciousness, spiritual guidance, and moral training. Although the young receive much of their consumer training within the family setting, the educational and religious systems reinforce this training by teaching economic and ethical concepts.

A fourth, frequently overlooked, social institution that plays a major role in the transfer of culture throughout society is the mass media. Given the extensive exposure of the American population to both print and broadcast media, as well as the easily ingested, entertaining format in which the contents of such media usually are presented, it is not surprising that the mass media are powerful vehicles for imparting a wide range of cultural values.

We are exposed daily to advertising, an important component of the media. Advertising not only underwrites, or makes economically feasible, the editorial or programming contents of the media, but also transmits much about our culture. Without advertising, it would be almost impossible to disseminate information about products, ideas, and causes. A leading historian noted that: ". . . advertising now compares with such long-standing institutions as the schools and the church in the magnitude of its social influence."[9]

Consumers receive important cultural information from advertising. For example, it has been hypothesized that one of the roles of advertising in sophisticated magazines such as *Vanity Fair* is to instruct readers how to dress, how to decorate their homes, and what foods and wines to serve guests; in other words, what types of behavior are most appropriate to their particular social class.

Thus, while the scope of advertising is often considered to be limited to influencing the demand for specific products or services, in a cultural context advertising has the expanded mission of reinforcing established cultural values and aiding in the dissemination of new tastes, habits, and customs. In planning their advertising, marketers should recognize that advertising is an important agent for social change in our society.

Culture Is Dynamic

To fulfill its need-gratifying role, culture continually must evolve if it is to function in the best interests of a society. For this reason, the marketer must carefully monitor the sociocultural environment in order to market an existing product more effectively or to develop promising new products.

This is not an easy task, because many factors are likely to produce cultural changes within a given society (new technology, population shifts, resource shortages, wars, changing values, and customs borrowed from other cultures). For example, a major ongoing cultural change in American society is the expanded role options open to women. Today, most women work outside the home, frequently in careers that once were considered exclusively male oriented (Figure 14-3). Also, women are increasingly active in social and ath-

If you have the will to succeed, we have about 200 ways.

As a woman in the Army, you will receive training in one of 188 military specialties. It's training that could prepare you for a career in high technology. You could learn guided missile technology or work with complex computer systems. You could manage communications and intelligence systems—all while working as a vital part of a team. And, if you qualify, you'll earn money for college, too. So come with the will to succeed. Today's Army will make a way. Call 1-800-USA-ARMY, ext. 447.

ARMY. BE ALL YOU CAN BE.

FIGURE 14-3

Depicting Women in an Expanded Role or Job
Courtesy of The Department of the U.S. Army and Army Reserve

letic activities outside the home. However, the 1980s stereotype of women striving to be "superwomen" (e.g., to juggle many demanding roles—full-time job or careers and full-time parenting responsibilities), is giving-way to a less stressful and more realistic goal of a balance between family and work.[10] Businesses need to be responsive to these shifting cultural and lifestyle forces. For instance, with a customer base comprised of more than 85 percent women, Hallmark Cards is changing its communication focus, as more of its female customers have less time to spend browsing in card shops. To bring them into Hallmark Card shops they have instituted a frequent buyer program to reward loyal customers.[11]

This and other changes mean that marketers have to consistently reconsider *who* are the purchasers and the users of their products (males only, females only, or both), when they do their shopping, *how* and *where* they can be reached by the media, and *what* new product and service needs are emerging. Marketers who monitor cultural changes also often find new opportunities to increase corporate profitability. For example, marketers of such products as life insurance, casual clothing, toy electric trains, and cigars are among those who have attempted to exploit the dramatically shifting sense of what is feminine.

THE MEASUREMENT OF CULTURE

A wide range of measurement techniques are used in the study of culture. Some of these techniques were described in Chapter 2. For example, the *projective tests* used by psychologists to study motivation and personality and the *attitude measurement techniques* used by social psychologists and sociologists are relatively popular tools in the study of culture.

In addition, **content analysis**, **consumer fieldwork**, and **value measurement instruments** are three research approaches that are frequently used to examine culture and spot cultural trends. There are also several commercial services that track emerging values and social trends for businesses and governmental agencies.

Content Analysis

Conclusions about a society, or specific aspects of a society, sometimes can be drawn from examining the content of its messages. *Content analysis*, as the name implies, focuses on the content of verbal, written, and pictorial communications (e.g., the copy and art composition of an ad).

Content analysis can be used as a relatively objective means of determining what social and cultural changes have occurred in a specific society. For instance, consumer researchers use content analysis to examine how African-Americans, women, the elderly, and animated spokes-characters have been depicted in the mass media. For example, researchers, using content analysis to study trends in the use of animated spoke-characters (e.g., Mickey Mouse, Flintstones, Bugs Bunny, Garfield the Cat, Speedy Alka-Seltzer, Elsie the Cow, or California Raisins), have found that the majority of animated spokes-characters are noncelebrity types and that their TV use tends to vary by time of day, type of program, and products (e.g., mornings, children's programs, and nondurable products).[12] Content analysis is also used to explore trends in the style and the layout of various types of advertising. For instance, a small California fragrance company has used content analysis to determine the most effective way to appeal to sophisticated urban adults through magazine advertising.[13] The research revealed that the product, together with a person and the logo, was the advertising format most frequently used by competing perfume makers. Meaning for the product was created through visual association with a person who has value to the consumer. Another study, this one a content analysis of Ms. magazine advertising during its first 15 years of publication (1973–1987), found that the portrayal of women as subordinate to men or as merely decorative had decreased over time.[14]

Content analysis is useful to both marketers and public-policy makers interested in comparing the advertising claims of competitors within a specific industry, as well as for evaluating the nature of advertising claims targeted to specific audiences (e.g., women, the elderly, or children).

Consumer Fieldwork

When examining a specific society, anthropologists frequently immerse themselves in the environment under study. As trained researchers, they are likely to select a small sample of people from a particular society and carefully observe their behavior. Based on their observations, researchers draw conclusions about the values, beliefs, and customs of the society under investigation. For example, if researchers were interested in how people select compact discs (CDs), they might position trained observers in record stores and note how specific types of CDs are selected (rap versus country, jazz versus classical, rock versus sound tracks). The researchers also may be interested in the degree of search that accompanies the choice; that is, how often consumers tend to take a CD off the display, read the description, and place it back again before selecting the CD they finally purchase.

The distinct characteristics of **field observation** are that (1) it takes place within a natural environment; (2) it is performed sometimes without the subject's awareness; and (3) it focuses on observation of behavior. Because the emphasis is on a natural environment and observable behavior, field observation concerned with consumer behavior often focuses on in-store shopping behavior and, less frequently, on in-home preparation and consumption (see the discussion on observational research in Chapter 2).

In some cases, instead of just observing behavior, researchers become **participant-observers** (i.e., they become active members of the environment that they are studying). For example, if a researcher were interested in examining how men select their shoes, he or she might take a sales position in a men's shoe department to observe directly and even to interact with customers in the transaction process.

Both field observation and participant-observer research require highly skilled researchers who can separate their own emotions from what they actually observe in their professional roles. Both techniques provide valuable insight that might not easily be obtained through survey research that simply asks consumers questions about their behavior.

In addition to fieldwork methods, *depth interviews* and *focus-group sessions* (see Chapter 2) are also often used by marketers to get a "first look" at an emerging social or cultural change. In the relatively informal atmosphere of focus group discussions, consumers are apt to reveal attitudes or behavior that may signal a shift in values that, in turn, may affect the long-run market acceptance of a product or service. For instance, one of the authors has been involved in a series of focus group studies concerned with identifying marketing programs that reinforce established customer loyalty and goodwill (i.e., relationship marketing). A common thread running throughout these studies showed that established customers, especially for services (e.g., investment and banking services), want to have their loyalty acknowledged in the form of *personalized* services. These observations have led various service and product companies to refine or establish loyalty programs that are more personalized in the way that they treat their established customers (e.g., by recognizing the individuality of such core customers). This is just one of numerous examples showing how focus groups and depth interviews are used to spot social trends.

Value Measurement Survey Instruments

Anthropologists have traditionally observed the behavior of members of a specific society and *inferred* from such behavior the dominant or underlying values of the society. In recent years, however, there has been a gradual shift to measuring values directly by means of survey (questionnaire) research. Researchers use data collection instruments called **value instruments** to ask people how they feel about such basic personal and social concepts as freedom, comfort, national security, and peace.

Research into the relationship between people's values and their actions as consumers still is in its infancy. It is an area that is destined to receive increased attention, however, for it taps a broad dimension of human behavior that could not be explored effectively before the availability of standardized value instruments.

A variety of popular value instruments have been used in consumer behavior studies, including: the **Rokeach Value Survey**, the **List of Values** (LOV), and the **Values and Lifestyles—VALS 2** (discussed in Chapter 3). The widely used Rokeach Value Survey is a self-administered value inventory that is divided into two parts, each part measuring different but complementary types of personal values (see Table 14-5 on page 418). The first part consists of 18 *terminal value* items, which are designed to measure the relative importance of **end-states of existence** (i.e., personal goals). The second part consists of 18 *instrumental value* items, which measure basic approaches an individual might take to reach end-state values. Thus, the first half of the measurement instrument deals with *ends*, and the second half considers *means*.

Using the Rokeach Value Survey, adult Brazilians were categorized into six distinctive value segments.[15] For example, Segment A (representing 13 percent of the sample) was most concerned with "world peace," followed by "inner harmony" and "true friendship." Members of this segment were found to be especially involved in domestic-oriented activities (e.g.,

table 14-5 The Rokeach Value Survey Instrument

TERMINAL VALUES	INSTRUMENTAL VALUES
A COMFORTABLE LIFE (a prosperous life)	AMBITIOUS (hard-working, aspiring)
AN EXCITING LIFE (a stimulating, active life)	BROAD-MINDED (open-minded)
A WORLD AT PEACE (free of war and conflict)	CAPABLE (competent, effective)
EQUALITY (brotherhood, equal opportunity for all)	CHEERFUL (lighthearted, joyful)
FREEDOM (independence and free choice)	CLEAN (neat, tidy)
HAPPINESS (contentedness)	COURAGEOUS (standing up for your beliefs)
NATIONAL SECURITY (protection from attack)	FORGIVING (willing to pardon others)
PLEASURE (an enjoyable life)	HELPFUL (working for the welfare of others)
SALVATION (saved, eternal life)	HONEST (sincere, truthful)
SOCIAL RECOGNITION (respect and admiration)	IMAGINATIVE (daring, creative)
TRUE FRIENDSHIP (close companionship)	INDEPENDENT (self-reliant, self-sufficient)
WISDOM (a mature understanding of life)	INTELLECTUAL (intelligent, reflective)
A WORLD OF BEAUTY (beauty of nature and the arts)	LOGICAL (consistent, rational)
FAMILY SECURITY (taking care of loved ones)	LOVING (affectionate, tender)
MATURE LOVE (sexual and spiritual intimacy)	OBEDIENT (dutiful, respectful)
SELF-RESPECT (self-esteem)	POLITE (courteous, well-mannered)
A SENSE OF ACCOMPLISHMENT (lasting contribution)	RESPONSIBLE (dependable, reliable)
INNER HARMONY (freedom from inner conflict)	SELF-CONTROLLED (restrained, self-disciplined)

gardening, reading, and going out with the family to visit relatives). Because of their less materialistic and nonhedonistic orientation, this segment also may be the least prone to experiment with new products. In contrast, Segment B (representing 9 percent of the sample) was most concerned with self-centered values such as self-respect, a comfortable life, pleasure, an exciting life, a sense of accomplishment, and social recognition. They were least concerned with values related to the family, such as friendship, love, and equality. These self-centered, achievement-oriented, pleasure seekers were expected to prefer provocative clothes in the latest fashion, to enjoy an active lifestyle, and to be more likely to try new products.

The results of this and other studies suggest that the Rokeach Value Survey can be used by marketers to segment markets by specific values and by perceptions of specific product attributes.[16] Such information is useful when developing new products for specific market segments.

The LOV is a related measurement instrument that is also designed to be used in surveying consumers' personal values. The LOV scale asks consumers to identify their two most important values from a nine-value list (e.g., "warm relationships with others," "a sense of belonging," or "a sense of accomplishment") that is based on the terminal value of the Rokeach Value Survey.[17]

The Yankelovich MONITOR®

The Yankelovich MONITOR® is a commercial research service that systematically tracks social trends designed to reflect a variety of cultural values. The Yankelovich MONITOR was first conducted in 1970 and has been updated annually ever since. The MONITOR currently tracks about fifty social trends (for examples, see Table 14-6) and provides

TREND NO. 3, PHYSICAL FITNESS AND WELL-BEING

MONITOR's measurement of Physical Fitness and Well-Being is based on a series of scaled items including: (1) the importance attributed to preventive (rather than therapeutic) health measures; (2) the concern about being in "top shape"; (3) the belief that without taking active measures, people tend to get "soft"; (4) the commitment to "taking care of oneself."

TREND NO. 12, NOVELTY AND CHANGE

MONITOR's measurement of Novelty and Change comprises a series of scaled items including: (1) recognition of a "hunger for a new experience" along with interest in catering to this hunger; (2) desire for a continuing pattern of "change in my life"; (3) the feeling that "there is too much change in the world today"; (4) the desire for things to "stay settled and stable"; (5) dislike of a lifestyle where "things remain the same over a period of time."

TREND NO. 32, CONCERN ABOUT ENVIRONMENT

MONITOR's measurement of Concern About Environment is based on a series of scaled items including: (1) concern about what the individual can do to protect our environment and natural resources; (2) willingness to pay more for basic consumer products that do not harm the environment; (3) willingness to boycott manufacturers whose products contribute to pollution; (4) willingness to forego convenience and services that adversely affect our environment.

TREND NO. 46, COMMITMENT TO BUY AMERICAN

The Commitment to Buy American is measured via several scaled items including: (1) concern that this country will lose its position as an economic leader; (2) the importance to the economy of buying only American-made products; (3) the perceived cost-benefit of buying American-made products; (4) belief about the relative uniqueness of American-made products vis-à-vis imports.

TREND NO. 47, RESPONSIVENESS TO FANTASY

MONITOR's measurement of Responsiveness to Fantasy is based on a series of scaled items including: (1) the need to remove oneself from one's daily experience by imagination and/or the pursuit of "unusual," out-of-the-ordinary activities; and (2) the preference for participatory entertainment experiences.

TREND NO. 52, ACCOMMODATION TO TECHNOLOGY

The Accommodation to Technology is measured via several scaled items including: (1) the pressing need to feel more comfortable with the new technologies; (2) agreement that people will be at a disadvantage in the future if they are "turned off" by the new technologies; and (3) sentiments regarding the need to adapt to technological change.

TREND NO. 59, NEED FOR CONTROL

MONITOR's measurement of the Need for Control is based on a series of scaled items including: (1) the need to feel in charge of all aspects of one's life; (2) the perceived importance of feeling personally self-sufficient; and (3) the active search for mechanisms to insure a better feeling of personal control.

Sources: The Yankelovich MONITOR® *Trend Reference Book*—Issued September 1995 (Yankelovich Partners, Inc., Norwalk, CT.), Appendix. Reprinted by permission.

detailed information about potential shifts in the size and direction of these trends, as well as implications for consumer marketing.[18]

By carefully interpreting social trends and determining which demographic segments are most affected by a particular group of trends, the MONITOR is capable of providing advance warning of likely shifts in demand for various product categories. The following are a few examples of marketing-related trends that impact executive decision making in various product and service areas:[19]

- *The* abatement of health and fitness concerns, *toward a long-term perspective on eating healthy and exercising occasionally. This replaces the Jane Fonda "feel the burn" that characterized the mid-1980s.*

- A decline in the need to acquire goods and services *at the frenetic pace of the 1980s. This attitude was driven not only by recessionary pressures but also by a reduced need to have so much "stuff." Rather than concern with having the latest and greatest, or the most expensive, consumers are looking for substance in the products and services they buy.*

- A lack of trust *in institutions. Rising cynicism and frustration has put business and government alike on the hot seat, making them quite susceptible to negative consumer reaction if their expectations are not met.*

- *An* increasing need to streamline or simplify our lives. *With demands on our time at an all-time high, we're looking for opportunities to delegate tasks to others, or simply prioritize (and cast out) those activities and/or responsibilities that are less important. There is increased recognition that we can't do and be everything.*

Armed with these insights, corporate executives are in a better position to make more enlightened decisions. For instance, a chain of fitness centers might decide to stress a more "moderate" program of physical exercise, given the older communities in which they are located, or a manufacturer of luxury luggage might de-emphasize department stores as outlets for its products in favor of its own direct marketing catalog department. Other marketers might see the wisdom of redesigning their point-of-purchase displays to facilitate consumer product selection.

DYG SCAN—A Scanning Program

Since 1986, DYG has conducted its annual *DYG SCAN* study. This research program tracks 38 social values (see Table 14-7) among various segments of the U.S. population (e.g., Hispanics, the affluent, teenagers, and opinion leaders), as well as business, government, and academic leaders.[20] Additionally, an optional service called *BrandLink* extends specific trends to the actual image assessment of a subscribing firm's brand. The sample can be selected from among the general public, users of specific products without regard to brand, users of the brand itself, or users of competitors' brands. The brand's image, as well as that of its closest competitors, can then be compared.

As these examples illustrate, standardized *value* and *social trend measurement instruments* are promising techniques for insightful consumer behavior research, especially segmentation analysis. When combined with other behavioral variables examined throughout this book, *values* can be used to predict shifts in consumption patterns. These insights are particularly useful when one is developing new product concepts, repositioning existing products, and adjusting a firm's general marketing efforts.

table 14-7   A Sample from the 38 Social Values Tracked by the DYG Scanning Program

SOCIAL VALUE	DESCRIPTION	TYPICAL MEASUREMENT SCALES
MATERIALISM	Measures the relative value placed on owning material possessions versus expenditures for intangible experiences, such as travel and dining out.	• An item that claims it is preferable to spend money on material possessions rather than on experiences • An item that claims that money should be spent on activities rather than on material things
AGE-GROUP FOCUS	Measures the positive orientation toward older individuals (i.e., values assigned to maturity) versus the positive orientation toward young people (i.e., placing a value primarily on youth).	• An item that claims that the nation's problems will best be solved by older citizens • An item that claims that the nation's problems will best be solved by younger citizens
SOCIAL MOBILITY	Measures the relative support for an open and mobile social, political, and economic system for all people.	• An item that acknowledges the difficulty of moving up the social ladder • An item that claims that upward social mobility is an achievable reality
PRESENT VERSUS FUTURE	Measures the relative value placed on living in the present versus planning for the future.	• An item that claims that it is most important to have an orientation toward the present and not to be concerned about the future • An item that asserts that it is more important for an individual to be oriented toward the future and not be preoccupied with the present
MATERIAL SUCCESS	Measures the extent money plays a role in measuring a person's relative success.	• An item that claims a successful person is one who earns a lot of money • An item that asserts that society places too much emphasis on money as the success criterion
HEALTH AND FITNESS	Measures the relative importance placed on focusing a great deal of attention on health and fitness versus focusing little attention on health and fitness.	• An item that emphasizes staying in shape and being health-conscious • An item that deemphasizes the importance of being concerned with fitness and health
APPEARANCE	Measures the relative value placed on paying little attention to body enhancement.	• An item that claims that an individual's appearance is always important • An item that expresses a lack of concern over individual appearance
RELATIONSHIP TO TECHNOLOGY	Measures the relative value placed on man's resistance or receptivity to technological advancement.	• An item that claims that new technologies are causing more problems than they are solving • An item that asserts an enthusiasm and openness to the possibilities of future technologies

Source: Courtesy of DYG SCAN^SM—A Trend Identification Program, DYG, Inc. Reprinted by permission.

AMERICAN CORE VALUES

What is the American culture? In this section, we identify a number of **core values** that both affect and reflect the character of American society. This is a difficult undertaking for several reasons. First, the United States is a diverse country, consisting of a variety of *subcultures* (religious, ethnic, regional, racial, and economic groups), each of which interprets and responds to society's basic beliefs and values in its own specific way. Second, America is a dynamic society that has undergone almost constant change in response to the development of new technology. This element of rapid change makes it especially difficult to monitor changes in cultural values. Finally, the existence of contradictory values in American society is somewhat confusing. For instance, Americans traditionally embrace *freedom of choice* and *individualism*, yet simultaneously they show great tendencies to conform (in dress, in furnishings, and in fads) to the rest of society. In the context of consumer behavior, Americans like to have a wide choice of products and prefer those that uniquely express their personal lifestyles. Yet, there is often a considerable amount of implicit pressure to conform to the values of family members, friends, and other socially important groups. It is difficult to reconcile these seemingly inconsistent values; their existence, however, demonstrates that America is a complex society with numerous paradoxes.

When selecting the specific core values to be examined, we were guided by three criteria:

1. *The value must be* pervasive. *A significant portion of the American people must accept the value and use it as a guide for their attitudes and actions.*

2. *The value must be* enduring. *The specific value must have influenced the actions of the American people over an extended period of time (as distinguished from a short-run trend).*

3. *The value must be* consumer-related. *The specific value must provide insights that help us to understand the consumption actions of the American people.*

Meeting these criteria are a number of basic values that expert observers of the American scene consider the "building blocks" of that rather elusive concept called the *"American character."*

Achievement and Success

In a broad cultural context, *achievement* is a major American value, with historical roots that can be traced to the traditional religious belief in the Protestant work ethic, which considers hard work to be wholesome, spiritually rewarding, and an appropriate end in itself. Indeed, substantial research evidence shows that the achievement orientation is closely associated with the technical development and general economic growth of American society.[21]

Individuals who consider a "sense of accomplishment" an important personal value tend to be achievers who strive hard for success. Although historically associated with men, especially male business executives, today *achievement* is very important for women, who are increasingly enrolled in undergraduate and graduate business programs and are more commonly seeking top level business careers.

Success is a closely related American cultural theme. However, achievement and success do differ. Specifically, achievement is its own direct reward (it is implicitly satisfying to the individual achiever), while success implies an extrinsic reward (such as luxury possessions, financial compensation, or status improvement).

Both achievement and success influence consumption. They often serve as social and moral justification for the acquisition of goods and services. For example, "You owe it to yourself," "You worked for it," and "You deserve it" are popular achievement themes used by advertisers to coax consumers into purchasing their products. Regardless of gender, achievement-oriented people often enjoy conspicuous consumption, because it allows them to display symbols of their personal achievement. Figure 14-4 presents an ad for Tumi, an elegant brand of status luggage and briefcases. The recognizable design and Tumi tag serve as a signal of the carrier's accomplishments and success. When it comes to personal development and preparation for future careers, the themes of achievement and success are also especially appropriate. Figure 14-5 on page 424 presents one in an ongoing series of ads for Hofstra University that stresses achievement with the tagline, "We Teach Success."

Activity

Americans attach an extraordinary amount of importance to being *active* or *involved*. Keeping busy is widely accepted as a healthy and even necessary part of the American lifestyle. The hectic nature of American life is attested to by foreign visitors, who frequently comment that they cannot understand why Americans are always "on the run" and seemingly unable to relax.

The premium placed on *activity* has had both a positive and a negative effect on the popularity of various products. For example, a principal reason for the enormous growth of fast-food chains, such as McDonald's and Kentucky Fried Chicken, is that so many people want quick, prepared meals when they are away from the house. Americans rarely eat a full breakfast, because they usually are too rushed in the morning to prepare and consume a traditional morning meal. In fact, microwaveable breakfast dishes that can be prepared quickly and easily before leaving the house in the morning have been gaining in popularity.

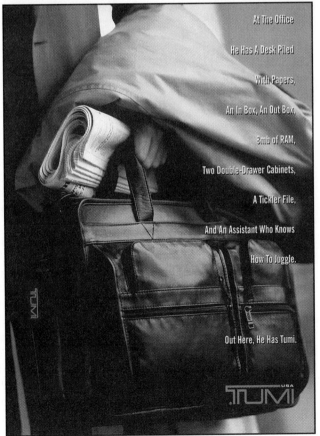

 FIGURE 14-4

Symbol of Accomplishment and Success
Courtesy of Tumi Luggage

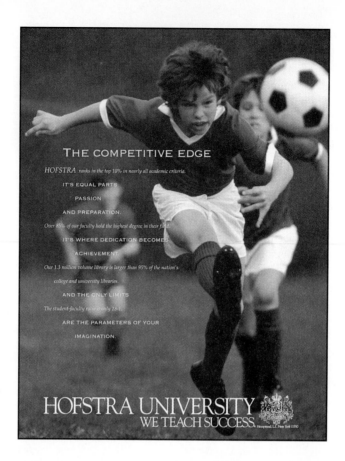

THE COMPETITIVE EDGE

HOFSTRA *ranks in the top 10% in nearly all academic criteria.*

IT'S EQUAL PARTS

PASSION

AND PREPARATION.

Over 85% of our faculty hold the highest degree in their field.

IT'S WHERE DEDICATION BECOMES

ACHIEVEMENT.

Our 1.3 million volume library is larger than 95% of the nation's

college and university libraries.

AND THE ONLY LIMITS

The student-faculty ratio is only 15-1.

ARE THE PARAMETERS OF YOUR

IMAGINATION.

HOFSTRA UNIVERSITY
WE TEACH SUCCESS. *Hempstead, L.I., New York 11550*

FIGURE 14-5 ▼

Incorporating Achievement and Success Appeals
Courtesy of Hofstra University

Efficiency and Practicality

With a basic philosophy of down-to-earth pragmatism, Americans pride themselves on being efficient and practical. When it comes to *efficiency*, they admire anything that saves time and effort. In terms of *practicality*, they generally are receptive to any new product that makes tasks easier and can help solve problems. For example, today it is possible for manufacturers of many product categories to offer the public a wide range of interchangeable components. Thus, a consumer can design his or her own "customized" wall unit from such standard components as compatible metals and woods, legs, door facings, and style panels at a cost not much higher than a completely standardized unit. The capacity of manufacturers to create mass-produced components offer consumers the practical option of a customized product at a reasonable price.

Another illustration of Americans' attentiveness to efficiency and practicality is the extreme importance attached to *time*. Americans seem to be convinced that "time waits for no one," which is reflected in their habitual attention to being prompt. Another sign of America's preoccupation with time is the belief that time is in increasingly short supply. Americans place a great deal of importance on getting there first, on the value of time itself, on the notion that time is money, and on the importance of not wasting time.

The frequency with which Americans look at their watches, and the importance attached to having an accurate timepiece, tend to support the American value of *punctuality*. Similarly, the broad consumer acceptance of the microwave oven and microwaveable foods are also examples of Americans' love affair with products that save time and effort by providing efficiency and practicality. This is especially important today, when so many female heads of household are in the work force. Similarly, in positioning its personal organizers, Mead stresses that its Cambridge brand day planners are "The Easiest Way To

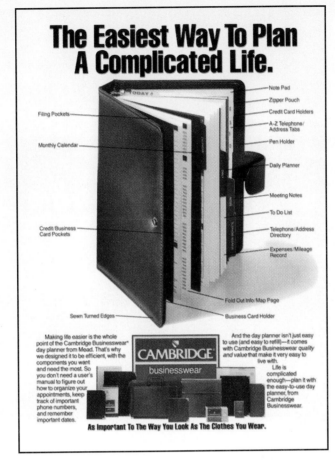

FIGURE 14-6

Punctuality as a Form
of Efficiency and
Effectiveness
Courtesy of The Mead Corporation

Plan A Complicated Life" (see Figure 14-6). Pulling out a planner at a business meeting is
a symbol that tells others at the meeting that you are organized and efficient.

Progress

Progress is another watchword of American society. Americans respond favorably to the
promise of "progress." Our receptivity to progress appears to be closely linked to other
core values already examined (*achievement* and *success*, *efficiency* and *practicality*) and to
the central belief that people can always improve themselves, that tomorrow should be better than today.

In a consumption-oriented society such as that of the United States, progress often
means the acceptance of change, new products or services designed to fulfill previously
undersatisfied or unsatisfied needs (Figure 14-7 on page 426). In the name of progress,
Americans appear to be receptive to product claims that stress "new," "improved,"
"longer-lasting," "speedier," "quicker," "smoother and closer," and "increased strength."
Figure 14-8 on page 427 presents an advertisement for "new-and-improved" Sun-Maid
Baking Raisins.

Material Comfort

For most Americans, *material comfort* signifies the attainment of "the good life," a life that
may include a new car, a dishwasher, a microwave oven, an air conditioner, a hot tub, and
an almost infinite variety of other convenience-oriented and pleasure-providing goods and

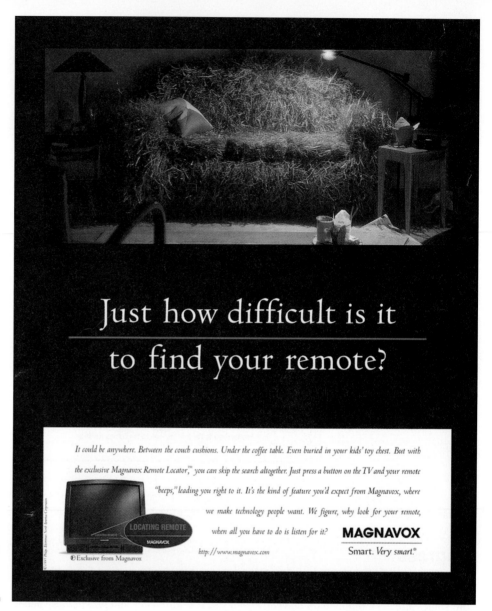

FIGURE 14-7

Progress in the Form of
Satisfying Unfulfilled
Needs
Courtesy of Magnavox Corporation

services. It appears that consumers' idea of material comfort is largely a *relative* view; that is, consumers tend to define their own satisfaction with the amount of material goods they have in terms of a comparison of what they have to what others have. If a comparison suggests that they have more than others do, then they are more likely to be satisfied.[22]

As many popular songs point out, the ownership of material goods does not always lead to happiness. In fact, some managers and professionals now acknowledge that the emphasis they have placed on career success and earning "lots of money" has not made them happy. Many say they would gladly trade income for more free time to spend with family and friends and for having fun.[23]

Individualism

Americans place a strong value on "being themselves." Self-reliance, self-interest, self-confidence, self-esteem, and self-fulfillment are all exceedingly popular expressions of *in-*

New.

Improved.

We've just developed a remarkable new kind of raisin for baking. Sun-Maid® Baking Raisins. They're juicier, all-natural raisins that make whatever you bake moister. Moister cookies, moister muffins, moister everything. Perfected in the kitchens of master chefs, Sun-Maid Baking Raisins eliminate the need to soak raisins before baking (a time-honored chore performed by the best bakers and most grandmothers). And after all, if you're taking the time to bake in the first place, don't you want to get the most delicious results you can? You'll get them with new Sun-Maid Baking Raisins.

≈ Sun-Maid's Raisin Oatmeal Classics ≈

3/4 cup butter or margarine, softened
1 cup firmly packed brown sugar
1/2 cup sugar
1 egg
1 teaspoon vanilla
1 cup all-purpose flour
1 teaspoon cinnamon
1/2 teaspoon baking soda
1/4 teaspoon salt
3 cups rolled oats
1 pkg. (1 cup) Sun-Maid Baking Raisins

Heat oven to 350°F. Grease cookie sheets. Combine butter, brown sugar, sugar, egg and vanilla; beat until well blended. Combine flour, cinnamon, baking soda and salt. Add to butter mixture; mix well. Stir in oats and Sun-Maid Baking Raisins. Drop by tablespoonfuls onto greased cookie sheets. Bake in upper third of oven at 350°F for 12 to 15 minutes. Remove from cookie sheets; cool on wire racks. Makes 3 dozen cookies.

©1994 Sun-Maid Growers of California

MOISTER   RAISINS   FOR   MOISTER   BAKING.

FIGURE 14-8

"New" and "Improved" Is a Progress Appeal
Courtesy of Sun-Maid Raisins

dividualism. Striving for individualism seems to be linked to the rejection of dependency; that is, it is better to rely on oneself than on others.

In terms of consumer behavior, an appeal to individualism frequently takes the form of reinforcing the consumer's sense of identity with products or services that both reflect and emphasize that identity. For example, advertisements for high-style clothing and cosmetics usually promise that their products will enhance the consumer's exclusive or distinctive character and set him or her apart from others.

Freedom

Freedom is another very strong American value, with historical roots in such democratic ideals as "freedom of speech," "freedom of the press," and "freedom of worship." As an outgrowth of these democratic beliefs in freedom, Americans have a strong preference for *freedom of choice*, the opportunity to choose from a wide range of alternatives. This preference is reflected in the large number of competitive brands and product variations that can be found on the shelves of the modern supermarket or department store. For many products, consumers can select from a wide variety of sizes, colors, flavors, features, styles, and even special ingredients (i.e., all-natural-ingredient toothpaste without sugar). It also explains why many companies offer consumers many choices: 100 Sony Walkmen, 800 Philips color TV sets, or 3,000 Seiko watches.

External Conformity

Although Americans deeply embrace *freedom of choice* and *individualism*, they nevertheless accept the reality of *conformity*. External conformity is a necessary process by which the individual adapts to society. It has been said that "no social organization, no culture, no form of institutionalized relationship whatever could exist without the process of interaction we call conformity."[24]

In the realm of consumer behavior, conformity (or uniformity) takes the form of standardized goods and services. Standardized products have been made possible by mass production. The availability of a wide choice of standardized products places the consumer in the unique position of being *individualistic* (by selecting specific products that close friends do not have) or of *conforming* (by purchasing a similar product). In this context, individualism and conformity exist side by side as choices for the American consumer.

An interesting example of the "ping-pong" relationship between seeking individualism and accepting conformity is the trend for more casual dressing in the workplace (already discussed in this chapter). For instance, male and female executives are conforming less to workplace dress codes (i.e., there are more dress options open to business executives). For instance, some male executives are wearing casual slacks and sport shirts to work; others are wearing blazers and slacks, rather than business suits. Greater personal confidence and an emphasis on comfort appear to be the reasons that many executives are wearing less traditional business attire. Nevertheless, in some companies the appearance of males executives in blue blazers and grey slacks does seem like a "business uniform" (which is a kind of conformity). Figure 14-9 presents the findings of consumer research that reveals the types of clothing that men and women wear to the office. Research reveals that the majority of American workers are wearing some type of casual clothing to work.[25] For men, it is commonly "everyday casual" (jeans, shorts, T-shirts, etc.); for women it is "casual" (casual pants with or without a jacket, sweaters, separates, and pantsuits). Moreover, more than 50 percent of workers surveyed feel that it increases their productivity to wear casual clothing to work.

Humanitarianism

Americans are generous when it comes to those in need. They support with a passion many humane and charitable causes, and they sympathize with the "underdog" who must overcome adversity to get ahead. They also tend to be charitable and willing to come to the aid of people less fortunate. Additionally, social issues have an impact on both what consumers buy and where they invest. For example, some investors prefer mutual funds that screen companies for such social concerns as military contracts, pollution problems, and equal-opportunity employment. Investments in socially conscious mutual funds are now quite commonplace.

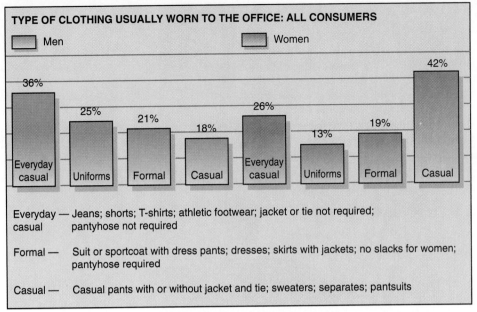

TYPE OF CLOTHING USUALLY WORN TO THE OFFICE: ALL CONSUMERS

☐ Men   ☐ Women

Men:
- Everyday casual: 36%
- Uniforms: 25%
- Formal: 21%
- Casual: 18%

Women:
- Everyday casual: 26%
- Uniforms: 13%
- Formal: 19%
- Casual: 42%

Everyday casual — Jeans; shorts; T-shirts; athletic footwear; jacket or tie not required; pantyhose not required

Formal — Suit or sportcoat with dress pants; dresses; skirts with jackets; no slacks for women; pantyhose required

Casual — Casual pants with or without jacket and tie; sweaters; separates; pantsuits

FIGURE 14-9

What Are Men and Women Wearing to the Office?
Source: KARI VAN HOOF, "Casual Clothing Are Workplace Trend," *Brandweek*, July 18, 1994, 17. © 1996 ASM Communications, Inc. Used with permission from Brandweek.

Many companies try to appeal to consumers by emphasizing their concern for environmental or social issues (see Chapter 20). AT&T, for example, a leader in long distance and wireless telecommunication services, makes it known to its consumers, through public service ads, that it donates money and employees' time to a wide range of ecological and environmental charities and causes.

Youthfulness

Americans tend to place an almost sacred value on *youthfulness*. This emphasis is a reflection of America's rapid technological development. In an atmosphere where "new" is constantly stressed, "old" is often equated with being "outdated." This is in contrast to traditional European, African, and Asian societies, in which the elderly are revered for having the wisdom of experience that comes with age.

Youthfulness should not be confused with youth, which describes an age grouping. Americans are preoccupied with *looking* and *acting* young, regardless of their chronological age. For Americans, youthfulness is a state of mind and a state of being, sometimes expressed as being "young at heart," "young in spirit," or "young in appearance." Figure 14-10 on page 430 presents an ad for Quaker Oats that features a profile of a mature woman who very much typifies an individual with a youthful state of mind.

A great deal of advertising is directed to creating a sense of urgency about retaining one's youth and fearing aging. Hand-cream ads talk about "young hands"; skin-treatment ads state "I dreaded turning 30 . . ."; fragrance and makeup ads stress looking "sexy and young" or "denying your age"; detergent ads ask the reader, "Can you match their hands with their ages?" These advertising themes, which promise the consumer the benefits of youthfulness, reflect the high premium Americans place on appearing and acting young.

Fitness and Health

Americans' preoccupation with *fitness* and *health* has emerged as a core value. This value has manifested itself in a number of ways, including tennis, racquetball, and jogging fads,

FIGURE 14-10

Appealing to
Youthfulness
Courtesy of Quaker Oats

and the continued increases in sales of vitamin's (growing at more than 10 percent, it is nearly a $2 billion industry).[26] Add to these trends an enhanced consciousness on the part of Americans that "You are what you eat (or drink)."

According to some, the fitness trend is an outgrowth of the "me generation." Today, a significant segment of the population engages in one or more athletic activities, which supports the growing market for health- and fitness-related products and services. Research reveals that almost half of white-collar working women find time to exercise each week.[27] They feel that working out provides them with physical benefits, while it bolsters their self-image. Table 14-8 shows the top-10 fitness and sports activities that they engage in.

Fitness and health are becoming lifestyle choices for many consumers. This trend has stimulated Reebok to open a $55 million exercise-retail complex in New York, seeking to build a cultural connection with consumers that goes beyond the normal marketing approach. The Reebok Sports Club/NY is a pilot for a possible chain of such clubs.[28] Traditional food manufacturers have begun modifying their ingredients to cater to the health-conscious consumer. For instance, Ragú Today's Recipe Pasta Sauces offer reduced fat and sodium to meet the demand for healthier foods; Slim-Fast, whose major product is a 190-calorie liquid substitute for meals, is the leader in the meal-replacement category. Frozen dinners have become more nutritious in recent years (see Figure 14-11 on page 432), and manufacturers of traditional "junk food" are trying to make it appear more healthful. "Light" or "fat-free" versions of snack chips or pretzels, along with "low-sodium," "no-cholesterol," "no-preservative" snack products, are an attempt to provide

table 14-8   Top 10 Fitness and Sports Activities for White-Collar Women

RANK	ACTIVITY	PERCENT
1	Walking	85%
2	Bicycling	63
3	Aerobics	61
4	Swimming	50
5	Bowling	33
6	Jogging/running	30
7	Calisthenics	30
8	Hiking/backpacking	26
9	Boating	22
10	Weightlifting	22

Source: DEBORAH BOSANKO, "Why Do Working Women Work Out?" *American Demographics*, February 1994, 12; and Women's Sports Foundation.

consumers with tasty and healthy options (estimated to be worth $12 billion). Even fast-food restaurants, whose foods are traditionally high in salt, fat, and cholesterol, are beginning to change. Taco Bell has introduced its reduced-fat "Border Lights" menu in response to its projections of increasing sales opportunities coming about with growth of the health-conscious market.[29]

Some of the biggest changes have occurred with respect to what people drink. Diet beverages are the super-growth segment of the soft-drink industry. Home coffee consumption has been declining since 1984. Americans are also abstaining from hard liquor. Over the past decade, the consumption of distilled spirits dropped 25 percent, and beer consumption also has declined. Nonalcoholic beer is the fastest growing segment of the United States beer market, and the consumption of bottled water has likewise flourished.

While there is no denying the *fitness and healthy living* trend in American society, there is evidence that consumers find it difficult "to be good." For instance, people miss their desserts. Research suggests that more than 75 percent of American consumers think about dessert between one and eight times a day. The main activities that seem to put people in the "mood" for desserts are: exercise, working, entertainment, eating, and studying.[30] Also, many Americans are unwilling to compromise on flavor for health benefits, with the result being a kind of reverse trend toward full-flavored, rich foods. For example, Frito-Lay has reported "marginal to disappointing" sales of its light versions of Cheetos and Doritos, and Haagen-Daz's new "Extraas" line of premium ice creams, including extra-rich flavors such as Chocolate Macadamia and Triple Brownie Overload, have increased the company's dollar share of the ice cream market. This counter-trend reveals the diversity of preferences that exist side by side within the marketplace. It points up that low-fat and low-cholesterol food products are not for everyone and that there is an important market segment whose members seek to indulge their taste buds and their waistlines.

Another manifestation of Americans' concern with health and fitness is the new fear of the perils of suntanning. Regular TV, magazine, and newspaper coverage of the dangers of suntans have motivated consumers to seek out sunscreen and sunblock products and have caused manufacturers to aggressively market such products, with protective ratings of 15, 20, 30, and even 50.

Core Values Are Not an American Phenomenon

The cultural values just examined are not all uniquely or originally American. Some were borrowed, particularly from European society, as people emigrated to the United States. Some values that originated in America are now part of the fabric of other societies. For example, there is evidence that "the good life" may be a universal notion and that global brands are used as an external sign of attaining "the good life."[31]

In addition, not all Americans necessarily accept each of these values. However, as a whole, these values do account for much of the American character. Table 14-9 summarizes a number of American core values and indicates their relevance to consumer behavior.

table 14-9 Summary of American Core Values

VALUE	GENERAL FEATURES	RELEVANCE TO CONSUMER BEHAVIOR
ACHIEVEMENT AND SUCCESS ACTIVITY	Hard work is good; success flows from hard work Keeping busy is healthy and natural	Acts as a justification for acquisition of goods ("You deserve it") Stimulates interest in products that are time-savers and enhance leisure time
EFFICIENCY AND PRACTICALITY	Admiration of things that solve problems (e.g., save time and effort) People can improve themselves; tomorrow should be better than today	Stimulates purchase of products that function well and save time Stimulates desire for new products that fulfill unsatisfied needs; ready acceptance of products that claim to be "new" or "improved"
MATERIAL COMFORT	"The good life"	Fosters acceptance of convenience and luxury products that make life more comfortable and enjoyable
INDIVIDUALISM	Being oneself (e.g., self-reliance, self-interest, self-esteem)	Stimulates acceptance of customized or unique products that enable a person to "express his or her own personality"
FREEDOM	Freedom of choice	Fosters interest in wide product lines and differentiated products
EXTERNAL CONFORMITY	Uniformity of observable behavior; desire for acceptance	Stimulates interest in products that are used or owned by others in the same social group
HUMANITARIANISM	Caring for others, particularly the underdog	Stimulates patronage of firms that compete with market leaders
YOUTHFULNESS	A state of mind that stresses being "young at heart" and having a youthful appearance	Stimulates acceptance of products that provide the illusion of maintaining or fostering youthfulness
FITNESS AND HEALTH	Caring about one's body, including the desire to be physically fit and healthy	Stimulates acceptance of food products, activities, and equipment perceived to maintain or increase physical fitness

summary

The study of culture is the study of all aspects of a society—its language, knowledge, laws, customs—that give that society its distinctive character and personality. In the context of consumer behavior, culture is defined as the sum total of learned beliefs, values, and customs that serve to regulate the consumer behavior of members of a particular society. Beliefs and values are guides for consumer behavior; customs are usual and accepted ways of behaving.

The impact of culture on society is so natural and so ingrained that its influence on behavior is rarely noted. Yet, culture offers order, direction, and guidance to members of society in all phases of human problem solving. Culture is dynamic and gradually and continually evolves to meet the needs of society.

Culture is learned as part of social experience. Children acquire from their environments a set of beliefs, values, and customs that constitute culture (i.e., they are encultured). These are acquired through formal learning, informal learning, and technical learning. Advertising enhances formal learning by reinforcing desired modes of behavior and expectations; it enhances informal learning by providing models for behavior.

Culture is communicated to members of society through a common language and through commonly shared symbols. Because the human mind has the ability to absorb and to process symbolic communication, marketers can suc-cessfully promote both tangible and intangible products and product concepts to consumers through mass media.

All the elements in the marketing mix serve to communicate symbolically with the audience. Products project an image of their own; so does promotion. Price and retail outlets symbolically convey images concerning the quality of the product.

The elements of culture are transmitted by three pervasive social institutions: the family, the church, and the school. A fourth social institution that plays a major role in the transmission of culture is the mass media, both through editorial content and through advertising.

A wide range of measurement techniques is used to study culture. The range includes projective techniques, attitude measurement methods, field observation, participant observation, content analysis, and value measurement survey techniques.

A number of core values of the American people are relevant to the study of consumer behavior. These include achievement and success, activity, efficiency and practicality, progress, material comfort, individualism, freedom, conformity, humanitarianism, youthfulness, and fitness and health.

Because each of these values varies in importance to the members of our society, each provides an effective basis for segmenting consumer markets.

discussion questions

1. Distinguish between beliefs, values, and customs. Illustrate how the clothing a person wears at different times or for different occasions is influenced by customs.

2. A manufacturer of fat-free granola bars is considering targeting school-age children by positioning its product as a healthy, nutritious snack food. How can an understanding of the three forms of cultural learning be used in developing an effective strategy to target the intended market?

3. The Citrus Growers of America is planning a promotional campaign to encourage the drinking of orange and grapefruit juice in situations in which many con-sumers normally consume soft drinks. Using the Rokeach Value Survey Instrument (Table 14-5), identify relevant cultural, consumption-specific, and product-specific values for citrus juices as an alternative to soft drinks. What are the implications of these values for an advertising campaign designed to increase the consumption of citrus juices?

4. Describe how a marketer can use some of the social trends examined by the Yankelovich Monitor Service (listed in Table 14-6) to position a microwave oven.

5. A national hotel chain that offers accommodations to several segments of travelers is considering subscribing to the Yankelovich MONITOR and/or the DYG

Scanning Program. Which of the trends tracked by these services (listed in Tables 14-6 and 14-7) should be of interest to the hotel chain? Why? How can the chain's management use such knowledge to design its services and marketing strategies?

6. For each of the products and activities listed below:

   a. Identify the core values most relevant to their purchase and use.

   b. Determine whether these values encourage or discourage use or ownership.

   c. Determine whether these core values are shifting and, if so, in what direction. The products and activities are:

1. Donating money to charities
2. Donating blood
3. Compact disc players
4. Telephone answering machines
5. Toothpaste
6. Diet soft drinks
7. Foreign travel
8. Suntan lotion
9. Cellular phones
10. Interactive TV home-shopping services
11. Fat-free foods
12. Products in recyclable packaging

exercises

1. Identify a singer or singing group whose music you like and discuss the symbolic function of the clothes that person (or group) wears.

2. Think of various routines in your everyday life (e.g., grooming or food preparation). Identify one ritual and describe it. In your view, is this ritual shared by others? If so, to what extent? What are the implications of your ritualistic behavior to the marketer(s) of the product(s) you use during your routine?

3. a. Summarize an episode of a weekly television series that you watched recently. Describe how the program transmitted cultural beliefs, values, and customs.

   b. Select and describe three commercials that were broadcast during the program mentioned above. Do these commercials create or reflect cultural values? Explain your answer.

4. a. Find two different advertisements for deodorants in two magazines that are targeted to different audiences. Content-analyze the written and pictorial aspects of each ad, using any core values discussed in this chapter. How are these values portrayed to the target audiences?

   b. Identify symbols used in these ads and discuss their effectiveness in conveying the desired product image or characteristics.

key words

- Acculturation
- American core values
- Consumer fieldwork
- Content analysis
- Culture
- DYG SCAN
- Enculturation

- Field observation
- Formal, informal, and technical learning of culture
- List of Values
- Participant-observers
- Rituals
- Ritualistic behavior

- Rokeach Value Survey
- Subculture
- Symbols
- Values and Lifestyles–VALS 2
- The Yankelovich MONITOR®

end notes

1. "Remember When Bras Were for Burning," *Business Week*, January 16, 1995, 37; and CYNDEE MILLER "A Casual Affair," *Marketing News*, March 13, 1995, 1; and "Casual Clothes are Workplace Trend," *Brandweek*, July 18, 1994, 17.

2. LARRY JABBONSKY, "Pepsi Sees If Consumers Wanna Guarana," *Beverage World*, June 30, 1995, 3.

3. GRETA ELEEM PENNELL, "Babes in Toyland: Learning an Ideology of Gender," in Chris T. Allen and Deborah Roedder John, eds., *Advances in Consumer Research* 21 (Provo, UT: Association for Consumer Research, 1994), 359–64.

4. GWEN RAE BACHMANN, DEBORAH ROEDDER JOHN, and AKSHAY RAO, "Children's Susceptibility to Peer Group Purchase Influence: An Exploratory Investigation," in Leigh McAlister and Michael L. Rothschild, eds., *Advances in Consumer Research* 20 (Provo, UT: Association for Consumer Research 1993), 463–68.

5. T. BETTINA CORNWELL, "T-Shirts as Wearable Diary: An Examination of Artifact Consumption and Garnering Related to Life Events," in Marvin E. Goldberg, Gerald Gorn, and Richard W. Pollay, eds., *Advances in Consumer Research* 17 (Provo, UT: Association for Consumer Research, 1990), 375–79; and also SUSAN H. GODAR, "The Cultural Meaning of Products as a Barrier to Adoption By Other Subcultures—Who Controls It?" in Rajan Varadarajan and Bernard Jaworski, eds., *1993 AMA Winter Educators' Proceedings* 4 (Chicago: American Marketing Association, 1993), 500–506.

6. DENNIS W. ROOK, "The Ritual Dimension of Consumer Behavior," *Journal of Consumer Research* 12, December 1985, 251–64.

7. DENNIS W. ROOK, "Ritual Behavior and Consumer Symbolism," in Thomas C. Kinnear, ed., *Advances in Consumer Research* 11 (Ann Arbor, MI: Association for Consumer Research, 1984), 279–84.

8. LISE HEROUX and NANCY J. CHURCH, "Wedding Anniversary Celebration and Gift-Giving Rituals: The Dialectic of Intimacy," in Robert L. King, ed., *Marketing: Perspectives for the 1990s* (Richmond, VA: Southern Marketing Association, 1992), 43–47.

9. DAVID M. POTTER, *People of Plenty* (Chicago: University of Chicago Press, 1954), 167.

10. CYNDEE MILLER, "Study Dispels '80s Stereotypes of Women," *Marketing News*, May 22, 1995, 3.

11. KATE FITZGERALD, "Hallmark Alters Focus as Life Styles Change," *Advertising Age*, October 31, 1994, 4.

12. M. F. CALLCOTT and WEI-NA LEE, "A Content Analysis of Animation and Animated Spokes-Characters in Television Commercials," *Journal of Advertising* 23, December 1994, 1–12.

13. SHAY SAYRE, "Content Analysis as a Tool for Consumer Research," *The Journal of Consumer Marketing* 9, Winter 1992, 15–25.

14. JILL HICKS FERGUSON, PEGGY J. KRESHEL, and SPENCER F. TINKHAM, "In the Pages of Ms.: Sex Role Portrayals of Women in Advertising," *Journal of Advertising* 19, 1990, 20–51.

15. WAGNER A. KAMAKURA and JOSE AFONSO MAZZON, "Value Segmentation: A Model for the Measurement of Values and Value Systems," *Journal of Consumer Research* 18, September 1991, 208–18.

16. J. MICHAEL MUNSON and SHELBY H. MCINTYRE, "Developing Practical Procedures for the Measurement of Personal Values in Cross-Cultural Marketing," *Journal of Marketing Research* 16, February 1979, 48–52; THOMAS J. REYNOLDS and JAMES P. JOLLY, "Measuring Personal Values: An Evaluation of Alternative Methods," *Journal of Marketing Research* 17, November 1980, 531–36; and L. J. SHRUM, JOHN A. MCCARTY, and TAMARA L. LOEFFLER, "Individual Differences in Value Stability: Are We Really Tapping True Values?" in Goldberg, Gorn, and Pollay, eds., *Advances in Consumer Research*, op. cit., 609–15.

17. LYNN R. KAHLE, ed., *Social Values and Social Change: Adaption of Life in America* (New York: Praeger, 1983); SHARON E. BEATTY, et al., "Alternative Measurement Approaches to Consumer Values: The List of Values and the Rokeach Value Survey," *Psychology & Marketing* 2, 1985, 181–200; and LYNN R. KAHLE and ROGER P. MCINTYRE, REID P. CLAXTON and DAVID B. JONES, "Empirical Relationships Between Cognitive Style and LOV: Implications for Values and Value Systems," in Frank R. Kardes and Mita Sujan, eds., *Advances in Consumer Research* 22 (Provo, UT: Association for Consumer Research 1995), 141–46.

18. *Yankelovich MONITOR: Tracking Consumer Attitudes Since 1971*, Yankelovich, Clancy Shulman, 1995.

19. PETER H. ROSE, *Personal Communication* (Westport, CT: Yankelovich Partners, May 6, 1995).

20. *DYG SCAN A Scanning Program, DYG, Inc., and Presentation for the Marketing Community*, DYG, Inc.

21. DAVID C. MCCLELLAND, *The Achieving Society* (New York: Free Press, 1961), 150–51.

22. RAMESH VENKAT and HAROLD J. OGDEN, "Material Satisfaction: The Effects of Social Comparison and Attribution," in Barbara B. Stern and George M. Zinkan, eds., *1995 AMA Educators' Proceedings* (Chicago: American Marketing Association, 1995), 314–19.

23. CAROL HYMOWITZ, "Trading Fat Paychecks for Free Time," *The Wall Street Journal*, August 5, 1991, B1.

24. ROBERT A. NISBET, *The Social Bond* (New York: Knopf, 1970), 69.

25. "Casual Clothes Are Workplace Trend," *Brandweek*, July 18, 1994, 17. Also, see: ELLEN NEUBORNE, "Fashion on Menu at T.G.I. Friday's," *USAToday*, February 27, 1996, B1.

26. KELLY SHERMACH, "Putting the 'Men' into Vitamin," *Marketing News*, February 27, 1995, 1, 39; and PAM WEISZ, "BeautiControl Is Latest to Enter Ever-Segmenting Vitamin Market," *Brandweek*, April 17, 1995, 9.

27. DEBORAH BOSANKO, "Why Do Working Women Work Out?" *American Demographics*, February 1994, 12–13.

28. ERIC HOLLREISER, "Reebok: The Club," *Brandweek*, February 20, 1995, 1.

29. JEANNE WHALEN, "Taco Bell Cuts the Fat, Aims for Hefty Sales," *Advertising Age*, February 13, 1995, 36. Also, see: JUDANN POLACK and MARK GLEASON, "Wendy's, McD's to Add Menu Sizzle," *Advertising Age*, February 12, 1996, 12; and JUDANN POLACK, "New-Product Feast Readied by Frito-Lay," *Advertising Age*, February 12, 1996, 1 and 37.

30. "The Big Scoop on Just Desserts," *Advertising Age*, October 2, 1995, 3.

31. GEORGE M. ZINKHAN and PENELOPE J. PRENSHAW, "Good Life Images and Brand Name Associations: Evidence from Asia, America, and Europe," in Chris T. Allen and Deborah Roedder John, eds., *Advances in Consumer Research* 21 (Provo, UT: Association for Consumer Research, 1994), 496–500.

Culture has a potent influence on all consumer behavior. Individuals are brought up to follow the beliefs, values, and customs of their society and to avoid behavior that is frowned upon or considered taboo. In addition to cultural segmentation, marketers segment larger societies into smaller subgroups (subcultures) that consist of people who are similar in terms of their ethnic origin, their customs, and/or the ways they behave. These subcultures provide important marketing opportunities for astute marketing strategists.

Our discussion of subcultures, therefore, has a narrower focus than the discussion of culture. Instead of examining the dominant beliefs, values, and customs that exist within an entire society, this chapter explores the marketing opportunities created by the existence of certain beliefs, values, and customs shared by members of specific subcultural groups within a society. These

To me, old age is always fifteen years older than I am.

—Bernard Baruch
Quoted in *The New York Times*
June 6, 1984

subcultural divisions are based on a variety of sociocultural and demographic variables, such as nationality, religion, geographic locality, race, age, sex, even working status.

What is Subculture?

The members of a specific **subculture** possess beliefs, values, and customs that set them apart from other members of the same society. In addition, they adhere to most of the dominant cultural beliefs, values, and behavioral patterns of the larger society. We define subculture, then, as *a distinct cultural group that exists as an identifiable segment within a larger, more complex society.*

Thus, the cultural profile of a society or nation is a composite of two distinct elements: (1) the unique beliefs, values, and customs subscribed to by members of specific subcultures; and (2) the central or core cultural themes that are shared by most of the population, regardless of specific subcultural memberships. Figure 15-1 presents a simple model of the relationship between two subcultural groups (teens and Xers) and the larger culture. As the figure depicts, each subculture has its own unique traits, yet both groups share the dominant traits of the overall American culture.

Let us look at it in another way: Each American is, in large part, a product of the "American way of life." Each American, however, is at the same time a member of various subcultures. For example, a 14-year-old boy may simultaneously be Hispanic, Catholic, a teenager, and a New Yorker. We would expect that membership in each different subculture would provide its own set of specific beliefs, values, attitudes, and customs. Table 15-1 lists typical subcultural categories and corresponding examples of specific subcultural groups. This list is by no means exhaustive: college graduates, feminists, Girl Scouts, and single parents—in fact, any group that shares common beliefs and customs—may be classified as a subculture.

Subcultural analysis enables the marketing manager to focus on sizable and "natural" market segments. When carrying out such analyses, the marketer must determine whether the beliefs, values, and customs shared by members of a specific subgroup make

FIGURE 15-1

Relationship Between Culture and Subculture

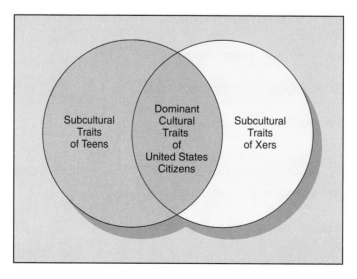

table 15-1   Examples of Major Subcultural Categories

CATEGORIES	EXAMPLES
Nationality (i.e., birthplace of ancestors)	French, Puerto Rican, Korean
Religion	Catholic, Hindu, Jew
Geographic region	Southeastern, midwestern, eastern
Race	African-American, Caucasian, Asian-American
Age	Teens, Xers, middle age, elderly
Gender	Female, male
Occupation	Engineer, cook, plumber
Social class	Lower, middle, upper

them desirable candidates for special marketing attention. Subcultures, therefore, are relevant units of analysis for market research.

The following sections examine a number of important subcultural categories: nationality, religion, geographic location, race, age, and sex. (Occupational and social-class subgroups were discussed in detail in Chapter 13.)

NATIONALITY SUBCULTURES

Although most U.S. citizens, especially those born in the United States, see themselves as Americans, they frequently retain a sense of identification and pride in the language and customs of their ancestors. When it comes to consumer behavior, this ancestral pride is manifested most strongly in the consumption of ethnic foods, in travel to the "homeland," and in the purchase of numerous cultural artifacts (ethnic clothing, art, music, foreign-language newspapers). Interest in these goods and services has expanded rapidly as younger Americans attempt to better understand and more closely associate with their ethnic roots. To illustrate the importance of ethnic origin as a subcultural market segment, the following section examines Hispanic-American subculture.

Hispanic Subcultures

Hispanic-Americans represent about 9 percent of the United States population (more than 25 million people, with buying power of $205 billion).[1] In contrast to other American population segments, Hispanic-Americans are younger (the median age of Hispanics is about 7 years younger than the median age of non-Hispanics), they are members of larger families, and they are more likely to live in an "extended family" household, with members consisting of several generations.

With a 53 percent population increase during the decade from 1980 to 1990 (and a 27 percent growth rate expected for the decade 1990 to 2000), Hispanic-Americans are projected to supplant African-Americans within 20 years as the largest American minority group. Indeed, Hispanics have already become the dominant minority in New York, Los Angeles, San Diego, Phoenix, San Francisco, and Denver, and they represent the majority in San Antonio, Texas.

This subcultural group can be considered as a single market, based on a common language and culture, or as separate subcultural markets that correspond to different Hispanic countries of origin. There are twelve Hispanic subgroups now identified in the United States. The three largest Hispanic subcultural groups consist of Mexican-Americans (about 60 percent of total Hispanic-Americans), Puerto Ricans (approximately 12 percent of the total), and Cubans (almost 5 percent of the total). These subcultures are heavily concentrated geographically, with more than 70 percent of their members residing in California, Texas, New York, and Florida.[2]

▲ **Understanding Hispanic Consumer Behavior** Available evidence indicates that Hispanic and Anglo consumers differ in terms of a variety of important buyer behavior variables. For instance, Hispanic consumers prefer well-established brands and traditionally prefer to shop at smaller stores. In the New York metropolitan area, Hispanic consumers spend 55 percent of their food budgets in over 8000 *bodegas* (relatively small food specialty stores), despite the fact that supermarket prices generally are lower. Table 15-2 presents, in list form, these and other distinctive characteristics of the overall Hispanic market.

While mindful of their tradition, Hispanic-Americans, like other major subcultural groups, are a dynamic and evolving portion of the overall society. For this reason, a growing number of Hispanic consumers are food shopping in nonethnic large American-style supermarkets. They appear to be engaged a process of acculturation, that is, they are gradually adopting the consumption patterns of the majority of United States consumers.[3] Similarly, other research indicates that when it comes to clothes shopping, Hispanic youths are more fashion-conscious and are more likely to seek out and be loyal to well-known brands and to generally like the act of shopping more than their non-Hispanic counterparts.[4]

▲ **Defining and Segmenting the Hispanic Market** Marketers who are targeting the diverse Hispanic subcultural groupings are concerned with finding the best ways to define and segment this market. In terms of definition, Table 15-3 presents six variables marketers have used to determine who is Hispanic. Of these measures, the combination of *self-identification* and *degree of identification* are particularly appealing, because they permit consumers to define or label themselves. Research shows that those who strongly identify with being Hispanic (i.e., *Strong Hispanic Identifiers*) are more frequent users of Spanish-

table 15-2   Traditional Characteristics of the Hispanic-American Market

Prefer well-known or familiar brands

Buy brands perceived to be more prestigious

Are fashion-conscious

Historically prefer to shop at smaller personal stores

Buy brands advertised by their ethnic-group stores

Tend *not* to be impulse buyers (i.e., are deliberate)

Increasingly clipping and using cents-off coupons

Likely to buy what their parents bought

Prefer fresh to frozen or prepared items

Tend to be negative about marketing practices and government intervention in business

table 15-3 Ways in Which "Hispanic" Has Been Defined

NAME OF INDICATOR	NATURE/SCOPE AND COMMENTARY
Spanish surname	Not a definitive, since a non-Hispanic person might have a Spanish surname, or an Hispanic person might have a non-Spanish surname.
Country of origin	The birthplace of persons born in the United States of Hispanic parents (e.g., of Puerto Rican parentage) would not reveal their Hispanic background.
Country of family ancestry	Includes those individuals who may not be Hispanic despite coming from a particular Spanish-Latin country (e.g., people of German parentage who may be brought up in a Latin country).
Spanish spoken at home	A significant minority of Hispanic households may speak English at home, yet consider themselves to be culturally Hispanic.
Self-identification	It is reasonable that if an adequate number of self-report choices are offered, a person might identify himself or herself as "Hispanic."
Degree of identification	This measure captures the "degree" of personal identification as "Hispanic" and augments the self-identification measure.

language media, are more brand loyal, are more likely to buy prestige brands, are more likely to seek the advice of another and to more often be influenced by friends or family, and are more likely to buy brands advertised to Hispanics than *Weak Hispanic Identifiers*.[5] This pattern suggests that the degree of Hispanic identification is a useful segmentation variable when one is targeting the Hispanic market.

In addition, the Hispanic market can be segmented by using a combination of *country of origin* and *geographic concentration in the United States* (e.g., 74 percent of Hispanic-Americans of Mexican origin are concentrated in California and Texas; almost 40 percent of those of Puerto Rican origin live in New York).[6] Some marketers feel that it is worthwhile to target each Hispanic-American market separately. Other marketers, including Procter & Gamble, Anheuser-Busch, Coca-Cola, American Honda, Sears, Coors, Colgate-Palmolive, McDonald's, Toyota, Philip Morris, and the "Big Three" United States car companies (GM, Ford, and Chrysler) have targeted the Hispanic market as a single market, using Spanish-language mass media.[7] Recently, Dannon introduced a variety of yogurts in flavors like guava, mango, papaya, and pineapple that are popular with Hispanic-American consumers.[8] Figure 15-2 on page 444 presents a recent Avon ad targeted at the Hispanic-American market.

The Spanish language is often regarded as the bridge that links the various Hispanic subcultures. Even with this common language, however, there is considerable variation among Hispanics regarding their language preferences (e.g., Spanish only, Spanish preferred, English only, or English preferred). This language framework provides still another basis for segmenting the Hispanic-American market. Recent research indicates that Hispanic-Americans spend the most time with mass media in the first language that they learn to speak. So those whose first language is Spanish tend to prefer TV, radio, magazines, and newspapers in Spanish, whereas those Hispanic-Americans who first learn English prefer their media exposure to be in English.[9]

Highlighting the potential importance of the Spanish language, the California Milk Processor Board uncovered, as part of focus group research designed to develop a separate campaign targeted at Hispanic-Americans, that its otherwise very successful tagline, "Got Milk," was misunderstood (it was misinterpreted as "Are you lactating?"). To correct this misperception, they had their Hispanic-market ad agency develop and test a separate Spanish-language campaign that was better suited to Mexican-American values and customs. The targeted campaign proposed: "Have you given them enough milk today?"[10] The new campaign has proven to be very successful.

Each of the major Hispanic subcultural groups appears to have some distinct beliefs, values, and customs; thus, a marketing strategy that may be successful with Puerto Ricans in New York might fail with Cubans in Miami. For this reason some marketers segment the Hispanic market by appealing to the distinct cultural values of a specific nationality. Others segment the Hispanic market in terms of the degree of *acculturation* to the dominant American cultural values, customs, artifacts, and rituals.

The Impact of Nationality Subcultures

The United States presently is in the midst of one of its largest immigration waves in decades. Although the 1990 census found almost 20 million foreign-born persons living in the United States, about 25 percent of them had arrived within the past 5 years. The almost 8 percent of the population that was foreign-born was the highest total in 40 years. Figure 15-3 shows where these immigrants come from, where they live, and where they are making the most impact.

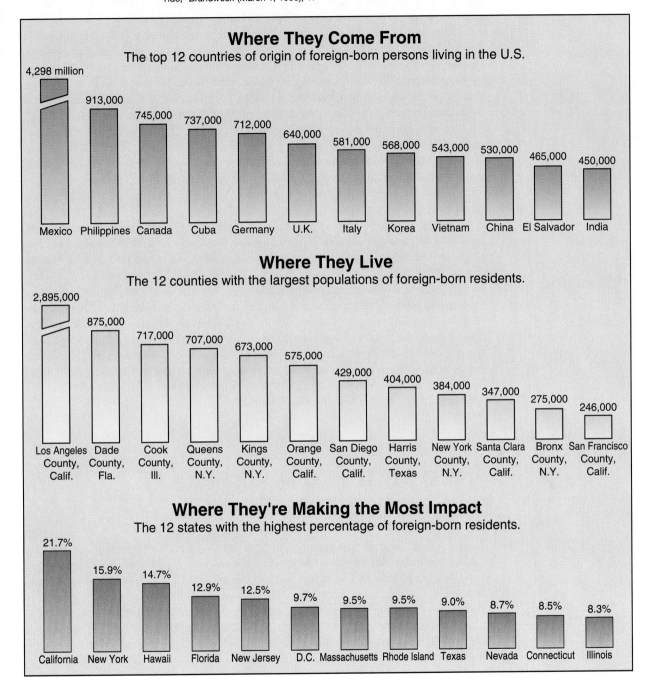

Where They Come From
The top 12 countries of origin of foreign-born persons living in the U.S.

Mexico	Philippines	Canada	Cuba	Germany	U.K.	Italy	Korea	Vietnam	China	El Salvador	India
4,298 million	913,000	745,000	737,000	712,000	640,000	581,000	568,000	543,000	530,000	465,000	450,000

Where They Live
The 12 counties with the largest populations of foreign-born residents.

Los Angeles County, Calif.	Dade County, Fla.	Cook County, Ill.	Queens County, N.Y.	Kings County, N.Y.	Orange County, Calif.	San Diego County, Calif.	Harris County, Texas	New York County, N.Y.	Santa Clara County, Calif.	Bronx County, N.Y.	San Francisco County, Calif.
2,895,000	875,000	717,000	707,000	673,000	575,000	429,000	404,000	384,000	347,000	275,000	246,000

Where They're Making the Most Impact
The 12 states with the highest percentage of foreign-born residents.

California	New York	Hawaii	Florida	New Jersey	D.C.	Massachusetts	Rhode Island	Texas	Nevada	Connecticut	Illinois
21.7%	15.9%	14.7%	12.9%	12.5%	9.7%	9.5%	9.5%	9.0%	8.7%	8.5%	8.3%

RELIGIOUS SUBCULTURES

The United States reportedly has more than 200 different organized religious groups. (Of this number, Protestant denominations, Roman Catholicism, and Judaism are the principal organized religious faiths.) The members of all these religious groups at times are likely to make purchase decisions that are influenced by their religious identity. Commonly, consumer behavior is directly affected by religion in terms of products that are *symbolically* and *ritualistically* associated with the celebration of various religious holidays. For example, Christmas has become the major gift-purchasing season of the year.

Very little consumer research has been devoted to examining how religious affiliation and commitment influence consumption preferences and the meaning of possessions. One stream of research that examined the leisure activities of individuals with different religious backgrounds found several interesting distinctions: Protestant and Catholic consumers possessed a stronger orientation toward solitary leisure pursuits, while Jewish consumers preferred activities that provided companionship and/or sensory stimulation.[11]

In our earlier discussion of the family (see Chapter 12), we indicated that husband-and-wife decision making also was related to religious orientation. When examining differences in proreligious and nonreligious Catholic and Jewish households, it was reported that husbands in proreligious and Catholic families were the major influence in making specific purchase decisions, while in nonreligious and Jewish families, husbands and wives shared equally in most decisions.[12]

Religious requirements or practices sometimes take on an expanded meaning beyond their original purpose. For instance, dietary laws for an observant Jewish family represent an obligation. For example, there is a Kosher lipstick manufactured by Cinema Beauté.[13] The "U" and "K" marks on food packaging are symbols that the food meets Jewish dietary laws. For nonobservant Jews and an increasing number of non-Jews, however, these marks often signify that the food is pure and wholesome—a kind of "Jewish *Good Housekeeping* Seal of Approval." In response to the broader meaning given to kosher-certified products, a number of national brands, such as Coors beer and Pepperidge Farm cookies, have secured kosher certification for their products.[14] Other marketers, like Krups (e.g., electric coffee makers) and Mont Blanc (e.g., fine writing instruments), have developed strong relationships with upscale Jewish customers, even though their products are not particularly linked to Jewish custom or ritual.[15]

GEOGRAPHIC AND REGIONAL SUBCULTURES

The United States is a large country, one that enjoys a wide range of climatic and geographic conditions. Given the country's size and physical diversity, it is only natural that many Americans have a sense of regional identification and use this identification as a way of describing others (e.g., "He is a true Southern gentleman"). These labels often assist us in developing a mental picture and supporting *stereotype* of the person in question.

Anyone who has traveled across the United States has probably noted many regional differences in consumption behavior, especially when it comes to food and drink. For example, a *mug* of black coffee typifies the West, while a *cup* of coffee with milk and sugar is preferred in the East. There also are geographic differences in the consumption of a staple food such as bread. Specifically, in the South and Midwest, soft white bread is preferred, while on the East and West Coasts, firmer breads (rye, whole wheat, and French and Italian breads) are favored.

A collection of research studies further document regional differences in consumption patterns. For instance, Table 15-4 illustrates that differences in product purchase, ownership, or usage levels occur between major metropolitan areas. Metropolitan areas can also be segmented between downtowns and edge cities.[16] This distinction helps redefine

table 15-4   Product Purchase/Usage by Leading Metropolitan Market

PRODUCT PURCHASE/USAGE	HIGHEST PURCHASE/USAGE	LOWEST PURCHASE/USAGE
New domestic car	Detroit	Los Angeles
New imported car	San Francisco	Detroit
Have life insurance	Cleveland	Los Angeles
Drink Scotch whiskey	New York	Detroit
Purchased men's jeans (regular and (designer) in past 12 months	Dallas Fort-Worth	Washington, D.C.
Have a videocassette recorder	Los Angeles	Washington, D.C.
Have a bowling ball	Cleveland	Boston
Use eyeliner	San Francisco	Washington, D.C.
Use artificial sweeteners	Dallas-Fort Worth	San Francisco
Used cough syrup (two-plus times in past 30 days)	Detroit	Los Angeles
Popcorn (two-plus bowls in past 30 days)	Detroit	Los Angeles
Lottery tickets (one-plus in past 30 days)	Cleveland	Washington, D.C.

Source: Based on 1995 Doublebase Mediamark Research, Inc. (New York: Mediamark Research, Inc. 1995). Reprinted by permission.

local markets in terms of specific urban lifestyle. Moreover, such regional variations provide additional support for marketers who argue that it is important to take geographic consumption patterns into account when planning marketing and promotional efforts.

As discussed in Chapter 3, Campbell's Soup Company is a strong advocate of regional marketing. For example, to cater to regional differences in consumer tastes, Campbell's designed a Cajun gumbo soup for the Mississippi Delta area and a spicy hot chili for the Southwest. When developing a canned nacho cheese sauce, Campbell's initially created a product that was too hot for the Eastern United States and too mild for the West and Southwest, then adjusted its formula to a range of values that would appeal to specific regional tastes. Further illustrating regional differences in consumer behavior, Table 15-5 on page 448 presents some comparative lifestyle and activity patterns for three major metropolitan markets: Atlanta, Miami-Ft. Lauderdale, and San Diego. As the results suggest, there are differences that provide each market with a particular "lifestyle flavor."

In general, large metropolitan areas, with a substantial number of affluent middle-age households, dominate most, but not all, consumer-spending categories.[17] Table 15-6 presents some examples of consumer-spending categories, identifies the corresponding hottest metro area, and suggests the likely reason for the market's dominance.

Consumer research into regional differences in purchase behavior reinforces the reality of geographic diversity and the need to segment consumer markets.

RACIAL SUBCULTURES

The major **racial subcultures** in the United States are Caucasian, African-American, Asian-American, and American Indian. Although differences in lifestyles and consumer-spending patterns exist among these groups, the vast majority of racially oriented consumer

table 15-5

Comparison of Lifestyle and Activity Patterns for Atlanta, Miami-Ft. Lauderdale, and San Diego

LIFESTYLE/ACTIVITY	ATLANTA	MIAMI-FT. LAUDERDALE	SAN DIEGO
Bible/devotional reading	139	75	80
Home furnishing/decorating	117	97	97
Foreign travel	108	156	153
Travel for business	137	92	104
Wines	112	117	136
Casino gambling	60	84	136
Boating/sailing	93	121	100
Recreation vehicles	81	61	122
Bicycling frequently	67	125	114
Physical fitness/exercise	110	101	121
Buy prerecorded videos	108	82	104
Military veteran in household	95	77	118
Home video games	107	92	104
Science fiction	104	99	123
Use an IBM-compatible computer	122	91	120
Base Index for U.S.: 100			

Source: From *The Lifestyle Market Analyst.* Data provided by National Demographics and Lifestyles. Published by SRDS. Copyright © 1996 by SRDS. Reprinted by permission.

table 15-6

Top-Ranked Metropolitan Areas for Selected Spending Categories

SPENDING CATEGORY	HOTTEST METRO	EXPLANATION
Alcohol	San Jose, CA	Affluent and somewhat younger
Apparel	San Jose	Affluent and somewhat younger
Cash contributions	Nassau-Suffolk, NY	Older and high-income
Education and reading	Nassau-Suffolk	College-aged kids
Entertainment	San Jose	Affluent and somewhat younger
Food	Nassau-Suffolk	Affluent, children present
Health	Sarasota-Bradenton, FL	Nonpoor elderly (most likely to spend out-of-pocket)
Insurance/pensions	Nassau-Suffolk	Middle-aged affluent
Owned homes	Nassau-Suffolk	Middle-aged affluent
Rented homes	Jacksonville, NC	Young and poor
Tobacco and smoking supplies	El Paso, TX	Young and poor
Transportation	Nassau-Suffolk	Middle-aged affluent (two-income)

Source: MARCIA MOGELONSKY, "America's Hottest Market," *American Demographics*, January 1996, 30. © 1996 American Demographics Magazine. Reprinted with permission.

research has focused on consumer differences between African-Americans and Caucasians. Only recently has particular research attention been given to Asian-American consumers.

The African-American Consumer

Consisting of about 30 million people, African-American consumers currently constitute the largest racial minority in the United States (approximately 12 percent of the population). With a purchasing power estimated to be between $250 and $270 billion, African-American consumers are sought after by marketers who target about $845 million in advertising and promotions to communicate specifically with them. However, this important subcultural grouping is frequently portrayed as a single, undifferentiated "African-American market," consisting of consumers who have a uniform set of consumer needs.[18] In reality they are a diverse group, consisting of numerous subgroups, each with distinctive backgrounds, needs, interests, and opinions. Therefore, just as the white majority has been divided into a variety of market segments, each with its own distinctive needs and tastes, so, too, can the African-American market be segmented.

▲ **Segmenting the African-American Market** The segmentation of the African-American market has largely been approached in terms of economics or social-class standing, that is, by divisions based on income, education, and occupation. Primary attention has been given to pinpointing the values and lifestyles of the African-American middle class. Most research has found that the value orientations of middle-class African-Americans are quite similar to those of middle-class Caucasians. Indeed, in many instances, middle-class African-Americans appear to be more committed to middle-class values than their white counterparts. For example, middle-class African-American consumers often are more dedicated than white middle-class consumers to *family security* (taking care of loved ones) and a *need for accomplishment* (making a lasting contribution)—both middle-class values.

African-Americans who are involved with the Internet and frequent black-oriented on-line sites are a particularly upscale group. A survey of subscribers to BOBC ("Black On Black Communications"), an "Afrocentric" newsletter delivered by e-mail, revealed that 77 percent have a four-year college degree and 45 percent have household incomes in excess of $50,000 (10 percent have incomes more than $100,000).[19] Further evidence of the advancement of increased numbers of African-Americans into the ranks of the middle class is the observation of researchers at Claritas (the research company that produces PRIZM geodemographic clusters) that their *Black Enterprise* cluster (which was portrayed in the last edition of this book) has been dispersed to a number of different middle-class and affluent clusters, each made up of a mix of different racial and ethnic subcultures. This redistribution can be interpreted as reflecting the economic progress of African-Americans.

▲ **Consumer Behavior Characteristics of African-American Consumers** Although there are many similarities between African-Americans and the rest of America in terms of consumer behavior, there are also some meaningful differences in terms of product preferences and brand purchase patterns. African-American consumers tend to prefer popular or leading brands, are brand loyal, and are unlikely to purchase private-label and generic products. Also, to satisfy a valid need in the marketplace, cosmetic and hair care companies have developed a stream of products aimed at African-American women, such as Almay's Darker Tones, African Pride's® Body Bar, Dark & Lovely's® hair color, Revlon's Herba Rich with oils and African herbs, and Maybelline's Shades of You.

Some meaningful differences exist among white, African- American, and Hispanic-American consumers in the purchase, ownership, and use of a diverse group of products (see Table 15-7 on page 450). For marketers, these findings confirm the wisdom of targeting racial market segments (see Figure 15-4 on page 451).

table 15-7
Comparison of Purchase Patterns of White, African-American, and Hispanic-American Households

PRODUCT/ACTIVITY	WHITE	AFRICAN-AMERICAN	HISPANIC-AMERICAN
Purchased men's jeans (regular and designer) in past 12 months	103	74	102
Dress shoes	100	99	89
Women's designer jeans	97	117	98
Regular women's jeans	102	83	96
Have a bowling ball	109	36	58
Have a rifle	111	29	56
Non-cola soft drink 2+ glasses in past 7 days	97	122	101
Diet-cola soft drink 2+ glasses in past 7 days	106	62	77
Cough syrup 2+ times in past 30 days	94	141	117
Baby powder 5+ times in past 7 days	96	129	106
Hair coloring past 6 months	100	93	117
Women's eyeliner	100	96	110

Index: All adults = 100

Source: Based on 1995 Doublebase Mediamark Research, Inc. (New York: Mediamark Research, Inc. 1995). Reprinted by permission.

▲ **Reaching the African-American Audience** A question of central importance to marketers is how to best reach **African-American consumers**. Traditionally, marketers have subscribed to one of two distinct marketing strategies. Some have followed the policy of running all their advertising in general mass media in the belief that African-Americans have the same media habits as whites; others have followed the policy of running additional advertising in selected media directed exclusively to African-Americans.

Both strategies may be appropriate in specific situations and for specific product categories. For products of very broad appeal (e.g., aspirin or toothpaste), it is possible that the mass media (primarily television) may effectively reach all relevant consumers, including African-American and white. For other products (e.g., personal grooming products or food products), marketers may find that mass media do not communicate effectively with the African-American market. Because the media habits of African-American consumers differ from those of the general population, media specifically targeted to African-Americans are likely to be more effective. As one African-American advertising executive remarked, "Black people are not dark-skinned white people—there are cultural values which cause us to be subtly different from the majority population."[20] This idea is supported by a Yankelovich survey in which a majority of African-Americans believe that most advertising is designed for white people.[21]

Many marketers supplement their general advertising with advertisements in magazines, newspapers, and other media directed specifically to African-Americans. For example, Segmented Marketing Services of Winston-Salem, North Carolina distributes packets of product samples through beauty salons to over 500,000 African-American women. Hanes Hosiery is one of the latest national marketers to take advantage of this channel to

FIGURE 15-4

Ad Targeting African-
American Consumers
Courtesy of Posner Laboratories

reach African-American women.[22] In recent years, major advertisers targeting the African-American market have increasingly used the specialized services of African-American advertising agencies. These specialized agencies generally provide marketers wanting to target African-Americans the distinctive advantage of access to a staff of African-American marketing professionals who thoroughly know the values and customs of this market and its specific subsegments.

Asian-American Consumers

The Asian-American population (primarily Chinese, Filipinos, Japanese, Asian-Indians, Koreans, and Vietnamese) is currently more than seven million in size and is the fastest-growing American minority. For example, between 1980 and 1990, the white, African-American, and Hispanic populations in the United States grew 6, 13, and 53 percent, respectively; during this same time period, the Asian population (which includes Pacific Islanders) grew by 108 percent.

The current Asian-American market which, according to the most recent census, accounts for about 3 percent of the United States population, is composed of almost 23 percent Chinese, 19 percent Filipino, 12 percent Japanese, 11 percent Asian-Indians, and 11 percent Korean, with the remainder being drawn from a variety of Asian countries. In fact, today almost 40 percent of all new immigrants to this country are from Asia. Because Asian-Americans are largely family-oriented, highly industrious, and strongly driven to achieve a middle-class lifestyle, they are an attractive market for increasing numbers of marketers.

▲ Where Are the Asian-Americans?

Where Are the Asian-Americans? Asian-Americans are largely urban people, who are presently concentrated in a small number of large American cities. About 58 percent of Asian-Americans live in Los Angeles, San Francisco, and Hawaii, while another 18 percent reside in New York, Philadelphia, and Washington, D.C. At present, more than 10 percent of California's population is Asian, an increase from 1.2 million in 1980 to 2.8 million in 1990. By the year 2000, approximately 5 million Asians will be living in California.[23] Marketers can be misled by these numbers if they treat the Asian-American market as one single market. For instance, the stereotype that most Chinese live in "Chinatown" is incorrect. Most Chinese, as well as most other Asian-Americans, do not live in downtown urban areas; they live in the suburbs.[24]

▲ Understanding the Asian-American Consumer

Understanding the Asian-American Consumer Local newspapers and weekly newsmagazines frequently portray the accomplishments of Asian-Americans, who have shown themselves to be hardworking, very family-oriented, and strivers for excellence in educational pursuits (for themselves and their children). Indeed, throughout the United States, Asian-American children have consistently won a substantial share of academic awards and scholarships.

Supporting this profile, United States Census Bureau data reveal that more Asian-Americans, on a per-capita basis, own their own businesses than non-Asian American minorities. Those who do not own their own businesses are largely in professional, technical, or managerial occupations. They also tend to be better educated and more computer-literate than the general population. Additionally, many Asian-Americans are young and live a good part of their lives in multi-income households.

▲ Asian-Americans as Consumers

Asian-Americans as Consumers Asian-Americans spend about $38 billion on consumer goods and services annually.[25] They value quality (frequently associated with well-known brands) and are willing to pay for it (see Figure 15-5). This population segment tends to be loyal customers, frequently more male-oriented when it comes to consumption decisions, and attracted to retailers who make it known that they welcome Asian-American patronage. Table 15-8 on page 454 presents comparative purchase information on African-American, Hispanic-American, and **Asian-American consumers**. It is important to remember that Asian-Americans are really drawn from diverse cultural backgrounds. Therefore, although Asian-Americans have many similarities, marketers should approach this overall group with caution, as they are not completely homogeneous. For example, Vietnamese-Americans are more likely to follow the traditional model wherein the man makes the decision for large purchases, whereas Chinese-American husbands and wives are more likely to share in the decision-making process.[26]

Retailers and other service businesses can benefit from niche marketing to specific subsegments of the overall Asian-American market. As an example of such niche marketing, a life insurance manager in Forest Hills, New York turned the agency into one of the top ten producing offices of MONY Financial Services by focusing on Asian-Indians.[27] However, with 29 major ethnic groups between the Indian subcontinent and the Pacific Ocean, Asian-Americans cannot be efficiently targeted as a single homogeneous group.

The use of Asian-American models in advertising is effective in reaching this market segment. A research study found that responses to an advertisement for stereo speakers featuring an Asian model were significantly more positive than responses to the same ad using a Caucasian model.[28]

AGE SUBCULTURES

Each major age subgrouping of the population (e.g., those 13 to 19, those 20 to 30, or those 65-plus) might be thought of as a separate subculture, because important shifts occur in the demand for specific types of products and services. We have already discussed young children and teenagers in Chapter 12; as part of our discussion of the family, here we will limit our examination of age subcultures to three additional groups: *Generation X, baby boomers,* and the *mature and elderly.* These three age segments have been singled out because their distinctive lifestyles qualify them for consideration as subcultural groups.

The Generation X Market

This age grouping, often referred to as *Xers, busters* or *slackers* (as opposed to boomers); and twentysomethings, consists of approximately 46 million 18- to 29-year-olds who spend about $125 billion yearly. Ironically, they do not like labels and do not want to be singled out and marketed to.

Unlike their parents, who are frequently baby boomers, they are in no rush to marry, start a family, or work excessive hours to earn high salaries. For **Generation X Consumers**, job satisfaction is typically much more important than salary. Xers reject the

table 15-8 A Comparison of Purchase Behavior of Three Minority Groups

PERCENT PURCHASING PRODUCTS IN A 30-DAY PERIOD			
PRODUCT	AFRICAN-AMERICANS (%)	HISPANIC-AMERICANS (%)	ASIAN-AMERICANS (%)
Regular coffee	54	72	49
Regular carbonated soft drinks	71	77	70
Powdered drink mix	35	35	14
Beer	31	38	44
Ready-to-eat cereal	72	78	44
Shampoo	76	93	89
Hair spray	15	27	29
Frozen breakfast foods	9	2	6
Dishwashing detergent	86	88	79
Canned vegetables	44	42	17
Solid air fresheners	24	12	13
Powdered cleaners	57	53	46
Liquid cleaners	61	57	43
Disposable diapers	7	16	9
Chocolate bars	33	23	36
Chewing gum	35	26	39
Packaged cheese	53	65	39
Packaged sliced meats	39	55	43
Microwave popcorn	23	16	18
Dried fruit products	14	14	17
Nonmenthol cigarettes	12	14	22
Cat food	10	7	5
Packaged cookies	46	42	44
Sunscreen	3	5	9
Antacids	20	29	13
Cough syrup	41	50	28
Stomach remedies	32	35	18
Jams and jellies	28	36	37
Ice cream	35	43	43

Source: CHRISTY FISHER, "Poll: Hispanics Stick to Brands." Reprinted with permission from the February 15, 1993 issue of *Advertising Age.* Copyright 1993 by Crain Communications.

values of older co-workers who may neglect their families while striving to secure higher salaries and career advancement. For Generation X, it is more important to enjoy life and to have a lifestyle that provides freedom and flexibility. Many Xers are much more interested in tennis shoes, furniture for their apartments, and camping equipment than in BMWs or oceanfront condos. Owning one's own home is often considered a negative that reduces an individual's flexibility. Although upward mobility has traditionally been the American dream, Xers often find good jobs either difficult or impossible to find.

▲ **Appealing to Generation X** Members of Generation X often pride themselves on their sophistication. Although they are not necessarily materialistic, they do purchase good brand names (e.g., Sony) but not necessarily designer labels. They want to be recognized by marketers as a group in their own right and not as mini-baby boomers. Therefore, advertisements targeted to this audience must focus on their style in music, fashions, and language (see Figure 15-6). One key for marketers appears to be sincerity. Xers are not against advertising but only opposed to insincerity.[29]

Katie, 8   KATHERINE, 29 AND HOLDING

You wanted Barbie's® life, the high rise Condo, the Clothes, the Sports Car, Ken.

NOW, YOU'RE TIRED OF VACUUMING, HIGH HEELS, INSURANCE AND TESTOSTERONE.

You can't count the hours you Spent jumping rope with Jenny.

NOW, YOU COUNT FAT GRAMS AND YOUR BEST FRIEND IS A STAIR MACHINE.

Your favorite Snack was Sweet, Crunchy and gooey all at the Same time.

IT STILL IS!

INTRODUCING TIGER CRUNCHIE
IT'S TIME TO START SNACKING LIKE A KID AGAIN

You have to grow up but you don't have to grow old. That's why Tiger's Milk created Tiger Crunchie. It's as sweet and crispy as the ones mom made and only has 3 grams of fat. Ask for it at **GNC**, NATURE FOOD CENTRES, fine health food retailers and chain drug stores. For more information or to place an order call 1-800-695-8888.

FIGURE 15-6

Ad Appealing to Generation X Consumers
Courtesy of GNC, Nature Food Centers

Baby boomer media does not work with Generation X members. For example, 18 to 24 year olds have the lowest percentage of daily newspaper readership of all age groups. Xers are the MTV generation and while the three major United States TV networks attract an average of only 18 percent of the 18-to-29 group, the Fox network claims that 38 percent of its viewers are in this age group. The success Fox has had with Xers may be due to such programs as "Married with Children," "The Simpsons," "In Living Color," and "Beverly Hills, 90210." Furthermore, a number of cable TV networks such as MTV, Comedy Central, and E! have been very successful in reaching this audience. It appears that a low-key approach works best in reaching this market segment.

The Baby Boomer Market

Marketers have found baby boomers a particularly desirable target audience because (1) they are the single largest distinctive age category alive today; (2) they frequently make important consumer purchase decisions; and (3) they contain a small subsegment of trend-setting consumers (sometimes known as *yuppies*, or young upwardly mobile professionals) who have influence on the consumer tastes of other age segments of society.[30]

▲ **Who Are the Baby Boomers?** The term **baby boomers** refers to the age segment of the population that was born between 1946 and 1964 (see Figure 15-7). Thus, baby boomers are in the broad age category that extends from about mid-30s to early-50s. Baby boomers represent more than 40 percent of the adult population. The magnitude of this statistic alone would make them a much sought-after market segment. However, they also are valued because they comprise about 50 percent of all those in professional and managerial occupations and more than one-half of those with at least a college degree.

▲ **Consumer Characteristics of Baby Boomers** Baby boomers tend to be motivated consumers. They enjoy buying for themselves, for their homes or apartments, and for others—they are consumption-oriented. As baby boomers age, the nature of the products and services they most need or desire changes. For example, because of the aging of this market segment, Levi Strauss is featuring "relaxed fit" jeans, sales of "lineless" bifocal glasses to new customers are up substantially, and sales of walking shoes have grown rapidly.[31] Recently, bank marketers and other financial institutions are also paying more attention to how boomers are preparing for retirement.[32]

▲ **Segmenting the Baby Boomer Market** Although an age segment unto itself, baby boomers can be further subdivided into two subsegments: (1) *younger boomers*, those in their mid-30s to early-40s; and (2) *older boomers*, those from mid-40s to early-50s. As might be expected, this age split is reflected in living arrangements and lifestyles. For instance, older boomers came of age in a period when it was much easier to start a career and

FIGURE 15-7

Baby Boomers Constitute the Largest Age Category

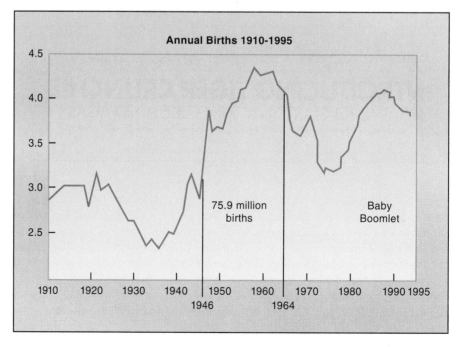

afford a home. Thus, although many younger boomers are well educated and aspire to "the good life," they have found it much more difficult to attain their dreams. Increased competition for a contracting number of desirable career opportunities has also made it more difficult for them to fulfill their expectations. Today, older boomers are facing reduced job security and opportunities, because many large organizations have gone through one or more bouts of downsizing.

▲ **Affluent Baby Boomers** Yuppies are by far the most sought-after subgroup of baby boomers. Although constituting only 5 percent of the population, they generally are well off financially, well educated, and in enviable professional or managerial careers. Table 15-9 presents a list of traits and characteristics that identify this affluent group of consumers.

Yuppies often are associated with status brand names, such as BMWs or Volvo station wagons, Rolex watches, cable TV, and Cuisinart food processors. Today, as many yuppies are maturing, it is not surprising that some are shifting their attention away from expensive status-type possessions to travel, physical fitness, planning for second careers, or some other form of new directions for their lives (see Figure 15-8 on page 458).

Mature and Elderly Consumer

America is aging. Baby boomers are starting to hit 50 (i.e., "mature adults"), there are plenty of preboomers (i.e., those 45 to 65 years), and the number of elderly consumers is growing twice as fast as the overall United States population. Thus, we will explore the 50-plus market and elderly market, two age subcultures.

▲ **The 50-Plus Market** As the population of America has grown older, there has been increased focus on the group of Americans who have reached their 50th birthdays. According to the Census Bureau, between 1990 and 2020, as the number of individuals less than

table 15-9 Demographic-Psychographic Traits of Affluent Baby Boomers

DEMOGRAPHIC TRAITS

Both males and females
35 to 45 years of age
Reside in major metropolitan areas
Single's income $50,000+; dual/family income $60,000+
Professional/managerial positions or self-employed
Four-year college education at minimum

PERSONALITY-PSYCHOGRAPHIC TRAITS

Achievement-oriented
High-fashion involvement
Recreational shoppers
Credit card users
Status brand purchasers
Physical-fitness concerns

FIGURE 15-8

Ad Appealing to Aging Baby Boomers
Courtesy of NordicTrack®

50 years old decreases, the 50-and-older population will grow by 76 percent. Not only do people over 50 have money, but also they tend to spend it. For example, they purchase 43 percent of all new cars, including 57 percent of all new Cadillacs. Typically, they dine out frequently and spend more than any other group on travel and recreation. When compared to the general population, members of the 50-plus segment watch more TV, read more newspapers, and listen to less radio. More specifically, the 50-plus market prefers both TV and radio news programs, game shows, and mature market magazines.[33]

▲ **Older Consumers** More than 30 million Americans are within the 65-plus age category, representing 12 percent of the country's population. This number is expected to more than double in the next 50 years, with the elderly segment eventually accounting for about 20 percent of the American population. This expected growth in the elderly population can be explained by the declining birthrate, the aging of the huge baby boomer segment, and improved medical diagnoses and treatment. One expert has called this phenomenon the "Age Wave."[34]

▲ **Who Are the Elderly?** In the United States, "old age" is officially assumed to begin with a person's 65th birthday (i.e., when the individual qualifies for full Social Security and Medicare). However, people who are 70 years old still tend to view themselves as "middle aged." Research consistently suggests that people's perceptions of their ages are more important in determining behavior than their chronological ages (i.e., the number of years lived).[35] In fact, people may at the same time have a number of different perceived or **cognitive ages**. Specifically, **elderly consumers** perceive themselves to be younger than their chronological ages on four perceived age dimensions: *feel age* (how old they feel); *look age* (how old they look); *do age* (how involved they are in activities favored by members of a specific age group); and *interest age* (how similar their interests are to those of members of a specific age group).[36] The results support other research that indicates that elderly consumers are more likely to consider themselves younger (i.e., have a younger cognitive age) than their chronological age.

There is evidence that with older consumers, the younger their cognitive ages, the more likely they are to be satisfied with their lives.[37] Most important, life satisfaction is not significantly related to older consumers' chronological ages but only to their cognitive or perceived ages. A study of women who were chronologically between 60 and 79 years of age found that women with younger cognitive ages had more self-confidence, had greater fashion interests, were more work-oriented, and were more likely to participate in entertainment and culturally related activities than women with older cognitive ages.[38]

For marketers, these findings underscore the importance of looking beyond chronological age to perceived or cognitive age when appealing to mature consumers and to the possibility that cognitive age might be used to segment the mature market (see Figure 15-9 on page 460).

▲ **Understanding the Elderly Market** Although marketers once avoided the older market, today they are anxious to know more about elderly consumers. They are especially interested in the very attractive subsegment of affluent elderly who have more discretionary income than any other adult-age segment (see Chapter 13). Today, with more and more elderly consumers receiving the benefits of private pension and retirement programs, in addition to Social Security and Medicare, and with an increasing percentage working longer, this age segment is even more likely to be able to afford new products and services in the future. Table 15-10 on page 461 presents a summary of the major myths and realities of the elderly as consumers.

▲ **Segmenting the Elderly Market** The elderly are by no means a homogeneous subcultural group. There are those who, as a matter of choice, do not have color TVs or touch-tone telephone service, whereas there are others who have the latest desktop computers and spend their time surfing the Internet.[39] One consumer gerontologist has suggested that the elderly are more diverse in interests, opinions, and actions than other segments of the adult population.[40] While this view runs counter to the popular myth that the elderly are uniform in terms of attitudes and lifestyles, both gerontologists and market researchers have repeatedly demonstrated that age is not necessarily a major factor in determining how older consumers respond to marketing activities.[41]

With an increased appreciation that the elderly constitute a diverse age segment, more attention is now being given to identifying ways to segment the elderly into meaningful groupings.[42] One relatively simple segmentation scheme partitions the elderly into three chronological age categories: the *young-old* (65 to 74 years of age), the *old* (those 75 to 84); and the *old-old* (those 85 years of age and older). This market segmentation approach provides useful consumer-relevant insights.

For instance, the members of the *young-old* subsegment tend to have both health and money and, therefore, comprise a profitable market for all types of discretionary and luxury items. In contrast, the members of the fast-growing *old-old* subsegment are in an age category that is likely to require various specialized housing and medical services.[43]

The elderly can also be segmented in terms of motivations and *quality-of-life orientation*. Table 15-11 on page 462 presents a side-by-side comparison of *new-age elderly*

FIGURE 15-9

Ad Appealing to
Cognitive Age
Courtesy of Acer America
Corporation

consumers and the more traditional older consumers. The increased presence of the new-age elderly suggests that marketers need to respond to the value orientations of older consumers whose lifestyles remain relatively ageless. Clearly, the new-age elderly are individuals who feel, think, and do according to a cognitive age that is younger than their chronological age. Still further, as Table 15-12 on page 463 shows, when it comes to "cyberseniors" or mature-older consumers who use the Internet, there seem to be two different segments of users: *technology users* and *technology lovers*. They are different in terms of computer behavior, resource availability, and personal characteristics. These differences provide additional support that it is often fruitful to identify meaningful segments of the overall mature-older market.

table 15-10   Five Myths About Older Consumers

MYTH 1: The Elderly Are Not a Separate Market
REALITY: The Elderly Have Distinguishing Traits

They are price/value conscious.
They are deal prone.
They like to shop—it has special meaning.
They are tuned in to the mass media.
They read direct mail, package labels, and package inserts.

MYTH 2: The Elderly Are One Homogeneous Group
REALITY: The Elderly Market Can Be Segmented into

Psychographic segments (isolationists, traditionalists, outgoers)
Chronological age segments (young-old, old, old-old)
Motivation and adjustment orientation (healthy adjustment, fair adjustment, poor
    adjustment)

MYTH 3: The Elderly Are Not a Substantial Market
REALITY: The American Population Is Aging Rapidly

There are approximately 18 million households headed by a person 65-plus
Median age rose quickly during the 1970s and early 1980s.
Rapid growth is expected through the year 2000-plus.
An aging population implies more older women.

MYTH 4: The Elderly Lack Buying Power
REALITY: The Elderly Have Money

Seven out of ten over-65s own their home.
Eighty-five percent of elderly homeowners have *no* mortgages.
Empty nests mean more discretionary income.
More older working women mean more two-income households and more
    discretionary income.

MYTH 5: The Elderly Are Not Innovative Consumers
REALITY: Under the Right Circumstances, the Elderly Are.

Source: ELAINE SHERMAN and LEON G. SCHIFFMAN (presentation before various academic and professional groups).

▲ **Shopping Experiences of the Older Consumer** Service organizations (e.g., retailers, financial institutions, and hotel and travel companies) have been especially attuned to the needs of elderly consumers and have been quickest to realize their value as customers. For instance, airlines frequently run ads that list three fares to each destination one for adults, one for children, and one for seniors, and vacation resorts have special reduced rate fares for American Association of Retired Persons (AARP) members. Look at the signs in some of the retail shops in your town, and you are likely to find that your local drugstore or dry cleaner offers seniors a discount for purchases made on a particular day of the week (e.g., a 10 percent discount on all clothing brought in for dry cleaning on Wednesday).

Research indicates that older consumers use credit cards less frequently; this may not be a function of a negative attitude toward credit but may simply reflect a reduced need for credit.[44] Another study suggests that the elderly's years of experience as consumers makes them more value conscious, more likely to use cents-off coupons, and just generally wiser shoppers.[45] Some elderly have been classified as "mall mavens," because they tend

table 15-11   Comparison of New-Age and Traditional Elderly

NEW-AGE ELDERLY	TRADITIONAL/STEREOTYPICAL ELDERLY
• Perceive themselves to be different in outlook from other people their age	• Perceive all older people to be about the same in outlook
• Age is seen as a state of mind	• See age as more of a physical state
• See themselves as younger than their chronological age	• See themselves at or near their chronological age
• Feel younger, think younger, and "do" younger	• Tend to feel, think, and do things that they feel match their chronological age
• Have a genuinely youthful outlook	• Feel that one should act one's age
• Feel there is a considerable adventure to living	
• Feel more in control of their own lives	• Normal sense of being in control of their own lives
• Have greater self-confidence when it comes to making consumer decisions	• Normal range of self-confidence when it comes to making consumer decisions
• Less concerned that they will make a mistake when buying something	• Some concern that they will make a mistake when buying something
• Especially knowledgeable and alert consumers	• Low-to-average consumer capabilities
• Selectively innovative	• Not innovative
• Seek new experiences and personal challenges	• Seek stability and a secure routine
• Less interested in accumulating possessions	• Normal range of interest in accumulating possessions
• Higher measured life satisfaction	• Lower measured life satisfaction
• Less likely to want to live their lives over differently	• Have some regrets as to how they lived their lives
• Perceive themselves to be healthier than most people their age	• Perceive themselves to be of normal health for their age
• Feel financially more secure	• Somewhat concerned about financial security

Source: Reprinted by permission of the publisher from "The Value Orientation of New-Age Elderly: The Coming of an Ageless Market" by Leon G. Schiffman and Elaine Sherman in *Journal of Business Research* 22 (April 1991), 187–94. Copyright 1991 by Elsevier Science Publishing Co., Inc.

to go to the local shopping mall almost daily. These individuals, generally male, go to the mall to meet other people when they have nothing else to do. The experience of shopping for themselves or their families, getting some healthy exercise (walking around the mall), and meeting others satisfies their needs for social activity and health and adds to their overall happiness.[46]

▲ **Communicating with the Elderly Consumer** When targeting products to the elderly, marketers must be careful not to embarrass them or make them feel uncomfortable about their age. In a classic marketing blunder, Heinz some years ago introduced a line of pureed "senior foods" when it learned that many elderly people with chewing difficulties were buying baby foods. The new product failed because elderly consumers were ashamed to

table 15-12 Cyberseniors: a Comparison of Technology
Users and Technology Lovers

	TECHNOLOGY USERS	TECHNOLOGY LOVERS
COMPUTER BEHAVIOR		
Time spent on-line	Less hours	More hours
On-line purchase behavior	Little	More
Other on-line activities	Less	More
RESOURCE AVAILABILITY		
Time available	No difference	No difference
Money available	No difference	No difference
Space available	No difference	No difference
Others (health, caregiver)	No difference	No difference
PERSONAL CHARACTERISTICS		
Attitudes	Less positive	More positive
Involvement	Less involvement	More involvement
Impact of computers	Less impact	More impact
Innovator	Less	More
Travel more than others	No difference	No difference
Happier than others	Less	More
Collector	No difference	No difference
Computers are magical	No difference	No difference
Financially better off than others	No	Yes
Healthier than others	No	Yes
Cog. age versus chron. age	The same	Younger
Computer experience	Less	More
Locus of control	Generally in control	Very much in control
Need for cognition	Less	More
Need for novelty	Less	More
Need to communicate	Perhaps (not computers)	Yes
Education	College	College
Life satisfaction	Less satisfied	More satisfied

Source: CHARLES A. McMELLON, LEON G. SCHIFFMAN, and ELAINE SHERMAN, "Consuming Cyberseniors: Some Personal and Situational Characteristics That Influence Their On-Line Behavior" (New York: Baruch College, Working Paper, 1996), 20.

admit that they required strained foods. Instead, they preferred to buy baby foods, which they could always pretend were for a grandchild. Table 15-13 on page 464 presents a list of frequent errors that marketers have made concerning the elderly consumer.

Visual messages targeted to the elderly should show the diversity of older consumers in the course of the campaign. Ads should avoid gender and lifestyle stereotypes (e.g., older men living alone do not do their own laundry or older women are unable to handle their own financial matters). Instead, they should feature positive intergenerational images (i.e., interactions with friends and relatives of various ages). Marketers should also recognize that some audio, visual, and processing loss is common among the elderly. Thus, when advertisers target the elderly, they should avoid high-frequency sounds, reduce clutter, use larger type sizes, and introduce fewer ideas per unit of time.[47]

The number of publications targeted directly to the elderly (or mature) market has increased in recent years. *Modern Maturity*, the leading publication, reaches more than 25

table 15-13 Mistakes Marketers Make Toward Mature/ Elderly Consumers

They ignore them.

They do not treat them with respect.

They treat them as undifferentiated consumers.

They place too much emphasis on chronological age.

They rely on traditional age categories.

They perceive older consumers as having little money to spend.

They perceive older consumers as set in their ways and noninnovative.

They use complex messages in their advertisements.

million members of the AARP. In addition, major direct marketers are beginning to target the elderly. Sears mails its "Mature Wisdom" catalog and J. C. Penney their "Easy Dressing Fashions" catalog to an elderly target audience.[48]

Sex as a Subculture

Because sex roles have an important cultural component, it is quite fitting to examine gender as a subcultural category.

Sex Roles and Consumer Behavior

All societies tend to assign certain traits and roles to males and others to females. In American society, for instance, aggressiveness, competitiveness, independence, and self-confidence often were considered traditional *masculine traits*; neatness, tactfulness, gentleness, and talkativeness were considered traditional *feminine traits*.[49] In terms of role differences, women have historically been cast as homemakers with responsibility for child care and men as the providers or breadwinners. Although such traits and roles are no longer relevant, or so strongly associated with members of a specific sex, some advertisers continue to appeal to such sex-linked roles.

▲ **Consumer Products and Sex Roles** Within every society, it is quite common to find products that are either exclusively or strongly associated with the members of one sex. In the United States, for example, shaving equipment, cigars, pants, ties, and work clothing were historically male products; bracelets, hair spray, hair dryers, and sweet-smelling colognes generally were considered feminine products. For most of these products, the sex link has either diminished or disappeared; for others, the prohibition still lingers. An interesting product category with regard to the blurring of a gender appeal is men's fragrances. Although men are increasingly wearing fragrances, it is estimated that 30 percent of men's fragrances are worn by women.[50] Also, although women have historically been the major market for vitamins, men are increasingly being targeted for vitamins exclusively formulated for men.[51]

Despite the fact that the line between "male only" and "female only" products has become blurred in recent years, consumers tend to impute a sex, or gender, to products. For this reason, advertising executives should consider not only the sex of their target market but also the *perceived sex* of the product category in the development of their advertising campaigns.

The Working Woman

Marketers and consumer researchers have been increasingly interested in the working woman, especially the married working woman. They recognize that married women who work outside of the home are a large and growing market segment, one whose needs differ from those of women who do not work outside the home (frequently self-labeled "stay-at-home-moms"). It is the size of the working woman market that makes it so attractive. Approximately 72 percent of American women work full time, and only 3.5 percent of American families consist of the traditional arrangement of a breadwinning husband and a homemaking wife.[52] Young women, with young children, have been the fastest-growing segment in the female work force. The number of working wives with children under the age of six has risen by more than 400 percent since 1948, and among those with children 6 to 17 years of age, the increase has been more than 200 percent. Figure 15-10 on page 466 shows an ad for a Motorola cellular phone that acknowledges the many roles and pressure of career or working women.

▲ **Segmenting the Working Woman Market** To provide a richer framework for segmentation, marketers have developed categories that differentiate the motivations of working and nonworking women. For instance, a number of studies have divided the female population into four segments: *stay-at-home* housewives; *plan-to-work* housewives; *just-a-job* working women; and *career-oriented* working women.[53] The distinction between "just-a-job" and "career-oriented" working women is particularly meaningful. "Just-a-job" working women seem to be motivated to work primarily by a sense that the family requires the additional income, whereas "career-oriented" working women, who tend to be in a managerial or professional position, are driven more by a need to achieve and succeed in their chosen careers.

▲ **Shopping Patterns of Working Women** Working women spend less time shopping than nonworking women. They accomplish this "time economy" by shopping less often and by being brand- and store-loyal. Not surprisingly, working women also are likely to shop during evening hours and on the weekend, as well as to buy through direct-mail catalogs.

▲ **Reaching the Working Woman** An examination of magazine advertisements appearing in general audience magazines concludes that the proportion of males shown as workers and co-workers remained almost constant from 1970 to 1988, whereas the proportion of women shown as workers or co-workers (as opposed to homemakers and/or mothers) nearly doubled.[54] A study examining advertising response to financial services concluded that the use of a "modern" positioning strategy (with a focus on career and family) proved more effective with women than a more traditional positioning strategy (which focused on nurturing and family).[55] However, there is a danger in positioning a married working woman as a "superwoman" (e.g., who perfectly "balances" her career and family responsibilities). The downside is to foster beyond reason striving, without regard to the stress that it produces. In contrast, advertisements that portray a "balance" between work and home obligation are likely to appreciated.

In the past few years, a number of companies have realized just how important it is for them to communicate appropriately with today's working women and mothers. Women's groups are quick to protest ads depicting them in bathing suits, such as the Old Milwaukee beer ad featuring the Swedish Bikini Team. Anheuser-Busch has stated it will no longer portray women as sex objects.[56]

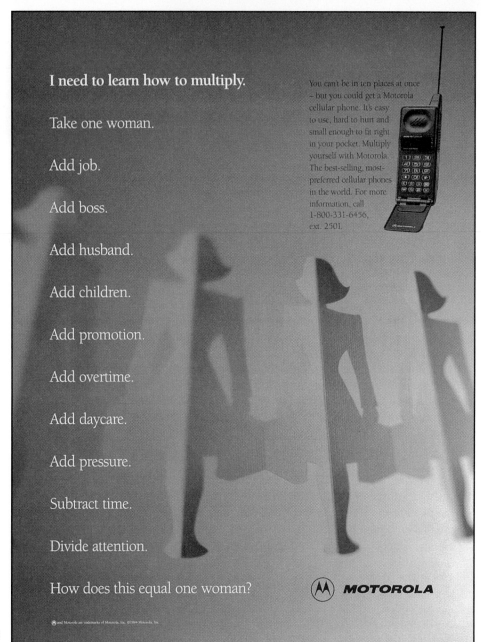

SUBCULTURAL INTERACTION

All consumers are simultaneously members of more than one subcultural segment (for example, a consumer may be an elderly African-American Baptist working wife living in the Pacific Northwest). For this reason, marketers should strive to understand how multiple subcultural memberships interact to influence target consumers' relevant consumption behavior. Promotional strategy should not be limited to target a single subcultural membership.

Subcultural analysis enables marketers to segment their markets to meet the specific needs, motivations, perceptions, and attitudes shared by members of a specific subcultural group. A subculture is a distinct cultural group that exists as an identifiable segment within a larger, more complex society. Its members possess beliefs, values, and customs that set them apart from other members of the same society; at the same time, they hold to the dominant beliefs of the overall society. Major subcultural categories in this country include nationality, religion, geographic location, race,

age, and sex. Each of these can be broken down into smaller segments that can be reached through special copy appeals and selective media choices. In some cases (e.g., the elderly consumer), product characteristics can be tailored to the specialized needs of the market segment. Because all consumers simultaneously are members of several subcultural groups, the marketer must determine for the product category how specific subcultural memberships interact to influence the consumer's purchase decisions.

1. Why is subcultural analysis especially significant in a country such as the United States?

2. Discuss the importance of subcultural segmentation to marketers of food products. Identify a food product for which the marketing mix should be regionalized. Explain why and how the marketing mix should be varied across geographic areas of the United States.

3. How can marketers of the following products use the material presented in this chapter to develop promotional campaigns designed to increase market share among African-American, Hispanic, and Asian-American consumers? The products are: (a) compact disc players, (b) ready-to-eat cereals, and (c) designer jeans.

4. Asian-Americans are a small proportion of the total United States population. Why are they an important market segment? How can a marketer of personal computers effectively target Asian-Americans?

5. Sony is introducing a new 27-inch TV with a picture-in-picture feature. How should the company position and advertise the product to: (a) Generation X consumers and (b) affluent Baby Boomers?

6. In view of the anticipated growth of the over-50 market, a leading cosmetics company is reevaluating the marketing strategy for its best-selling moisturizing face cream for women. Should the company market the product to younger (under-50) as well as older women? Would it be wiser to develop a new brand and formula for consumers over 50 rather than target both age groups with one product? Explain your answer.

7. Marketers realize that people of the same age often exhibit very different lifestyles. Using the evidence presented in this chapter, discuss how developers of retirement housing can use older Americans' lifestyles to more effectively segment their markets.

8. a. How should marketers promote products and services to working women? What appeals should they use? Explain.

   b. As the owner of a Saturn automobile dealership, what kind of marketing strategies would you use to target working women?

1. Using one of the subculture categories listed in Table 15-1, identify a group that can be regarded as a subculture within your university or college.

   a. Describe the norms, values, and behaviors of the subculture's members.

   b. Interview five members of that subculture regarding attitudes toward the use of credit cards.

   c. What are the implications of your findings for marketing credit cards to the group you selected?

2. Interview one Baby Boomer and one Generation X consumer regarding the purchase of a car. Prepare a report on the differences in attitudes between the two individuals. Do your findings support the text's discussion of the differences between "boomers" and "busters"? Explain.

3. Many of *your* perceptions regarding price versus value are likely to be different from those of your parents or grandparents. Researchers attribute such differences to "cohort effects," which are based on the premise that consumption patterns are determined early in life. Therefore, individuals who experienced different economic, political, and cultural environments during their youth are likely to be different types of consumers as adults. Describe instances in which your parents or grandparents disagreed with or criticized purchases you had made. Describe the cohort effects that explain each party's position during these disagreements.

4. Find two good and two bad examples of advertising directed toward elderly consumers. To what degree are these ads stereotypical? Do they depict the concept of perceived age? How could these ads be improved by applying some of this chapter's guidelines for advertising to elderly consumers?

key words

- African-American consumers
- Age subcultures
- Asian-American consumers
- Baby Boomers
- Cognitive ages
- Elderly consumers

- Gender subcultures
- Generation X consumers
- Hispanic subcultures
- Nationality subcultures
- Racial subcultures
- Regional subcultures

- Religious subcultures
- Sex roles
- Subcultural categories
- Subcultural interaction
- Subculture
- Working woman subcultures

end notes

1. JEFFERY D. ZBAR, "Hispanics Attract Publishers' Notice," *Advertising Age*, October 2, 1995, 12.
2. MARK S. HOFFMAN, ed., *The World Almanac and Book of Facts: 1995* (New York: Pharos Books, 1993); and OTTO JOHNSON, ed., 1995 *Information Please Almanac* (Boston: Houghton Mifflin, 1995).
3. MARILYN LAVIN, "Acculturating the Hispanic Consumer: The Grocery Shopping Experience, *1995 AMA Winter Educators' Conference Proceedings* (Chicago: American Marketing Association, 1995), 359–64.
4. SOYEON SHIM and KENNETH C. GEHRT, "Native American and Hispanic Adolescent Consumers: Examination of Shopping Orientation, Socialization Factors and Social Structure Variables," in Barbara B. Stern and George M. Zinkan, eds., *1995 AMA Educators' Proceedings* (Chicago: American Marketing Association, 1995), 297–98.
5. ROHIT DESHPANDE, WAYNE D. HOYER, and NAVEEN DONTHU, "The Intensity of Ethnic Affiliation: A Study of the Sociology of Hispanic Consumption," *Journal of Consumer Research* 13, September 1986, 214–20; and CYNTHIA WEBSTER, "The Role of Hispanic Ethnic Identification on Reference Group Influence," in Chris T. Allen and Deborah Roedder John, eds., *Advances in Consumer Research* 21 (Provo, UT: Association for Consumer Research, 1994), 458–63.
6. OTTO JOHNSON, ed., *1995 Information Please Almanac*. op. cit.
7. KAREN BENEZRA, "Coke Kicks in World Cup Hispanic Promo, Packaging," *Brandweek*, March 7, 1994, 12. Also, see: BETSY SPETHMANN, "Kraft Bumps Ethnic Umbrella to $24M, Rolls Demo-Specific Lines," *Brandweek*, November 27, 1995, 4.
8. BETSY SPETHMANN, "Dannon Sees Oasis in Dessert Yogurt Track," *Brandweek*, March 20, 1995, 8.
9. MARCIA MOGELONSKY, "First Language Comes First," *American Demographics*, October 1995, 21.
10. LEON E. WYNTER, "Group Finds Right Recipe for Milk Ads in Spanish," *The Wall Street Journal*, March 6, 1996, B1.
11. ELIZABETH C. HIRSCHMAN, "Ethnic Variation in Leisure Activities and Motives," in Bruce J. Walker et al., eds., *An Assessment of Marketing Thought and Practice* (Chicago: American Marketing Association, 1982), 93–98; and ELIZABETH C. HIRSCHMAN, "American Jewish Ethnicity: Its Rela-

tionship to Some Selected Aspects of Consumer Behavior," *Journal of Marketing* 45, Summer 1981, 102–10.
12. NEJDET DELENER and LEON G. SCHIFFMAN, "Family Decision Making: The Impact of Religious Factors," in Gary Frazier et al., eds., *1988 AMA Educators' Proceedings* (Chicago: American Marketing Association, 1988), 80–83.
13. MARCIA MOGELONSKY, "Kiss Me, You Kosher Fool," *American Demographics*, May 1994, 17.
14. LAURA BIRD, "Major Brands Look for the Kosher Label," *Adweek's Marketing Week*, April 1, 1991, 18–19; and JUDITH WALDROP, "Everything's Kosher," *American Demographics*, March 1991, 4.
15. KAREN BURKA, "Mazel Tov," *Direct*, April 1994, 75.
16. JOEL GARREAU, "Edge Cities in Profile," *American Demographics*, February 1994, 24–33.
17. MARCIA MOGELONSKY, "America's Hottest Market," *American Demographics*, January 1996, 20–31,55.
18. MARK S. HOFFMAN, ed., *The World Almanac and Book of Facts: 1995* op. cit.; and LAURIE M. GROSSMAN, "After Demographic Shift, Atlanta Mall Restyles Itself as Black Shopping Center," *The Wall Street Journal*, February 26, 1992, B1.
19. LEON E. WYNTER, "Group Finds Right Recipe for Milk Ads in Spanish," *The Wall Street Journal*, March 6, 1996, B1.
20. MARIE SPADONI, "Marketing to Blacks—How to Media Segment the Target Audience," *Advertising Age*, November 19, 1984, 43.
21. KARI VAN HOOF, "Surveys Point to Group Differences," *Brandweek*, March 7, 1994, 32–33.
22. PAM WEISZ and ELAINE UNDERWOOD, "Hanes' Ethnic Sampler," *Brandweek*, June 26, 1995, 1.
23. DAN FOST, "California's Asian Market," *American Demographics* (October, 1990), 34–37; and LISA MARIE PETERSEN, "Advertisers Look to Asian Immigrants," *Mediaweek*, November 30, 1992, 2; and WILLIAM P. O'HARE, WILLIAM H. FREG, and DAN FOST, "Asians in the Suburbs," *American Demographics*, May 1994, 32–38.
24. Ibid., 35.
25. MARIA SHAO, *Business Week*, June 17, 1991, 54–55.
26. JOHN STEERE, "How Asian-Americans Make Purchase Decisions," *Marketing News*, March 13, 1995, 9.
27. HARVEY BRAUM, "Marketing to Minority Consumers," *Dis-*

count Merchandiser, February 1991, 44–46, 74; CHUI LI, "The Asian-American Market for Personal Products," *Drug and Cosmetic Industry*, November 1992, 32–36; and ASHOK PRADHAN, "Ethnic Markets: Sales Niche of the Future," *National Underwriter*, November 6, 1989, 18.

28. JUDY COHEN, "White Consumer Response to Asian Models in Advertising," *Journal of Consumer Marketing*, Spring 1992, 17–27.

29. KAREN RICHIE, "Marketing to Generation X," *American Demographics*, April 1995, 34–39.

30. "Boomer Facts," *American Demographics*, January 1996, 14. Also see: DIANE CRISPELL, "U.S. Population Forecasts Decline for 2000, but Rise Slightly for 2050," *The Wall Street Journal*, March 25, 1996, B3.

31. PETER KERR, "Shift for Marketers: Yup to Grump," *The New York Times*, August 27, 1991, D1, D6; and SUSAN MITCHELL, "How Boomers Save," *American Demographics*," September 1994, 22–28,52.

32. Ibid, 22-23.

33. "The Slo-Go's and the No-Go's," *The New York Times*, May 28, 1991, A20; and "Mature American in the 1990s," A Publication of the AARP, 1992, The Roper Organization.

34. For a discussion of various demographic trends affecting the elderly, see KEN DYCHTWALD and JOE FLOWER, *Age Wave* (Los Angeles: Jeremy P. Tarcher, 1989); and KEN DYCHTWALD, "Baby Boomers Catch the Age Wave," *Marketing Review*, January 1996, 16-19. Also, see GEORGE P. MOSCHIS, "Consumer Behavior in Later Life Multidisciplinary Contributios and Implications for Research," *Journal of the Academy of Marketing Science*, 1994, 195–204.

35. KELLY TEPPER, "The Role of Labeling Processes in Elderly Consumers' Responses to Age Segmentation Cues, *Journal of Consumer Research*, March 1994, 503-519; and CANDACE CORLETT, "Building a Successful 50+ Marketing Program," *Marketing Review*, January 1996, 10–11, 19.

36. BENNY BARAK and LEON G. SCHIFFMAN, "Cognitive Age: A Nonchronological Age Variable," in Kent B. Monroe, ed., *Advances in Consumer Research* 8 (Ann Arbor, MI: Association for Consumer Research, 1981), 602–606; PHILIP D. COOPER and GEORGE MIAOULIS, "Altering Corporate Strategic Criteria to Reflect the Changing Environment: The Role of Life Satisfaction and the Growing Senior Market," *California Management Review*, Fall 1988, 87–97; and STUART VAN AUKEN and THOMAS E. BARRY, "An Assessment of the Trait Validity of Cognitive Age," *Journal of Consumer Psychology*, 1995, 107–32.

37. ELAINE SHERMAN, LEON G. SCHIFFMAN, and WILLIAM R. DILLON, "Age/Gender Segments and Quality of Life Differences," in Stanley Shapiro and A. H. Walle, eds., *1988 Winter Educators' Conference* (Chicago: American Marketing Association, 1988), 319–20.

38. ROBERT E. WILKES, "A Structural Modeling Approach to the Measurement and Meaning of Cognitive Age," *Journal of Consumer Research*, September 1992, 292–301.

39. CHAD RUBEL, "Mature Market Often Misunderstood," *Marketing News*, August 28, 1995, 28–29.

40. Professor Elaine Sherman, quoted in DAVID B. WOLFE, "The Ageless Market," *American Demographics*, July 1987, 26–28 and 55–56.

41. GEORGE P. MOSCHIS, "Marketing to Older Adults: An Overview and Assessment of Present Knowledge and Practice," *Journal of Consumer Marketing*, Fall 1991, 33–41.

42. CAROL M. MORGAN and DORAN J. LEVY, "Understanding Mature Consumers," *Marketing Review*, January 1996, 12–13, 25.

43. ELAINE SHERMAN and LEON G. SCHIFFMAN, "Quality-of-Life (QOL) Assessment of Older Consumers: A Retrospective Review," *Journal of Business and Psychology*, Fall 1991, 107–119.

44. ANIL MATHUR and GEORGE P. MOSCHIS, "Use of Credit By Older Adults," in Robert P. Leone and V. Kumor, et al., eds., 1992 *AMA Educators' Proceedings* 3 (Chicago: American Marketing Association, 1992), 454.

45. JANE W. LICATA, ABHIJIT BISWAS, and BALAJI KRISHNAN, "Consumer Experience: Is It the Basis for Differences Between Elder and Nonelder Consumers?" in Barbara B. Stern and George M. Zinkan, eds., 1995 *AMA Educators' Proceedings* (Chicago: American Marketing Association, 1995), 308–09.

46. ROYCE ANDERSON, "The Elderly Mall Maven: In Pursuit of Quality of Life," in M. Joseph Sirgy, et al., *Developments in Quality-of-Life Studies in Marketing* (Blacksburg, VA: Academy of Marketing, 1992), 12–15.

47. ROSE L. JOHNSON and CATHY J. COBB-WALGREN, "Aging and the Problems of Television Clutter," *Journal of Advertising Research*, July/August 1994, 54–62; and PATRICIA BRAUS, "Vision in an Aging America," *American Demographics*, June 1995, 34–39.

48. HELEN MUNDELL, "Direct Marketers Discover the Elderly, *American Demographics*, June 1994, 8, 20.

49. INGE K. BROVERMAN, SUSAN RAYMOND VOGEL, DONALD M. BROVERMAN, FRANK E. CLARKSON, and PAUL S. ROSENKRANTZ, "Sex Role Stereotypes: A Current Appraisal," *Journal of Social Issues* 28, 1972, 63.

50. MAXINE WILKIE, "Scent of a Market," *American Demographics*, August 1995, 40–49.

51. KELLY SHERMACH, "Putting the 'Men' into Vitamin," *Marketing News*, February 27, 1995, 1, 39.

52. "America's Vanishing Housewife," *Adweek's Marketing Week*, June 24, 1991, 28–29.

53. THOMAS BARRY, MARY GILLY, and LINDLEY DORAN, "Advertising to Women with Different Career Orientations," *Journal of Advertising Research* 25, April-May 1985, 26–35.

54. BERT J. KELLERMAN, "An Update on the Role Portrayal of Men and Women in Magazine Advertising," in Robert L. King, ed., *Developments in Marketing Science* (Richmond, VA: Academy of Marketing Science, 1991), 298–302.

55. LYNN J. JAFFE, "Impact of Positioning and Sex-Role Identity on Women's Responses to Advertising," *Journal of Advertising Research*, June-July 1991, 57–64.

56. "Automakers Learn Better Roads to Women's Market," *Marketing News*, October 12, 1992, 2; IRA TEINOWITZ, "This Bud's for Her," *Advertising Age*, October 28, 1991, 1; and CYNDEE MILLER, "Liberation for Women in Ads," *Marketing News*, August 17, 1992, 1–2; and LEAH RICKARD, "Subaru, GMC Top Push to Win Over Women," *Advertising Age*, April 3, 1995, S-24.

the

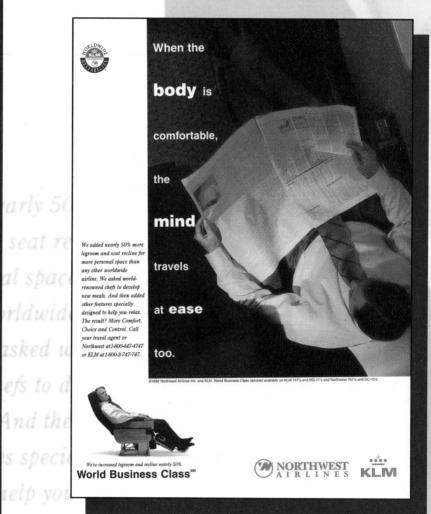

too.

In our examination of psychological, social, and cultural factors, we have consistently pointed out how various segments of the American consuming public differ. If so much diversity exists among segments of a single society, then even more diversity is likely to exist among the members of two or more societies. To succeed, international marketers must understand the "cross-cultural" differences among the consumers of different societies, so that they can develop targeted marketing strategies to penetrate each foreign market of interest.

In this chapter, we broaden our scope of analysis and consider the marketing implications of cultural differences and similarities that exist between the people of two or more nations. We also compare the views that pit a global marketing perspective—one that stresses the *similarities* of consumers worldwide—against a localized marketing strategy that stresses the *diversity* of consumers in

You can tell the ideals of a nation by its advertisements.

—Norman Douglas, 1930

different nations and their specific cultural orientations. Our own view is that marketers must be aware of and sensitive to cross-cultural similarities and differences that can provide expanded sales and profit opportunities. Multinational marketers must be ready to tailor their marketing mixes to the specific customs of each nation that they want to target.

THE IMPERATIVE TO BE MULTINATIONAL

Today, almost all major corporations are actively marketing their products beyond their original homeland borders, many are engaged in global marketing. In fact, the issue is generally not *whether* to sell a brand in other countries but rather *how* to do it (e.g., the same product, the same global advertising campaign, or "tailored" products and localized ads for each country).

This challenge has been given special meaning by the efforts of the **European Community** (EC) to form a single market. Although the movement of goods and services among community members has been eased, it is unlikely that this diverse market will be transformed into a single market of homogeneous "Euroconsumers" with the same wants and needs.[1] The opening up of Eastern Europe to capitalism also presents a major opportunity and challenge to marketers. Firms like Coca-Cola, General Motors, Nabisco, Gillette, and R.J. Reynolds are now investing extensive sums on product development and marketing to satisfy the needs of awakening Eastern European consumer markets.[2]

The **North American Free Trade Agreement** (NAFTA), which currently consists of the United States, Canada, and Mexico, is the world's second largest regional trading bloc after the EC, providing free-market access to 360 million consumers representing a $6 trillion market.[3] The emerging Association of Southeast Asian Nations (ASEAN), consisting of Indonesia, Singapore, Thailand, the Philippines, Malaysia, and Brunei, is another important economic alliance that offers marketers new global markets.[4]

Many firms are developing strategies to take advantage of these and other emerging economic opportunities. A substantial number of firms are now jockeying for market share in foreign markets. Pepsi, for example, has introduced a new electric-blue packaging that it will gradually roll out worldwide. The packaging and a globally consistent taste are two actions designed to achieve a better level of in-store visibility and a more favorable comparison with the red packaging of its archrival Coca-Cola. Its decision is also driven by research that suggests that the blue can provides Pepsi with a more positive image in the global marketplace.[5]

With the buildup of this multinational fever and the general attractiveness of multinational markets, products originating in one country are increasingly being sought out by consumers in other parts of the world. For instance, young Japanese children flock to the L. L. Bean store in Tokyo for casual American styles and are attracted to other American products as well (see Table 16-1).[6] French and British teenagers have adopted mainstream American popular culture products, such as baseball caps; 18,000 local "Avon ladies" sell cosmetics in China; and the French are even buying selected English supermarket products, because they judge them as being of good value and convenient.[7]

Firms are selling their products worldwide for a variety of reasons. First, many firms have learned that overseas markets represent the single most important opportunity for

table 16-1 Product Trends That Appeal to Young Japanese Consumers

TREND	IMPRESSION
Value	Newcomer L. L. Bean delivers value; so does Dell Computer.
Casual Fashion	J. Crew, Levi's, Gap knockoffs: simple styles appeal to young consumers.
"Green Chic"	Ecology orientation makes Body Shop products more popular than fragrance and beauty aids from Chanel.
Ease of Use	Simplicity of Macintosh computers makes them more appealing than souped-up PCs from NEC.
Assertiveness	Pepsi-Cola scores big here: its comparison ads against Coke offend older Japanese but delight younger consumers.

Source: Adapted from KAREN LOWRY MILLER, "You Just Can't Talk to These Kids," *Business Week* (April 19, 1993), 104, 106. Reprinted from April 19, 1993 issue of *Business Week* by Special permission, copyright © 1993 by McGraw-Hill Companies

their future growth when their home markets reach maturity. This realization is propelling them to expand their horizons and seek consumers scattered all over the world. Moreover, consumers all over the world are increasingly eager to try "foreign" products that are popular in different and far-off places.

Acquiring Exposure to Other Cultures

As more and more consumers come in contact with the material goods and lifestyle of people living in other parts of the world, they have the opportunity to adopt these different products and practices. How consumers in one culture secure exposure to the goods of other people living in other cultures is an important part of consumer behavior. It impacts the well-being of consumers worldwide and of marketers trying to gain acceptance for their products in countries that are often quite different from their home country.

A portion of consumers' exposure to different cultures tends to come about through consumers' own initiatives—their travel, their living and working in foreign countries, or even their immigration to a different country.[8] Additionally, consumers obtain a "taste" of different cultures from contact with foreign movies, theater, art and artifact and, most certainly, exposure to unfamiliar and different products. This second major category of cultural exposure is often undertaken by marketers seeking to expand their markets by "bringing" new products, services, practices, and ideas to potential consumers residing in a different country and possessing a different cultural view. Within this context, international marketing provides a form of "culture transfer."

Country-of-Origin Effects

When consumers are making purchase decisions, they may take into consideration the countries-of-origin of their choices. Researchers have shown that consumers use their knowledge of where products are made in the evaluation of their purchase options.[9] Such a "country-of-origin" effect seems to come about because consumers are often aware that a particular firm- or brand-name is associated with a particular country (e.g., Swatch is associated with Switzerland, and Jeep is associated with the United States). Moreover, consumers tend to have an *attitude* or even a preference when it comes to a particular product being made in a particular country. This attitude might be positive, negative, or neutral, depending on perceptions or experience. For instance, a consumer in one country might positively value a particular product made in another country (e.g., "Affluent American consumers may feel that German luxury automobiles are a worthwhile investment").[10] In contrast, another consumer might be negatively influenced when he learns that a shirt he is looking at in a store is made in a country he does not associate with fine shirts (e.g., "Hugo Boss shirts from a country other than Germany or Italy"). Such "country-of-origin" effects influence how consumers rate quality, and sometimes which brands they will ultimately select.[11]

CROSS-CULTURAL CONSUMER ANALYSIS

To determine whether and how to enter a foreign market, marketers need to conduct some form of **cross-cultural consumer analysis**. Within the scope of this discussion, cross-cultural consumer analysis is defined as *the effort to determine to what extent the consumers of two or more nations are similar or different*. Such analyses can provide marketers with an understanding of the psychological, social, and cultural characteristics of the foreign consumers they wish to target, so that they can design effective marketing strategies for each of the specific national markets involved.

In a broader context, cross-cultural consumer analysis might also include a comparison of subcultural groups (see Chapter 15) within a single country (e.g., English and French Canadians, Mexican-Americans and Anglos, or Protestants and Catholics in Northern Ireland). For our purposes, however, we will limit our discussion of cross-cultural consumer analysis to comparisons of consumers of *different* countries.

Similarities and Differences Among People

A major objective of cross-cultural consumer analysis is to determine how consumers in two or more societies are similar and how they are different. For instance, Table 16-2 presents the insights of two Japanese advertising executives on the difference between Japanese and American cultural traits. Such an understanding of the similarities and differences that exist between nations is critical to the multinational marketer, who must devise appropriate strategies to reach consumers in specific foreign markets. The greater the similarity between nations, the more feasible it is to use relatively similar strategies in each nation. On the other hand, if the cultural beliefs, values, and customs of specific target countries are found to differ widely, then a highly *individualized* marketing strategy is indicated for each country. To illustrate, Table 16-3 presents a comparison of the United States and a few Latin-American neighbors in terms of their similarities and differences when it comes to selected forms of consumer behavior. Specifically, the results reveal that whereas United States consumers are substantially more likely to use credit cards, they are less likely to buy children's clothing, less likely to take vacations, and less likely to use a cellular phone than consumers in several Latin-American countries.[12] Similarly, the management of the Discovery Channel (i.e., the cable TV channel) found, in their effort to bring the correct programming to viewers in specific countries, that they should emphasize history and architecture in Mexico; military technology in China and Brazil; a do-it-yourself series in Russia; and science and technology in Australia.[13]

A firm's success in marketing a product or service in a number of foreign countries is likely to be influenced by how similar the beliefs, values, and customs are that govern the use of the product in the various countries. For example, the worldwide TV commer-

table 16-2 — Observations on the Differences Between Japan and American Cultural Traits

JAPANESE CULTURE, TRAITS	AMERICAN CULTURE, TRAITS
• Japanese language	• English language
• Homogeneous	• Diverse
• Harmony to be valued and preserved	• Fight for one's beliefs/positions
• Group, not individual, important	• Individualistic
• Ambiguous	• Clearcut
• General	• Specific
• Unspoken agreement	• Get the facts straight
• Hold back emotions in public	• Display emotions in public
• Process-oriented	• Result-oriented
• Pun-oriented	• Humor-oriented
• Make a long story short	• Make a short story long
• Nonverbal communication important	• Verbal communication important
• Interested in *who* is speaking	• Interested in *what* is spoken

Source: HIDEO ISHIKAWA and KOICH NAGANUMA, "Exploring Differences in Japanese. U.S. Culture," *Advertising Age,* September 18, 1995, I-8. Reprinted with permission from the September 18, 1995 issue of *Advertising Age.* Copyright 1995 by Crain Communications.

cials of major international airlines (American Airlines, Continental Airlines, Air France, Lufthansa, SAS, Sabena, Swissair, United Airlines, USAir/British Airways, etc.) tend to depict the luxury and pampering offered their business-class and first-class international travelers. Figure 16-1 presents an ad that reflects Northwest and KLM's joint approach to

table 16-3 — Differences in Latin-Americans and United States Consumer Spending Preferences

	U.S.	ARGENTINA	BRAZIL	MEXICO	VENEZUELA
Bought clothes for self	48%	38%	30%	46%	41%
Used credit card	44	21	13	16	17
Bought clothes for child/teen	32	36	25	40	27
Did job-related work at home	25	32	11	39	28
Bought recorded music	22	23	9	19	10
Went away for weekend	20	15	16	35	21
Sent/received fax at work	15	7	3	11	7
Used car/cellular phone	14	5	2	10	16
Shopped for used car	11	11	8	18	9
Looked at new cars	11	9	7	15	7
Made international phone call	8	11	4	18	14
Went away for 4+ days	6	14	8	19	10

Sourc: IGNACIO GALCERAN and JON BERRY, "A New World of Consumers," *American Demographics,* March 1995, 26–33. © 1995 American Demographics Magazine. Reprinted with permission.

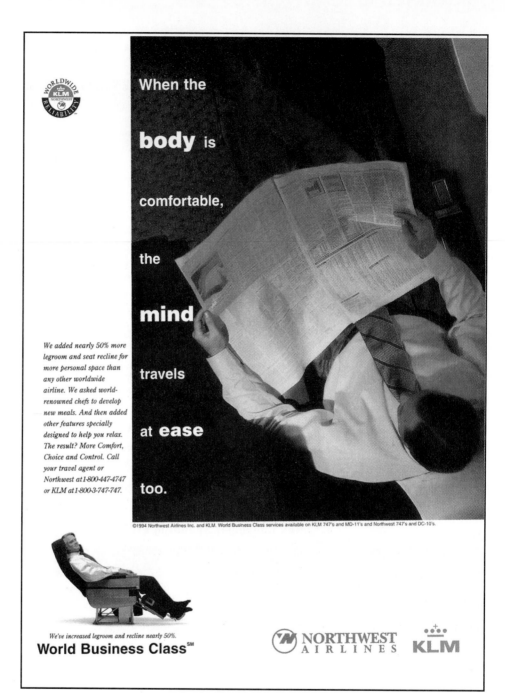

FIGURE 16-1

Appealing to the
Frequent International
Traveler
Courtesy of Northwest Airlines

communicating with this select group of "world-class" consumers. The reason for its general cross-cultural appeal is that it speaks to the same type of individual worldwide—the upscale international business traveler.

The Growing Global Middle Class

The growing middle class in developing countries is a phenomenon that is very attractive to global marketers who are often eager to identify new customers for their products. The news media has given considerable coverage to the idea that the rapidly expanding middle class in countries of Asia, South America, and Eastern Europe is based on the reality that while per capita income may be low, there is nevertheless considerable buying power in a country like China, where $1500 of income is largely discretionary income. This means that a Chinese family with $1500 is middle class and is a target customer for TVs, VCRs, and computers. Indeed, this same general pattern of the growing middle class has also been observed in many parts of South America, Asia, and Eastern Europe.[14] Table 16-4 presents information on ten Latin-American countries that dramatically illustrates the rapid expansion of the middle class in countries that, historically, were associated with having a small group of rich people, almost no middle class, and a very large proportion of the population who lived at or below the poverty level.

Acculturation Is a Needed Marketing Viewpoint

Too many marketers, contemplating international expansion, make the strategic error of believing that "if it is liked by local or domestic consumers, then everyone will like it." This biased viewpoint increases the likelihood of marketing failures abroad. It reflects a lack of appreciation of the unique psychological, social, cultural, and environmental characteristics of distinctly different cultures. To overcome such a narrow and culturally myopic view, marketers must also go through a kind of *acculturation process*. They must learn everything that is relevant about the usage or potential usage of their products and product categories in the foreign countries in which they plan to operate. Take the Chinese culture, for example. For Western marketers to succeed in China it is important for them to take into consideration *guo qing* (pronounced "gwor ching"), which means "to consider the special situation or character of China."[15] An example of *guo qing* for Western marketers is the Chinese policy of limiting families to one child. An appreciation of this policy means that foreign businesses will understand that Chinese families are open to particularly high-quality baby products for their single child (i.e., "the little emperor").[16]

In a sense, cross-cultural **acculturation** is a dual process for marketers. First, marketers must thoroughly orient themselves to the values, beliefs, and customs of the new society to appropriately position and market their products (being sensitive to and consistent

table 16-4   Growing Latin-American Middle Class*

	UPPER CLASS	MIDDLE-TO-UPPER CLASS	MIDDLE CLASS	LOWER CLASS AND SUBSISTENCE LEVEL
Argentina	2%	9%	35%	55%
Brazil	3	16	29	53
Chile	2	6	42	50
Colombia	2	8	37	53
Ecuador	2	15	22	61
Mexico	2	12	30	56
Paraguay	3	12	34	51
Peru	3	8	33	56
Uruguay	8	20	36	36
Venezuela	1	4	36	59

* Note: Class designations correspond in Socioeconomic Strata (SES) segments.

Source: CHIP WALKER, "The Global Middle Class," *American Demographics*, September 1995, 42. © 1995 American Demographics Magazine. Reprinted with permission.

with traditional or prevailing attitudes and values). Second, to gain acceptance for a culturally new product in a foreign society, they must develop a strategy that encourages members of that society to modify or even break with their own traditions (to change their *attitudes* and possibly alter their *behavior*). To illustrate the point, a social marketing effort designed to encourage consumers in developing nations to secure smallpox vaccinations for their children would require a two-step acculturation process. First, the marketer must obtain an in-depth picture of a society's present attitudes and customs with regard to preventive medicine and related concepts. Then, the marketer must devise promotional strategies that will convince the members of a target market to have their children vaccinated, even if doing so requires a change in current attitudes.

▲ **Distinctive Characteristics of Cross-Cultural Analysis** It is often difficult for a company planning to do business in foreign countries to undertake **cross-cultural consumer research**. For instance, it is difficult in the Islamic countries of the Middle East to conduct Western-style market research. In Saudi Arabia it is illegal to stop people on the streets, and focus groups are impractical, because most gatherings of four or more people (with the exception of family and religious gatherings) are outlawed.[17] American firms desiring to do business in Russia have found a limited amount of information regarding consumer and market statistics. Similarly, marketing research information on China is generally inadequate, and surveys that ask personal questions arouse suspicion.

▲ **Applying Research Techniques** Although the same basic research techniques used to study domestic consumers are useful in studying consumers in foreign lands (see Chapter 2), in cross-cultural analysis an additional burden exists, because language and word usage often differ from nation to nation. Another issue in international marketing research concerns scales of measurement. In the United States, a 5- or 7-point scale may be adequate, but in other countries, a 10- or even 20-point scale may be needed.

To avoid such research measurement problems, consumer researchers must familiarize themselves with the availability of research services in the countries they are evaluating as potential markets, and must learn how to design marketing research studies that will yield useful data. Researchers must also keep in mind that cultural differences may make "standard" research methodologies inappropriate. Table 16-5 identifies basic issues that multinational marketers must consider when planning cross-cultural consumer research.

ALTERNATIVE MULTINATIONAL STRATEGIES: GLOBAL VERSUS LOCAL

Some marketers have argued that world markets are becoming more and more similar and that standardized marketing strategies are, therefore, becoming more feasible. In contrast, other marketers feel that differences between consumers of various nations are far too great to permit a standardized marketing strategy. In a practical sense, a basic challenge for many executives contemplating multinational marketing is to decide whether to use *shared needs and values* as a segmentation strategy (i.e., to appeal to consumers in different countries in terms of their "common" needs, values, and goals) or to use *national borders* as a segmentation strategy (i.e., to use relatively different, "local," or specific marketing strategies for members of distinctive cultures or countries).[18]

table 16-5 Basic Research Issues in Cross-Cultural Analysis

FACTORS	EXAMPLES
Differences in language and meaning	Words or concepts (e.g., "personal checking account") may not mean the same in two different countries.
Differences in market segmentation opportunities	The income, social class, age, and sex of target customers may differ dramatically in two different countries.
Differences in consumption patterns	Two countries may differ substantially in the level of consumption or use of products or services (e.g., mail catalogs).
Differences in the perceived benefits of products and services	Two nations may use or consume the same product (e.g., yogurt) in very different ways.
Differences in the criteria for evaluating products and services	The benefits sought from a service (e.g., bank cards) may differ from country to country.
Differences in economic and social conditions and family structure	The "style" of family decision making may vary significantly from country to country.
Differences in marketing research and conditions	The types and quality of retail outlets and direct-mail lists may vary greatly among countries.
Differences in marketing research possibilities	The availability of professional consumer researchers may vary considerably from country to country.

Favoring a "World Brand"

An increasing number of firms have created *world brands* products that are manufactured, packaged, and positioned in exactly the same way regardless of the country in which they are sold. Playtex has moved from a local strategy of nation-by-nation advertising to a global advertising strategy. Other multinational companies, such as General Motors, Gillette, Estée Lauder, Unilever, Parker Pen, and Fiat, also use global advertising for various products and services. Advertising for the Gillette Sensor Excel for Women Shaving System is an example of a global advertising campaign. As Figure 16-2 on page 480 reveals, the only difference in the ads running in France and Sweden is the language in which they are executed; the illustration and headline are the same. Similarly, a very well reviewed advertising campaign, designed with a global orientation, is the corporate advertising of IBM (Figure 16-3), which offers "Solutions for a Small Planet." The frames from the TV commercials show that the only real difference is one of language. Still further, the print ads in Figure 16-4 on page 481 reveal that Campbell's uses a relatively standardized format in its advertising and packaging throughout the world; however, it does vary the ingredients of its products, both regionally and nationally, so as to better satisfy local taste preferences.

Adaptive Global Marketing

In contrast to the marketing communication strategy that stresses a common message, some firms embrace a strategy that adapts their advertising messages to the specific values of particular cultures. McDonald's is an example of a firm that tries to localize its advertising to consumers in each of the cross-cultural markets in which it operates (see Figure 16-5 on page 482). Levi's and Reebok also tend to follow strategies that calculate cultural differences in creating brand images for their products. Levi's tends to position its jeans for American consumers, stressing a social-group image, whereas it uses a much more individualistic, sexual image when communicating with European consumers. Similarly, Reebok

FIGURE 16-2

An Advertising Campaign with a Global Appeal
Courtesy of The Gillette Company

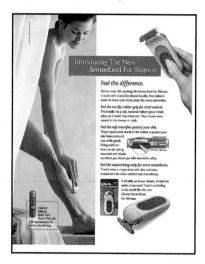 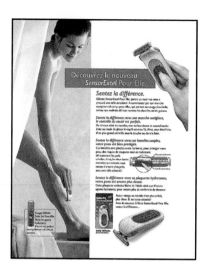 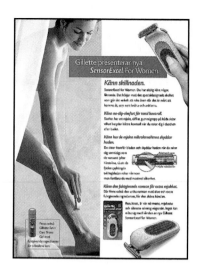

tries to use a combined lifestyle and athletic appeal when speaking to American consumers and appeals to performance and athletics when communicating with European consumers.[19]

Other marketers, too, feel that the world-brand concept may be going too far. Procter & Gamble has four brands that are marketed under the same name worldwide (Camay soap, Crest toothpaste, Head & Shoulders shampoo, and Pampers diapers), but the flavor and scent of each product are likely to vary from country to country. The company believes that globally standardized products may not be desirable. *Cosmopolitan* magazine, besides publishing in 12 languages, also tailors the editorial content of its 28 international editions to suit the local market.[20] In a similar fashion, *Forbes* magazine targets business readers in

FIGURE 16-3

Appealing to Consumers Worldwide
Courtesy of IBM

FIGURE 16-5 ▼ Point-of-Purchase Displays for "Happy Meals" are
Localized by McDonald's for Different Markets
Courtesy of McDonald's Corporation

a number of different languages, using customized editorial content that sets them apart from the United States magazine (Figure 16-6).

These marketing case histories suggest that differences between countries are often sufficiently glaring to make *localized* marketing more appropriate than a global approach, which may sometimes prove to be too costly. For example, Hoover Ltd., the British subsidiary of the United States company, decided to sell washing machines in other European nations. When research indicated that consumers in other countries wanted a host of different features, the company ultimately decided to drop its expansion plans, because a localized product strategy would have been too costly.

FIGURE 16-6

Forbes Offers International Advertisers a Variety of Advertising Options

Credit: Reprinted by Permission of Forbes Magazine © Forbes Inc., 1994.

When people get serious about business, they start reading FORBES. Worldwide.

FORBES • !FORBES von Burda • FORBES Nihonban • FORBES Zibenjia

German, Japanese, Chinese-speaking business executives...they're also reading FORBES. Month after month, FORBES delivers influential readers in these key markets. With a key difference -- these aren't just translated versions of FORBES' U.S. magazine. They're original publications in their own right, written in their countries' indigenous language: !FORBES von Burda, FORBES Nihonban, and FORBES Zibenjia. Each with the FORBES' editorial flavor.

So when you place an ad in FORBES, your message has an unrivaled level of authority, integrity and believability. Because, suddenly you can reach over 1,000,000 executives in the language they understand best. Their own.

Call Christian Frost, FORBES' International Advertising Liason at (212) 620-2423. And don't forget to ask for our Global Advantage media kit. **FORBES. Global Management. Global Solutions.**

Forbes
CAPITALIST TOOL

Following a "mixed" strategy, firms such as Coca-Cola, Unilever, Playtex, and Black & Decker have augmented their global strategies with local execution. In taking such an adaptive approach, global advertisers with a knowledge of cross-cultural differences can tailor their supplemental messages more effectively to suit individual local markets. For example, an analysis of TV commercials in the United States, France, and Taiwan reveals that while strong product identification, use of celebrities, and testimonials are acceptable in the United States, consumers in France and Taiwan are more accustomed to subtle and symbolic advertising with very few direct and reasoned arguments.[21] Similarly, an analysis of print advertising indicated that French ads make greater use of emotion, humor, and sex than do ads in the United States.[22] Following this mixed or hybrid strategy, knowledgeable multinational marketers adapt their advertising accordingly.

Frameworks for Assessing Multinational Strategies

Multinational marketers face the challenge of creating marketing and advertising programs capable of communicating effectively with a diversity of target markets. To assist in this imposing task, various frameworks have been developed to determine the degree to which marketing and advertising efforts should be globalized or localized.

To enable international marketers to assess the positions their products enjoy in specific foreign markets, Table 16-6 presents a five-stage continuum that ranges from mere awareness of a foreign brand in a local market area to complete global identification of the brand; that is, the brand is accepted "as is" in almost every market, and consumers do not think about its country of origin.

Table 16-7 on page 486 presents a framework that focuses on four marketing strategies available to a firm planning to do business on a global basis. A firm might decide either to standardize or localize its product and either standardize or localize its communications program (e.g., forming a two-by-two matrix). The four possibilities that this decision framework considers range from a company's merely "exporting" its present marketing mix (i.e., standardizing both product and communications program) to developing a completely new product and communications program. All four cells may represent growth opportunities for the firm. To determine which cell represents the firm's best strategy, the marketer must conduct cross-cultural consumer analysis to obtain consumer reactions to alternative product and promotional executions. To illustrate the strategic importance of product uniformity, Frito-Lay, the United States snack-food giant, is presently standardizing quality and reducing the dozens of local brand names of potato chip companies that it owns throughout the world. This effort will mean a common global visual appearance that features the Lay's logo. Its efforts are driven by research that reveals that potato chips are a snack-food that has widespread appeal throughout much of the world.[23]

A recent study of international advertising messages found that possibly one in three campaigns has global potential. This study also suggested that advertising standardization opportunities for American and other admired foreign products are more likely to occur in less affluent and developing markets. On the other hand, products introduced into affluent and highly competitive foreign markets that have many discriminating consumers should have promotional messages that are consistent with the "tastes" of the particular market.[24]

Figure 16-7 on page 486 presents another framework that may be used to evaluate the degree of global standardization feasible for a particular product or service. This framework may help a company decide between using a standardized approach, in which all decisions are made on a global basis, or a localized approach, in which a strategy is customized for each nation.[25] Although a local strategy is appealing because it enables a firm to truly target a particular country's population, a firm taking that approach may forfeit possible economic and marketing synergies among the nations in which it markets. Ac-

table 16-6 A Product Recognition Continuum for Multinational Marketing

FACTORS	EXAMPLES
STAGE ONE	Local consumers have heard or read of a brand marketed elsewhere but cannot get it at home; a brand is "alien" and unavailable but may be desirable [e.g., Rover (English autos), Havana cigars (made in Cuba), or medicine not approved by the FDA but sold in Europe].
STAGE TWO	Local consumers view a brand made elsewhere as "foreign," made in a particular country but locally available (e.g., Saab autos, French wine). The fact that the brand is foreign makes a difference in the consumer's mind, sometimes favorable, sometimes not).
STAGE THREE	Local consumers accord imported brand "national status"; that is, its national origin is known but does not affect their choice (e.g., Molson beer in United States, Ford autos in southern Europe).
STAGE FOUR	Brand owned by a foreign company is made (wholly or partly) domestically and has come to be perceived by locals as a local brand; its foreign origins may be remembered but the brand has been "adopted" ("naturalized"). Examples are Sony in the United States, Coca-Cola in Europe and Japan.
STAGE FIVE	Brand has lost national identity and consumers everywhere see it as "borderless" or global; not only can people not identify where it comes from but they never ask this question. Examples include the Associated Press and CNN news services, Nescafe, Bayer aspirin.

Source: Adapted from George V. Priovolos, "How to Turn National European Brands into Pan-European Brands," Working paper, Hagan School of Business, Iona College, New Rochelle, NY.

cording to the framework, the following factors must be considered when determining the strategy orientation that would be most fruitful: (1) characteristics of the target market, (2) assessment of the firm's market position, (3) attributes of the product, (4) specific environmental issues, and (5) organizational style and concerns.

A final scheme for assessing whether to use a **global versus local marketing** strategy concentrates on a *high-tech to high-touch* continuum. **Product standardization** appears to be most successful for high-involvement products that approach either end of the high-tech/high-touch continuum. In other words, products that are at either extreme are more suitable for positioning as global brands. In contrast, low-involvement products in the mid-range of the high-tech/high-touch continuum are more suitably marketed as local brands, using market-by-market executions.[26]

For example, on a worldwide basis, consumers interested in high-tech products share a common language (e.g., "bytes" and "microprocessors"). In contrast, advertisements for high-touch products tend to use more emotional appeals and emphasize image. The high-tech positioning is used for such products as computers, cameras, and telecommunication products and services; while the high-touch positioning strategy is used for products that are more image-oriented (e.g., perfumes and fine wristwatches).

table 16-7 Alternative International Marketing Strategies

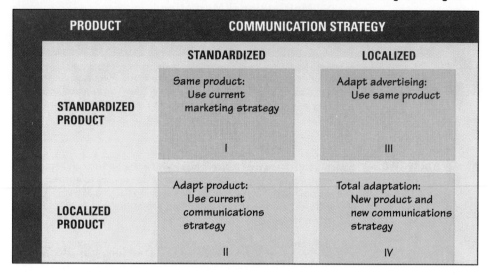

PRODUCT	COMMUNICATION STRATEGY	
	STANDARDIZED	**LOCALIZED**
STANDARDIZED PRODUCT	Same product: Use current marketing strategy I	Adapt advertising: Use same product III
LOCALIZED PRODUCT	Adapt product: Use current communications strategy II	Total adaptation: New product and new communications strategy IV

Source: Adapted from Linda J. Coleman, Ernest F. Cooke, and Chandra M. Kochunny, "What Is Meant by Global Marketing?" in J. M. Haws and G. B. Gilsan, eds., *Developments in Marketing Science* 10 (Akron, Ohio: Academy of Marketing Science, 1987), 176.

Figure 16-7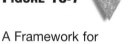

A Framework for Determining Standardization of Marketing Strategy
Source: From "Figure Out the Russian Consumer" by Stuart Elliot in *The New York Times*, April 1, 1992. Copyright © 1992 by The New York Times Company. Reprinted by permission.

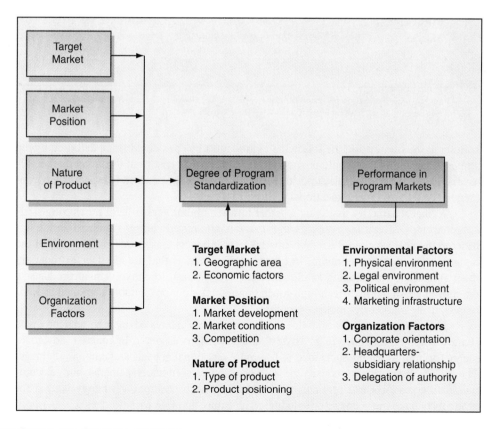

CROSS-CULTURAL PSYCHOGRAPHIC SEGMENTATION

The paradox in cross-cultural consumer research is that while worldwide consumers may be similar in many ways (e.g., the increased number who work outside of the home), any differences in attitudes or behavior can be crucial in determining the satisfaction and may provide an opportunity for segmenting consumers in terms of cultural differences.[27] For example, while more than 50 percent of Japanese and American women work outside of the home (which has made them recognize the need for many convenience and time-saving products), Japanese women have been slower to embrace the liberated attitudes of their counterpart working women in the United States.[28] Seen in this light, the determination as to whether or not to market a time-saving cleaning device as a world brand is a critical strategic decision. Some firms might attempt to establish a global branding strategy, whereas others would design an individual or local marketing strategy, one that treats Japanese and American working women differently. One marketing authority aptly summed up the issues as follows: "The only ultimate truth possible is that humans are both deeply the same and obviously different. . . ."[29]

This book is based on the same thesis. Earlier chapters have described the underlying similarities that exist between people and the external influences that serve to differentiate them into distinct market segments. If we believe in tailoring marketing strategies to specific segments of the American market, it follows then that we also believe in tailoring marketing strategies to the needs—psychological, social, cultural, and functional—of specific foreign segments.

Global psychographic research often reveals cultural differences of great importance to marketers. For example, Roper Starch Worldwide, a major multinational marketing research company, recently completed a 40-country cross-cultural psychographic segmentation study consisting of some 37,743 consumer interviews that are projectable to 1.97 billion adults worldwide.[30] The results revealed that the following four major shopping styles dominate worldwide consumers: "Deal makers," "Price seekers," "Brand loyalists," and "Luxury innovators." Table 16-8 on page 488 presents a brief description of each of these psychographic-oriented global market segments. The Gallup Organization, another leading marketing research company, has also recently completed a regional multinational segmentation study of the metropolitan areas of the following five Latin-American countries: Argentina, Brazil, Chile, Colombia, and Mexico.[31] This segmentation model identified the following eight segments: "Emerging Professional Elite," "Traditional Elite," "Progressive Upper Middle Class," "Self-Made Middle Class," "Skilled Middle Class," "Self-Skilled Lower Middle Class," "Industrial Working Class," and "Struggling Working Class" (see Table 16-9 on page 489).

As a final example, Table 16-10 on page 490 presents a countrywide psychographic segmentation scheme that sorts Russians into five groups that differ in terms of outlook, behavior, and openness to Western products.[32]

MARKETING MISTAKES: A FAILURE TO UNDERSTAND DIFFERENCES

In most cases, the gamble for marketers in international marketing is not knowing whether the product, the promotional appeal, the pricing policy, or the retail channels that are

table 16-8 Four Global Consumer Market Segments

SEGMENT NAME	GLOBAL SIZE (%)	U.S. SIZE (%)	DESCRIPTION
Deal makers	29	37	They concentrate on the process of buying. Demographically they are in a well-educated group, median age 32, with average affluence and employment.
Price seekers	27	36	They place primary value on the product and price. This group has the highest proportion of retirees, the lowest education level, skews female, and has an average level of affluence.
Brand loyalists	23	11	They are the least affluent. The segment is mostly male, median age 36, who hold average education and employment.
Luxury I innovators	21	17	They seek new, prestigious brands and are the most educated and affluent shoppers, with the highest proportion of executives and other professionals. The group is mostly male with a median age of 32.

Source: Adapted from KELLY SHERMACH, "Portrait of the World," *Marketing News,* August 28, 1995, 20–21. Reprinted by permission of American Marketing Association.

effective in one country will work in other countries and trying to determine what specific changes should be made to ensure acceptance in each foreign market. The following examples of some international marketing blunders illustrate that failure to adapt marketing strategy to the target market's distinctive cultural traits can lead to costly mistakes.

Product Problems

International marketers frequently neglect to modify their products to meet local customs and tastes. American marketers, selling food products in Japan, frequently learn the hard way (through poor sales performance) that they must alter traditional product characteristics. For example, recently Snapple failed to sustain sales momentum in Japan because consumers preferred clearer, less sweet iced tea. It appears that Snapple was unwilling or too slow to alter its ingredients to conform to local Japanese tastes.[33] Kellogg's, the giant cereal company, in pursuing international expansion, has attempted to avoid the numerous "cultural traps" that are associated with cross-cultural marketing of food stuff. It has learned to draw careful distinctions between the Irish, who consume 17 pounds of cereal per person per year (the highest rate in the world), and the French, Italians, and Greeks, whose meager breakfasts tend not to include cereal.[34] Still another example showed that, when Oreos were introduced in Japan, Nabisco reduced the amount of sugar in the cookie batter (the box promoted them as having a "bitter twist") to meet Japanese tastes. However, some Japanese consumers still considered them too sweet and told the company that they "just wanted to eat the base" without the cream. Nabisco belatedly introduced new Petit Oreo Non-Cream cookies that consisted of single wafers without the cream.[35] To

table 16-9

Eight Socioeconomic-Psychographic Segments of the Latin American Market

BEYOND NATIONAL BOUNDARIES

Gallup's eight socioeconomic segments of Latin American consumers:

EMERGING PROFESSIONAL ELITE

14% of total; occupies top professional, executive positions:
- 51% graduated from university or technical college.
- 55% are married.
- 98% have color TV; 96%, VCR; 97% car; 98%, credit card; 90% vacuum cleaner.

TRADITIONAL ELITE

11%; almost half in top professional, executive positions:
- 53% finished secondary education.
- 54% married.
- All have color TV; 91%, VCR; 89%, car; 60%, credit card; 60% vacuum cleaner.

PROGRESSIVE UPPER MIDDLE CLASS

13%; 36% in top or middle management:
- 75% studied beyond primary education, 30% studied beyond secondary school.
- 48% married.
- 99% have a color TV; 77%, VCR; 74%, car; 31%, credit card; 30% vacuum cleaner.

SELF-MADE MIDDLE CLASS

11%; skills gained through entrepreneurship:
- Most ended education with primary school, "virtually none" went beyond secondary school.
- Half married.
- 98% have color TV; 72%, VCR; 81%, car; 46%, credit card; 51%, vacuum cleaner.

SKILLED MIDDLE CLASS

9%; 45% have top operational jobs, 14% own small businesses:
- 60% completed secondary education, 18% completed university or technical college.
- Half married.
- 96% have color TV; 60%, VCR; 28%, car; 29%, credit card; 32%, vacuum cleaner.

SELF-SKILLED LOWER MIDDLE CLASS

13%; 58% employed in operational jobs:
- 42% went beyond primary school, 11% went beyond secondary education.
- Half married.
- 97% have color TV; 50%, VCR; 4%, car; 8%, credit card; none, vacuum cleaner.

INDUSTRIAL WORKING CLASS

14%; a third are in skilled worker positions and another third in average operational jobs:
- 16% went beyond secondary school, 26% completed secondary, 35% completed primary.
- 57% married.
- 92% have color TV; 13%, VCR; 5%, credit card; 15%, vacuum cleaner.

STRUGGLING WORKING CLASS

15%; most in operational, skilled and unskilled jobs:
- 29% completed primary school, 24% completed secondary school.
- 53% married.
- 63% have color TV; no more than 10% have VCR, car, credit card or vacuum cleaner.

Source: Jeffrey D. Zbar, "Gallup Offers New Take On Latin America," *Advertising Age*, November 13, 1995, 21.
Reprinted with permission from the November 13, 1995 issue of *Advertising Age*. Copyright 1995 by Crain Communications.

avoid such problems, marketers must ascertain in advance whether the physical characteristics of their products will be acceptable to the new market.

McDonald's, which has been very successful in its ongoing efforts to bring fast-food to the world, has reached a point at which its international operations now bring in more

table 16-10   Five Psychographic Segments of the Russian Market

	"KUPTSI" OR MERCHANTS	"COSSACKS"	STUDENTS	BUSINESS EXECUTIVES	"RUSSIAN SOULS"
PERCENT OF ALL MEN	30%	10%	10%	25%	25%
PERCENT OF ALL WOMEN	45	10	5	10	30
DOMINANT TRAITS	Reliant Nationalistic Practical Seeks value	Ambitious Independent Nationalistic Seeks status	Passive Scraping by Idealistic Practical	Ambitious Western-oriented Busy Concerned with status	Passive Follows others Fears choices Hopeful
LIKELY PREFERENCES Car Cigarettes Liquor	Volkswagen Chesterfield Stolichnaya	BMW Dunhill Rémy Martin	Citroën 2CV Marlboro Local vodka in Smirnoff bottles	Mercedes Winston Johnnie Walker	Lada Marlboro Smirnoff

Source: STUART ELLIOT, "Figuring Out the Russian Consumer," *The New York Times* (April 1, 1992), D1, D19. Copyright © 1992 by The New York Times. Reprinted by permission.

than half of its operating income. Its international expansion plans are ambitious: it currently anticipates opening more than 600 outlets in China and has just finished developing a vegetable-and-fish burger that is designed to be culturally acceptable to India's 800 million non-meat-eating Hindus.[36]

Color is also a critical variable in international marketing, because the same color often has different meanings in different cultures. For example, consider the color blue. In Holland, it stands for warmth; in Iran, it represents death; in Sweden, it connotes coldness; in India, it means purity. Furthermore, yellow, which represents warmth in the United States, connotes infidelity in France.[37] Pepsodent erred when it tried to sell its toothpaste in Southeast Asia by promising white teeth. In that part of the world, chewing betel nuts is considered an elite habit and, consequently, brownish-red teeth are viewed as a status symbol. Thus, Pepsodent's slogan, "You'll wonder where the yellow went" did not help to sell the product.[38] It is critical that the colors of products and packages convey the proper meaning in the countries in which they are marketed.

Promotional Problems

When communicating with consumers in different parts of the world, the promotional message must be consistent with the language and customs of the particular target society. International marketers have faced various problems in communicating with widely different customer groups. For example, the Seven-Up Company's highly successful "uncola" theme, developed for the United States market, was considered inappropriate for many foreign markets because it did not translate well into other languages. Similarly, something got lost, when IBM had translated, from English to Japanese, its global theme "Solutions for a small planet." It came out as "Answers that make people smaller"—not a very pleasant portrayal.[39] Learning from earlier mistakes, multinational firms like P&G and Ford

FIGURE 16-8

Names That Work in
One Culture May Bomb
in Another
Source: STEVE RIVKIN, "The Name
Game Heats Up," *Marketing
News*, April 22, 1996, 6.

now work harder to be responsive to particular tastes and values of local markets. For instance, they recently withdrew their sponsorship of television programming in some countries when the sex and violence of the shows were judged to be too strong.[40]

Product names and promotional phrases can also cause considerable problems for international marketers (see Figure 16-8). The word "clock" in Chinese sounds like the word "death." The Chevrolet Nova did not sell well in Latin America because in Spanish the word "nova" means "It doesn't run." GM also blundered with its "body by Fisher" tag line, which in Flemish translates into "corpse by Fisher." The United States government made a miscalculation recently when it moved to drop the word "North" from North American Free Trade Agreement (i.e., to move from NAFTA to AFTA) so as to make it more inclusive. The trouble began when Brazil pointed out that in Portuguese "AFTA" sounded like the words that mean "an open mouth sore."[41]

International direct marketing has increased in recent years.[42] For example, the famed British retailer Harrods invited consumers to participate in a transatlantic shopping spree by means of a toll-free 800 number. American direct marketers who now enter overseas markets are likely to have a competitive edge over those who follow in future years. These firms, however, must be aware of the differences in doing business in other countries.

Pricing and Distribution Problems

International marketers must adjust their pricing and distribution policies to meet local economic conditions and customs. For instance, in many developing nations, small-sized product packages often are a necessity, because consumers cannot afford the cash outlay required for the larger sizes popular in the United States and other affluent countries. Even in developed nations, important differences do exist. For example, supermarkets are very popular in Switzerland, but in France, which is just across the border, consumers prefer smaller and more intimate stores for grocery shopping.

Japan's traditional distribution system differs from the United States in that a close, complex relationship exists among the larger Japanese manufacturers and their distributors and retailers. For example, it took 24 years from the time Japan allowed the introduction of United States apples, until they actually reached the marketplace where Japanese consumers could buy them.[43] Thus, marketers must vary their distribution channels by nation.

summary

With so much diversity present among the members of just one nation (as in the United States), it is easy to appreciate that numerous larger differences may exist between citizens of different nations having different cultures, values, beliefs and languages. If international marketers are to satisfy the needs of consumers in potentially very distinct markets effectively, they must understand the relevant similarities and differences that exist between the peoples of the countries they decide to target.

When consumers make purchase decisions, they seem to take into consideration the countries-of-origin of the brands that they are assessing. Consumers frequently have specific *attitudes* or even preferences for products made in particular countries. These "country-of-origin" effects influence how consumers rate quality and, sometimes, which brands they will ultimately select.

As increasing numbers of consumers from all over the world come in contact with the material goods and lifestyle of people living in other countries, and as the number of middle-class consumers grows in developing countries, marketers are eager to locate these new customers and to offer them their products. The rapidly expanding middle class in countries of Asia, South American, and Eastern Europe possess relatively substantial buying power because their incomes are largely discretionary (for necessities like housing and medical care are often provided by the state, at little or no costs).

For some international marketers, acculturation is a dual process: First, they must learn everything that is relevant to the product and product category in the society in which they plan to market, then they must persuade the members of that society to break with their traditional ways of doing things to adopt the new product. The more similar a foreign target market is to a marketer's home market, the easier the process of acculturation. Conversely, the more different a foreign target market, the more difficult the process of acculturation.

Some of the problems involved in cross-cultural analysis include differences in language, consumption patterns, needs, product usage, economic and social conditions, marketing conditions, and market research opportunities. There is an urgent need for more systematic and conceptual cross-cultural analyses of the psychological, social, and cultural characteristics concerning the consumption habits of foreign consumers. Such analyses would identify increased marketing opportunities that would benefit both international marketers and their targeted consumers.

discussion questions

1. Will the elimination of trade barriers among the countries of the European Community change consumer behavior in these countries? How can United States companies take advantage of the economic opportunities emerging in Europe?

2. With all the problems facing companies that go global, why are so many companies choosing to expand internationally? What are the advantages of expanding beyond the domestic market?

3. Are the cultures of the world becoming more similar or more different? Discuss.

4. What is cross-cultural consumer analysis? How can a multinational company use cross-cultural research to design each factor in its marketing mix? Illustrate your answer with examples.

5. What are the advantages and disadvantages of global promotional strategies?

6. Should Head & Shoulders shampoo be sold worldwide with the same formulation? In the same package? With the same advertising theme? Explain your answers.

7. a. If you wanted to name a new product that would be acceptable to consumers throughout the world, what cultural factors would you consider?

   b. What factors might inhibit an attempt by Apple to position a new laptop computer as a "world brand"?

8. An American company is introducing a line of canned soups in Poland. (a) How should the company use cross-cultural research? (b) Should the company use the same marketing mix it uses in the United States to target Polish consumers? (c) Which, if any, marketing mix components should be designed specifically for marketing canned soups in Poland? Explain your answers.

9. Mercedes-Benz, a West-German car manufacturer, is using cross-cultural psychographic segmentation to develop marketing campaigns for a new two-seater, sports car directed at consumers in different countries. How should the company market the car in the United States? How should it market the car in Japan?

10. What advice would you give to an American retailer who wants to sell women's clothing in Japan?

11. Select two of the marketing mistakes discussed in the text. Discuss how these mistakes could have been avoided if the companies involved had adequately researched some of the issues listed in Table 16-5.

1. Have you ever traveled outside the United States? If so, please identify some of the differences in values, behavior, and consumption patterns you noted between people in a country you visited and Americans.

2. Interview a student from another culture about his or her use of: (a) credit cards, (b) fast-food restaurants, (c) shampoo, and (d) sneakers. Compare your consumption behavior to that of the person you interviewed and discuss any similarities and differences you found.

3. Much has been written about the problems at Euro Disney, the Walt Disney Company's theme park and resort complex which opened in France in April of 1992. These difficulties were largely attributed to Disney's lack of understanding of European (particularly French) culture, and the company's failure to modify its American theme-park concept to fit the preferences and customs of European visitors. Discuss how the Walt Disney Company could have used input from cross-cultural analysis in bet-

ter designing and operating Euro Disney, using a computerized literature search about Euro Disney from your school's library.

4. Select one of the following countries: Mexico, Brazil, Germany, Italy, Israel, Kuwait, Japan, or Australia. Assume that a significant number of people in the country you chose would like to visit the United States and have the financial means to do so. Now, imagine you are a consultant for your state's tourism agency and that you have been charged with developing a promotional strategy to attract tourists from the country you chose. Conduct a computerized literature search of the databases in your school's library and select and read several articles about the lifestyles, customs, and consumption behavior of people in the country you chose. Prepare an analysis of the articles and, on the basis of what you read, develop a promotional strategy designed to persuade tourists from that country to visit your state.

- **Acculturation**
- **Cross-cultural consumer analysis**
- **Cross-cultural consumer research**
- **Cross-cultural psychographic segmentation**
- **European Community**
- **Global-versus-localized marketing**
- **Multinational strategies**
- **North American Free Trade Agreement**
- **Product standardization**
- **World brands**

1. GIANLUIGI GUIDO, "What U.S. Marketers Should Consider in Planning a Pan-European Approach," *Journal of Consumer Marketing* 9, Spring 1992, 29–33.

2. BETSY MCKAY and STEVEN GUTTERMAN, "For Ads, Russian Revolution Lives," *Advertising Age*, March 7, 1994, 40.

3. SYED TARIQ ANWAR, "How NAFTA Provisions Will Affect Marketers," *Marketing News* 27, May 24, 1993, 14, 18.

4. CARL SPIELVOGEL, "The Challenge of Vietnam," *Advertising Age*, January 18, 1993, 24.

5. ROBERT FRANK, "Seeing Red Abroad, Pepsi Rolls Out a New Blue Can," *The Wall Street Journal*, April 2, 1996, B1 and B6; and "Canny Pepsi Repackaging Sings the Cola Blue," *Brandweek*, April 8, 1996, 8.

6. KAREN LOWRY MILLER, "You Just Can't Talk to These Kids," *Business Week*, April 19, 1993, 104, 106.

7. WILLIAM E. SCHMIDT, "In Europe, America's Grip on Pop

Culture Is Fading," *The New York Times*, March 28, 1993, L3; SHERYL WUDUNN, "Booming China Is Dream Market for West," *The New York Times*, February 15, 1993, A1, A6; and PAM WEISZ, "Avon Continues Assault on Dept. Store Scents," *Brandweek*, July 24, 1994, 14.

8. MARY C. GILLY, "Consumer Acculturation: Immigrants, Migrants and Expatriates," in Frank R. Kardes and Mita Sujan, eds., *Advances in Consumer Research* 22 (Provo UT: Association for Consumer Research, 1995), 505; LISA PENALOZA, "Immigrant Consumer Acculturation," *Advances in Consumer Behavior* 16 (Provo UT: Association for Consumer Research, 1989), 110–118; and LISA PENALOZA, "Atravesando Fronteras/Border Crossings: A Critical Ethnographic Exploration of the Consumer Acculturation of Mexican Immigrants," *Journal of Consumer Research*, 1994, 32–54.

9. SHARYNE MERRITT and VERNON STAUBB, "A Cross-Cultural Exploration of Country-of-Origin Preference," in David W. Stewart and Naufel J. Vilcassim, eds., *1995 AMA Winter Educators' Proceedings* (Chicago: American Marketing Association, 1995), 380.

10. TERENCE A. SHIMP, SAEED SAMIEE, and THOMAS J. MADDEN, "Countries and Their Products: A Cognitive Structure Perspective," *Journal of the Academy of Marketing Science* 21(4), 1993, 323–30.

11. DURAIRA MAHESWARAN, "Country-of-Origin as a Stereotype: Effects of Consumer Expertise and Attribute Strength of Product Evaluation," *Journal of Consumer Research* 21, September 1994, 354–56.

12. IGNACIO GALCERMAN and JON BERRY, "A New World of Consumers," *American Demographics*, 1995, 26–33.

13. WAYNE WALLEY, "Programming Globally—With Care," *Advertising Age*, September 18, 1995, I-14.

14. CHIP WALKER, "The Global Middle Class," *American Demographics*, September 1995, 40–46; PAULA KEPHART, "How Big Is the Mexican Market?," *American Demographics*, October 1995, 17–18; and RAHUL JACOB, "The Big Rise," *Fortune*, May 30, 1994, 74–90.

15. RICK YAN, "To Reach China's Consumers, Adapt to Guo Qing," *Harvard Business Review*, September-October 1994, 66–67.

16. SALLY D. GOLL, "China's (Only) Children Get the Royal Treatment," *The Wall Street Journal*, February 8, 1995, B1.

17. TARA PARKER-POPE, "Nonalcoholic Beer Hits the Spot in Mideast," *The Wall Street Journal*, December 6, 1995, B1.

18. NIRAJ DAWAR and PHILIP ARKER, "Marketing Universals: Consumers' Use of Brand Name, Price, Physical Appearance, and Retailer Reputation as Signals of Product Quality," *Journal of Marketing* 58, April 1994, 81-95; and MADHU AGRAWAL, "Review of a 40-Year Debate in International Advertising," *International Marketing Review*, 12(1), 1995, 26–48.

19. MARTIN S. ROTH, "The Effects of Culture and Socioeconomics on the Performance of Global Brand Image Strategies," *Journal of Marketing Research* 32, 1995, 163–75.

20. SUZANNE CASSIDY, "Defining the Cosmo Girl: Check Out the Passport," *The New York Times*, October 12, 1992, D8.

21. FRED ZANDPOUR, CYPRESS CHANG, and JOELLE CATALANO, "Stories, Symbols, and Straight Talk: A Comparative Analysis of French, Taiwanese, and U.S. TV Commercials," *Journal of Advertising Research* 32, January/February 1992, 25–38.

22. ABHIJIT BISWAS, JANEEN E. OLSEN, and VALERIE CARLET, "A Comparison of Print Advertisements from the United States and France," *Journal of Advertising* 21, December 1992, 73–81.

23. ROBERT FRANK, "Potato Chips To Go Global—Or So Pepsi Bets," *The Wall Street Journal*, November 30, 1995, B1.

24. WILLIAM L. JAMES and JOHN S. HILL, "International Advertising Messages: To Adapt or Not to Adapt (That Is the Question)," *Journal of Advertising Research*, June/July 1991, 65–71.

25. SUBHASH C. JAIN, "Standardization of International Marketing Strategy: Some Research Hypotheses," *Journal of Marketing* 53, January 1989, 70–79. See also GEORGE S. YIP, "Global Strategy . . . In a World of Nations?" *Sloan Management Review*, Fall 1989, 29–41.

26. TERESA DOMZAL and LYNETTE UNGER, "Emerging Positioning Strategies in Global Marketing," *Journal of Consumer Marketing* 4, Fall 1987, 27–29.

27. For a comprehensive discussion, see: A. COSKUM SAMLI, *International Consumer Behavior* (Westport, CT: Quorum Books, 1995); and SALAH S. HASSAN and ROGER D. BLACKWELL, *Global Marketing: Perspectives and Cases* (Orlando, FL: Dryden Press, 1994).

28. JACK RUSSEL, "Working Women Give Japan Culture Shock," *Advertising Age*, January 16, 1995, I-24.

29. SIDNEY J. LEVY, "Myth and Meaning in Marketing," in Ronald C. Curhan, ed., *1974 Combined Proceedings* (Chicago: American Marketing Association, 1975), 555–56.

30. KELLY SHERMACH, "Portrait of the World," *Marketing News*, August 28, 1995, 20–21.

31. JEFFREY D. ZBAR, "Gallup Offers New Take on Latin America," *Advertising Age*, November 13, 1995, 21.

32. STUART ELLIOT, "Figuring Out the Russian Consumer," *The New York Times*, April 1, 1992, D1, D19.

33. NORIHIKO SHIROUZU, "Snapple in Japan: Splash Dried Up," *The Wall Street Journal*, April 15, 1996, B1 and B6.

34. JOHN TAGLIABUE, "Spoon-to-Spoon Combat Overseas," *The New York Times*, January 7, 1995, 17.

35. YUMIKO ONO, "Some Kids Won't Eat the Middle of an Oreo," *The Wall Street Journal*, November 20, 1991, B1.

36. JEANNE WHALEN, "McDonald's Cooks Worldwide Growth," *Advertising Age International*, July 17, 1995, I-1.

37. LINDA J. COLEMAN, ERNEST F. COOKE, and CHANDRA M. KOCHUNNY, "What Is Meant by Global Marketing?" in J. M. Hawes and G. B. Gilsan, eds., *Developments in Marketing Science* (Akron, OH: Academy of Marketing Science, 1987), 10, 178.

38. Ibid., 179.

39. Bradley Johnson, "Global Thinking Paces Computer Biz," *Advertising Age*, March 6, 1995, 10.

40. Deborah Klosky, "Spanish Viewership Cries 'Foul' on Lurid TV," *Advertising Age*, April 17, 1995, I-20.

41. David E. Sanger, "An Epidemic Adverted: Foot-in-Mouth Disease," *The New York Times*, December 11, 1994, 22.

42. James S. Gould, "Preferences for Promotion Programs, A Study of Japanese Consumers," in M. Joseph Sirgy, Kenneth D. Bahn, and Tune Erem, eds, *World Marketing Congress*, 6 (Blackburg, VA: Academy of Marketing Science, 1993), 351-354.

43. Lisa A. Petrison, Masaru Ariga, and Paul Wang, "Strategies for Penetrating the Japanese Market", *Journal of Direct Marketing* 8, Winter 1994, 44–58; and Sheryl WuDunn, "Japan Tastes Once-Forbidden Fruit," *The New York Times*, January 11, 1995, A3.

PART FOUR

The Consumer's

Decision-Making

Process

PART **4**

EXPLORES VARIOUS

ASPECTS OF

CONSUMER

DECISION MAKING.

T BEGINS WITH A DISCUSSION OF PERSONAL INFLUENCE and opinion

leadership, and then examines the diffusion of innovations. This section

offers the reader a simple model of consumer decision making that ties

together the psychological, social, and cultural concepts examined

throughout the book.

the mall."

"Let's hit the mall."

"The mall? I've got better things to do with my money."

"Girl, please! Every dime you get goes on your back."

"Not anymore. When I shop E STYLE, a lot of those dimes go to the UNCF."

Call now for a free fashion and home catalog

1 800 2 E STYLE
(1 800 237-8953)
ask for offer 3781

Style that speaks your Body's Language

E STYLE

from Ebony® and Spiegel®

When choosing products and services, consumers often are influenced by advice from other people. The power and importance of personal influence is encapsulated in the following comment by an ad agency executive: "Perhaps the most important thing for marketers to understand about word of mouth is its huge potential economic impact."[1]

Buying-decision influences from others include which computer printer is the "best buy," which tennis racket would improve one's tennis game, and which restaurant might be most suitable for a Saturday night date. Opinion leadership involves so much social interaction about so many products and services that it is often difficult for consumers to remember the extent to which they have participated in informal communications that have influenced either their consumption behavior or the consumption behavior of others.

The art of conversation is the art of hearing as well as of being heard.

—William Hazlitt
"On the Conversations of Authors," *The Plain Speaker* (1826)

This chapter describes the influence that friends, neighbors, acquaintances, co-workers, and others have on the individual's consumption behavior. It examines the nature and dynamics of this influence, called the **opinion leadership** process, and the personality and motivations of those who influence (*opinion leaders*) and those who are influenced (*opinion receivers*).

WHAT IS OPINION LEADERSHIP?

Opinion leadership is *the process by which one person (the opinion leader) informally influences the actions or attitudes of others, who may be opinion seekers or merely opinion recipients.* This influence is informal and usually verbal, but it may take the form of nonverbal behavior observed by others. The informal flow of consumption-related influence between two people is sometimes referred to as product-related conversation, or **word-of-mouth** communication.

The key characteristic of word-of-mouth communication is that it is interpersonal and informal and takes place between two or more people, none of whom represents a commercial selling source that would gain directly from the sale of something. Word-of-mouth implies personal, or face-to-face, communication, although it may also take place in a telephone conversation or in the context of chat group on the Internet.

One of the parties in an informal product-related communications encounter usually offers advice or information about a specific product or product category, such as which of several brands is best, or how a particular product may be used. This person, the **opinion leader**, may become an *opinion receiver* when another product or product category is brought up as part of the discussion.

Individuals who actively seek information and advice about products sometimes are called **opinion seekers**. For purposes of simplicity, the terms *opinion receiver* and *opinion recipient* will be used interchangeably in the following discussion to identify both those who actively seek product information from others and those who receive unsolicited information. Simple examples of opinion leadership at work include the following:

1. *During dinner, one friend mentions the desire to purchase a new fax machine, and the other recommends a particular brand.*
2. *A person shows a co-worker photographs of his recent California vacation, and the co-worker suggests that a different type of film might produce better pictures of outdoor scenery.*
3. *A woman who recently moved into a new house wants more light in her kitchen and calls her neighbor for the name of "a good electrician."*

Most studies of opinion leadership are concerned with the identification and measurement of the behavioral impact that opinion leaders have on the consumption habits of others. A recent article, for example, suggests that "influentials" are almost four times more likely than others to be asked about political and government issues, as well as how to handle teens, three times more likely to be asked about computers or investments, and twice as likely to be asked about heath issues and restaurants.[2]

Dynamics of the Opinion Leadership Process

The opinion leadership process is very dynamic. This section discusses the specific dimensions of opinion leadership that make it such a powerful consumer force.

Opinion Leaders Are Persuasive

As informal communication sources, opinion leaders are remarkably effective at influencing consumers in their product-related decisions. Some of the reasons for the effectiveness of opinion leaders are discussed below.

▲ **Credibility** Opinion leaders are highly credible sources of product-related information, because they usually are perceived as objective concerning the information or advice they dispense. Their intentions are perceived as being in the best interests of the opinion recipients, because they receive no compensation for the advice and apparently have no "ax to grind." Because opinion leaders often base their product comments on firsthand experience, their advice reduces for opinion receivers the perceived risk or anxiety inherent in buying new products.

▲ **Positive and Negative Product Information** Information provided by marketers is invariably favorable to the product. Thus, the very fact that opinion leaders provide both favorable and unfavorable information adds to their credibility. An example of an unfavorable or negative product comment is: "The problem with those little subnotebook computers is that they have external disk drives that you have to stop and hook-up." Compared with positive or even neutral comments, negative comments are relatively uncommon. For this reason, consumers are especially likely to note such information and to avoid products or brands that receive negative evaluations.[3]

▲ **Information and Advice** Opinion leaders are the source of both information and advice. They may simply talk about their *experience* with a product, relate what they know about a product, or, more aggressively, *advise* others to buy or to avoid a specific product. The kinds of product (or service-)related information that opinion leaders are likely to transmit during a conversation include the following:

1. *Which of several brands is best:*
   "In my opinion, Bose speakers are the best speakers you can buy."
2. *How to best use a specific product:*
   "I find that ink-jet printers work best when you use specially formulated ink-jet paper."
3. *Where to shop:*
   "When Bloomingdale's has a sale, the values are terrific."
4. *Who provides the best service:*
   "I've been taking my cars to Goodyear for tune-ups, brakes, tires, and shocks for the past 10 years, and I think their service can't be beat."

▲ **Opinion Leadership Is Category-Specific** Opinion leadership tends to be *category-specific*; that is, opinion leaders often "specialize" in certain product categories about which they offer information and advice. When other product categories are discussed, however, they are just as likely to reverse their roles and become opinion receivers. A person who is considered particularly knowledgeable about bicycles may be an opinion leader in terms of this subject, yet when it comes to purchasing a VCR, the same person may seek advice from someone else—perhaps even from someone who has sought his advice on bicycles.

▲ **Opinion Leadership Is a Two-Way Street** As the example above suggests, consumers who are opinion leaders in one product-related situation may become opinion receivers in another situation, even for the same product. Consider the following example. Jim, a new homeowner contemplating the purchase of a lawn mower, may seek information and advice from other people to reduce his indecision about which brand to select. Once the lawn mower has been bought, however, he may experience **postpurchase dissonance** (see Chapter 9) and have a compelling need to talk favorably about the purchase to other people to confirm the correctness of his own choice. In the first instance, he is an opinion receiver (seeker); in the second, he assumes the role of opinion leader.

An opinion leader may also be influenced by an opinion receiver as the result of a product-related conversation. For example, a person may tell a friend about a favorite hotel getaway in the Bahamas and, in response to comments from the opinion receiver, come to realize that the hotel is too small, too isolated, and offers vacationers fewer amenities than other hotels.

The Motivation Behind Opinion Leadership

To understand the phenomenon of opinion leadership, it is useful to examine the motivation of those who provide and those who receive product-related information.

▲ **The Needs of Opinion Leaders** What motivates a person to talk about a product or service? Motivation theory suggests that people may provide information or advice to others to satisfy some basic need of their own (see Chapter 4). However, opinion leaders may be unaware of their own underlying motives. As suggested earlier, opinion leaders may simply be trying to reduce their own *postpurchase dissonance*. For instance, if Fred buys a new large-screen color TV and then is uncertain that he made the right choice, he may try to reassure himself by "talking up" the TV's advantages to others. In this way, he relieves his own psychological discomfort. Furthermore, when he can influence a friend or neighbor to also buy that brand, he confirms his own good judgment in selecting the product first. Thus, the opinion leader's true motivation may really be self-confirmation or self-involvement. Furthermore, the information or advice that an opinion leader dispenses may provide all types of tangential personal benefits: it may confer attention; imply some type of status, grant superiority; demonstrate awareness and expertise, and give the feeling of possessing inside information and the satisfaction of "converting" less adventurous souls.

In addition to *self*-involvement, the opinion leader may also be motivated by *product* involvement, *social* involvement, and *message* involvement. Opinion leaders who are motivated by *product* involvement may find themselves so pleased or so disappointed with a product that they simply must tell others about it.

Those who are motivated by *social* involvement need to share product-related experiences. In this type of situation, opinion leaders use their product-related conversations as expressions of friendship, neighborliness, and love.

The pervasiveness of advertising in our society encourages *message* involvement. Individuals who are bombarded with advertising messages and slogans tend to discuss them and the products they are designed to sell. Such word-of-mouth conversation is typified by the popular use in everyday conversation of slogans such as Nike's "Just do it," the Army's "Be all that you can be," or Mountain Dew's "Been there, done that."

▲ **The Needs of Opinion Receivers** Opinion receivers satisfy a variety of needs by engaging in product-related conversations. First, they obtain new-product or new-usage information. Second, they reduce their perceived risk by receiving firsthand knowledge from a user about a specific product or brand. Third, they reduce the search time entailed in the identification of a needed product or service. Moreover, opinion receivers can be certain of receiving the approval of the opinion leader if they follow that person's product endorsement or advice and purchase the product. For all of these reasons, people often look to friends, neighbors, and other acquaintances for product information. Indeed, when a recent study examined the importance of four specific information sources on a hypothetical $100 purchase of consumer services, advice from others proved to be more important than the combined impact of sales representatives, advertising and promotion, and other sources.[4]

The type of person from whom opinion receivers tend to seek their information varies, depending on cultural background. Some researchers found that white American and British consumers tended to select close friends of similar age as sources of advice, whereas Chinese consumers preferred to seek advice from individuals who had acquired authority and respect (e.g., as a group standard bearer or as the male head of family). In contrast, African-Americans were drawn to individuals who had achieved a degree of notoriety or who were typecast by the press as charismatic. Finally, Asian-Indians were likely to select individuals recognized as possessing strong philosophical outlooks.[5] These findings suggest that subcultural and cross-cultural factors (see Chapters 15 and 16) are likely to influence the traits judged desirable in an opinion leader.

A recent study also concludes that women and men differ with respect to the types of products and services they are likely to seek advice about. For example, while an approximately equal percentage of men and women will seek advice about a new doctor, where to eat out, and what movies to see, significantly more women will seek advice about where to get their hair cut (24 percent versus 10 percent for men) and what car to buy (22 percent versus 15 percent).[6] In general, as Table 17-1 on page 504 shows, women are more likely to trust the advice of other individuals, especially other women.

Researchers have also examined the influence of "purchase pals" as information sources who actually accompany consumers on shopping trips. Although purchase pals were used only 9 percent of the time for grocery items, they were used 25 percent of the time for purchases of electronic equipment (e.g., computers, VCRs, TV sets).[7] Interestingly, male purchase pals are more likely to be used as sources of product category expertise, product information, and retail store and price information. Female purchase pals are more often used for moral support and to increase confidence in the buyer's decisions. Similarly, research evidence suggests that when a weak tie exists between the purchase pal and the shopper (e.g., neighbor, classmate, or work colleague), the purchase pal's main contribution tends to be functional—the source's specific product experiences and general marketplace knowledge are being relied on. In contrast, when strong ties exist (e.g., mother, son, husband, or wife), what is relied on is the purchase pal's familiarity and understanding of the buyer's individual characteristics and needs (e.g., tastes and preferences).[8] Table 17-2 on page 505 compares the motivations of opinion receivers with those of opinion leaders.

Measurement of Opinion Leadership

Consumer researchers are interested in identifying and measuring the impact of the opinion leadership process on consumption behavior. In measuring opinion leadership, the researcher has a choice of four basic measurement techniques: (1) the **self-designating**

table 17-1   Whose Advice Do Men and Women Trust?

	FIRST-RANKED	PERCENT CHOOSING	SECOND-RANKED	PERCENT CHOOSING	THIRD-RANKED	PERCENT CHOOSING
PERCENT OF MEN AND WOMEN WHO CHOOSE SELECTED PEOPLE AS SINGLE MOST-TRUSTED SOURCE FOR SELECTED PRODUCTS AND SERVICES, FOR THREE MOST-TRUSTED SOURCES, 1995						
New doctor:						
Men	female relative	26%	no one	18%	male friend	17%
Women	female relative	29	female friend	20	no one	14
Where to get hair cut						
Men	no one	38%	male friend	25%	female relative/friend	12%
Women	female friend	45	no one	26	female relative	22
What car to buy:						
Men	no one	31%	male friend	26%	male relative	22%
Women	male relative	46	male friend	20	no one	19
Car mechanic:						
Men	male friend	40%	no one	26%	male relative	21%
Women	male relative	50	male friend	30	no one	10
Where to get legal advice:						
Men	male relative	26%	male friend	23%	no one	17%
Women	male relative	31	male friend	16	female relative	14
Where to get personal loan:						
Men	no one	29%	male friend	20%	male relative	18%
Women	male relative	33	no one	21	professional advisor	12
What movies to see:						
Men	male friend	27%	no one	22%	female friend	18%
Women	female friend	40	no one	19	female relative	15
Where to eat out:						
Men	female friend	26%	female relative	21%	male friend	21%
Women	female friend	42	female relative	18	no one/male relative	11

Source: CHIP WALKER, "Word of Mouth," *American Demographics*, July 1995, 44. © 1995 American Demographics Magazine. Reprinted with permission.

method, (2) the **sociometric method**, (3) the **key informant method**, and (4) the **objective method**. We will briefly review each of these measurement methods in terms of strengths, weaknesses, and applications to consumer research.

Self-Designating Method

In the **self-designating method**, respondents are asked to evaluate the extent to which they have provided others with information about a product category or specific brand or have otherwise influenced the purchase decisions of others.

Figure 17-1 shows two types of self-designating question formats that can be used to determine a consumer's opinion leadership activity. The first consists of a single question, while the second consists of a series of questions. The use of multiple questions enables the researcher to determine a respondent's opinion leadership more reliably, because the statements are interrelated.[9]

When researchers use the self-designating method, they usually divide consumer respondents into two categories: those who influence others (opinion leaders) and those who do not. Although this two-category classification scheme is simple and easy to use, it does not realistically reflect the extent to which an individual might function as an opinion leader. Some people classified as nonleaders may truly have no influence on others, while others so classified may actually influence the consumption decisions of other people to

table 17-2

A Comparison of the Motivations of Opinion Leaders and Opinion Receivers

OPINION LEADERS	OPINION RECEIVERS
SELF-IMPROVEMENT MOTIVATIONS	
• Reduce postpurchase uncertainty or dissonance • Gain attention or status • Assert superiority and expertise • Feel like an adventurer • Experience the power of "converting" others	• Reduce the risk of making a purchase commitment • Reduce search time (e.g., avoid the necessity of shopping around)
PRODUCT-INVOLVEMENT MOTIVATIONS	
• Express satisfaction or dissatisfaction with a product or service	• Learn how to use or consume a product • Learn what products are new in the marketplace
SOCIAL-INVOLVEMENT MOTIVATIONS	
• Express neighborliness and friendship by discussing products or services that may be useful to others	• Buy products that have the approval of others, thereby ensuring acceptance
MESSAGE-INVOLVEMENT MOTIVATIONS	
• Express one's reaction to a stimulating advertisement by telling others about it	

some degree. Therefore, it would be more appropriate to employ a classification scheme that explicitly considers a range of opinion-leading activity: those who *never* or *infrequently* influence others, those who sometimes influence others, and those who *frequently* influence others.

The self-designating technique is used more often than other methods for measuring opinion leadership because consumer researchers find it easy to include in market research questionnaires. Because this method relies on the respondent's self-evaluation, however, it

---

FIGURE 17-1

Self-Designating Questions for Measuring Opinion Leadership

SINGLE-QUESTION APPROACH:

1. In the last 6 months have you been asked your advice or opinion about *golf equipment*?*

    Yes _____   No _____

MULTIPLE-QUESTION APPROACH:
(Measured on a 5-point bipolar "Agree"/"Disagree" scale)

1. Friends and neighbors frequently ask my advice about *golf equipment.*
2. I sometimes influence the types of *golf equipment* friends buy.
3. My friends come to me more often than I go to them about *golf equipment.*
4. I feel that I am generally regarded by my friends as a good source of advice about *golf equipment.*
5. I can think of at least three people whom I have spoken to about *golf equipment* in the past six months.

*Researchers can insert their own relevant product-service or product-service category.

may be open to bias, should respondents perceive "opinion leadership" (even though the term is not used) to be a desirable characteristic and thus overestimate their own roles as opinion leaders.

As mentioned in Chapter 5, consumer researchers have recently developed a companion instrument designed to provide consumers with an opportunity to reveal their susceptibility to influence by others. Table 17-3 presents the 12-item scale used to capture a consumer's degree of susceptibility to interpersonal influence. The scale is based on the assumption that a person who is highly responsive to the opinions of others is more likely to conform to the expectations of those others and to emulate their behavior or seek information from them.[10]

Sociometric Method

The sociometric method measures the person-to-person informal communication of consumers concerning products or product categories. In this method, respondents are asked to identify (a) the specific individuals (if any) to whom they provided advice or information about the product or brand under study and (b) the specific individuals (if any) who provided *them* with advice or information about the product or brand under study. In the first instance, if respondents identify one or more individuals to whom they have provided some form of product information, they are tentatively classified as opinion leaders. The researcher seeks to validate this determination by interviewing the individuals named by the primary respondents and asking them to recall whether they did, in fact, receive such product information.

In the second instance, respondents are asked to identify the individuals (if any) who provided them with information about a product under investigation. Individuals desig-

table 17-3   A Scale for Measuring Consumer Susceptibility to Interpersonal Influence*

1. I rarely purchase the latest fashion styles until I am sure my friends approve of them.
2. It is important that others like the products and brands I buy.
3. When buying products, I generally purchase those brands my friends expect me to buy.
4. If other people can see me using a product, I often purchase the brand they expect me to buy.
5. I like to know what brands and products make good impressions on others.
6. I achieve a sense of belonging by purchasing the same products and brands that others purchase.
7. If I want to be like someone, I often try to buy the same brands that person buys.
8. I often identify with other people by purchasing the same products and brands they purchase.
9. To make sure I buy the right product or brand, I often observe what others are buying and using.
10. If I have little experience with a product, I often ask my friends about the product.
11. I often consult other people to help choose the best alternative available from a product category.
12. I frequently gather information from friends or family about a product before I buy.

*Measured on a seven-point bipolar Agree/Disagree scale.

Source: WILLIAM O. BEARDEN, RICHARD NETEMEYER, and JESSE TEEL, "Measurement of Consumer Susceptibility to Interpersonal Influence," *Journal of Consumer Research* 15 (March, 1989), 477.

nated by the primary respondent are tentatively classified as opinion leaders. Again, the researcher attempts to validate this determination by asking the individuals named whether they did, in fact, provide the relevant product information.

Thus, if Eric reports that information or advice concerning a specific product was received from Jamie, Jamie must confirm that such information or advice was given to Eric. In this way, the sociometric method *confirms* the opinion leaders and opinion receivers in product-related conversations.

Figure 17-2 illustrates the type of questioning used in the sociometric research approach. It presents a series of questions that might, for example, be used in a study of opinion leadership among residents of a college dormitory (the "quad"). The objective of such a study might be to identify the opinion leaders of a recently released movie (e.g., *Goldeneye*).

▲ **Sociometric Research Designs** In using the sociometric method, researchers can study a self-contained community, or they can study a more widespread respondent sample. In the first instance (such as a study of all the residents in a particular retirement community in West Palm Beach, Florida or the student residents of a university-operated dormitory), it is relatively simple to verify consumer-related conversations. With a more widespread respondent sample, researchers must be prepared to trace the web of word-of-mouth contacts by seeking out all individuals named by the primary respondent group, regardless of location. Because this research often is costly and difficult to manage, most sociometric consumer studies focus on *intact* or self-contained communities.

FIGURE 17-2

An Illustration of the Sociometric Measurement Approach

PROVIDING INFORMATION TO OTHERS

1. Within the past week, did you tell anyone living here in the Quad about the new movie *Goldeneye*?   Yes _____   No _____

If "yes,"

2. Which person did you first tell about the movie *Goldeneye*?
   First Name _____   Family Name _____   Room or Floor _____

3. Which other people, living in the Quad, did you tell about the movie *Goldeneye*?
   _____
   _____

4. Did you suggest that they see or not see the movie *Goldeneye*?
   See _____   Not See _____   Other _____

RECEIVING INFORMATION FROM OTHERS

1. What was the first thing you remember hearing about the movie *Goldeneye*?

2. Do you remember who made this first comment about the movie *Goldeneye*?
   Yes _____   No _____

3. If "yes," what was his or her name?
   First Name _____   Family Name _____   Room or Floor _____

4. Does this person live in the Quad?   Yes _____   No _____

5. Did this person recommend that you see or not see the movie *Goldeneye*?
   See _____   Not See _____   Other _____

6. Did this conversation occur before or after you saw the movie *Goldeneye*?
   Before _____   After _____   Do not remember _____

7. Can you name any other persons, living in the Quad, who have mentioned the movie *Goldeneye*?
   _____
   _____

▲ **Consumer Behavior Applications** The sociometric approach to determining opinion leadership has useful applications to the study of consumer behavior. For example, consider the flow of opinion leadership among college students living in university housing. Each school year, dormitory students must select a long-distance telephone company. With this in mind, it would be useful for a long-distance company (e.g., AT&T, MCI, or Sprint) to undertake a sociometric study on a particular college campus to determine how word-of-mouth influences the selection of a long-distance telephone company. This information would provide the basis for subsequent promotional campaigns. On a more general level, any intact community (a college or an apartment house development, for example) provides an opportunity to measure and evaluate the flow of word-of-mouth communications concerning a new product and its subsequent impact on product trial.

Key Informant Method

Opinion leadership can also be measured through the use of a **key informant**, a person who is keenly aware or knowledgeable about the nature of social communications among members of a specific group. The key informant is asked to identify those individuals in the group who are most likely to be opinion leaders.

The key informant does not have to be a member of the group under study. For example, a professor may serve as the key informant for a college class, identifying those students who are most likely to be opinion leaders with regard to a particular issue. This research method is relatively inexpensive, because it requires that only one individual or at most several individuals be intensively interviewed, whereas the self-designating and sociometric methods require that a consumer sample or entire community be interviewed. However, the key informant method is generally not used by marketers because of the difficulties inherent in identifying an individual who can *objectively* identify opinion leaders in a relevant consumer group.

The key informant method would seem to be of greatest potential use in the study of industrial or institutional opinion leadership. For example, a firm's salespeople might serve as key informants in the identification of specific customers who are most likely to influence the purchase decisions of other potential customers. Similarly, the purchasing agent of a specific firm might serve as a key informant by providing a supplier's salesperson with the names of those persons in the firm who are most likely to influence the purchase decision. In the study of consumers, possible key informants include knowledgeable community members, such as the president of the women's club, the head of the local school board, or a prominent local businessperson.

Objective Method

The objective method of determining opinion leadership is much like a controlled experiment: It involves placing new products or new product information with selected individuals and then tracing the resulting "web" of interpersonal communication concerning the relevant product(s).

An intriguing classic study designed to measure the influence of opinion leaders on household matters provides a unique example of the objective method.[11] First, the individual members of fifteen women's friendship groups living in a self-contained community were interviewed via the sociometric method to assess their levels of opinion leadership in household management matters. The women who scored *highest* as opinion leaders in each of nine groups were chosen to serve as opinion leader "confederates" (i.e., to cooperate with the researcher). In each of the other six groups, the women who scored lowest in opinion leadership also were chosen to serve as opinion leader confederates. This research design enabled the researcher to compare the influence exerted by those identified as opinion leaders with the influence exerted by those identified as nonleaders, when all were placed in a "controlled" situation to serve as opinion leaders.

All fifteen participants selected to function as opinion leaders were provided with new freeze-dried food items and were asked to serve them to their families. They also were asked to give samples of the new food products to all other members of their friendship groups and to suggest that they, in turn, serve the items to their families.

The results indicated that those individuals who received the new food items from "natural" opinion leaders tended to echo this leader's opinions concerning the new product. Conversely, those individuals who received samples of the new food items from artificially created opinion leaders shifted away from these "leader's" sentiments. These findings suggest that true opinion leaders are capable of altering group members' opinions in the direction of their own opinions, while nonleaders (those who score low in opinion leadership studies) may have an adverse effect on those they attempt to influence.

Table 17-4 presents an overview of each of the four methods of measuring opinion leadership, together with advantages and limitations.

table 17-4   Methods of Measuring Opinion Leadership: Advantages and Limitations

OPINION LEADERSHIP MEASUREMENT METHOD	DESCRIPTION OF METHOD	SAMPLE QUESTIONS ASKED	ADVANTAGES	LIMITATIONS
SELF-DESIGNATING METHOD	Each respondent is asked a series of questions to determine the degree to which he or she perceives himself or herself to be an opinion leader.	"Do you influence other people in their selection of products?"	Measures the individual's own perceptions of his or her opinion leadership.	Depends on the objectivity with which respondents can identify and report their personal influence.
SOCIOMETRIC METHOD	Member of a social system are asked to identify to whom they give advice and to whom they go for advice and information about a product category.	"Whom do you ask?" "Who asks you for information about that product category?"	Sociometric questions have the greatest degree of validity and are easy to administer.	It is very costly and analysis often is very complex. Requires a large number of respondents. Not suitable for sample design where only a portion of the social system is interviewed.
KEY INFORMANT METHOD	Carefully selected key informants in a social system are asked to designate opinion leaders.	"Who are the most influential people in the group?"	Relatively inexpensive and less time consuming than the sociometric method.	Informants who are not thoroughly familiar with the social system are likely to provide invalid information.
OBJECTIVE METHOD	Artificially places individuals in a position to act as opinion leaders and measures results of their efforts.	"Have you tried the product?"	Measures individual's ability to influence others under controlled circumstances.	Requires the establishment of an experimental design and the tracking of the resulting impact on the participants.

Source: Adapted with the permission of The Free Press, a division of Simon & Schuster, from *Diffusion of Innovations,* Fourth Edition by Everett M. Rogers. Copyright © 1995 by Everett M. Rogers.

A Profile of the Opinion Leader

Just who are opinion leaders? Can they be recognized by any distinctive characteristics? Can they be reached through specific media? Marketers have long sought answers to these questions, for if they are able to identify the relevant opinion leaders for their products, they can target their promotional efforts to them, confident that the opinion leaders will, in turn, influence the consumption behavior of others. For this reason, consumer researchers have attempted to develop a realistic profile of the opinion leader. This has not been easy to do. As pointed out earlier, opinion leadership tends to be category-specific; that is, an individual who is an opinion *leader* in one product category may be an opinion *receiver* in another product category. Thus, the generalized profile of opinion leaders is likely to be influenced by the context of specific product categories.

Knowledge and Interest

Opinion leaders tend to possess a high level of interest in the product or service category in which they provide advice or information. For this reason, they are likely to seek information about the product category, and because of their knowledge, others may turn to them for product advice. Chief among the characteristics that distinguish opinion leaders from nonleaders is their degree of *involvement* with the subject. Compared with nonleaders in a particular product category, opinion leaders read more about related consumer issues, are more knowledgeable about related new-product developments, participate more often in related consumer activities, and derive greater satisfaction from these product-related activities. For example, financial opinion leaders are more involved in tracking their investments than nonleaders and, thus, they are "media omnivorous;" that is, they make extensive use of print, electronic, and subscription newsletter financial information sources.[12]

Consumer Innovators

Opinion leaders tend to be consumer innovators. Consistent with their keen interest in a product category, they are likely to try new products in the category as soon as they are introduced. Thus, on the basis of first-hand knowledge, opinion leaders tend to speak with some authority when providing information or advice to others about new products and services.

Studies of consumer innovators for a variety of products and services (e.g., stereo equipment, solar-energy devices, car care services, or telephone equipment) have found that individuals identified as innovators also function as opinion leaders by recommending specific products or services based on their own experiences or by showing the products to others. Consumer innovators often feel that others to whom they have spoken about new products or services have bought the specific products or services because of them.

Research conducted on behalf of the film industry confirms the close link between innovators and opinion leadership.[13] For example, frequent moviegoers who attend a movie within the first two weeks of its release tend to influence the attendance of their friends. This and other studies indicate that consumer innovators are likely to be opinion leaders in their areas of innovation.

Personal Characteristics

Although opinion leaders generally possess certain similar *personality traits*, other personal characteristics, such as *social status* and *demographic characteristics*, often are linked to the product or service category in which they "specialize."

▲ **Personality Traits** Several personality characteristics of opinion leaders appear to bridge specific product-related contexts. Among these are *self-confidence* and *gregariousness* (i.e., sociability). To advise others, individuals first must have confidence in themselves and their own opinions. Also, opinion leaders must generally be socially inclined, i.e., have friendships, enjoy the company of others, and be somewhat outspoken. These traits are not surprising, for individuals must be involved in social interaction to function as opinion leaders.

Researchers have also linked another personality trait, *cognitive differentiation*, to opinion leadership. Specifically, there is evidence that individuals who naturally take an opinion leadership role within a group setting are likely to score high on cognitive differentiation (defined as possessing a well-developed cognitive structure that enables such individuals to be more attuned to others in a social exchange).[14] Interestingly, the research also indicates that, for individuals who score low on cognitive differentiation to function as opinion leaders (i.e., they are "undifferentiated" individuals), they must possess a considerable amount of knowledge and interest in the area in which they will serve as opinion leader. This heightened knowledge and interest does not seem to be a requirement for those opinion leaders with high cognitive differentiation scores.

▲ **Social Class** As with other personal characteristics, the social status of the opinion leader appears to depend on the topic of interest. In most marketing studies, however, the opinion leader was found to belong to the same socioeconomic group as the opinion receiver. This is not surprising; it would seem reasonable to expect an individual to turn for advice to a person with whom he or she feels comfortable, someone within the same social class. Similarly, opinion leaders are most likely to give information or advice to those people with whom they regularly engage in informal communication, the people within their own social stratum.

▲ **Demographic Characteristics** Consumers tend to seek information and advice from people whom they perceive to be highly knowledgeable. In the context of physician selection, for example, older people may be perceived as having more information and experience. In the context of women's fashions, younger people, those with higher incomes, and/or those with higher occupational status are often perceived as more knowledgeable. A recent study, for example, found that women who were opinion leaders on business and clothing tended to work outside the home, had higher family incomes, and valued self-fulfillment. In contrast, women who valued belonging and who were self-described "traditionals" were more likely to serve as opinion leaders for such topics as babies, children, and cooking.[15]

In summary, it is difficult to construct a generalized profile of the opinion leader outside the context of a specific category of interest. However, on the basis of the limited evidence available (see Table 17-5), opinion leaders across all product categories generally

table 17-5 Profile of Opinion Leaders

GENERALIZED ATTRIBUTES ACROSS PRODUCT CATEGORIES	CATEGORY-SPECIFIC ATTRIBUTES
Innovativeness	Interest
Willingness to talk	Knowledge
Self-confidence	Special-interest media exposure
Gregariousness	Same age
Cognitive differentiation	Same social status
	Social exposure outside group

exhibit the following attributes: innovativeness, greater willingness to talk, self-confidence, gregariousness, and cognitive differentiation. Within the context of specific subject areas, opinion leaders possess greater interest in and knowledge of the product category and are more exposed to relevant special-interest media. They also usually belong to the same socioeconomic and age groups as their opinion receivers.

Media Habits

Like consumer innovators, opinion leaders are likely to read special-interest publications devoted to the specific topic or product category in which they "specialize." For example, fashion opinion leaders read publications such as *Vogue, Harpers Bazaar*, and *Elle*. These special-interest magazines serve not only to inform fashion-oriented consumers about new clothing and accessories that may be of personal interest but also provide them with the specialized knowledge that enables them to make recommendations to relatives, friends, and neighbors. Thus, the opinion leader tends to have greater exposure to media specifically relevant to his or her area of interest than the nonleader.

To take advantage of this point, mass and targeted (special-interest) media like to point out the impact that their particular audience has on influencing the tastes and buying behavior of others. As an example of such a media message, Figure 17-3 presents a print ad for *Car and Driver* magazine that informs prospective advertisers of its audience's influence on the consumption behavior of others. The advertisement notes that *Car and Driver* readers "pass their opinions along to others—more than half of those given advice by our subscribers follow it and buy the recommended vehicle." Also, some magazines include as part of their advertising kits research information that demonstrates the extent to which their readers serve as opinions when it comes to a variety of products and services (see Table 17-6 on page 514).

FREQUENCY AND OVERLAP OF OPINION LEADERSHIP

Opinion leadership is not a rare phenomenon. Often, more than one-third of the people studied in a consumer research project are classified as opinion leaders with respect to some self-selected product category. The frequency of consumer opinion leadership suggests that people are sufficiently interested in at least one product or product category to talk about it and give advice concerning it to others.

This leads to the interesting question: Do opinion leaders in one product category tend to be opinion leaders in other product categories? Consumer researchers have concerned themselves with answers to this question in their search for a richer profile of the opinion leader.

Overlap of Opinion Leadership

Opinion leadership tends to overlap across certain combinations of *interest areas*. Overlap is likely to be highest among product categories that involve similar interests (e.g., televisions and VCRs, high-fashion clothing and cosmetics, household cleansers and detergents, hunting gear and fishing tackle). Thus, opinion leaders in one product area often are opinion leaders in related areas in which they are also interested.

However, research does suggest the existence of a special category of opinion leader, the **market maven**.[16] These consumers possess a wide range of information about many

For almost 7 million readers, *Car and Driver* represents the first stop on the way to the showroom. There simply isn't a more effective way to impact the decision-making process about buying a new car. And, *Car and Driver* readers pass their opinions along to others—more than half of those given advice by our subscribers follow it and buy the recommended vehicle.

For more information, call our nearest sales office, New York: (212) 767-6089, Detroit: (810) 816-0136, Los Angeles: (213) 954-4843.

Sources: Spring 1996 MRI Car and Driver Subscriber Study

CAR AND DRIVER

FIGURE 17-3

Car and Driver Informs
Advertisers of Audience
Opinion Leadership
Courtesy of *Car and Driver*

different types of products, retail outlets, and other dimensions of markets. They both initiate discussions with other consumers and respond to requests for market information. Market mavens like to shop, and they also like to share their shopping expertise with others. However, although they appear to fit the profile of opinion leaders in that they have high levels of brand awareness and tend to try more brands, unlike opinion leaders their influence extends beyond the realm of high-involvement products. For example, market mavens may help diffuse information on such low-involvement products as razor blades and laundry detergent.[17]

table 17-6   *Car and Driver* Research Supporting Subscribers Are Opinion Leaders

AREA OF OPINION LEADERSHIP	GIVEN ADVICE PAST 12 MONTHS (%)	AVERAGE NO. OF PEOPLE ADVISED*	AVERAGE NO. WHO FOLLOWED SUBSCRIBERS' ADVICE	AVERAGE NO. WHO SUBSEQUENTLY BOUGHT*
Gave advice in past year	69			
Passenger cars	53	7.8	2.7	3.2
Pickups, SUV's, Vans	31	4.5	1.2	1.5
Automotive parts	24	20.5	17.2	18.3
Maintenance/appearance products	28	18.2	14.8	15.8
Tires	32	8.3	6.7	7.0
Auto sound equipment	17	8.2	3.7	4.0
Other electronic accessories	24	6.2	3.1	3.4

*Among those who gave advice (i.e., 69 percent). Base: Total subscribers (multiple responses)

Source: *Car and Driver*, Subscriber Profile. Reprinted by permission.

Market mavens are also distinguishable from other opinion leaders because their influence stems not so much from product experience but from a more general knowledge or market expertise that leads them to an early awareness of a wide array of new products and services. Part of this early awareness may come from the fact that market mavens have a more favorable attitude than nonmavens toward direct mail as a source of information. An initial investigation suggests that market mavens play an important role in helping other consumers evaluate the differences among specific brands and models of a product.[18] The ad for *Popular Mechanics* shown in Figure 17-4 characterizes its typical reader as "The Must-Know Man . . . a man others turn to for information and authoritative advice." This depiction is very similar to the "market maven."

Who are these "Must-Know Men"? According to a recent study sponsored by *Popular Mechanics*, Must-Know Men constitute approximately 21 percent of the adult male population of the United States. In terms of demographics, 54 percent of Must-Know Men are members of households with incomes of $50,000 or more, and 51 percent are between 30 and 49 years of age (28 percent are over 50 years of age).[19] Must-Know Men were defined in terms of the following nine characteristics:

1. *They want to know how things work/they are mechanically inclined*

2. *They want to know the latest developments in technology*

3. *They are "do-it-yourselfers"*

4. *They enjoy teaching others how do things*

5. *They are interested/involved in automobiles*

6. *They are interested/involved in home repairs and maintenance*

7. *They are interested/involved in outdoor activities*

8. *They are interested/involved in computers and electronics*

9. *They are interested/involved in science, space travel, and defense technology*

When it comes to influencing others, the research reveals that the Must-Know Man scores high.[20] Eighty-seven percent report that at least sometimes others come to them for information and advice on home improvement, automobiles, and mechanical things in general.

FIGURE 17-4

The "Must-Know Man" Is a "Market Maven"
Courtesy of *Popular Mechanics*. *Popular Mechanics* is a publication of Hearst
Magazines, a Division of the Hearst Corporation. © The Hearst Corporation.

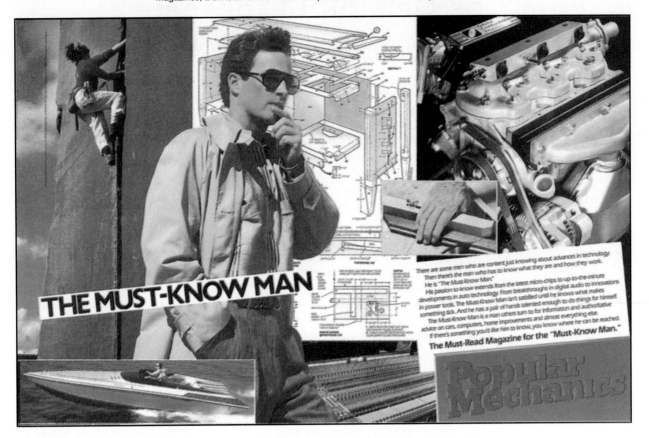

The research also indicates that the Must-Know Man is "frequently/sometimes" asked for
information or advice about a specific *brand* in a fairly wide range of product categories
(see Table 17-7). Clearly, these Must-Know Men are opinion leaders.

table 17-7 "Must-Know Man" Provides Information and Advice

WHICH BRAND OF . . .	FREQUENTLY/SOMETIMES ASKED FOR INFORMATION/ ADVICE ABOUT BRANDS (%)
Outdoors sporting equipment to buy	62
Building and maintenance products	73
Automobiles, trucks, or RVs to buy	74
Tools and equipment to buy	82
Boats and boating equipment to buy	40
Computers and software to buy	63
Major household appliances to buy	64
Auto and video equipment to buy	72

Source: Popular Mechanics research information provided as part of promotional literature.

The Situational Environment of Opinion Leadership

Product-related discussions between two people do not take place in a vacuum. Two people are not likely to meet and spontaneously break into a discussion in which product-related information is sought or offered. Rather, product discussions generally occur *within relevant situational contexts*, e.g., when a specific product or a similar product is used or served or as an outgrowth of a more general discussion that touches on the product category. Thus, if two couples are planning a joint skiing vacation in Vail, Colorado, and one of the individuals asks, "How dressed up do you think we'll have to get at night to eat in a nice restaurant?", the discussion might eventually lead to one person asking another for advice on the appropriateness of a new style or fashion. In this situation, the opinion leader would provide information to the opinion receiver as an outgrowth of a conversation concerning the vacation that they are planning together.

Opinion Leaders Are Friends or Neighbors

It is not surprising that opinion leaders and opinion receivers often are friends, neighbors, or work associates, for existing friendships provide numerous opportunities for conversation concerning product-related topics. Close *physical proximity* is likely to increase the occurrences of product-related conversations.[21] A community center, for example, or even the local supermarket, provides opportunities for neighbors to meet and engage in informal communications about products or services. Opinion leadership based on physical proximity is important to marketers when it comes to door-to-door selling (Avon), party selling (Tupperware), and direct-marketing efforts based on geodemographic clusters.

In a similar fashion, the rapid growth in the use of the Internet is also creating a type of close "electronic proximity," one in which people of like minds, attitudes, concerns, backgrounds, and experiences are coming together in "chat sessions" to explore their common interests. It has been our experience that a fair amount of information and advice, especially as to the strengths and limitations of products and services, is offered in these chat sessions. Within this context, the Internet is proving to be a fertile environment for word-of-mouth communications of the kind that consumer marketers are interested in impacting.

The Interpersonal Flow of Communication

How does information provided by the mass media reach and influence the total population? Several theories suggest that the opinion leader is a vital link in the transmission of information and influence.

Two-Step Flow of Communication Theory

A classic study of voting behavior concluded that ideas often flow from radio and print media to opinion leaders and from them to the general public.[22] This so-called **two-step flow of communication theory** portrays opinion leaders as direct receivers of information from impersonal mass-media sources, who in turn transmit (and interpret) this information to the masses. This theory views the opinion leader as a *middleman* between the impersonal mass media and the majority of society.

The major contribution of the two-step flow of communication theory is that it highlights the idea that social interaction between people serves as the principal means by which information is transmitted, attitudes are developed, and behavior is stimulated. The theory rejects the notion that mass media alone influence the sale of products, political candidates, and ideas to a mass audience.

Figure 17-5 presents a model of the two-step flow of communication theory. Information is depicted as flowing in a single direction (i.e., one way) from the mass media to opinion leaders (Step 1), and then from the opinion leaders (who interpret, legitimize, and transmit the information) to friends, neighbors, and acquaintances, who constitute the "masses" (Step 2).

The two-step flow of communication theory is insightful because it illustrates how people acquire information about issues of interest. However, it is not a particularly accurate portrayal of the flow of information and influence. The need for modification of this theory is in large part based on the following observations:

1. *Mass media may inform both opinion leaders and opinion receivers; however, the opinion receiver is more likely to be influenced by the opinion leader than by the media.*

2. *Not all interpersonal communication is initiated by opinion leaders and directed to opinion receivers. Very often, those who are receivers may initiate the interpersonal communication by requesting information or advice from the opinion leaders.*

3. *Those who receive information and advice from others (i.e., opinion receivers) are more likely to offer advice to others (including opinion leaders) than those who do not receive advice from others.*

4. *Opinion leaders are more likely than those who are nonleaders to both receive and seek advice from others.*

Multistep Flow of Communication Theory

A more comprehensive model of the interpersonal flow of communication depicts the transmission of information from the media as a *multistep flow*. The revised model takes into account the fact that information and influence often are two-way processes in which opinion leaders both influence and are influenced by opinion receivers. Figure 17-6 on page 518 presents a model of the **multistep flow of communication theory**. Steps 1a and 1b depict the flow of information from the mass media simultaneously to opinion leaders, opinion receivers/seekers, and information receivers (who neither influence nor are influenced by others). Step 2 shows the transmission of information and influence from opinion leaders to opinion receivers/seekers. Step 3 reflects the transfer of information and influence from opinion receivers to opinion leaders.

FIGURE 17-5

Two-Step Flow of Communication Theory

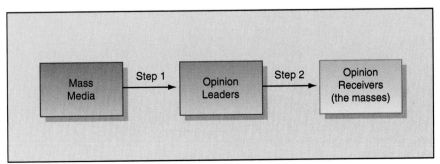

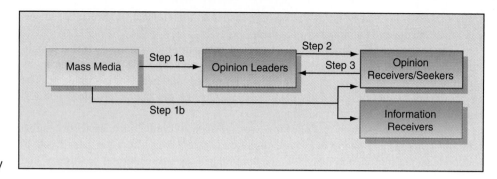

FIGURE 17-6

Multistep Flow of
Communication Theory

A Broader Approach to Interpersonal Communication

Measures of opinion leadership and opinion seeking can be *combined* to form a richer picture of the interpersonal communication process than is possible by examining opinion leadership alone.[23] The resulting **four-way categorization of interpersonal communication** (see Figure 17-7) classifies individuals as:

1. *Socially Integrated:*
   Those who score high *on both opinion leadership and opinion seeking*

2. *Socially Independent:*
   Those who score high *on opinion leadership and* low *on opinion seeking;*

3. *Socially Dependent:*
   Those who score low *on opinion leadership and* high *on opinion seeking;*

4. *Socially Isolated:*
   Those who score low *on both opinion leadership and opinion seeking.*

   This typology is basically consistent with the multistep flow of communication theory. The four interpersonal communication groups are formed by cross-classifying consumers in terms of their responses to questions designed to establish the extent to which they are opinion leaders and/or opinion seekers. The advantage of this four-way classification over the traditional two-way classification (i.e., opinion leaders versus nonleaders) is that it distinguishes those consumers who transmit and/or seek information and advice from those who neither transmit nor seek information and advice. A review of the results of available consumer behavior studies concerning the interpersonal communications schema reveals that most consumers are involved in some form of product-related conversation and that the percentage of respondents in each of the four groups tends to vary by product category.

FIGURE 17-7

Four-Way Categorization of Interpersonal Communication

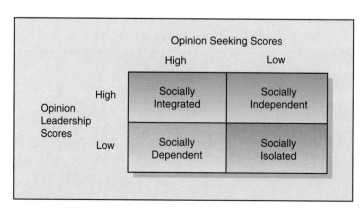

OPINION LEADERSHIP AND THE FIRM'S PROMOTIONAL STRATEGY

Marketers have long been aware of the power that opinion leadership exerts on consumers' preferences and actual purchase behavior. For this reason many marketers look for an opportunity to encourage word-of-mouth communications and other favorable informal conversations concerning their products because they recognize that consumers place more credibility in informal communications sources than in paid advertising or a company's salespeople (see Chapter 10). Seeking product information and advice tends to be the most widely used consumer strategy for reducing perceived risk.[24]

New product designers take advantage of the effectiveness of word-of-mouth communication by deliberately designing products to have word-of-mouth potential. A new product should give customers something to talk about. Examples of products and services that have had such word-of-mouth appeal include the Polaroid camera, the Sony Walkman, the Water Pik, Cabbage Patch dolls, Swatch watch, American on Line, and Microsoft Windows 95. These revolutionary products have attained market share because consumers "sell" them to each other by means of word-of-mouth. Motion pictures also appear to be one form of entertainment in which word-of-mouth operates with some degree of regularity and a large degree of impact. It is very common to be involved directly or overhear people discussing which movies they liked and which movies they advise others to skip. Proof of the power of word-of-mouth are those cases in which critics hate a movie and the viewing public like it and tell their friends.

In instances where informal word of mouth does not spontaneously emerge from the uniqueness of the product or its marketing strategy, some marketers have deliberately attempted to *stimulate* or to *simulate* opinion leadership.

Programs Designed to Stimulate Opinion Leadership

Advertising and promotional programs designed to persuade consumers to "tell your friends how much you like our product" are one way in which marketers encourage consumer discussions of their products or services. Figure 17-8 on page 520 is a recent outdoor poster for Daffy's, an off-price retailer operating in the New York metropolitan area. The ad poster, designed for bus shelters and subway stations, boldly states that "Friends don't let friends pay retail." The implication is that you should share your knowledge and experience with others.

In introducing the LH range of cars, Chrysler undertook a direct-marketing program designed specifically to provoke word-of-mouth communication.[25] Chrysler dealers in twenty-five geographic areas offered the new cars for a weekend of use to influential community and business leaders. The results were measured in terms of exposures. Chrysler reported that more than 6,000 influentials took advantage of the offer, which was estimated to equal approximately 32,000 exposures among drivers, secondary drivers, and passengers, in a 3-month period.

Similarly, in a campaign for Hennessy Cognac, actors were paid to visit Manhattan bars and nightclubs and order Cognac martinis, made with Hennessy. Although they were instructed to act as if they were ordering a new fad drink, in reality they were attempting to *create a new fad drink.*[26] Finally, it has even been noted that Starbucks, the rapidly expanding chain of gourmet coffee bars, has "established a major presence through word-of-mouth."[27] The objective of a promotional strategy of *stimulation* is to run advertisements or a direct marketing program that is sufficiently interesting and informative to provoke consumers into discussing the benefits of the product with others.

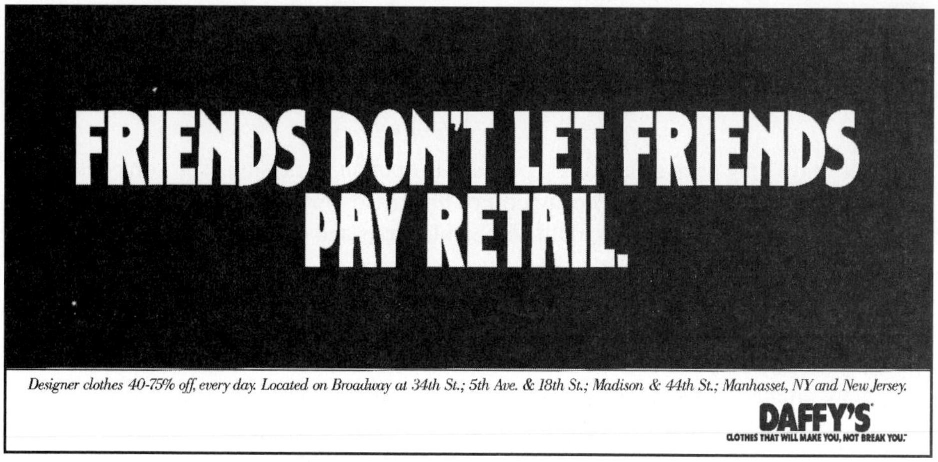

FIGURE 17-8

Poster That Suggests
the Consumer Should
Act as an Opinion
Leader
Courtesy of Daffy's

Advertisements Simulating Opinion Leadership

A firm's advertisements can also be designed to *simulate* product discussions by portraying people in the act of informal communication. This promotional tactic suggests that it is appropriate to discuss a particular subject or product. For example, simulated informal communications encounters between two or more women are often portrayed in TV advertising for personal-care products to persuade women to discuss their use or contemplated use. Because these simulations often function as convenient substitutes, they reduce the need for consumers to actually seek product advice from others.

A recent advertisement for Herrera for Men cologne (see Figure 17-9) captures the "give-and-take" of two women carrying on a discussion that asks the question "Did you ever notice how good he smells?" When it comes to the marketing of a men's cologne, what more need be said! In a somewhat similar manner, Figure 17-10 on page 522 presents an ad for E STYLE, a joint venture of Johnson Publishing, publisher of Ebony Magazine, and the direct marketer Spiegel, that depicts two African-American women in a conversation in which one is telling the other about the virtue of shopping Spiegel's catalog for E STYLE fashions.

Word-of-Mouth May Be Uncontrollable

Although most marketing managers believe that word-of-mouth communication is extremely effective, one problem that they sometimes overlook is the fact that informal communication is difficult to control.[28] Negative comments frequently in the form of rumors that are untrue can sweep through the marketplace to the detriment of a product.

Indeed, a recent study by the White House Office of Consumer Affairs found that 90 percent or more of unhappy customers will not do business again with the company that is the source of their dissatisfaction. To make matters even worse, each dissatisfied customer will share his or her grievance with at least nine other people, and 13 percent of unhappy customers will tell more than twenty people about the negative experience.[29]

Some common rumor themes that have plagued marketers in recent years and unfavorably influenced sales include the following: (1) The product was produced under unsanitary conditions. (2) The product contained an unwholesome or culturally unacceptable ingredient. (3) The product functioned as an undesirable depressant or stimulant. (4) The product included a cancer-causing element or agent. (5) The firm was owned or influenced by an unfriendly or misguided foreign country, governmental agency, or religious cult.

"*Did you ever notice how good he smells?*"

GEORGIA: *I finally went out to dinner with him last night.*

JACKIE: *Just the two of you? Where did you go?*

GEORGIA: *Mario's.*

JACKIE: *Mario's? The food is terrible.*

GEORGIA: *I didn't notice. I don't really even know what I ate.*

JACKIE: *Really?*

GEORGIA: *You should have seen him. He was so sweet. He spilled his wine all over my dress.*

JACKIE: *Adorable.*

GEORGIA: *And then when he reached over to give me his napkin, he knocked over his water glass.*

JACKIE: *Hilarious.*

GEORGIA: *Well, it was. We couldn't stop laughing. We just had to get out of there. We laughed all the way back to my place.*

JACKIE: *Your place?*

GEORGIA: *Well, I was soaked. And besides...*

JACKIE: *Besides.*

GEORGIA: *Did you ever notice how good he smells?*

JACKIE: *Frankly, no.*

GEORGIA: *He wears the most wonderful cologne.*

JACKIE: *Dare I ask what it is?*

GEORGIA: *Well, it comes in a box with dots.*

JACKIE: *Dots?*

GEORGIA: *Dots.*

JACKIE: *So. Now we're back at your place...*

GEORGIA: *Jackie, how's your mother?*

Herrera for Men

Carolina Herrera
New York

FIGURE 17-9

Ad That Simulates
Word-of-Mouth
Communication
Courtesy of Compar

Some marketers have used toll-free telephone numbers in an attempt to head off negative word-of-mouth, displaying an 800 number prominently on their products' labels. Customer relations managers want dissatisfied customers to call their companies' 800 numbers and receive "satisfaction," instead of telling their complaints to friends and relatives.

As further support of the importance of marketer responsiveness to dissatisfied consumers, research reveals that negative word-of-mouth is less common when consumers

FIGURE 17-10

Ad That Simulates
Word-of-Mouth
Communication
Courtesy of Spiegel

perceive the seller to be responsive to consumer complaints.[30] In such instances, dissatisfied consumers are likely to voice their complaints directly to the service provider, because such complaining is perceived to be "worth the effort." Consequently, consumer "hotlines" and other ways of handling consumer complaints promptly and courteously have been shown to reduce negative word-of-mouth about products or services.

Creation of Opinion Leaders

Marketing strategists agree that promotional efforts would be significantly improved if they could segment their markets into opinion leaders and opinion receivers. Then they could direct their promotional messages directly to the people most likely to "carry the word" to the masses. Because of the difficulties inherent in identifying appropriate opinion leaders, however, some researchers have suggested that it might be more fruitful to "create" product-specific opinion leaders.

In one classic study, a group of socially influential high school students (class presidents and sports captains) were asked to become members of a panel that would rate newly released records. As part of their responsibilities, panel participants were encouraged to discuss their record choices with friends. Preliminary examination suggested that these influentials would not qualify as opinion leaders for records because of their relatively meager ownership of the product category.[31] However, some of the records the group evaluated made the top-10 charts in the cities in which the members of the group lived; these same records did not make the top-10 charts in any other city. This study suggests that product-specific opinion leaders can be created by taking socially involved or influential people and deliberately *increasing their enthusiasm* for a product category.

summary

Opinion leadership is the process by which one person (the opinion leader) informally influences the actions or attitudes of others, who may be opinion seekers or merely opinion recipients. Opinion receivers perceive the opinion leader as a highly credible, objective source of product information who can help reduce their search time and perceived risk. Opinion leaders, in turn, are motivated to give information or advice to others in part because doing so enhances their own status and self-image and because such advice tends to reduce any postpurchase dissonance that they may have. Other motives include product involvement, "other" involvement, and message involvement.

Market researchers identify opinion leaders by such methods as self-designation, key informants, the sociometric method, and the objective method. Studies of opinion leadership indicate that this phenomenon tends to be product-specific; that is, individuals "specialize" in a product or product category in which they are highly interested. An opinion leader for one product category may be an opinion receiver for another.

Generally, opinion leaders are gregarious, self-confident, innovative people who like to talk. Additionally, they may feel differentiated from others and choose to act differently (i.e., public individuation). They acquire information about their areas of interest through avid readership of special-interest magazines and by means of new-product trials. Their interests often overlap adjacent product areas; thus, their opinion leadership may extend into related areas. The *market maven* (and the Must-Know Man) is an intensive case of such a person. These consumers possess a wide range of information about many different types of products, retail outlets, and other dimensions of markets. They both initiate discussions with other consumers and respond to requests for market information over a wide range of products and services. Market mavens are also distinguishable from other opinion leaders, because their influence stems not so much from product experience but from a more general knowledge or market expertise that leads them to an early awareness of a wide array of new products and services.

The opinion leadership process usually takes place among friends, neighbors, and work associates who have frequent physical proximity and, thus, have ample opportunity to hold informal product-related conversations. These conversations usually occur naturally in the context of the product-category usage.

The two-step flow of communication theory highlights the role of interpersonal influence in the transmission of information from the mass media to the population at large. This theory provides the foundation for a revised multistep-flow-of-communication model, which takes into account the fact that information and influence often are two-way processes and that opinion leaders both influence and are influenced by opinion receivers.

Marketers recognize the strategic value of segmenting their audiences into opinion leaders and opinion receivers for their product categories. When marketers can direct their promotional efforts to the more influential segments of their markets, these individuals will transmit this information to those who seek product advice. Marketers try to both simulate and stimulate opinion leadership. They have also found that they can create opinion leaders for their products by taking socially involved or influential people and deliberately increasing their enthusiasm for a product category.

discussion questions

1. **a.** Why is an opinion leader a more credible source of product information than an advertisement for the same product?

    b. Are there any circumstances in which information from advertisements is likely to be more influential than word-of-mouth?

2. Why would a consumer who has just purchased an expensive fax machine for home use attempt to influence the purchase behavior of others?

3. Is an opinion leader for 35-mm cameras likely to be an opinion leader for Spandex clothing? Discuss.

4. A company that owns and operates health clubs across the country is opening a health club in your town. The company has retained you as its marketing research consultant and has asked you to identify opinion leaders for its service. Which of the following identification methods would you recommend: the self-designating method, the sociometric method, the key informant method, or the objective method? Explain your selection. In your answer, be sure to discuss the advantages and disadvantages of the four techniques as they relate to the marketing situation described above.

5. Emerging telecommunications technology relying on cable transmission of video, audio, and control signals will allow broadcasters to send thousands of channels to every television set. This transmission system also permits interactive television, which offers viewers the ability to interact with other viewers or the broadcaster. Companies such as Time Warner, Sony, and Disney are developing multimedia services that include interactive video games, home shopping, and "on-demand" movie viewing from a vast video library. Identify and discuss specific characteristics of opinion leaders that you feel would be particularly useful for introducing multimedia services to the public.

6. The two-step flow of communication theory has been modified to portray more accurately the flow of information. Briefly describe this modification and explain its relevance to the marketing strategist.

7. Do you have any "market mavens" among your friends? Describe their personality traits and behaviors. Describe a situation in which a market maven has given you advice regarding a product or service and discuss what you believe was his or her motivation for doing so.

8. How can marketers combat negative word-of-mouth?

exercises

1. For each of the following products and services, indicate who you would go to for information and advice: (1) the latest fashion in clothes, (2) banking, (3) air travel, (4) the "hottest" night clubs, (5) vacation destinations, and (6) personal copiers. For each situation, indicate the person's relationship to you and your reasons for selecting him or her as the source of information and advice.

2. Describe two situations in which you *served* as an opinion leader and two situations in which you *sought* consumption-related advice/information from an opinion leader. Indicate your relationship to the persons with whom you interacted. Are the circumstances during which you engaged in word-of-mouth communications consistent with those in the text's material? Explain.

3. **a.** Find ads that simulate and ads that stimulate opinion leadership and present them in class.

    b. Can you think of negative rumors that you have heard recently about a company or a product? If so, present them in class.

key words

- **Four-way categorization of interpersonal communication**
- **Key informant**
- **Key informant method**
- **Market mavens**
- **Multistep flow of communication theory**
- **Objective method**
- **Opinion leader**
- **Opinion leadership**
- **Opinion receiver**
- **Opinion seeker**
- **Self-designating method**
- **Simulating opinion leadership**
- **Sociometric method**
- **Stimulating opinion leadership**
- **Two-step flow of communication theory**
- **Word-of-mouth communication**

1. CHIP WALKER, "Word of Mouth," *American Demographics*, July 1995, 40.
2. Ibid., 42.
3. AVICHAI SHUV-AMI and LEON G. SCHIFFMAN, "Time Perception in the Diffusion of Safety Hazard Information," *Psychology & Marketing* 3, 1986, 211–21.
4. PAMALA L. ALRECK and ROBERT B. SETTLE, "The Importance of Word-of-Mouth Communications to Service Buyers," in David W. Stewart and Naufel J. Vilcassim, eds., *1995 AMA Winter Educators' Proceedings* (Chicago: American Marketing Association, 1995), 188–193.
5. LAWRENCE F. FEICK, LINDA L. PRICE, and ROBIN A. HIGIE, "People Who Use People: The Other Side of Opinion Leadership," in Richard J. Lutz, ed., *Advances in Consumer Research* 13 (Provo, UT: Association for Consumer Research, 1986), 301–5; and RONALD E. GOLDSMITH, MELVIN T. STITH, and J. DENNIS WHITE, "Race and Sex Differences in Self-Identified Innovativeness and Opinion Leadership," *Journal of Retailing* 63, Winter 1987, 411–25.
6. CHIP WALKER, op. cit, 40–41.
7. CATHY L. HARTMAN and PAMELA L. KIECKER, "Marketplace Influencers at the Point of Purchase: The Role of Purchase Pals in Consumer Decision Making," in Mary C. Gilly and F. Robert Dwyer, et al., eds., *1991 AMA Educators' Proceedings* (Chicago: American Marketing Association, 1991), 461–67.
8. PAMELA KIECKER and CATHY L. HARTMAN, "Predicting Buyers' Selection of Interpersonal Sources: The Role of Strong Ties and Weak Ties," in Chris T. Allen and Deborah Roedder John, eds., *Advances in Consumer Research* 21 (Provo, UT: Association for Consumer Research, 1994), 464–69.
9. LEISA REINECKE FLYNN, RONALD E. GOLDSMITH, and JACQUELINE K. EASTMAN, "The King and Summers Opinion Leadership Scale: Revision and Refinement," *Journal of Business Research* 31, 1994, 55–64.
10. WILLIAM O. BEARDEN, RICHARD NETEMEYER, and JESSE TEEL, "Measurement of Consumer Susceptibility to Interpersonal Influence," *Journal of Consumer Research* 15, March 1989, 473; and "Further Validation of the Consumer Susceptibility to Interpersonal Influence Scale," in Marvin E. Goldberg, Gerald Gorn, and Richard W. Pollay, eds., *Advances in Consumer Research* 17 (Provo, UT: Association for Consumer Research, 1990), 770–76.
11. JOHN G. MYERS, "Patterns of Interpersonal Influence in the Adoption of New Products," in Raymond M. Haas, ed., *Proceedings* (Chicago: American Marketing Association, 1966), 750–57.
12. BARBARA STERN and STEPHEN GOULD, "The Consumer as Financial Opinion Leader," *Journal of Retail Banking* 10, Summer 1988, 47–49.
13. ALJEAN HARMETZ, "For Films, Word of Mouth Means Success," *The New York Times*, November 27, 1978, C13.
14. JOEL N. GREENE, RICHARD E. PLANK, and LEON G. SCHIFFMAN, "Using Cognitive Personality Theory to Predict Opinion Leadership Behavior," in K. Grant, ed., *Proceedings of the World Marketing Congress* VII-I (Melbourne, Australia: Academy of Marketing Science, 1995), 6/83–6/91.
15. GREGORY M. ROSE, LYNN R. KAHLE, and AVIV SHOHAM, "The Influence of Employment-Status and Personal Values on Time Related Food Consumption Behavior and Opinion Leadership," in Frank R. Kardes and Mita Sujan, eds., *Advances in Consumer Research* 22 (Provo, UT: Association for Consumer Research 1995), 367–72.
16. LAWRENCE F. FEICK and LINDA L. PRICE, "The Market Maven: A Diffuser of Marketplace Information," *Journal of Marketing* 51, January 1987, 85.
17. MICHAEL T. ELLIOTT and ANNE E. WARFIELD, "Do Market Mavens Categorize Brands Differently?," in Leigh McAlister and Michael L. Rothschild, eds., *Advances in Consumer Research* 20 (Provo, UT: Association for Consumer Research 1993), 202–8; and FRANK ALPERT, "Consumer Market Beliefs and Their Managerial Implications: An Empirical Examination," *Journal of Consumer Marketing* 10 (2), 1993, 56–70. ·
18. FEICK and PRICE, Op cit, 85, 87. See also DONALD R. LICHTENSTEIN and SCOTT BURTON, "An Assessment of the Moderating Effects of Market Mavenism and Value Consciousness on Price-Quality Perception Accuracy," in Marvin E. Goldberg, Gerald Gorn, and Richard W. Pollay, eds., *Advances in Consumer Research* 17 (Provo, UT: Association for Consumer Research, 1990), 53–59; and MARK E. SLAMA and TERRELL G. WILLIAMS, "Generalizations of the Market Maven's Information Provision Tendency Across Product Categories," in Goldberg, Gorn and Pollay, eds., *Advances in Consumer Research*, 48–52; and KENNETH C. SCHNEIDER and WILLIAM C. ROGERS, "Generalized Marketplace Influencers' (Market Mavens') Attitudes Toward Direct Mail as a Source of Information," *Journal of Direct Marketing* 7, Autumn 1993, 20–28.
19. *Popular Mechanics* research information provided as part of promotional literature.
20. Ibid.
21. For example, see WILLIAM H. WHITE, "The Web of Word-of-Mouth," *Fortune*, November 1954, 140–43; and LINDA L. PRICE and LAWRENCE F. FEICK, "The Role of Interpersonal Sources in External Search: An Informational Perspective," in Thomas C. Kinnear, ed., *Advances in Consumer Research* 9 (Ann Arbor, MI: Association for Consumer Research, 1984), 250–55.
22. PAUL F. LAZARSFELD, BERNARD BERELSON, and HAZEL GAUDET, *The People's Choice*, 2nd ed. (New York: Columbia University Press, 1948), 151.
23. LEISA REINECKE FLYNN, RONALD E. GOLDSMITH, and JACQUELINE K. EASTMAN, "Opinion Leaders and Opinion Seekers: Two New Measurement Scales," *Journal of the Academy of Marketing Science* 24, Spring 1996, 137–47.
24. JULIA M. BRISTOR, "Enhanced Explanations of Word-of-Mouth Communications: The Power of Relationships," in *Research in Consumer Behavior* 4, 1990, 51–83.
25. JOHN P. CORTEZ, "Put People Behind the Wheel," *Advertising Age*, March 22, 1993, S-28; also, see CHIP WALKER, op. cit., 44.
26. "In the News: Ploys," *The New York Times Magazine*, February 13, 1994, 19.
27. ALICE Z. CUNEO, "Starbucks' Word-of-Mouth Wonder," *Advertising Age*, March 7, 1994, 12.
28. BARRY L. BAYUS, "Word-of-Mouth: The Indirect Effects of Marketing Efforts," *Journal of Advertising Research* 25, June-July 1985, 31–38.
29. WALKER, Op cit., 40.
30. JAGDIP SINGH, "Voice, Exit, and Negative Word-of-Mouth Behaviors: An Investigation Across Three Service Categories," *Journal of the Academy of Marketing Sciences* 18(1), Winter 1990, 1–15. See also VICTORIA BUSH and EMIN BABAKUS, "Explaining Consumer Complaint Behavior Via the Learned Helplessness Paradigm," in Robert P. Leone and V. Kumor, et al., eds., *1992 AMA Educators' Proceedings 3* (Chicago: American Marketing Association, 1992), 389–90.
31. JOSEPH R. MANCUSO, "Why Not Create Opinion Leaders for New Product Introduction?" *Journal of Marketing* 33, July 1969, 20–25.

Now the hardest thing about shipping is mastering the complexities of the double click.

Introducing FedEx Ship, the revolutionary new desk-top shipping software from FedEx. Now with FedEx Ship, you can handle virtually any aspect of shipping a package with just a few clicks of your mouse.

Using your modem, the software connects your computer directly to FedEx. It creates shipping labels and prints them on your own laser printer. Maintains a data base of your customers. Schedules pickups, tracks and confirms delivery of your packages. All faster and easier than ever before. Without so much as picking up the phone. FedEx Ship. Once you get the double click down, it's a whole new way of shipping packages. For a free copy of FedEx Ship software for Windows™ or Macintosh® just call 1-800-GO-FEDEX.®

FedEx
Federal Express
Our Most Important Package Is Yours.®

JUST POINT, CLICK AND SHIP.

This chapter examines a major issue in marketing and consumer behavior, the acceptance of new products and services. The introduction of new products and services is vital to the consumer, the marketer, and the world economy. For the consumer, new products and services represent increased opportunities to satisfy personal, social, and environmental needs. For the marketer, new products and services provide an important mechanism for keeping the firm competitive and profitable. For entire countries or geographic regions or even the *world*, new products and services represent potential improvements in the *quality of life* for billions of people.

The framework for exploring consumer acceptance of new products is drawn from the area of research known as the **diffusion of innovations**. Consumer researchers who specialize in the diffusion of innovations are primarily interested in understanding two

W

e have learned so well how to absorb novelty that receptivity itself has turned into a kind of tradition, the tradition of the new.

—Richard Hofstadter
Anti-Intellectualism in American Life (1993)

closely related processes: the diffusion process and the adoption process. In the broadest sense, diffusion is a *macro* process concerned with the spread of a new product (an innovation) from its source to the consuming public. In contrast, adoption is a *micro* process that focuses on the stages through which an individual consumer passes when deciding to accept or reject a new product. In addition to an examination of these two interrelated processes, we present a profile of **consumer innovators**, those who are the first to purchase a new product. The ability of marketers to identify and reach this important group of consumers plays a major role in the success or failure of new product introductions.

THE DIFFUSION PROCESS

The **diffusion process** is concerned with how innovations spread, that is, how they are assimilated within a market. More precisely, diffusion is *the process by which the acceptance of an innovation* (a new product, new service, new idea, or new practice) *is spread by communication* (mass media, salespeople, or informal conversations) *to members of a social system* (a target market) *over a period of time*. This definition includes the four basic elements of the diffusion process: (1) the innovation, (2) the channels of communication, (3) the social system, and (4) time.

The Innovation

No universally accepted definition of the terms "product innovation" or "new product" exists. Instead, various approaches have been taken to define a *new product* or a *new service*; these can be classified as **firm-**, **product-**, **market-**, and **consumer-oriented definitions of innovations**.

▲ **Firm-Oriented Definitions** A *firm-oriented* approach treats the newness of a product from the perspective of the company producing or marketing it. When the product is "new" to the company, it is considered *new*. This definition ignores whether or not the product is actually new to the marketplace (i.e., to competitors or consumers). Consistent with this view, copies or modifications of a competitor's product would qualify as new. Although this definition has considerable merit when the objective is to examine the impact that a "new" product has on the firm, it is not very useful when the goal is to understand consumer acceptance of a new product.

▲ **Product-Oriented Definitions** In contrast to firm-oriented definitions, a *product-oriented* approach focuses on the features inherent in the product itself and on the effects these features are likely to have on consumers' established usage patterns. One product-oriented framework considers the extent to which a new product is likely to disrupt established behavior patterns. It defines the following three types of product innovations:[1]

1. *A **continuous innovation** has the least disruptive influence on established patterns. It involves the introduction of a modified product, rather than a totally new product. Examples include the redesigned 1996 Ford Taurus, the HP Laserjet 5 printer (replacing the HP Laserjet 4), and reduced-fat Oreo cookies. See Figure 18-1 for a BOSE ad that reflects how the radio is even today a continuous innovation.*

FIGURE 18-1

The Radio as an Example of a Continuous Innovation
Courtesy of BOSE Corporation

---

2. A **dynamically continuous innovation** *is somewhat more disruptive than a continuous innovation but still does not alter established behavior patterns. It may involve the creation of a new product or the modification of an existing product. Examples include 8-mm camcorders, compact disc players, erasable-ink pens, and disposable diapers.*

3. A **discontinuous innovation** *requires consumers to adopt new behavior patterns. Examples include fax machines, cellular telephones, home computers, videocassette recorders, medical self-test kits, and the Internet.*

Figure 18-2 shows how the telephone, a discontinuous innovation of major magnitude, has produced a variety of both dynamically continuous and continuous innovations and has even stimulated the development of other discontinuous innovations. The QuoTrek device shown in Figure 18-3 is an interesting example of a dynamically continuous innovation that is an outgrowth of the telephone. The unit is capable of providing real-time stock market quotes, headline news, and sports scores.

Another product-oriented definition suggests that extent of product "newness" can be measured in terms of how much impact its physical features or attributes are likely to have on user satisfaction. Thus, the more satisfaction a consumer derives from a new product, the higher it ranks on the scale of "newness." This concept leads to the classification of products as *artificially new*, *marginally new*, or *genuinely new*. A genuinely new product has features that satisfy the user in a manner that differs significantly from that of an older product. New products that have enough "newness" to qualify as genuinely new include fax machines, CD-ROM players, cellular telephones, in-home medical test kits, and digital still cameras.

▲ **Market-Oriented Definitions** A *market-oriented* approach judges the newness of a product in terms of how much exposure consumers have to the new product. Two market-oriented definitions of product innovation have been used extensively in consumer studies:

1. *A product is considered new if it has been purchased by a relatively small (fixed) percentage of the potential market.*

FIGURE 18-2

The Telephone Has Led
to Related Innovations

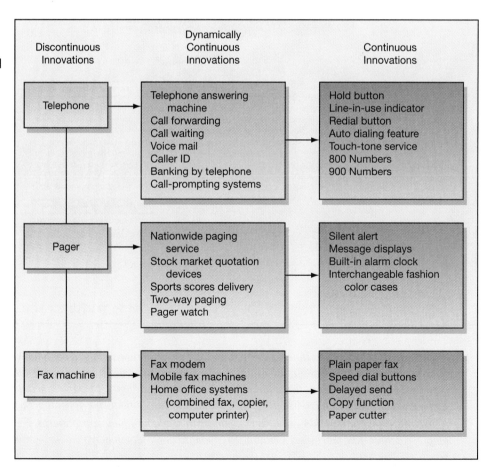

FIGURE 18-3

A Dynamically Continuous Innovation
Courtesy of Data Broadcasting Company

2. *A product is considered new if it has been on the market for a relatively short (specified) period of time.*

Both of these market-oriented definitions are basically subjective, because they leave the researcher with the task of establishing the degree of sales penetration within the market that qualifies the product as an innovation (e.g., the first 5 percent of the potential market to use the new product) or how long the product can be on the market and still be considered "new" (e.g., the first three months that the product is available).

▲ **Consumer-Oriented Definitions** Although each of the three approaches described above have been useful to consumer researchers in their study of the diffusion of innovations, some researchers have favored a *consumer-oriented* approach in defining an innovation.[2] In this context, a "new" product is any product that a potential consumer judges to be new. In other words, newness is based on the consumer's *perception* of the product, rather than on physical features or market realities. Although the consumer-oriented approach has been endorsed by some advertising and marketing practitioners, it has received little systematic research attention.

Additionally, it should be pointed out that although this chapter deals primarily with what might be described as "purchase" innovativeness (i.e., time of adoption), a second type of innovativeness, "use-innovativeness," has been the subject of a number of recent articles. A consumer is being use-innovative when he or she uses a previously adopted product in a novel or unusual way. In one study that dealt with the adoption of VCRs and PCs, early adopters showed significantly higher use-innovativeness than did members of the early majority group.[3]

▲ **Product Characteristics That Influence Diffusion** All products that are "new" do not have equal potential for consumer acceptance. Some products seem to catch on almost overnight (e.g., cordless telephones), while others take a very long time to gain acceptance or never seem to achieve widespread consumer acceptance (e.g., trash compactors).

The uncertainties of product marketing would be reduced if marketers could anticipate how consumers will react to their products. For example, if a marketer knew that a product contained inherent features that were likely to inhibit its acceptance, the marketer could develop a promotional strategy that would compensate for these features or decide not to market the product at all. Although there are no precise formulas by which marketers can evaluate a new product's likely acceptance, diffusion researchers have identified five product characteristics that seem to influence consumer acceptance of new products: (1) relative advantage, (2) compatibility, (3) complexity, (4) trialability, and (5) observability.[4]

RELATIVE ADVANTAGE The degree to which potential customers perceive a new product as superior to existing substitutes is its **relative advantage**. For example, although many people carry beepers so that their business offices or families can contact them, receiving a "beep" signal still requires the user to find a telephone (and working public telephones are not always close at hand) and place a return call. In contrast, a cellular telephone enables users to be in nearly instant communication with the world and allows users to both receive and place calls.

An outstanding example of an innovation that offers users a significant relative advantage in their ability to communicate is the fax machine. Why has the fax machine diffused so rapidly? Clearly, its relative advantage is great. A document can be transmitted in as little as 15 to 18 seconds at minimal cost. A document sent by overnight express will not arrive until the next morning, and the cost may be 10 times higher than a fax. In the case of international mail (e.g., between Europe and the United States), a courier service such as Federal Express or DHL might provide two-day service, while a fax provides almost instantaneous delivery.

In addition to unique product features, a promotional program (including, for example, cents-off coupons, two-for-one sales, a seal of approval, or a variety of special services) also may be perceived as offering a relative advantage and can lead to increased acceptance.

COMPATIBILITY The degree to which potential consumers feel a new product is consistent with their present needs, values, and practices is a measure of its *compatibility*. For example, it is not too difficult to imagine men making the transition from permanent razors involving disposal of only the blade to fully disposable razors that are completely discarded after the blade becomes dull. Indeed, it is not even too difficult to accept the idea that men might *return* to using a superior shaving system such as Gillette's Sensor Excel, where the blade head is disposable and the handle is permanent. These changes are fully compatible with the established wet-shaving rituals of many men. However, it is difficult to imagine male shavers shifting to a new depilatory cream designed to remove facial hair. Although potentially simpler to use, a cream would be basically *incompatible* with most men's current values regarding daily shaving practices.

A study of purchasers of CD players and other high-tech products (such as computers, VCRs, and telephone answering machines) found that the key factors inhibiting product adoption were incompatibility with existing values and poor product quality.[5]

COMPLEXITY Complexity, the degree to which a new product is difficult to understand or use, affects product acceptance. Clearly, the easier it is to understand and use a product, the more likely it is to be accepted. For example, the acceptance of such convenience foods as frozen french fries, instant puddings, and microwave dinners is generally due to their ease of preparation and use. A couple spending a week aboard a Caribbean cruise ship might prefer playing blackjack or the slot machines because they are easier to understand (less complex) than craps or roulette. Also, although VCRs can be found in most American homes, millions of adults still need help from their children in programming the machine to record a particular television program. The recognition of this need has made the VCR Plus+ device a huge success.

The issue of complexity is especially important when attempting to gain market acceptance for high-tech consumer products. Four predominant types of "technological fear" act as barriers to new product acceptance: (1) fear of technical complexity, (2) fear of rapid obsolescence, (3) fear of social rejection, and (4) fear of physical harm. Of the four, *technological complexity* was the most widespread concern of consumer innovators.[6] Figure 18-4 presents an advertisement for FedEx, claiming: "Now the hardest thing about shipping is mastering the complexities of the double click." (FedEx trademarks used by permission.)

FIGURE 18-4

As Designed to Lower the "Fear" of Technological Complexity
Courtesy of Federal Express Corporation

TRIALABILITY **Trialability** refers to the degree to which a new product is capable of being tried on a limited basis. The greater the opportunity to try a new product, the easier it is for consumers to evaluate it and ultimately adopt it. In general, frequently purchased household products tend to have qualities that make trial relatively easy. For instance, for many supermarket products, consumers can make a trial purchase of a new brand in a smaller quantity than they might usually purchase. Marketers of such products recognize that smaller-than-average sizes tend to stimulate new-product trial. Because a computer program cannot be packaged in a smaller size, many computer software companies offer free working models of their latest software to encourage computer users to try the program and subsequently buy the program. Even better, Delphi Internet is offering a 10-hour free trial of their Internet service (see Figure 18-5).

FIGURE 18-5

An Offer to Stimulate Product Trial
Courtesy of Delphi Internet Services Corporation

In the case of products such as CD players, *trialability* was found to be most salient to the potential consumer's overall decision process.[7] To try CD players, all a shopper has to do is visit a retailer for a demonstration.

Aware of the importance of trial, marketers of new supermarket products commonly use substantial cents-off coupons or free samples to provide consumers with direct product experience. These promotions provide consumers with little- or no-risk opportunities to try new products. On the other hand, durable items, such as refrigerators or ovens, are difficult to try without making a major commitment. This may explain why publications such as *Consumer Reports* are so widely consulted for their ratings of infrequently purchased durable goods.

OBSERVABILITY Observability (or communicability) is the ease with which a product's benefits or attributes can be observed, imagined, or described to potential consumers. Products that have a high degree of social visibility, such as fashion items, are more easily diffused than products that are used in private, such as a new type of toothbrush. Similarly, a tangible product is promoted more easily than an intangible product (i.e., a service).

It is important to recognize that each of these product attributes—relative advantage, compatibility, complexity, trialability, and observability—depends on consumer perception. A product that is *perceived* as having a strong relative advantage, as fulfilling present needs and values, as easy to try on a limited basis, and as simple to understand and to see (and/or examine) is more likely to be purchased than a product that is not so perceived. A particular innovation may diffuse differently throughout different cultures. For example, although shelf-stable milk (i.e., milk that does not require refrigeration) has been successfully sold for years in Europe, Americans thus far have resisted the aseptic milk package.[8]

▲ **Resistance to Innovation** What makes some new products almost instant successes, while others must struggle to achieve consumer acceptance? To help answer such a question, a model of innovation resistance has been developed that attempts to provide further insights into the adoption and diffusion processes.[9] The product characteristics of an innovation help to determine the extent of consumer resistance, which increases when perceived relative advantage, perceived compatibility, trialability, and communicability are low, and perceived complexity is high. Indeed, the term "innovation overload" is used to describe the situation in which the increase in information and options available to the consumer are so great that they seriously impair decision making. As a result, the consumer finds it difficult to make comparisons among the available choices. In a world in which consumers often find themselves with too little time and too much stress, the increasing complexity of products wastes time and may delay the diffusion of innovations.[10]

Figure 18-6 on page 536 presents a model of innovation resistance, set in the context of cultural, situational, and social factors. As shown by the model, each of these factors can affect resistance.

The Channels of Communication

How quickly an innovation spreads through a market depends to a great extent on communications between the marketer and consumers, as well as communication among consumers (e.g., word-of-mouth communication). Of central concern is the uncovering of the relative influence of impersonal sources (e.g., advertising and editorial matter) and interpersonal sources (salespeople and informal opinion leaders).

In recent years, a variety of new channels of communication have been developed to inform consumers of innovative products and services. Consider the growth of *interactive marketing messages*, in which the consumer becomes an important part of the

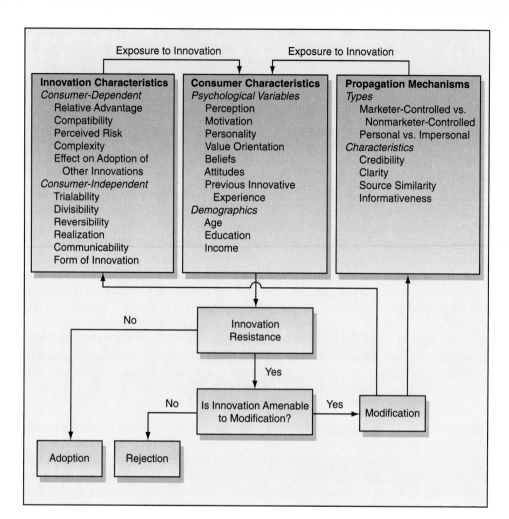

FIGURE 18-6

A Model of Innovation Resistance

Source: S. RAM, "A Model of Innovation Resistance," in M. Wallendorf and P. F. Anderson, eds., *Advances in Consumer Research* 14 (1987), 209.

communication, rather than just a "passive" message recipient. For example, for the past several years, an increasing number of companies, such as the Ford Motor Company, General Motors, and other major automobile manufactures, have used floppy discs or CD-ROMS to promote their products. Another example of a new channel of communication is beauty parlors in New York City. An organization, Women in Crisis, has found it to be fast and efficient to disseminate information about AIDS *through* hair stylists. Consequently, AIDS educators working for this organization spend their days visiting beauty parlors in Harlem and the South Bronx, where they inform hair stylists who, in turn, inform their customers.[11]

Consumer shows and exhibits are also growing in popularity as a channel for assisting consumers in making increasingly complex decisions. Specifically, research that examined boat show attendees' reactions to an innovative marine engine control found that the act of attending the show encouraged both the decision to purchase at the show and an information search after the show.[12] Additionally, it was found that early adopters engaged in more at-show activities, obtained more detailed product information, used more retail sources of postshow information and attributed greater relative advantage to the innovation, than did later adopters.

The Social System

The diffusion of a new product usually takes place in a social setting frequently referred to as a **social system**. In the context of consumer behavior, the terms *market segment* and *target market* are synonymous with the term *social system* used in diffusion research. A *social system is a physical, social, or cultural environment to which people belong and within which they function*. For example, for a new hybrid seed corn, the social system might consist of all farmers in a number of local communities. For a new drug, the social system might consist of all physicians within a specific medical specialty (e.g., all allergists). For a new special-diet product, the social system might include all residents of a geriatric community. As these examples indicate, the social system serves as the *boundary* within which the diffusion of a new product is examined.

The orientation of a social system, with its own special *values* or *norms*, is likely to influence the acceptance or rejection of new products. When a social system is *modern* in orientation, the acceptance of innovations is likely to be high. In contrast, when a social system is *traditional* in orientation, innovations that are perceived as radical or as infringements on established customs are likely to be avoided. According to one authority, the following characteristics typify a **modern social system**:[13]

- ■ *A positive attitude toward change*
- ■ *An advanced technology and skilled labor force*
- ■ *A general respect for education and science*
- ■ *An emphasis on rational and ordered social relationships, rather than on emotional ones*
- ■ *An outreach perspective, in which members of the system frequently interact with outsiders, thus facilitating the entrance of new ideas into the social system*
- ■ *A system in which members can readily see themselves in quite different roles*

The orientations of a social system (either modern or traditional) may be national in scope and may influence members of an entire society or may exist at the local level and influence only those who live in a specific community. The key point to remember is that a social system's orientation is the climate in which marketers must operate to gain acceptance for their new products. For example, in recent years, the United States has experienced a decline in the demand for beef. The growing interest in health and fitness throughout the nation has created a climate in which beef is considered too high in fat and caloric content. At the same time, the consumption of chicken and fish has increased, because these foods satisfy the prevailing nutritional values of a great number of consumers.

Time

Time is the backbone of the diffusion process. It pervades the study of diffusion in three distinct but interrelated ways: (1) **the amount of purchase time**, (2) the identification of **adopter categories**, and (3) the **rate of adoption**.

▲ **Purchase Time** Purchase time refers to the amount of time that elapses between consumers' initial awareness of a new product or service and the point at which they purchase or reject it. Table 18-1 on page 538 illustrates the scope of purchase time by tracking a hypothetical consumer's purchase of a large-screen (i.e., 40-inch or larger) rear projection TV.

Table 18-1 illustrates not only the length and complexity of consumer decision making but also how different information sources become important at successive steps in the process. Purchase time is an important concept because the average time a consumer takes to adopt a new product is a predictor of the overall length of time it will take for the new

table 18-1

Time Line for Selecting a New Large-Screen TV Set

WEEK	PRECIPITATING SITUATIONS/FACTORS
0	Current family room 19-inch TV set works fine but is 10 years old and cannot access a number of the cable channels. The wife has recently purchased a new sofa and new carpeting for the family room, and she and her husband have spoken about possibly having a cabinet built for the wall opposite the sofa that would contain the TV, stereo, tape deck, CD player, and VCR. Several friends have purchased large screen TVs and have turned their family rooms into home entertainment centers. Couple decides, therefore, to also look at projection TVs.
	DECISION PROCESS BEGINS
1-4	Consumer senses a need to learn more about the features and availability of large screen TVs, both those with conventional picture tubes (up to 35-inches in picture size) and projection TVs (40- to 52-inch picture sizes).
	THE TV IS OUT OF MIND
5-8	The transmission in the older of the couple's two cars, a 1987 Honda, begins to shift erratically. Because of the expense of this repair (the transmission had to be replaced), the hunt for a new TV is put on the back burner.
	INTEREST IS RETRIGGERED
9	The wife reads an article in one of the magazines that she periodically buys at the supermarket about a family that purchased a Zenith 52-inch projection TV for their family room and created a home entertainment center. She shows the article to her husband.
	CONSUMER ACQUIRES A MENTOR (OPINION LEADER)
	The husband asks a neighbor to serve as a mentor (opinion leader) with regard to home entertainment centers. He agrees.
	FEATURES AND BRAND OPTIONS ARE REVIEWED
10	With the advice of the mentor, the decision is made to use a projection TV in the 46 to 50-inch range as the nucleus of the home entertainment center. The couple visits several department store and appliance store TV departments and narrows down its choices to projection units from Pioneer, Sony, and Zenith.
	OBTAINING MORE FOCUSED INFORMATION ABOUT OPTIONS
11-12	The toll-free 800 numbers of the three TV manufacturers (which were featured in ads) are called to request additional detailed information (brochures and booklets).
	PERIOD OF SELF-STUDY
13-14	After reading the brochures and discussing the pros and cons of the alternatives with their mentor (comparing models with regard to features such as picture-in-picture and surround sound capability), a decision is made.
	The 46-inch Sony is selected because of a magazine review that gave it very high marks in terms of its screen brightness and sharpness, and because it offered colored picture-in-picture.
	ORDERING THE TV
	Sunday's newspaper contains an advertisement from a local appliance store chain stating that any projection TV purchased within the next week can be paid for with 6 monthly payments, at no interest charge—the first payment beginning 6 months after the TV is installed. The couple decides to drive to the store and talk to a salesperson about this deal. When the salesperson agrees to lower the price of the Sony 46-inch set to match the lowest price the couple had been quoted, they decide to make the purchase.
	The TV arrives in the appliance dealer's trunk and is installed in the couple's family room.

product to achieve widespread adoption. For example, when the individual purchase time is short, a marketer can expect that the overall rate of diffusion will be faster than when the individual purchase time is long.

▲ **Adopter Categories** The concept of *adopter categories* involves a classification scheme that indicates where a consumer stands in relation to other consumers in terms of time (i.e., *when* he or she adopts a new product). Five adopter categories are frequently cited in the diffusion literature: **innovators**, **early adopters**, **early majority**, **late majority**, and **laggards**. Table 18-2 describes each of these adopter categories and estimates their relative proportions within the total population that eventually adopts the new product.

As Figure 18-7 on page 540 indicates, the adopter categories are generally depicted as taking on the characteristics of a normal distribution (a bell-shaped curve) that describes the total population that ultimately adopts a product. Some argue that the bell curve is an erroneous depiction, because it may lead to the inaccurate conclusion that 100 percent of the members of the social system under study (the target market) eventually will accept the product innovation. This assumption is not in keeping with marketers' experiences, because

table 18-2   Adopter Categories

ADOPTER CATEGORY	DESCRIPTION	RELATIVE PERCENTAGE WITHIN THE POPULATION THAT EVENTUALLY ADOPTS
Innovators	*Venturesome*—very eager to try new ideas; acceptable if risk is daring; more cosmopolite social relationships; communicates with other innovators	2.5%
Early Adopters	*Respect*—more integrated into the local social system; the persons to check with before adopting a new idea; category contains greatest number of opinion leaders; are role models	13.5
Early Majority	*Deliberate*—adopt new ideas just prior to the average time; seldom hold leadership positions; deliberate for some time before adopting	34.0
Late Majority	*Skeptical*—adopt new ideas just after the average time; adopting may be both an economic necessity and a reaction to peer pressures; innovations approached cautiously	34.0
Laggards	*Traditional*—the last people to adopt an innovation; most "localite" in outlook; oriented to the past; suspicious of the new	16.0
		100.0%

Source: Adapted/Reprinted with the permission of The Free Press, a division of Simon & Schuster, from *Diffusion of Innovations*, 3rd edition, by Everett M. Rogers. Copyright © 1962, 1971, 1983 by The Free Press.

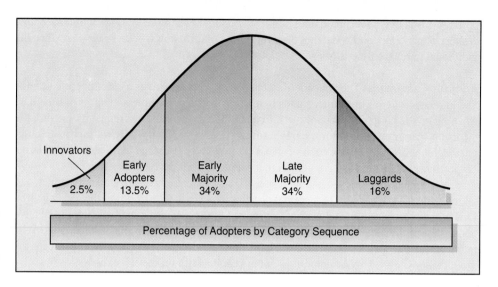

FIGURE 18-7

The Sequence and
Proportion of Adopter
Categories among the
Population that
Eventually Adopts
Source: Adapted/Reprinted with
the permission of The Free Press,
a division of Simon & Schuster,
from *Diffusion of Innovations*, 3rd
edition, by Everett M. Rogers.
Copyright © 1962, 1971, 1983 by
The Free Press.

very few, if any, products fit the precise needs of all potential consumers. For example, all purchasers of prerecorded music could theoretically be expected to use (or try) compact disks (CDs). In fact, however, only a small percentage of cassette users have adopted CDs, and it is unrealistic for the music industry to expect all prerecorded cassette purchasers to do so. For this reason, it is appropriate to add an additional category, that of **nonadopters**. The "nonadopter" category is in accord with marketplace reality, for not all potential consumers adopt a product innovation.

Instead of the classic five-category adopter scheme, many consumer researchers have used other classification schemes, most of which consist of two or three categories that compare *innovators* or *early triers* with *later triers* or *nontriers*. As we will see, this focus on the innovator or early trier has produced several important generalizations that have practical significance for marketers planning the introduction of new products.

Another classification scheme differentiates between five different types of non-adopters: (1) the **unaware group**, which consists of those consumers who do not know about the innovation or do not yet have enough information to make a decision about it; (2) **symbolic rejectors**, who know of the product but have decided it is not for them; (3) **symbolic adopters**, who believe the product might be for them but have yet to try it; (4) **trial adopters**, who have tried the product but have not made an actual purchase (or re-purchase); and (5) **trial rejectors**, who have tried the product but found it to be lacking.[14]

▲ **Rate of Adoption** The rate of adoption is concerned with *how long it takes a new product or service to be adopted by members of a social system*; that is, how quickly it takes a new product to be accepted by those who will ultimately adopt it. The general view is that the rate of adoption for new products is getting faster or shorter. Fashion adoption is a form of diffusion, one in which the rate of adoption is important. Cyclical fashion trends or "fads" are extremely "fast," whereas "fashion classics" may be extremely slow or "long" cycles.[15]

The diffusion of television sets illustrates this trend. Figure 18-8 compares the growth in the total number of United States households with the growth in television-owning households for the period from 1950 to 1995. Note the very rapid rate of adoption of television sets between 1950 and 1958, and the emergence of multiset homes as an important market segment since 1958. The figure shows that color television sets had a very low rate of adoption in the 10-year period from 1955 to 1964, probably because of their high

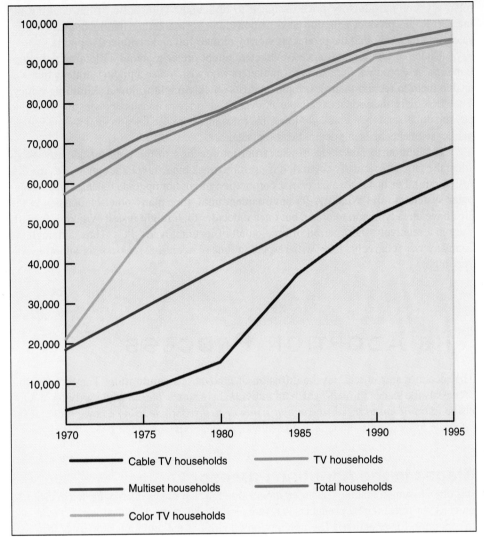

FIGURE 18-8

The Diffusion of
Television (1970–1995)
Source: "Trends in Television: A
Research Trend Reports"
(Television Bureau of Advertising,
Inc.), 1995.

Chart legend:
- Cable TV households
- Multiset households
- Color TV households
- TV households
- Total households

sales price, lack of color programming, and consumers' perceived functional risk. Since 1965, however, there has been a dramatic acceleration in the acceptance of color television sets.

Similarly, the diffusion of products worldwide is becoming a more rapid phenomenon. For example, it took black-and-white TVs about 12 years longer to reach the same level of penetration in Europe and Japan as in the United States. For color TVs, the lag time dropped to about five years for Japan and several more years for Europe. In contrast, for VCRs there was only a three- or four-year spread, with the United States (with its emphasis on cable TV) lagging behind Europe and Japan. Finally, for compact disc players, penetration levels in all three countries were about even after only three years.[16] The diffusion patterns of other electronic products provide rather forceful evidence that differences in the cross-cultural rate of adoption for certain types of goods are declining rather swiftly in consumer-oriented societies.

The objective in marketing new products is usually to gain wide acceptance of the product as quickly as possible. Marketers desire a rapid rate of product adoption to penetrate the market and quickly establish market leadership (obtain the largest share of the market) before competition takes hold. A **penetration policy** is usually accompanied by a relatively low introductory price designed to discourage competition from entering the market. Rapid product adoption also demonstrates to marketing intermediaries (wholesalers and retailers) that the product is worthy of their full and continued support.

Under certain circumstances, marketers might prefer to avoid a rapid rate of adoption for a new product. For example, marketers who wish to use a pricing strategy that will enable them to recoup their development costs quickly might follow a **skimming policy**: They first make the product available at a very high price to consumers who are willing to pay top dollar, and then gradually lower the price in a stepwise fashion to attract additional market segments at each price reduction plateau.

In addition to how long it takes from introduction to the point of adoption (e.g., when the purchase actually occurs), it is useful to track the *extent* of adoption (i.e., the diffusion rate). For instance, a particular corporation might not upgrade its employees' computer systems to the Windows 95 environment until after many other companies in the area have already begun to do so, but once it decides to, it might install Windows 95 software in a relatively short period of time on all of its employees' PCs. Thus, although the company was relatively "late" with respect to *time* of adoption, its *extent* of adoption was very high.

THE ADOPTION PROCESS

The second major process in the diffusion of innovations is **adoption**. The focus of this process is the stages through which an individual consumer passes while arriving at a decision to *try or not to try or to continue using or to discontinue using* a new product. (The *adoption process* should not be confused with *adopter categories*.)

Stages in the Adoption Process

It is often assumed that the consumer moves through five stages in arriving at a decision to purchase or reject a new product: (1) awareness, (2) interest, (3) evaluation, (4) trial, and (5) adoption (or rejection). The assumption underlying the adoption process is that consumers engage in an extensive information search (see Chapter 7), while consumer involvement theory suggests that for some products, a limited information search is more likely (i.e., "low-involvement products"). The stages in the adoption process can be described as follows:

1. *Awareness. During the first stage of the adoption process, consumers are exposed to the product innovation. This exposure is somewhat neutral, for they are not yet sufficiently interested enough to search for additional product information.*

2. *Interest. When consumers develop an interest in the product or product category, they search for information about how the innovation can benefit them.*

3. *Evaluation. Based on their information, consumers draw conclusions about the innovation or determine whether further information is necessary. The evaluation stage represents a kind of "mental trial" of the product innovation. When the evaluation is satisfactory, the consumer will actually try the product innovation; when the mental trial is unsatisfactory, the product will be rejected.*

4. *Trial. At this stage, consumers use the product on a limited basis. Their experience with the product provides them with the critical information that they need to adopt or reject.*

5. *Adoption (Rejection)*. Based on their trials and/or favorable evaluation, consumers decide to use the product on a full, rather than limited basis, or they decide to reject it.

Although the traditional adoption process model is insightful in its simplicity, it does not adequately reflect the full complexity of the consumer adoption process. For one, it does not adequately acknowledge that there is quite often a need or problem-recognition stage that consumers face before acquiring an awareness of potential options or solutions (i.e., a need recognition preceding the awareness stage). Moreover, the adoption process does not adequately provide for the rejection of a product after its trial (i.e., a consumer may reject the product after trial or never use the product on a continuous basis). Similarly, it does not adequately recognize that evaluation occurs throughout the decision-making process and not solely at the evaluation stage. Finally, it does not explicitly include post-purchase evaluation, which can lead to a strengthened commitment or to a decision to discontinue use.

As a partial solution to these shortcomings, consumer researchers have added two additional stages between trial and adoption: *direct product experience* (consequences) and *product evaluation* (confirmation). This proposed modification to the adoption process is shown in Figure 18-9. The adoption process starts with *awareness* (stage 1), which leads to *interest* (stage 2) and *evaluation* (stage 3). The product can then be rejected or *tried* (stage 4) before or after purchase. The trial provides *direct product experience* (stage 5), and the consequences of that experience serve to confirm the *product evaluation* (stage 6), leading to subsequent rejection or *adoption* (stage 7).

The adoption of some products and services may have minimal consequences, while the adoption of other innovations may lead to major behavioral and lifestyle changes. Examples of innovations with such major impact on society include the automobile, the telephone, the electric refrigerator, the television, and the PC computer.

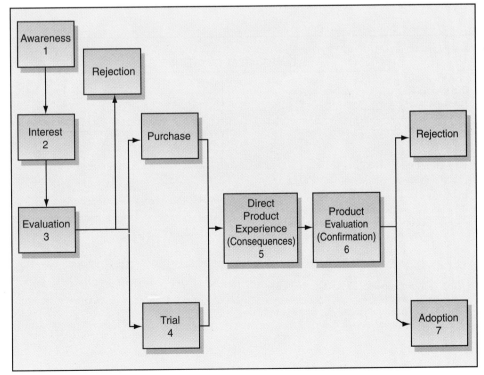

FIGURE 18-9

A Proposed Modification to the Trial-Adoption Process
Source: Adapted from JOHN ANTIL, "New Product or Service Adoption: When Does it Happen?" *Journal of Consumer Marketing* 5 (Spring, 1988), 9.

The Innovation Decision Process

To overcome the limitations discussed above, the traditional adoption process model has been updated into a more general decision-making model, the **innovation decision process**. The five stages of the revised adoption process model are:

1. **Knowledge**. *Consumer is exposed to the innovation's existence and gains some understanding of how it functions.*

2. **Persuasion** *(attitude formation). Consumer forms favorable or unfavorable attitudes toward the innovation.*

3. **Decision**. *Consumer engages in activities that lead to a choice to adopt or reject the innovation.*

4. **Implementation**. *Consumer puts the innovation into use.*

5. **Confirmation**. *Consumer seeks reinforcement for the innovation decision but may reverse this decision if exposed to conflicting messages about the product.*[17]

Figure 18-10 diagrams the operation of the innovation decision process. Briefly, the model suggests that a number of prior conditions (e.g., felt needs and social-system norms) and characteristics of the decision-making unit (e.g., socioeconomic status and personality factors) influence the reception of information about the product innovation during the *knowledge* stage. At the *persuasion* (attitude formation) stage, the consumer is further influenced by communications channels (sources) and by perceptions of the characteristics of the innovation (its relative advantage, compatibility, complexity, trialability, and observability). Additional information received during the *decision* stage enables the consumer to assess the innovation and decide whether to adopt or reject it. During the *implementation* stage, further communication is received as the consumer puts the innovation to use. The final stage, *confirmation*, also is influenced by communications sources. It is at this stage that consumers evaluate their purchase experiences, look for support for their behavior, and decide to continue or discontinue using the product.

FIGURE 18-10

The Innovation Decision Process
Source: Adapted/Reprinted with the permission of The Free Press, a division of Simon & Schuster, from *Diffusion of Innovations*, Third Edition, by EVERETT M. ROGERS. Copyright © 1962, 1971, 1983 by The Free Press

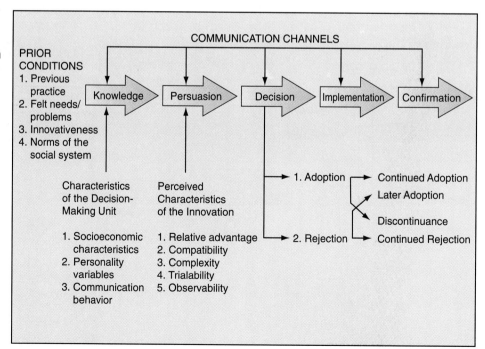

The innovation decision process model is more comprehensive than the earlier adoption process model and overcomes many of its basic limitations. It is also much more attuned to the realities faced by the marketer launching a new product.

The Adoption Process and Information Sources

The adoption process provides a framework for determining which types of information sources consumers find most important at specific decision stages. For example, early subscribers to a computer-linked data service, such as CompuServe, might first become aware of the service via *mass-media sources* (magazines and radio publicity). Then, these early subscribers' final pretrial information might be an outcome of informal discussions with *personal sources*. The key point is that impersonal mass-media sources tend to be most valuable for creating initial product awareness; as the purchase decision progresses, however, the relative importance of these sources declines while the relative importance of interpersonal sources (friends, salespeople, and others) increases. Figure 18-11 depicts this relationship.

A PROFILE OF THE CONSUMER INNOVATOR

Who is the consumer innovator? What characteristics set the innovator apart from later adopters and from those who never purchase? How can the marketer reach and influence the innovator? These are key questions for the marketing practitioner about to introduce a new product or service.

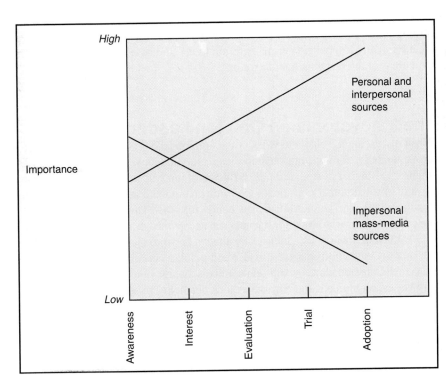

FIGURE 18-11

The Relative Importance of Different Types of Information Sources in the Adoption Process

Defining the Consumer Innovator

Consumer innovators can be defined as *the relatively small group of consumers who are the earliest purchasers of a new product*. The problem with this definition, however, concerns the concept "earliest," which is, after all, a relative term. Sociologists have treated this issue by sometimes defining innovators as the first 2.5 percent of the social system to adopt an innovation. In many marketing diffusion studies, however, the definition of the consumer innovator has been derived from the status of the new product under investigation. For example, if researchers define a new product as an innovation for the first three months of its availability, then they define the consumers who purchase it during this period as "innovators." Other researchers have defined innovators in terms of their *innovativeness,* that is, their purchase of some minimum number of new products from a selected group of new products. For instance, in the adoption of new fashion items, innovators can be defined as those consumers who purchase more than one fashion product from a group of ten new fashion products. Noninnovators would be defined as those who purchase none or only one of the new fashion products. In other instances, researchers have defined innovators as those falling within an arbitrary proportion of the total market (e.g., the first 10 percent of the population in a specified geographic area to buy the new product).

Interest in the Product Category

Not surprisingly, consumer innovators are much more interested than either later adopters or nonadopters in the product categories that they are among the first to purchase. If what is known from diffusion theory holds true in the future, the earliest purchasers of small electric automobiles are likely to have substantially greater interest in automobiles (they will enjoy looking at automotive magazines and will be interested in the performance and functioning of automobiles) than those who purchased conventional small cars during the same period or those who purchased small electric cars during a later period.

Consumer innovators are more likely than noninnovators to seek information concerning their specific interests from a variety of informal and mass media sources. They are more likely to give greater deliberation to the purchase of new products or services in their areas of interest than noninnovators.

The Innovator Is an Opinion Leader

When discussing the characteristics of the opinion leader (see Chapter 17), we indicated a strong tendency for consumer opinion leaders to be innovators. In the present context, an impressive number of studies on the diffusion of innovations have found that consumer innovators provide other consumers with information and advice about new products, and that those who receive such advice frequently follow it. Thus, in the role of opinion leader, the consumer innovator often influences the acceptance or rejection of new products.

When innovators are enthusiastic about a new product and encourage others to try it, the product is likely to receive broader and quicker acceptance. When consumer innovators are dissatisfied with a new product and discourage others from trying it, its acceptance will be severely limited and may die a quick death. For products that do not generate much excitement (either positive or negative), consumer innovators may not be sufficiently motivated to provide advice. In such cases, the marketer must rely almost entirely on mass media and personal selling to influence future purchasers; the absence of *informal* influence is also likely to result in a somewhat slower rate of acceptance (or in rejection) of the new product. Because motivated consumer innovators can influence the rate of acceptance or rejection of a new product, they influence its eventual success or failure.

Personality Traits

In Chapter 5, we examined the *personality traits* that distinguish the consumer innovator from the noninnovator. In this section, we will briefly highlight what researchers have learned about the personality of the consumer innovator.

First, consumer innovators generally are *less dogmatic* than noninnovators. They tend to approach new or unfamiliar products with considerable openness and little anxiety. In contrast, noninnovators seem to find new products threatening, to the point where they prefer to delay purchase until the product's success has been clearly established.

Consistent with their open-mindedness, consumer innovators are also *inner-directed*; that is, they rely on their own values or standards when making a decision about a new product. In contrast, noninnovators are *other-directed*, relying on others for guidance on how to respond to a new product, rather than trusting their own personal values or standards. Thus, the initial purchasers of a new line of automobiles might be inner-directed, whereas the later purchasers of the same automobile might be other-directed. This suggests that as acceptance of a product progresses from early to later adopters, a gradual shift occurs in the personality type of adopters from inner-directedness to other-directedness.

Researchers have isolated a link between *variety seeking* and purchase behavior that provides insights into consumer innovators. Variety-seeking consumers tend to be brand switchers and purchasers of innovative products and services. They also possess the following innovator-related personality traits: they are open-minded (i.e., low in dogmatism), extroverts, liberal, low in authoritarianism, able to deal with complex or ambiguous stimuli, and creative.[18]

To sum up, consumer innovators seem to be more receptive to the unfamiliar; they are more willing to rely on their own values or standards than on the judgment of others. They also are willing to run the risk of a poor product choice to increase their exposure to new products that will be satisfying. For the marketer, the personality traits that distinguish innovators from noninnovators suggest the need for separate promotional campaigns for innovators and for later adopters.

Consumer innovators are more likely to react favorably to informative or fact-oriented advertising in the product category that appeals to their strong interest and to readily evaluate the merits of a new product on the basis of their own personal standards. To reach noninnovators, sophisticated marketers feature reference group settings (e.g., a group of smiling people having fun at a party) in their advertising and use recognized and trusted experts or celebrities to appeal to such consumers responsiveness to authority figures.

There also appears to be a link between *optimum stimulation level* and consumer innovativeness. Specifically, individuals who seek a lifestyle rich with novel, complex, and unusual experiences (i.e., high optimum stimulation levels) are more willing to risk trying new products, to be innovative, to seek purchase-related information, and to accept new retail facilities.

▲ **Perceived Risk** *Perceived risk*, which is discussed in detail in Chapter 6, is another measure of a consumer's likelihood to try new brands or products. Perceived risk is the degree of *uncertainty* or *fear* about the consequences of a purchase that a consumer feels when considering the purchase of a new product. For example, consumers experience uncertainty when they are concerned that a new product will not work properly or as well as other alternatives. Research on perceived risk and the trial of new products overwhelmingly indicates that the consumer innovator is a low-risk perceiver; that is, they experience little fear of trying new products or services. Consumers who perceive little or no risk in the purchase of a new product are much more likely to make innovative purchases than consumers who perceive a great deal of risk. In other words, high-risk perception limits innovativeness. One study on the adoption of in-house computers, for example, found that perceived risk and self-confidence were the only two variables that significantly differentiated between those adopting early and those adopting late.[19]

▲ **Venturesomeness** *Venturesomeness* is a broad-based measure of a consumer's willingness to accept the risk of purchasing new products. Measures of venturesomeness have been used to evaluate a person's general values or attitudes toward trying new products. A typical measurement scale might include such items as:

- *I prefer to (try a toothpaste when it first comes out) (wait and learn how good it is before trying it).*
- *When I am shopping and see a brand of paper towels I know about but have never used, I am (very anxious or willing to try it), (hesitant about trying it), (very unwilling to try it).*
- *I like to be among the first people to buy and use new products that are on the market (measured on a five-point "agreement" scale).*

Research that has examined venturesomeness has generally found that consumers who indicate a willingness to try new products tend to be consumer innovators (as measured by their actual purchase of new products). On the other hand, consumers who express a reluctance to try new products are, in fact, less likely to purchase new products. Therefore, venturesomeness seems to be an effective barometer of actual innovative behavior.

Consistent with their greater venturesomeness and lower risk perception, consumer innovators are likely to learn about innovations earlier than others. They also are more intrigued with the prospect of "newness" than are noninnovators. The question remains, however, as to whether an individual's purchase of an early example of an innovation has any relationship to his or her purchase of later innovations within the same product class. For example, does an innovator's purchase of the original computer spreadsheet program, VisiCalc, affect the buying of Lotus 1-2-3, Microsoft Excel, or Quattro Pro at a later date? According to the *innovator buying cycle* depicted in Figure 18-12, consumer innovators eventually end up as noninnovators. They progress through the following three states: (1) embracing innovations, (2) innovation satiation, and (3) innovator no more. In effect, they eventually "burn out" of their innovator's role.

FIGURE 18-12 ▼

The Innovator Buying Cycle

Source: FRANK ALPERT, "Innovator Buying Over Time and the Cumulative Effects of Innovations," in Robert P. Leone and V. Kumer et al., eds., 1992, *AMA Educators' Proceedings* 3 (Chicago: American Marketing Association, 1992), 298. Reprinted by permission.

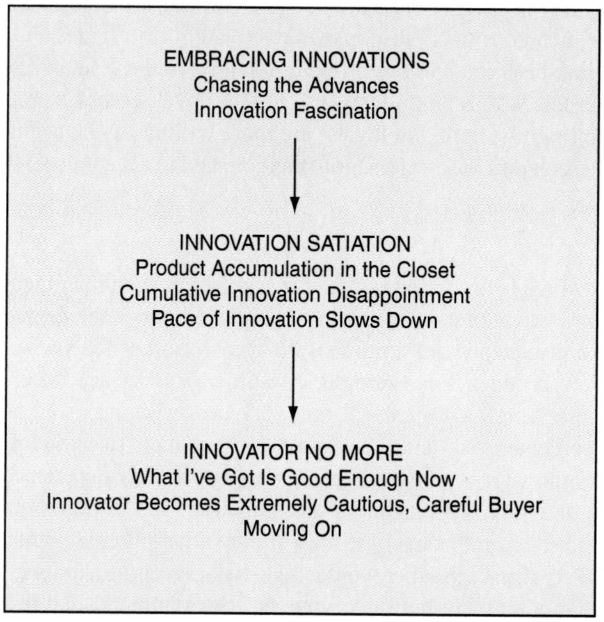

EMBRACING INNOVATIONS
Chasing the Advances
Innovation Fascination

↓

INNOVATION SATIATION
Product Accumulation in the Closet
Cumulative Innovation Disappointment
Pace of Innovation Slows Down

↓

INNOVATOR NO MORE
What I've Got Is Good Enough Now
Innovator Becomes Extremely Cautious, Careful Buyer
Moving On

▲ **Need for Uniqueness** There is support for the notion that innovative behavior is an expression of a person's *need for uniqueness*.[20] Those new products, both branded and unbranded, that represent a greater change in a person's consumption habits were viewed as superior when it came to satisfying the *need for uniqueness*. Therefore, to gain more rapid acceptance of a new product, marketers might consider appealing to a consumer's need for uniqueness.

Purchase and Consumption Characteristics

Consumer innovators possess purchase and usage traits that set them apart from noninnovators. For example, consumer innovators are *less* brand loyal; that is, they are more apt to switch brands. This is not surprising, for brand loyalty would seriously impede a consumers' willingness to try new products.

Consumer innovators are more likely to be *deal-prone* (e.g., to take advantage of special promotional offers such as free samples and cents-off coupons). Consumer innovators are also likely to be *heavy users* of the product category in which they innovate. Specifically, they purchase larger quantities and consume more of the product than noninnovators. Finally, for products like VCRs, PCs, microwave ovens, 35-mm cameras, and food processors, usage variety is likely to be a relevant dimension of new product diffusion. An understanding of how consumers might be "usage-innovators"—that is, finding or "inventing" new uses for an innovation)—might create entirely new market opportunities for the marketers' products.

To sum up, a positive relationship exists between innovative behavior and heavy usage. Consumer innovators are not only an important market segment from the standpoint of being the first to use a new product, but also they represent a substantial market in terms of product volume. However, their propensity to switch brands or to use products in different or unique ways, as well as their positive response to promotional deals, also suggest that innovators will continue to use a specific brand only as long as they do not perceive that a new and potentially better alternative is available.

Media Habits

Comparisons of the media habits of innovators and noninnovators across such widely diverse areas of consumption as fashion clothing and new automotive services suggest that innovators have somewhat greater total exposure to magazines than noninnovators, particularly to *special-interest* magazines devoted to the product category in which they innovate. For example, fashion innovators are more likely to read magazines such as *Gentlemen's Quarterly* and *Vogue* than noninnovators; financial services innovators have greater exposure to such special-interest magazines as *Money* and *Financial World*.

Consumer innovators are also less likely to watch television than noninnovators. This view is consistently supported by research that over the past decade or so has compared the magazine and TV exposure levels of consumer innovators. The evidence indicates that consumer innovators have higher-than-average magazine exposure and lower-than-average TV exposure. Studies concerning the relationship between innovative behavior and exposure to other mass media, such as radio and newspapers, have been too few, and the results have been too varied to draw any useful conclusions.

Social Characteristics

Consumer innovators are more socially accepted and socially involved than noninnovators. For example, innovators are more socially integrated into the community, better accepted by others, and more socially involved; that is, they belong to more social groups and organizations than noninnovators. This greater social acceptance and involvement of consumer innovators may help explain why they function as effective opinion leaders.

Demographic Characteristics

It is reasonable to assume that the age of the consumer innovator is related to the specific product category in which he or she innovates; however, research suggests that consumer innovators tend to be younger than either later adopters or noninnovators. This is no doubt because many of the products selected for research attention (e.g., fashion, convenience grocery products, or new automobiles) are particularly attractive to younger consumers.

Consumer innovators have more formal education, higher personal or family incomes, and are more likely to have higher occupational status (to be professionals or hold managerial positions) than later adopters or noninnovators. In other words, innovators tend to be more upscale than other consumer segments and can, therefore, better afford to make a mistake, should the innovative new product or service being purchased prove to be unacceptable. For example, while only about 5 percent of United States households owned cellular telephones in 1993, almost 14 percent of households with annual incomes of $75,000 or more had one.[21]

Are There Generalized Consumer Innovators?

Do consumer innovators in one product category tend to be consumer innovators in other product categories? The answer to this strategically important question is a guarded "No." The overlap of innovativeness across product categories, like opinion leadership, seems to be limited to product categories that are closely related to the same basic interest area. Consumers who are innovators of one new food product or one new appliance are more likely to be innovators of other new products in the same general product category. In other words, although no single or generalized consumer-innovativeness trait seems to operate *across* broadly different product categories, evidence suggests that consumers who innovate *within* a specific product category will innovate again within the same product category. For example, up to the point of "innovator burn out" (again, see Figure 18-12), a person who was an innovator in buying a Sony Walkman probably was again an innovator in buying a portable CD player and is likely to again be an innovator when it comes to a portable minidisk player or DAT (digital audio tape) Walkman player. For the marketer, such a pattern suggests that it is generally a good marketing strategy to target a new product to consumers who were the first to try other products in the same basic product category.

However, there is some recent evidence that suggests that a new type of more generalized "high-tech" innovator does exist, that is, the "change leader."[22] Such individuals tend to embrace and popularize many of the innovations that are ultimately accepted by the mainstream population, such as computers, cellular telephones, and fax machines. They tend to have a wide range of personal and professional contacts representing different occupational and social groups; most often, these contacts tend to be "weak ties" or acquaintances. Change leaders also appear to fall into one of two distinct groups: a **younger group** that can be characterized as being stimulation-seeking, sociable, and having high levels of fashion awareness or a **middle-aged group** that is highly self-confident and have very high information-seeking needs. Table 18-3 presents the six personality traits of change leaders and corresponding attributes of the new media (e.g., interactive information services or computer networks) they use to communicate among themselves and with other nonchange leaders.

Similar to change leaders, "technophiles" are individuals who purchase technologically advanced products soon after their market debut. Such individuals tend to be technically curious people. Also, another group responding to technology are adults who are categorized as "techthusiasts"—people who are most likely to purchase or subscribe to emerging products and services that are technologically oriented. These consumers are typically younger, better educated, and more affluent.[23]

table 18-3 Change Leader Attributes and New Media Attributes

CHANGE LEADER ATTRIBUTES	NEW MEDIA ATTRIBUTES
Novelty-seeking	Great content diversity
Stimulation-seeking	Interactivity
Information-seeking	Wide archive, service access
Individualistic	Personalized, user-controlled
Sociable	Connectivity, networking
Fashionable	Timely, lifestyle focus

Source: BRUCE MACEVOY, "Change Leaders and the New Media," *American Demographics*, January 1994, 44. © 1994 American Demographics Magazine. Reprinted with permission.

Table 18-4 summarizes the major differences between consumer innovators and later adopters or noninnovators. The table includes the major distinctions examined in the presentation of the **consumer innovator profile**.

table 18-4 Comparative Profiles of the Consumer Innovator and the Noninnovator or Later Adopter

CHARACTERISTIC	INNOVATOR	NONINNOVATOR (OR LATER ADOPTER)
PRODUCT INTEREST	More	Less
OPINION LEADERSHIP	More	Less
PERSONALITY		
Dogmatism	Open-minded	Closed-minded
Social character	Inner-directed	Other-directed
Optimum stimulation level	Higher	Lower
Venturesomeness	More	Less
Perceived risk	Less	More
PURCHASE AND CONSUMPTION TRAITS		
Brand loyalty	Less	More
Deal proneness	More	Less
Usage	More	Less
MEDIA HABITS		
Total magazine exposure	More	Less
Special-interest magazines	More	Less
Television	Less	More
SOCIAL CHARACTERISTICS		
Social integration	More	Less
Social striving (e.g., social, physical, and occupational mobility)	More	Less
Group Memberships	More	Less
DEMOGRAPHIC CHARACTERISTICS		
Age	Younger	Older
Income	Higher	Lower
Education	More	Less
Occupational status	Higher	Lower

summary

The diffusion process and the adoption process are two closely related concepts concerned with the acceptance of new products by consumers. The diffusion process is a macro process that focuses on the spread of an innovation (a new product, service, or idea) from its source to the consuming public. The adoption process is a microprocess that examines the stages through which an individual consumer passes when making a decision to accept or reject a new product.

The definition of the term "innovation" can be firm-oriented (new to the firm), product-oriented (a continuous innovation, a dynamically continuous innovation, or a discontinuous innovation), market-oriented (how long the product has been on the market or an arbitrary percentage of the potential target market that has purchased it), or consumer-oriented (new to the consumer). Market-oriented definitions of innovation are most useful to consumer researchers in the study of the diffusion and adoption of new products.

Five product characteristics influence the consumer's acceptance of a new product: relative advantage, compatibility, complexity, trialability, and observability (or communicability).

Diffusion researchers are concerned with two aspects of communication: the channels through which word of a new product is spread to the consuming public and the types of messages that influence the adoption or rejection of new products. Diffusion is always examined in the context of a specific social system, such as a target market, a community, a region, or even a nation.

Time is an integral consideration in the diffusion process. Researchers are concerned with the amount of purchase time required for an individual consumer to adopt or reject a new product, with the rate of adoption, and with the identification of sequential adopters. The five adopter categories are innovators, early adopters, early majority, late majority, and laggards.

Marketing strategists try to control the rate of adoption through their new-product pricing policies. Marketers who wish to penetrate the market to achieve market leadership try to achieve wide adoption as quickly as possible by using low prices. Those who wish to recoup their developmental costs quickly use a skimming pricing policy but lengthen the adoption process.

The traditional adoption process model describes five stages through which an individual consumer passes to arrive at the decision to adopt or reject a new product: awareness, interest, evaluation, trial, and adoption. The newer innovation-decision-process model is a more general decision-making model that focuses on five stages of adoption: knowledge, persuasion, decision, implementation, and confirmation. Both models offer a framework for determining the importance of various information sources to consumers at the various decision stages.

New product marketers are vitally concerned with identifying the consumer innovator so that they may direct their promotional campaigns to the people who are most likely to try new products, adopt them, and influence others.

Consumer research has identified a number of consumer-related characteristics and personality traits that distinguish consumer innovators from later adopters. These serve as useful variables in the segmentation of markets for new-product introductions.

discussion questions

1. What are the essential differences between firm-, product-, market-, and consumer-oriented definitions of a new product? Which definition do you feel is most suitable for the marketer of a Caller ID telephone service that displays the caller's telephone number on the phone of the person being called? Explain your answer.

2. Would you classify each of the following as a continuous innovation, a dynamically continuous innovation, or a discontinuous innovation? Explain your answers.
   a. Sony's Video Walkman (a portable TV and VCR)
   b. A PC fax/modem that enables the user to send and receive faxes directly from a personal computer

c. A pocket-size cellular telephone

d. A plain paper laser desktop fax

e. Procter & Gamble's Tide free of dyes and perfumes

f. A Timex watch with a luminescent dial

g. An interactive TV home shopping service that offers consumers a video "mall of stores" and allows them to try clothing on electronic mannequins

h. Nonalcoholic beer

3. Select three of the products listed in Question 2 and describe the diffusion pattern that you expect each product to have. Justify your answers.

4. Describe how a manufacturer might use knowledge of the following product characteristics to speed up the acceptance of pocket-sized cellular telephones:

a. Relative advantage

b. Compatibility

c. Complexity

d. Trialability

e. Observability

5. Toshiba has introduced a new laptop computer that weighs seven pounds, has a color screen, and a powerful processor, into which a full-size desktop screen and keyboard can be easily plugged. How can the company use the diffusion-of-innovations framework to develop promotional, pricing, and distribution strategies targeted to:

a. Innovators

b. Early adopters

c. Early majority

d. Late majority

e. Laggards

6. Is the curve which describes the sequence and proportion of adopter categories among the population (Figure 18-7) similar in shape to the product life cycle curve? Explain your answer. How would you use both curves to develop a marketing strategy?

7. Compare and contrast the adoption and diffusion processes. Discuss each process in terms of the market acceptance of fax machines.

8. Sony is introducing a 27-inch TV with a built-in VCR, a picture-in-picture feature, and a feature that allows the viewer to simultaneously view frozen frames of the last signals received from twelve channels.

a. What recommendations would you make to Sony regarding the initial target market for the new TV model?

b. How would you identify the innovators for this product?

c. Select three characteristics of consumer innovators (as summarized in Table 18-4). Explain how Sony might use each of these characteristics to influence the adoption process and speed up the diffusion of the new product.

d. Should Sony follow a penetration or a skimming policy in introducing the product? Why?

exercises

1. Identify a product, service, or style that recently was adopted by you and/or some of your friends. Identify what type of innovation it is and describe its diffusion process up to this point in time. What are the characteristics of people who adopted it first? What types of people did not adopt it? What features of the product, service, or style are likely to determine its eventual success or failure?

2. With the advancement of digital technology, some companies plan to introduce interactive TV systems that will allow viewers to select films from "video libraries" and view them on demand. Among people you know, identify two who are likely to be the innovators for such a new service and construct consumer profiles using the characteristics of consumer innovators discussed in the text.

key words

- Adopter categories
- Adoption
- Adoption process
- Compatibility
- Complexity
- Consumer innovator profile
- Consumer innovators
- Continuous innovation
- Diffusion of innovations
- Diffusion process
- Discontinuous innovation
- Dynamically continuous innovation

- Early adopters
- Early majority
- Firm-, product-, market-, and consumer-oriented definitions of innovations
- Innovation-decision process
- Innovators
- Late majority
- Laggards
- Modern social system
- Nonadopters
- Observability
- Penetration policy

- Purchase time
- Rate of adoption
- Relative advantage
- Skimming policy
- Social system
- Stages in the adoption process
- Symbolic adopters
- Symbolic rejectors
- Trial adopters
- Trial rejectors
- Trialability

end notes

1. THOMAS S. ROBERTSON, "The Process of Innovation and the Diffusion of Innovation," *Journal of Marketing* 31, January 1967, 14–19.

2. EVERETT M. ROGERS, *Diffusion of Innovations*, 4th ed. (New York: Free Press, 1995); and HUBERT GATIGNON and THOMAS S. ROBERTSON, "Innovative Decision Processes," in Thomas S. Robertson and Harold H. Kassarjian, eds., *Handbook of Consumer Behavior* (Englewood Cliffs, NJ: Prentice Hall, 1991), 316–48.

3. S. RAM and HYUNG-SHIK JUNG "Innovativeness in Product Usage: A Comparison of Early Adopters and Early Majority," *Psychology and Marketing* 11, January-February 1994, 57–67; A. R. PETROSKY, "Gender and Use Innovation: An Inquiry Into the Socialization of Innovative Behavior," in Barbara B. Stern and George M. Zinkan, eds., *1995 AMA Educators' Proceedings* (Chicago: American Marketing Association, 1995), 299-307; KYUNGAE PARK and CARL L. DYER, "Consumer Use Innovative Behavior: An Approach Toward Its Causes," in Frank R. Kardes and Mita Sujan, eds., *Advances in Consumer Research* 22 (Provo, UT: Association for Consumer Research 1995), 566–72.

4. ROGERS, op. cit., 15–16.

5. TINA M. LOWREY, "The Use of Diffusion Theory in Marketing: A Qualitative Approach to Innovative Consumer Behavior," in Rebecca H. Holman and Michael R. Solomon, eds., *Advances in Consumer Research* 18 (Provo, UT: Association for Consumer Research, 1991), 644–50.

6. SUSAN H. HIGGINS and WILLIAM L. SHANKLIN, "Seeding Mass Market Acceptance for High Technology Consumer Products," *Journal of Consumer Marketing* 9, Winter 1992, 5–14.

7. LOWREY, op. cit., 649.

8. RICHARD GIBSON, "Shelf Stable Foods Seek to Freshen Sales," *The Wall Street Journal*, November 2, 1990, B1.

9. S. RAM, "A Model of Innovation Resistance," in M. Wallendorf and P. F. Anderson, eds., *Advances in Consumer Research* 14 (Provo, UT: Association for Consumer Research, 1987), 208–12.

10. PAUL A. HERBIG and HUGH KRAMER, "The Effect of Information Overload on the Innovation Choice Process," *Journal of Consumer Marketing* 11 (2), 1994, 45–54.

11. DOUGLAS MARTIN, "Lessons in AIDS Come with a Curl," *The New York Times*, March 14, 1992, B1.

12. GLORIA J. BARCZAK, DANIEL C. BELLO, and EVERETT S. WALLACE, "The Role Of Consumer Shows in New Product Adoption," *Journal of Consumer Marketing* 9, Spring 1992, 55–67.

13. EVERETT M. ROGERS and F. FLOYD SHOEMAKER, *Communication of Innovations*, 2nd ed. (New York: Free Press, 1971), 32–33; see also ELIZABETH C. HIRSCHMAN, "Consumer Modernity, Cognitive Complexity, Creativity and Innovativeness," in Richard P. Bagozzi et al., eds., *Mar-*

keting in the 80's: Changes and Challenges (Chicago: American Marketing Association, 1980), 135–39.

14. Suresh Subramanian and Robert A. Mittelstaedt, "Managing the New Product Introduction Process: Focusing on the Nonadopters of Innovations," in David W. Cravens and Peter R. Dickson, eds., *1993 AMA Educators' Proceedings* 4 (Chicago: American Marketing Association, 1993), 169–74.

15. Christopher M. Miller, Shelby H. McIntyre, and Murali K. Mantala, "Toward Formalizing Fashion Theory," *Journal of Marketing Research* 30, May 1993, 143.

16. Kenichi Ohmae, "Managing in a Borderless World," *Harvard Business Review*, May-June 1989, 152–61.

17. Rogers, op. cit., 162.

18. Wayne D. Hoyer and Nancy M. Ridgway, "Variety Seeking as an Explanation for Exploratory Purchase Behavior: A Theoretical Model," in Thomas C. Kinnear, ed., *Advances in Consumer Research* 11 (Provo, UT: Association for Consumer Research, 1984), 114–19.

19. Herbig and Kramer, op cit., 50.

20. David J. Burns and Robert F. Krampf, "A Semiotic Perspective on Innovative Behavior," in Robert L. King, ed., *Developments in Marketing Science* (Richmond, VA: Academy of Marketing Science, 1991), 32–35.

21. Peter Francese, "Cellular Consumers," *American Demographics*, August 1994, 30–56.

22. Bruce MacEvoy, "Change Leaders and the New Media," *American Demographics*, January 1994, 42–48.

23. Susan Mitchell, "Technophiles and technophobes," *American Demographics*, February 1994, 36–42.

This chapter draws together many of the psychological, social, and cultural concepts developed throughout the book into an overview framework for understanding how consumers make decisions. Unlike Chapter 18, which examined the dynamics of *new* product adoption, this chapter takes a broader perspective and examines consumer decision making in the context of all types of *consumption choices*, ranging from the consumption of new products to the use of old and established products. Also, it considers consumers' decisions not as the end point, but rather as the beginning point of a consumption process.

N*othing is more difficult, and therefore more precious, than to be able to decide.*

—Napoleon I

WHAT IS A DECISION?

Every day, each of us makes numerous decisions concerning every aspect of our daily lives. However, we generally make these decisions without stopping to think about *how* we make them and what is involved in the particular decision-making process itself. In the most general terms, a decision is the *selection of an option from two or more alternative choices*. In other words, for a person to make a decision, a choice of alternatives must be available. When a person has a choice between making a purchase and not making a purchase, a choice between brand X and brand Y, or a choice of spending time doing "A" or "B," that person is in a position to make a decision. On the other hand, if the consumer has no alternatives from which to choose and is literally *forced* to make a particular purchase or take a particular action (e.g., use a prescribed medication), then this single "no-choice" does not constitute a decision, such a no-choice decision is commonly referred to as a "Hobson's choice."

In actuality, no-choice purchase or consumption situations are fairly rare. You may recall from our discussion of core American cultural values (Chapter 14) that for consumers, *freedom* often is expressed in terms of a wide range of product choices. Thus, if there is almost always a choice, then there is almost always an opportunity for consumers to make decisions. Moreover, experimental consumer research reveals that providing consumers with a choice when there was originally none can be a very good business strategy, one that can substantially increase sales.[1] For instance, when a direct mail electrical appliance catalog displayed two coffee makers instead of just one (e.g., the original coffee maker at $149 and a "new" only slightly larger one at $229), the addition of the second *comparison* coffee maker seemed to stimulate consumer evaluation that significantly increased the sales of the original coffee maker.

Table 19-1 summarizes various types of consumption and purchase-related decisions. Although not exhaustive, this list does serve to demonstrate that the scope of consumer decision making is far broader than the mere selection of one brand from a number of brands.

LEVELS OF CONSUMER DECISION MAKING

Not all consumer decision-making situations receive (or require) the same degree of information search. If all purchase decisions required extensive effort, then consumer decision making would be an exhausting process that left little time for anything else. On the other hand, if all purchases were routine, then they would tend to be monotonous and would provide little pleasure or novelty. On a continuum of effort ranging from very high to very low, we can distinguish three specific levels of consumer decision making: **extensive problem solving**, **limited problem solving**, and **routinized response behavior**.[2]

Extensive Problem Solving

When consumers have no established criteria for evaluating a product category or specific brands in that category or have not narrowed the number of brands they will consider to a small, manageable subset, their decision-making efforts can be classified as *extensive problem solving*. At this level, the consumer needs a great deal of information to establish a set of criteria on which to judge specific brands and a correspondingly large amount of information concerning each of the brands to be considered.

table 19-1 Types of Purchase or Consumption Decisions

DECISION CATEGORY	ALTERNATIVE A	ALTERNATIVE B
BASIC PURCHASE OR CONSUMPTION DECISION	To purchase or consume a product (or service)	Not to purchase or consume a product (or service)
BRAND PURCHASE OR CONSUMPTION DECISIONS	To purchase or consume a specific brand	To purchase or consume another brand
	To purchase or consume one's usual brand	To purchase or consume another established brand (possibly with special features)
	To purchase or consume a basic model	To purchase or consume a luxury or status model
	To purchase or consume a new brand	To purchase or consume one's usual brand or some other established brand
	To purchase or consume a standard quantity	To purchase or consume more or less than a standard quantity
	To purchase or consume an on-sale brand	To purchase or consume a nonsale brand
	To buy or consume a national brand	To buy or consume a store brand
CHANNEL PURCHASE DECISIONS	To purchase from a specific type of store (e.g., a department store)	To purchase from some other type of store (e.g., a discount store)
	To purchase from one's usual store	To purchase from some other store
	To purchase in-home (by phone or catalog)	To purchase in-store merchandise
	To purchase from a local store	To purchase from a store requiring some travel (outshopping)
PAYMENT PURCHASE DECISIONS	To pay for the purchase with cash	To pay for the purchase with a credit card
	To pay the bill in full when it arrives	To pay for the purchase in installments

Limited Problem Solving

At this level of problem solving, consumers already have established the basic criteria for evaluating the product category and the various brands in the category. However, they have not fully established preferences concerning a select group of brands. Their search for additional information is more like "fine-tuning"; they must gather additional brand information to discriminate among the various brands.

Routinized Response Behavior

At this level, consumers have some experience with the product category and a well-established set of criteria with which to evaluate the brands they are considering. In some situations, they may search for a small amount of additional information; in others, they simply review what they already know.

Just how extensive a consumer's problem-solving task is depends on how well established his or her criteria for selection are, how much information he or she has about each brand being considered, and how narrow the set of brands is from which the choice will be made. Clearly, extensive problem solving implies that the consumer must seek more information to make a choice, while routinized response behavior implies little need for additional information.

MODELS OF CONSUMERS: FOUR VIEWS OF CONSUMER DECISION MAKING

Before presenting an overview model of how consumers make decisions, we will consider several schools of thought that depict consumer decision making in distinctly different ways. The term **models of consumers** refers to a general "view" or perspective as to how (and why) individuals behave as they do. Specifically, we will examine *models of consumers* in terms of the following four views: (1) an **economic view**, (2) a **passive view**, (3) a **cognitive view**, and (4) an **emotional view**.

An Economic View

In the field of theoretical economics, which portrays a world of perfect competition, the consumer has often been characterized as making *rational decisions*. This model, called the *economic man* theory, has been criticized by consumer researchers for a number of reasons. To behave rationally in the economic sense, a consumer would have to: (1) be aware of all available product alternatives, (2) be capable of correctly ranking each alternative in terms of its benefits and disadvantages, and (3) be able to identify the one best alternative. Realistically, however, consumers rarely have all of the information, or sufficiently accurate information, or even an adequate degree of involvement or motivation, to make the so-called "perfect" decision.

According to a leading social scientist, the classical economic model of an all-rational consumer is unrealistic for the following reasons: (a) people are limited by their existing skills, habits, and reflexes; (b) people are limited by their existing values and goals; and (c) people are limited by the extent of their knowledge.[3] Consumers operate in an imperfect world in which they do not maximize their decisions in terms of economic considerations, such as price-quantity relationships, marginal utility, or indifference curves. Indeed, the consumer generally is unwilling to engage in extensive decision-making activities and will settle, instead, for a "satisfactory" decision, one that is "good enough."[4] For this reason, the economic model is often rejected as too idealistic and simplistic.

A Passive View

Quite opposite to the rational economic view of consumers is the *passive* view that depicts the consumer as basically submissive to the self-serving interests and promotional efforts of marketers. In the passive view, consumers are perceived as impulsive and irrational purchasers, ready to yield to the aims and arms of marketers. At least to some degree, the passive model of the consumer was subscribed to by the hard-driving supersalesmen of old, who were trained to regard the consumer as an object to be manipulated. The following excerpt from a 1917 salesmanship text dramatically illustrates the long-held belief in the dominance of the salesman over the unresisting, somewhat passive consumer:

> *In the development of the selling process, there are four distinct stages. First, the salesman must secure the prospect's undivided attention. Secondly, this attention must be sustained and devel-*

oped into interest. Thirdly, this interest must be ripened into desire. And fourthly, all lingering doubts must be removed from the prospect's mind, and there must be implanted there a firm resolution to buy; in other words, the sale must be closed.[5]

The principal limitation of the passive model is that it fails to recognize that the consumer plays an equal, if not dominant, role in many buying situations—sometimes by seeking information about product alternatives and selecting the product that appears to offer the greatest satisfaction and at other times impulsively selecting a product that satisfies the mood or emotion of the moment. All that we have studied about motivation (see Chapter 4), selective perception (Chapter 6), learning (Chapter 7), attitudes (Chapters 8 and 9), communication (Chapter 10), and opinion leadership (Chapter 17) serves to support the proposition that consumers are rarely objects of manipulation. Therefore, this simple and single-minded view should also be rejected as unrealistic.

A Cognitive View

The third model portrays the consumer as a *thinking problem solver*. Within this framework, consumers frequently are pictured as either receptive to or actively searching for products and services that fulfill their needs and enrich their lives. The cognitive model focuses on the *processes* by which consumers seek and evaluate information about selected brands and retail outlets. Figure 19-1 on page 562 presents a basically cognitive appeal to American Express card users to consider the proposed advantages of the MasterCard Corporate card. In similar fashion, the ad also reminds current MasterCard Corporate card customers of the comparative value of their own card.

Within the context of the cognitive model, consumers are viewed as *information processors*. Information processing leads to the formation of preferences and, ultimately, to purchase intentions. Consumers also may use a *preference formation strategy* that is "other based," in which they allow another person (i.e., a trusted friend, an interior decorator, or an expert retail salesperson) to make the selection for them.[6]

In contrast to the economic view, the cognitive view recognizes that the consumer is unlikely to even attempt to obtain all available information about every choice. Instead, consumers are likely to cease their information-seeking efforts when they perceive that they have *sufficient information* about some of the alternatives to make a "satisfactory" decision. As this information-processing viewpoint suggests, consumers often develop short-cut decision rules (called **heuristics**) to facilitate the decision-making process. They also use decision rules to cope with exposure to too much information (i.e., **information overload**).[7]

The cognitive, or problem-solving, view describes a consumer who falls somewhere between the extremes of the economic and passive views, who does not (or cannot) have total knowledge about available product alternatives and therefore cannot make *perfect* decisions, but who nonetheless actively seeks information and attempts to make *satisfactory* decisions.

The cognitive model seems to capture the essence of a well-educated and involved consumer who seeks information on which to base consumption decisions. Our discussions, throughout the book, of specific aspects of consumer decision making have frequently depicted a consumer who is consistent with the cognitive, or problem-solving, view.

An Emotional View

Although long aware of the *emotional* or *impulsive* model of consumer decision making, marketers frequently prefer to think of consumers in terms of either economic or passive models. In reality, however, each of us is likely to associate deep feelings or emotions,

FIGURE 19-1

Ad Appealing to "Cognitive Man"
Courtesy of MasterCard

such as joy, fear, love, hope, sexuality, fantasy, and even a little "magic," with certain purchases or possessions. These feelings or emotions are likely to be highly involving. For instance, a person who misplaces a favorite fountain pen might go to great lengths to look for it, despite the fact that he or she has six others at hand. During World War II, there were many stories of how American GIs attributed protective powers to their Zippo cigarette lighters. Some even credited the lighters with saving their lives.

Possessions also may serve to preserve a sense of the past and act as familiar transitional objects when one is confronted with an uncertain future. For example, members of the armed forces invariably carry photographs of "the girl (or guy) back home," their families, and their lives in earlier times. These memorabilia frequently serve as hopeful reminders that normal activities will someday resume.[8]

If we were to reflect on the nature of our recent purchases, we might be surprised to realize just how impulsive some of them were. Rather than carefully searching, deliberating, and evaluating alternatives before buying, we are jut as likely to have made many of these purchases on impulse, on a whim, or because we were "emotionally driven."

When a consumer makes what is basically an *emotional* purchase decision, less emphasis is placed on the search for prepurchase information. Instead, more emphasis is placed on current mood and feelings ("Go for it!"). This is not to say that *emotional* decisions are not rational. As Chapter 4 pointed out, buying products that afford emotional satisfaction is a perfectly rational consumer decision. Furthermore, in the case of a good number of products, the choice of one brand over another has little to do with rationality.

For instance, many consumers buy designer label clothing, not because they *look* any better in them, but because status labels make them *feel* better. When a woman chooses between two dresses, it is quite natural that she decides in favor of the one that makes her *feel* better. This is a rational decision. Of course, if a man with a wife and three children purchases a two-seater Mazda Miata for himself, the neighbors might wonder about his level of rationality (although some might think it was deviously high). No such question would arise if the same man selected Grey Poupon mustard instead of Heinz mustard, although in both instances, each might be an impulsive, emotional purchase decision. Advertisers are recognizing with renewed interest the importance of emotional or *feeling-oriented* advertising. For instance, the ad in Figure 19-2 for Riviera by Buick is emotional in its message.

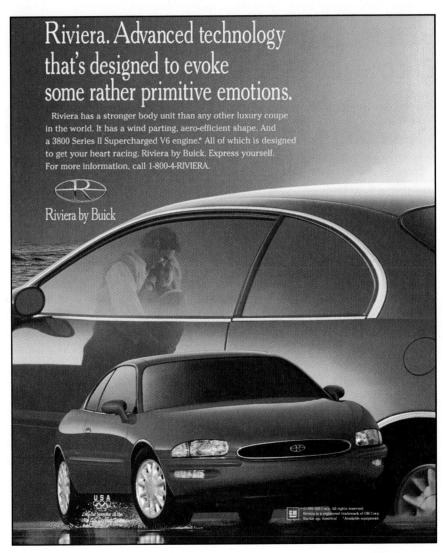

 FIGURE 19-2

An Emotional Appeal to Car Buyers
Reprinted with the permission of Buick Motor Division

Consumers' **moods** are also important to decision making. Mood can be defined as a "feeling state" or state of mind.[9] Unlike an emotion, which is a response to a particular environment, a mood is more typically an unfocused, *preexisting* state—already present at the time a consumer "experiences" an advertisement, a retail environment, a brand, or a product.[10]

Mood appears to be important to consumer decision making, because it impacts on *when* consumers shop, *where* they shop, and *whether* they shop alone or with others. It also is likely to influence *how* the consumer responds to actual shopping environments (i.e., at point of purchase).[11] Some retailers attempt to *create* a mood for shoppers, even though shoppers enter the store with a preexisting mood. Research suggests that a store's image or atmosphere can affect shoppers' moods; in turn, shoppers' moods can influence how long they stay in the store, as well as other behavior that retailers wish to encourage.[12]

In general, individuals in a positive mood recall more information about a product than those in a negative mood. As the results of one study suggest, however, inducing a positive mood at the point-of-purchase decision (e.g., through background music, point-of-purchase displays, etc.) is unlikely to have a meaningful impact on specific brand choice unless a previously stored brand evaluation already exists.[13]

A MODEL OF CONSUMER DECISION MAKING

This section presents an overview model of consumer decision making that reflects the *cognitive* (i.e., *problem-solving*) consumer and, to some degree, the *emotional consumer*. The model is designed to tie together many of the ideas on consumer decision making and consumption behavior discussed throughout the book. It does not presume to provide an exhaustive picture of the complexities of consumer decision making. Rather, it is designed to synthesize and coordinate relevant concepts into a significant whole. The model, presented in Figure 19-3, has three major components: input, process, and output.

Input

The *input* component of our consumer decision-making model draws on external influences that serve as sources of information about a particular product and influence a consumer's product-related values, attitudes, and behavior. Chief among these input factors are the **marketing mix activities** of organizations that attempt to communicate the benefits of their products and services to potential consumers, and the nonmarketing **sociocultural influences**, which, when internalized, affect the consumer's purchase decisions.

▲ **Marketing Inputs** The firm's marketing activities are a direct attempt to reach, inform, and persuade consumers to buy and use its products. These inputs to the consumer's decision-making process take the form of specific marketing mix strategies that consist of the product itself (including its package, size, and guarantees); mass-media advertising, direct marketing, personal selling, and other promotional efforts; pricing policy; and the selection of distribution channels to move the product from the manufacturer to the consumer.

Ultimately, the impact of a firm's marketing efforts in large measure is governed by the consumer's perception of these efforts. Thus, marketers do well to remain diligently alert to consumer perceptions by sponsoring consumer research, rather than to rely on the *intended* impact of their marketing messages.

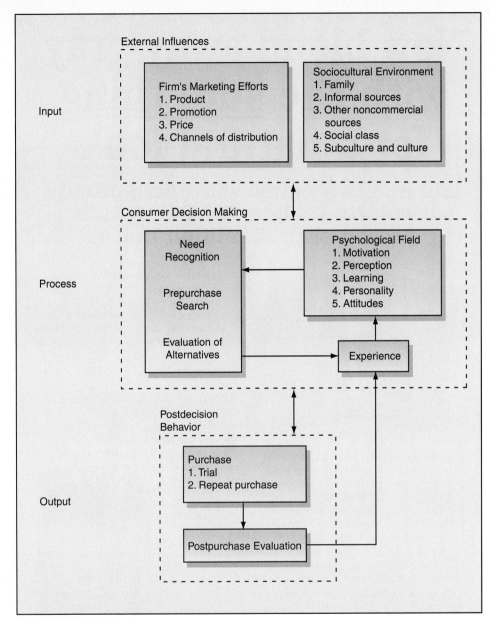

FIGURE 19-3

A Simple Model of
Consumer Decision
Making

▲ **Sociocultural Inputs** The second type of input, the *sociocultural environment*, also exerts a major influence on the consumer. Sociocultural inputs (examined in Part III) consist of a wide range of noncommercial influences. For example, the comments of a friend, an editorial in the newspaper, usage by a family member, or an article in *Consumer Reports* are all specific and direct noncommercial sources of information. The influences of social class, culture, and subculture, although less tangible, are important input factors that are internalized and affect how consumers evaluate and ultimately adopt (or reject) products.

The unwritten codes of conduct communicated by culture subtly indicate which consumption behavior should be considered "right" or "wrong" at a particular point in time. For example, until the 1970s, most men would not have considered using a hair coloring or hairspray. Now, use of these products is fairly commonplace among men (Figure 19-4).

FIGURE 19-4

Sociocultural Changes Impact on a Product's Acceptance
Courtesy of Combé Inc.

Unlike the firm's marketing efforts, sociocultural inputs do not necessarily *support* the purchase or consumption of a specific product but may influence consumers to *avoid* a product. For example, in some areas of the country and in some circles, animal rights activists have discouraged women from buying and wearing furs.

The cumulative impact of each firm's marketing efforts; the influence of family, friends, and neighbors; and society's existing code of behavior are all inputs that are likely to affect what consumers purchase and how they use what they buy. Because these influences may be directed to the individual or actively sought by the individual, a two-headed arrow is used to link the *input* and *process* segments of the model (Figure 19-3).

Process

The *process* component of the model is concerned with how consumers make decisions. To understand this process, we must consider the influence of the psychological concepts examined in Part II. The **psychological field** represents the internal influences (motivation, perception, learning, personality, and attitudes) that affect consumers' decision-making processes (what they need or want, their awareness of various product choices, their information-gathering activities, and their evaluation of alternatives). As pictured in the *process* component of the overview decision model (Figure 19-3), the act of making a consumer decision consists of three stages: (1) **need recognition**, (2) **prepurchase search**, and (3) **evaluation of alternatives**.

▲ **Need Recognition** The *recognition of a need* is likely to occur when a consumer is faced with a "problem." For example, consider the case of a newly retired couple, Arthur and Joanne, who have recently sold their home in a suburb of Boston and relocated to Tampa, Florida. Although Arthur is looking forward to spending time on the golf course, Joanne (a former kindergarten teacher) has been promising herself for the past 2 years that she was going to learn how to send and receive e-mail and access the Internet, using their home computer (which was formally used only for letter writing and for making birthday cards to send to the couple's grandchildren). Some of her friends who are already retired have told her how convenient and inexpensive it is to keep in touch via e-mail, and they have also spoken to her about the wealth of free information available on the Internet—everything from apple pie recipes to zoo visiting hours. One friend in particular, Robert (who is also a retired teacher), a "technology lover" (a person heavily interested in technology, including computers and the Internet), has been encouraging Joanne "to take the plunge and subscribe to an on-line service." Recent research exploring older consumers' on-line computer behavior has revealed two different types of "cyberseniors"—technology lovers versus technology users. Table 19-2 on page 568 presents a comparative portrait of cybersenior technology lovers, like Robert, and technology users (who are less involved with computers and on-line usage).[14]

Now, let us return to Joanne. She is also interested in being able to check on the performance of the couple's current investments in several stocks and mutual funds. Moreover, her friends have told her that the easiest way to gain access to e-mail and the Internet is by subscribing to an on-line service. (Joanne has *recognized a possible need* for an on-line service.)

Because Joanne had been talking about subscribing to an on-line service for a while, for Mother's Day her children and grandchildren presented her with a new, external 28,800 bps modem, and they even attached it to her computer and telephone line for her.

Among consumers, there seem to be two different need or problem recognition styles. Some consumers are *actual state* types, who perceive that they have a problem when a product fails to perform satisfactorily (e.g., a wristwatch no longer keeps accurate time). In contrast, other consumers are *desired state* types, for whom the desire for something new may trigger the decision process.[15] (Joanne, in her consideration of an on-line service, appears to be a *desired state* consumer.)

Need or problem recognition also can be viewed as either *simple* or *complex*. Simple problem recognition refers to needs that occur frequently and that can be dealt with almost automatically, such as becoming hungry and purchasing a candy bar from a vending machine. Complex problem recognition, however, is characterized as a state in which a problem develops over time, as the *actual state* and the *desired state* gradually move apart.[16] For example, after several years of driving a car, the owner may begin to consider trading it in for a new one to avoid growing repair bills. Figure 19-5 on page 569 shows an ad for the Psion palmtop, which presents the product as a perfect solution for a messy, heavy, and "disorganized" organizer.

table 19-2   Comparison Cybersenior Technology Lovers Versus Technology Users

	TECHNOLOGY USERS	TECHNOLOGY LOVERS
COMPUTER BEHAVIOR		
Time spent on-line	Less hours	More hours
On-line purchase behavior	Little	More
Other on-line activities	Less	More
RESOURCE AVAILABILITY		
Time available	No difference	No difference
Money available	No difference	No difference
Space available	No difference	No difference
Others (health, caregiver)	No difference	No difference
PERSONAL CHARACTERISTICS		
Attitudes	Less positive	More positive
Involvement	Less involvement	More involvement
Impact of computers	Less impact	More impact
Innovator	Less	More
Travel more than others	No difference	No difference
Happier than others	Less	More
Collector	No difference	No difference
Computers are magical	No difference	No difference
Financially betteroff	No	Yes
Healthier than others	No	Yes
Cognitive age vs. chronological age	The same	Younger
Computer experience	Less	More
Locus of control	Generally in control	Very much in control
Need for cognition	Less	More
Need for novelty	Less	More
Need to communicate	Perhaps (not computers)	Yes
Education	College	College
Life satisfaction	Less satisfied	More satisfied
Lifestyles	No differences	No differences

Source: CHARLES MCMELLON, LEON SCHIFFMAN, and ELAINE SHERMAN, "Consuming Cyberseniors: Some Personal and Situational Characteristics That Influence Their On-Line Behavior," Working Paper, City University of New York, Baruch College, 1996, 5.

▲ **Prepurchase Search** *Prepurchase search* begins when a consumer perceives a need that might be satisfied by the purchase and consumption of a product. The recollection of past experiences (drawn from long-term memory storage) might provide the consumer with adequate information to make the present choice. On the other hand, when the consumer has had no prior experience, he or she may have to engage in extensive search of the outside environment for useful information on which to base a choice.

The consumer usually searches his or her memory (the **psychological field** depicted in the model) before seeking external sources of information regarding a given consumption-related need. Past experience is considered an *internal* source of information. The greater the relevant past experience, the less external information the consumer is likely to need to reach a decision. Many consumer decisions are based on a combination of past experience (internal sources) and marketing and noncommercial information (external

FIGURE 19-5 ▼

An Ad Presenting a Product as a Solution to a Consumer's Need
Courtesy of Psion Inc.

sources). The degree of perceived risk can also influence this stage of the decision process (see Chapter 6). In high-risk situations, consumers are likely to engage in complex information search and evaluation; in low-risk situations, they are likely to use very simple search and evaluation tactics.

An examination of the external search effort associated with the purchase of different product categories (e.g., TVs, VCRs, or personal computers) found that, as the amount of total search effort increased, consumer attitudes toward shopping became more positive, and more time was made available for shopping. Not surprisingly, the external search effort was greatest for consumers who had the least amount of product category knowledge.[17] It follows that the less consumers know about a product category and the more important the purchase is to them, the more time they will make available and the more extensive their prepurchase search activity is likely to be. Additionally, by conducting focus groups and other consumer research on how expectations of a product influence consumers' subsequent interpretation and evaluation of product information, firms are assisted in their efforts to devise better products and to promote their products' strongest points.[18]

How much information a consumer will gather also depends on various situational factors. Consider the case of Joanne, the retired kindergarten teacher who has *recognized a need* for an on-line computer service. Although she has little exposure to such services (simply hearing about these services from friends and neighbors), she believes that such a service would provide her with the link she needs to the Internet and make it easy for her to send and receive e-mail and to keep track of her family's investments. If she feels that she must make an immediate purchase decision, then she might call each on-line vendor's 800 number, speak to a customer service representative, and select one on that basis alone. On the other hand, this type of rapid decision making does not suit everyone. Many consumers prefer to approach a new and somewhat complex decision with more deliberation and consideration of the options (i.e., considering competitors' services and/or options that can be added onto the core service). In addition to calling the on-line services to find out about the features and services offered by each, Joanne might go to the local library and try to find a number of magazine articles that have reviewed these services. She might also talk to some friends, neighbors (former and present), and/or relatives who she thinks subscribe to one or more on-line services. On the basis of selective perception, Joanne might start seeing ads and direct mail for computer on-line services (Figure 19-6).

As Table 19-3 on page 572 indicates, a number of factors are likely to increase consumers' prepurchase search. In the specific case of a computer on-line service, a service that is relatively new and evolving, Joanne does not have ongoing experience on which to draw. Furthermore, an on-line service is essentially a discretionary purchase, rather than a necessity, so there is no rush to make a decision.

Let's consider several of the prepurchase search alternatives open to a prospective subscriber to an on-line service. At the most fundamental level, search alternatives can be classified as either personal or impersonal. *Personal* search alternatives include more than a consumer's past experience with the product or service. They also include asking for information and advice from friends, relatives, co-workers, and sales representatives. For instance, Joanne might speak with a former colleague at the elementary school she taught at and ask her what she knows about on-line services. Because several of these services have been in existence for a number of years, Joanne might investigate whether *Consumer Reports, PC Magazine*, and/or some other publications might have rated the various on-line services.

Table 19-4 presents some of the sources of information that Joanne might use as part of her prepurchase search. Any or all of these sources might be used as part of a consumer's search process.

▲ **Evaluation of Alternatives** When evaluating potential alternatives, consumers tend to use two types of information: (1) a "list" of brands from which they plan to make their selection (the evoked set) and (2) the criteria they will use to evaluate each brand. Making a selection from a *sample* of all possible brands is a human characteristic that helps simplify the decision-making process.

EVOKED SET Within the context of consumer decision-making, the **evoked set** refers to the specific brands a consumer considers in making a purchase within a particular product category. (The evoked set is also called the *consideration set*.) A consumer's evoked set is distinguished from his or her **inept set**, which consists of brands the consumer excludes from purchase consideration because they are felt to be unacceptable (e.g., they are seen as "inferior"), and from the **inert set**, which consists of brands the consumer is indifferent toward because they are perceived as not having any particular advantages. Regardless of the

total number of brands in a product category, a consume's evoked set tends to be quite small on average, often consisting of only three to five brands.[19]

The evoked set consists of the small number of brands the consumer is familiar with, remembers, and finds acceptable. Figure 19-7 on page 573 depicts the evoked set as a subset of all available brands in a product category. As the figure indicates, it is essential that a product be part of a consumer's evoked set if it is to be considered at all. The five terminal positions in the model that do *not* end in purchase would appear to have perceptual problems. For example: (1) Brands may be *unknown* because of the consumer's selective exposure to advertising media and selective perception of advertising stimuli: (2) Brands may be *unacceptable* because of poor qualities or attributes or inappropriate positioning in either advertising or product characteristics: (3) Brands may be perceived as not having any special benefits and are regarded *indifferently* by the consumer: (4) Brands may be *overlooked* because they have not been clearly positioned or sharply targeted at the consumer market segment under study: and (5) Brands may not be selected because they are perceived by consumers as *unable to satisfy* perceived needs as fully as the brand that is chosen.

In each of these instances, the implication for marketers is that promotional techniques should be designed to impart a more favorable, perhaps more relevant product image to the target consumer. This may also require a change in product features or attributes (more or better features).

CRITERIA USED FOR EVALUATING BRANDS The criteria consumers use to evaluate the brands that constitute their evoked sets usually are expressed in terms of important

table 19-3 Factors That Are Likely to Increase Prepurchase Search

PRODUCT FACTORS

Long interpurchase time (a long-lasting or infrequently used product)
Frequent changes in product styling
Frequent price changes
Volume purchasing (large number of units)
High price
Many alternative brands
Much variation in features

SITUATIONAL FACTORS

Experience
   First-time purchase
   No past experience because the product is new
   Unsatisfactory past experience within the product category
Social Acceptability
   The purchase is for a gift
   The product is socially visible
Value-Related Considerations
   Purchase is discretionary rather than necessary
   All alternatives have both desirable and undesirable consequences
   Family members disagree on product requirements or evaluation of alternatives
   Product usage deviates from important reference group
   The purchase involves ecological considerations
   Many sources of conflicting information

PRODUCT FACTORS

Demographic Characteristics of Consumer
   Well-educated
   High-income
   White-collar occupation
   Under 35 years of age
Personality
   Low dogmatic
   Low-risk perceiver (broad categorizer)
   Other personal factors, such as high product involvement and enjoyment of
      shopping and search

table 19-4 Alternative Prepurchase Information Sources for an On-Line Service

PERSONAL	IMPERSONAL
Friends	Newspaper articles
Neighbors	Magazine Articles
Relatives	Consumer Reports
Co-workers	Direct mail brochures and trial offer from
Computer store salespeople	on-line vendors
Calling (800-number) the on-line vendor	Information from product advertisements

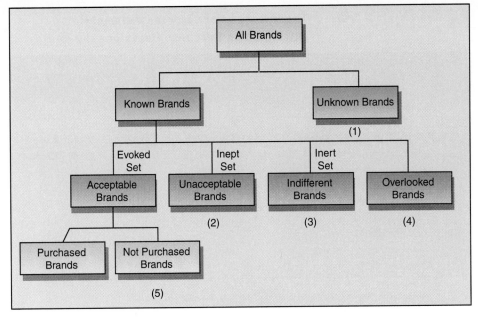

FIGURE 19-7

The Evoked Set as a Subset of All Brands in a Product Class

product attributes. Examples of product attributes that consumers have used as criteria in evaluating nine product categories are listed in Table 19-5.

Table 19-6 on page 574 presents a comparison of consumers by different age groups in terms of their ratings of attributes that "strongly influence" their automobile purchase

table 19-5   Possible Product Attributes Used as Purchase Criteria for Nine Product Categories

PERSONAL COMPUTERS	SNEAKERS	WRISTWATCHES
Processing speed	Styling	Watchband
Price	Color	Alarm feature
Type of display	Price	Price
Hard-disk size	Air-sole	Water-resistant
Amount of memory	Hightop or lowtop	Quartz movement
Laptop or desktop	Purpose (e.g., basketball, tennis)	Size of dial

TELEPHONES	COLOR TVS	FROZEN DINNERS
Size	Picture quality	Taste
Warranty	Length of warranty	Type of main course
Memory dialing	Cable-ready	Type of side dishes
Hold button	Price	Speakerphone
Cabinet style	Size of screen	Preparation requirements

35-MM CAMERAS	FOUNTAIN PENS	MEN'S DRESS SHIRTS
Autofocus	Balance	Size
Built-in flash	Price	Fabric
Automatic film loading	Gold nib	Color
Lens type	Smoothness	Collar style
Size and weight	Ink reserve	Cuff style

table 19-6   The Influence of Selected Automobile Attributes on Purchase Decisions (by Age)

	PERCENT RATING AS "STRONGLY INFLUENCE": AGE CATEGORIES		
	16–29	30–49	50+
Reliable, works like it should	68	85	73
Long-lasting, durable	63	78	72
Easy to fix, maintain	39	49	53
Low price	40	42	30
Easy to use	38	40	46
Easy to purchase	33	31	25
Known, trusted brand name	26	32	43
Latest technology, styles	20	13	14
Many options, features	18	11	13

Source: LAURIE PETERSON, "The Strategic Shopper," *Adweek's Marketing Week* (March 30, 1992), 18.

decisions. Although all consumers, regardless of age, value cars that are reliable and durable, there are some age differences. For instance, while the youngest car buyers (those from 16 to 29 years of age) are more concerned with owning cars that offer the latest technology, the oldest car buyers (those 50 years of age and older) appear to be the *least* price-conscious, to rely more on trusted brand names, and to value "easy-to-use" factors. Because baby boomers are moving into this older-age cohort, automobile makers are increasingly human engineering their cars to make them easier to get into and out of, as well as easier to use.

When a company knows that consumers will be evaluating alternatives, they sometimes advertise in a way that recommends the criteria that consumers should use in assessing product or service options. For example, an ad for The Bank of New York (Figure 19-8) challenges the reader to compare the home equity credit lines offered by different banks in terms of a number of specific criteria.

We have probably all gone through the experience of comparing or evaluating different brands or models of a product and finding the one that just feels, looks, and/or performs "right." Interestingly, research shows that when consumers discuss such "right products," there is little or no mention of price; brand names are not often top-of-mind; items often reflect personality characteristics or childhood experiences; and it is often "love at first sight." In one recent study, the products claimed by research participants to "just feel right" included Big Bertha golf clubs, old leather briefcases, Post-it notes, and the Honda Accord.[20]

Let's return for a moment to Joanne, the retiree who is contemplating subscribing to a computer on-line service. After calling the major on-line service companies for literature on their services, reading the direct mail she received at home and a number of magazine articles, and talking to a few knowledgeable friends, Joanne's evoked set might consist of America Online, Prodigy, and CompuServe.

On the basis of her recently acquired information, Joanne has tentatively decided that the on-line service she subscribes to should have the following three features: local telephone number access, the ability to "surf the net," and the availability of stock market and mutual fund information that she would need to monitor her investments. Evaluating the information supplied by each of the on-line services, Joanne might mentally or on

FIGURE 19-8

Ad Suggesting Criteria
for Decision Making
Courtesy of The Bank of New
York

SPRING LOAN SALE *Apply Today!*

We're so confident we've got the best home equity credit line, we're not afraid to help you shop around.

The Bank of New York		Your bank	
Low 6-mo. intro. variable rate (6.95%*A.P.R.)	✔		
Low regular rate (Prime + 1.40%*)	✔		
Low rate fixed cap**	✔		
No points, fees or closing costs	✔		
Tax deductibility***	✔		
No other banking relationship required	✔		
Same low rates for any size credit line	✔		
60 minute approval	✔		
Apply by phone 1-800-HOUR-LOAN Mon.-Sat. 8:30AM-9PM and Sunday 1PM-8PM	✔		

THE BANK OF NEW YORK
MEMBER FDIC

We're making it hard to bank anywhere else.

Another bank		Yet another bank	

An Equal Housing Lender — New accounts only. Response in 60 minutes or less. *Variable introductory A.P.R. offer of Prime -2.05% is based on the Prime Rate published on the last Monday of each month in The Wall Street Journal. Following the introductory period, the rate without closing costs for houses and condominiums will be calculated at 1.40% above Prime. Introductory A.P.R. is 6.95% and regular A.P.R. is 10.40% based on Prime Rate of 9.00% — current as of April 4, 1995. For co-ops, the rate following the introductory period will be calculated at 1.80% above Prime. Regular A.P.R. for co-ops is currently 10.80%. All rates current as of April 4, 1995. Rates subject to change without notice. **Rate cap of 16.50% applies to houses and condominiums only. ***Consult your tax advisor to determine the deductibility of your finance charges. Deductibility may not apply to co-op loans. Application fee of $250.00 will not be refunded if your application is declined, withdrawn or canceled. Property must be owner-occupied. (Co-op accounts available only in NY.) EquityLink is a registered service mark of The Bank of New York. ©1995 The Bank of New York. Member FDIC

paper construct a table that compares the availability of specific features of the three services in her evoked set (see Table 19-7).

As part of her search process, Joanne also has acquired information about other relevant issues (or attributes) that could influence her final choice (again, see Table 19-7). For example, she has learned that both America Online and Prodigy offer 24-hour, 7-days-a-week technical support; CompuServe offers more business and reference features; and America Online has the most user-friendly interface. Additionally, whereas America Online and CompuServe will allow her to use her modem at its highest speed of 28,000 bps, Prodigy's maximum user speed was at the time of her decision only 14,400 bps.[21]

CONSUMER DECISION RULES Consumer decision rules often referred to as *heuristics, decision strategies*, and *information-processing strategies* are procedures used by consumers to facilitate brand (or other consumption-related) choices. These rules reduce the burden of making complex decisions by providing guidelines or routines that make the process less taxing.

Consumer decision rules have been broadly classified into two major categories: **compensatory** and **noncompensatory decision rules**. In following a *compensatory decision rule*, a consumer evaluates brand options in terms of each relevant attribute and computes a weighted or summated score for each brand. The computed score reflects the brand's relative merit as a potential purchase choice. The assumption is that the consumer will select the brand that scores highest among the alternatives evaluated. Referring to Table 19-8, it is clear that using a compensatory decision rule, America Online scores highest.

A unique feature of a compensatory decision rule is that it allows a positive evaluation of a brand on one attribute to balance out a negative evaluation on some other attribute. For example, a positive assessment of the energy-savings made possible by a particular brand or type of light bulb may offset an unacceptable assessment in terms of the bulb's diminished light output.

table 19-7

Comparison of Selected Characteristics of Three Competitive On-Line Services*

FEATURE	AMERICA ONLINE	COMPUSERVE	PRODIGY
Monthly fee	$9.95/5 hr	$9.95/5 hr	$9.95/5 hr
Additional hours	$2.95	$2.95	$2.95
Maximum connect speed	28,800 bps	28,800 bps	14,400 bps
24-hour, 7 days/week technical support	Yes	No	Yes
On-line banking	Yes	No	Yes
Full Internet connection	Yes	Yes	Yes
Allows use of good Web browsing software	Yes	No	No
Can check stocks and mutual funds	Yes	Yes	Yes
Personalized investment news & services	No	Yes (Executive News Service 25¢/min to download)	Yes (Quote Track, $2.95/h4)

*As of May 30, 1996.

table 19-8   Hypothetical Ratings for On-Line Services*

FEATURE**	AMERICA ONLINE	COMPUSERVE	PRODIGY
Monthly fees	6	6	6
Maximum connect speed	10	10	5
24-hour, 7 days/week technical support	7	5	7
On-line banking	6	4	6
Full Internet connection	9	9	9
Allows use of good Web browsing software	10	5	5
Can check stocks and mutual funds	10	10	10
Personalized investment news & services	5	7	7
Totals	63	56	55

*Evaluations are on a ten-point scale; a higher number indicates a higher rating.

**As of May 30, 1996.

In contrast, *noncompensatory decision rules* do not allow consumers to balance positive evaluations of a brand on one attribute against a negative evaluation on some other attribute. For instance, in the case of an energy-saving light bulb, the product's negative (unacceptable) rating on its light output would not be offset by a positive evaluation of its energy savings. Instead, this particular light bulb would be disqualified from further consideration. If Joanne's choice of an online service was based on maximum connection speed (refer again to Table 19-7), a noncompensatory decision rule would have eliminated Prodigy.

Three noncompensatory rules are considered briefly here: the *conjunctive* rule, the *disjunctive* rule, and the *lexicographic* rule.

In following a **conjunctive decision rule**, the consumer establishes a separate, minimally acceptable level as a cutoff point for each attribute. If any particular brand falls below the cutoff point on any one attribute, the brand is eliminated from further consideration. Because the conjunctive rule can result in several acceptable alternatives, it becomes necessary in such cases for the consumer to apply an additional decision rule to arrive at a final selection; for example, to accept the first satisfactory brand. The conjunctive rule is particularly useful in quickly reducing the number of alternatives to be considered. The consumer can then apply another, more refined decision rule to arrive at a final choice.

The **disjunctive rule** is the "mirror image" of the conjunctive rule. In applying this decision rule, the consumer also establishes a separate, minimally acceptable level as the cutoff point for each attribute (which may be higher than the one normally established for a conjunctive rule). In this case, if a brand alternative meets or exceeds the cutoff established for any one attribute, it is accepted. Here again, a number of brands might exceed the cutoff point, producing a situation in which another decision rule is required. When this occurs, the consumer may accept the first satisfactory brand as the final choice or apply some other, perhaps more suitable, decision rule.

In following a **lexicographic decision rule**, the consumer first ranks the attributes in terms of perceived relevance or importance. The consumer then compares the various brand alternatives in terms of the single attribute that is considered most important. If one brand scores sufficiently high on this top-ranked attribute (regardless of the score on any of the other attributes), it is selected and the process ends. When there are two or more surviving brand alternatives, the process is repeated with the second highest-ranked attribute (and so on), until reaching the point that one of the brands is selected because it exceeds the others on a particular attribute.

With the lexicographic rule, the highest-ranked attribute (the one applied first) may reveal something about the individual's basic consumer (or shopping) orientation. For instance, a "buy the best" rule might indicate that the consumer is *quality oriented*; a "buy the most prestigious brand" rule might indicate that the consumer is *status oriented*; a "buy the least expensive" rule might reveal that the consumer is *economy minded*. The ad for Saab presented in Figure 19-9 appeals to those consumers who especially value *safety and*

FIGURE 19-9

Saab Appealing to Consumers Who Appreciate Safety and Practicality
Courtesy of Saab Cars USA, Inc.

practicality in an automobile, yet do not assume that such a car also cannot be exciting and fun to drive.

A variety of decision rules appear quite commonplace. According to a consumer survey, nine out of ten shoppers who go to the store for frequently purchased items possess a specific shopping strategy for saving money. The consumer segment and the specific shopping rules that these segments employ are:[22]

1. Practical loyalists—*those who look for ways to save on the brands and products they would buy anyway.*

2. Bottom-line price shoppers—*those who buy the lowest-priced item, with little or no regard for brand.*

3. Opportunistic switchers—*those who use coupons or sales to decide among brands and products that fall within their evoked set.*

4. Deal hunters—*those who look for the best "bargain" and are not brand-loyal.*

We have considered only the most basic of an almost infinite number of consumer decision rules. Most of the decision rules described here can be combined to form new variations, e.g., conjunctive-compensatory, conjunctive-disjunctive, or disjunctive-conjunctive. It is likely that for many purchase decisions, consumers maintain in long-term memory overall evaluations of the brands in their evoked sets. This would make assessment by individual attributes unnecessary. Instead, the consumer would simply select the brand with the highest perceived overall rating. This type of synthesized decision rule is known as the **affect referral decision rule** and may represent the simplest of all rules.

Table 19-9 summarizes the essence of many of the decision rules considered in this chapter, in terms of the kind of mental statements that Joanne, our retired school teacher, might make in selecting an on-line information service.

LIFESTYLES AS A CONSUMER DECISION STRATEGY An individual's or family's decisions to be committed to a particular lifestyle (e.g., devoted followers of a particular religion) impacts on a wide range of specific everyday consumer behavior. For instance, The Trends Research Institute has identified "voluntary simplicity" as one of the top 10 lifestyle trends of the 1990s.[23] They estimate that by the year 2000, 15 percent of all "boomers" will be seeking a simpler lifestyle with reduced emphasis on ownership and possessions. Voluntary simplifiers are making do with less clothing, fewer credit cards (with no outstanding balances), and moving to smaller, yet still adequate homes or apartments, in less populated communities. Most importantly, it is not that these consumers can

table 19-9   Hypothetical Use of Popular Decision Rules in Making an On-Line Service Decision

DECISION RULE	MENTAL STATEMENT
Compensatory rule	"I selected the on-line service that came out best when I balanced the good ratings against the bad ratings."
Conjunctive rule	"I picked the on-line service that had no bad features."
Disjunctive rule	"I selected the on-line service that excelled in at least one attribute."
Lexicographic rule	"I looked at the feature that was the most important to me and chose the on-line service that ranked highest on that attribute."
Affect referral rule	"Everything they do is outstanding, so I decided to buy their on-line service."

no longer afford their affluence or "lifestyle of abundance"; rather, they are seeking new, "reduced," less extravagant lifestyles. As part of this new lifestyle commitment some individuals are seeking less stressful and lower salary careers or jobs. In a recent telephone survey, for example, 33 percent of those contacted claimed that they would be willing to take a 20 percent pay cut in return for working fewer hours.[24]

INCOMPLETE INFORMATION AND NONCOMPARABLE ALTERNATIVES In many choice situations, consumers face incomplete information on which to base decisions and must use alternative strategies to cope with the missing elements. Missing information may result from advertisements or packaging that mentions only certain attributes, the consumer's own imperfect memory of attributes for nonpresent alternatives, or because some attributes are experiential and can only be evaluated after product use.[25] There are at least four alternative strategies that consumers can adopt for coping with missing information:[26]

1. *Consumers may delay the decision until missing information is obtained. This strategy is likely to be used for high-risk decisions.*

2. *Consumers may ignore missing information and decide to continue with the current decision rule (e.g., compensatory or noncompensatory), using the available attribute information.*

3. *Consumers may change the customarily used decision strategy to one which better accommodates missing information.*

4. *Consumers may infer ("construct") the missing information.*

In discussing consumer decision rules, we have assumed that a choice is made from among the brands evaluated. Of course, a consumer also may conclude that none of the alternatives offers sufficient benefits to warrant purchase. If this were to occur with a necessity, such as a refrigerator, the consumer would probably either lower his or her expectations and settle for the best of the available alternatives or seek information about additional brands, hoping to find one that more closely meets predetermined criteria. On the other hand, if the purchase is more discretionary (e.g., a second or third pair of jeans), the consumer probably would postpone the purchase. In this case, information gained from the search up to that point would be transferred to long-term storage (in the psychological field) and retrieved and reintroduced as input if and when the consumer regains interest in making such a purchase.

It should be noted that, in applying decision rules, consumers may at times attempt to compare dissimilar (noncomparable) alternatives. For example, a consumer may be undecided about whether to buy a new car or remodel her kitchen, because she can afford either, but not both, expenditures. Another example: A consumer may try to decide between buying a new raincoat or a new pair of shoes. When there is great dissimilarity in the alternative ways of allocating available funds, consumers abstract the products to a level in which comparisons are possible.[27] In the examples cited above, a consumer might weigh the alternatives (new car versus remodeled kitchen or raincoat versus shoes) in terms of which alternative would offer the most pleasure or which, if either, is more of a "necessity."

A SERIES OF DECISIONS Although we have discussed the purchase decision as if it were a single decision, in reality, a purchase can involve a number of decisions. For example, when purchasing an automobile, consumers are involved in multiple decisions such as choosing the make or country of origin of the car (e.g., foreign versus domestic), the dealer, the financing, and particular options. In the case of a replacement automobile, these decisions must be preceded by a decision as to whether or not to trade in one's current car. A study found that the attitudes and search behavior of consumers who replace their cars after only a few years (early replacement buyers) differ greatly from those who replace their cars after many years (late replacement buyers). In particular, early car replacement buyers were more concerned with the car's styling and image or status and were less concerned with cost. In contrast, late car replacement buyers undertook a greater amount of information and dealer search and were greatly influenced by friends.[28]

DECISION RULES AND MARKETING STRATEGY An understanding of which decision rules consumers apply in selecting a particular product or service is useful to marketers concerned with formulating a promotional program. A marketer familiar with the prevailing decision rule can prepare a promotional message in a format that would facilitate consumer information processing. The promotional message might even suggest how potential consumers should make a decision. For instance, a direct mail piece for a new computer notebook might tell potential consumers "what to look for in a new notebook." This mail piece might specifically ask consumers to consider the attributes of screen size, battery life, price, weight, pointing device, and amount of memory in their purchase decision process.

CONSUMPTION VISION Researchers have recently proposed "consumption vision" as a nonorthodox, but potentially accurate, portrayal of decision making for those situations in which the consumer has little experience and problems are not well-structured, as well as in which there is a considerable amount of emotion. Under such circumstances, the consumer may turn to a *"consumption vision,"* a mental picture or visual image of specific usage outcomes and/or consumption consequences."[29] Such visions (e.g., a prospective bride envisioning a garden wedding versus a wedding taking place on a boat or a consumer visualizing a skiing vacation versus a Caribbean vacation) allow consumers to imagine or vicariously participate in the consumption of the product or service *prior* to making an actual decision. After "trying out" a number of different alternatives in one's mind, so to speak, the consumer then makes his or her decision.[30]

Output

The *output* portion of the consumer decision-making model concerns two closely associated kinds of postdecision activity: **purchase behavior** and **postpurchase evaluation**. The objective of both activities is to increase the consumer's satisfaction with his or her purchase.

▲ **Purchase Behavior** Consumers make three types of purchases: *trial purchases, repeat purchases*, and *long-term commitment purchases*. When a consumer purchases a product (or brand) for the first time and buys a smaller quantity than usual, this purchase would be considered a trial. Thus, a trial is the exploratory phase of purchase behavior in which consumers attempt to evaluate a product through direct use. For instance, when consumers purchase a new brand of mouthwash about which they may be uncertain, they are likely to purchase smaller trial quantities than if it were a familiar brand. Consumers can also be encouraged to try a new product through such promotional tactics as free samples, coupons, and/or sale prices. A recent study by the Promotion Marketing Association of America found that coupons substantially influenced initial trial of products like ready-to-eat cereal, bar soap, and salted snacks.[31]

When a new brand in an established product category (toothpaste, chewing gum, or cola) is found by trial to be more satisfactory or better than other brands, consumers are likely to repeat the purchase. Repeat purchase behavior is closely related to the concept of *brand loyalty*, which most firms try to encourage, because it contributes to greater stability in the marketplace (see Chapter 7). Unlike trial, in which the consumer uses the product on a small scale and without any commitment, a repeat purchase usually signifies that the product meets with the consumer's approval and that he or she is willing to use it again and in larger quantities.

Trial, of course, is not always feasible. For example, with most durable goods (clothes dryers, freezers, or microwave ovens), a consumer usually moves directly from evaluation to a long-term commitment (through purchase), without the opportunity for an actual trial.

Consider Joanne and her decision concerning the selection of an on-line service. If she wanted to personally try each of the services in her evoked set—America Online, Prodigy, and CompuServe—she could receive a free trial disk and several free hours of usage from each of these on-line vendors. However, she feels that setting up software for each service on her home computer would be just too much of a hassle for her. Instead, she asks around her retirement community and finds individuals who subscribe to each. She then visits each of these individuals' homes to see, firsthand, each on-line service. (Joanne discovers that users of on-line services delight in showing others their computer systems and what their on-line services have to offer.) Joanne is especially impressed with how easy it is to "surf the net," using the version of browser software that America Online users can download and use for free. So she decides that she will try America Online, using the disk that she received in the mail that offers her 10 free hours of trial usage.

▲ **Postpurchase Evaluation** As consumers use a product, particularly during a trial purchase, they evaluate its performance in light of their own expectations. There are three possible outcomes of these evaluations: (1) Actual performance matches expectations, leading to a neutral feeling: (2) Performance exceeds expectations, causing what is known as **positive disconfirmation of expectations** (which leads to satisfaction): and (3) Performance is below expectations, causing **negative disconfirmation of expectations** and dissatisfaction.[32] For each of these three outcomes, consumers' expectations and satisfaction are closely linked; that is, consumers tend to judge their experience against their expectations when performing a *postpurchase evaluation*. The two go hand in hand.

An important component of postpurchase evaluation is the reduction of uncertainty or doubt that the consumer might have had about the selection. As part of their postpurchase analyses, consumers try to reassure themselves that their choice was a wise one; that is, they attempt to reduce **postpurchase cognitive dissonance**. As Chapter 9 indicated, they do this by adopting one of the following strategies: they may rationalize the decision as being wise; they may seek advertisements that support their choice and avoid those of competitive brands; they may attempt to persuade friends or neighbors to buy the same brand (and thus confirm their own choice); or they may turn to other satisfied owners for reassurance.

The degree of postpurchase analysis that consumers undertake depends on the importance of the product decision and the experience acquired in using the product. When the product lives up to expectations, they probably will buy it again. When the product's performance is disappointing or does not meet expectations, however, they will search for more suitable alternatives. Thus, the consumer's postpurchase evaluation "feeds back" as *experience* to the consumer's psychological field and serves to influence future related decisions.

What was Joanne's postpurchase evaluation of America Online? Joanne was pleasantly surprised at how easy it was to install America Online on her computer. She just followed the directions on the disk and then followed the directions on the screen, and within about 10 minutes she was on-line and had her own e-mail address and password. In no more than about 30 minutes from the time she first put the America Online install disk in her disk drive, she had composed e-mail messages to several of her friends and had sent them; in fact, she could not wait to start receiving their replies, now that they would have her e-mail address.

She also had even more fun "surfing the net" than she ever thought she would. Joanne also found the experience of being able to send e-mail to her many friends (and some relatives) anywhere in the world to be a great time and cost saver. Additionally, she was very impressed with the amount of investment information she could obtain from

America Online—information that would help her both select and keep track of her stocks, bonds, and mutual funds. Although America Online did not offer her specialized, extra-cost investment news and services, she found that the investment services it did offer were more than adequate for her needs. For example, she found that she could enter up to 100 investments into her America Online "portfolio" and each time she opened her portfolio screen she would find updated quotes for each one.

In summary, Joanne is thus far thrilled with her experiences as an America Online user, and she wonders how she ever got along without it!

CONSUMER GIFTING BEHAVIOR

In terms of both dollars spent each year and how they make givers and receivers feel, gifts are a particularly interesting part of consumer behavior. Products and services chosen as gifts represent more than ordinary "everyday" purchases. Because of their symbolic meaning, they are associated with such important events as Mother's day, births and birthdays, engagements, weddings, graduations, and many other accomplishments and milestones.

Gifting behavior has been defined as "the process of *gift exchange* that takes place between a giver and a recipient."[33] The definition is broad in nature and embraces gifts given voluntarily (e.g., "Just to let you know I'm thinking of you"), as well gifts that are an obligation (e.g., "I had to get him a gift").[34] It includes gifts given to (and received from) others and gifts to oneself, i.e., **self-gifts**.

Still further, gifting is an act of symbolic communication, with explicit and implicit meanings ranging from congratulations, love, and regret to obligation and dominance. The nature of the relationship between gift giver and gift receiver is an important consideration in choosing a gift. Table 19-10 presents a model of the relationships between various combinations of gift givers and gift receivers in the consumer gifting process. The model reveals the following five gifting subdivisions: (1) intergroup gifting, (2) intercategory gifting, (3) intragroup gifting, (4) interpersonal gifting, and (5) intrapersonal gifting.

Intergroup gifting behavior occurs whenever one group exchanges gifts with another group (e.g., one family and another). You will recall from Chapter 12 that the process and outcome of family decision making is different from individual decision making. Similarly, gifts given to families will be different than those given to individual family members. For example, a "common" wedding gift for a bride *and* a groom may include products for setting up a household, rather than a gift that would personally be used by either the bride or the groom. When it comes to *intercategory gifting*, either an individual is

table 19-10   Five Giver-Receiver Gifting Subdivisions

GIVERS	RECEIVERS		
	"OTHER"		
	INDIVIDUAL	GROUP	SELF*
INDIVIDUAL	Interpersonal gifting	Intercategory gifting	Intrapersonal gifting
GROUP	Intercategory gifting	Intergroup gifting	Intragroup gifting

*This "SELF" is either singular self ("me") or plural self ("us").

Source: Based on Deborah Y. Cohn, and Leon G. Schiffman, "Gifting: A Taxonomy of Private Realm Giver and Recipient Relationships," Working Paper, City University of New York, Baruch College, 1996, 2–7.

giving a gift to a group (e.g., a single friend is giving a couple an anniversary gift) or a group is giving an individual a gift (e.g., friends chip in and give another friend a joint birthday gift). The gift selection strategies "Buy for joint recipients" or "Buy with someone" (creating intercategory gifting) are especially useful when it comes to a difficult recipient situation (e.g., "Nothing seems to satisfy her").[35] These strategies can also be applied to reduce some of the time pressure associated with shopping for the great many gifts exchanged during the American Christmas season gift-giving ritual. For example, a consumer may choose to purchase five intercategory gifts for five aunt and uncle pairs (intercategory gifting), instead of buying ten personal gifts for five aunts and five uncles (interpersonal gifting). In this way, less time, money, and effort may be expended. Figure 19-10 shows a Radio Shack ad, targeted at grandparents, that describes a service, Gift Express®, in which gifts are gift wrapped and FedExed to the recipient for a nominal charge.

FIGURE 19-10

Radio Shack Is
Targeting Grandparents
as Gift-Givers
Courtesy of Tandy Corporation

An *intragroup gift* can be characterized by the sentiment "we gave this to ourselves," that is, a group gives a gift to itself or its members. For example, a dual-income couple may find that their demanding work schedules limit leisure time spent together as husband and wife. Therefore, an anniversary gift ("to us") of a "getaway weekend" would be an example of a intragroup gift. It would also remedy the couple's problem of not spending enough time together. In contrast, *interpersonal gifting* occurs between just two individuals, a gift-giver and gift-receiver. By their very nature, interpersonal gifts are "intimate" because they provide an opportunity for a gift-giver to reveal what he/she thinks of the gift-receiver.[36] Successful gifts are those which communicate that the giver knows and understands the receiver, and their relationship.[37] For example, a sweater given to a friend in just the right color and size can be viewed as "she really knows me." In contrast, a clock radio given as a Valentine's Day gift, when the recipient is expecting a more "intimate" gift can mean a deterioration of a relationship.[38] Still further, researchers that have explored the gender of gift-givers and their feelings about same-sex gifting (i.e., female-to-female or male-to-male) and opposite-sex gifting (i.e., male-to-female or female-to-male) have found that both male and female gift-givers feel more comfortable in giving gifts to the same sex; however, they also reported that they felt more intense feeling with respect to gifts given to members of the opposite sex.[39] Knowledge of such gender differences are useful for marketers to know, because they imply that additional support might be appreciated at the point of purchase (e.g., while in a store) when a consumer is considering a gift for an opposite-sex recipient.

Intrapersonal gifting or a self-gift (also called "monadic giving") occurs when the giver and the receiver are the same individual.[40] To some extent a self-gift is a "state of mind." If a consumer sees a purchase as the "buying of something I need," then it is simply a "purchase." On the other hand, if the same consumer sees the same purchase as a "self-gift," then it is something special, with special meaning. Consumers may "treat" themselves to *self-gifts* that are products (e.g., clothing, compact discs, or jewelry), services (e.g., hair styling, restaurant meals, spa membership), or experiences (e.g., socializing with friends).[41] Such *intrapersonal* gifts have their own special range of meaning and context. Table 19-11 illustrates specific circumstances and motivations that might lead a consumer to engage in self-gift behavior. Research focusing on college students' self-gifting behavior

table 19-11 Reported Circumstances and Motivations for Self-Gift Behavior

CIRCUMSTANCES	MOTIVATIONS
Personal accomplishment	To reward oneself
Feeling down	To be nice to oneself
Holiday	To cheer up oneself
Feeling stressed	To fulfill a need
Have some extra money	To celebrate
Need	To relieve stress
Had not bought for self in awhile	To maintain a good feeling
Attainment of a desired goal	To provide an incentive toward a goal
Others	Others

Source: DAVID GLEN MICK and MITCHELLE DEMOSS, "To Me from Me: A Descriptive Phenomenology of Self-Gifts," in Marvin E. Goldberg, Gerald Gorn, and Richard W. Pollay, eds., *Advances in Consumer Research* 17 (Provo, UT: Association for Consumer Research, 1990), 677–82. Reprinted by permission.

table 19-12   Gifting Relationship Categories: Definitions and Examples

GIFTING RELATIONSHIP	DEFINITION	EXAMPLE
Intergroup	A group giving a gift to another group	A Christmas gift from one family to another family
Intercategory	An individual giving a gift to a group or a group giving a gift to an individual	A group of friends chips in to buy a new mother a baby gift
Intragroup	A group giving a gift to itself or its members	A family buys a VCR for itself as a Christmas gift
Interpersonal	An individual giving a gift to another individual	Valentine's Day chocolates presented from a boyfriend to a girlfriend
Intrapersonal	Self-gift	A woman buys herself jewelry to cheer herself up

Source: Adapted from: DEBORAH Y. COHN and LEON G. SCHIFFMAN, "Gifting: A Taxonomy of Private Realm Giver and Recipient Relationships," Working Paper, City University of New York, Baruch College, 1996, 2.

found that when they had the money to spend and when they either felt good or wished to cheer themselves up, they were particularly likely to purchase self-gifts.[42]

Finally, Table 19-12 summarizes the five gifting behavior subdivisions explored above.

BEYOND THE DECISION: CONSUMING AND POSSESSING

Historically, the emphasis in consumer behavior studies has been on product, service, and brand choice decisions. As shown throughout this book, however, there are many more facets to consumer behavior. The experience of using products and services, as well as the sense of pleasure derived from *possessing, collecting*, or *consuming* "things" and "experiences" (e.g., a VCR, rare stamps or coins, or a faraway vacation), contribute to consumer satisfaction and overall quality of life. These consumption outcomes or experiences, in turn, affect consumers' future decision processes.

Thus, given the importance of possessions and experiences, a broader perspective of consumer behavior might view consumer choices as the *beginning* of a **consumption process**, not merely the *end* of a consumer decision-making effort. In this context, the choice or purchase decision is an *input* into a process of consumption. The input stage includes the establishment of a *consumption set* (an assortment or portfolio of products and/or their attributes) and a *consuming style* (the "rules" by which the individual or household fulfills consumption requirements). The *process* stage of a simple model of consumption might include (from the consumer's perspective) the *using, possessing* (or having), *collecting*, and *disposing* of things and experiences. The *output* stage of this process would include changes in a wide range of feelings, moods, attitudes, and behavior, as well as reinforcement (positive or negative) of a particular lifestyle (e.g., a devotion to physical fitness), enhancement of a sense of self, and the level of consumer satisfaction and quality of life.[43] Figure 19-11 presents a simple **model of consumption** that reflects ideas discussed above and throughout the book.

Products Have Special Meaning and Memories

Consuming is a diverse and complex concept.[44] It includes the simple utility derived from the continued use of a superior toothpaste, the stress reduction of an island holiday, the stored memories of a video reflecting one's childhood, the "sacred" meaning or "magic" of a grandparent's wristwatch, the symbol of membership gained from wearing a school tie, the pleasure and sense of accomplishment that comes from building a model airplane, and the fun and even financial rewards that come from collecting almost anything (e.g., jokers from decks of cards). In fact, one man's hobby of collecting old earthenware drain tiles has become the "Mike Weaver Drain Tile Museum."[45]

Some possessions (e.g., photographs, souvenirs, trophies, and everyday objects) serve to assist consumers in their effort to create "personal meaning" and to maintain a sense of the *past*, which is essential to having a sense of self.[46] For instance, "objects of the past" are often acquired and retained intentionally (some become antiques or even heirlooms) to "memorialize" pleasant or momentous times and people in one's past.

Why are some consumers so interested in the past? It has been suggested that nostalgia permits people to maintain their identity after some major change in their life. This nostalgia can be based on family and friends, on objects such as toys, books, jewelry, and/or cars, or on special events, such as graduations, weddings, and holidays.[47] Providing

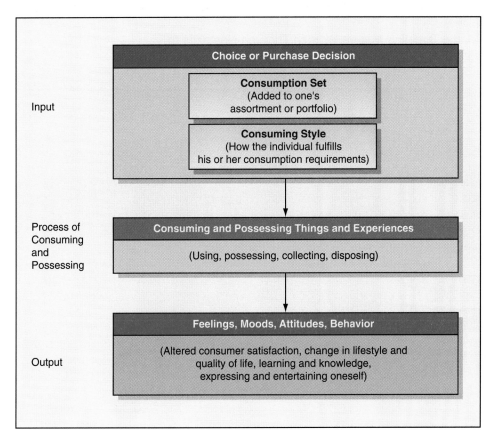

FIGURE 19-11

A Simple Model of Consumption

the triple benefits of a sense of nostalgia, the fun of collecting and the attraction of a potential return on investment, there is a strong interest in collecting Barbie dolls. It is estimated that there are currently some 100,000 Barbie doll collectors, who are dedicated to hunting down rare and valuable Barbies to add to their collections. To encourage interest in Barbie collecting, Mattel has an ad campaign that plays-up the nostalgia and fun of collecting Barbies—there is even a Barbie collectors' 800 hotline (Figure 19-12).[48]

ELATIONSHIP MARKETING

We will complete our discussion of consumer decision making with a brief consideration of **relationship marketing**. Many firms have established relationship marketing programs (sometimes called _loyalty programs_) to foster usage loyalty and a commitment to their company's products and services. Relationship marketing is exceedingly logical when we think that credit card research has shown that "75 percent of college students keep their first card for 15 years, and 60 percent keep that card for life."[49] This kind of loyalty is enhanced by relationship marketing, which at its heart is all about building _trust_ (between the firm and its customers) and keeping _promises_ ("making promises," "enabling promises," and "keeping promises" on the part of the firm and, possibly, on the part of the customer).[50]

Indeed, it is the aim of relationship marketing to create strong, lasting relationships with a core group of customers. The emphasis is on developing _long-term bonds_ with customers by making them feel good about how the company interacts (i.e., does business) with them and by giving them some kind of "personal connection" to the business.[51] A review of the composition of 66 consumer relationship marketing programs revealed three elements

FIGURE 19-12 Mattel Targeting Mature Women Through Nostalgia to Ignite Interest in Barbies
Courtesy of Mattel, Inc.

shared by more than 50 percent of the programs. They are: (1) Fostering ongoing communication with customers (73 percent of the programs), (2) Furnishing loyalty by building extras like upgrades and other peaks (68 percent of the programs); and (3) Stimulating a sense of belonging by providing a "club membership" format (50 percent of the programs).[52]

An analogy can be drawn between two individuals who build an interpersonal relationship and the type of relationship marketers attempt to build between the company (or its products) and the consumer. Like personal relationships between individuals who are willing to do favors for each other, "relationship" marketers offer loyal customers special services, discounts, increased communications, and attention beyond the core product or service, *without* expecting an immediate payback. However, they are hoping that, over time, they will reap the advantages of sustained and increasing transactions with a core group of loyal customers.

Although direct marketing, sales promotion, and general advertising may be used as part of a relationship marketing strategy, relationship marketing stresses long-term commitment to the individual customer. Advances in technology (e.g., UPC scanning equipment, relational databases) have provided techniques that make tracking customers simpler, thus influencing the trend toward relationship marketing.[53]

As illustrated in Table 19-13, relationship marketing can be seen in a wide variety of product and service categories. Many companies call their relationship programs a "club,"

table 19-13   Examples of Relationship Marketing Techniques

COMPANY	PROGRAM TYPE AND MEMBERSHIP CRITERIA	BENEFITS
AT&T	"True Rewards" points earned for dollars spend on long distance calling (no fee to join)	Points may be redeemed for free minutes, frequent flyer miles, and other rewards. Toll-free number for member questions, quarterly point statement, and informational mailings.
American Express	Platinum Card Program "By invitation only" Offered to the top 1 percent of AmEx cardholders (fee to join)	Invitations to special cultural, culinary, and artistic events based on member's personal profile.
Road Runner Sports (catalog that caters to runners, bikers, and other sports)	"Run America Club" (fee to join)	Discounts on merchandise and "shoe analysis program," quarterly newsletter "Running Shorts," free shipping upgrades, and travel and car rental discounts.
World Yacht (restaurant and cruises)	"World Yacht club" "flags" earned each time a member dines aboard World Yacht	"Flags" redeemed for awards such as free brunch, caviar, champagne, and discounts on dinner cruises. Five "flags" earn VIP status for preferred seating and additional discounts.
Neiman Marcus	"InCircle" point system (minimum purchases of $3,000 per year to join)	Quarterly newsletter, travel discounts, credit card registration, perfume, magazine subscriptions, special offer mailings, and dedicated toll-free telephone number.
Pacific Bell	"California Gold" points earned for dollars spent	Newsletter, toll-free customer service number, and third party discounts.

Source: Adapted by Mary M. Long, Drexel University, from issues of *Colloquy*.

and some even charge a fee to join. Membership in a club may serve as a means to convey to customers the notions of permanence and exclusivity inherent in a "committed relationship."[54] Additionally, those firms that charge a fee (e.g., the American Express Platinum card) increase customers' investment in the relationship that may, in turn, lead to greater commitment to the relationship and increased usage loyalty. A remarkably alluring relationship club, one with branches in several continents and with members from all over the world, is the Swatch Collectors' Club (i.e., "Swatch the Club"). For an $80 annual membership fee, participants (i.e., "Swatchers") receive an exclusive membership Swatch watch, a member's pin and card, journals and newsletters, and a variety of other materials all designed to inform and entertain collectors of Swatch watches (Figure 19-13).

Airlines and major hotel chains, in particular, use relationship marketing techniques by awarding points to frequent customers that can be used to obtain additional goods or services from the company. This kind of point system may act as an exit barrier, because starting a new relationship would mean giving up the potential future value of the points and starting from ground zero with a new service provider. Moreover, companies have recently been broadening the scope of such relationship programs. For example, Table 19-14 lists the many products and services offered to participants in the American Airlines AAdvantage Mileage Program.

Ultimately, it is to a firm's advantage to develop long-term relationships with existing customers, because it is easier and less expensive to make an additional sale to an existing customer than to make a new sale to a new consumer.[55] However, the effort involved for the firm in developing and maintaining a customer relationship must be weighed against the expected long-term benefits. Marketers must determine the "lifetime value" of a customer to ensure that the costs of obtaining, servicing, and communicating with the customer do not exceed the potential profits.[56] Figure 19-14 portrays some of the characteristics of the relationship between the firm and the customer within the "spirit" of relationship marketing.

FIGURE 19-13

Part of a Direct
Marketing Campaign to
Promote Swatch the
Club
Courtesy of Swatch

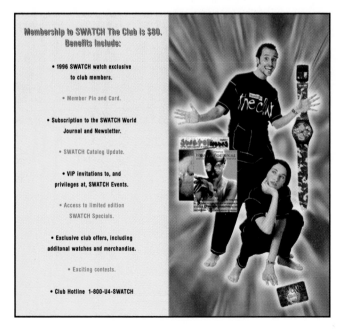

table 19-14   A Broad-based Relationship Program

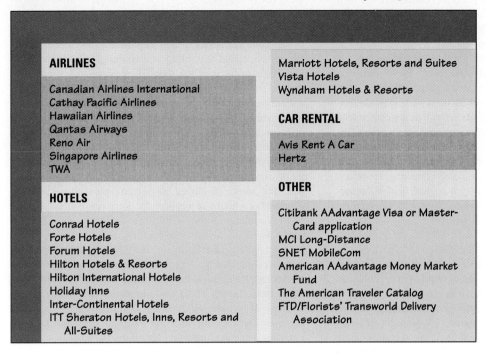

AIRLINES

Canadian Airlines International
Cathay Pacific Airlines
Hawaiian Airlines
Qantas Airways
Reno Air
Singapore Airlines
TWA

HOTELS

Conrad Hotels
Forte Hotels
Forum Hotels
Hilton Hotels & Resorts
Hilton International Hotels
Holiday Inns
Inter-Continental Hotels
ITT Sheraton Hotels, Inns, Resorts and
    All-Suites

Marriott Hotels, Resorts and Suites
Vista Hotels
Wyndham Hotels & Resorts

CAR RENTAL

Avis Rent A Car
Hertz

OTHER

Citibank AAdvantage Visa or Master-
    Card application
MCI Long-Distance
SNET MobileCom
American AAdvantage Money Market
    Fund
The American Traveler Catalog
FTD/Florists' Transworld Delivery
    Association

Source: JENNIFER LAWRENCE, "Yet Another Way to Pedal Frequent Flier Miles," *Advertising Age*, March 7, 1994, 8.
Reprinted with permission from the March 7, 1994 issue of *Advertising Age*. Copyright 1994 by Crain Communications.

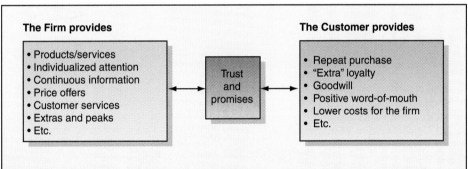

The Firm provides

• Products/services
• Individualized attention
• Continuous information
• Price offers
• Customer services
• Extras and peaks
• Etc.

Trust
and
promises

The Customer provides

• Repeat purchase
• "Extra" loyalty
• Goodwill
• Positive word-of-mouth
• Lower costs for the firm
• Etc.

FIGURE 19-14

A Portrayal of the
Characteristics of
Relationship Marketing

Source: In part, this portrayal was inspired by: MARY LONG, LEON SCHIFFMAN, and ELAINE SHERMAN, "Understanding the Relationships in Consumer Marketing Relationship Programs: A Content Analysis," in K. Grant and Walker, eds., *Proceedings of the World Marketing Congress* VII-II (Melbourne, Australia: Academy of Marketing Science, 1995), 10/27-10/32; LEONARD L. BERRY, "Relationship Marketing of Services—Growing Interest, Emerging Perspectives," *Journal of the Academy of Marketing Science*, 23, Fall 1995, 236–45; and MARY JO BITNER, "Building Service Relationships: It's All About Promises" *Journal of the Academy of Marketing Science*, 23, Fall 1995, 246–51.

summary

The consumer's decision to purchase or not to purchase a product or service is an important moment for most marketers. It can signify whether a marketing strategy has been wise, insightful, and effective, or whether it was poorly planned and missed the mark. Thus, marketers are particularly interested in

the consumer's decision-making process. For a consumer to make a decision, more than one alternative must be available. (The decision not to buy is also an alternative.)

Theories of consumer decision making vary, depending on the researcher's assumptions about the nature of humankind.

The various "models of man" (economic man, passive man, cognitive man, and emotional man) depict consumers and their decision-making processes in distinctly different ways.

An overview consumer decision-making model ties together the psychological, social, and cultural concepts examined in Parts Two and Three into an easily understood framework. This decision model has three sets of variables: input variables, process variables, and output variables.

Input variables that affect the decision-making process include commercial marketing efforts, as well as noncommercial influences from the consumer's sociocultural environment. The decision process variables are influenced by the consumer's psychological field, including the evoked set (i.e., the brands in a particular product category considered in making a purchase choice). Taken as a whole, the psychological field influences the consumer's recognition of a need, prepurchase search for information, and evaluation of alternatives.

The output phase of the model includes the actual purchase (either trial or repeat purchase) and postpurchase evaluation. Both prepurchase and postpurchase evaluation feed back in the form of experience into the consumer's psychological field, and serve to influence future decision processing.

The process of *gift exchange* is an important part of consumer behavior. Various gift-giving and gift-receiving relationships are captured by the following five specific gifting classification scheme: (1) intergroup gifting (i.e., a group gives a gift to another group); (2) intercategory gifting (i.e., an individual gives a gift to a group or a group gives a gift to an individual); (3) intragroup gifting (i.e., a group gives a gift to itself or its members), (4) interpersonal gifting (i.e., an individual gives a gift to another individual), and (5) intrapersonal gifting (i.e., a self-gift).

Consumer behavior is not just making a purchase decision or the act of purchasing; it also includes the full range of experiences associated with using or *consuming* products and services. It also includes the sense of pleasure and satisfaction derived from *possessing* or *collecting* "things." The *outputs* of consumption are changes in feelings, moods, or attitudes; reinforcement of lifestyles; an enhanced sense of self; satisfaction of a consumer-related need: belonging to groups; expressing and entertaining oneself.

Among other things, consuming includes the simple utility of using a superior product, the stress reduction of a vacation, the sense of having a "sacred" possession, and the pleasures of a hobby or a collection. Some possessions serve to assist consumers in their effort to create "personal meaning" and to maintain a sense of the *past*.

Relationship marketing impacts consumers' decisions and their consumption satisfaction. Firms establish relationship marketing programs (sometimes called "loyalty programs") to foster usage loyalty and a commitment to their products and services. At its heart, relationship marketing is all about building *trust* (between the firm and its customers), and keeping *promises* made to consumers. Therefore, the emphasis in relationship marketing is almost always on developing *long-term bonds* with customers by making them feel "special" and by providing them with personalized services.

discussion questions

1. Compare and contrast the economic, passive, cognitive, and emotional models of consumer decision making.

2. What kinds of marketing and sociocultural inputs would influence the purchase of: (a) a TV with a built-in VCR, (b) a concentrated liquid laundry detergent, and (c) fat-free ice cream? Explain your answers.

3. Define extensive problem solving, limited problem solving, and routinized response behavior. What are the differences between the three decision-making approaches? What type of decision process would you expect most consumers to follow in their first purchase of a new product or brand in each of the following areas: (a) chewing gum; (b) sugar; (c) men's aftershave lotion; (d) carpeting; (e) paper towels; (f) a cellular telephone; and (g) a luxury car. Explain your answers.

4. a. Identify three different products that you believe require a reasonably intensive prepurchase search by a consumer. Then, using Table 19-3 as a guide, identify the specific characteristics of these products that make an intensive prepurchase search likely.

   b. For each of the products that you listed, identify the perceived risks that a consumer is likely to experience before a purchase. Discuss how the marketers of these products can reduce these perceived risks.

5. Let's assume that this coming summer you are planning to spend a month touring Europe and are therefore in need of a good 35-mm camera. (a) Develop a list of product attributes that you will use as the purchase criteria in evaluating various 35-mm cameras. (b) Distinguish the differences that would occur in your decision process if you were to use compensatory versus noncompensatory decision rules.

6. How can a marketer of very light, very powerful laptop computers use its knowledge of customers expectations in deigning a marketing strategy?

7. How do consumers reduce postpurchase dissonance? How can marketers provide positive reinforcement to consumers after the purchase to reduce their dissonance?

8. The Gillette Company, which produces the highly successful Sensor shaving blade, has recently introduced a clear gel antiperspirant and deodorant for men. Identify the perceived risks associated with the purchase of this new product and outline a strategy designed o reduce these perceived risks during the product's introduction.

9. Albert Einstein once wrote that "the whole of science is nothing more than a refinement of everyday thinking." Do you think that this quote applies to the development of the consumer decision-making model presented in Figure 19-4?

1. Find two print advertisements, one that illustrates the cognitive model of consumer decision making and one that illustrates the emotional model. Explain your choices. In your view, why did the marketers choose the approaches depicted in the advertisements?

2. Describe the need recognition process that took place before you purchased your last can of soft drink. How did it differ from the process that preceded the purchase of a new pair of sneakers? What role, if any, did advertising play in your need recognition?

3. List the colleges that you considered when choosing which college or university to attend, and the criteria that you used to evaluate them. Describe how you acquired information on the different colleges along the different attributes that were important to you and how you made your decision. Be sure to specify whether you used compensatory or noncompensatory decision rules.

4. Select one of the following product categories: (a) compact disc players, (b) fast-food restaurants, or (c) shampoo, and: (1) write down the brands that constitute your evoked set, (2) identify brands that are not part of your evoked set, and (3) discuss how the brands included in your evoked set differ from those that are not included in terms of important attributes.

5. Select a newspaper or magazine advertisement that attempts: (a) to provide the consumer with a decision strategy to follow in making a purchase decision or (b) to reduce the perceived risk(s) associated with a purchase. Evaluate the effectiveness of the ad you selected.

- Affect referral decision rule
- Cognitive model of man
- Compensatory decision rules
- Conjunctive decision rule
- Consumer decision making
- Consumption process
- Disjunctive rule
- Economic model of man
- Emotional model of man
- Evaluation of alternatives
- Evoked set
- Extensive problem solving
- Gifting behavior
- Heuristics
- Inept set
- Inert set
- Information overload
- Levels of decision making
- Lexicographic decision rule
- Limited problem solving
- Marketing mix activities
- Moods
- Model of consuming
- Need recognition
- Noncompensatory decision rules
- Passive model of man
- Perceived risk: functional, physical, financial, social, psychological, and time risks
- Positive (or negative) disconfirmation of expectations
- Postpurchase cognitive dissonance
- Postpurchase evaluation
- Prepurchase search
- Problem-solving consumer
- Psychological field of the decision process
- Purchase behavior
- Relationship marketing
- Routinized response behavior
- Self-gifts
- Sociocultural influences in decision making

1. ITAMAR SIMONSON, "Shoppers' Easily Influenced Choices," *The New York Times*, November 6, 1994, 11.

2. JOHN A. HOWARD and JAGDISH N. SHETH, *The Theory of Buyer Behavior* (New York: Wiley, 1969), 46–47. See also: JOHN HOWARD, *Consumer Behavior in Marketing Strategy* (Englewood Cliffs, NJ: Prentice Hall, 1989).

3. HERBERT A. SIMON, *Administrative Behavior*, 2nd ed. (New York: Free Press, 1965), 40.

4. JAMES G. MARCH and HERBERT A. SIMON, *Organizations* (New York: Wiley, 1958), 140–41.

5. JOHN G. JONES, *Salesmanship and Sales Management* (New York: Alexander Hamilton Institute, 1917), 29.

6. RICHARD W. OLSKAVSKY, "Towards a More Comprehensive Theory of Choice," in Elizabeth C. Hirschman and Morris B. Holbrook, eds., *Advances in Consumer Research* 12 (Provo, UT: Association for Consumer Research, 1985), 465–70.

7. ROBERT S. OWEN and CURTIS P. HAUGTVEDT, "Time and Consumer Information Load," in Michael Levy and Dhruv Grewal, eds., *Developments in Marketing Science* (Coral Gables, FL: Academy of Marketing Science, 1993), 55–59.

8. RUSSELL W. BELK, "The Role of Possessions in Constructing and Maintaining a Sense of Past," in Marvin E. Goldberg, Gerald Gorn, and Richard W. Pollay, eds., *Advances in Consumer Research* 17 (Provo, UT: Association for Consumer Research, 1990), 669–76.

9. MERYL PAULA GARDNER, "Mood States and Consumer Behavior: A Critical Review," *Journal of Consumer Research* 12, December 1985, 281–300; and ROBERT A. PETERSON and MATTHEW SAUBER, "A Mood Scale for Survey Research," in Patrick E. Murphy, et al., eds., *1983 AMA Educators' Proceeding* (Chicago: American Marketing Association, 1983), 409–14.

10. BARRY J. BABIN, WILLIAM R. DARDEN, and MITCH GRIFFIN, "Some Comments on the Role of Emotions in Consumer Behavior," in Robert P. Leone and V. Kumor, et al., eds., *1992 AMA Educators' Proceedings* (Chicago: American Marketing Association, 1992), 130–39; and PATRICIA A. KNOWLES, STEPHEN J. GROVE, and W. JEFFREY BURROUGHS, "An Experimental Examination of Mood Effects on Retrieval and Evaluation of Advertisement and Brand Information," *Journal of the Academy of Marketing Science* 21, Spring 1993, 135–42.

11. GARDNER, op. cit.

12. RUTH BELK SMITH and ELAINE SHERMAN, "Effects of Store Image and Mood on Consumer Behavior: A Theoretical and Empirical Analysis," in Leigh McAlister and Michael L. Rothschild, eds., *Advances in Consumer Behavior* 20 (Provo, UT: Association for Consumer Research, 1993), 631.

13. KNOWLES, GROVE, and BURROUGHS, op. cit.

14. CHARLES MCMELLON, LEON SCHIFFMAN, and ELAINE SHERMAN, "Consuming Cyberseniors: Some Personal and Situational Characteristics That Influence Their On-Line Behavior," Working Paper, City University of New York, Baruch College, 1996, 5.

15. GORDON C. BRUNER, II, "The Effect of Problem-Recognition Style on Information Seeking," *Journal of the Academy of Marketing Science* 15, Winter 1987, 33–41.

16. GORDON C. BRUNER, II, and RICHARD J. POMAZAL, "Problem Recognition: The Crucial First Stage of the Consumer Decision Process," *Journal of Consumer Marketing* 5, Winter 1988, 53–63.

17. SHARON E. BEATTY and SCOTT M. SMITH, "External Search Effort: An Investigation Across Several Product Categories," *Journal of Consumer Research* 14, June 1987, 83–95.

18. MOONKYU LEE and FRANCIS M. ULGADO, "Alternative Models of Cognitive Processes Underlying Consumer Reactions to Conjunction Categories," in Chris T. Allen and Deborah Roedder John, eds., *Advances in Consumer Research* 21 (Provo, UT: Association for Consumer Research, 1994), 483–88.

19. AYN E. CROWLEY and JOHN H. WILLIAMS, "An Information Theoretic Approach to Understanding the Consideration Set/Awareness Set Proportion," in Rebecca H. Holman and Micheal R. Solomon, eds., *Advances in Consumer Research* 18 (Provo, UT: Association for Consumer Research, 1991), 780–87; JOHN R. HAUSER and WERNERFELT BIRGER, "An Evaluation Cost Model of Consideration Sets," *Journal of Consumer Research* 19, March 1990, 393–408; and PRAKASH NEDUNGADI, "Recall and Consumer Consideration Sets: Influencing Choice Without Altering Brand Evaluations," *Journal of Consumer Research* 17, December 1990, 263–76.

20. JEFFREY F. DURGEE, "Why Some Products 'Just Fell Right', Or, The Phenomenology of Product Rightness," in Frank R. Kardes and Mita Sujan, eds., *Advances in Consumer Research* 22 (Provo, UT: Association for Consumer Research, 1995), 650–52.

21. Given the very rapid changes occurring in the on-line services industry, it is likely that by the time you read this book the rate plans for these services and other features will have changed. However, for illustration purposes, the relevance of the examples is still appropriate.

22. LAURIE PETERSON, "The Strategic Shopper," *Adweek's Marketing Week*, March 30, 1992, 18–20.

23. CAREY GOLDBERG, "Choosing the Joys of a Simplified Life, *The New York Times*, September 21, 1995, C1 and C9.

24. Ibid.

25. SANDRA J. BURKE, "The Effects of Missing Information on Decision Strategy Selection," in Goldberg, Gorn, and Pollay, eds., *Advances in Consumer Research*, 250–56.

26. SARAH FISHER GARDIAL and DAVID W. SCHUMANN, "In Search of the Elusive Consumer Inference," in Goldberg, Gorn, and Pollay, eds., *Advances in Consumer Research*, op. cit., 283–87. See also BURKE, ibid.

27. MICHAEL D. JOHNSON, "Consumer Choice Strategies for Comparing Noncomparable Alternatives," *Journal of Consumer Research* 11, December 1984, 741–50.

28. BARRY L. BAYUS, "The Consumer Durable Replacement Buyer," *Journal of Marketing* 55, January 1991, 42–51.

29. DIANE M. PHILLIPS, JERRY C. OLSON, and HANS BAUMGARTNER, "Consumption Visions in Consumer Decision Making," in Frank R. Kardes and Mita Sujan, eds., *Advances in Consumer Research* 22 (Provo, UT: Association for Consumer Research, 1995), 280.

30. Ibid., 280–84.

31. "Promotion Influence Spurs Buyers to Try Something New," *Brandweek*, March 21, 1994, 32–33.

32. ERNEST R. CADOTTE, ROBERT B. WOODRUFF, and ROGER L. JENKINS, "Expectations and Norms in Models of Con-

sumer Satisfaction," *Journal of Marketing Research*, August 24, 1987, 305–14.

33. DEBORAH Y. COHN and LEON G. SCHIFFMAN, "Gifting: A Taxonomy of Private Realm Giver and Recipient Relationships," Working Paper, City University of New York, Baruch College, 1996, 2.

34. RUSSELL W. BELK and GREGORY S. COON, "Gift Giving as Agapic Love: An Alternative to the Exchange Paradigm Based on Dating Experiences," *Journal of Consumer Research* 20, December 1993, 393–417.

35. CELE OTNES, TINA M. LOWREY, and YOUNG CHAN KIM, "Gift Selection for Easy and Difficult Recipients: A Social Roles Interpretation," *Journal of Consumer Research* 20, September 1993, 229–44.

36. CAROLE B. BURGOYNE and DAVID A. ROUTH, "Constraints on the Use of Money as a Gift at Christmas: The Role of Status and Intimacy," *Journal of Economic Psychology* 12, 1991, 47–69; and DAVID CHEAL, "'Showing Them You Love Them': Gift Giving and the Dialectic of Intimacy," *Sociological Review*, 1987, 35, 150–69.

37. SUSAN SCHULTZ-KLEINE, ROBERT E. KLEINE, III, and CHRIS T. ALLEN, "How Is a Possession 'Me' or 'Not Me'? Characterizing Types and an Antecedent of Material Possession Attachment," *Journal of Consumer Research* 22, December 1995, 327–43; and BARRY SCHWARTZ, "The Social Psychology of the Gift," *The American Journal of Sociology*, 73, July 1967, 1–11.

38. JOHN F. SHERRY, JR., "Reflections on Giftware and Giftcare: Whither Consumer Research?" in Cele Otnes and Richard F. Beltramini, eds, *Gift Giving: An Interdisciplinary Anthology* (Bowling Green, KY: Popular Press, 1996), 220.

39. STEPHEN J. GOULD and CLAUDIA E. WEIL, "Gift-Giving and Gender Self-Concepts," *Gender Role* 24, 1991, 617–37.

40. For a really interesting article on self-gifts, see: JOHN F. SHERRY, JR., MARY ANN MCGRATH, and SIDNEY J. LEVY, "Monadic Gifting: Anatomy of Gifts Given to the Self," in John F. Sherry, Jr., ed., *Contemporary Marketing and Consumer Behavior* (Thousand Oaks, CA: Sage, 1995), 399–432.

41. DAVID GLEN MICK and MITCHELLE DEMOSS, "To Me from Me: A Descriptive Phenomenology of Self-Gifts," in Goldberg, Gorn, and Pollay, eds., *Advances in Consumer Research*, op. cit., 677–82.

42. KIM K. R. MCKEAGE, MARSHA L. RICHINS, and KATHLEEN DEBEVEC, "Self-Gifts and the Manifestation of Material Values," in Leigh McAlister and Michael L. Rothschild, eds., *Advances in Consumer Research* 20 (Provo, UT: Association for Consumer Research 1993), 359–64.

43. KATHLEEN M. RASSULI and GILBERT D. HARRELL, "A New Perspective on Choice," in Goldberg, Gorn, and Pollay, eds., *Advances in Consumer Research*, op. cit., 737–44.

44. For an interesting article on "consumption practices," see: DOUGLAS B. HOLT, "How Consumers Consume: A Typology of Consumer Practices," *Journal of Consumer Research* 22, June 1995, 1–16.

45. JAMES M. PERRY, "Mike Weaver Proves That Everything Can Be a Collection," *The Wall Street Journal*, August 16, 1995, 1.

46. RUSSELL W. BELK, "The Role of Possessions in Constructing and Maintaining a Sense of Past," in Goldberg, Gorn, and Pollay, eds., *Advances in Consumer Research*, op. cit., 669–76.

47. STACEY MENZEL BAKER and PATRICIA F. KENNEDY, "Death by Nostalgia: A Diagnosis of Context-Specific Cases," in Chris T. Allen and Deborah Roedder John, eds., *Advances in Consumer Research* 21 (Provo, UT: Association for Consumer Research, 1994), 169–74.

48. JOSEPH PEREIRA, "Behind the Great Barbie Shortage Are Those Meanie Doll Collectors," *The Wall Street Journal*, December 7, 1995, B1.

49. ROBERT BRYCE, "Here's a Course in Personal Finance 101, the Hard Way," *The New York Times*, April 30, 1995, F11.

50. LEONARD L. BERRY, "Relationship Marketing of Services—Growing Interest, Emerging Perspectives," *Journal of the Academy of Marketing Science* 23, Fall 1995, 236–45; and MARY JO BITNER, "Building Service Relationships: It's All About Promises" *Journal of the Academy of Marketing Science* 23, Fall 1995, 246–51.

51. AIMEE L. STERN, "Courting Consumer Loyalty with the Feel-Good Bond," *The New York Times*, January 17, 1993, F10.

52. MARY LONG, LEON SCHIFFMAN, and ELAINE SHERMAN, "Understanding the Relationships in Consumer Marketing Relationship Programs: A Content Analysis," in K. Grant and Walker, eds., *Proceedings of the World Marketing Congress* VII-II (Melbourne, Australia: Academy of Marketing Science, 1995), 10/27-10/32.

53. JONATHAN R. COPULSKY and MICHAEL J. WOLF, "Relationship Marketing: Positioning for the Future," *The Journal of Business Strategy*, July/August 1990, 16–20.

54. MARY M. LONG, *Relationship Marketing: A Causal Model* (New York: City University of New York, unpublished position paper, 1993).

55. JAGDISH N. SHETH and ATUL PARVATIYAR, "Relationship Marketing in Consumer Marketing: Antecedents and Consequences," *Journal of the Academy of Marketing Science* 23, Fall 1995, 255–271.

56. ROBERT F. DWYER, "Customer Lifetime Valuation to Support Marketing Decision Making," *Journal of Direct Marketing* 3, 1989, 8–15; JONATHAN R. COPULSKY and MICHAEL J. WOLF, op. cit.; and PHILIP KOTLER, "Marketing's New Paradigm: What's Really Happening Out There," *Planning Review*, September-October 1992, 50–52.

PART FIVE

Consumer

Behavior and

Society

PART 5

ADDRESSES THE

ROLE OF CONSUMER

BEHAVIOR IN OUR

SOCIETY.

T DEMONSTRATES THE APPLICATION OF CONSUMER BEHAVIOR principles

to the marketing of profit and not-for-profit services, including health

care marketing, political marketing, environmental ("green")

marketing, and the marketing of social causes. The book concludes

with an examination of public policy issues and a discussion of

consumer behavior research priorities.

CONSUMER BEHAVIOR

APPLICATIONS TO PROFIT AND

NOT-FOR-PROFIT MARKETING

THE SAFEKEEPING OF OUR NATIONAL PARKS
IS AN INVESTMENT EVERY AMERICAN SHOULD MAKE.

Charles Schwab

In addition to the impetus given to the study of consumer behavior by developments in marketing philosophy and practice, the field has grown in response to the extension of marketing concepts from products to services, and from the private sector to the public sector. This chapter will discuss the applications of consumer behavior research findings to health care marketing, political marketing, and the marketing of social causes, examining in depth the growth in cause-related marketing for a major consumer concern—protection of the environment.

A *cause is like champagne and high heels—one must be prepared to suffer for it.*

—Arnold Bennett (1867–1931)

HEALTH CARE MARKETING

The provision of health care services is a major component of the nonprofit sector, with annual expenditures for health care skyrocketing in 1993 to almost $885 billion dollars.[1] Until recently, hospitals and physicians (the traditional health care providers) knew little, if anything, about marketing, and they thought it unprofessional to market their services. However, as the incidence of third-party payers (insurance companies, employers, and government programs such as Medicare and Medicaid) increased and medical costs soared, the health care environment changed dramatically. In 1993, while the Clinton administration was trying to devise a broader, more cost-efficient health care system that would provide universal health insurance to all Americans, the insurance companies took the matter into their own hands and set up managed health care programs that were almost totally dependent on marketing. The insurance companies targeted physicians, hospitals, pharmaceutical companies, and other health care providers and intermediaries to persuade them to join managed care networks on a salary, fixed fee, or volume basis in order to put together a comprehensive service that, in turn, they could market to employers and to individuals. Pressures were placed on hospitals to reduce inpatient care and on network doctors to reduce costly medical testing and specialist referrals.

The new health care delivery system was designed to take care of all an enrolled patient's health care needs for a predetermined annual fee (paid either by the patients themselves or by their employers.) One type of managed care network is the *health maintenance organization*, or HMO, in which enrolled patients must accept care from a preestablished set of doctors, hospitals, medical laboratories, and other providers in order to receive reimbursement; any health care service obtained outside the network must be paid for privately. The patient must first see a primary-care physician (a "gatekeeper") before he or she may see a specialist.

A less restrictive managed care network is called a *preferred provider organization* (or PPO), in which the patient receives lower rates when he or she uses the doctors and hospitals included on a list of preferred providers. Patients enrolled in a PPO may see a specialist without a referral from a primary-care physician and may see other providers outside of the network. A third type of managed care network, called *point-of-service* (POS), bridges the concept of an HMO and a PPO by permitting patients to see doctors outside of their network for traditional fee-for-service payments, while offering them the incentive to receive lower rates by using a plan doctor.

Despite the fact that managed care has begun to limit the costs of health care, there is a growing concern that the quality of care is being compromised when patients are denied access to specialists by gatekeepers or denied coverage for certain experimental or expensive procedures. Further complicating the issue is the fact that managed care plans are often privately owned by investor groups, whose profit-making goals may conflict with patients' needs for medically necessary services. A national debate is under way, making the marketing of health care in this competitive atmosphere enormously challenging.

Market Segmentation

To position themselves to best meet consumer demands in a highly competitive market place, health care providers are marketing to end-users (i.e., patients), as well as to other health care intermediaries. Hospitals are conducting demographic analyses, compiling physician profiles, and establishing affiliation agreements with other organizations. Independent community hospitals are conducting surveys of local community health needs ("community health assessments") to assist in their decision making as to which services to add, cut, or expand to best maximize revenues.

Health care organizations are looking for niches to satisfy consumer demand for services. Consumers are segmented by their unique needs, and then programs and services are created to best satisfy those needs. For example, the needs of certain patient groups (e.g., drug addicts, alcoholics, AIDS patients, pregnant teenagers) have led to specially tailored programs. The growing needs of the aging population have led to increased provision of geriatric services and long-term care facilities. The managed care emphasis on preventive care and outpatient treatments has led to hospitals offering health education programs to the community and expanding their outpatient clinics. The financial disincentives of high-cost hospitalization and the recognition that many medical treatments can be given in patients' homes have led to the development and expansion of home care services.

▲ **Marketing to Intermediaries** The ultimate consumer of the health care delivery system is the patient. However, intermediaries play a major role in influencing the usage of medical services: *physicians* who order tests, admit patients, and who may be part of a managed care network; *insurers* and *managed care networks*, who may direct their enrollees to use specific physicians or facilities; the *government*, which may control where Medicare and Medicaid patients and government employees seek treatment; and *employers*, who offer health care plans to their employees and retirees. Health care organizations have dramatically increased their marketing efforts to appeal to all of these groups in order to increase patient volume at a time when admission rates and length of stay are declining.

Health care organizations—both hospitals and managed care networks—are marketing to physicians, especially primary-care physicians, in order to establish referral sources for their specialized services and inpatient care. They provide the doctors with resources to assist them in caring for patients, such as high-technology equipment and access to specialists. To attract both doctors and patients, many hospitals advertise "physician referral centers," which direct inquiring consumers to associated physicians to meet their medical needs. Some hospitals provide office space to associated physicians in adjacent medical office buildings at which office management and group purchasing services are available.

Large medical centers are actively "courting" physician group practices and regional hospitals in order to generate patient referrals to their high-technology services and specialists. Use of innovative marketing media, such as the Internet and the World Wide Web, has allowed hospitals to extend their geographic reach to physicians in outlying areas. For example, the Mayo Clinic has targeted physicians by creating continuing education programs in digital formats; Mayo hopes that closer bonds will be forged with these physicians, leading to consults and referrals.[2]

Hospitals are cutting costs and marketing themselves as "low-cost providers" to insurers and managed care networks. They are reducing overhead by methods such as reorganizing their management structures and reducing staff, by streamlining admissions and billing processes, and by purchasing supplies in bulk to achieve economies of scale. Critics have raised concerns that some cost-cutting measures are compromising the quality of patient care, so administrators must weigh the trade-offs involved in balancing the needs of both patients and intermediaries.

Insurers and managed care networks are actively marketing to the federal and state governments to provide low-cost managed care to government employees and people on government assistance. In fact, there is a rapid increase in the number of Medicare and Medicaid managed care plans designed for this population group, and a growing number of individuals are enrolling in such programs.

Because employers influence the selection of managed health care plans offered to their employees, managed care networks and hospitals are targeting these employers directly with information about their medical services. One hospital distributes a quarterly "Employer Newsletter" to "better inform area employers of our low-cost, high quality services and programs"; this newsletter is sent to the President/CEO, Vice President of

Human Resources, and Benefits Administrator of more than 5000 regional companies meeting certain size criteria.[3]

▲ **Marketing to Patients** Many hospitals conduct *patient satisfaction surveys* to assist them in improving patient care and the perception of patients about the quality of their care. The surveys aim to identify the parts of the service delivery system that matter most to the patients; the hospitals then try to improve efficiency in these areas to achieve a corresponding increase in patient satisfaction. These surveys are usually taken after the patient is discharged from the hospital. It has been shown that self-administered questionnaires, rather than telephone surveys, yield the most constructive comments and are less costly to administer.[4]

In addition to actual treatment received, *perceptions* of care are ultimately responsible for whether a patient is willing to return to that hospital or to refer other people. Improved communication with patients while they are in the hospital, both through staff education and a responsive complaint process, can positively improve the hospital experience.[5] Family and friends of the patient may be harder to satisfy than the patient, and addressing the concerns of these individuals can positively influence future decisions to use the hospital's services again.[6]

As a by-product of patient satisfaction surveys, hospitals are emphasizing *customer service*. Seminars are being held for employees to teach empathy, thoughtfulness, politeness, and basic etiquette.[7] New positions and programs are being created to reinforce this patient-focused approach. By satisfying both patients and their insurers, hospitals hope to generate an expanded patient base.

A number of marketing techniques are practiced by innovative hospitals to increase and/or impress their patient population. Physician referral centers, health information hot lines, and health fairs have become popular methods of developing bonds with potential patients. Some hospitals are providing "hotel accommodations" for family members of patients. Others have improved their food service and have even added ethnic foods to satisfy certain patient market segments.

Columbia Presbyterian Medical Center, an academic medical center located in an inconvenient area of New York City, added an ambulatory care center in a high-demand location and provides shuttle service to its main facility when specialized services are needed.[8] Cleveland Clinic Foundation has an annual "Senior Health Day" to market its services and help develop loyalty among potential patients. This health fair has generated new business, provided health education, and promoted goodwill in the community.[9]

Beth Israel Medical Center in New York City opened a new state-of-the-art outpatient clinic in 1996 to appeal to patients, physicians, and managed care networks alike.[10] The clinic is located in a convenient location near a busy subway station and is designed to appeal to a broad range of potential patients. It provides comprehensive medical services and physician offices under one roof, and has cost efficiencies designed into the system. The staff has even taken classes to "treat patients as customers." Beth Israel hopes that these efforts will encourage managed care networks to assign their enrollees to Beth Israel, thereby broadening the medical center's patient base and increasing revenues.

Marketing on the Internet is proving to be a cost-effective way to educate, inform, and communicate with both patients and intermediaries. For example, to develop closer bonds with potential patients (and their doctors), the Mayo Clinic developed "The Mayo Clinic Family Health Book" in book form and on CD-ROM; sales have been a good revenue source and image builder among consumers.[11]

Employers are eager to switch their employees and retirees from fee-for-service insurance to managed care networks in order to control the costs of providing health care benefits. To provide incentives, both the employers and networks are emphasizing features of the managed care plans which surveys indicate are most likely to appeal to these individuals. For example, retirees are being enticed by such features as cheaper prescription drugs, lower or no copayments, and affiliated facilities in retirement locations such as Florida.

▲ **Demarketing Versus Remarketing Health Care Services** A marketing strategy called **de-marketing** was introduced in 1987 for the purpose of reducing the utilization of health care services. It was based on the assumption that health care providers could discourage the consumption of some services by such methods as increasing prices and reducing their availability and convenience. The purpose of *selective demarketing* is to reduce demand by "parts of the market which are less profitable or less in need of service."[12] Critics believe this marketing approach is both ethically questionable and professionally risky, and causes more problems than it solves. For example, a Kaiser HMO found that even though demarketing did achieve control over utilization and costs, it created customer dissatisfaction and caused enrollees to drop out of the HMO.[13]

In another approach, called **remarketing**, health care providers seek to lower demand for certain services by offering and promoting better alternatives than the services they wish to discourage. Examples include encouraging preventive care (exercise, dieting, and other wellness programs), promoting the cessation of smoking and alcohol consumption, advising consultation with pharmacists to answer drug questions and recommend over-the-counter medicines, and promoting the use of bicycle and motorcycle helmets to reduce head injuries. The key to remarketing is offering preferable options that increase consumer satisfaction while reducing the demand for more expensive or less desirable alternatives.

Health Care Advertising

Hospitals have increased their advertising budgets to promote their medical staff credentials, their specialized diagnostic and treatment services, their affiliation agreements with other organizations, and their caring approach. Critics question whether such consumer-oriented advertising campaigns are ethical and whether such dollars are being wasted, since managed care networks have greater influence than patients over the selection of facilities.[14] Proponents claim that advertising is justified because consumers often select a managed care network based on which hospitals and physicians are associated with it; thus "educating" consumers helps them make an informed choice.[15] Health care providers target advertising to special consumer markets, such as women (see Figure 20-1 on page 604), and promote specialized services to patients requiring such treatment as orthopedics, cosmetic surgery, or laser eye surgery.

Providers have found that they can increase their advertising effectiveness by reducing the perceived risk of making a health care purchase decision. Elements that reduce patients' perceived risk include assurance (trust and confidence in the staff), reliability (ability to provide the service as promised), empathy (personal attention), responsiveness (promptness and ability to answer questions thoroughly), and tangibles such as the physical appearance of the facility and state-of-the-art equipment.[16]

Pharmaceutical companies have created advertising campaigns that have dual goals: to market certain products and to improve their image among consumers by describing their research and development efforts and their community involvement (see Figure 20-2 on page 605). These manufacturers attempt to persuade consumers that they are getting more by paying more for the advertised trademark brands than for generic products.

Nonprofit organizations also conduct blood donation drives in an attempt to encourage consumers to "contribute to the community's well-being" by adding to the nation's blood supply. Organ donation is marketed as a way to "ease the emotional trauma of losing a loved one" and to foster the healing process.

FIGURE 20-1

Hospitals Target
Special Segments
Courtesy of Mt. Sinai Hospital

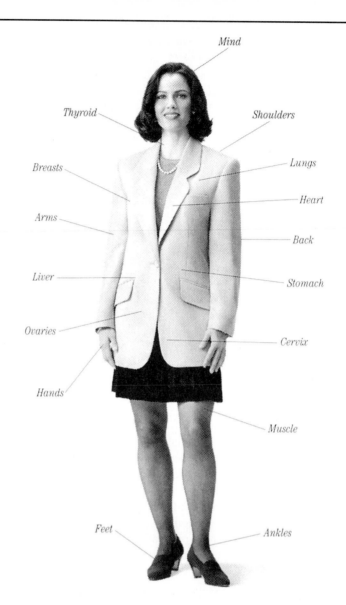

WE'VE CREATED A MEDICAL PROGRAM
DEVOTED TO AREAS WHERE
WOMEN REQUIRE SPECIAL ATTENTION.

Like their arms and legs. Their shoulders and back. Their bones and internal organs. Even the unique complexities of their emotional needs.

Because at Mount Sinai, women's health care has gone well beyond a Pap test and a pelvic exam.

In addition to having access to the expert staff at the Women's Health Program of the Kravis Women's and Children's Center, you can also develop a relationship with one Mount Sinai physician who's devoted to all your medical needs.

And since most of the physicians at the Women's Health Program are women, we can easily provide you with a female doctor if you'd prefer one.

So call (212) 241-8818 for an appointment. We've taken the traditional concept of women's health to an entirely new place. The rest of your body.

Mount Sinai

WOMEN'S HEALTH PROGRAM
OF THE KRAVIS WOMEN'S AND CHILDREN'S CENTER
5 EAST 98TH STREET FIFTH FLOOR NEW YORK, N.Y.

Can we arrest the disease that robs people of their minds?

Over 4 million people suffer from it, and nearly half of all nursing home patients are its victims.

It's Alzheimer's, the disease that steals a person's mind, takes away dignity and independence, and costs the average family $18,000 a year just for home care.

Leading the way in the search for relief from this mysterious disease is the pharmaceutical industry, which is making the nation's largest investment in drug research.

Since 1988 alone, the industry has been conducting research on over 40 medicines for Alzheimer's, and currently has 13 in test. While these efforts hold hope for breakthroughs, the process is long and difficult, with only a few of the thousands of compounds developed ever achieving success.

This exhaustive, high risk research increases the industry's cost of doing business, and in turn the price of drugs. But it also leads to the kind of discoveries that can break the grip of a tragic disease like Alzheimer's.

To learn more about research in progress for Alzheimer's and other diseases of aging, and what it means to you, call or write for our free booklet, "Good Medicine."

The Pharmaceutical Manufacturers Association, 1100 15th St., N.W., Box IR, Wash., D.C. 20005. 1-800-221-2157.

PHARMACEUTICALS
Good Medicine For A Better Life.

FIGURE 20-2

Pharmaceutical Industry Uses Human Interest Ads
Courtesy of The Pharmaceutical Manufacturers Association

Special interest groups conduct **advocacy advertising** to influence consumer opinion and impact legislative action. Often, the public is unaware of who is funding these groups, because the special interests use a "front group" with an innocuous name. When the Clinton administration was promoting universal health care insurance, the threatened insurance industry conducted the "Harry and Louise" campaign, in which actors portrayed a yuppie couple who were concerned about the proposed Clinton initiative. This campaign has been credited with helping turn the grounds well of public opinion against the administration's plan.[17]

Advocacy advertising is being practiced by groups opposed to the proliferation of managed care (see Figure 20-3 on page 606). Health care unions are trying to strengthen their members' image and medical importance by appealing directly to the public through advocacy advertising. For example, a nurses' association advertised directly to consumers that registered nurses are critical to good quality care, and advised them to avoid hospitals that use low-cost labor alternatives (see Figure 20-4 on page 607).

POLITICAL MARKETING

Political marketing has become a very sophisticated, consumer-oriented marketing process in which the creation of a party's political platform is based on extensive consumer research. All major political parties conduct consumer (i.e., voter) research. They use the

First in a series:

Managed Care Is Poor Public Policy

**Managed Care Insurance Companies Use
Financial Penalties And Rewards To Influence Their
Doctors' Decisions About Your Health Care**

*Questions You Should Ask Your Benefits Coordinator
Before You Accept Any Insurance Policy*

1. Does your insurance company financially reward your doctor for not hospitalizing you or for discharging you from the hospital quickly?

2. Does your insurance company penalize your doctor for ordering "too many" tests, asking for "too many" consultations or seeing you "too often"?

3. Does your insurance company financially reward your doctor for not using certain drugs, not obtaining specialist consultation, and not using certain hospitals?

4. Does your insurance company "capitate" your doctor, making him or her financially responsible for all your care, placing your doctor in the role of insurer and setting up strong financial incentives to withhold care?

5. Does your insurance company encourage physician investment in their company, making their profits part of your doctor's motivation?

6. Does your insurance company come between you and your doctor by insisting on pre-hospital certification, phone consultations with insurance nurses about therapy, and limitations on hospital stays?

Your Doctor Is Your Advocate.

Doctors Should Always Be Their Patients' Advocates.

Don't Let The Insurance Industry Try To Make Them Theirs!

Let your legislators know how you feel.
Managed Care is meddlesome care that severely restricts my choices. Managed Care interferes with my physician's ability to administer care, and it strains our relationship on every level. Please pass legislation that will end the insurance industry's ability to influence medical decisions, and return that power to the patients and their physicians.

CODE BLUE
DEDICATED TO RESUSCITATING A DYING HEALTH CARE SYSTEM

For more information or to support this effort, Call (914) 686-4900, Fax (914) 686-4968
Code Blue Inc., P.O. Box 44, Irvington, NY 10533

FIGURE 20-3

Advocacy Ad in Opposition to Managed Care
Courtesy of Code Blue, Inc.

findings of *quantitative* surveys (e.g., polls) to segment voters according to their specific needs and interests and to identify, quantify, and qualify voters' opinions and values on a variety of issues. They use the findings of *qualitative* research (i.e., focus groups) to focus campaign themes more precisely to reflect voter attitudes and interests.

Voter Research

Political research has long been in the forefront of consumer research, using sophisticated sampling methods and computer analyses with great skill and creativity. Voter surveys (i.e., political polling) became a major force in the 1972 presidential election; since that time all candidates, and even elected officials, employ polling experts to help them determine voter reactions to issues on a day-to-day basis.

Polls help politicians gain insight into the minds of the American public and enable them to forecast where public opinion is heading. Political researchers conduct demographic and psychographic surveys to segment the voter population by various criteria (e.g., age, sex, race, family income, party affiliation) in order to tailor appropriate issues to each segment.

Polling is designed to yield findings that can be projected to the entire population. For example, a random sample of 1200 people can be statistically representative of the

total American population. One way that pollsters obtain a random sample is by using a list of all telephone prefixes; then a computer randomly generates the last four digits, so that theoretically everyone in the country has a chance of being called. Well-conducted surveys make an effort to call back anyone who has not answered the first time to avoid skewing the results. Overnight surveys (conducted over one evening) do not permit call backs to unanswered phones, and thus do not adequately represent the population.

Special interest groups sometimes use questionable polling methods to achieve "findings" that support their own positions. Selection of a nonrandom sample, or defects in selecting a random sample, and the use of "leading" survey questions can all bias survey results. For example, professional pollsters identified two major flaws in a mail-in survey used by Presidential candidate Ross Perot: a skewed sample (based on the self-selection process of *TV Guide* readers to a mail-in survey published in the magazine) and biased (i.e., leading) questions.[18] The same questions were posed to a nationwide random sample, and a more neutrally worded version was given to still another nationwide random sample; each version yielded dramatically different findings from Perot's survey (see Figure 20-5 on page 608).

Focus groups enable campaign consultants to elicit detailed opinions from voters that help them shape their candidate's image and issues. Although focus groups are not representative of the voter population, they provide important insights into the thought processes and attitudes behind voter decision making. Focus group participants are chosen by independent research agencies that do not identify campaign sponsorship—which in itself might bias response. In some instances, participants are paid to watch videos of the

FIGURE 20-5

Samplng Errors and Biased Questions Distort Research Findings

Source: "The Question of Questions: An Experiment in Polling," *The New York Times*, September 7, 1993, C11. Copyright © 1993 by The New York Times. Reprinted by permission.

The Question of Questions: An Experiment in Polling

Results of H. Ross Perot's mail-in survey in the 1992 Presidential campaign are compared with those for the same question given to a national sample by Yankelovich & Partners, a more neutrally worded version of the question submitted to a national sample, and still another version given to another national sample by the Gordon Black Corporation.

Question 1. Perot/ TV Guide mail-in sample: *Do you believe that for every dollar of tax increase there should be $2 in spending cuts with the savings ear-marked for deficit and debt reduction?*

Perot question/ Yankelovich sample: Same wording.

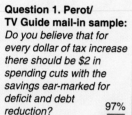

Yankelovich question/ Yankelovich sample: *Would you favor or oppose a proposal to cut spending by $2 for every dollar in new taxes, with the savings earmarked for deficit reduction, even if that meant cuts in domestic programs like Medicare and education?*

Black's redo of Perot question/ Black Sample: *Which of the following deficit reduction approaches would you prefer? a) A program that relies entirely on tax increases, with no spending cuts, b) a program that requires $1 of spending cuts for every $1 of tax increases, or c) a program that requires at least $2 of more spending cuts for every $1 of tax increases.*

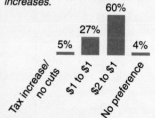

Question 2. Perot/ TV Guidemail-in sample: *Should laws be passed to eliminate all possibilities of special interests giving huge sums of money to candidates?*

Perot question/ Yankelovich sample: Same wording.

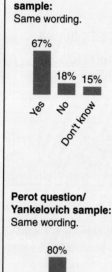

Yankelovich question/ Yankelovich sample: *Should laws be passed to prohibit interest groups from contributing to campaigns, or do groups have a right to contribute to the candidate they support?*

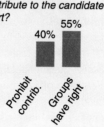

Black's redo of Perot question/ Black Sample: *Please tell me whether you favor or oppose the proposal: The passage of new laws that would eliminate all possibility of special interests giving large sums of money to candidates.*

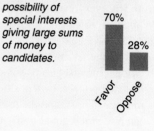

---

candidates and to answer questions posed by a moderator about everything from choice of issues, to the candidates' clothing, to use of words and jargon. The sessions are frequently observed behind one-way mirrors and are videotaped for further analysis.

▲ **Issue Positioning** One of the purposes of political research is to determine which issues are most important in the voters' minds. For example, the Republican's "Contract with America" was thoroughly tested in focus groups before it was introduced to the public in 1993. Political advisors tested different versions of the "contract" on different voters to determine the relative importance of various positions. This led to the decision to put "balanced budget" (ostensibly the most popular issue) at the top of the list and "term limits" (the second most popular issue) at the bottom of the list, so that voters scanning the "contract" would see things they liked. The "G.O.P." in the original name "G.O.P. Contract with America" was also dropped as a result of focus group input.[19]

From 1952 to 1992, foreign policy was perceived by voters as more critical than domestic issues. The Cold War and nuclear proliferation were at the forefront, and voters were most concerned with selecting a President that they felt they could trust in handling foreign affairs. Presidents Eisenhower, Kennedy, Johnson, Nixon, Carter, and Bush were all seen as able foreign policy experts. Although President Reagan was viewed as having limited foreign policy experience, his congenial personality, combined with his strong support of the military, gave voters confidence that he could be "trusted."[20]

The dissolution of the Soviet Union led to a change in the political climate of the 1990s, with domestic policy issues taking precedence over foreign policy. Political researchers discovered through focus groups that the general public was concerned about the domestic economy, the loss of jobs, the depletion of savings, and the high cost of health care. It was in this atmosphere that then-Governor Clinton, who had no foreign policy experience whatever and a record of avoiding military service during the Vietnam War, was able to become President. Clinton emphasized domestic issues in his campaign platform, while the incumbent President Bush, flush with the victory of the Persian Gulf War, would not even acknowledge the deepening economic recession. President Bush's failure to achieve reelection has been attributed to his apparent lack of empathy or even recognition of voter concerns about the domestic economy. Although foreign issues commanded headline attention in the 1996 election campaign, domestic concerns continued to dominate the minds of the American public during this period.

The imagery invoked in campaign rhetoric is most important. For example, the 1996 campaign debate had Democrats accusing the Republicans of wanting to "cut Medicare spending" while the Republicans claimed they just wanted to "increase spending at a slower rate." Republicans talked about "balancing the budget to protect future generations," while Democrats declared that balancing the budget would "hurt ordinary people, while the wealthy get tax breaks."[21]

Although actual debate over conflicting issues is complex, most voters make up their minds based on a few key words or phrases. The relative importance of the issues and responses to specific wording are tested in focus groups. For example, during the 1996 election process, both President Clinton and Senator Dole used the word "values" in many of their speeches. President Clinton also used the term "common ground" as a rhetorical device to connect to the American community, and claimed that Republicans were "outside the mainstream" or "too extreme." These phrases were carefully selected and frequently used, until it was believed that the terms had become cliches.[22]

The immediacy of major issues affects voter turnout, especially with the young. Almost 90% of youths aged 18 to 29 years old (some 21% of the electorate) voted in the 1992 election. This young group was motivated by the issues of abortion, gay rights, and the environment. The issues of Social Security, welfare, and taxation, which dominated the 1994 election, however, did not foster a sense of urgency among the young; their percent of the voting electorate dropped to only 14%.[23]

Political Imagery

Imagery and positioning play increasingly pivotal roles in the "packaging" of political candidates. Ever since 1960, when the televised Kennedy-Nixon debates gave voters a sense of personal access to the candidates, charisma, charm, and good looks have tended to overshadow substantive issues. Since then, politicians have recognized that the packaging of candidates is all important.

In the 1984 Presidential contest, Ronald Reagan's television commercials showed beautiful sunsets, parades of high school bands, pretty girls, and waving flags; challenger Walter Mondale's commercials painted images of nuclear destruction, starvation, and poverty. Reagan's theme was nostalgia, patriotism, and the opportunities America offers its young citizens; Mondale talked about raising taxes. Reagan, a former actor and professional communicator, projected a warm, likable, sincere manner on television; Mondale appeared lifeless and uncomfortable. Reagan's verbal imagery included words like prosperity, opportunity, respect, and growth; Mondale used words like debt, unfairness, and fear. After the political frustrations of the 1960s and 1970s, voters welcomed a candidate who reflected the notions of nostalgia, love of country, self-improvement, hope, and pride. Reagan's campaign advisers demonstrated a solid understanding of the demographic and psychographic trends in the nation.

The importance of imagery was even more apparent in the 1988 Presidential election. Republican strategists repackaged an awkward, stilted George Bush to appear relaxed, confident, genial, likable, and engaging. The Democratic candidate, Michael Dukakis, with his emphasis on competence and administration, appeared serious, solemn, taciturn, and unapproachable. As one pollster said, ". . . competence is only a part of image. A President has [to appear] to be open and caring, as well as tough and hard. He must project a comfortable image."[24] The 1988 Presidential campaign was totally dominated by television imagery and television ads. It was also the first time in American history that Presidential candidates used at least as much negative advertising to slander their opponents as they used positive advertising to promote themselves. It was estimated that more than half the ads for both camps were negative.

Many voters were outraged at the lack of substantive discussion of issues by either side in the 1988 campaign. They recognized that the candidates appeared in staged events created solely for the television cameras, avoided probing questions, and relied on "spin-doctors" (glorified public relations people) to interpret the impact of their remarks and debates for public consumption. The timing and substance of televised debates were carefully negotiated between the parties; questions and questioners were prescreened and preapproved, and politically correct answers were rehearsed. No opportunities were made available for extemporaneous discussions or spontaneous question-and-answer sessions.

The 1992 Presidential race changed all that. Ross Perot, the Texas billionaire who established his own political party, began appearing on popular talk shows and made himself accessible to questions from the public through electronic "town halls" that he initiated. Soon candidate Clinton also appeared on late-night talk shows, and even played his saxophone on television to show that he was a man of the people. President Bush was forced to become somewhat more accessible, but still maintained his slightly patrician air. On a campaign visit to a supermarket, his absolute amazement at seeing the product scanners at the checkout counters caused voter derision at how out of touch he was with everyday living.

In 1992, when Democratic campaign strategists discovered, through a national survey and a round of focus groups, that 40% of the voters did not much like their Presidential candidate and his wife Hillary, they set out to create a totally new image for the Clinton family. The "General Election Project," as the plan was called, set forth the thematic message Mr. Clinton would deliver (that he was an aggressive, middle-class-oriented agent of change ready to stand up to special-interest groups), and the tactics by which he would drive that point home (town hall-style forums, live television talk shows, and a series of speeches directly challenging specific interest groups). On a personal level, the plan offered the image of Mr. Clinton as a child whose "father died before he was born, whose mother worked and struggled, who later interceded to stop an alcoholic stepfather who abused his brother and his mother, and who went on to oppose institutionalized racism and the perpetuation of a failed welfare system."[25] During the 1996 election, President Clinton was "repackaged" to appear more distinguished and more "presidential" than his opponents and firmly in control of the nation. While Dole emphasized his military service and sacrifice in World War II and offered a "bridge" to a long-ago "gentler" era, Clinton portrayed a youthful vigor in offering voters a bridge to the 21st century.

To the American public, a candidate's family is just as important as the candidate. To this end, Hillary Clinton has constantly redefined her image. Early in the 1992 election process, her image evoked intelligence, competence, and a partnership with her husband. Then, to appeal to a broader spectrum of women and to make herself seem less imposing to men, Mrs. Clinton emphasized her interest in children and family, and even revealed a favorite cookie recipe. Once her husband was elected President and placed her in charge of developing a new national health care plan, Mrs. Clinton ignored the softer image and again stressed her intelligence and competence. After the health care plan failed, Hillary Clinton was once again repositioned with a softened image that made her appear more likable, with a renewed interest in women's and children's issues.

Political Advertising

For years, the dominant issues in political advertising research have been the impact of advertising on voter beliefs, affect, and behavior (i.e., the three components of attitudes) and the ways that voters cognitively process political ads.[26]

Positive advertisements often feature photo opportunities of the candidates and their families, indicate patriotism, and are "warm and fuzzy." Rarely do these ads present substantive issues, and they have little effect on voters.[27] On the other hand, *negative advertisements* that attack the opponent seem to elicit a more vigorous viewer response. Some tracking polls have shown that people who see a negative ad at least eight times begin to shift away from the attacked candidate.[28] Positive ads increase voter turnout; negative ads are known to discourage potential voters of all parties from voting at all. In fact, negative ads have been used by some campaign strategists as a way of ensuring low turnout when they believe high turnout would be to their candidate's disadvantage.[29]

Research on the use of comparative political advertisements (sponsor-positive and opponent-negative, or simple opponent-negative) found that negative ads produced negative reactions from voters, reflected negatively on the ad sponsor, and had less impact on the opposing candidate than sponsor-positive ads.[30] Widespread negative advertising has been found to reduce all candidates in the eyes of the public, as well as their believability across all issues.[31]

▲ **Political Persuasion** Political strategists are masters of the art of persuasion. Researchers who have studied political persuasion techniques have noted that many political advertisements are really unfair appeals to bias and emotion. Of course, that description also applies to much nonpolitical advertising, but unfortunately, none of the restrictions on deceptive product advertising (see Chapter 21) apply to political advertising, leaving the opportunity open for great abuse.

A 1992 study of election year persuasion methods examined the impact of an entire range of communication techniques on political campaigning. These include fear appeals, attack ads, one-sided arguments, two-sided arguments, the "granfalloon," and agenda-setting.[32]

Fear appeals play on voters' fears that various misfortunes will befall the country (or state or city) if the opponent is elected. (Example: Elect Candidate X and the country will plunge into depression.)

An *attack ad* makes a strong negative claim about an opponent, especially in the last days of a campaign when there is little time for the attack target to refute it. The main impact of attack ads is among undecided voters: they tend to discourage these voters from voting altogether.

With *one-sided arguments*, the candidate argues in generalities that a particular course of action is the correct one, but gives no details with which the audience can analyze, discuss, or rebut the argument. In *two-sided arguments*, the candidate says something favorable as to the reasonableness of an opponent's position before attacking it. This technique boosts the credibility of those who use it, because it suggests to the audience that the candidate is objective, open-minded, and fair in examining the issues.

The *granfalloon*, a frequently used propaganda device, is a term coined by the writer Kurt Vonnegut to mean a false and arbitrary sense of belonging to a group. The granfalloon creates a false sense of "we" and "they," and is frequently used by candidates to align themselves with their audiences while portraying their opponents as the enemy. (Example: We must hold fast against those slick Washington insiders.)

In *agenda setting*, candidates or political parties proclaim the one issue they are interested in as crucial and all others as irrelevant. This technique establishes the candidate as the "champion" of a specific popular issue and downgrades the issues supported by the opposing party.

Clearly, it is important for voters to find ways to *inoculate* themselves against the propaganda techniques used in political advertising. It is also important for a candidate to provide voters with *counterarguments* to opponents' claims.

Political marketing is by far the most controversial area in which behavioral research is conducted. The potential for manipulation of the voter by politicians or special interest groups is undeniable. On the other hand, like other areas of consumer behavior research, voter behavior studies offer the promise of a deeper understanding of voter needs and the development of improved voter communications programs.

THE MARKETING OF SOCIAL CAUSES

Profit and not-for-profit organizations increasingly use the findings of consumer behavior to advance social causes. Objectives can be as varied as supporting social, cultural, political, and philanthropic organizations to correcting social ills and altering negligent consumer behavior, from fund-raising for education and the arts and to providing programs to fight societal problems such as teenage crime, addiction, drunk driving, adolescent pregnancy, and AIDS.

Several studies have examined the effectiveness of advertising campaigns designed to promote socially desirable behavior. For example, consumer behavior studies have been conducted to determine the kinds of messages that are most effective in conveying the dangers of taking drugs, and advertising research has been conducted to assess the effects of specific ads on changing attitudes toward drugs.

Social Marketing and Corporate Philanthropy

Many corporations have integrated philanthropy into their overall corporate goals. The trend is to support specific societal goals, such as safer streets, better schools, fewer people on welfare, and less alcohol and drug addiction.[33] Education receives the largest share of total corporate support; in 1992 it reached almost $1 billion.[34] This type of support is depicted in Figures 20-6A and B. Figure 20-7 on page 614 presents a corporate ad supporting vocational education and training.

FIGURE 20-6A  Corporate Support of Education
Courtesy of AT&T

FIGURE 20-6B Coors Combats Illiteracy
Courtesy of Coors Brewing Company and Uniworld Group, Inc.

Corporations that practice social responsibility usually allocate a percentage of their annual budgets to a variety of preferred philanthropic causes to which they contribute money, expertise, or promotional know-how. Figure 20-8 on page 615 reflects the strong personal commitment of Charles Schwab, Founder and Chairman of Charles Schwab & Co., Inc., to support the National Parks System. Socially responsible activities can only enhance the image and stature of the company among its many publics. Thus, such activities indirectly contribute to the company's commercial objectives, creating a win-win situation for the company and for society.

The Benetton Corporation for years has run highly controversial ads designed to raise public awareness of social issues, such as AIDS and multicultural diversity. Their corporate philosophy is that advertising can provoke political discourse and public debate, which in turn will lead to social change. They use stark, provocative photographs to dramatize a cause, and only identify themselves with an inconspicuous Benetton logo in a corner of the photo.[35] (The company has come under sharp attack from some European retailers who do not want the merchandise they carry to be associated with controversial issues.) Other companies prefer to support noncontroversial causes, such as promoting sports and fitness, discouraging underage drinking, and honoring role models (see Figure 20-9 on page 615).

Many corporations include in their philanthropic budgets the sponsorship of fundraising events for nonprofit organizations. The cosmetics and fragrance industry sponsors the March of Dimes annual "Beauty Ball."[36] Coca-Cola and Adidas are among the many sponsors of the Special Olympics World Games.[37]

Today, these students will learn HOW TO DISSECT AN ENGINE. Frogs everywhere breathe A SIGH OF RELIEF.

Students at Automotive High School in Brooklyn, New York learn auto-engineering skills through the Toyota Technical Education Network.

EVERY YEAR, Toyota donates vehicles, equipment and training to schools and colleges across America, helping students with an interest in automotive careers get a head start in the job world. But our commitment to education doesn't end with cars. Over the last four years Toyota invested more than $50 million in worthwhile educational organizations like National Center for Family Literacy, United Negro College Fund and hundreds of other projects across America. As America's fourth-largest manufacturer of vehicles, it's only natural that we should be helping to prepare students for the long road ahead.

INVESTING IN THE THINGS WE ALL CARE ABOUT. **TOYOTA**

For more information about Toyota in America write Toyota Motor Corporate Services, 9 West 57th Street, Suite 4900-P10, New York, NY 10019

FIGURE 20-7

Corporate Philanthropy Supports Vocational Training
Courtesy of Toyota

Many marketers volunteer their services to promote social causes. Some companies design and sell special products and donate the proceeds to a charitable cause. Other companies "donate" their employees' time or encourage employee participation in volunteer activities. For example, in 1996 the Bayer Corporation, headquartered in Pittsburgh, lent an executive to a local university's Small Business Development Center.[38]

The fashion industry has actively supported such causes as AIDS and cancer research (see Figure 20-10 on page 616). Country music performers and record companies have

FIGURE 20-8

Corporate Promotion
Reflects Social
Responsibility
Courtesy of Charles Schwab

FIGURE 20-9 Corporate Social Responsibility Highlights Role Models
Courtesy of Timberland

FIGURE 20-10

Cause-related
Marketing
Courtesy of CTFA Foundation, Inc.

joined together to help in the battle against AIDS by donating the profits of musical record-ings to support anti-AIDS programs and public service announcements.[39] The Campbell Soup Company and Chrysler/Plymouth help to sponsor "Make-A-Difference Day," in which local residents around the country are encouraged to volunteer one day a year to a volunteer activity of their choice. The companies' sponsorship contributions range from running ads in support of the program to encouraging their own employees to become involved.[40] Other corporations support The United Way's annual "Day of Caring" by allowing employees to participate in local community projects during company time. Figure 20-11 shows an ad by General Motors' GMC Truck division that reports their support for The Nature Conservancy.

When *nonprofit organizations* undertake social marketing, their purposes invariably are to fulfill specific objectives in their stated missions. Thus, the American Cancer Soci-

ety raises money for cancer research, disseminates preliminary cancer research findings, and urges women to have annual mammograms. The March of Dimes conducts a walk-a-thon ("WalkAmerica") and an annual ball to help fund research and community outreach programs that support its mission to eliminate birth defects (see Figure 20-12 on page 618). Mothers Against Drunk Driving (MADD) urges people not to drink and drive (see Figure 20-13 on page 619). The Gay Men's Health Crisis lobbies government and raises money for AIDS research. These are social causes that fulfill the prime objectives of the nonprofit organizations that sponsor them; marketing these causes is their major reason for being.

Cause-related Marketing and Corporate Promotion

Cause-related marketing is a new form of corporate promotion based on the rationale of profit-motivated charitable contributions.[41] Companies use cause-related marketing as a way to motivate socially aware consumers to buy their products; the cause becomes the peg to which a promotional program is linked. This form of marketing is known to increase sales and market share, boost employee morale, enhance corporate and brand image, and generate goodwill and positive publicity.

While some companies point proudly to their cause-related marketing programs as examples of corporate philanthropy, critics point out that the companies often spend more in promoting these programs (and thereby stimulating demand for their products) than they spend on actual contributions to the associated cause. There are also concerns that the nonprofit organization's social mission may become lost through the commercialization of their corporate fund-raising affiliations, and that potential donors may feel that they—and

FIGURE 20-12

The March of Dimes
Focuses Promotion on
Social Causes
Courtesy of March of Dimes

the affiliated charities—are being exploited. A study determined that when corporate donations were small, consumers felt that the nonprofit organization was being exploited; when corporate donations were high, they felt that the cause-related marketing tie-in was beneficial.[42]

It is revealing to note that corporate contributions to a cause-related marketing program usually come from the company's promotional budget, rather than from its philanthropic budget. Cause-related marketing is designed to promote goodwill and to increase sales and market share; the contribution to the cause is simply the cost of obtaining these objectives.

The Special Olympics World Games tried to broaden its visibility (and the message that the mentally and physically challenged have much to offer) and expand its fund-raising potential by televising the 1995 games on national TV. To attract corporate sponsorship of the event, they needed to increase attendance at the games, and were advised by marketing consultants to add attractions such as concerts, fireworks, and dances. These unrelated activities ran the risk of drowning out the true purpose of the games, namely, watching and cheering on the participants in the Special Olympics sports events. To avoid upstaging the sporting events, the World Games organizers placed the commercial activities between the tracks, stadiums, and pools where the games were taking place, so that people would be drawn to watch the games. Some sponsors were content with just giving cash contributions to support the World Games, while others, such as Coca-Cola and

Tie one on.

This holiday season, some 150 million people will tie a simple red ribbon on their car antennas, to express their commitment to safe, sober driving. It's part of the "Tie One On For Safety"™ campaign sponsored by Mothers Against Drunk Driving (MADD) and The Good Hands People of Allstate.
See your Allstate agent now for your complimentary red ribbon. Together we can help ensure a safe and jolly holiday. And many more happy new years.

Allstate
You're in good hands.

For more tips on being a responsible, safe driver, write to: Allstate, Dept. DD,
P.O. Box 7660, Mt. Prospect, IL 60056-9961. © 1992 Allstate Insurance Company, Northbrook, IL.

FIGURE 20-13 ▼

Allstate Joins Mothers
Against Drunk Driving
in Cause-related Social
Marketing
Courtesy of Allstate Insurance
Company

Adidas, also marketed their products. The president of the World Games, Timothy Shriver, noted: "It's walking a tightrope. We don't want to lose the integrity of the cause. We're not just a commercial property. . . . something that is up for sale."[43]

▲ **Affinity Group Marketing** *Affinity group marketing* is a type of cause-related marketing that capitalizes on the loyalty that individuals often show to the causes in which they believe or the organizations to which they belong. The rationale is that when service offerings are all similar, consumers would just as soon support specific causes or groups. For example, Visa encourages use of its credit card over other cards by promising to make a donation to the U.S. Olympic Team every time a consumer makes a Visa purchase (see Figure 20-14 on page 620).

FIGURE 20-14

Affinity Group
Marketing
Courtesy of Visa USA, Inc.

Banks and telephone companies frequently use *affinity group* marketing affiliations
to obtain new customers and to build brand loyalty. In return for access to their membership lists, the companies offer nonprofit organizations a percentage of the ensuing credit
card or telephone charges made by organization members; the credit card or calling card
identifies the nonprofit organization as the sponsor of the card. To maximize its potential
income, the nonprofit (e.g., a university alumni association) promotes the card(s) to its
membership. The arrangement provides added income to the nonprofit partner, and the
bank or telephone company benefits by gaining access to a special-interest market niche.[44]

Working Assets Funding Service, a company that resells both credit card and long-
distance telephone services, successfully uses affinity group marketing. The company's
premise is that generosity to charitable causes is easy and painless when it is linked to bills
that people normally pay. The company accumulates a philanthropic fund in three ways:
(1) credit card holders donate a nickel for each purchase made; (2) telephone customers
contribute 1% of their monthly bill; and (3) telephone customers are encouraged to round
their payments upward by $5 to $10 (the proceeds of the round-ups are tax-deductible for
the customers). Once a year, all Working Assets customers vote to select the charitable
causes that the company's philanthropic fund will support; the company directors narrow
the choices down to several dozen groups. In 1992, Working Assets donated one million
dollars to charitable causes.[45]

When for-profit organizations undertake *social marketing*, it is an expression of their
companies' sense of social responsibility toward the improvement of society. However,
when such organizations undertake *cause-related marketing*, they do so to achieve specific
commercial objectives. The opportunity to support a worthy cause indirectly is a strong in-

centive for many consumers to select the cause-related product over competing brands. Thus, in cause-related marketing, it is the consumer who displays social responsibility, not the sponsoring company. As pointed out earlier, cause-related marketing is simply a hook on which to hang a promotional program.

ENVIRONMENTAL MARKETING: A CAUSE-RELATED GROWTH INDUSTRY

Since Rachel Carson wrote *The Silent Spring* in 1962, there has been a growing awareness in the United States and in other industrialized nations of the fragility of the environment, and of the need to protect the natural resources that earlier generations had taken for granted: clean air, clean water, unspoiled earth, and a self-renewing ecosystem.[46]

Consumer environmental groups have adopted as their dual missions the need to educate the public and to lobby government to take appropriate actions to protect the environment. After a slow start in the 1970s and 1980s, the early 1990s experienced spectacular growth in the size of the consumer segment concerned with protecting and preserving the environment. While many consumers, corporations, and countries practice safer environmental practices today, the sense of urgency that marked consumer environmental activism has slowed down, perhaps an indication of consumers' satisfaction with the positive steps already achieved.

Marketers saw increasing consumer interest in the environment as a marketing opportunity to target ecologically-concerned consumers. They redesigned products and packaging, both voluntarily and in response to public pressure, and were quick to announce these improvements on package labels and in company advertisements. The burgeoning environmental movement was dubbed the *green movement*; environmentally aware consumers called *green consumers*; products designed to protect the environment called *green products*; and, not surprisingly, marketing that uses environmental claims called *green marketing* (see Figure 20-15 on page 622).

A number of businesses and industry groups have responded to environmental concerns by integrating environmental issues into their corporate policies. The Xerox Corporation includes environmental protection among its core company values and objectives. AT&T and Intel have formulated a joint program to develop benchmarks for corporate pollution prevention programs.[47] A number of travel companies, including Hertz, American Airlines, British Airways, and Inter-Continental Hotels, have agreed to develop recycling and air quality guidelines under the auspices of the World Travel and Tourism Council.[48] MasterCard has launched a "Forests For Our Future" program that promises to plant a tree every time MasterCard is used to make a catalog purchase; *Business Week* promises to plant a tree for every new paid subscription it receives.

Unfortunately, the growing consumer interest in protecting the environment has also attracted so-called *green marketeers*, who were quick to join the green marketing movement with deceptive or misleading packaging and advertisements proclaiming or implying environmental safety. Even respected companies got drawn into this vortex. For example, the Mobil Corporation put "biodegradable" on its Hefty plastic trash bags, neglecting to note that they were only degradable in sunlight, not when buried in landfills. Procter & Gamble ran ads for its Pampers disposable diapers that showed a tree seedling planted in a tub of rich soil under the headline "Ninety days ago this was a disposable diaper," despite

SEEMS OUR MOST ORIGINAL IDEAS

ARE RECYCLED.

Bluer sky, greener grass, cleaner air. These are elements we see in the vehicles we're developing at FORD MOTOR COMPANY. Like the Synthesis 2010. A car whose body is made of 100% RECYCLABLE aluminum. Which is just as strong as steel, yet gentler on the gas pump. Today, Ford is an industry LEADER in aluminum fabrication and RECYCLED plastics. It's all part of our continuing effort to build ENVIRONMENTALLY RESPONSIBLE cars that combine even better fuel economy and HIGH RECYCLABILITY. We believe this visionary thinking, powered by the latest technology, will make cars and trucks safe on the road and the ENVIRONMENT. Which has always been our original idea.

· FORD · FORD TRUCKS · · LINCOLN · MERCURY ·

QUALITY IS JOB 1.

FIGURE 20-15

Green Marketing
Courtesy of Ford Motor Company

the fact that diapers cannot be fully composted and that not all states have composting facilities.[49] Marketers of products that are totally unrelated to the environment (e.g., Rolex watches) have also tied their advertising to the environment.

Regulation of Environmental Marketing Claims

Several nonprofit organizations have sought to establish product environmental certification programs in the United States. Under such a program, a product that passes specified environmental criteria would merit an environmental seal, similar to the Underwriters Laboratories' UL seal of approval. The European Community has already put a "green" seal of approval in place: its *eco* label (consisting of a cheerful flower logo with an E for a pistil) is designed to counter the plethora of dubious, unregulated green marketing ads that have sprouted in Europe.[50]

Most major United States companies are fighting third-party product certification; they would prefer self-regulation without outside interference in product or package design. However, most consumers support product certification, because it provides some shopping assurance as to which products are less damaging to the environment than others. The federal government has taken a hands-off attitude on this issue, hoping the market will regulate itself, and that consumers will somehow determine which products are "green" and which are harmful to the environment without government intervention. Many consumers have already switched to so-called natural cleaning products (such as baking soda, vinegar, and lemon juice), which require more effort and may not be as effective as chemical-based cleaners. This "green cleaning trend" illustrates a major shift in consumer behavior. Throughout much of the 1980s, consumers were motivated mainly by convenience and performance; in the late 1990s, they are more concerned about polluted waste water or exposing their children to harmful chemicals.[51]

Consumers' Environmental Concerns and Behavior

On April 22, 1970, American environmentalists declared the first celebration of Earth Day to call attention to the dangers of pollution. Since that time, there has been a surge in the consumers' environmental learning curve. People understand the concepts of "degradable," "recyclable," "reusable," and "environmentally friendly" products and manufacturing processes.

Figure 20-16 illustrates the relative concern that consumers have for environmental issues. Solid waste disposal has become the most important issue, overtaking concern

FIGURE 20-16

Consumer Concern for Environmental Issues
Source: From Consumer Solid Waste Awareness Attitude and Behavior Study conducted by Gerstman+Meyers Inc., New York. Reprinted by permission.

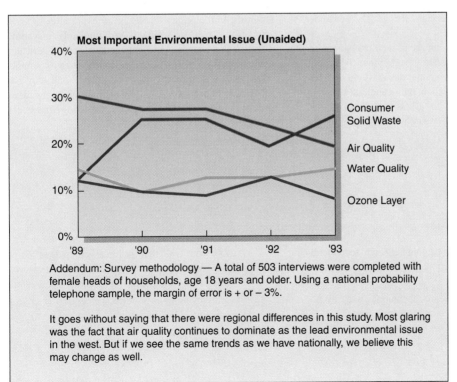

Most Important Environmental Issue (Unaided)

- Consumer Solid Waste
- Air Quality
- Water Quality
- Ozone Layer

Addendum: Survey methodology — A total of 503 interviews were completed with female heads of households, age 18 years and older. Using a national probability telephone sample, the margin of error is + or − 3%.

It goes without saying that there were regional differences in this study. Most glaring was the fact that air quality continues to dominate as the lead environmental issue in the west. But if we see the same trends as we have nationally, we believe this may change as well.

about air quality and the atmosphere.[52] Almost three-quarters of survey respondents said that their brand selection is affected by the company's environmental reputation, and almost half reported that they made a negative purchase decision over the past year because of environmental concerns.[53]

Clearly, there is a need for public policymakers to enact appropriate laws and regulations to protect the environment. However, there is also a need for policymakers to enact laws and regulations that protect the consumer from deceptive environmental claims, a need for regulatory agencies to police the marketplace to ensure that environmental claims are truthful, and a need for consumer education that enables naive consumers to understand the difference. The following chapter will discuss the role of consumer research in the development of public policy designed to protect the public interest and promote the public welfare.

summary

Consumer behavior research has become an important basis for profit and not-for-profit marketing by both the private and public sectors. Despite dramatic changes in the health care delivery system in the United States, many health care providers continue to monitor the perceptions of their patients regarding the delivery of services and their overall satisfaction in order to improve the quality of the services that they provide. Employers monitor the perceptions of their employees regarding their general satisfaction with company-sponsored managed care networks. Some health care providers use research findings to develop innovative outpatient services that satisfy consumer needs.

Political strategists are very intense users of consumer behavior research. They are constantly surveying the public through voter polls and focus group interviews, trying to determine voters' beliefs and attitudes about their candidates and opposing candidates, and trying to assess the feelings and cognitions of the voting public. Research findings provide the basis for positioning candidates and their families and, where necessary, reformulating negative images. Although political marketing is by far the most controversial area in which behavioral research is conducted, voter behavior studies offer the promise of a deeper understanding of voter needs and the development of improved voter communications programs.

Consumer behavior findings are used increasingly by profit and not-for-profit organizations to advance social causes and to fight social ills. Nonprofit organizations use social marketing to fulfill specific objectives in their stated missions; for-profit corporations do so as an expression of social responsibility, to create goodwill, and ultimately (and sometimes directly) to increase sales and market share. Marketers have recognized that environmental protection is an important social cause with widespread consumer support, and they have responded with products and promotional campaigns focused on the environment. So-called "green marketing" has become an important growth industry in America.

discussion questions

1. How can hospitals use consumer research to: (a) improve their services and (b) market their services effectively?

2. a. Describe two voter research techniques used by political strategists to develop marketing strategy.

   b. Do you feel that political campaigns emphasize image at the expense of issues? Illustrate your answer with examples from recent political campaigns.

3. "In politics as in commerce, perception is more potent than reality." Discuss.

4. **a.** How can politicians use consumer research to create more persuasive messages?

    b. Describe five communication techniques frequently used by political candidates in their efforts to persuade voters.

5. You are developing a campaign promoting the concept of "Don't drink and drive" among 18 to 24 year olds. Would you recommend segmenting the target market on the basis of demographics, lifestyles, or the benefits that people seek from drinking alcohol? Explain.

6. Do commercial companies have an obligation to promote causes that are beneficial to society? Why or why not?

7. Compare and contrast corporate social marketing and cause-related marketing.

8. "Get government out of the business of regulating environmental marketing claims. Marketers will police themselves." Please respond to this statement.

exercises

1. Does your doctor or dentist apply the marketing concept in providing his or her service? Explain your answer.

2. Find one example (e.g., advertisement, coupons, package) of social marketing and one example of cause-related marketing. Explain the differences between the two in terms of the objectives and missions of the sponsoring organizations. Does the cause-related marketing example that you chose constitute corporate philanthropy or corporate promotion? Explain.

3. Think back to a political campaign in your state or town in which you voted. (a) How did advertising and/or other forms of persuasive communications influence your voting decision? (b) In your opinion were any of the ads or messages used in the course of this campaign deceptive? Discuss.

4. Conduct a survey of twenty consumers and identify those who have purchased green products or taken other environment-friendly actions during the recent past. How do their demographics, lifestyle characteristics, and media habits distinguish these green consumers from the rest of the sample?

key words

- Advocacy Advertising
- Agenda setting
- Attack ads
- Affinity group marketing
- Counterarguments
- Cause-related marketing
- De-marketing
- Environmental marketing
- Granfalloon

- Green Consumers
- Green Marketing
- Green Products
- Health Care Intermediaries
- Marketing of Social Causes
- Not-for-profit marketing
- One-sided vs. two-sided arguments
- Political imagery

- Political marketing
- Political polling
- Positive and negative advertising
- Re-marketing
- Social marketing
- Social responsibility
- Voter research

end notes

1. U.S. DEPARTMENT of COMMERCE *Statistical Abstract of the United States* (115th Edition). 1995.
2. RON WINSLOW, "A Trip to the Mayo Clinic via Information Highway," *The Wall Street Journal*, October 17, 1994, B1.
3. SHADYSIDE HOSPITAL, Pittsburgh, PA, *Working Together*, Winter 1995.
4. MELVIN F. HALL, "Patient Satisfaction or Acquiescence," *Journal of Health Care Marketing* 15(1), Spring 1995, 54–61.
5. M. C. GOLDBERG, "If We Are Lucky the Patient Will Complain," *American Journal of Nursing*, February 1995, 52–54.
6. STEPHEN STRASSER, SHARON SCHWEIKHART, GERALD E. WELSH II, M.D., and JEAN C. BURGE, "Satisfaction with Medical Care," *Journal of Health Care Marketing* 15(3), Fall 1995, 34–42.
7. ESTHER B. FEIN, "Competing, Hospitals Are Nicer to Patients," *The New York Times*, July 24, 1995, B1.
8. MELINDA HENNEBERGER, "Hospitals Learning the Not-Subtle Art of Self-Promotion," *The New York Times*, July 4, 1994, 1.
9. MARTIN J. GORBIEN, M.D., SALLY BRASFIELD SIMMONS, and JON R. CANTANESE, "Senior Health Day," *Journal of Health Care Marketing* 15(2), Summer 1995, 58–60.
10. ESTER B. FEIN, "Region's Hospitals Have Seen the Future, and It's an Outpatient Clinic," *The New York Times*, February 19, 1996, B1.
11. WINSLOW, op. cit.
12. PHILLIP KOTLER and SIDNEY LEVY, "Demarketing, Yes, Demarketing," *Harvard Business Review*, 1987, as quoted in SCOTT MACSTRAVIC, "Remarketing, Yes, Remarketing Health Care," *Journal of Health Care Marketing* 15(4), Winter 1995, 57–58.
13. Ibid., SCOTT MACSTRAVIC.
14. HENNEBERGER, op. cit.
15. PATTY TASCARELLA, "Hospitals Woo Patients, as Competition Grows Intense," *Pittsburgh Business Times*, July 3, 1995, 4.
16. KENNETH E. CLOW, "Advertising Health Care Services," *Journal of Health Care Marketing* 15(2) Summer 1995, 9.
17. ELIZABETH KOLBERT, "Special Interests' Special Weapon," *The New York Times*, March 26, 1995, 20.
18. DANIEL GOLEMAN, "Pollsters Enlist Psychologists in Quest for Unbiased Results," *The New York Times*, September 7, 1993, C1.
19. ELIZABETH KOLBERT and FRANK LUNTZ, "The Vocabulary of Votes," *The New York Times Magazine*, March 26, 1995, 46–49.
20. R. W. APPLE, JR., "Post-Cold War Candidates Find No Place Like Home," *The New York Times*, February 20, 1996, A14.
21. ELIZABETH KOLBERT, "Shifting Public Opinion by a Turn of Phrase," *The New York Times*, June 5, 1995, A1.
22. ALISON MITCHELL, "Consult Polls. Choose Phrase. Repeat," *The New York Times*, December 3, 1995, D3.
23. WENDY BOUNDS and ERIC NORTON, "Disaffected Youth Are Truant from Polls," *The Wall Street Journal*, November 16, 1994, B1.
24. RICHARD STENGEL, "The Likability Sweepstakes," *Time Magazine*, October 24, 1988.
25. MICHAEL KELLY, "The Making of a First Family: A Blueprint," *The New York Times*, November 12, 1992, 1, 9.
26. RONALD PAUL HILL, "An Exploration of Voter Responses to Political Advertisements," *Journal of Advertising* 18(4), 1989, 14–22; RICHARD M. PERLOFF and DENNIS KINSEY, "Political Advertising as Seen by Consultants and Journalists," *Journal of Advertising Research*, May/June 1992, 53–60.
27. ROGER STONE, "Positively Negative," *The New York Times*, February 26, 1996, A13.
28. Ibid.
29. STEPHEN ANSOLABEHERE and SHANTO IYENGAR, *Going Negative* (New York: The Free Press, 1996).
30. HILL, op. cit.
31. Ibid.
32. ANTHONY PRATKANIS and ELLIOT ARONSON, *Age of Propaganda: Uses and Misuses of Persuasion* (W. H. Freeman and Company, 1992).
33. BARBARA CLARK O'HARE, "Good Deeds Are Good Business," *American Demographics*, September 1992, 38–42.
34. *Annual Survey of Corporate Contributions* (New York: The Conference Board, 1993).
35. MICHAEL JANOFSKY, "Advertising: A Revolutionary Benetton Campaign Uses the Real Thing," *The New York Times*, July 29, 1993.
36. "Marching Toward a Future Without Birth Defects," *Advertising Supplement* to *The New York Times Magazine*, April 2, 1995.
37. KIRK JOHNSON, "Selling of the Special Olympics," *The New York Times*, June 23, 1995, B1.
38. *Pittsburgh Business Times*, March 4, 1996.
39. STUART ELLIOTT, "Advertising: The Country Music Industry Climbs on the Anti-AIDS Bandwagon," *The New York Times*, August 24, 1993, D18.
40. STUART ELLIOTT, "Advertising: Campbell Soup and Chrysler Support a Day of Volunteerism," *The New York Times*, October 24, 1994.
41. The term "cause-related marketing" has been copyrighted by the American Express Company.
42. DARREN W. DAHOL and ANNE M. LAVACK, "Cause-Related Marketing: Impact of Size of Corporate Donation and Size of Cause-Related Promotion on Consumer

Perceptions and Participation," *American Marketing Association*, Winter 1995, 476–81.

43. JOHNSON, op. cit.

44. See SCOTT M. SMITH and DAVID S. ALCORN, "Cause Marketing: A New Direction in the Marketing of Corporate Responsibility," *Journal of Services Marketing* 5(4), Fall 1991, 21–37.

45. JANE GROSS, "Profile: Laura S. Scher—She Took One Look at the Age of Greed and Made a Quick Left," *The New York Times*, November 7, 1993, 8.

46. RACHEL CARSON, *The Silent Spring* (Boston: Houghton Mifflin Company, 1962).

47. WALTER CODDINGTON, *Environmental Marketing: Positive Strategies for Reaching the Green Consumer* (New York: McGraw-Hill, 1993).

48. "Taking the Green Road," *The Wall Street Journal*, March 25, 1993, A1.

49. JOSEPH M. WINSKI, "Big Prizes, but No Easy Answers," *Advertising Age*, October 28, 1991, GR3.

50. MARLISE SIMONS, "12 Countries, 340 Million Shoppers, One Planet," *The New York Times*, April 11, 1993, E5.

51. KATHLEEN DEVENY, "For Growing Band of Shoppers, Clean Means Green," *The Wall Street Journal*, April 6, 1992, B1.

52. GERSTMAN+MEYERS INC, Consumer Solid Waste Awareness Attitude and Behavior Study.

53. Ibid.

The previous chapter explored the growing application of consumer research findings to profit and not-for-profit social marketing, and the marketing of social causes. This final chapter examines the application of consumer behavior research to the development of public policy.

PUBLIC POLICY AND CONSUMER PROTECTION

Public policy (or social policy, as it has been called) intersects the field of consumer behavior when public policymakers believe that **government intervention** in the process or outcome of marketing exchanges (i.e., between marketers and consumers) will benefit society as a whole. New social policies that affect marketing usually are the outgrowth of marketplace abuses brought to the attention of policymakers through the media, through consumer advocacy groups, through consumers themselves, or through public recognition of the need for economic or social welfare (e.g., the provision of shelter to the homeless, medical treatment to the poor, cultural enrichment to the public.)

When Ralph Nader, thought by many to be the "father" of the modern consumerist movement, wrote his first book, *Unsafe at Any Speed* in 1965, the common wisdom was that "you can't fight City Hall and you can't fight Big Business." In the book he accused General Motors of ignoring dangerous flaws in its Chevrolet Corvair. Nader achieved folk hero status when he survived General Motors' attempt to discredit him by investigating his private life, and won a sizable invasion-of-privacy suit against GM. Nader showed consumers that it *was* possible to "beat Big Business." The money he was awarded served to fund the first of his public advocacy organizations, the Center for Study of Responsive Law.[1] Among the highlights of his consumer advocacy accomplishments are the creation of the National Highway Traffic Safety Administration (1970), amendments that strengthened the Freedom of Information Act (1974), and the requirement that all new cars must have airbags (1984).

In its public advocacy role, the government usually uses three types of intervention: *regulation, consumer education*, and the provision of *incentives* to encourage desired behaviors. Through **regulation**, policymakers can prohibit certain types of marketing practices (e.g., the sale of unsafe products), they can influence the nature of certain practices (e.g., the information provided on a food label), and they can proscribe certain practices (misleading or deceptive advertising). Government can foster desired consumer behavior through **consumer education** (e.g., the provision of booklets on such topics as the importance of prenatal care or how to select a home building contractor), and by providing information on the dangers of certain consumption behaviors (e.g., taking drugs). Figure 21-1 shows a Department of Transportation ad that urges parents to have their children use seat belts. Government can also encourage certain types of consumption behavior deemed to be in the public interest through the use of **incentives**, such as tax deductions for charitable contributions or homestead rebates to encourage home ownership. Figure 21-2 on page 632 is an example of a government advertisement encouraging new parents to buy U.S. Savings Bonds for their baby's college tuition, promising the interest would be tax-free when the money is used for the child's education. Figure 21-3 on page 633 promises college tuition assistance and skill training to people who join the U.S. Air Force.

Marketing abuses have caused growing concern among policymakers at every level of government. Indeed, some critics complain that a knowledge of consumer behavior simply enables marketers to better exploit vulnerable and naive consumers. For example, as Chapter 20 pointed out, many marketers have sought the respect and loyalty of environmentally aware consumers by reducing waste, by recycling, and by reformulating products and packaging. Others have targeted the same market niche for the same objectives by using deceptive claims and misleading promotions.

Consider the growing consumer interest in nutritious foods. A number of food processors have made a concerted effort to address consumer concerns about nutrition and health by reducing the caloric content of foods, by eliminating fats, and by reducing

FIGURE 21-1

Consumer Safety
Information
Courtesy of the U.S. Department
of Transportation

sodium. Others have deceptively applied the terms "light," "low cholesterol," or "fat-free" to their food labels to attract the same market segment, but without making the appropriate changes in their products. Other marketplace abuses include deceptive and misleading advertising, false or misleading labeling, packaging-to-price deceptions, and exploitative advertising to children.

Many people believe that it is the government's responsibility to promote and to protect the public interest, and to provide for the general welfare. Table 21-1 on page 634 summarizes the role of the Executive Branch departments in fulfilling these responsibilities. Over the years, Congress has enacted *consumer-oriented legislation* in response to public outcries about dishonest or unethical business practices. In a number of areas they have also established *independent regulatory agencies* (see Table 21-2 on page 634), whose missions consist of policing specific industries, enacting rules and regulations designed to prevent or eliminate industry abuses, and enforcing industry compliance with these regulations. Because compliance costs are ultimately borne by the consumer, legislators and government officials have begun to weigh the costs and benefits of enacting and enforcing consumer protection legislation. Such cost/benefit analyses are said to underlie the increasing move towards deregulation and relaxed enforcement of existing statutes.

For these reasons, and because consumer legislation is so rarely based on empirical consumer research findings, the effectiveness of consumer legislation in safeguarding consumer rights has proved to be somewhat uneven. The Truth-in-Lending law, for example, was enacted to ensure that consumers are aware of the true rates of interest they are

FIGURE 21-2

Federal Savings
Incentive
Courtesy of the Department of
the Treasury

charged for buying on credit. The law was intended to aid low-income consumers in particular, who most often rely on credit purchases. However, subsequent research found that only 34 percent of those who had made a credit purchase after passage of the law could report the true interest charges they had agreed to pay; moreover, low-income shoppers were among those who were the least aware of finance charges.[2] Further research discovered that low-income consumers were more concerned with the size and frequency of installment repayments than with the amount of interest they were charged. Many policymakers

FIGURE 21-3

Air Force Recruitment
Incentives
Courtesy of the United States Air
Force

now concede that legislation like Truth-in-Lending, although well intentioned, was passed with little consideration or understanding of actual consumer behavior. They agree that research into consumer attitudes, habits, and purchase behavior should be a necessary precondition to the enactment of consumer legislation, and should be the requisite basis for remedying flaws in current laws.

The **Federal Communications Commission (FCC)**, established by the Communications Act of 1934, is an independent regulatory agency that regulates the United States communications industry. The FCC has an immense impact on almost every communications medium. It has opened the airwaves to cellular phones and direct-broadcast satellites; it has auctioned off billions of dollars worth of broadcast licenses, and it has defined the terms of competition for television, radio, satellites, and phone services. Its Mass Media Bureau enforces rules on obscene programming, commercials aimed at children, and political ads; its Cable Services Bureau enforces the Cable Television Consumer Protection and Competition Act of 1992 by regulating cable companies' prices and business practices.[3]

The **Federal Trade Commission (FTC)** is empowered to regulate the *substance* of commercial communications (i.e., advertising), and retains broad powers to define and regulate unfair or deceptive advertising claims.[4] Because the Federal Trade Commission Act gives the agency (through its Commissioners) enormous latitude in deciding what is unfair, deceptive, or unlawful, the level of enforcement usually depends on the philosophy

table 21-1

Executive Branch Departments Promote and Protect the Public Interest and Provide for the General Welfare

PROMOTING THE PUBLIC INTEREST

Department of Commerce
Department of Agriculture
Department of the Interior

PROTECTING THE PUBLIC INTEREST

Department of State
Department of Defense
Department of Justice

PROVIDING FOR THE GENERAL WELFARE

Department of Treasury
Department of Labor
Department of Energy
Department of Housing and Urban Development
Department of Health and Human Services
Department of Transportation
Department of Veterans Affairs

of the incumbent administration, as reflected in Presidential appointments to the Commission. During the Reagan and Bush years, the FTC eased its advertising substantiation requirements in an effort to balance both industry and consumer demands, while keeping down the costs of products. The FTC still requires substantiation of advertised claims about a product's safety, performance, quality, and comparative prices.[5] Under the chairman appointed by President Clinton in the mid-1990s, the agency has been working to combat an earlier reputation for pursuing only the most blatant cases and for focusing their

table 21-2

Independent Regulatory Agencies Protect the Public Interest

Federal Trade Commission (FTC)
Food and Drug Administration (FDA)
Consumer Products Safety Commission (CPSC)
Environmental Protection Agency (EPA)
Federal Communications Commission (FCC)
Interstate Commerce Commission (ICC)
Federal Maritime Commission (FMC)
Securities and Exchange Commission (SEC)
Commodity Futures Trade Commission (CFTC)
International Trade Commission (ITC)

enforcement efforts on smaller advertisers, who were less able and less likely to dispute FTC directives than giant corporations.

In addition to FTC oversight, deceptive advertising among major advertisers is usually limited by competitive reaction. For example, many large advertisers have challenged advertising claims made by competitors and have sued each other because of conflicting superiority claims. In a dispute between oil companies, Castrol Inc. sued the Pennzoil Company over Pennzoil's claims to outperform "any leading motor oil against viscosity breakdown." The Gillette Company sued Wilkinson Sword Inc. for claiming that its Ultra Glide Blades were superior to Gillette's Atra Plus blades. The Coors Brewing Company sued Anheuser-Busch for running a commercial that pointed out that the Coors Light Beer sold in the Northeast was made from Virginia water, despite Coors' claim of using pure Rocky Mountain spring water. Coors lost the suit, and Anheuser-Busch countersued to ban Coors from using the Rocky Mountain image in future advertising.[6]

State attorneys general have begun to take an important enforcement role in monitoring deceptive advertising. For example, the makers of Mazola Corn Oil were accused by a group of State attorneys general of making untrue product claims about the beneficial effects of Mazola Oil on cholesterol levels. The Sara Lee Corporation agreed to drop the word "light" from its whipped dessert products after nine State attorneys general challenged the claim as misleading. The Quaker Oats Company was sued in Texas over claims that its oat bran cereals decreased the risk of heart attacks.[7] Many consumer groups believe that stricter regulation is needed to protect consumers, and they support increased FTC enforcement of business compliance.

Deceptive Advertising and Consumer Research

An *unfair* ad is one in which the advertiser withholds information that, when not disclosed, could result in injuries to consumers; a *deceptive* ad contains explicit or implied claims or omissions that are likely to "mislead a consumer acting reasonably under the circumstances."[8] Despite these general definitional standards, over the years no single definition of deception in advertising has evolved. Cases brought before either the FTC or the **Food and Drug Administration (FDA)** have been decided on an *ad hoc* basis—that is, each on its own merits—so that advertisers have had difficulty in discerning broad regulatory guidelines as to what is considered improper or deceptive advertising. To remedy this situation, consumer behavior studies have been conducted to clarify the meaning of deceptive advertising. One study distinguished three categories of deception: (1) *unconscionable lies*, in which completely false claims are made intentionally; (2) *claim/fact discrepancies*, in which some relevant qualifications of a claim are omitted, resulting in misrepresentation; and (3) *claim/belief discrepancies*, in which no deceptive claim is made explicitly, but a deceptive belief is created.[9]

Of the three categories, the one that is probably the most insidious is the last— claim/belief discrepancies. Industry watchdog agencies frequently guard against outright lies and inadequately documented claims, but the clever manipulation of words to foster a misleading belief is more difficult to police. For example, a candy bar that is portrayed in advertising as "wholesome" implies that it meets basic FDA requirements for vitamins and other nutrients, whether or not it actually does. Another example: Despite the fact that no clinical tests had been conducted to support the claim that Anacin was superior to other analgesic medications, consumers assumed that the advertised claim was based on research evidence, even though the advertising made no explicit claim that such superiority had been proved. As a result, the FTC ruled that comparative advertising claims for over-the-counter pain relievers that do not refer to specific medical proof must be supported by test evidence, or must be qualified by a disclosure that the claim has not been proved or that there are "substantial questions" about its validity.[10]

Still another example of claim/belief discrepancies can be found in food labeling. The phrase "no preservatives, no artificial ingredients" obscures the fact that coloring agents may be added to enhance the food's appearance (e.g., onion soup often contains caramel powder to make it look darker and richer). The FDA accused the Perrier Group of misleading labeling because of its "calorie-free" claim (no water contains calories) and of deceptive labeling because some Perrier samples exceeded FDA standards for products labeled "sodium-free." The FDA also banned the Perrier claim that its water was "naturally sparkling" and required it to list water and carbon dioxide as separate ingredients.[11]

How can the FTC or the FDA determine whether a false belief has been created among consumers? Consumer behavior research offers some promising answers but requires some creativity in design. A technique is needed that would enable researchers to spot the existence of false beliefs and trace those beliefs to specific ads. This would enable advertisers to pretest their advertising prior to widespread media release, and to revise any ads that research indicated might be misleading. Such a technique would also enable the FTC and the FDA to predetermine the strength of a misleading advertising case before deciding whether or not to prosecute.

Research has shown that consumers routinely make inferences from advertisements and then believe the inferences to have been directly stated in the advertisement. Highly involved consumers are likely to make invalid inferences about a brand on the basis of *incomplete-comparison* claims at the time of information processing and to indicate greater purchase intentions than do low-involvement consumers, who tend to be deceived by *inconspicuous-qualification* claims, which cannot be noted without detailed processing of the advertisement.[12]

Corrective Advertising and Consumer Research

In situations where the FTC has determined that an advertisement is deceptive, it has ordered the advertiser to cancel the ad and to run a series of corrective ads in an effort to eliminate any residual effects of the misleading claims on consumers. The main purpose of **corrective advertising** is to dispel mistaken impressions created by *misleading advertising*, and thus to help consumers make more informed product decisions. (An implicit purpose is to impose sanctions designed to discourage marketers from deliberately or thoughtlessly sponsoring such ads.)

Volvo Cars of North America was required to run corrective ads for *deceptive advertising* when it was discovered that the company had altered cars for a "monster truck-crushing" commercial that showed the only car to be left unharmed was the Volvo (see Figure 21-4).[13] The corrective ad took the form of a letter "to all interested consumers" from the company's president, acknowledging that the advertising "inaccurately characterized the event as a car-crushing exhibition when in fact it was a dramatization. . . ."

Consumer behavior research into the effectiveness of corrective advertising in achieving its primary purpose has produced some mixed results. Although deceptive claims are less widely believed after corrective advertising has been run, some consumers tend to ignore the corrective ads. For example, the Warner-Lambert Company was ordered to run corrective advertising for a period of 17 months to correct its claims that Listerine was an effective cold remedy. The corrective ads stated that Listerine did not help to prevent colds or sore throats or lessen their severity. In a follow-up study of Listerine's corrective advertising, the FTC found that although the ads had some impact, many people continued to use the product as a remedy for sore throats and colds.

FIGURE 21-4

Deceptive Advertising
Source: HOWARD SCHLOSSBERG, "The Simple Truth: Ads Will Have to Be Truthful," *Marketing News*, December 14, 1990, 6. Reprinted by permission of AP/Wide World Photo.

A series of research studies undertaken to assess the real-world effects of three corrective advertising campaigns found that corrective ads are not uniformly effective, but that they have the "potential to provide consumers with useful information which may change beliefs or modify purchase behavior."[14] It appears that corrective advertising can be overly effective as well as ineffective. Some consumers tend to overgeneralize the corrective message, so that they disbelieve all subsequent advertising claims for the brand and for the product category.

Research is needed to determine consumer responses to proposed corrective ads *before the fact* to ensure that the corrective ads fulfill their intended purpose. A comprehensive review of corrective advertising indicates how difficult it is to create a corrective message that will capture the attention of consumers, sustain their interest, alter previous beliefs, and form new beliefs that consumers will remember. This is particularly difficult, given the fact that corrective messages usually are buried within the context of regularly scheduled advertising. For example, examination of the storyboard for the Listerine corrective commercial discussed above shows the corrective message buried in the middle of the commercial. It is used neither in the opening frame of the commercial nor in its close; either position would have heightened consumer awareness of the corrective information (see the discussion of order effects in Chapter 10).

Packaging-to-Price Deceptions

Today almost all "pound" containers of coffee contain only 13 ounces, with the incredible rationale—as stated on the Maxwell House label—that the 13-ounce can "makes as many cups as one full pound." Consumer critics have been quick to note that only one full pound can make "as many cups as one full pound." This same type of **packaging-to-price deception** is practiced by many packagers of household goods. For example, in recent years there have been six reductions in the size of a roll of Bounty paper towels—from 85 square feet to 60 square feet—with no change in price. The package proclaims the product to be "more absorbent than ever." Another example: A "new, improved" bottle of Triaminic Syrup for colds and allergies contains the same number of ounces and costs the same price as the previous version, but the key ingredient has been halved, so that the consumer gets half as much medicine for the same price. The label accounts for that by giving a new dosage regimen, doubling the required dosage.[15] Clearly, a Truth-in-Packaging law is needed, but Congress is unlikely to act unless there is a concerted consumer outcry about packaging abuses.

CONSUMER EDUCATION

In addition to protective legislation and regulation, consumers need information and education to enable them to make wise buying decisions. Increasingly, government policy-makers and consumer advocates recognize that they cannot protect consumers against every possible marketing abuse, and that the consumer's best defense is better product knowledge. Today, many federal, state, and local agencies offer consumer education programs and disseminate consumer information. Figure 21-5 presents an ad sponsored by several Federal agencies advising consumers to eat low-cholesterol foods.

Some major firms have been involved with consumer education for a number of years, in the belief that educated consumers make better customers. Indeed, the Syms off-price clothing chain's motto is "An Educated Consumer Is Our Best Customer." Safeway has a Nutrition Awareness Program and distributes the *Food Pyramid Guide to Daily Food Choices* developed by the U.S. Department of Agriculture to customers. The American Express Company has distributed various types of educational pamphlets since 1982, including *Women's Credit Rights* and *Mail Order Rights*; the Coca-Cola Company distributes a pamphlet called *How to Talk to a Company and Get Action*, which explains the best ways to approach a company with a complaint or a request. Follow-up studies have shown that most consumers who received these pamphlets saved them for future reference and gave copies to friends.[16]

Educational materials distributed by corporations help them to increase their direct contacts with customers (a goal of relationship marketing) while reducing contact with third-party consumer groups. A number of companies have worked with the Consumer Information Center to distribute educational materials, including American Honda, AT&T, Fidelity Investments, Goodyear Tire and Rubber, and Gulf Oil. Sponsoring companies are permitted to use their names and logos, but they cannot use brand names or trademarks, which would imply an endorsement.[17]

One proposal to advance consumer education involves the development of computerized data banks containing product information (e.g., local prices, availability, and product test results) and general educational information (e.g., the meaning of nutritional information.) Consumers could tap into such information banks by means of home computers or cable television.

Consumer advocates recommend that consumer education programs be made mandatory in the public school system. At present, only a few states have such programs, and the content varies widely. Many companies, recognizing the estimated $100 billion worth of goods that children and teenagers buy each year, have stepped into the breach by providing booklets and other materials to schools, with very clear commercial intent. For example, Revlon, which targets teenagers for some of its products, sent a guide to 29,000 home economics teachers that includes exercises asking students to list the three hair-care products they would "have to have" if stranded on a desert island. Weyerhauser, the wood products company, distributes a teacher's guide on forestry that poses such "thought-pro-voking" questions as "What innovative practices has Weyerhauser introduced in recent years?" Despite the fact that health experts advise that individuals should consume no *more* than 30 percent of calories from fat, the National Dairy Council distributes materials to classrooms that say children should consume no *less* than 30 percent of calories from fat.[18] As noted in an earlier chapter, Channel One, owned by KIII Communications, carries a daily 12-minute news program that more than 8 million students in almost 12,000 schools are required to watch, including two minutes of commercials for such products as Clearasil, Reebok sneakers, Gatorade, and Pepsi. The schools that subscribe to Channel One receive a fixed-band satellite dish, two videocassette recorders, and a video monitor

There's No Wrong Way To Eat,
As Long As You Eat Right.

Eating right means eating food
low in saturated fat and cholesterol,
which will help lower your blood
cholesterol level and reduce your risk
of heart disease. So whether you eat
with silverware, chopsticks or a straw,
remember, there's no wrong way to
eat, as long as you eat right. For more
information and for free recipes,
call 1-800-575-WELL.

A Low Fat Diet. Good Food.
Good For Your Heart.

National Cholesterol Education Program
National Heart, Lung, and Blood Institute;
National Institutes of Health; Public Health Service;
U.S. Department of Health and Human Services

FIGURE 21-5

Consumer Education
Courtesy of the National Heart
Lung Blood Institute

for each classroom—although the satellite dish can only receive Channel One.[19] The unfortunate fact is that so many schools are strapped for cash and short on textbooks that the teachers gladly accept the new, slick pamphlets that companies distribute. And of course, the companies recognize that, for many children, an early product or brand introduction is likely to result in a lifetime of product loyalty.

Consumer behavior researchers could make a substantive contribution to the field of consumer education by designing appropriate curricula for such programs. Because parents play such an essential role in the consumer socialization of children, it is especially important that parents acquire as much product information as possible.

Nutritional Labeling

The concept of **nutritional labeling** covers a broad spectrum of programs and proposals for telling consumers about the nutritional value of the foods they buy. Consumers depend on food labels as their most useful source for nutrition information, but often do not understand or agree on the meanings of frequently-used descriptive terms, such as "light," "low-calorie," "low-sodium," or "cholesterol-free."[20]

The 1990 Nutritional Labeling and Education Act makes labeling mandatory for all processed foods and calls for voluntary labeling of seafood and commonly consumed fruits and vegetables. It also requires the FDA to define a wide range of nutritional terms frequently used on food labels. The Act exempts food sold in restaurants, and does not cover meat and poultry products, which are regulated by the Department of Agriculture. Most other foods now are required to carry labels that show the number of calories per serving, total fat, saturated fat, and cholesterol. The labels also must show data on total sodium, sugar, dietary fiber, protein, carbohydrates, complex carbohydrates, and important vitamins and minerals. The label offers consumers a way to compare the nutrients found in a specific processed food with recommended daily dietary requirements.

Consumer advocates have proposed that food labels be required to adopt uniformity in the *recommended serving size* for which nutritional information is given. By reducing the recommended size of a serving, a food producer may imply that the caloric content of its product is lower than that of competitive brands. To illustrate, Brand X salad dressing may list its recommended serving size as one teaspoon, with a caloric content per serving of 17 calories, while Brand Y uses a tablespoon as the standard measure, with a caloric content of 25 calories per serving. The diet-conscious consumer is likely to choose Brand X for its apparently lower caloric content and actually end up with increased calorie consumption. Although the FTC has adopted a policy for regulating food advertising claims, its policy is much less restrictive than the rules established by the FDA and the Department of Agriculture for food labels.[21] Consumer advocates have asked the FTC to require the same nutritional standards in food advertising as mandated for food labeling, but so far have been unsuccessful.

Consumer advocates have also proposed a mandatory labeling program for all goods to certify *quality*. A cooperative effort by government officials, business people, consumer spokespersons, and academic researchers is needed to establish the standards to be summarized on such labels. Unfortunately, many consumers lack the background to understand the meaning of the nutritional content of foods, and without more education, they may not benefit from nutritional labeling requirements.

Studies show that women are more likely to read food labels than men and that nonworking women are the most likely to read ingredients (48 percent) or nutritional information (41 percent).[22] Shoppers aged 50 or older read ingredients 48 percent of the time, while 18 to 24 year olds do so only 31 percent of the time. Midwesterners are the least likely to read labels, and those in the South are most likely to check food expiration dates.

The FDA prohibits health claims on food labels. However, enforcement of this prohibition sometimes can be difficult. For example, Kellogg's noted on its package of All-Bran cereal that eating high-fiber foods (such as bran cereals) could reduce the incidence of several types of cancer. Despite the fact that the statement implied that All-Bran prevents cancer, the company maintained that its package did not make a health claim; rather, it was simply disseminating information provided by the National Cancer Institute.[23] This is a perfect example of a company fostering a *claim/belief discrepancy*, described earlier as the most insidious of the three forms of advertising deception.

CONSUMER BEHAVIOR RESEARCH PRIORITIES

There is no question that marketing plays an essential role in our economy. In its most basic form, the marketing process identifies unfulfilled or unsatisfied human needs, and develops and delivers products and services designed to satisfy those needs in ways that satisfy organizational and societal objectives. Consumer research and market segmentation ensure a better "fit" between products and consumers, and enable marketers to communicate more efficiently with their target markets. For this reason, it is incumbent upon public policymakers to support, and academic consumer researchers to design and implement, research studies that identify and document areas in need of government intervention. For example, as Chapter 20 pointed out, there is growing consumer concern about the restrictive practices of many health maintenance organizations. As a result, the Public Advocate's Office of the City of New York undertook a year-long study of 12 commercial health maintenance organizations. Its 128 page report, *What Ails HMOs—A Consumer Diagnosis and RX*, contains such consumer-relevant information as the number of network doctors and hospitals in a plan, rules on seeing specialists, the kinds of specialists each HMO has, how much physicians are paid, restrictions and "secret" criteria for Emergency Room visits. This booklet is available at no cost to consumers and enables them to make informed choices among HMOs.[24]

A foremost marketing scholar, in exhorting consumer researchers to engage in **social policy** research, has said that in many ways the field of social policy research presents "the best of all possible worlds to the research scholar," because of the many issues that are "both fundamental to the discipline of consumer behavior and relevant to the information needs of public policymakers."[25] Public policymakers look to such research for two kinds of input: the detection of problems that are in need of public intervention and help in setting priorities.[26] To make strategic decisions regarding government intervention, they need to know (1) the frequency and severity of market problems in need of potential intervention, (2) the availability and potential costs of possible solutions (to all parties, including producers and sellers), and (3) the likelihood that proposed solutions will have the desired effect.[27]

There is no question that consumer researchers have made an enormous contribution to our knowledge and understanding of consumer behavior in the marketplace. They are now in a unique position to make an even greater contribution by providing empirically based insights into the impact of marketing on the consumer and on society, in the short run and over the longer term. Some of the many consumer behavior questions that should be explored through consumer research are presented in Table 21-3 on page 642 and 643. Scholarly, objective research findings should provide the basis for enlightened public policy that ensures positive consequences for all marketing activity and an enhanced quality of life for future generations of consumers.

table 21-3   Consumer Research Priorities for the 1990s

1. How might the marketplace be improved so that consumers make better decisions as to what they buy?

2. How might the marketplace be improved so that consumers are more satisfied with their consumption experiences?

3. Do consumers have adequate, undistorted information on which to base choices? Are they subject to undue pressures?

4. Do consumers have appropriate opportunities to secure reimbursement or compensation when products or services don't perform as promised?

5. Are there specific segments of consumers that are systematically or routinely discriminated against by the marketing process?

6. In what ways do marketing exchanges place consumers at risk in terms of their lives or physical well-being?

7. In what ways can economic and social welfare transactions lead to greater consumer satisfaction?

8. Are there unidentified economic or social welfare needs that are not currently being met?

9. Are there unidentified economic or social welfare transactions that should be avoided because of their potentially negative consequences?

10. How do specific government-sponsored consumer laws impact on consumers' quality of life?

11. How have the marketing programs of selected not-for-profit organizations (e.g., civic centers, museums, preventive health programs) impacted on consumers' quality of life?

12. How do consumers' past successes (and failures) at complaining impact on attitudes and intentions toward future complaint actions?

13. How does the concept of "blame" (i.e., "self-blame" or "blame of others") affect consumers' attitudes and behavior with respect to dissatisfaction with products and services?

14. How does the amount of prepurchase search (e.g., a little or a great deal) influence consumers' sense of self-blame or blaming others?

15. What are the underlying motivations (i.e., punitive or self-protective) that account for consumers' decisions to boycott specific products or outlets?

16. How do consumers acquire their personal strategies to improve the effectiveness of their complaining actions?

17. How do recent immigrants fare when it comes to market discrimination? Are there differences across or within immigrant groups?

18. How does declining physiological functioning among the "old-elderly" affect their marketplace attitudes and behavior?

19. Are there personality differences for high-involvement issues such as family planning decisions, dieting plans, or cancer detection practices?

20. How is consumer compliance obtained for products and practices that are of individual or social benefit (e.g., wearing seat belts, giving blood, undergoing disfiguring medical treatment, safe sexual behavior) but which meet with considerable consumer distaste?

21. How do marketing communications affect human values and the priorities in which they are held?

22. How should deceptive advertising and misleading advertising be defined and identified?

(continued)

table 21-3 (Continued)

23. How can corrective advertising more effectively mitigate the learning of misleading or deceptive advertising?

24. Do consumers develop evaluative criteria from ads? What kind of "critical mass" is necessary for such learning to occur?

25. What is the role of marketing communications in shaping cultural "traditions," such as Mother's Day, Valentine's Day, and Christmas?

26. Does the value hierarchy implicit in advertising correlate with society's value hierarchy? Does it correlate with the value hierarchy of certain segments of society? Which ones?

27. Is there cultural drift toward the values endorsed by advertising?

28. What is the impact of marketing communications on developing countries?

29. What is the impact of the advertising of luxury goods on underprivileged youth?

30. What impact do the symbolism and the scenes depicted in advertising have on the national character?

31. What formative influences does advertising have on our culture? What are the effects of such influences?

32. What are the unintended consequences of advertising on our society?

33. What are the impacts of advertising role models on behavior?

34. To what extent does advertising alter personal values and morality?

35. Does advertising encourage unsafe behavior? Antisocial behavior?

36. To what extent does advertising develop inappropriate standards for choice?

37. Has advertising replaced such institutions as the family and the church as social guide?

38. To what extent does advertising contribute to racial, age, and gender stereotypes?

39. To what extent does advertising cause social dissatisfaction?

40. Do large companies "get away" with deceptive advertising more easily than small companies because of uneven FTC enforcement?

Source: Questions have been drawn in part from ALAN R. ANDREASEN, "Consumer Behavior Research and Social Policy," in Thomas S. Robertson and Harold S. Kassarjian, eds., *Handbook of Consumer Behavior* (Englewood Cliffs, NJ: Prentice Hall, 1991), 459–506; and RICHARD W. POLLAY, "The Distorted Mirror: Reflections on the Unintended Consequences of Advertising," *Journal of Marketing* 50 (April 1986), 18–36.

summary

Public policy intersects the field of consumer behavior when policymakers believe that government intervention in the process or outcome of marketing exchanges will benefit society as a whole. The three types of intervention used by government include regulation, consumer education, and the provision of incentives to encourage marketing transactions that benefit society.

Congress has enacted consumer-oriented legislation in response to marketing abuses, and has created independent regulatory agencies whose function is to protect the public interest by policing the relevant industry, enacting needed rules and regulations, and enforcing industry compliance. The Federal Trade Commission is charged with the responsibility for policing the marketplace and preventing deceptive or misleading advertising. In situations in which the FTC has determined that an advertisement is deceptive, it has ordered the advertiser to cancel the ad and to run a series of corrective advertisements to correct misperceptions that the deceptive ad may have created.

In addition to protective legislation, consumers need information and education to enable them to make wise buying decisions. Increasingly, government policymakers and consumer advocates recognize that they cannot protect consumers against all marketing abuses and that the consumer's best defense is better product knowledge. Nutritional labels, monitored by the Food and Drug Administration, are an important source of consumer information.

Because consumption is the most pervasive human activity, it is incumbent upon public policymakers to support, and academic consumer researchers to design and implement, consumer behavior studies that identify and document areas in need of government intervention. Consumer behavior research findings should provide the basis for consumption-related public policy.

discussion questions

1. Describe how public policymakers use consumer research in proposing consumer-oriented legislation.

2. A mouthwash marketer advertises that its product eliminates 50 percent more plaque than other brands. (Actually, it eliminates 3 percent of the plaque on teeth, whereas other brands eliminate 2 percent—a difference that dentists agree is insignificant.) Does the marketer's claim constitute (1) an unconscionable lie, (2) a claim/fact discrepancy, (3) a claim/belief discrepancy, or (4) none of these? Explain your answer.

3. "Consumers need to be informed about products and services so that they can make better consumption decisions." Discuss this statement in relation to consumer use of nutritional information on labels.

4. Why have consumers been confused by the serving sizes listed on food labeling? What can the government do to reduce this confusion?

5. A number of corporations have been providing schools with promotional materials (in the guise of educational materials) concerning their products. Discuss the promotional value to the companies of distributing such materials. Do you think this practice is ethical or unethical? Explain your answer.

exercises

1. Visit a supermarket and find examples of packaging-to-price deceptions. Present them in class and discuss whether and how a Truth-in-Packaging law would eliminate such deceptions.

2. Conduct a survey of 20 to 30 consumers regarding their use of nutritional information on labels when they purchase food products. Identify the demographics, lifestyle characteristics, and media habits that distinguish consumers who use the labels in making product choices from those who do not.

3. Visit a supermarket and find examples of two competitive products that list different serving sizes and different caloric contents per serving on their nutritional labels. Present your examples in class and discuss (a) the impact, if any, on consumers and (b) whether the government should consider some form of intervention.

key words

- Consumer advocates
- Claim/belief discrepancy
- Claim/fact discrepancy
- Consumer education
- Consumer-oriented legislation
- Consumer protection
- Corrective advertising
- Deceptive or misleading advertising
- Federal Communications Commission (FCC)
- Federal Trade Commission (FTC)
- Food and Drug Administration (FDA)
- Government incentives
- Government intervention
- Government regulation
- Independent regulatory agencies
- Nutritional labeling
- Packaging-to-price deceptions
- Public policy
- Social policy
- Unconscionable lies in advertising
- Unfair advertising

end notes

1. ANTHONY RAMIREZ, "Consumer Crusader Feels a Chill in Washington," *The New York Times*, December 31, 1995, 1, 10–11.

2. GEORGE S. DAY, "Assessing the Effects of Information Disclosure Requirements," *Journal of Marketing* 40, April 1976, 46; and HOMER KRIPKE, "Gesture and Reality in Consumer Credit Reform," in David A. Aaker and George S. Day, eds., *Consumerism: Search for the Consumer Interest*, 2nd ed. (New York: Free Press, 1974), 218–24.

3. EDMUND L. ANDREWS, "Has the FCC Become Obsolete?" *The New York Times*, June 12, 1995, D1.

4. The FTC enforcement authority derives from Section 5 of the FTC Act, which was amended to read: "Unfair methods of competition in or affecting commerce, and unfair or deceptive acts or practices in or affecting commerce, are declared unlawful."

5. THOMAS J. MARONICK, "Copy Tests in FTC Deception Cases: Guidelines for Researchers," *Journal of Advertising Research*, December 1991, 9.

6. CHUCK ROSS, "What Does It Take to Get a Commercial on the Air?" *The New York Times*, September 27, 1992, F10.

7. HOWARD SCHLOSSBERG, "The Simple Truth: Ads Will Have to Be Truthful," *Marketing News*, December 24, 1990, 6.

8. MARONICK, op. cit.

9. DAVID M. GARDNER, "Deception in Advertising: A Conceptual Approach," *Journal of Marketing* 39, January 1975, 42.

10. DEBRA L. SCAMMON and RICHARD J. SEMENIK, "The FTC's 'Reasonable Basis' for Substantiation of Advertising: Expanded Standards and Implications," *Journal of Advertising* 12, 1983, 4–11.

11. LAURA BIRD, "Perrier's Launch Stalled—Again—Over Health Concerns," *Adweek's Marketing Week*, April 30, 1990, 5.

12. GITA VENKATARAMANI JOHASR, "Consumer Involvement and Deception from Implied Advertising Claims," *Journal of Marketing Research*, August 1995, 267–79.

13. RAYMOND SERAFIN and GARY LEVIN, "Ad Industry Suffers Crushing Blow," *Advertising Age*, November 12, 1990, 1, 76.

14. ALAN R. ANDREASEN, "Consumer Behavior Research and Social Policy," in Thomas S. Robertson and Harold H. Kassarjian, eds. *Handbook of Consumer Behavior* (Englewood Cliffs, New Jersey: Prentice Hall, 1991), 468.

15. IRWIN LANDAU, "Why a Pound of Coffee Weighs 13 Oz," *The New York Times*, May 23, 1993, F13.

16. JUDITH WALDROP, "Educating the Consumer," *American Demographics*, September 1991, 44–47.

17. Ibid.

18. MICHAEL F. JACOBSON, "Now There's a Fourth R: Retailing," *The New York Times*, January 29, 1995, F9.

19. Ibid.

20. WILLIAM MUELLER, "Who Reads the Label?" *American Demographics*, January 1991, 36–41.

21. MARIAN BURROS, "Minding the Store on Food Ad Claims," *The New York Times*, November 23, 1994, B8.

22. MARIAN BURROS, "Ad Campaign for New Federal Food Label Is Putting Washington in the Big Leagues," *The New York Times*, May 1, 1994, 1, 30.

23. MARIAN BURROS, "Health Claims on Food Put FDA in a Corner," *The New York Times*, February 19, 1986, C1.

24. MARK GREEN, "HMOs: What You Need to Know," *Advocate's Alert*, 2(1) (New York: Public Advocate for the City of New York, Winter 1996), 1, 4.

25. ANDREASEN, op. cit.

26. ALAN R. ANDREASEN, "Unethical Seller Practices: A Neglected Issue in Consumer Satisfaction and Dissatisfaction Research," *Advances in Consumer Research* 20, 1993, 109–112.

27. Ibid.

GLOSSARY

Absolute Threshold. The lowest level at which an individual can experience a sensation.

Acculturation. The learning of a new or "foreign" culture.

Achievement Need. The need for personal accomplishment as an end in itself.

Acquired Needs. Needs that are learned in response to one's culture or environment (such as the need for esteem, prestige, affection, or power). Also known as *psychogenic* or *secondary needs*.

Actual Self-Image. The image that an individual has of himself or herself as a certain kind of person, with certain characteristic traits, habits, possessions, relationships, and behavior.

Adaptation. Process by which an individual becomes accommodated to a certain level of stimulation.

Adopter Categories. A sequence of categories that describes how early (or late) a consumer adopts a new product in relation to other adopters. The five typical adopter categories are innovators, early adopters, early majority, late majority, and laggards.

Adoption Process. The stages through which an individual consumer passes in arriving at a decision to try (or not to try), to continue using (or discontinue using) a new product. The five stages of the traditional adoption process are awareness, interest, evaluation, trial, and adoption.

Advertising Wearout. Overexposure to repetitive advertising that causes individuals to become satiated and their attention and retention to decline.

Advertorials. Print advertisements that are laid out to resemble editorial material, often making it difficult for readers to distinguish between the two.

Affective Component. The part of the tricomponent attitude model that reflects a consumer's emotions or feelings with respect to an idea or object.

Affect Referral Decision Rule. A simplified decision rule by which consumers make a product choice on the basis of their previously established overall ratings of the brands considered, rather than on specific attributes.

Affiliation Need. The need for friendship, for acceptance, and for belonging.

Affinity Group Marketing. A type of cause-related marketing targeted to members of a specific group or organization.

Affluent Consumers. Consumers with household incomes that provide them with a disproportionately large share of all discretionary income.

Age Subcultures. Age subgroupings of the population.

Aggressive Personality. One of three personality types identified by Karen Horney. The aggressive person is one who moves against others (e.g., competes with others).

Aided Recall and Recognition. A research technique in which the consumer is shown a specific advertisement and is asked whether he or she remembers seeing it and can recall its content.

AIOs. Psychographic variables that focus on activities, interests, and opinions. Also referred to as Lifestyle.

Approach Object. A positive goal toward which behavior is directed.

Arousal of Motives. Motives are often aroused on the basis of physiological, emotional, cognitive, or environmental factors.

Aspirational Group. A group to which a nonmember would like to belong.

Assimilation-Contrast Theory. A theory of attitude change that suggests that consumers are likely to accept only moderate attitude changes. If the change suggested is too extreme, the contrast with presently held attitudes will cause rejection of the entire message.

Attitude. A learned predisposition to behave in a consistently favorable or unfavorable manner with respect to a given object.

Attitude-Toward-Behavior Model. A model that proposes that a consumer's attitude toward a specific behavior is a function of how strongly he or she believes that the action will lead to a specific outcome (either favorable or unfavorable).

Attitude-Toward-Object Model. A model that proposes that a consumer's attitude toward a product or brand is a function of the presence of certain attributes and the consumer's evaluation of those attributes.

Attitude-Toward-the-Ad Model. A model that proposes that a consumer forms various feelings (affects) and judgments (cognitions) as the result of exposure to an advertisement, which, in turn, affect the consumer's *attitude toward the ad* and *beliefs and attitudes toward the brand*.

Attribution Theory. A theory concerned with how people assign causality to events and form or alter their attitudes as an outcome of assessing their own or other people's behavior.

Audience Profile. Psychographic/demographic profile of the audience of a specific medium.

Autonomic (Unilateral) Decision. A purchase decision in which either the husband or the wife makes the final decision.

Avoidance Group. A group with which a nonmember does not wish to be identified.

Avoidance Object. A negative goal from which behavior is directed away.

Baby Boomers. Individuals born between 1946 and 1964 (approximately 45% of the adult population).

Balance Theory. An attitude-change theory that postulates that individuals avoid inconsistency and seek harmony (consistency) by changing the weaker conflicting attitude to agree with the stronger attitude.

Behavioral Learning Theories. Theories based on the premise that learning takes place as the result of observable responses to external stimuli. Also known as *stimulus response theory*.

Beliefs. Mental or verbal statements that reflect a person's particular knowledge and assessment about some idea or thing.

Benefit Segmentation. Segmentation based on the kinds of benefits consumers seek in a product.

Brand Equity. The value inherent in a well-known brand name.

Brand Loyalty. Consistent preference and/or purchase of the same brand in a specific product or service category.

Brand Personification. Specific "personality-type" traits or characteristics ascribed by consumers to different brands.

Cause-Related Marketing. A form of corporate promotion in which companies try to motivate socially-aware consumers to buy their products by promising to contribute a portion of the sale to a specific cause.

Central and Peripheral Routes to Persuasion. A promotional theory that proposes that highly involved consumers are best reached through ads that focus on the specific attributes of the product (the central route) while uninvolved consumers can be attracted through peripheral advertising cues such as the model or the setting (the peripheral route).

Chapin's Social Status Scale. A social class rating scheme that focuses on the presence or absence of certain items of furniture and accessories in the home.

Claim/Belief Discrepancy. Deceptive advertising in which no deceptive claim is made explicitly, but a deceptive belief is created.

Claim/Fact Discrepancy. Deceptive advertising in which some relevant qualifications of a product are falsified or omitted.

Classical Conditioning. (See Conditioned Learning.)

Closure. A principle of Gestalt psychology that stresses the individual's need for completion. This need is reflected in the individual's subconscious reorganization and perception of incomplete stimuli as complete or whole pictures.

ClusterPLUS. A geodemographic segmentation service that employs a 47-category classification scheme.

Cognitions. Knowledge that is acquired by a combination of direct experience and related information from various sources.

Cognitive Age. An individual's perceived age (usually 10 to 15 years younger than his or her chronological age).

Cognitive Component. A part of the tricomponent attitude model that represents the knowledge, perception, and beliefs that a consumer has with respect to an idea or object.

Cognitive Dissonance. The discomfort or dissonance that consumers experience as a result of conflicting information. (See Balance Theory.)

Cognitive Learning Theory. A theory of learning based on mental information processing, often in response to problem solving.

Cognitive Man Model. A model of man that portrays consumers as active seekers of information that enables them to make appropriate purchase decisions.

Cognitive Arousal. A motivating situation in which mental or visual cues (e.g., specific thoughts or an ad) lead to awareness of a need.

"Common-Man" Appeals. The use of a stereotypical actor or model in an ad to demonstrate to prospective customers that someone "just like them" is satisfied with the advertised product or service.

Communication. The transmission of a message from a sender to a receiver by means of a signal of some sort sent through a channel of some sort.

Communication Feedback. The response (or nonresponse) of the targeted audience to a message.

Comparative Advertising. Advertising that explicitly names or otherwise identifies one or more competitors of the advertised brand for the purpose of claiming superiority, either on an overall basis or in selected product attributes.

Comparative Reference Group. A group whose norms serve as a benchmark for highly specific or narrowly defined types of behavior. (See also Normative Reference Group.)

Compatibility. The degree to which potential consumers feel that a new product is consistent with their present needs, values, and practices.

Compensatory Decision Rule. A type of decision rule in which a consumer evaluates each brand in terms of each relevant attribute and then selects the brand with the highest weighted score.

Complexity. The degree to which a new product is difficult to comprehend and/or use.

Compliant Personality. One of three personality types identified by Karen Horney. The compliant person is one who moves toward others (e.g., one who desires to be loved, wanted, and appreciated by others).

Composite Variable Index. An index that combines a number of socio-economic variables (such as education, income, occupation) to form one overall measure of social class standing. (See also Single Variable Index.)

Compulsive Consumption. Consumers who are compulsive buyers have an addiction; in some respects, they are out of control and their actions may have damaging consequences to them and to those around them.

Conative Component. A part of the tricomponent attitude model that reflects a consumer's likelihood or tendency to behave in a particular way with regard to an attitude-object. Also referred to as "intention to buy."

Concentrated Marketing. Targeting a product or service to a single market segment with a unique marketing mix (price, product, promotion, method of distribution).

Concept. A mental image of an intangible trait, characteristic, or idea.

Conditioned Learning. According to Pavlovian theory, conditioned learning results when a stimulus paired with another stimulus that elicits a known response serves to produce the same response by itself.

Conditioned Response. Automatic response to a situation built up through repeated exposure.

Conformity. The extent to which an individual adopts attitudes and/or behavior that is consistent with the norms of a group to which he or she belongs or would like to belong.

Conjunctive Rule. A noncompensatory decision rule in which consumers establish a minimally acceptable cutoff point for each attribute evaluated. Brands that fall below the cutoff point on any one attribute are eliminated from further consideration.

Construct. A term that represents or symbolizes an abstract trait or characteristic, such as motivation or aggression.

Consumer Behavior. The behavior that consumers display in searching for, purchasing, using, evaluating, and disposing of products, services, and ideas.

Consumer Boycotts. Concerted (but nonmandatory) refusals by groups of consumers to do business with one or more companies to express disapproval of certain policies and to attempt to coerce the target companies to modify their policies.

Consumer Decision Rules. Procedures adopted by consumers to reduce the complexity of making product and brand decisions.

Consumer Ethnocentrism. A consumer's predisposition to accept or reject foreign-made products.

Consumer Innovativeness. The degree to which consumers are receptive to new products, new services, or new practices.

Consumer Learning. The process by which individuals acquire the purchase and consumption knowledge and experience they apply to future related behavior.

Consumer Materialism. A personality-like trait of individuals who regard possessions as particularly essential to their identities and lives. (See also Materialistic Consumers.)

Consumer-Oriented Definition of Innovation. Any product that a potential consumer judges to be new. Newness is based on the consumer's *perception* of the product, rather than on physical features or market realities.

Consumer-Oriented Legislation. Legislation enacted to protect the public from dishonest or unethical business practices.

Consumer Profile. Psychographic/demographic profile of actual or proposed consumers for a specific product or service.

Consumer Research. Methodology used to study consumer behavior.

Consumer Research Process. The consumer research process generally consists of six steps: defining objectives, collecting secondary data, developing a research design, collecting primary data, analyzing the data, and preparing a report on the findings.

Consumers. A term used to describe two different kinds of consuming entities: *personal consumers* (who buy goods and services for their own use or for household use) and *organizational consumers* (who buy products, equipment, and services in order to run their organizations).

Consumer Socialization. The process, started in childhood, by which an individual first learns the skills and attitudes relevant to consumer purchase behavior.

Contactual Group. A formal or informal group with which a person has regular face-to-face contact and with whose values, attitudes, and standards he or she tends to agree.

Content Analysis. A method for systematically analyzing the content of verbal and/or pictorial communication. The method is frequently used to determine prevailing social values of a society.

Continuous Innovation. A new product entry that is an improved or modified version of an existing product rather than a totally new product. A continuous innovation has the least disruptive influence on established consumption patterns.

Copy Pretests. A test of an advertisement before the ad is run to determine which, if any, elements of the advertising message should be revised before major media expenses are incurred.

Copy Posttests. Posttests are used to evaluate the effectiveness of an advertisement that has already appeared and to see which elements, if any, should be revised to improve the impact of future advertisements.

Corrective Advertising. Advertising designed to eliminate the residual effects of misleading advertising claims.

Countersegmentation Strategy. A strategy in which a company combines two or more segments into a single segment to be targeted with an individually tailored product or promotion campaign.

Cross-Cultural Consumer Analysis. Research to determine the extent to which consumers of two or more nations are similar in relation to specific consumption behavior.

Cross-Cultural Psychographic Segmentation. Tailoring marketing strategies to the needs (psychological, social, cultural, and functional) of specific foreign segments.

Cues. Stimuli that give direction to consumer motives, i.e., that suggest a specific way to satisfy a salient motive.

Cultural Anthropology. The study of human beings that traces the development of core beliefs, values, and customs passed down to individuals from their parents and grandparents.

Culture. The sum total of learned beliefs, values, and customs that serve to regulate the consumer behavior of members of a particular society.

Customs. Overt modes of behavior that constitute culturally acceptable ways of behaving in specific situations.

Deceptive Advertising. Advertising that presents or implies false or misleading information to the consumer.

Decision. A choice made from two or more alternatives.

Decision Time. Within the context of the diffusion process, the amount of time required for an individual to adopt (or reject) a specific new product.

Decoding. Receivers interpret the messages they receive on the basis of their personal experience and personal characteristics.

Defense Mechanisms. Methods by which people mentally redefine frustrating situations to protect their self-images and their self-esteem.

Defensive Attribution. A theory that suggests consumers are likely to accept credit for successful outcomes (internal attribution) and to blame other persons or products for failure (external attribution).

Demographic Segmentation. The division of a total market into smaller subgroups on the basis of such objective characteristics as age, sex, marital status, income, occupation, or education.

Deontology. An ethical philosophy that places greater weight on personal and social values than on economic values.

Dependent Variable. A variable whose value changes as the result of a change in another (i.e., independent) variable. For example, consumer purchases are a dependent variable subject to level and quality of advertising (independent variables).

Depth Interview. A lengthy and relatively unstructured interview designed to uncover a consumer's underlying attitudes and/or motivations.

Detached Personality. One of three personality types identified by Karen Horney. The detached person is one who moves away from others (e.g., who desires independence, self-sufficiency, and freedom from obligations).

Differential Threshold. The minimal difference that can be detected between two stimuli. Also known as the *j.n.d.* (*just noticeable difference*). (See also Weber's Law.)

Differentiated Marketing. Targeting a product or service to two or more segments, using a specifically tailored product, promotional appeal, price, and/or method of distribution for each.

Diffusion Process. The process by which the acceptance of an innovation is spread by communication to members of a social system over a period of time.

Direct Mail. Advertising that is sent directly to the mailing address of a target consumer.

Direct Marketing. A marketing technique that uses various media (mail, print, broadcast, telephone) to solicit a direct response from a consumer. Also known as database marketing.

Disclaimant Group. A group in which a person holds membership, but with whose values, attitudes, and behavior he or she does not wish to be associated.

Discontinuous Innovation. A dramatically new product entry that requires the establishment of new consumption practices.

Disjunctive Rule. A noncompensatory decision rule in which consumers establish a minimally acceptable cutoff point for each relevant product attribute; any brand meeting or surpassing the cutoff point for any one attribute is considered an acceptable choice.

Distributed Learning. Learning spaced over a period of time to increase consumer retention. (See also Massed Learning.)

Dogmatism. A personality trait that reflects the degree of rigidity a person displays toward the unfamiliar and toward information that is contrary to his or her own established beliefs.

Drive. An internal force that impels a person to engage in an action designed to satisfy a specific need.

DYG SCAN. A scanning program that tracks 37 social values among various segments of the United States population (e.g., Hispanics, the affluent, teenagers, and opinion leaders), as well as business, government, and academic leaders.

Dynamically Continuous Innovation. A new product entry that is sufficiently innovative to have some disruptive effects on established consumption practices.

Economic Man Theory. Assumes that consumers are perfectly rational beings who objectively evaluate and rank each product alternative and select the alternative that gives the best value.

Effective Reach. Minimum of three confirmed vehicle exposures to an individual member of a target group over an agreed-upon time period.

Effective Reach Threshold. Measurement that suggests that 45 percent of the target group should be reached over the agreed-upon time period.

Ego. In Freudian theory, the part of the personality that serves as the individual's conscious control. It functions as an internal monitor that balances the impulsive demands of the *id* and the sociocultural constraints of the *superego*.

Ego-Defensive Function. A component of the functional approach to attitude-change that suggests that consumers want to protect their self-concepts from inner feelings of doubt.

Elaboration Likelihood Model (ELM). A theory that suggests that a person's level of involvement during message processing is a critical factor in determining which route to persuasion is likely to be effective. (See also Central and Peripheral Routes to Persuasion.)

Electronic Shopping. Direct marketing that generates an electronic database of buyers through home-shopping TV channels, interactive cable, home computers, and stand-alone shopping kiosks.

Embeds. Disguised stimuli (often sexual in nature) that are "planted" in print advertisements to subconsciously influence consumers to buy the advertised products.

Emotional Arousal. Motives aroused through emotional factors (e.g., anger).

Emotional Man Model. A model of man that suggests consumers make decisions based on subjective criteria, such as love, pride, fear, affection, or self-esteem, rather than objective evaluation.

Emotional Motives. The selection of goals according to personal or subjective criteria (e.g., the desire for individuality, pride, fear, affection, status).

Encoding. The process by which individuals select and assign a word or visual image to represent a perceived object or idea.

Enculturation. The learning of the culture of one's own society.

Endorsements. Celebrities who may or may not be users of a particular product or service may lend their names to advertisements for such products or services for a fee.

Environmental Marketing. Marketing targeted to ecologically concerned consumers.

Environmental Arousal. Motives activated at a particular time by specific cues in the environment.

Evaluation of Alternatives. A stage in the consumer *decision-making process* in which the consumer appraises the benefits to be derived from each of the product alternatives being considered.

Evoked Set. The specific brands a consumer considers in making a purchase choice in a particular product category.

Executive Spokesperson. A corporate executive who speaks on behalf of his or her company's product or service.

Expected Self-Image. How individuals expect to see themselves at some specified future time.

Experientialism. An approach to the study of consumer behavior that focuses on the consumption experience. (See also Interpretivism and Postmodernism.)

Expert Appeals. The promotional use of a person who, because of his or her occupation, special training, or experience, is able to speak knowledgeably to the consumer about the product or service being advertised.

Extended Family. A household consisting of a husband, wife, offspring, and at least one other blood relative.

Extended Self. Modification or changing of the self by which consumers use self-altering products or services to conform to or take on the appearance of a particular type of person (e.g., a biker, a physician, a lawyer, a college professor).

Extensive Problem Solving. A search by the consumer to establish the necessary product criteria to evaluate knowledgeably the most suitable product to fulfill a need.

External Attribution. A theory that suggests that consumers are likely to credit their success to outside sources.

Extinction. The point at which a learned response ceases to occur because of lack of reinforcement. (See also Wearout.)

Extrinsic Cues. Cues external to the product (such as price, store image, or brand image) that serve to influence the consumer's perception of a product's quality.

Family. Two or more persons related by blood, marriage, or adoption who reside together.

Family Branding. The practice of marketing several company products under the same brand name.

Family Gatekeeper. A family member who controls the flow of information to the family about products or services, thereby regulating the related consumption decisions of other family members.

Family Influencer. A family member who provides product-related information and advice to other members of the family, thereby influencing related consumption decisions.

Family Life Cycle. Classification of families into significant stages. The five traditional stages are Bachelorhood, Honeymooners, Parenthood, Postparenthood, and Dissolution.

Family Life Cycle (FLC) Analysis. A strategic tool that enables marketers to segment families in terms of a series of stages spanning the life course of a family unit.

Federal Trade Commission (FTC). Federal agency empowered to regulate the substance of commercial communications (i.e., advertising).

Field Observation. A cultural measurement technique that takes place within a natural environment that focuses on observing behavior (sometimes without the subjects' awareness).

Figure and Ground. A Gestalt principle of perceptual organization that focuses on contrast. Figure is usually perceived clearly because, in contrast to (back) ground, it appears to be well defined, solid, and in the forefront, while the ground is usually perceived as indefinite, hazy, and continuous. Music can be figure or (back) ground.

Financial Risk. The perceived risk that the product will not be worth its cost.

Firm-Oriented Definition of Innovation. Treats the newness of a product from the perspective of how new it is for the company producing or marketing it.

Fixated Consumers. Have a passionate interest in a specific product category.

Focus Group. A qualitative research method in which about eight to ten persons participate in an unstructured group interview about a product or service concept.

Foot-in-the-Door Technique. A theory of attitude change that suggests individuals form attitudes that are consistent with their own prior behavior.

Formal Group. A group that has a clearly defined structure, specific roles and authority levels, and specific goals (e.g., a political party).

Formal Interpersonal Communication. Direct communication between a person representing a profit or non-profit organization and one or more others (e.g., a discussion between a salesman and a prospect).

Four-Way Categorization of Interpersonal Communication. Classification of individuals on the basis of opinion leadership scores as socially integrated, socially independent, socially dependent, and socially isolated.

Frequency. How often advertisements are run during a specified period of time.

Freudian Theory. A theory of personality and motivation developed by the psychoanalyst Sigmund Freud. (See Psychoanalytic Theory.)

Freud's Stages of Personality Development. Freud postulated that an individual's personality is formed as he or she passes through the following stages of infant and childhood development: oral, anal, phallic, latent, and genital.

Functional Approach. An attitude-change theory that classifies attitudes in terms of four functions: utilitarian, ego-defensive, value-expressive, and knowledge functions.

Functional Risk. The perceived risk that the product will not perform as expected.

Functions of the Family. Traditional functions of the family include the provision of: economic well-being, emotional support, suitable family lifestyles, and childhood socialization.

Generation X. The 18- to 29-year-old post baby-boomer segment (also referred to as *Xers* or *busters*).

Generic Goals. The general classes or categories of goals that individuals select to fulfill their needs. (See also Product-Specific Goals.)

Geodemographic Clusters. A composite segmentation strategy that uses both geographic variables (zip codes, neighborhoods, or blocks) and demographic variables (e.g., income, occupation, value of residence) to identify target markets.

Geographic Segmentation. The division of a total potential market into smaller subgroups on the basis of geographic variables (e.g., region, state, or city).

Gestalt. A German term meaning "pattern" or "configuration" that has come to represent various principles of perceptual organization. (See also Perceptual Organization.)

Goals. The sought-after results of motivated behavior. A person fulfills a need through achievement of a goal.

"Granfalloon." Term coined by writer Kurt Vonnegut to mean a false and arbitrary sense of belonging to a group.

Green Consumers. Environmentally aware consumers.

Green Marketing. Marketing that employs environmental claims.

Green Movement. The burgeoning environmental movement.

Green Products. Products designed to protect the environment.

Group. Two or more individuals who interact to accomplish either individual or mutual goals.

Group Cohesiveness. The extent to which group members tend to "stick together" and follow group norms.

Grouping. A Gestalt theory of perceptual organization that proposes that individuals tend to group stimuli automatically so that they form a unified picture or impression. The perception of stimuli as groups or chunks of information, rather than as discrete bits of information, facilitates their memory and recall.

Group Norms. The implicit rules of conduct or standards of behavior which members of a group are expected to observe.

Habit. A consistent pattern of behavior performed without considered thought. Consistent repetition is the hallmark of habit.

Halo Effect. A situation in which the perception of a person on a multitude of dimensions is based on the evaluation of just one (or a few) dimensions (e.g., a man is trustworthy, fine, and noble because he looks you in the eye when he speaks).

Hemispheral Lateralization. Learning theory in which the basic premise is that the right and left hemispheres of the brain "specialize" in the kinds of information that they process. Also called Split Brain theory.

Heuristics. (See Consumer Decision Rules.)

Hierarchy of Needs. (See Maslow's Need Hierarchy.)

High Involvement. A situation where consumers judge a purchase decision to be important enough for them to engage in an extensive information search prior to making the decision.

Hypothesis. A tentative statement of relationship between two or more variables.

Hypothetical Construct. (See Construct.)

Id. In Freudian theory, the part of the personality that consists of primitive and impulsive drives that the individual strives to satisfy.

Ideal Self-Image. How individuals would *like* to perceive themselves (as opposed to Actual Self-Image—the way they *do* perceive themselves).

Impersonal Communication. Communication directed to a large and diffuse audience, with no direct communication between source and receiver. Also known as Mass Communication.

Independent Variable. A variable that can be manipulated to effect a change in the value of a second (i.e., dependent) variable. For example, price is an independent variable that often affects sales (the dependent variable).

Index of Status Characteristics (ISC). A composite measure of social class that combines occupation, source of income (not amount), house type, and dwelling area into a single weighted index of social class standing. Also known as *Warner's ISC.*

Indirect Reference Group. Individuals or groups with whom a person identifies but does not have direct face-to-face contact, such as movie stars, sports heroes, political leaders, or TV personalities.

Inept Set. Brands that a consumer excludes from purchase consideration.

Inert Set. Brands that a consumer is indifferent towards because they are perceived as having no particular advantage.

Infomercial. Thirty-minute commercials that appear to the average viewer as documentaries and thus command more attentive viewing than obvious commercials would receive.

Informal Group. A group of people who see each other frequently on an informal basis, such as weekly poker players or social acquaintances.

Informal Interpersonal Communication. Direct communication between two or more persons who are friends, neighbors, relatives, or co-workers.

Informal Learning of Culture. Situations in which a child learns primarily by imitating the behavior of selected others (family, friends, TV heroes).

Information Overload. A situation in which the consumer is presented with too much product- or brand-related information.

Information Processing. A cognitive theory of human learning patterned after computer information processing that focuses on how information is stored in human memory and how it is retrieved.

Innate Needs. Physiological needs for food, water, air, clothing, shelter, and sex. Also known as biogenic or primary needs.

Inner-Directed Consumers. Consumers who tend to rely on their own "inner" values or standards when evaluating new products and who are likely to be consumer innovators.

Innovation Decision Process. An update of the traditional *adoption process* model consisting of the following four stages: knowledge, persuasion, decision, and confirmation.

Innovativeness. A measure of a consumer's willingness to try new products.

Innovator. An individual who is among the earliest purchasers of a new product.

Institutional Advertising. Advertising designed to promote a favorable company image rather than to promote specific products.

Instrumental Conditioning. A behavioral theory of learning based on a trial-and-error process, with habits formed as the result of positive experiences (reinforcement) resulting from certain responses or behaviors. (See also Conditioned Learning.)

Intermediary Audiences. Wholesalers, distributors, and retailers who are sent *trade advertising* designed to persuade them to order and stock merchandise, and relevant professionals (such as architects or physicians) who are sent *professional advertising* in the hopes that they will specify or prescribe the marketers' products.

Interpersonal Communication. Communication that occurs directly between two or more people by mail, by telephone, or in person.

Interpretivism. A postmodernist approach to the study of consumer behavior that focuses on the act of consuming rather than on the act of buying.

Intrinsic Cues. Physical characteristics of the product (such as size, color, flavor, or aroma) that serve to influence the consumer's perceptions of product quality.

Involvement Theory. A theory of consumer learning which postulates that consumers engage in a range of information processing activity from extensive to limited problem solving, depending on the relevance of the purchase.

Joint Decisions. Family purchase decisions in which the husband and wife are equally influential. Also known as Syncratic Decisions.

Jungian Personality Types. Carl Jung's theories and insights concerning personality types that are specially relevant to consumer behavior, particularly the dimensions of sensing-intuiting, thinking-feeling, extroversion-introversion, and judging-perceiving.

Just Noticeable Difference (j.n.d.). The minimal difference that can be detected between two stimuli. (See also Differential Threshold and Weber's Law.)

Key Informant Method. A method of measuring various aspects of consumer behavior (such as opinion leadership or social class) by which a knowledgeable person is asked to classify individuals with whom he or she is familiar into specific categories.

Knowledge Function. A component of the functional approach to attitude-change theory that suggests that consumers have a strong need to know and understand the people and things with which they come into contact.

Learning. The process by which individuals acquire the knowledge and experience they apply to future purchase and consumption behavior.

Lexicographic Rule. A noncompensatory decision rule in which consumers first rank product attributes in terms of their importance, then compare brands in terms of the attribute considered most important. If one brand scores higher than the other brands, it is selected; if not, the process is continued with the second ranked attribute, and so on.

Licensing. The use by manufacturers and retailers of well-known celebrity or designer names (for a fee) to acquire instant recognition and status for their products.

Lifestyle. (See Psychographic Characteristics.)

Lifestyle Profiles of Social Classes. A constellation of specific lifestyle factors (shared beliefs, attitudes, and behavior) that tend to distinguish the members of each class from the members of all other social classes.

Likert Scale. A summated attitude scale.

Limited Problem Solving. A limited search by a consumer for a product that will satisfy his or her basic criteria from among a selected group of brands.

Long-Term Store. In information-processing theory, the stage of real memory where information is organized, reorganized and retained for relatively extended periods of time.

Low Involvement. A situation where consumers judge a purchase decision to be so unimportant or routine that they engage in little information search prior to making a decision.

Manufacturer's Image. The way in which consumers view (i.e., perceive) the "personality" of the firm that produces a specific product.

Market Mavens. Individuals whose influence stems from a general knowledge or market expertise that leads to an early awareness of new products and services.

Marketing. Activities designed to enhance the flow of goods, services, and ideas from producers to consumers in order to satisfy consumer needs and wants.

Marketing Concept. A consumer-oriented philosophy that suggests that satisfaction of consumer needs provides the focus for product development and marketing strategy to enable the firm to meet its own organizational goals.

Marketing Mix. The unique configuration of the four basic marketing variables (product, promotion, price, and channels of distribution) that a marketing organization controls.

Marketing of Social Causes. Advertising campaigns designed to promote socially desirable behavior.

Market-Oriented Definitions of Innovativeness. Judges the newness of a product in terms of how much exposure consumers have had to the new product.

Market Segmentation. The process of dividing a potential market into distinct subsets of consumers and selecting one or more segments as a target market to be reached with a distinct marketing mix.

Maslow's Need Hierarchy. A theory of motivation that postulates that individuals strive to satisfy their needs according to a basic hierarchical structure, starting with physiological needs, then moving to safety needs, social needs, egotistic needs, and finally self-actualization needs.

Mass Communication. (See Impersonal Communication.)

Massed Learning. Compressing the learning schedule into a short time span to accelerate consumer learning. (See also Distributed Learning.)

Mass Marketing. Offering the same product and marketing mix to all consumers.

Materialistic Consumers. Consumers who value the acquisition and public display of possessions.

Media Demassification. Publishers shifting their focuses from large, general-interest audiences to smaller, more specialized audiences.

Media Strategy. An essential component of a communications plan, which calls for the placement of advertisements in the specific media read, viewed, or heard by selected target markets.

Medium. A channel through which a message is transmitted (e.g., a television commercial, a newspaper advertisement, or a personal letter). The plural is Media.

Membership Group. A group to which a person either belongs or qualifies for membership.

Message. The thought, idea, attitude, image, or other information that a sender wishes to convey to an intended audience.

Message Comprehension. The amount of meaning accurately derived from the message.

Message Framing. Positively constructed messages (those that specify benefits to be *gained* by using a product) are more persuasive than negatively constructed messages that specify benefits *lost* by not using a product).

Micromarketing. Highly regionalized marketing strategies that use advertising and promotional campaigns specifically geared to local market needs and conditions.

Model. A simplified representation of reality designed to show the relationships between the various elements of a system or process under investigation.

Modeling. (See Observational Learning.)

Models of Man. (See Economic Man, Passive Man, Cognitive Man, and Emotional Man Models.)

Mood/Affect. An individual's subjectively perceived "feeling state."

Motivation. The driving force within individuals that impels them to action.

Motivational Research. Qualitative research designed to uncover consumers' subconscious or hidden motivations. The basic premise of motivational research is that consumers are not always aware of, or may not wish to reveal, the basic reasons underlying their actions.

Multiattribute Attitude Models. Attitude models that examine the composition of consumer attitudes in terms of selected product attributes or beliefs.

Multistep Flow of Communication Theory. A revision of the traditional two-step theory that shows multiple communication flows: from the mass media simultaneously to opinion leaders, opinion receivers, and information receivers (who neither influence nor are influenced by others); from opinion leaders to opinion receivers; and from opinion receivers to opinion leaders.

National Subcultures. Nationality subcultures in a larger society in which members often retain a sense of identification and pride in the language and customs of their ancestors.

Need for Cognition. The personality trait that measures a person's craving for or enjoyment of thinking.

Need Recognition. The realization by the consumer that there is a difference between "what is" and "what should be."

Negative Motivation. A driving force away from some object or condition.

Negative Reinforcement. An unpleasant or negative outcome that serves to encourage a specific behavior. (Not to be confused with punishment, which discourages repetition of a specific behavior.)

Neo-Freudian Personality Theory. A school of psychology that stresses the fundamental role of social relationships in the formation and development of personality.

Noncompensatory Decision Rule. A type of consumer decision rule by which positive evaluation of a brand attribute does not compensate for (i.e., is not balanced against) a negative evaluation of the same brand on some other attribute.

Nonprofit Marketing. The use of marketing concepts and techniques by not-for-profit organizations (such as museums or government agencies) to impart information, ideas, or attitudes to various segments of the public.

Nontraditional FLC Stages. A family life-cycle categorization that includes nontraditional household configurations such as divorced or widowed young adults, homosexual couples, couples without children, unmarried couples, etc.

Normative Reference Group. A group that influences the general values or behavior of an individual. (See Comparative Reference Group.)

Not-for-Profit-Marketing. (See Nonprofit Marketing.)

Nuclear Family. A household consisting of a husband and wife and at least one offspring.

Objective Measurement of Social Class. A method of measuring social class whereby individuals are asked specific socioeconomic questions concerning themselves or their families. On the basis of their answers, people are placed within specific social-class groupings.

Observability. The ease with which a product's benefits or attributes can be observed, visualized, or described to potential customers.

Observational Learning. A process by which individuals observe the behavior of others, remember it, and imitate it. Also known as Modeling.

Observational Research. Research that relies on observation of consumers in the process of buying and using products.

One-Sided Versus Two-Sided Messages. A one-sided message tells only the benefits of a product or service; a two-sided message also includes some negatives, thereby enhancing the credibility of the marketer.

Opinion Leader. A person who informally gives product information and advice to others.

Opinion Leadership. The process by which one person (the *opinion leader*) informally influences the consumption actions or attitudes of others, who may be *opinion seekers* or *opinion recipients*.

Opinion Receiver (Recipient). An individual who either actively seeks product information from others or receives unsolicited information.

Optimizing Decision Strategy. A strategy whereby a consumer evaluates each brand in terms of significant product criteria. (See also Simplifying Decision Strategy.)

Optimum Stimulation Level (OSL). A personality trait that measures the level or amount of novelty or complexity that individuals seek in their personal experiences. High OSL consumers tend to accept risky and novel products more readily than low OSL consumers.

Organizational Consumer. A business, government agency, or other institution (profit or nonprofit) that buys the goods, services, and/or equipment necessary for the organization to function.

Other-Directed Consumers. Consumers who tend to look to others for direction and for approval.

Packaging-to-Price Deceptions. Deception practiced by some marketers who maintain the size and price of their product packages but decrease the quantity in the package.

Participant Observers. Researchers who participate in the environment that they are studying without notifying those who are being observed.

Passive Man Theory. A theory of man that depicts the consumer as a submissive recipient of the promotional efforts of marketers.

Perceived Age. (See Cognitive Age.)

Perceived Quality. Consumers often judge the quality of a product or service on the basis of a variety of informational cues that they associate with the product; some of these cues are intrinsic to the product or service; others are extrinsic, such as price, store image, service environment, brand image, and promotional messages.

Perceived Risk. The degree of uncertainty perceived by the consumer as to the consequences (outcome) of a specific purchase decision.

Perception. The process by which an individual selects, organizes, and interprets stimuli into a meaningful and coherent picture of the world.

Perceptual Blocking. The subconscious "screening out" of stimuli that are threatening or inconsistent with one's needs, values, beliefs, or attitudes.

Perceptual Defense. The process of subconsciously distorting stimuli to render them less threatening or more consistent with one's needs, values, beliefs, or attitudes.

Perceptual Interpretation. The interpretation of stimuli based on an individual's expectations in light of previous experiences, on the number of plausible explanations that he or she can envision, and on motives and interests at the time of perception.

Perceptual Mapping. A research technique that enables marketers to plot graphically consumers' perceptions concerning product attributes of specific brands.

Perceptual Organization. The subconscious ordering and perception of stimuli into groups or configurations according to certain principles of Gestalt psychology.

Personal Consumer. The individual who buys goods and services for his or her own use, for household use, for the use of a family member, or for a friend. (Also referred to as the Ultimate Consumer or End User.)

Personality. The inner psychological characteristics that both determine and reflect how a person responds to his or her environment.

Personality Scale. A series of questions or statements designed to measure a single personality trait.

Personality Test. A pencil-and-paper test designed to measure an individual's personality in terms of one or more traits or inner characteristics.

Physical Risk. The perceived physical risk to self and others that the product may pose.

Physiological Needs. Innate (i.e., biogenic needs), including the needs for food, water, air, clothing, shelter, and sex. Also known as Primary Needs.

Political Marketing. The use of marketing concepts and techniques by candidates for political office and by those interested in promoting political causes.

Positioning. Establishing a specific image for a brand in relation to competing brands. (See also Product Positioning.)

Positive Motivation. A driving force toward some object or condition.

Positive Reinforcement. A favorable outcome to a specific behavior that strengthens the likelihood that the behavior will be repeated.

Positivism. A consumer behavior research approach that regards the consumer behavior discipline as an applied marketing science. Its main focus is on consumer decision making.

Positivist Research. Research primarily concerned with predicting consumer behavior.

Postivists. Researchers who endorse the assumptions on which positivism (modernism) is based.

Postpurchase Dissonance. Cognitive dissonance that occurs after a consumer has made a purchase commitment. Consumers resolve this dissonance through a variety of strategies designed to confirm the wisdom of their choice. (See Cognitive Dissonance.)

Postpurchase Evaluation. An assessment of a product based on actual trial after purchase.

Power Need. The need to exercise control over one's environment, including other persons.

Prepotent Need. An overriding need, from among several needs, that serves to initiate goal-directed behavior.

Prepurchase Search. A stage in the consumer decision-making process in which the consumer perceives a need and actively seeks out information concerning products that will help satisfy that need.

Price-Quality Relationship. The perception of price as an indicator of product quality (e.g., the higher the price, the higher the perceived quality of the product).

Primacy Effect. A theory that proposes that the first (i.e., the earliest) message presented in a sequential series of messages tends to produce the greatest impact on the receiver. (See also Recency Effect.)

Primary Group. A group of people who interact (e.g., meet and talk) on a regular basis, such as members of a family, neighbors, or coworkers.

Primary Needs. (See Innate Needs.)

Primary Research. Original research undertaken by individual researchers or organizations to meet specific objectives. Collected information is called Primary Data.

Private Label Brand. A distributor's or retailer's brand.

PRIZM (Potential Rating Index by Zip Market). A composite index of geographic and socioeconomic factors expressed in residential zip-code neighborhoods from which geodemographic consumer segments are formed.

Product Line Extension. A marketing strategy of adding related products to an already established brand based on the Stimulus Generalization Theory).

Product Positioning. A marketing strategy designed to project a specific image for a product.

Product-Specific Goals. The specifically branded or labeled products that consumers select to fulfill their needs. (See also Generic Goals.)

Projective Techniques. Research procedures designed to identify consumers' subconscious feelings and motivations. These tests often require consumers to interpret ambiguous stimuli such as incomplete sentences, cartoons, or inkblots.

Psychoanalytic Theory. A theory of motivation and personality that postulates that unconscious needs and drives, particularly sexual and other biological drives, are the basis of human motivation and personality.

Psychogenic Needs. (See Acquired Needs.)

Psychographic Characteristics. Intrinsic psychological, sociocultural, and behavioral characteristics that reflect how an individual is likely to act in relation to consumption decisions. Also referred to as Lifestyle or Activities, Interests, and Opinions (AIOs).

Psychographic Instrument. A series of written statements designed to capture relevant aspects of a consumer's personality, buying motives, interests, attitudes, beliefs, and values.

Psychological Characteristics. The inner or intrinsic qualities of the individual consumer.

Psychological Noise. A barrier to message reception (i.e., competing advertising messages or distracting thoughts).

Psychological Segmentation. The division of a total potential market into smaller subgroups on the basis of intrinsic characteristics of the individual, such as personality, buying motives, lifestyle, attitudes, or interests.

Psychology. The study of the intrinsic qualities of individuals, such as their motivations, perception, personality, and learning patterns.

Purchase Behavior. Behavior that involves two types of purchases: *trial purchases* (the exploratory phase in which consumers attempt to evaluate a product through direct use) and *repeat purchases*, which usually signify that the product meets with consumer's approval and that the consumer is willing to use it again.

Purchase Time. The amount of time that elapses between consumers' initial awareness of a new product or service and the point at which they purchase or reject it.

Rank-Order Scale. An attitude scale in which subjects are asked to rank items such as products (or retail stores or companies) in order of performance in terms of some criterion, such as overall quality or value for the money.

Rate of Adoption. The percentage of potential adopters within a specific social system who have adopted a new product within a given period of time.

Rate of Usage. The frequency of use and repurchase of a particular product.

Rational Motives. Motives or goals based on economic or objective criteria, such as price, size, weight, or miles-per-gallon.

Reach. The number of different people or households that are exposed to an advertisement (either because they hear or watch the program or read the newspaper or magazine).

Reactance Theory. A theory that postulates that when an individual's freedom to engage in a specific behavior is threatened, the threatened behavior becomes more attractive.

Recency Effect. A theory that proposes that the last (i.e., most recent) message presented in a sequential series of messages tends to be remembered longest. (See also Primacy Effect.)

Reference Group. A person or group that serves as a point of comparison (or reference) for an individual in the formation of either general or specific values, attitudes, or behavior.

Regional Subcultures. Groups who identify with the regional or geographical areas in which they live.

Rehearsal. The silent, mental repetition of material. Also, the relating of new data to old data to make the former more meaningful.

Reinforcement. A positive or negative outcome that influences the likelihood that a specific behavior will be repeated in the future in response to a particular cue or stimulus.

Relationship Marketing. Marketing aimed at creating strong, lasting relationships with a core group of customers by making them feel good about the company and by giving them some kind of personal connection to the business.

Relative Advantage. The degree to which potential customers perceive a new product to be superior to existing alternatives.

Reliability. The degree to which a measurement instrument is consistent in what it measures.

Repeat Purchase. The act of repurchasing a product or brand purchased earlier.

Repositioning. Changing the way a product is perceived by consumers in relation to other brands or product uses.

Reputational Measurement of Social Class. A method of measuring social class by which a knowledgeable community member is asked to classify the other members of the community into status groupings. (See Key Informant Method.)

Response. The reaction of an individual to a specific stimulus or cue.

Retention. The ability to retain information in the memory.

Retrieval. The stage of information processing in which individuals recover information from long-term storage.

Ritual. A type of symbolic activity consisting of a series of steps (multiple behaviors) occurring in a fixed sequence and repeated over time.

Rokeach Value Survey. A self-administered inventory consisting of eighteen "terminal" values (i.e., personal goals) and eighteen "instrumental" values (i.e., ways of reaching personal goals).

Role. A pattern of behavior expected of an individual in a specific social position, such as mother, daughter, teacher, lawyer. One person may have a number of different roles, each of which is relevant in the context of a specific social situation.

Routinized Response Behavior. A habitual purchase response based on predetermined criteria.

Seal of Approval. An ostensibly objective product rating that serves as a positive endorsement to encourage consumers to act favorably toward certain products (i.e., *Good Housekeeping* magazine's Seal of Approval).

Secondary Data. Data that has been collected for reasons other than the specific research project at hand.

Secondary Needs. (See Acquired Needs.)

Secondary Research. Research conducted for reasons other than the specific problem under study. Resulting data are called Secondary Data.

Segmentation Bases. Eight major categories provide the most popular bases for market segmentation: geographic factors, demographic factors, psychological characteristics, sociocultural variables, use-related characteristics, use-situational factors, benefits sought, and hybrid segmentation forms (such as demographic/psychographic profiles, geodemographic factors, and values and lifestyles [VALS2]).

Selective Attention. A heightened awareness of stimuli relevant to one's needs or interests. Also called Selective Perception.

Selective Exposure. Conscious or subconscious exposure by the consumer to certain media or messages, and the subconscious or active avoidance of others.

Selective Perception. (See Selective Attention.)

Self Concept. (See Self-Image.)

Self-Designating Method. A method of measuring some aspect of consumer behavior (such as opinion leadership) in which a person is asked to evaluate or classify his or her own attitudes or actions.

Self-Perception Theory. A theory that suggests that consumers develop attitudes by reflecting on their own behavior.

Self-Report Attitude Scales. The measurement of consumer attitudes by self-scoring procedures, such as Likert scales, semantic differential scales, or rank-order scales.

Self Reports. Pen-and-pencil "tests" completed by individuals concerning their own actions, attitudes, or motivation in regard to a subject or product under study.

Semantic Differential Scale. A series of bipolar adjectives (such as good/bad, hot/cold) that are anchored at the ends of an odd-numbered (e.g., 5- or 7-point) continuum. Respondents are asked to evaluate a concept (e.g., a product or company) on the basis of each attribute by checking the point on the continuum that best reflects their feelings or beliefs.

Semiotics. The study of symbols and the meanings they convey. Often used to discover the meanings of various consumption behaviors and rituals.

Sensation. The immediate and direct response of the sensory organs to simple stimuli (e.g., color, brightness, loudness, smoothness).

Sensory Adaptation. "Getting used to" certain sensations; becoming accommodated to a certain level of stimulation.

Sensory Receptors. The human organs (eyes, ears, nose, mouth, skin) that receive sensory inputs.

Sensory Store. The place in which all sensory inputs are housed very briefly before passing into the short-term store.

Shopping Group. Two or more people who shop together.

Short-Term Store. The stage of real memory in which information received from the sensory store for processing is retained briefly before passing into the long-term store or forgotten.

Single-Component Attitude Model. An attitude model consisting of just one overall affective, or "feeling," component. Also called Working Memory.

Single Variable Index. The use of a single socioeconomic variable (such as income) to estimate an individual's relative social class. (See also Composite Variable Index.)

Sleeper Effect. The tendency for persuasive communication to lose the impact of source credibility over time (i.e., the influence of a message from a high credibility source tends to *decrease* over time; the influence of a message from a low credibility source tends to *increase* over time).

Slice-of-Life Commercials. Television commercials that depict a typical person or family solving a problem by using the advertised product or service. They focus on "real-life" situations with which the viewer can identify.

Social Character. In the context of consumer behavior, a personality trait that ranges on a continuum from inner-directedness (reliance on one's own "inner" values or standards) to other-directedness (reliance on others for direction).

Social Class. The division of members of a society into a hierarchy of distinct status classes, so that members of each class have either higher or lower status than members of other classes.

Social Judgment Theory. An individual's processing of information about an issue is determined by his or her involvement with the issue.

Social Marketing. The use of marketing concepts and techniques to win adoption of socially beneficial ideas.

Social Psychology. The study of how individuals operate in a group.

Social Risk. The perceived risk that a poor product choice may result in social embarrassment.

Social Self-Image. How consumers feel others see them.

Social System. A physical, social, or cultural environment to which people belong and within which they function.

Societal Marketing Concept. A revision of the traditional marketing concept that suggests that marketers adhere to principles of social responsibility in the marketing of their goods and services; that is, they must endeavor to satisfy the needs and wants of their target markets in ways that preserve and enhance the well-being of consumers and society as a whole.

Sociocultural Segmentation. The division of a total potential market into smaller subgroups on the basis of sociological or cultural variables, such as social class, stage in the family life cycle, religion, race, nationality, values, beliefs or customs.

Socioeconomic Status Scores (SES). A multivariable social class measure used by the United States Bureau of the Census that combines occupational status, family income, and educational attainment into a single measure of social class standing.

Sociology. The study of groups.

Sociometric Method. A method of measuring opinion leadership by which the actual pattern or web of person-to-person informal communications is traced.

Source. The initiator of a message.

Source Credibility. The perceived honesty and objectivity of the source of the communication.

Spokesperson. A celebrity or company executive who represents a product, brand, or company over an extended period of time, often in print, on television, and in personal appearances.

SRI Values and Lifestyle Program (VALS/I&II). A research service that tracks marketing-relevant shifts in the beliefs, values, and lifestyles of psychographic segments of the American population.

Starch Readership Service. A syndicated service that evaluates the effectiveness of magazine advertisements.

Status. The relative prestige accorded to an individual within a specific group or social system.

Stereotypes. Individuals tend to carry "pictures" in their minds of the meanings of various kinds of stimuli. These stereotypes serve as expectations of what specific situations or people or events will be like and are important determinants of how such stimuli are subsequently perceived.

Stimulus. Any unit of input to any of the senses. Examples of consumer stimuli include products, packages, brand names, advertisements, and commercials. Also known as Sensory Input.

Stimulus Discrimination. The ability to select a specific stimulus from among similar stimuli because of perceived differences.

Stimulus Generalization. The inability to perceive differences between slightly dissimilar stimuli.

Storage. The stage in information processing in which individuals organize and reorganize information in long-term memory received from the short-term store.

Store Image. Consumers' perceptions of the "personality" of a store and the products it carries.

Subculture. A distinct cultural group that exists as an identifiable segment within a larger, more complex society.

Subjective Measurement of Social Class. A method of measuring social class by which people are asked to estimate their own social-class position.

Sublimation. The manifestation of repressed needs in a socially acceptable form of behavior; a type of defense mechanism.

Subliminal Perception. Perception of very weak or rapid stimuli received below the level of conscious awareness.

Substitute Goal. A goal that replaces an individual's primary goal when that goal cannot be achieved or acquired.

Superego. In Freudian theory, the part of the personality that reflects society's moral and ethical codes of conduct. (See also Id and Ego.)

Supraliminal Perception. Perception of stimuli at or above the level of conscious awareness.

Symbol. Anything that stands for something else.

Symbolic Group. A group with which an individual identifies by adopting its values, attitudes, or behavior despite the unlikelihood of future membership.

Targeting. The selection of a distinct market segment at which to direct a marketing strategy.

Technical Learning of Culture. Learning in which teachers instruct the child in an educational environment about *what* should be done, *how* it should be done, and *why* it should be done.

Teleology. An ethical philosophy which considers the moral worth of a behavior as determined by its consequences. (See also Utilitarianism.)

Testimonials. A promotional technique in which a celebrity that has used a product or service speaks highly of its benefits in order to influence consumers to buy.

Theory of Reasoned Action. A comprehensive theory of the interrelationship among attitudes, intentions, and behavior.

Theory of Trying. Recasts the theory-of-reasoned-action model by replacing *behavior* with *trying to behave* (i.e., consume) as the variable to be explained and/or predicted.

Three Hit Theory. A theory which proposes that the optimum number of exposures to an advertisement to induce learning is three: one to gain consumers' awareness, a second to show the relevance of the product, and a third to show its benefits.

Time Risk. The perceived risk that the time spent in product search may be wasted if the product does not perform as expected.

Trait. Any distinguishing, relatively enduring way in which one individual differs from another.

Trait Theory. A theory of personality that focuses on the measurement of specific psychological characteristics.

Trialability. The degree to which a new product is capable of being tried by consumers on a limited basis (e.g., through free samples or small-size packages).

Tricomponent Attitude Model. An attitude model consisting of three parts: a cognitive (knowledge) component, an affective (feeling) component, and a conative (doing) component.

Two-Step Flow of Communication Theory. A communication model that portrays opinion leaders as direct receivers of information from mass media sources who, in turn, interpret and transmit this information to the general public.

Unaided Recall. An advertising measurement technique in which respondents are asked to recall advertisements they have seen, with no cues as to the identity or product class of the advertisements to be recalled. Often used to measure the influence of timing on learning schedules.

Unconscionable Lies in Advertising. Deceptive advertisements in which completely false claims are made intentionally.

Unfair Advertising. Advertising in which the advertiser withholds information that could result in injuries to consumers.

Unfounded Rumors. Negative comments that are untrue that can sweep through the marketplace to the detriment of a product or service.

Unintended Audiences. Includes those people who are exposed to an advertising message who are not specifically targeted by the source.

Use-Related Segmentation. Popular and effective form of segmentation that categorizes consumers in terms of product, service, or brand usage characteristics, such as usage rate, awareness status, and degree of brand loyalty.

Use-Situation Segmentation. Segmentation that is based on the idea that the occasion or situation often determines what consumers will purchase or consume (i.e., certain products for certain situations, special usage occasions).

Utilitarian Function. A component of the functional approach to attitude-change theory that suggests consumers hold certain attitudes partly because of the brand's utility.

Utilitarianism. A teleological theory summarized best by the idea of "the greatest good for the greatest number."

Validity. The degree to which a measurement instrument accurately reflects what it is designed to measure.

VALS. (See SRI Values and Lifestyle Program [VALS/I&II].)

Value-Expressive Function. A component of the functional approach to attitude-change theory that suggests that attitudes express consumers' general values, lifestyles, and outlook.

Value Measurement Instruments. Data-collection instruments used to ask people how they feel about basic personal and social concepts such as freedom, comfort, national security, or peace.

Values. Relatively enduring beliefs that serve as guides for what is considered "appropriate" behavior and that are widely accepted by the members of a society.

Variable. A thing or idea that may vary (i.e., assume a succession of values).

Variety-Novelty Seeking. A personality trait similar to OSL, which measures a consumer's degree of variety seeking.

Venturesomeness. A personality trait that measures a consumer's willingness to accept the risk of purchasing innovative products.

Verbal Communication. A message based on either the spoken or written word.

Verbalizers. Consumers who prefer verbal or written information and products, such as membership in book clubs or audiotape clubs.

Visual Communication. Nonverbal stimuli such as photographs or illustrations commonly used in advertising to convey or add meaning to a message or to reinforce message arguments.

Visualizers. Consumers who prefer visual information and products that stress the visual, such as membership in a videotape cassette club.

Warner's Index of Status Characteristics. (See Index of Status Characteristics [ISC].)

Weber's Law. A theory concerning the perceived differentiation between similar stimuli of varying intensities (i.e., the stronger the initial stimulus, the greater the additional intensity needed for the second stimulus to be perceived as different).

Wearout. (See Advertising Wearout.)

Word-of-Mouth Communication. Informal conversations concerning products or services.

World Brands. Products that are manufactured, packaged, and positioned the same way regardless of the country in which they are sold.

Yankelovich Monitor™. A research service that tracks more than fifty social trends and provides information as to shifts in size and direction, and resulting marketing implications.

COMPANY INDEX

Jacobson, Michael F., 645
Jacoby, Jacob, 189, 191, 229
Jaffe, Lynn J., 469
Jaffe, Morton I., 141
Jain, Subhash C., 494
James, Karen E., 314
James, William L., 494
Janiszewski, Chris, 228
Janofsky, Michael, 626
Jaworski, Bernard, 343, 436
Jenkins, John R.G., 313
Jenkins, Roger L., 594
Jensen, Jeff, 313
Jensen, Thomas D., 343
Joachimsthaler, Erich A., 142
Johar, J.S., 143
Johasr, Gita Venkataramani, 645
John, Deborah Roedder, 373, 402, 436, 437, 468, 525, 594, 595
Johnson, Bradley, 495
Johnson, Hugh, 228
Johnson, Keren A., 229
Johnson, Kirk, 626, 627
Johnson, Lyndon B., 609
Johnson, Madeline, 255
Johnson, Michael D., 229, 594
Johnson, Otto, 468
Johnson, Rose L., 190–191, 469
Jolly, James P., 436
Jones, David B., 436
Jones, Edward E., 277
Jones, John G, 593
Jung, Carl Gustav, 113, 120–122, 141
Jung, Hyung-Shik, 142, 554

Kahle, Lynn R., 231, 255, 436, 525
Kahn, Barbara E., 142
Kalra, Ajay, 190
Kalya-Naram, Gurumurthy, 229
Kamakura, Wagner A., 436
Kamins, Michael A., 191
Kanner, Bernice, 121
Kant, Immanuel, 13, 20
Kanuk, Lesie Lazar, 111, 277
Kao, Chuan Feng, 230
Kapferer, Jean-Noel, 231
Kardes, Frank R., 134, 143, 229, 255, 314, 343, 371, 373, 436, 494, 525, 554, 594
Karsahi, Nili, 314
Kassarjian, Harold, 20, 42, 228, 255, 276, 554, 643, 645
Katz, Daniel, 276
Kaufman, Carol Felker, 313
Kavas, Alican, 255
Keaveney, Susan M., 191
Kellaries, James J., 190–191
Keller, Kevin Lane, 191, 229, 230
Kellerman, Bert J., 469
Kelley, Bill, 343
Kelley, Harold H., 277
Kelly, Michael, 626
Kennedy, John F., 15, 609
Kennedy, Patricia F., 595
Kent, Robert J., 229
Kephart, Paula, 494
Kernan, Jerome B., 189, 229
Kerr, Peter, 469
Key, Wilson Bryan, 189
Kiam, Victor, 336
Kiecker, Pamela L., 343, 525
Kim, John, 314
Kim, Young Chan, 595
King, Robert L., 343, 436, 469, 555
Kinnear, Thomas C., 142, 189, 229, 230, 231, 436, 525, 555
Kinsey, Dennis, 626
Kipling, Rudyard, 375
Kirchler, Erich, 372
Kisielius, Jolita, 314
Klein, Calvin, 306
Klein, Howard J., 111
Kleine, Robert E., III, 595
Kleinfield, N.R., 77, 189
Klosky, Deborah, 495

Knowles, Patricia A., 343, 594
Kochunny, Chandra M., 486, 494
Kolbert, Elizabeth, 626
Koranteng, Juliana, 373
Korman, Abraham K., 111
Kotler, Philip, 16, 21, 29, 595, 626
Kover, Arthur J., 313
Kraft, Kenneth L., 21
Kramer, Hugh, 554, 555
Kramp, Robert F., 555
Kreshel, Peggy J., 436
Kripke, Homer, 645
Krishnan, Balaji, 469
Kron, Joan, 402
Krugman, Herbert E., 230
Kuhfeld, Warren F., 43
Kumor, V., 142, 469, 525, 548, 594
Kwai-Choli, Christina, 372

Laczniak, Gene R., 21, 189
Landau, Irwin, 645
Lane, Paul M., 313
Langmeyer, Daniel, 343
Langmeyer, Lynn, 343
Laoretti, Larry, 331
Larson, Jan, 403
Lastovicka, John L., 142
LaTour, Michael S., 315, 372
Laurent, Gilles, 231
Lautman, Martin R., 343
Lavack, Anne M., 626
Lavenka, Mark, 190
Lavin, Marilyn, 372, 468
Lawrence, Jennifer, 591
Lazarsfeld, Paul F., 525
Lee, Cynthia, 111
Lee, Moonkyu, 594
Lee, Myung Soo, 231, 255
Lee, Wei-Na, 340, 343, 436
Lefton, Terry, 373
Leigh, James H., 189
Leone, Robert P., 142, 469, 525, 548, 594
Levesque, Terrence, 77
Levin, Gary, 645
Levin, Rosalyn S., 315
Levine, Davie, 277
Levy, Doran J., 469
Levy, Michael, 372, 594
Levy, Sidney J., 43, 494, 595, 626
Lewin, Kurt, 111
Li, Chui, 469
Licata, Jane W., 469
Lichtenstein, Donald R., 139, 143, 255, 525
Liechtenstein, Richard G., 190
Lindbergh, Anne Morrow, 279
Lindsay, Peter H., 230
Lingle, John H., 230
Lipman, Joanne, 314
Locander, William B., 255
Locke, Edwin A., 111
Loeffler, Tamara L., 436
Lofflin, John, 189
London, Steve, 402
Long, Mary M., 58, 589, 591, 595
Lord, Kenneth R., 229, 230, 255
Louis-Dreyfuss, Julia, 334
Lowe, Charles A., 314
Lowrey, Tina M., 314, 554, 595
Lumsdaine, Arthur A., 313
Luntz, Frank, 626
Lurch, Robert F., 189
Lutz, Richard, 42, 373, 525
Lysonski, Steven, 255

Macadams, Elizabeth A., 372
McAlister, Leigh, 142, 143, 276, 343, 372, 373, 436, 525, 594, 595
McCarthy, Michael J., 190, 343
McCarty, John A., 436
McCaulley, Mary H., 141
McClelland, David C., 96, 111, 436
McCorkle, Denny E., 402–403
McCracken, Grant, 343, 410

McCrohan, Kevin, 36
McCullough, Jim, 371
McDonald, William J., 43
McDougall, Gordon H.G., 36, 77
MacEvoy, Bruce, 551, 555
McGrath, Mary Ann, 371, 595
McIntyre, Roger P., 143, 436
McIntyre, Shelby H., 436, 555
McKay, Betsy, 493
McKeage, Kim K.R., 595
MacKenzie, Scott B., 141, 255, 277
Mackintosh, N.J., 228
Macklin, M. Carole, 372
MacLachlan, James, 299, 314
McMellon, Charles, A., 436, 568, 594
McNeal, James U., 372
McQuarrie, Edward F., 231
Macstravic, Scott, 626
McWilliams, Michael, 111
Madden, Thomas J., 255, 494
Madill-Marshall, Judith J., 373
Madonna, 331
Maheswasran, Durairaj, 190, 229, 314, 494
Malhotra, Narish K., 229
Mancuso, Joseph R., 525
Manderlink, George, 111
Manning, Kenneth C., 314
Mantala, Murali K., 555
March, James G., 593
Markoff, John, 313, 315
Marks, Lawrence J., 20
Markus, Hazel, 143
Marmorstein, Howard, 229, 230, 313, 314
Maronick, Thomas J., 645
Marriott, Bill, 336
Marshall, Roger, 372
Martin, Claude R., Jr., 189
Martin, Douglas, 554
Martineau, Pierre, 111, 379
Martins, Marielza, 190
Maslow, Abraham H., 68, 95, 111
Mathur, Anil, 255, 469
Mathur, Mahima, 313
Matthews, Robert, 372
Mayer, Robert, 372
Mayo, Michael A., 20
Mazursky, David, 191, 313
Mazzon, Jose Afonso, 436
Meeker, Marchia, 403
Menelly, Nancy E., 313
Menon, Staya, 142
Meredith, Geoffrey, 77
Meric, Havva J., 143
Merikle, Philip M., 189
Merritt, Sharyne, 494
Meyers-Levy, Joan, 229, 314
Miaoulis, George, 469
Mick, David Glen, 43, 111, 313, 595
Mifflin, Lawrie, 77
Miller, Christopher M., 555
Miller, Cyndee, 77, 373, 436, 469
Miller, Karen Lowry, 473, 493
Milner, Laura M., 120, 141
Miniard, Paul W., 314
Mitchell, Alison, 626
Mitchell, Andrew, 343
Mitchell, Susan, 469, 555
Mittal, Banwari, 230, 231
Mittelstaedt, Robert A., 142, 143, 402, 555
Mogelonsky, Marcia, 448, 468
Mondale, Walter, 610
Monroe, Kent B., 180, 190, 276, 469
Moore, Roy L., 372
Moore, William L., 230
Moore-Shay, Elizabeth S., 373
Morawaski, David M., 141
Morgan, Amy J., 143
Morgan, Carol M., 469
Morganosky, Michelle A., 314
Morris, Kathrine J., 230
Morrow, Kathleen, 77
Moschis, George P., 20, 372, 469
Mothersbaugh, David L, 343

Smith, Scott M., 594, 627
Smith, Stephen M., 315
Snook-Luther, Daviod C., 315
Soloman, Michael R., 123, 141, 255, 276, 314, 343, 372, 373, 412, 554, 594
Sonsone, Carol, 111
Spadoni, Marie, 468
Spangenberg, Eric R., 371
Spethmann, Betsy, 468
Spielvogel, Carl, 493
Spiggle, Susan, 43
Spreng, Richard A., 277
Srinivasan, V., 231
Srull, Thomas K., 142, 230, 276
Staelin, Richard, 190, 191, 229
Stahl, Michael J., 111
Starch, Daniel, 95
Starr, Valerie, 314
Staubb, Vernon, 494
Stayman, Douglas M., 141
Steenkamp, Jan-Benedict E.M., 142
Steere, John, 468
Steiner, Gary, A., 189
Stengel, Richard, 626
Stephens, Debra, 255
Stern, Aimee, 595
Stern, Barbara B., 143, 255, 343, 436, 468, 469, 525, 554
Sternthal, Brian, 42, 230, 313, 314
Stevenson, Adlai, 81
Stewart, David W., 120, 141, 143, 494, 525
Stiller, Jerry, 331
Stinson, Kandi M., 373
Stith, Melvin T., 525
Stoltman, Jeffrey J., 314
Stone, Robert N., 231
Stone, Roger, 626
Stopeck, Madeline H., 189
Stout, Patricia A., 313
Strasser, Stephen, 626
Strate, Lance, 412
Strathman, Alan J., 277
Strom, Stephanie, 77
Stutts, Mary Ann, 372
Subramanian, Suresh, 142, 555
Sujan, Mita, 134, 143, 255, 340, 343, 371, 373, 436, 494, 525, 554, 594
Sullivan, Harry Stack, 122
Swinyard, William R., 313
Synodinos, Nicolas E., 189

Tabouret, Gerard J., 276
Tagliabue, John, 494
Talpade, Salil, 372
Tankersley, Clint B., 77
Tannenbaum, Jeffrey A., 402
Tanner, John F., Jr., 315
Tanshuhaj, Patriya, 371
Tascarella, Patty, 626
Tashchian, Armen, 231

Tate, Allen, 23
Taylor, Elizabeth, 334, 398
Taylor, Shirley, 190
Taylor, Steven A., 190
Teel, Jesse E., 142, 506, 525
Teinowitz, Ira, 469
Tepper, Kelly, 469
Theus, Kathryn, T., 189
Thomas, Dave, 336, 338
Till, Brian D., 314, 343
Tinkham, Spencer F., 436
Tobias, Randall D., 43
Topol, Martin T., 313
Trachtenberg, Jeffrey A., 343
Traylor, Mark B., 230
Trevino, Lee, 331
Triplett, Tim, 141
Tripp, Carolyn, 343
Tsal, Yehoshua, 314
Tull, Donald S., 33
Twible, Jacquelyn L, 255
Tyagi, Pradeep K., 141
Tybout, Alice M., 20, 42, 141, 230

Uehling, Mark D., 314
Ulgado, Francis M., 594
Underhill, Paco, 372
Underwood, Elaine, 468
Unger, Lynette, 494
Unnava, H. Rao, 228, 229, 255, 314
Urbany, Joel E., 191

Valence, Gilles, 134
Van Auken, Stuart, 469
Van Hoof, Kari, 429, 468
Varadarajan, Rajan, 343, 436
Velez, David A., 276
Venkat, Ramesh, 436
Venkatesh, Alladi, 42, 43
Vilcassin, Naufel J., 120, 141, 143, 494, 525
Vitell, Scott, 20, 21
Vogel, Susan Raymond, 469
Voli, Patricia K., 343
Von Pechmann, Frederick and Frederick E., Jr., 33
Vonnegut, Kurt, 612

Wahlers, Russell G., 142
Wald, Matthew L., 314
Waldrop, Judith, 73, 77, 468, 645
Walker, Bruce J., 231, 468
Walker, Chip, 477, 494, 504, 525
Walker, Mary, 343
Wallace, Everett S., 554
Wallendorf, Melanie, 43, 189, 229, 230, 536, 554
Walley, Wayne, 494
Walsh, Doris, 315
Wang, Paul, 495
Wansink, Brian, 276
Ward, Scott, 372
Warfield, Anne E., 525

Warlop, Luk, 228
Warner, Fara, 229
Warner, W. Lloyd, 387, 403
Warren, Wendy L., 228
Warshaw, Paul R., 255
Webb, Peter H., 314
Weber, Ernst, 148, 149, 150
Webster, Cynthia, 372, 468
Wegener, Barry, 189
Weil, Claudia E., 595
Weil, Frank A., 12
Weinberg, Charles B., 189
Weinberg, Peter, 111
Weinberger, Marc G., 315
Weisendancer, Betsy, 143
Weisz, Pam, 437, 468, 494
Welsh, Gerald E., II, 626
Whalen, Jeanne, 437, 494
White, J. Dennis, 525
White, William H., 525
Wildt, Albert R., 190
Wilkens, Henry T., 189
Wilkes, Robert E., 373, 469
Wilkie, Maxine, 77, 469
Williams, John H., 594
Williams, Terrel G., 525
Wilson, Edmund, 23
Winski, Joseph, M., 627
Winslow, Ron, 626
Winters, Lewis C., 313
Wisenblit, Joseph Z., 143, 315
Witte, Carl L., 189
Wittmanyer, Cecelia, 402
Wittrock, Merlin C., 230
Wolf, Michael J., 595
Wolfe, David B., 469
Woodruff, Robert B., 594
Woodside, Arch G., 141
Wudunn, Sheryl, 494, 495
Wynter, Leon E., 468

Yadav, Manjit S., 190
Yan, Rick, 494
Yankelovich, Clancy Shulman, 436
Yi, Yougae, 276
Yip, George S., 494
Young, Charles E., 314
Young, Meliss J., 314

Zachary, Lacey J., 141
Zaichkowsky, Judith L., 231
Zandpour, Fred, 494
Zanna, Mark P., 276
Zbar, Jeffery D., 468, 494
Zeithaml, Valerie A., 178, 179, 190
Zimmer, Mary R., 229
Zinkhan, George M., 143, 255, 313, 343, 436, 437, 468, 469, 554
Zollo, Peter, 372, 373
Zuckerman, Lawrence, 77

Interpersonal communication, 280, 288–289
    four-way categorization of, 518
    multistep flow theory, 517–518
    two-step flow theory, 516–517
Interpretation in perception, 168–170
Interpretivism, 8, 11
Interpretivist research, 25
    combining with positivist research, 25–27
Interstate Commerce Commission (ICC), 634
Interviews
    depth, 25, 30, 120, 417
    field, 38
    personal, 34
Inventories, 35
Involvement, level of, 287
Involvement theory, 195, 207, 215–222, 299–301
Inwardly-directed ego, 99
Irrelevant cues, 169–170
ISC. *See* Index of Status Characteristics
Issue positioning, 608–609
ITC. *See* International Trade Commission

j.n.d. (just noticeable difference), 148–152
Japanese, 451, 473, 475, 487, 491
Jews, 445–446, 356, 357
Joint decision making, 355
Jumping to conclusions, 170
Jungian personality types, 120–122, 123, 124
Just noticeable difference (j.n.d.), 148–152

Key informant method of opinion leadership measure-
    ment, 508, 509
Knowledge function of attitude change, 265
Koreans, 451

Labeling, 630, 631, 640–641
Laggards in adopter category, 539–540
Language, 409, 411
    English, 443
    Spanish, 60, 443, 444
Latchkey kids, 358
Late majority in adopter category, 539–540
Latency stage, 117
Latin-Americans, 475, 477, 489
Learned predispositions, attitudes as, 337
Learning, 55, 192–231
    of associations, 198
    of attitudes, 258–259, 337
    behavioral theories, 196–207
    of culture, 408–412
    definition of, 194–196
    formal, informal, and technical, 408
    massed and distributed, 206
    observational or vicarious, 206
Left hemisphere, 215, 216, 217, 222
Legislation, consumer-oriented, 631
Leisure, 398
Level of involvement, 55, 287
Levels of aspiration, 89
Lexicographic decision rules, 577–578
Licensing, 170, 185, 202–203
Life cycle, family, 360–369
Lifestyles
    affluent, 397
    analysis of, 56–59, 67
    and decision making, 579–580
    factors of, 387
    and family, 348–349
    profiles of, 387–390
Likert scale, 35, 36
Limited problem solving in decision making, 559
List of Values (LOV), 417, 418
Logical empiricism, 24
Logical positivism, 24
Long-term commitment purchases, 581
Long-term storage, 209, 211
Loss framing, 300–301
LOV. *See* List of Values
Low-involvement purchases, 216–221
Low-risk perceivers, 184
Loyalty programs, 588

MADD. *See* Mothers Against Drunk Driving
Magazines, 289, 295, 304

Magnuson-Moss Warranty/FTC Improvement Act,
    16
Mail surveys, 34–35
Makers, 71, 72, 73
"Mall mavens," 461–462
Managed health care systems, 600
Managerial marketing strategy, 8
Manufacturer's image, 181–182
Marital status, 55
Market maven, 512–514
Market segmentation, 9, 44–77, 641
    of African-Americans, 449
    of baby boomers, 456–457
    bases for, 48–71
    definition of, 46–48
    of elderly, 459–460
    in health care marketing, 600–603
    of Hispanics, 442–444
    identification of, 71, 73
    implementing strategies, 74–75
    multinational strategies, 478–486
    and need hierarchy, 102
    psychographic, 487, 488, 489, 490
    and social class, 376
    targeting of, 71–74
Marketing
    abuses in, 630–631
    and affinity groups, 619–621
    ambush, 304
    cause-related, 266, 617–621
    concentrated, 74–75
    countersegmentation strategy in, 74–75
    development of concept, 10–11
    differentiated, 74–75
    distribution problems in, 491
    diversity in, 4–10
    environmental, 621–623
    ethics in, 11–17
    of health care, 600–605
    interactive, 535–536
    market-oriented approach to, 82
    mistakes in, 487–491
    multinational strategies in, 478–486
    niche. *See* Niche marketing
    political, 605–612
    pricing problems in, 491
    product problems in, 488–490
    product-oriented approach to, 82
    promotional problems in, 490–491
    relationship, 295–296, 588–591
    of social causes, 612–621
    See also Direct marketing
Marketing mix activities, 564
Market-oriented approach, 82
Market-oriented innovations, 530–531
Masculine traits, 464
Maslow's hierarchy of needs, 95–102
Mass marketing, 46
Mass media. *See* Media
Mass Media Bureau, 633
Massed learning, 206
Material comfort as core value, 425–426
Materialism, 126, 132
Mature and elderly consumers, 457–464
Mature-adult market, 52–53
Media
    and adoption process, 545
    and attitude formation, 262
    and communication, 281
    and consumer innovator, 549
    diversity in, 4
    and first language, 443
    high- and low-involvement, 215–216
    as institution, 414
    and market segmentation, 48
    and opinion leaders, 512
Media strategy, 291–296
Medicaid, 600, 601
Medicare, 458, 459, 600, 601, 609
Medium for communication, 280–281
Mega-brands, 226
Membership groups, 321
Memory, 208–210

Men
    and encoding, 210
    as homemakers, 54
    and opinion leadership, 503, 504
Mental images, 406
Message
    comprehension of, 286–287
    initiator (source) of, 282–286
    and mood, 287
    one-sided versus two-sided, 301
    presentation of, 297–304
    verbal or nonverbal, 281
Message framing, 300–301
Message strategies, 296–309
Mexican-Americans, 442
Micromarketing. *See* Niche marketing
Middle class, global, 476–477
Middle-aged, 7
Misleading advertising, 631, 636
Mission statement, 15
Mobility in social class, 390–392
Modeling, 206
Models of consumers, 560–564
Modern social system, 537
Mood
    in emotional model of consumers, 564
    and message decoding, 287
Moral absolutism, 14
Motivation, 55, 80–111
    arousal of, 92–94
    definition of, 83
    dynamic nature of, 87–94
    in learning, 195
    measurement of, 105–106
    of opinion leaders and seekers, 505
    positive and negative, 86, 87
    rational and emotional, 86–87
    research on, 24–25, 106–109
Multiattribute attitude model, 242–247, 267–270
Multinational marketing strategies, 478–486
Multinational markets, 409, 470–495
Multiple selves, 136–137
Multistep flow of communication theory, 517–518
Murray's list of psychogenic needs, 96
"Must-Know Men," 514, 515
Myers-Briggs Type Indicators, 120–122

NAFTA. *See* North American Free Trade Agreement
National advertising, 284
National borders, 478
National Commission on Consumer Finance, 16
National Environmental Policy Act, 16
National Highway Traffic Safety Administration, 630
National Traffic and Safety Act, 16
Nationality subcultures, 441–444
Natural sciences, 24
Naturalism, 25
Need recognition in decision making model, 567
Needs, 55, 80–111
    biological, 4–5, 96
    for cognition, 130–131
    and culture, 407–408
    definition of, 84
    dynamic nature of, 87–94
    multiplicity of, 92
    of opinion leaders, 502, 505
    of opinion seekers, 503, 505
    types and systems of, 94–105
Negative disconfirmation of expectations, 582
Negative motivation, 86, 87
Negative political advertising, 611
Negative product information, 501, 520–522
Negative reinforcement, 206
Neighborhood quality, 384
Neo-Freudian personality theory, 122–125
Neo-Pavlovian theory, 198
New learning, 214
New product development, 9
New-age elderly, 459–460, 462
Niche marketing, 50, 182, 261
Noise, psychological, 288
Nonadopters in adopter category, 540
Nonaffluent consumers, 397